Jamaica Highlights

The nature of any Jamaican vacation is defined as much by individual tastes as by the amount of time you have on the island. The Caribbean's third-largest island affords simple pleasures and rigorous activities, tranquil beaches and ear-shattering sound-system parties, water sports and fiery jerk chicken. The vacation menu is varied, and the more you sample – be it a bush-medicine tour, a zip-line ride over a waterfall or a visit to a pulsating market – the more nourishing your stay.

G JOHNSTON

1 NEGRIL

We unzip our tent at Roots Bamboo (p229) on Seven Mile Beach to a glorious morning, with neighbors climbing the coconut trees for fresh breakfasts. After sunning ourselves and scrambling along Booby Cay (p226), a quick motorboat ride from the beaches of Negril, and getting just a touch woozy on the boat ride back to shore, we find our land legs at the beachside bar stands, before heading to hear live reggae at De Buss (p239).

Jay Cooke, Lonely Planet staff, USA

DOUG PEARSON / © JON ARNOLD IMAGES LTD

2 KINGSTON

Pay tribute to the master who brought reggae to the masses at the Bob Marley Museum (p79).

Jay Cooke, Lonely Planet staff, USA

JERRY ALEX

3 BLUE MOUNTAIN COFFEE

You can summit Jamaica's most famous mountain range (p111), fueled by its signature crop: Blue Mountain coffee.

Jay Cooke, Lonely Planet staff, USA

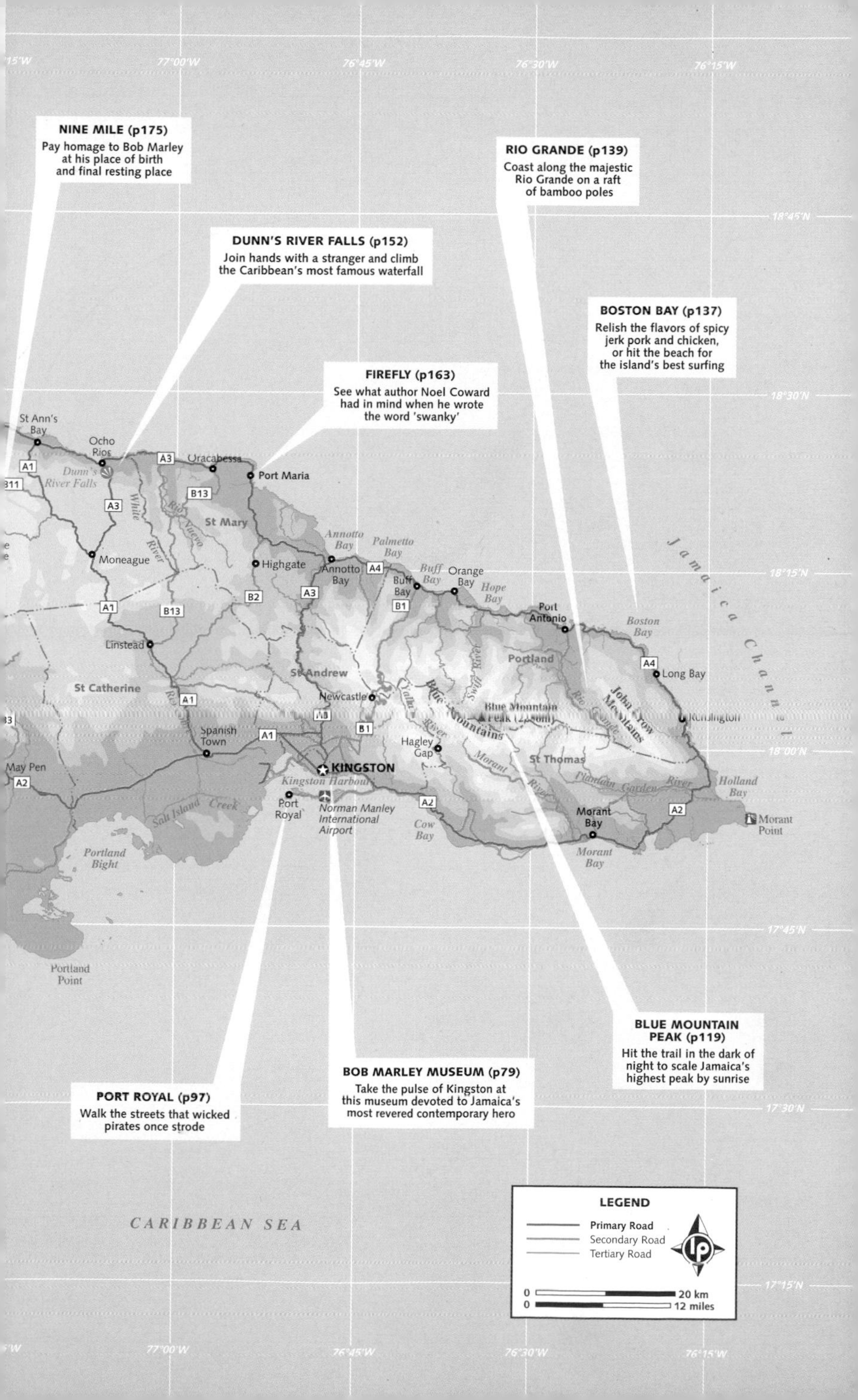

NINE MILE (p175)
Pay homage to Bob Marley at his place of birth and final resting place

RIO GRANDE (p139)
Coast along the majestic Rio Grande on a raft of bamboo poles

DUNN'S RIVER FALLS (p152)
Join hands with a stranger and climb the Caribbean's most famous waterfall

BOSTON BAY (p137)
Relish the flavors of spicy jerk pork and chicken, or hit the beach for the island's best surfing

FIREFLY (p163)
See what author Noel Coward had in mind when he wrote the word 'swanky'

St Ann's Bay
Ocho Rios
Dunn's River Falls
Oracabessa
Port Maria
St Mary
Annotto Bay
Palmetto Bay
Highgate
Moneague
Buff Bay
Orange Bay
Hope Bay
Port Antonio
Boston Bay
Long Bay
Jamaica Channel
Linstead
St Catherine
St Andrew
Portland
Newcastle
Blue Mountains
Blue Mountain Peak (2256m)
John Crow Mountains
Kensington
Spanish Town
May Pen
KINGSTON
Kingston Harbour
Hagley Gap
St Thomas
Plantain Garden River
Holland Bay
Port Royal
Norman Manley International Airport
Cow Bay
Morant Bay
Morant Point
Portland Bight
Portland Point
Salt Island Creek
CARIBBEAN SEA

BLUE MOUNTAIN PEAK (p119)
Hit the trail in the dark of night to scale Jamaica's highest peak by sunrise

BOB MARLEY MUSEUM (p79)
Take the pulse of Kingston at this museum devoted to Jamaica's most revered contemporary hero

PORT ROYAL (p97)
Walk the streets that wicked pirates once strode

LEGEND
Primary Road
Secondary Road
Tertiary Road
0 — 20 km
0 — 12 miles

On the Road

RICHARD KOSS Coordinating Author

My love affair with jerk seasoning took me to Walkerswood (p166), where one of the best versions is produced. Here I am pounding its ingredients with a pestle and growing hungrier by the moment. I like this photo because you can see my car, which spent the previous day in a repair shop in St Ann's Bay.

MY FAVORITE TRIP

I'd kick off in Kingston (p67), taking in the Bob Marley Museum and a sound-system jam, then spend a few recuperative days hiking in the Blue Mountains (p111). Descending, I'd make my way north to Robin's Bay (p143), the most unspoiled part of the island, to follow a trail with a bush-medicine doctor. From there, I'd head for Portland, basing myself in Boston Bay (p137), where – when not savoring the island's best jerk chicken – I'd go rafting on the Rio Grande and caving in the river's valley. On the way back to Kingston, I'd make the trek out to the Morant Point Lighthouse (p122), the island's easternmost point.

Robin's Bay
Boston Bay
Blue Mountain Peak
Rio Grande
Kingston
Morant Point

ABOUT THE AUTHOR

Ever since he first saw *The Harder They Come*, Richard dreamed of becoming a 'rude boy.' And although the prospect of life as a Jamaican gangster lost its appeal over time, Richard's infatuation with the island and all things Jamaican grew. A collector of vintage reggae, an aficionado of rum and an ardent lover of jerk (some might call him a jerk lover), he leapt at the opportunity to cover Jamaica. A native New Yorker, Richard has also worked on Lonely Planet's *New England* and *Caribbean Islands* guides.

CLIMBING DUNN'S RIVER FALLS

It's probably dangerous and it's touristy as hell, but the climb up Dunn's River Falls (p152) in Ocho Rios is deservedly popular. Starting at the bottom of the falls, you, your trusty local guide and a dozen or so strangers conquer the cascade hand-in-hand, slipping, sliding and squealing your way to the top of the falls. The waterfall is stunning, and the cool water and dense jungle-y shade offer relief from the Caribbean heat. The biggest highlight, though, was meeting our excellent guide, who was so calm and reassuring that even the scariest sections seemed fun!

Janet Brunckhorst, traveler, Australia

4

GREG JOHNSTON

THE WILD SOUTH COAST

The south coast (p246) is where you really get off the beaten track. Trek the tangled mangrove forests that teem with wildlife, cool off in natural swimming holes or retreat to the undulating hills of the peaceful central highlands.

Anne Davis, traveler, Canada

5

JERRY ALEXANDER

HOLGER LEUE

6

A STAGE SHOW IN BLACK RIVER

Christmas sees an outbreak of outdoor dancehall shows (p62), with all-star lineups taking the stage for marathon concerts across the island. I went to one in Black River (p250), at the invitation of a local.

The show took place in a field, and there must have been several thousand people in attendance. Some of the biggest names played – Bounty Killer, Tyrus Riley, Capleton, Sizzla, Ninja Man – in addition to local acts. Fireworks went off, flares were fired (some landing very close to the stage) and the air was suffused with the smell of ganja. It was hard to stand for so long, but harder to sit, as each new set recharged the crowd. At one point, I looked across the field and was impressed by how bright the fireworks had made the sky – only to realize it was the sun coming up.

At 6am, Beenie Man, the headliner, came on stage. We lasted through half an hour before finally leaving. The show might still be going on.

Richard Koss, Lonely Planet author

JERK SEASONINGS AT WALKERSWOOD

Jerk – Jamaica's great culinary gift to the world – is all over the island. It drenches meats and seafood at roadside shacks and insinuates its piquancy into elaborate dishes at upscale fusion restaurants. But if you want to know just how the seasoning is made, Jamaicans are cagey. They each have a special recipe, and it wouldn't be special anymore if they told you.

Walkerswood (p166) reveals all. On a sunny November day, I toured a small farmer's co-op there and saw how they grow and gather 14 different spices, including pimento (allspice), nutmeg, cinnamon and the tongue-scorching Scotch bonnet pepper, then grind them in a wooden bowl with a pestle (best part of the tour – they let you have a go pulverizing your own mix) to make the seasoning. After that, I visited the factory where it's converted into a variety of marinades to be sold all over the world. Anything this delicious is meant to be shared.

Richard Koss, Lonely Planet author

7

JERRY ALEX

JON DAVISON

8 PORT ANTONIO

Many think it's one of the loveliest ports in the world; it attracts the beautiful and the famous, but it's still a sleepy little place to wander in at your own leisurely pace, watching the color and life of Jamaica unfold before your eyes. The world will discover Portie (p124) one day; drop by before that happens.

Anne Davis, traveler, Canada

JAMAICAN FOOD & DRINK

Jamaica might not strike you as a dining destination, but there are some serious culinary highlights to be enjoyed (p42). Jerk fish and Red Stripe beer are a grand lunch, and rum is de rigueur, but it's your breakfast coffee that will make your heart sing. Freshly ground, expertly brewed Blue Mountain coffee is one of Jamaica's greatest joys. Grab a souvenir pack to take home – and while you're at it, pick up a bottle of duty-free vanilla essence. It's nothing short of sensational; my chocolate-chip cookies have never been better!

Janet Brunckhorst, traveler, Australia

9

JERRY ALEX

Contents

Regional Map Contents

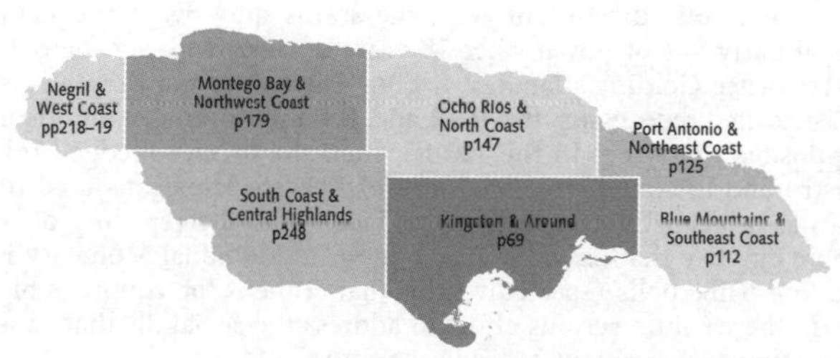

Destination Jamaica

Despite its location almost smack in the center of the Caribbean Sea, the island of Jamaica doesn't blend in easily with the rest of the Caribbean archipelago. To be sure, it boasts the same addictive sun rays, sugary sands and pampered resort-life as most of the other islands, but it is also set apart historically and culturally.

Nowhere else in the Caribbean is the connection to Africa as keenly felt. Kingston was the major nexus in the New World for the barbaric triangular trade that brought slaves from Africa and carried sugar and rum to Europe, and the Maroons (runaways who took to the hills of Cockpit Country and the Blue Mountains) safeguarded many of the African traditions – and introduced jerk seasoning to Jamaica's singular cuisine. St Ann's Bay's Marcus Garvey founded the back-to-Africa movement of the 1910s and '20s; Rastafarianism took up the call a decade later, and reggae furnished the beat in the 1960s and '70s. Little wonder many Jamaicans claim a stronger affinity for Africa than for neighboring Caribbean islands.

FAST FACTS

Population: 2,780,200

Area: 10,992 sq km

Length of coastline: 1022km

GDP (per head): US$4600

Inflation: 5.8%

Unemployment: 11.3%

Average annual rainfall: 78in

Number of orchid species found only on the island: 73 (there are more than 200 overall)

Amount of rum produced annually: 50 million liters

And less wonder that today's visitors will appreciate their trip to Jamaica all the more if they embrace the island's unique character. In addition to the inherent 'African-ness' of its population, Jamaica boasts the world's best coffee, world-class reefs for diving, offbeat bush-medicine hiking tours, congenial fishing villages, pristine waterfalls, cosmopolitan cities, wetlands harboring endangered crocodiles and manatees, unforgettable sunsets – in short, enough variety to comprise many utterly distinct vacations.

As Jamaica's largest industry, tourism reveals a great deal about the forces at play here. Some of the country's biggest assets – its glorious beaches and waterfalls, for example – are facing serious challenges of survival. Sewage pours into the coastal waters of all the major resort towns while the concerns of local communities are often ignored. Profits hightail it out of the country to feed the bottom line of foreign consortia. Many hotel workers live in degrading conditions, but are still expected to smile for guests; quite a few will tell you that they are lucky to have a low-paying job at all. As more and more tourists come, the resort towns sink deeper into urban blight. This is more than irony: it's a potent recipe for social unrest and the accelerated decline of Jamaica's most important industry. The government continues to offer reactionary 'solutions' to tourism's woes, while at the same time approving ever more large-scale resorts. Fortunately, sustainable tourism is beginning to make inroads, and while the impact is still very small, there are grounds for guarded optimism.

In 2007, public discontent with the status quo swept the People's National Party out of power after 18 years of rule. However, new Prime Minister Bruce Golding's Jamaica Labour Party does not present a stark contrast to its predecessor; the PNP and JLP are no longer the ideological opposites they were in the 1970s, when the former pledged fidelity to Castro and the latter professed love of Reagan. Jamaicans tend to see politics as a localized arena, in which issues like the repaving of roads are more emotive than, say, the repaying of International Monetary Fund loans. And while polls repeatedly show that crime is the country's biggest concern, there's little serious effort to address the social ills that cause it, and no popular movement to bring them to the fore.

Behind this backdrop of governmental neglect and popular resignation is a country infused with pride in its unique history, stunning landscape and influential culture. All this is the 'real Jamaica'.

Getting Started

Of course, Jamaican vacations are as varied as the island itself, and there are numerous ways to visit. You can leave little to chance by booking a week in an all-inclusive resort, or you can leave *everything* to chance, traveling from town to town by route taxi, and choosing your lodgings and the next destination as you go along.

You can lead a carefree lifestyle at a secluded retreat, enjoy the stylish luxury of a boutique hotel or stay in a brightly painted, candlelit shack with no electricity and a refreshing outdoor cool-water shower. You'll rarely have trouble finding suitable accommodation on any budget.

Good Jamaican cooking can be had for economical prices just about everywhere you go. The country's fertile soil produces excellent and plentiful vegetables and a seemingly endless array of tropical fruits. If you love fish and seafood you'll be in heaven. In the resort areas, you'll find cosmopolitan fare and some 'nouvelle' Jamaican chefs who are pushing the culinary envelope.

If you don't like reggae music (you can't escape it!), can't cope with poverty or power outages and hate being approached by hustlers, then Jamaica is definitely not for you. To savor Jamaica properly, to appreciate what it is that makes people passionate about the place, it pays to enjoy the idiosyncratic. To rest content here you have to 'get' Jamaica, to take the punches in your stride. If you can handle that, if you like travel with a raw edge, you'll love it.

WHEN TO GO

Jamaica is a year-round destination, though there are seasonal differences to consider. Weather-wise, temperature isn't an important factor: winter is usually warm by day and mild to cool by night, and summer months are hot. The rainy season extends from May to November, with peaks in May, June, October and November. Rain usually falls for short periods (normally in the late afternoon), and it's quite possible to enjoy sunshine for most of your visit during these months. However, note that in Portland parish, it can rain for days on end.

See Climate Charts (p277) for more information.

Tourism's high, or 'winter,' season runs from early-December to mid-April, when hotel prices are highest. Many hotels charge peak-season rates during Christmas and Easter.

DON'T LEAVE HOME WITHOUT...

- your passport: new regulations require visitors from the USA to carry one
- sunscreen: it's crazily expensive in Jamaica, and it's not widely available outside resort areas
- sports sandals: all-terrain all-weather sandals are essential footwear on beach and trail (but not at the disco, please!)
- hot-weather clothing: choose light, quick-dry fabrics to help you cope with Jamaica's sometimes unrelenting heat and humidity
- snorkeling gear: a pain to carry on the plane, but great to have on the beach (rentals are expensive and often of poor quality)
- a flashlight (torch) for those not-so-well-lit Jamaican streets, and the occasional cave
- an extra pair of sunglasses to wear at the sound-system jam.

COSTS & MONEY

How much you spend depends on your sense of style. Even hard-core budget travelers will need to spend at least US$35 a day. Roadside stalls and budget restaurants sell patties for less than US$1 and jerk pork and other local meals for as little as US$2. A hand of bananas or half a dozen mangoes will cost about US$1. More touristy restaurants, however, can be expensive, as many of the ingredients they use are imported: expect to pay at least US$10 per person and, for the finest restaurants, as much as US$60.

Car rentals begin at about US$45 a day for the smallest vehicle. Public transport is inordinately cheap, although the tourist taxis can get very expensive (usually US$8 minimum for even the shortest journey).

The budget accommodations cost US$20 or more, even for spartan conditions. Midrange hotels range from about US$60 to US$150, while luxury resorts can charge US$300 or more. All-inclusive hotels can offer tremendous bargains, as everything you consume or participate in is included in room rates.

To save money, visit in 'summer,' or low season (mid-April to mid-December), when hotel prices plummet and airfares are often reduced.

HOW MUCH?

Taxi from Montego Bay's Donald Sangster International Airport to the 'Hip Strip' US$8

Guided snorkeling trip US$30

Rio Grande raft trip US$60

Fresh fish in a touristy restaurant US$12

Fresh fish in a local restaurant US$5

TRAVEL LITERATURE

There are numerous excellent books about Jamaica's eminently rich cultural, historical and natural landscape. See the History and Culture chapters for more book suggestions.

Several memoirs and novels by foreigners seek to capture the essence of life on the island. Swashbuckling Hollywood hero Errol Flynn, who lived in Jamaica for many years, recalls his colorful experiences in his autobiography *My Wicked, Wicked Ways*. Anthony Winckler's *Going Home to Teach* tells of the novelist's time in Jamaica as a teacher during an epoch of anti-white sentiment in the tension-filled late 1970s. Russell Banks' *The Book of Jamaica*

INTRODUCTION TO JAMAICA

Montego Bay Also called 'MoBay,' the principal gateway to Jamaica and the main tourist center, with several public beaches and a good choice of hotels and all-inclusive resorts. A fistful of interesting historic sites lies close at hand, as do bamboo-raft trips and, for hardy hikers, Cockpit Country.

Negril Jamaica's liveliest resort, with the longest (and one of the most stunning) beaches on the island. Live reggae shows, spectacular sunsets and a let-your-hair-down attitude make this a favorite of budget and college-age travelers. Negril is also renowned for scuba diving and water sports.

Ocho Rios Also called 'Ochi,' the main destination for cruise ships. The town itself is unappealing despite its two beaches, but it's a good base for exploring Dunn's River Falls, several botanical gardens and other attractions within a few minutes' drive.

Runaway Bay This is a secluded resort midway between MoBay and Ochi, famous for its coral reefs. It has nice beaches, but the one-street town itself has no appeal whatsoever, and tourist infrastructure – and nightlife – is minimal.

Port Antonio Secluded at the lush northeastern tip of Jamaica, a center for bamboo-raft trips and hiking in the Rio Grande Valley. Its highlights are its fully staffed, upscale villas and deluxe resorts tucked into coves east of town.

South Coast Appealing for its isolation and a lifestyle that still revolves around fishing. The best all-around destination is Treasure Beach, an in-vogue spot for travelers seeking an offbeat experience. Near at hand lie the Great Morass (a swamp area good for crocodile-spotting safaris), the YS Falls, Appleton Rum Estate and Lover's Leap.

Kingston The nation's bustling capital, more of a business locale than a tourism center. However, it *is* the center of island culture, with museums, art galleries, important historic buildings and a pulsing nightlife.

Blue Mountains Rising east of Kingston and offering an idyllic escape from the package-tour syndrome. The Blue Mountains-John Crow National Park has well-developed hiking trails.

Mandeville A historic agricultural and residential town in the cool upland interior. It appeals to visitors who shun the beach resorts in favor of birding, scenic mountain drives, hiking and interaction with local families.

TOP 10

JAMAICA
•Kingston

MOST ATMOSPHERIC LODGING

The following hotels and guest houses, spanning all price ranges, share one key ingredient: ambience.

1. Strawberry Hill (p114)
2. Jake's Place (p271)
3. River Lodge (p144)
4. Shafston Estate Great House (p249)
5. Great Huts (p137)
6. Richmond Hill Inn (p195)
7. Zion Country (p139)
8. Banana Shout (p234)
9. Caves (p235)
10. High Hope Estate (p169)

OUTDOOR PURSUITS

If you've seen only the beaches, you haven't seen Jamaica. The following are your best bets for adventures in 'de bush.'

1. Climbing Blue Mountain Peak (p119)
2. Exploring the Black River Great Morass (p253)
3. Diving and snorkeling near Montego Bay (p189)
4. Caving in the Cockpits (p213)
5. Hiking in the Rio Grande Valley (p140)
6. Biking the hills of Negril (p226)
7. Rafting the Martha Brae (p205)
8. Biking down from the high Blue Mountains (p113)
9. Riding a horse into the sea (p153)
10. Fishing at Treasure Beach (p269)

tells the story of an American expatriate college professor who delves into Jamaica and Maroon culture of Cockpit Country with unexpected results. A perceptive look at the rise of the island's tourist industry is afforded by Frank Fonda Taylor's *To Hell with Paradise*.

Understanding Jamaican Patois by Emilie Adams provides an understanding of English as it is spoken in Jamaica, and Cassidy and RB LePage's *Dictionary of Jamaican English* is the definitive lexicon on Jamaican patois.

Macmillan Caribbean (in the UK ☎ 1865 405841; www.macmillan-caribbean.com), a division of Macmillan Press, publishes a wide range of books about the Caribbean.

INTERNET RESOURCES

Afflicted Yard (http://afflictedyard.com) Edgy culture site with entertainment listings.

Dancehall Reggae (www.dancehallreggae.com) The place to go for *the* latest on the island's music scene.

Insiders Jamaica (www.insidersjamaica.com) Tourist-board site focusing on inns and villas in Jamaica.

Jamaica Gleaner (www.jamaica-gleaner.com) Best news source from the island's most reliable newspaper.

Jamaica National Heritage Trust (www.jnht.com) Excellent guide to Jamaica's history and heritage.

Jamaica Yellow Pages (www.jamaicayp.com) Handy online presentation of the Jamaican phone directory.

See p281 for information about getting online in Jamaica.

Jamaicans (www.jamaicans.com) Eclectic and informative site seeking to reflect the Jamaican experience.

LonelyPlanet.com (www.lonelyplanet.com) Succinct summaries on travel in Jamaica, plus the popular Thorn Tree bulletin board, travel news and a complete online store.

Visit Jamaica (www.visitjamaica.com) The tourist board's presentation of Jamaica to travelers, with plenty of destination, attractions and lodging information.

What's On Jamaica (www.whatsonjamaica.com) Calendar-based event and entertainment listings.

Events Calendar

Having given the rest of the world reggae, jerk seasoning and the finest rum on earth, Jamaicans have much to celebrate, and they certainly do… mainly with reggae, jerk and rum. From exuberant islandwide bashes to local fiestas, Jamaica is home to a large variety of events, and while most are centered on the tourist meccas of Negril, Montego Bay and Ocho Rios, some of the more intriguing yam festivals and African-heritage celebrations occur off the beaten track. We've compiled a calendar of the major events, but you should also check for local affairs on the radio and street posters, or consult the Jamaican Tourist Board (www.visitjamaica.com) for the island's lesser-known fiestas.

JANUARY

ACCOMPONG MAROON FESTIVAL 6 Jan

This spirited festival, held on the anniversary of the Maroons' 1739 treaty with the English, celebrates the legacy of the proud runaway slaves in Cockpit Country.

AIR JAMAICA JAZZ & BLUES FESTIVAL late Jan

Locally and internationally acclaimed artists perform a variety of musical genres (not just jazz and blues) in a splendid outdoor setting near Rose Hall, Montego Bay. See www.airjamaicajazzandblues.com.

FEBRUARY

BOB MARLEY'S BIRTHDAY CELEBRATION 6 Feb

Even if you have only a casual interest in Bob Marley, you'll find it hard to resist this celebration, held in Nine Mile, of the birth of the great Tuff Gong.

FAT TYRE FESTIVAL 2nd weekend of Feb

Relocated from Negril to Ocho Rios after a one-year absence, this rip-roaring mountain-biking race and festival is not for the weak of heart.

FI WI SINTING 3rd weekend of Feb

A moving celebration of Jamaica's African heritage with music, crafts and food, held in Buff Bay. See www.fiwisinting.com for more.

PINEAPPLE CUP MONTEGO BAY RACE 1st week of Feb

This is ocean racing's most complete test…a 1290km race held biennially on the odd year in Montego Bay. It's also an excuse for four days of partying. Check out www.montegobayrace.com for details.

MARCH

JAMAICAN CARNIVAL Easter week

Not as renowned as Trinidad's bacchanalian fest, Jamaica's version draws thousands of costumed revelers to the streets of Kingston and Ochi. Head to www.jamaicacarnaval.com for more information.

TRELAWNY YAM FESTIVAL Easter Mon

In Albert Town: yam-balancing races, best-dressed goat and donkey, the crowning of the Yam King and Queen – how can you resist?

APRIL

JAMAICA BEACHFEST mid-Apr

This massive spring-break celebration lures thousands of North Americans to Negril for live music, parties and booze – and the uninhibited behavior it arouses.

MAY

CALABASH INTERNATIONAL LITERARY FESTIVAL 3rd week of May

This highly innovative literary festival draws creative voices from near and far to Treasure Beach. Head to www.calabashfestival.org for more information.

JUNE

OCHO RIOS JAZZ FESTIVAL mid-Jun

One of the world's top jazz extravaganzas, the eight-day Ocho Rios Jazz Festival draws some of the biggest names in jazz and stages concerts under the stars. Tours to this event including transport, tickets and lodging are offered by It's Your Tour (www.itsyourtour.com). Check out www.ochoriosjazz.com for further details.

JULY

NATIONAL DANCE THEATER COMPANY'S SEASON OF DANCE
One of the year's cultural highlights, Jamaica's premier dance troupe puts on a display of modern interpretive dance; held across the month in Kingston.

PORTLAND JERK FESTIVAL 1st Sun of Jul
A food festival in Port Antonio for folks in love with the hot and spicy.

INTERNATIONAL DANCEHALL QUEEN CONTEST last weekend of Jul
This raucous extravaganza attracts dancehall fanatics the world over to Montego Bay for a contest that ends with the crowning of the world's dancehall queen.

REGGAE SUMFEST last week of Jul
The mama of all reggae festivals, in Montego Bay, brings the top acts to the masses for this four-day affair. See www.reggaesumfeset.com for more.

AUGUST

DENBIGH AGRICULTURAL SHOW 1st week of Aug
From gargantuan yams to gussied-up livestock, Jamaica's farming finest is on display in May Pen.

APPLETON TREASURE ISLAND 1st weekend of Aug
This major beach party in Negril is well-oiled by rum from the island's famous distillery.

SEPTEMBER

MONTEGO BAY MARLIN TOURNAMENT last week of Sep
Big fish, big party.

OCTOBER

JAMAICA COFFEE FESTIVAL 1st week of Oct
As if you need an excuse to get jacked up on Jamaica's world-famous coffee! Held in Kingston. Thousands of coffee lovers converge on the spacious lawns of Devon House in the first week of October to slurp up Jamaica's world-famous coffee in an orgy of beverages, liqueurs, ice cream, cigars and classic Jamaican chow.

PORT ROYAL SEAFOOD FESTIVAL 3rd Mon of Oct
A rollicking good time in Port Royal with local vendors selling scrumptious seafood.

NOVEMBER

HARMONY HALL ANNIVERSARY CRAFTS FAIR 26 Nov
Excellent variety and quality crafts in a wonderful setting; in Ocho Rios.

NEGRIL JERK FESTIVAL last Sun of Nov
Jerkmasters from all over the island descend on Negril to show off their fiery wares.

DECEMBER

LTM NATIONAL PANTOMIME Dec – Jan
Irreverent social satire is presented at this annual song-and-dance revue in Kingston. Providing social commentary that may well leave you speechless, the Jamaican take on pantomime is front and center at the Ward Theatre each year from December through January. It continues through to April at the Little Theater.

REGGAE STING Dec – Jan
This annual reggae show/raunchfest in Portmore is regarded by many islanders as the best.

FIREWORKS ON THE WATERFRONT 31 Dec
Ring in the new year on the Kingston waterfront with 100,000 others. Jamaicans travel from across the island to celebrate with fireworks over the harbor and celebratory stage entertainment.

ANNUAL NATIONAL EXHIBITION Dec – Feb
The National Gallery showcases the work of Jamaica's newcomers and old hands at this annual display that's the highpoint of the island's arts season.

Itineraries
CLASSIC ROUTES

NORTH COAST HOLIDAY
Two Weeks/Montego Bay to Ocho Rios

Start in **Montego Bay** (p178), a swirling vortex of tourism. Hit **Doctor's Cave Beach** (p187) for water sports, head downtown to historic **Sam Sharpe Square** (p184), and take to the hills to **Rocklands Bird Feeding Station** (p209).

Heading east, tour **Rose Hall** (p201), or the more authentic **Greenwood Great House** (p201). Take a walking tour of **Falmouth** (p202) for its crumbling Georgian buildings, a night-time boating expedition on the **Glistening Waters** (p205) or a rafting trip on the **Martha Brae River** (p205).

Between Falmouth and Ocho Rios are pretty landscapes and historical sites. Tour the **Green Grotto Caves** (p174), where the Spanish resistance and runaway slaves took refuge. Enjoy excellent scuba diving in **Runaway Bay** (p172). At **Chukka Cove** (p170), choose from tours including horseback rides into the sea.

In **St Ann's Bay**, where Christopher Columbus was marooned for a year, learn the history behind sites such as the **Maima Seville Great House & Heritage Park** (p168) and see the **Columbus and Marcus Garvey monuments** (p168).

In Ocho Rios, climb **Dunn's River Falls** (p152), learn about **reggae music** (p149) and check out the latest art exhibit at **Harmony Hall** (p153) before finishing the day with a sublime dinner in the hall's restaurant.

This 108km trip is perfect for sampling the most popular attractions and activities of the north central coast. You'll get your fill of fun, sun and sand, and there are kid-friendly attractions all along the way.

KINGSTON, BLUE MOUNTAINS & PORTLAND

Three Weeks/Kingston to Manchioneal

Touch down in **Kingston** (p67) for three days of sightseeing, excellent food and rip-roaring nightlife. Don't miss the **National Gallery** (p72) and the fascinating **downtown walking tour** (p82). Take in historic **Devon House** (p78) and lunch at one of Jamaica's famous restaurants, **Norma's on the Terrace** (p90). Whether or not you're a reggae fan, there's much to see at the **Bob Marley Museum** (p79). After hours, enjoy some of the liveliest **nightlife** (p90) in the Caribbean. For a captivating day trip, visit **Port Royal** (p97), the earthquake-shattered former haunt of pirates and privateers.

Those hills looming over the city are calling, so slip into the **Blue Mountains** (p111). Pamper your mind and body at **Strawberry Hill** (p114), one of Jamaica's most excellent hotels, or spend the night in an economical hut perched on the side of a mountain. Enjoy the breathtaking scenery and crisp mountain air from hiking trails in **Blue Mountains–John Crow National Park** (p115). See how the Caribbean's most prized coffee rises from humble beginnings at the **Old Tavern Coffee Estate** (p116). Make an early-morning ascent of **Blue Mountain Peak** (p119), Jamaica's highest mountain, or, if you are truly adventurous, whiz down from the highlands on a **bicycle tour** (p113).

Descend from the Blue Mountains to **Portland parish** (p123), on the prettiest stretch of the north coast. Walk the atmospheric streets of **Port Antonio** (p124), taking lodging in one of the many intimate spots to the east of town in **Drapers** or **Fairy Hill**. Make a foray into the gorgeous **Rio Grande Valley** (p139) for river rafting or hiking. **East of Port Antonio** (p133), you'll find appealing communities with stellar beaches and attractive places to stay. Don't miss **Boston Bay** (p137) for jerk and surf, or **Manchioneal** (p137), a terrific base for visiting Reach Falls.

On this whirlwind adventure you'll experience the extremes of the city, mountains and sea, with an appealing mix of cosmopolitan pursuits, breathtaking high-mountain scenery and classic beach-bumming on stretches of white sand.

ROADS LESS TRAVELED

A TASTE OF COCKPIT COUNTRY

One Week/Falmouth to Albert Town

Explore the once-grand port of **Falmouth** (p202), then leave the coast behind. Spend an afternoon rafting on the **Martha Brae** (p205) or at **Good Hope Estate** (p213), a beautiful great house and working plantation. Enjoy horseback riding, lunch on the terrace and tremendous views.

On narrow roads, travel through cane fields as you start your ascent to **Windsor** (p214). Check into a modest lodge and take a well-earned rest. Wake to the sound of birds, and head off to explore **Windsor Caves** (p214) with a Rastafarian guide, or pay a visit to the **Windsor Great House** (p214) to learn about its environmental protection and bird-banding efforts.

Get ready for some challenging but rewarding **hiking** (p213). From Windsor or Albert Town, you can hire a guide and walk the old military trail connecting Windsor (in the north) with Troy (in the south)…but be ready for some gnarly trails.

Exhausted and exhilarated, head east to Clark's Town, then to **Albert Town** (p215), passing through prime sugarcane country. This part of the journey is less about destinations and activities, and more about just soaking up the scenery. In Albert Town coordinate a **homestay** (p212) with the Southern Trelawny Environmental Agency.

Return to the north coast or continue south to Mandeville or the south coast. It's possible to get around on this tour via route taxi, but you'll get the most out of it by renting a 4WD vehicle.

This wild and woolly 52km backcountry tour suits a temperament that loves mountains, caves and trails at least as much as beaches. You'll be traveling through Jamaica's most rugged country and into its richest ecosystems. Allow one week or longer, depending on how deep you want to go.

EXPLORE THE SOUTHWEST

Two Weeks/Negril to Alligator Pond

Let your hair down – or get it braided – in **Negril** (p217) for a few days, until you've had your fill of peach-colored sunsets and rockin' reggae.

Starting out early, head to **Roaring River Park** (p244) near Savanna-la-Mar for a day of incredible scenery and soaking in turquoise mineral pools. Spend the night in a rustic cottage, or head further down the coast to **Bluefields** (p247), where you'll find comfortable guest houses, an exceptional great house to stay in, and the **mausoleum of reggae star Peter Tosh** (p247).

After a good night's slumber, linger on one of the quiet fishing beaches or continue on to **Black River** (p250), a sleepy port town with interesting historic buildings and vintage hotels. This is the gateway for boat travel into the mangrove swamps of the **Black River Great Morass** (p253), a gorgeous wetlands where crocodile sightings are common.

In the morning head north to **Middle Quarters** (p254) for an unforgettable lunch of pepper shrimp at a crossroads eatery and an afternoon at the lovely **YS Falls** (p256). Wet your whistle at the **Appleton Rum Estate** (p258), then head south to **Treasure Beach** (p267). Check into a hospitable guest house or idiosyncratic boutique hotel and stay awhile in the welcoming embrace of this tight-knit community. Be sure to take a boat trip to one of the planet's coolest watering holes, the **Pelican Bar** (p271), perched on stilts on a sandbar 1km out to sea.

From Treasure Beach, visit **Lover's Leap** (p273) for an astonishing view of the coastlands. Continue along the coast to the fishing village of **Alligator Pond** (p273). Far from packaged tourism, here you can enjoy traditional village life and unspoiled scenery at its best. You'll also enjoy a delicious seafood feast at a truly extraordinary beachside restaurant, **Little Ochie** (p274).

This 152km, two-week tour has it all. Start with a few days of maximum repose in Negril, then slip into the less touristy, wide-open lands of the southwestern coast. You'll pass through fishing villages and a quiet port town, travel by boat into the Great Morass, enjoy celebrated waterfalls and get to know the locals.

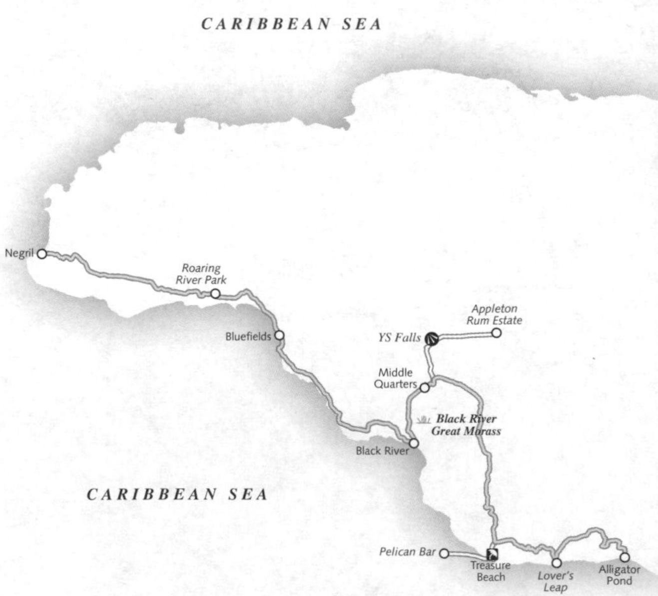

TAILORED TRIPS

HONORING THE ANCESTORS

Black history is *the* history of Jamaica. This itinerary will shed light on the horrors of slavery, as well as the resistance and triumph of African slaves.

Start in **Montego Bay** (p178), taking time to visit the **Museum of St James** (p184). With great poignancy, it details how Sam Sharpe counseled fellow slaves to refuse to work at Christmas in 1831, sparking the Christmas Rebellion.

Traveling east, visit the port town of **Falmouth** (p202), where human beings were once offloaded from ships and sold at auction. Traveling up into the hills, visit the beautiful **Good Hope Estate** (p213), remembering that many of the stately buildings here were built by slave labor.

Climb further into Cockpit Country to **Accompong**, where the Leeward Maroons, a band of runaway slaves led by Cujo, fought so effectively against the British in a protracted insurgency. See the nearby **Peace Cave**, where the 1739 treaty granting the Maroons autonomy was signed.

On the coast again, move into Portland parish and up into the **Rio Grande Valley** (p139), home to the Windward Maroons. Their leader Nanny's contribution is honored in **Moore Town** (p141).

Travel around the eastern tip of Jamaica to **Morant Bay** (p121), where National Hero Paul Bogle led the Morant Bay Rebellion of 1865.

Conclude your trip in Kingston at **National Heroes Park** (p75), where you can pay your respects at the grave of Black-consciousness leader Marcus Garvey.

IN THE FOOTSTEPS OF A LION

Begin your Bob Marley pilgrimage where it all started, in **Kingston** (p67). Visit the **Bob Marley Museum** (p79), where he lived and recorded at the height of his career, and the **'government yard in Trench Town'** (p76), where he lived as a child. Visit **Tuff Gong Recording Studios** (p77), started by Marley and now run by his son Ziggy. Browse record stores and dub-plate studios on **Orange St** (p93). If you've got the stamina, check out a **sound-system party** (see the boxed text, p92).

Hit the road for **Ocho Rios** (p146), stopping at **Reggae Beach** (p160) on the way; if you're in luck there may be a show that night. In Ochi follow the trajectory of reggae music at the **Reggae Xplosion** (p149) museum. Head into the hills on a pilgrimage to **Nine Mile** (p175), Bob Marley's birthplace and final resting place.

East of Montego Bay, visit the **Bob Marley Experience** (p200) for Jamaica's best collection of reggae t-shirts and a documentary film. If you've timed it right, enjoy the world's best reggae festival, **Reggae Sumfest** (p18). Hightail it to **Negril** (p239), where smokin' live reggae is featured nearly every night. Finally, weave your way down to Belmont in Westmoreland to pay respects to Marley's fellow Wailer at the **Peter Tosh Mausoleum** (p247).

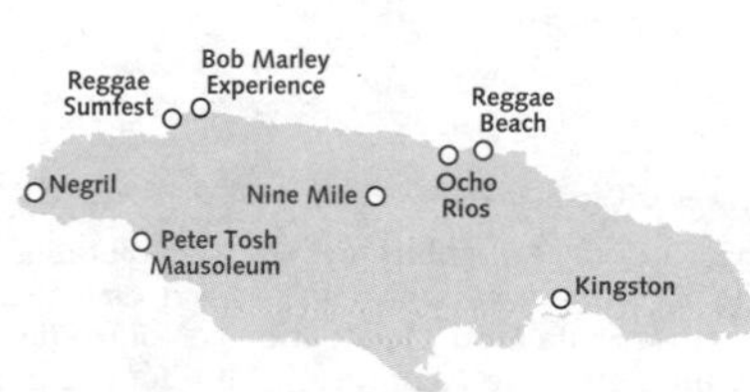

History

> Out of the past of fire and suffering and neglect, the human spirit has survived – patient and strong, quick to anger, quick to forgive, lusty and vigorous, but with deep reserves of loyalty and love and a deep capacity for steadiness under stress and for joy in all the things that make life good and blessed.
>
> *Norman Manley, Jamaica's first prime minister*

Ever since the Spanish conquered the peaceful Arawaks in the early 16th century, Jamaica has endured a painful history tinged with an undercurrent of violence. Yet it's also the story of epic resistance to tyranny and a passion for freedom. It's this passion, and the perseverance of the Jamaican people that have made the island and its inimitable culture so vital.

XAYMACA

An Amerindian group, the Arawaks (also known as the Tainos), settled the island around AD 700 to 800. The Arawaks are believed to have originated in the Guianas of South America perhaps 2000 years earlier. After developing seafaring skills, they gradually moved north through the Caribbean island chain.

The Arawaks believed that, after death, the soul went to a joyful land called Coyaba, a place of perpetual feasting and dancing.

Once settled, they made their homes in conical thatched shelters. Their communal villages were made up of several family clans, which were headed by a *cacique* (chief). Subsistence farmers to the core, the women gathered food, while the men tilled the fields, hunted and fished. Jamaica's fertile soils yielded yams, maize, beans, spices and cassava, which the Arawaks leached of poison and baked into cakes and fermented into beer. The Arawaks called the island 'Xaymaca,' meaning 'land of wood and water.'

Having neither the wheel nor a written language, the Arawaks did not use beasts of burden or metals (except for crude gold ornamentation). They honed skills as potters, carvers, weavers and boat builders. (Columbus was impressed with the scale of their massive canoes hewn from silk cotton trees.) They were particularly adept at spinning and weaving cotton into clothing and hammocks – the latter an Amerindian invention.

For recreation, the Arawaks got fired up with maize alcohol, smoked dried leaves and snorted a powdered drug through a meter-long tube they called a *tabaco.* They worshipped a variety of gods believed to control rain, sun, wind and hurricanes, and who were represented by *zemes,* idols of humans or animals.

TIMELINE

1494

Christopher Columbus first lands on Jamaica, which he names Santa Jago – it later becomes his personal property.

1503

Columbus is irresistibly drawn to Jamaica, returning for the fourth time, convinced he can forge a passage to Asia. However, his return is disastrous. His decrepit ships are ruined and he and his party become stranded.

1517

Jamaica's brutal African slave trade is begun by the Spanish, who enslave West Africans to do their bidding on the island in place of the Arawaks, whose population has been decimated by European disease and appalling treatment.

COLUMBUS & SPANISH SETTLEMENT

Jamaica's first tourist was none other than Christopher Columbus, who landed on the island in 1494 on the second of his four voyages to the New World. Anchoring offshore in Bahía Santa Gloria (modern-day St Ann's Bay), Columbus sailed down the coast to a horseshoe-shaped cove (Discovery Bay), where he had his men fire crossbows at a group of Arawaks that failed to welcome him. He also set a fierce dog – the first the Arawaks had ever seen – on them, establishing the vicious tone of future colonial occupation. Columbus claimed the island for Spain and christened it Santo Jago. The Arawaks soon reappeared with peace offerings and feasted the strange newcomers throughout their brief stay.

On May 9 Columbus sailed on to El Golfo de Buen Tiempo (the Gulf of Good Weather, now Montego Bay) and then on to Cuba. He returned later that year and explored the west and south coasts before again departing.

Like so many later visitors to Jamaica, Columbus could not keep away. In 1503 he returned on his fourth and final voyage, still hell-bent on finding that elusive passage to Asia. Unfortunately, his worm-eaten ships were falling apart. He abandoned one, the *Gallega,* off Panama. Another sank off Hispaniola. Later, as he headed back to Hispaniola, storms forced him to seek shelter in Jamaica and he barely made it to Bahía Santa Gloria. The two remaining vessels were so worm-riddled that Columbus and his 120 crew were forced to abandon ship and watch both vessels sink.

Jamaica National Heritage Trust (www.jnht.com) provides a guide to Jamaica's history and heritage.

The hapless explorers spent almost a year marooned and suffered desperately from disease and malnutrition. Finally, two officers paddled a canoe 240km to Hispaniola, where they chartered a ship to rescue the now broken explorer and his men. On June 29, 1504, Columbus sailed away (see the boxed text, p170).

Though he'd had enough of the New World to never again leave the Old, Jamaica became Columbus' personal property. When he died in 1506, it passed to his son Diego, whose descendants carry the honorary title of Marquis of Jamaica to this day. Diego appointed as governor one of his father's lieutenants, Don Juan de Esquivel, who established a capital called Nueva Sevilla (New Seville) near present-day Ocho Rios.

From their arrival the Spaniards had exacted tribute from the Arawaks, whom they enslaved and killed off through hard labor and ill-treatment. European diseases decimated the Amerindians too, for they had no resistance to the common cold, influenza and such deadly European exports as syphilis. By Esquivel's time, the Indian population had been virtually wiped out, and to replenish the labor pool, the Spaniards began importing slaves from West Africa to Jamaica, the first arriving in 1517.

In 1534 the Spanish uprooted and created a new settlement on the south coast, Villa de la Vega (Spanish Town). However, the Spaniards never

1655

The English capture Jamaica from the Spanish, who retreat to Cuba.

1670

At the Treaty of Madrid, the Spanish relinquish all claim to the island, ceding Jamaica (as well as the Cayman Islands) to the English. Both nations agree to cease trading in each others territories.

1692

Port Royal slides into the harbor after an earthquake. More than 2000 people die.

developed their Jamaican colony and it languished as a post for provisioning ships en route between Spain and Central America.

THE ENGLISH INVASION

In 1654, Oliver Cromwell, Lord Protector of England, devised his ill-fated 'Grand Western Design' to destroy the Spanish trade monopoly and amass English holdings in the Caribbean. He assembled a fleet, jointly led by Admiral William Penn and General Robert Venables, to conquer the Spanish-held Caribbean islands. The ill-equipped expedition was repulsed in April 1655 by Spanish forces on Hispaniola.

David Howard's *Kingston* is an engaging exploration of the capital's history, from Spanish to modern times.

Deciding on an easier target, Penn and Venables then sailed to weakly defended Jamaica. On May 10, 1655, this expeditionary force of 38 ships landed 8000 troops near Villa de la Vega. The Spaniards retreated north over the mountains, from where they set sail to Cuba.

In a rare act of benevolence, the departing Spanish freed their slaves – encouraging them to harass the English, who promptly destroyed the Spanish capital. These *cimarrones* (wild runaways) took to the hills, where they mastered the tactics of guerrilla warfare and fiercely defended their freedom. A small band of Spanish loyalists under General Cristobal Ysassi also fought a guerrilla war against the English with less success. The decisive battle at Rio Bueno (outside Ocho Rios) in 1660 was won by the English under Colonel Edward D'Oyley.

In December 1656, some 1600 English arrived to settle the area around Port Morant near the eastern tip of Jamaica. The region proved too swampy: within a year, three-quarters of the settlers had succumbed to disease. Other settlers fared better and a viable economy began to evolve.

By 1662, there were 4000 colonists on the island, including exiled felons as well as impoverished Scots and Welshmen, who arrived as indentured laborers. Settlement hastened as profits began to accrue from cocoa, coffee and sugarcane production.

THE AGE OF THE BUCCANEERS

Throughout the 17th century, Britain was constantly at war with France, Spain or Holland. The English sponsored privateers to capture enemy vessels, raid their settlements and contribute their plunder to the Crown's coffers. These privateers, or buccaneers (from *boucan*, a French word for smoked meat, of which the privateers were fond), evolved as a motley band of seafaring miscreants, political refugees and escaped criminals who decided their ill-gotten gains were better off in their own pockets. They formed the Confederacy of the Brethren of the Coast, committed to a life of piracy. Gradually they replaced their motley vessels with captured ships and grew into a powerful and ruthless force, feared throughout the Antilles – even by their English sponsors.

1693

Kingston is officially founded. Before that it had been known as Hog Crawle on account of the small pig-raising settlement that had emerged there since the arrival of English settlers in 1655.

1700

There are more than five slaves for every English settler on Jamaica. The practise of slavery creates enormous economic bounty for English at terrible cost to the slaves, who share none of Jamaica's new riches.

1814

Jamaican sugar production peaks at 34 million pounds. During the latter half of the eighteenth century and the first half of the nineteenth, Jamaica is the world's largest produces of sugar.

Initially, the newly appointed governor of Jamaica, Sir Thomas Modyford, joined with the Spanish in attempts to suppress the buccaneers. But the outbreak of the Second Dutch War against Holland and Spain in March 1664 forced England to rethink its policy. Modyford contrived for the Brethren to defend Jamaica. Port Royal and Kingston Harbour became their base. Their numbers swelled astronomically, and within a decade Port Royal was Jamaica's largest city – a den of iniquity and prosperity.

With England at peace with Spain, buccaneers were now regarded merely as pirates. Mother Nature lent a hand in their suppression when a massive earthquake struck Port Royal on June 7, 1692, toppling much of the city into the sea. More than 2000 people – one-third of the Port Royal population – perished.

Port Royal Project (http://nautarch.tamu.edu/portroyal) is a site that offers a fascinating look at the work of maritime archaeologists in the submerged historic neighborhoods of Port Royal, which have lain underwater since the great earthquake of 1692.

THE SLAVE TRADE

Meanwhile, Jamaica's English planters grew immensely wealthy from sugar, and English merchants from the sordid market in slaves – whose lot marked a brutal contrast. Wrenched from the Ashanti, Cormorante, Mandingo and Yoruba tribes of West Africa, they were bought from African slave traders

A PIRATE HALL OF INFAMY

Even after they were forced out of Port Royal following the 1692 earthquake, pirates contributed to the colony's problems, plundering ships of all nations and coming ashore to raid the sugar plantations sprouting all over Jamaica. Several pirates chased booty across the Spanish Main, rising to infamy for their cruelty, daring and, occasionally, their colorful ways.

The most flamboyant was undoubtedly Blackbeard (whose real name was Edward Teach). This brutal giant terrorized foes by going into battle wearing flaming fuses in his matted beard and hair. Do not try this at home.

A ruthless young Welshman, Henry Morgan, established his supremacy and guided the buccaneers to their pinnacle. Morgan pillaged Spanish towns throughout the Americas before crowning an illustrious career by sacking Panama City. Eventually Morgan became lieutenant governor of Jamaica and was ordered to suppress privateering. Even so, he caroused in Port Royal, where he succumbed to dropsy (edema) and was entombed at Port Royal in 1688.

'Calico Jack' Rackham, although equally ruthless, became known more for his soft spot for calico underwear...and rum. The latter weakness played a role during his capture in 1720 (see boxed text, p220), when, in the midst of his revels in Bloody Bay near Negril, he was subdued by English soldiers. 'Calico Jack' was hanged the next day, his body hung on an iron frame on a small cay off Port Royal (the cay is still called Rackham's Cay).

In the course of Rackham's capture, the English were surprised to discover that two bloodthirsty, machete-wielding comrades of his were actually women in disguise. Mary Read and Anne Bonney were tried by an admiralty court and, like Rackham, sentenced to hang. The two women warriors got a reprieve due to the fact that both were pregnant. Bonney was later pardoned but Read died in prison in 1721, and was buried in St Catherine parish.

1834

Slavery is abolished throughout the British Empire, causing economic chaos in Jamaica.

1845

A railroad is built connecting Spanish Town and Kingston. It is the first one built outside North America and Europe.

1872

The administrative capital of Jamaica is moved from Spanish Town to Kingston, which retains the title until independence in 1962 makes it the capital.

and shipped across the Atlantic to Kingston, where they were auctioned off. Estimates as to the number transported from Africa run as high as 20 million slaves.

Many never made it that far. The 'Middle Passage' across the Atlantic lasted anywhere from six to 12 weeks. The captives were crammed so tight in the festering holds that there wasn't room enough to lie down; many died of disease.

Those slaves who were still alive at the end of the voyage were fattened up as the boat reached port, and oiled to make them appear healthy before being auctioned. Their prices varied between £25 and £75 for unskilled slaves. Slaves who had been trained as carpenters or blacksmiths fetched a premium – often £300 or more. The most wretched had a worth of no more than a shilling.

Kingston served as the main distribution point for delivery to other islands. Of the tens of thousands of slaves shipped to Jamaica every year, the vast majority was re-exported. The slave ships then returned to England carrying cargoes of sugar, molasses and rum.

MAROON RESISTANCE

By the end of the 17th century, Jamaica was also under siege from within. The first major slave rebellion occurred in 1690 in Clarendon parish, where many slaves escaped and joined the descendants of slaves who had been freed by the Spanish in 1655 and had eventually coalesced into two powerful bands (called Maroons, from the Spanish word *cimarrón*): one in the remote Blue Mountains and one in the almost impenetrable Cockpit Country of southern Trelawny, from where they raided plantations and attracted runaway slaves. The eastern community became known as the Windward Maroons; those further west were called Leeward Maroons.

Mavis Campbell's *The Maroons of Jamaica* is a serious study of the origins of the Maroons and their evolution as a culture through to the late-19th century.

In 1729 the English launched the First Maroon War offensive to eradicate the Maroons. The thickly jungled mountains, however, were ill-suited to English-style open warfare and the Maroons had perfected ambush-style guerrilla fighting. Nonetheless, after a decade of costly campaigning, the English gained the upper hand.

On March 1, 1739, Colonel Guthrie and Cudjoe, the leader of the Maroons of Cockpit Country, signed a peace treaty granting the Maroons autonomy and 1500 acres of land. In return, the Maroons agreed to chase down runaway slaves and return them to the plantations and to assist the English in quelling rebellions.

The Maroons of the Blue Mountains, under a leader named Quao, signed a similar treaty one year later.

KING SUGAR

During the course of the 18th century, Jamaica became the largest sugar producer in the world. The island was jointly ruled by a governor

1887

Marcus Garvey, the main proponent of the 'back to Africa' movement, is born. He dies in 1940.

1891

The Great Exhibition is held in Kingston, drawing over 300,000 visitors – the largest attendance of its time in proportion to the local population.

1907

A great earthquake topples much of Kingston on January 14th, causing widespread destruction and killing more than 800 people.

JAMAICA'S NATIONAL HEROES

Jamaica has its equivalent of George Washington and Joan of Arc – individuals deemed worthy of special status as national heroes, earning the honorific title 'the Right Excellent'. There are seven national heroes:

- Paul Bogle (unknown–1865) led the march on Morant Bay in 1865 that spun out of control and became the Morant Bay Rebellion.
- Alexander Bustamante (1884–1977) was a firebrand trade unionist and founder of the Jamaica Labour Party, who became the independent nation's first prime minister, 1962–67.
- Marcus Garvey (1887–1940) is considered the father of 'Black power' and was named Jamaica's first national hero in 1980.
- George William Gordon (1820–65), a mixed-race lawyer, assemblyman and post-emancipation nationalist, was a powerful advocate of nationalism and the rights of the poor.
- Norman Manley (1893–1969) founded the People's National Party, fought for political and became the self-governing island's first prime minister (1959–62), prior to independence.
- Nanny (dates unknown) was a leader of the Windward Maroons in the 18th century. Folklore attributes her with magical powers.
- Sam 'Daddy' Sharpe (1801–32), a town slave and Baptist deacon who was hanged by British authorities for his role in leading the 1831 slave rebellion that engulfed the western parishes.

Curiously, the world's most famous Jamaican is not among this venerable pantheon, though a movement is afoot to confer National Hero status on Robert Nesta Marley (1945–1981).

(appointed by the English monarch) and an elected assembly of planters. Jamaica was divided into the same 13 parishes that exist today. The Crown's interests at the parish level were looked after by an appointed custos (the Crown's local representative).

The planters built sturdy 'great houses' in Georgian fashion high above their cane fields. Many planters were absentee landlords who lived most of the year in England, where they formed a powerful political lobby. In Jamaica the planters lived a life of indolence, with retinues of black servants. Many overindulged in drink and sexual relations with slave mistresses, frequently siring mulatto children known as 'free coloreds,' who were accorded special rights.

The economic and political life of the times was an exclusively male arena. The planters' wives spent much of their time playing cards, arranging balls and other events, and otherwise socializing, while the day-to-day care of their children was undertaken by wet nurses, who were often female slaves.

The Story of the Jamaican People by Philip Sherlock and Hazel Bennett offers a new interpretation of Jamaica's history that eschews the imperial perspective, instead looking to Africa for the keys to understanding the island's complex culture.

1915

Hurricanes devastate the island, and again during 1916 and 1917, natural disasters that compound the hardships being experienced as a result of the demise of trade during WWI.

1930

Haile Selassie is crowned emperor of Ethiopia, encouraging the rise of Rastafarianism in Jamaica.

1938

Jamaica's first political party, the People's National Party, is formed by Norman Manley, who works with the Bustamante Trade Union to position working-class issues at the front and centre of Jamaican politics for the first time.

THE MORANT BAY REBELLION

Following emancipation in 1834, the local black population faced widescale unemployment and extreme hardship, conditions exacerbated by heavy taxation and the harshness of local magistrates. In the 1860s Paul Bogle, a Black Baptist deacon in the hamlet of Stony Gut, preached passive resistance against the oppression and injustice of the local authorities and planters in St Thomas. He was supported by George William Gordon, a wealthy mulatto planter who had become an assemblyman.

On October 11, 1865, Bogle and 400 supporters marched to the Morant Bay courthouse to protest the severe punishment meted out to a vagrant who had been arrested on a petty charge. An armed militia shot into the crowd and a riot ensued in which 28 people were killed, and the courthouse and much of the town center were razed. The countryside erupted in riots. Bogle fled with a £2000 bounty on his head, but was soon captured by Maroons (who had agreed in their peace treaty with the British to act as bounty hunters) and hanged the same day from the center arch of the burned-out courthouse. Gordon was arrested in Kingston, ferried to Morant Bay, condemned by a kangaroo court and also hanged.

Governor Edward Eyre ordered reprisals. The militia swept through St Thomas, razing more than 1000 houses and summarily executing more than 430 people. The British government was outraged by Eyre's reaction (a tribunal found that the punishments were 'excessive...reckless... and...at Bath positively barbarous') and forced the Jamaica House of Assembly to relinquish its power to the British parliament. Thus the island became a Crown colony, leading to reforms of the harsh judicial system.

THE CRUELTY OF SLAVERY

Slavery dominated Jamaican life. By 1700 there were perhaps 7000 English and 40,000 slaves in Jamaica. A century later, the number of whites had tripled and they ruled over 300,000 slaves. Tens of thousands were worked to death. Many were put to work building factories, houses and roads. Others were domestic servants, cooks, footmen, butlers and grooms.

During their few free hours, the slaves cultivated their own tiny plots. Sunday was a rest day and slaves gathered to sell yams and other produce at the bustling markets. In rare instances, slaves might save enough money to buy their freedom, which masters could also grant as they wished.

Before his execution on May 23, 1832, Sam Sharpe is quoted as saying 'I would rather die upon yonder gallows than live in slavery.'

The planters ran their estates as vicious fiefdoms under the authority of an overseer (the *busha*), who enjoyed relatively free rein. Some planters showed kindness and nurtured their slaves, but most resorted to violence to terrorize the slave population into obedience. The extreme treatment was eventually regulated by slave codes, but plantation society remained tied to the rule of the whip.

REVOLT

New slaves kept arriving, most of them put to work on sugar plantations in appalling conditions. Bloody slave insurrections occurred with frightening

1945

Reggae superstar Bob Marley (d 1981) is born in Nine Mile in St Ann's Parish.

1962

Jamaica becomes an independent nation within the British Commonwealth.

1963

At the height of the ska era in Jamaican music, Clement Dodd begins recording Bob Marley and the Wailers.

frequency. The last and largest of the slave revolts in Jamaica was the 1831 Christmas Rebellion, inspired by 'Daddy' Sam Sharpe, an educated slave and lay preacher who incited passive resistance. The rebellion turned violent, however, as up to 20,000 slaves razed plantations and murdered planters. When the slaves were tricked into laying down arms with a false promise of emancipation – and then 400 were hanged and hundreds more whipped – there was a wave of revulsion in England, causing the Jamaican assembly finally to abolish slavery in 1834.

The resulting transition from a slave economy to one based on wage labor caused economic chaos, with most slaves rejecting the starvation wages offered on the estates and choosing to fend for themselves. Desperation over conditions and injustice finally boiled over in the 1865 Morant Bay Rebellion, led by a black Baptist deacon named Paul Bogle (see the boxed text, p188).

BANANA BOOM & BUST

In 1866 a Yankee skipper, George Busch, arrived in Jamaica and loaded several hundred stems of bananas, which he transported to Boston and sold at a handsome profit. He quickly returned to Port Antonio, where he encouraged production and soon had himself a thriving export business. Captain Lorenzo Dow Baker followed suit in the west, with his base at Montego Bay. Within a decade the banana trade was booming. Production peaked in 1927, when 21 million stems were exported.

To help pay the passage south to Jamaica, banana traders promoted the island's virtues and took on passengers. Thus, the banana-export trade gave rise to the tourism industry.

BIRTH OF A NATION

With the Depression of the 1930s, sugar and banana sales plummeted, and the vast majority of Jamaicans were unemployed and destitute. Strikes and riots erupted, spilling over in 1938 when a demonstration at the West Indies Sugar Company factory at Frome, in Westmoreland, got out of hand. A battle between police and the unemployed seeking work left several people dead. The situation was defused when a locally born labor leader, Alexander Bustamante, mediated the dispute.

Amid the clamor, the charismatic Bustamante, son of an Irish woman and a mulatto man, formed the Bustamante Industrial Trade Union (BITU) in 1938. That same year, Bustamante's cousin Norman Manley formed the People's National Party (PNP), the first political party in the colony. Separately they campaigned for economic and political reforms. As historians Philip Sherlock and Barbara Preston observed, 'Bustamante swept the Jamaican working class into the mainstream of Jamaican political life and Norman Manley secured the constitutional changes that put political power

Tony Sewall's *Garvey's Children: The Legacy of Marcus Garvey* provides a look at the rise of Black Nationalism inspired by national hero Marcus Garvey.

1966

On the second stop of his Caribbean trip, HIM Haile Selassie I is greeted by nearly 100,000 chanting Rastafarians at the airport. He refuses to leave the plane until his security is assured.

1976

In the lead up to the election, tensions between Jamaica's two political parties erupt into open warfare in the street between politically aligned gangs. A state of emergency is declared; Jamaica teeters on the brink of civil war.

1978

The One Love Peace concert is held in Kingston, following Bob Marley's homecoming. A ceasefire between the People's National Party and the Jamaica Labour Party is declared in honor of the event. 100,000 people attend the concert.

ONE GOD, ONE AIM, ONE DESTINY

Marcus Garvey was born of working-class parents in St Ann's Bay on August 17, 1887. As a young man he traveled extensively throughout Costa Rica, Panama and England. He returned well educated and a firm believer in self-improvement. Inspired to raise the consciousness and well-being of the African diaspora, he founded the Universal Negro Improvement Association (UNIA) in 1914 to unite 'all the Negro peoples of the world to establish a state exclusively their own.' When Jamaica proved largely unreceptive to his message, he moved in 1916 to the US, where he formed a branch of the UNIA in New York. At its peak in the 1920s, the UNIA had five million members. Garvey, a gifted orator, established a weekly newspaper, the *Negro World*, and built an enormous following under the slogan 'One God! One Aim! One Destiny!'

Garvey set up the Black Star Line, a steamship company, with the aim of eventually repatriating Blacks to Africa. The company, however, failed due to poor management.

The American and British governments considered Garvey a dangerous agitator. They conspired against him, and in 1922 they arrested him on mail-fraud charges. He served two years in Atlanta Federal Prison before being deported to Jamaica. Back in his homeland, the Black Nationalist founded the reformist People's Political Party. Universal franchise did not then exist in Jamaica, and he failed to gather enough support at the polls. In 1935 he departed for England, where he died in poverty in 1940.

His remains were repatriated to Jamaica in 1984 and interred with state honors in National Heroes Park (p75).

in their hands.' Not content with trade union activism, Bustamante formed Jamaica Labour Party (JLP) in 1943.

Adult suffrage for all Jamaicans, and a new constitution that provided for an elected government, were introduced in 1944, and Bustamante's JLP won Jamaica's first election. In 1947 virtual autonomy was granted, though Jamaica remained a British colony under the jurisdiction of Parliament and the Crown – a prelude to full independence.

On August 6, 1962, Jamaica finally gained its independence (while remaining part of the British Commonwealth). At midnight the Union Jack came down, replaced by Jamaica's new flag with three new colors: black (for the people), green (for the land) and gold (for the sun).

Jamaica carries a debt to foreign banks exceeding US$800 billion. *Life & Debt*, a documentary film by Stephanie Black, takes a provocative look into the island's burden.

TURBULENT YEARS

Postindependence politics have been largely dominated by the legacies of Bustamante and Manley. Manley's son Michael led the PNP toward democratic socialism in the mid-'70s, his policy of taxation to fund social services deterring foreign investment and causing a capital flight at a time when Jamaica could ill afford it. Bitterly opposed factions engaged in open urban warfare before the 1976 election. A controversial state of emergency was declared and the nation seemed poised on the edge of civil war, but the

1980

The Jamaica Labour Party's Edward Seaga is elected to power, and begins transforming Jamaica's foreign engagement, cutting ties with Cuba, and positioning himself as a friend of the Reagan administration.

1988

Hurricane Gilbert slams Jamaica, killing 45 people and causing damage estimated at up to US$1 billion.

1992

The Blue Mountains-John Crow National Park is established. Formed during the Cretaceous Period (c144–65million years ago), the mountain range itself is the island's oldest geological feature.

PNP won the election by a wide margin and Manley continued with his socialist agenda.

Unsurprisingly, US government was hostile to the Jamaica's socialist turn, and when Manley began to develop close ties with Cuba, the CIA purportedly planned to topple the Jamaican government. Businesses pulled out, the economy (tourism in particular) went into sharp decline and the country was under virtual siege. Almost 800 people were killed in the lead-up to the 1980 elections, which were won by the JLP's Edward Seaga. Seaga restored Jamaica's economic fortunes somewhat, severed ties with Cuba and became a staunch ally of the Reagan Administration – even dispatching Jamaican troops to assist in the invasion of Grenada in 1983. Relatively peaceful elections in 1989 returned a reinvented 'mainstream realist' Manley to power; he retired in 1992, handing the reins to his deputy, Percival James Patterson – Jamaica's first black prime minister.

Pieces of the Past (www.jamaica-gleaner.com/pages/history) is a compendium of thematic essays about Jamaican history.

RECENT YEARS

The Patterson-led PNP romped in the 1993 and 1997 elections. In spring 1999, the country erupted in nationwide riots after the government announced a 30% increase in the tax on gasoline. Kingston and Montego Bay, where sugarcane fields were set ablaze, were particularly badly hit. After three days of arson and looting, the government thought better of it and rescinded the tax.

In the lead-up to the 2002 elections, violence in West Kingston soared to new heights as criminal posses battled to control electoral turf and profit from the largesse that victory at the polls in Jamaica brings. Rival political gangs turned the area into a war zone, forcing residents to flee and schools, businesses and even Kingston Public Hospital to close.

In 2004, Hurricane Ivan bounced off Jamaica en route to the Cayman Islands, causing widespread damage, and Edward Seaga – still representing the JLP as opposition leader – retired after over three decades of life in politics. Two years later, Prime Minister Patterson resigned in 2006, giving way to Portia Simpson-Miller. Jamaica's first female prime minister, 'Mama P' was initially popular with the masses, but 18 years of PNP rule bred gradual voter disillusionment with the party. In the 2007 elections, Bruce Golding of the JLP carried the day.

The Jamaica Golding inherits faces several battles, and most Jamaicans will tell you the greatest is crime (the 2007 murder rate was 17% higher than the previous year's). Illiteracy is also a grave concern (according to UNESCO, over 90% of 15 to 24 year olds couldn't both read and write in 2004) as are threats to the environment through deforestation and overdevelopment (see p51). In the meantime, the Jamaican people face the future with resolve and a measure of good humor – they've endured so much worse in the past.

2004

At least 15 people are killed by Hurricane Ivan, with Negril being particularly hard hit. The banana-tree population is ravaged, and the following year banana exports drop by 68%.

2006

Portia Simpson-Miller, of the People's National Party, becomes Jamaica's first female prime minister. But the people are cynical of change after PNP's 18 years in power, and the Jamaica Labour Party wins the 2007 elections.

2007

The Cricket World Cup is held in the West Indies, with opening ceremonies held in Falmouth. Won by Australia, the tournament was overshadowed by the death of Pakistani coach Bob Woolmer, apparently of heart failure.

The Culture

Although many of the package tourists that descend on Jamaica for some fur in the sun nurture packaged visions of the locals beyond the walls of thei all-inclusive resorts, Jamaicans are as diverse a people as the island's geog-raphy is varied. Far from being confined to the dreadlocked, spliff-puffing Rastafarian vibing to reggae or the violent 'rude boy' of the ghetto, Jamaican comprise many social and demographic strata. It's up to the tourist to scratcl the surface, to become a traveler.

Traditional folk healing is still very much alive. Healers, called 'balmists,' rely on concoctions of native herbs – bush medicines, the recipes for which span many generations.

To be sure, street-level Jamaica can be daunting at first. Poverty blight Jamaica's towns, and tourists mean money. Nevertheless, with reasonabl precaution, you'll soon fall under the spell of Jamaica's inimitable charms Violence rarely impinges on foreigners; it is mostly restricted to drug war and political gang feuds in the claustrophobic ghettoes of Kingston, Spanisl Town and sections of Montego Bay that you're highly unlikely ever to se foot in.

What emerges is a panoply of communities: from the sleepy fishing hamlets that line all the coasts to the cosmopolitan business sector of th capital, from the bustling market towns to the autonomous Maroon hillsid villages. And while you can of course meet Rastas happy to smoke ganj with you, you'll also encounter proud matriarchs presiding over the family owned rum shop; dancehall enthusiasts delighted to take you to the loca sound-system party; bush-medicine doctors who can explain the benefit of every local root, herb and flower; or students who know as much abou your own country as you do.

You'll learn to greet strangers with the local salutation 'blessed', and b the time you leave Jamaica, you'll realize you have been.

THE NATIONAL PSYCHE

Many Jamaicans will tell you their island is not part of the Caribbean, bu Africa. And while the vestiges of the slave era unsurprisingly weigh heavil on the national psyche, over the last century the rise of Jamaican national ism and an explosion in homegrown culture have engendered a proud an vibrant contemporary culture.

The devious spider Anancy, Jamaica's leading folk hero, derives from folktales that originated with the Ashanti tribe of Ghana. Over centuries they have become localized.

Jamaicans are an intriguing contrast. Much of the population comprise the most gracious people you'll ever meet: hard-working, happy-go-lucky helpful, courteous, genteel and full of humility. If you show them kindness they will give it back in return. However, charged memories of slavery an racism have continued to bring out the spirit of anarchy latent in a forme slave society divided into rich and poor. Jamaicans struggling hard agains poverty are disdainful of talk about a 'tropical paradise.'

Jamaicans love to debate, or 'reason.' You'll not meet many Jamaican without strong opinions, and they tend to express themselves forcefully turning differences of opinion into voluble arguments with some confound ing elliptical twists and stream-of-consciousness associations.

Jamaicans' sarcasm and sardonic wit is legendary. The deprecating humo has evolved as an escape valve that hides their true feelings. The saying tha 'everyt'ing irie' is black humor, because life is a problem. Often Jamaican wi is laced with sexual undertones. Jamaicans like to make fun of others, ofte in the subtlest yet no-punches-pulled way, but they accept being the sourc of similar humor in good grace. Individual faults and physical abnormali ties inspire many a knee-slapping jibe. If directed at you, take it in the goo humor it's proffered.

VISITORS DOS & DON'TS

- Don't ignore beggars, hustlers or higglers. Offer a firm but polite 'not interested,' 'sorry' or 'no thank you' where appropriate; simply walking past is taken as an insult that might soon be broadcast up and down the street.
- Do relax. Tropical time happens at a slower pace. 'Soon come' is a favorite expression often taken at face value by foreigners – in fact it means 'it'll happen when it happens.'
- Do empathize. Try to understand the hardships that the majority of Jamaicans face. Don't try to take advantage of an individual's plight.
- Don't call Jamaicans 'natives.' The term is laden with racial connotations and can be taken as a slur. 'Islanders' or simply 'Jamaicans' is more appropriate.
- Do be formal with strangers. Jamaicans are more formal than many foreigners, particularly North Americans, who are used to quickly reaching a first-name basis. To show respect, address people you meet with 'Mr' or 'Miss,' or even 'Sir' or 'Lady.' Using a first name can be taken as treating someone as inferior.
- Do ask before snapping a photo. Many Jamaicans enjoy being photographed, sometimes for a small fee, but others prefer not to pose for tourists and can respond angrily.

LIFESTYLE

Many Jamaicans live in the hills, out of sight of tourists: some get by quite adequately, living in homes made of aged wooden houses in Caribbean style or concrete cinder block in Western style. Others eke out a marginal existence in ramshackle villages and rural shacks, sometimes in pockets of extreme poverty, as in Kingston's ghettoes and shanties. Many low income Jamaicans have been unable to find a way out of poverty, so they hustle. They hang out on the streets waiting for an opportunity to present itself. A general malaise prevalent among a large segment of the male underclass is fired by a belief that a subtle apartheid force is purposely holding them back. The average per capita income is only US$3500, slightly lower than that of Guatemala.

Jamaica has a significant middle class, which lives a lifestyle familiar to its counterparts in Europe and North America. Middle-class Jamaicans are, as a whole, well educated; they have vivacious and well-honed intellects, are entrepreneurial and contemporary looking, and exhibit a preference for shopping trips to Miami or New York. But many of the middle class live with a surprising lack of contact with the harsh reality in which the majority of Jamaicans live, and they seem to be able to muster little empathy. Not infrequently you'll hear defensive denials that poverty even exists in Jamaica.

Jamaican proverbs are a proud celebration of heritage and dialect. A sample: 'So cow a grow so him nose hole a open.' This roughly translates to 'Live and learn.'

Sex & Family Life

To the outsider, Jamaicans are sexually active at an early age. Uncommitted sexual relationships are not unusual, especially among the poorer classes. Approximately 80% of children are born out of wedlock, and the local lexicon is full of terms related to the theme ('jacket,' for example, refers to a child fathered by someone other than a woman's husband). And while middle-class Jamaicans mores are decidedly less permissive, visitors to the island are ever-conscious of its aura of sexual freedom.

Sadly, Jamaican free-spirited attitudes do not extent to acceptance of gays. The island is an intensely homophobic place, and you are extremely unlikely to see displays of public intimacy between same sex locals. For advice to gay travelers, see p280.

POPULATION

Jamaica's population is currently estimated at a little over 2.7 million, out of which about 750,000 live in Kingston. At least another two million live abroad, generally in the US, UK or Canada. Some 91% of the population are classified as being of pure African descent; 7.3% are of Afro-European descent; the remainder are white (0.2%), East Indian and Middle Eastern (1.3%), and Afro-Chinese and Chinese (0.2%).

MULTICULTURALISM

The nation's motto, 'Out of Many, One People,' reflects the diverse heritage of Jamaica. Tens of thousands of West Africans, plus large numbers of Irish, Germans and Welsh, arrived throughout the colonial period, along with Hispanic and Portuguese Jews and those whom Jamaicans call 'Syrians' (a term for all those of Levantine extraction). In 1838, following emancipation, Chinese and Indian indentured laborers arrived from Hong Kong and Panama.

Jamaica proclaims itself a melting pot of racial harmony. Still, insecurities of identity have been carried down from the plantation era. Class divisions in Jamaica are still related to color and there is much lingering resentment – as well as prejudice – against whites, particularly among the poorer segment of society.

RELIGION

Jamaica professes to have the greatest number of churches per square kilometer in the world, with virtually every imaginable denomination represented. Although most foreigners associate the island with Rastafarianism, more than 80% of Jamaicans identify themselves as Christian.

Christianity

Many Jamaican elders still observe Nine Nights, a 'wake' held on the ninth night after someone's death to ensure that the spirit of the deceased departs to heaven (and doesn't hang around to haunt the living!).

On any day of the week, but most notably on weekends, it's common to see adults and children walking along country roads holding Bibles and dressed in their finest outfits – the girls in white, the men and boys in somber suits, and the women in heels, hats and bright satins. On Sundays every church in the country seems to overflow with the righteous, and the old fire-and-brimstone school of sermonizing is still the preferred mode. Bible-waving congregations sway to and fro, and wail and shriek 'Hallelujah!' and 'Amen, sweet Jesus!' while guitars, drums and tambourines help work the crowds into a frenzy.

The most popular denomination, the Anglican Church of Jamaica, accounts for 43% of the population. About 5% of the population today is Catholic. Fundamentalists have made serious inroads in recent years because of aggressive proselytizing.

Revivalist Cults

Jamaica has several quasi-Christian, quasi-animist sects that are generically named Revivalist cults after the postemancipation Great Revival, during which many blacks converted to Christianity. The most important Revivalist cult is Pocomania, which mixes European and African religious heritages.

The cults are derived from West African animist beliefs (animism has nothing to do with animal spirits; the name is derived from the Latin word *anima,* soul) based on the tenet that the spiritual and temporal worlds are a unified whole. A core belief is that spirits live independently of the human or animal body and can inhabit inanimate objects and communicate themselves to humans; how humans call them determines whether they will be a force of good or evil.

Rastafarianism

Rastafarians, with their uncut, uncombed hair grown into long sun-bleached tangles known as 'dreadlocks' or 'dreads,' are as synonymous with the island as reggae. There are perhaps as many as 100,000 Rastafarians in Jamaica. A faith rather than a church, Rastafarianism has no official doctrine or dogmatic hierarchy and is composed of a core of social and spiritual tenets that are open to interpretation. Not all Rastafarians wear dreads, for example, and others do not smoke ganja. All adherents, however, accept that Africa is the black race's spiritual home to which they are destined to return.

The Sympathetic Dread: The Rastafarians of Jamaica by Joseph Owens and *Rasta Heart: A Journey Into One Love* by Robert Roskind are noteworthy books on Jamaica's most talked-about creed.

Rastafarianism evolved as an expression of poor, black Jamaicans seeking fulfillment in the 1930s, a period of growing nationalism and economic and political upheaval. It was boosted by the 'back to Africa' zeal of Marcus Garvey's Universal Negro Improvement Association, founded in 1914 (see the boxed text, p32). Rastafarians regard Garvey as a prophet. He predicted that a black man – a 'Redeemer' – would be crowned king in Africa. Haile Selassie's crowning as emperor of Abyssinia (now Ethiopia) on November 2, 1930, fulfilled Garvey's prophecy and established a fascination with Ethiopia that lies at the core of Rastafarianism.

One charismatic leader, Leonard Percival Howell, developed the tenets of Rastafarianism and, in 1940, established the first Rastafarian community, the Pinnacle, at Sligoville, northwest of Kingston. His followers adopted the 'dreadlocked' hairstyle of several East African tribes – an allegory of the mane of the Lion of Judah.

Howell's document 'Twenty-One Points' defined the Rastafarian philosophy and creed. One tenet was that the African race was one of God's chosen races, one of the Twelve Tribes of Israel descended from the Hebrews and displaced. Jamaica is Babylon (named after the place where the Israelites were enslaved) and their lot is in exile in a land that cannot be reformed. A second tenet states that God, whom they call Jah, will one day lead them from Babylon – any place that 'downpresses' the masses – to Zion (the 'Promised Land,' or Ethiopia). A third addresses Selassie's status as the Redeemer chosen to lead Africans back to Africa.

Rastafarian leaders continue to petition Queen Elizabeth II to repatriate them to Africa. While she mulls over their appeal, they wait for redemption.

Rastafarians believe that ganja provides a line of communication with God. Again, they look to the Bible, specifically Psalm 146:8, which says of God:

A UNIQUE LEXICON

One of the 21 tenets of Rastafarianism is the belief that God exists in each person, and that the two are the same. Thus the creed unifies divinity and individuality through the use of personal pronouns that reflect the 'I and I.' ('One blood. Everybody same, mon!') 'I' becomes the id or true measure of inner divinity, which places everyone on the same plane. Thus 'I and I' can mean 'we,' 'him and her,' 'you and them.' (The personal pronoun 'me' is seen as a sign of subservience, of acceptance of the self as an 'object'.)

Rastafarians have evolved a whole lexicon that has profoundly influenced 'Jamaica talk' (for more information, see the Language chapter) and is laced with cryptic intent and meaning. This revisionist 'English' is inspired by Rastafarian reasoning that sees the English language as a tool in the service of Babylon designed to 'downpress' the black people. In short, they believe the language is biased. Every word is analyzed, and in this frame even the most insignificant word can seem tainted. The well-meant greeting 'Hello!' may elicit the response: 'Dis not 'ell and I not low!'

'Who covereth the heaven with clouds, and prepareth rain for the earth. Who maketh grass to grow on the mountains, and herbs for the service of men.'

Most but not all adherents smoke ganja copiously from cigar-size spliffs (reefers) and the 'holy chalice,' a bamboo pipe made of a goat's horn. Through it they claim to gain wisdom and inner divinity through the ability to 'reason' more clearly. The search for truth – 'reasoning' – is integral to the faith and is meant to see through the corrupting influences of 'Babylon.'

Despite its militant consciousness, the religion preaches love and nonviolence, and adherents live by strict biblical codes that advocate a way of life in harmony with Old Testament traditions. They are vegetarians and teetotalers who shun tobacco and the trappings of Western consumption.

SPORTS

Jamaica is a leader on the international athletics scene, regularly producing outstanding track-and-field athletes dating back to sprinter Arthur Wint, Jamaica's first Olympic gold-medal winner (in 1948). At the time of writing, Asafa Powell is the fastest man on the planet, thanks to his world-record time of 9.74 seconds in the 100m sprint, set in September 2007.

Jamaica is cricket mad, and you'll come across small fields in even the most remote backwaters, where boys with makeshift bats practice the bowling and swings that may one day bring them fortune and fame. In 2007, the World Cup was held in the West Indies, with opening ceremonies held at a brand-new stadium in Falmouth. Games between leading regional and international teams are played frequently at **Sabina Park** (☎ 967-0322; South Camp Rd) in Kingston.

One of the most electrifying voices of Jamaican dub poetry is that of Mutabaruka. Learn about his work and read his poems at www.mutabaruka.com.

Soccer is Jamaica's second sport. It was given a huge boost by the success of the Reggae Boyz – Jamaica's national soccer team – in qualifying for the 1998 World Cup. And though they've had little success since, the reappointment of the '98 team's Brazilian coach Rene Simoes in 2007 has rekindled hopes of a return to glory. Weekend games between village teams draw decent crowds. International matches are played at the **National Stadium** (☎ 929-4970; Arthur Wint Dr) in Kingston.

MEDIA

Since 1834 the **Jamaica Gleaner** (www.jamaica-gleaner.com) has been regarded as the high-standard newspaper in the Caribbean region, while the **Observer** (www.jamaicaobserver.com) offers a more populist counterpoint.

It's radio, however, that best captures the nation's pulse. Jamaica has some 30 stations, the most popular being **Irie Fm** (www.iriefm.net), the island's reggae and dancehall soundtrack. Call-in talk shows are popular, and there is considerable political debate on the air. As the island is so small and parochial, radio serves as a kind of community-service grapevine. Deaths, for example, are announced with somber details (and muted funereal music in the background) followed by a roll call of relatives and friends requested to attend the funeral.

There are seven Jamaican TV stations. News coverage dwells largely on sensational stories of traffic deaths, vigilantism, ghetto politics and good Samaritans. International news is covered broadly, with much attention devoted to the news from Africa.

The Jamaican Woman: A Celebration by Joanne Simpson provides biographies of 200 women who have made major contributions to Jamaican society.

WOMEN IN JAMAICA

While Jamaican society can appear oppressively macho to outsiders accustomed to dancehall lyrics, women tend to be strong and independent (in 40% of households, a woman is the sole provider). This spirit often translates into the self-assurance so apparent in Portia Simpson-Miller, former prime minister (2006–2007) and current leader of the PNP opposition. Jamaican women attain far higher grades in school and have higher literacy rates than Jamaican men, and middle-class women have attained levels of respect and career performance that are commensurate with their counterparts in North America and Europe. Women also make up about 46% of Jamaica's labor force, although the majority are in extremely low-paying jobs.

Jamaica has had strong links to James Bond movies ever since novelist Ian Fleming concocted the suave macho spy 007 at his home near Oracabessa. The Bond movies *Dr No* and *Live and Let Die* were both shot on location along Jamaica's north coast.

ARTS

Literature

Through the years Jamaican literature has been haunted by the ghosts of slave history and the ambiguities of Jamaica's relationship to Mother England. The classic novels tend to focus on survival in a grim colonial landscape and escape to Africa, which often proves to be even grimmer. Best known, perhaps, is Herbert de Lisser's classic *White Witch of Rose Hall.* This plantation-era tale – now an established part of Jamaican lore – tells of Annie Palmer, the wicked mistress of Rose Hall (see the boxed text, p201) who supposedly murdered three husbands and several slave lovers. The actual truth is less lurid.

Perry Henzell's *Power Game* is a tale of power politics based on real events in the 1970s, told by the director of the movie *The Harder They Come* (see below). The poignant novel of that name, written by Michael Thewell, recounts the story of a country boy who comes to Kingston, turns into a 'rude boy,' (armed thug) and becomes fatally enmeshed in the savage drug culture. The mean streets of Kingston are also the setting for the gritty novels of Roger Mais, notably *The Hills Were Joyful Together* and *Brother Man.* Orlando Patterson's *The Children of Sisyphus* mines the same bleak terrain from a Rastafarian perspective.

In recent years, a number of Jamaican female writers have gained notice: they include Christine Craig *(Mint Tea)*, Patricia Powell *(Me Dying Trial)*, Michelle Cliff *(Abeng, Land of Look Behind)* and Vanessa Spence *(Roads Are Down)*.

Jamaica's most celebrated theater company is the National Dance Theater Company, which performs at the Little Theater in Kingston.

Film

Jamaica has produced some excellent films (often pronounced 'flims' in Jamaica), most notably cult classic *The Harder They Come* (1973), starring Jimmy Cliff as a 'rude boy' in Kingston's ghettoes. *Rockers* (1978), another music-propelled, socially poignant fable is a Jamaican reworking of the *Bicycle Thief* featuring a cast of reggae all-stars.

Rick Elgood's emotionally engaging 1997 film *Dancehall Queen* found an international audience for its tale of redemption for a struggling, middle-aged street vendor, who escapes the mean streets of Kingston through the erotic intoxication of dancehall music. Jamaica's highest-grossing film of all time is Chris Browne's 2000 crime drama *Third World Cop*, in which old friends straddling both sides of the law must come to terms with each other.

Reggae Routes by Wayne Chen and Kevin O'Brien Chang is required reading. This copious, lavishly illustrated volume is an insider's guide to reggae and popular Jamaican music in general, demystifying the music and correcting many misconceptions.

Music

Music is everywhere – and it's loud! The sheer creativity and productivity of Jamaican music has produced a profound effect around the world. As reggae continues to attract and influence a massive international audience, Jamaica's sound system-based dancehall culture continues to inform contemporary rap, rave and hip-hop cultures.

Reggae is the heartbeat of Jamaica, and it is as strongly identified with the island as R&B is with Detroit or jazz with New Orleans. But reggae is actually only one of several distinctly Jamaican sounds, and the nation's musical heritage runs much deeper. Inspired by the country's rich African folk heritage, music spans mento (a folk calypso), ska, rocksteady, 'roots' music and contemporary dancehall and ragga. Kingston is the 'Nashville of the Third World,' with recording studios pumping out as many as 500 new titles each month.

The legacy of reggae superstar Bob Marley continues to thrive, as witnessed in the month-long celebration held in Ethiopia in early 2005 marking the 60th anniversary of his birth. There's long been talk about elevating Marley to National Hero status, a mantle reserved only for the nation's most pivotal figures.

The term dancehall, although used to mean a sound-system venue, is also used specifically to refer to a kind of Caribbean rap music that focuses on earthly themes dear to the heart of young male Jamaicans, principally 'gal business,' gunplay and ganja. This is hardcore music, named for the loosely defined outdoor venues at which outlandishly named 'toasters' (rapper DJs) set up mobile discos with enormous speakers, and singers and DJs pumped-up with braggadocio perform live over instrumental rhythm tracks. See p59 for more on Jamaican music.

Jamaica Art by Kim Robinson and Petrine Archer Straw is a well-illustrated treatise on the evolution of the island's art scene. Likewise, *Modern Jamaican Art* by David Boxer and Veerle Poupeye provides an illustrated overview of the works of 82 Jamaican painters and sculptors.

Painting & Sculpture

Jamaican art has its origins in the 18th and 19th centuries, when itinerant artists roamed the plantations, recording life in a Eurocentric, romanticized light that totally ignored the African heritage. English satirist William Hogarth was one of few artists to portray the hypocrisy and savagery of plantation life.

THE BIRTH OF VISUAL NATIONALISM

Until the early 20th century, Jamaica's visual, literary and performing arts largely sought to reflect British trends and colonial tastes. With the call for Jamaica's independence, leaders like Norman Manley eloquently called for the articulation of a new national culture. In 1939 Manley wrote, 'National culture is national consciousness reflected in the painting of pictures of our own mountains and our own womenfolk, in building those houses that are the most suitable for us to live in, in writing plays of our adventures and poetry of our wisdom, finding ourselves in the wrestle with our own problems.'

Manley's wife, Edna, an inspired sculptor and advocate for 'indigenous' Jamaican art, became a leading catalyst for change. Edna Manley's bitter opposition to the 'anaemic imitators of European traditions' pushed her to aspire to an 'expression of the deep-rooted, hidden pulse of the Country – that thing which gives it its unique life.' Through the example of seminal works like *Negro Aroused* (1935), which can be seen in the National Gallery (p72) in Kingston, and *Pocomania* (1936), which synthesized African and Jamaican archetypes within a deeply personal vision of the national psyche, Manley provided an electrifying example of the potential of Jamaican art. On a grass-roots level, Manley organized free art classes and volunteer-run training courses to energize and organize rising talent.

Out of this fertile ground emerged – almost simultaneously – three of Jamaica's great painters. Self-taught artist John Dunkley was 'discovered' by Manley in his brilliantly decorated Kingston barber shop. His inimitable style, articulated through brooding landscapes of sinister tropical foliage, never-ending roads and furtive reptiles and rodents, brought visual form to an apocalyptic vision that resonated with the historical traumas of the Jamaican people. At the National Gallery, keep an eye out for the particularly powerful paintings *Jerboa* and *Back to Nature*. In contrast, Albert Huie produced intricately detailed and beautifully composed works like *Crop Time* and *Coconut Piece*, depicting an idyllic dreamscape of rural scenes far removed from the urban strife of Kingston, where he lived and worked. More rooted in his immediate surroundings, David Pottinger's primary interest is in the urban landscape. His portrayals of downtown life, such as *Trench Town*, reveal the desolate melancholy of poverty while also suggesting the indomitable spirit of life.

In the 1920s artists of the so-called Jamaican School began to develop their own style shaped by realities of Jamaican life. The Jamaican School evolved into two main groups: the painters who were schooled abroad, and island-themed 'intuitives' – self-taught artists such as Bishop Mallica 'Kapo' Reynolds (1911–89) and John Dunkley (1891–1947).

Jamaica's foremost sculptor this century is undoubtedly Edna Manley (see the boxed text, opposite), the multitalented wife of ex-prime minister Norman Manley. Her works in wood, metal and stone are displayed in a magnificent collection in the National Gallery in Kingston. In addition to fine artists, thousands of self-taught woodcarvers hew intuitive carvings.

The Afflicted Yard (http://afflictedyard.com) is an edgy website out of Kingston featuring commentary and photography.

Food & Drink

From a simple roadside shack to the kitchen of a five-star hotel, Jamaican cuisine is both delicious and completely original. It is a vast stew, which the Arawaks began with callaloo, cassava, corn, sweet potatoes and many tropical fruits. The Spanish tossed in their influence, dishes of the African homelands of slaves jumped in, Indian curries and roti made an appearance, as did Middle Eastern flair, the Chinese touch, and even the coarser meat-pie-dominated food of the British.

But what really makes Jamaican cuisine special, to borrow a phrase from furious dancehall remixes, is that all these distinct ethnic foods got the Jamaican 'one-drop.' They were radically reinvented with homegrown spark and funk. Jamaicans love to give playful one-drop names for unique food creations, such as 'solomon grundy' for pickled herring, 'blue drawers' for duckunoo pudding, 'mannish water' for goat soup and 'fevergrass' for a type of herbal tea.

A top Jamaican food website is www.jamaicans.com/cooking which serves up a wide selection of dishes, kept fresh by a recipe of the month.

Let your taste buds run free. Ackee and saltfish for breakfast, curried goat for lunch and a light I-tal vegetarian dinner will teach you more about Jamaica than a month at an all-inclusive resort.

STAPLES & SPECIALTIES

Main Dishes

Jamaicans typically forsake cornflakes for more savory fare at breakfast: ackee and saltfish is typical. The ackee fruit bears an uncanny resemblance to scrambled eggs when cooked. Served with johnny cakes, callaloo and escoveitched fish, it is the breakfast of the gods.

Lunch is generally a light meal in Jamaica. You might try pepperpot stew, fried fish, 'jerk' pork or various island ingredients simmered in coconut milk and spices.

The ubiquitous escoveitch fish was first brought to Jamaica by Jews who immigrated during Spanish rule.

The island staple is rice and 'peas' (red beans), most often served with pork. Goat is another common ingredient, usually curried and chopped into small bits with meat on the bone. It is also the main ingredient of mannish water, a soup made from the head of a goat. Jamaican soups are thick, more like stews, and loaded with vegetables and 'breadkind.' 'Dip and fall back' is a salty stew served with bananas and dumplings.

Vegetables

Many meals are accompanied by starchy vegetables or 'breadkinds' such as plantains and yam, or other bread substitutes such as pancake-shaped cassava bread (also known as bammy) and johnny cakes (delicious fried dumplings, an original Jamaican fast food).

The yam is ubiquitous in Jamaica. In addition to fulfilling its time-honored role as a side dish, for special occasions it's made into wine, punch, buns and cakes, pudding and yam chops. There are about a dozen different types of yam on the island.

Jerk: Barbecue from Jamaica by Helen Willinsky brings to life the visceral joy of preparing a toothsome jerk marinade. You can almost smell the wood smoke and pimento (allspice).

Callaloo is a spinachlike vegetable, usually served shredded and steamed or lightly boiled. It also finds its way into spicy pepperpot stew.

Cho cho (also known as christophine) is a pulpy squashlike gourd served in soups and as an accompaniment to meats; it is also used for making hot pickles.

The most notorious vegetable is the Scotch bonnet pepper, celebrated for its delicious citrus sparkle just before your entire mouth and head go up in flames. Scotch bonnets are small hot peppers that come in yellow, orange and red, the very same colors that emanate from your head when you eat one!

Fruit

'All fruits ripe' is a Jamaican expression meaning 'all is well,' which is also the state of Jamaican fruit. This island is a tropical-fruit heaven. Sampling them all and finding your favorites is a noble, healthy and rewarding task. Don't just taste the obvious, like coconut, banana, papaya and mango. Savor your first star apple, soursop, ortanique, naseberry, ugli or tinkin' toe.

Get the lowdown on Pickapeppa, Jamaica's favorite condiment, at www.pickapeppa.com.

DRINKS

You'll never go thirsty in Jamaica. If you're not temperate, you may never go sober either.

Nonalcoholic Drinks

COFFEE

Jamaican Blue Mountain coffee is considered among the most exotic coffees in the world. It's also the most expensive (see the boxed text, p117).

The coffee is relatively mild and light-bodied with a musty, almost woody flavor and its own unmistakable aroma. Most upscale hotels and restaurants serve it as a matter of course. The majority of lesser hotels serve lesser coffees from other parts of the country or – sacrilege! – powdered instant coffee. Be careful if you ask for white coffee (with milk), which Jamaicans interpret to mean 50% hot milk and 50% coffee.

Be warned! The ubiquitous ackee fruit is poisonous if eaten before it's fully mature. Never open an ackee pod; when the fruit is no longer deadly, the pod will open itself and ask to be eaten.

TEA

'Tea' is a generic Jamaican term for any (usually) hot, nonalcoholic drink, and Jamaicans will make teas of anything. Irish moss is often mixed with rum, milk and spices. Ginger, mint, ganja and even fish are brewed into teas. Be careful

JAMAICAN FRUIT PRIMER

Ackee Its yellow flesh is a tasty and popular breakfast food, invariably served with saltfish.
Guava A small ovoid or rounded fruit with an intense, musky sweet aroma. It has a pinkish granular flesh studded with regular rows of tiny seeds. It is most commonly used in nectars and punches, syrups, jams, chutney and even ice cream.
Guinep A small green fruit (pronounced gI-nep) that grows in clusters, like grapes, and can be bought from July through November. Each 'grape' bears pink flesh that you plop into your mouth whole. It's kind of rubbery and juicy, and tastes like a cross between a fig and a strawberry. Watch for the big pip in the middle.
Jackfruit A yellow fruit from the large pods of the jackfruit tree. Jackfruit seeds can be roasted or boiled.
Mango A lush fruit that comes in an assortment of sizes and colors, from yellow to black. Massage the glove-leather skin to soften the pulp, which can be sucked or spooned like custard. Select your mango by its perfume.
Naseberry A sweet, yellow and brown fruit that tastes a bit like peach and comes from an evergreen tree. Also known as sapodilla.
Ortanique An unusual citrus discovered in the Christiana market, believed to be a cross between a sweet orange and a tangerine.
Papaya Cloaks of many colors (from yellow to rose) hide a melon-smooth flesh that likewise runs from citron to vermilion. The central cavity is a trove of edible black seeds. Tenderness and sweet scent are key to buying papayas.
Soursop An ungainly, irregularly shaped fruit with cottony pulp that is invitingly fragrant yet acidic. Its taste hints at guava and pineapple.
Star apple A leathery, dark-purple, tennis-ball-sized gelatinous fruit of banded colors (white, pink, lavender, purple). Its glistening seeds form a star in the center. The fruit is mildly sweet and understated.
Sweetsop A heart-shaped, lumpy fruit packed with pits and a sweet, custardlike flesh.
Tinkin' Toe The Jamaican name for a popular brown fruit that smells like stinky feet. Its scientific name is *Hymenaea courbaril*. Consider it the durian of Jamaica!
Ugli A fruit that is well named. It is ugly on the vine – like a deformed grapefruit with warty, mottled green or orange skin. But the golden pulp is delicious: acid-sweet and gushingly juicy.

TRAVEL YOUR TASTE BUDS

- Escoveitched fish: tangy fish pickled in vinegar, then fried and simmered with peppers and onions. As they say in Portland, 'it wicked.'
- Rundown chicken: cooked in spicy coconut milk, and is usually enjoyed for breakfast with johnny cakes. Some say the dish is named for the method by which the chicken is caught.
- Curried goat: with goats running around everywhere in Jamaica, it's no surprise to find one on the dinner menu.
- Spicy fish tea: 'warm up yuh belly' with this favorite local cure.
- Matrimony: a Christmas dessert made from purple star apples, which ripen in the winter.
- Mannish water is...let's just say it's not for everybody.

if tempted by 'mushroom tea'; the fungus in question is hallucinogenic, so unless you're in search of an LSD-like buzz, steer clear.

Duckanoo (or 'blue drawers' or 'tie-a-leaf') is a dessert made of cornmeal, green bananas and coconut, jacked up with sugar and spices and tied up in a banana leaf.

COLD DRINKS

A Jamaican favorite for cooling off is 'skyjuice': a shaved-ice cone flavored with sugary fruit syrup and lime juice, sold at streetside stalls, usually in a small plastic bag with a straw. You may also notice 'bellywash,' the local name for limeade. Be wary, though of drinking unpurified water.

Ting, a bottled grapefruit soda, is Jamaica's own soft drink. But the best way to quench a thirst is to drink coconut water straight from the nut. They're sold for about US$1 from streetside vendors.

Roots tonics, made from the roots of plants such as raw moon bush, cola bark, sarsaparilla and dandelion, are widely available in small shops, or sold roadside from handmade batches. They taste like dirt...but in a good way.

With all the food that is consumed at celebrations in Jamaica, it's only natural that food itself gets celebrated from time to time with events such as the Portland Jerk Festival, the Jamaica Coffee Festival and the Trelawny Yam Festival.

Alcoholic Drinks

No country's liquor cabinet boasts a wider array of rums than that of Jamaica's, ranging from rums seasoned with such flavors as coconut and peppermint, to those aged like Appleton Special to an amber tint in oak barrels for premium smoothness, to the knockout blow of Overproof (151 proof) white rum. While you may sample and savor these varieties in fruit punches, on the rocks or in daiquiris as the mood takes you, be very careful with Overproof: it may come in a shot glass, but it's not a shot and is best enjoyed mixed with Ting, a local grapefruit drink. Downing shots of Overproof will bring you nothing but an early night.

Red Stripe is Jamaica's famous beer, the one crisp and sweet antidote to spicy jerk creations. If you hear locals calling for 'policemen,' don't panic: the beer is named for the 'natty trim' – a conspicuous red seam – on the trouser legs of the uniform of the Jamaican police force. Should you tire of Red Stripe, Real Rock is a slightly heavier, tastier local lager, while the malty Dragon Stout is also popular. Heineken and Guinness are both brewed under license locally.

For something light, try a ginger wine over ice; it's available at most rum shops.

Jamaica produces many liqueurs, mostly of rum, but also of coffee beans and fruits. The original coffee liqueur is Tia Maria.

For the latest word on rum, check out the Ministry of Rum (www.ministryofrum.com).

CELEBRATIONS

No Jamaican needs a reason to throw a party, but some celebrations require days of planning. Some are cause for the slaughter of an animal, usually a goat or a pig. At weddings, funerals or milestone birthdays, a fattened goat is the victim. The meat is used to make a curry, but the head (and sometimes the testicles) is saved to make mannish water, a soup that also includes beans, onions and dumplings and is said to be an aphrodisiac.

WHERE TO EAT & DRINK

The options for dining in Jamaica range from wildly expensive restaurants to humble roadside stands where you can eat simple fare for as little as US$1. Don't be put off by their basic appearance (unless they're overtly unhygienic). Most serve at least one vegetarian meal, which is often called 'I-tal,' a Rastafarian inspiration for 'pure' or health food.

Watch for sorrel, a traditional bright red Christmas drink made from flower petals.

The most popular snack in Jamaica is a patty – a thin, tender yet crisp crust filled with highly spiced, well-seasoned beef or vegetables. Each town has at least one patty shop. Be warned: they're highly addictive. American fast-food joints are starting to figure prominently in small towns. The local equivalents are Mother's, King Burger and Juici-Beef Patties.

Most hotels proudly – and often exclusively – incorporate Jamaican dishes in their menus. Every town has several small restaurants and cookshops selling standard Jamaican fare.

Food at grocery stores is usually expensive, as many canned and packaged goods are imported. Dirt-cheap fresh fruits, vegetables and spices sell at markets and roadside stalls islandwide. Wash all produce thoroughly!

You can usually buy fish (and lobster, in season) from local fishermen.

From the Foods of the Worlds Series, Norma Benghiat and John Demers's *Food of Jamaica: Authentic Recipes from the Jewel of the Caribbean* is a comprehensive exploration of the island's cuisine.

VEGETARIANS & VEGANS

Thanks to the Rastafarians, Jamaica is veggie-friendly. The Rastafarian diet is called I-tal (for 'vI-tal') cooking, and in its evolved form has an endless index of no-nos. For instance: no salt, no chemicals, no meat or dairy and, for that matter, no alcohol, cigarettes or drugs (ganja doesn't count). Fruits, vegetables, soy, wheat gluten and herbs prevail. Because of the popularity of the I-tal diet most restaurants offer I-tal options.

EATING WITH KIDS

Any all-inclusive resort that accepts children keeps the little ones in mind when laying out the all-you-can-eat buffet, but most menus in Jamaica do not include 'kids' meals.'

Children seem to particularly enjoy seeing and tasting fruit from the tree and there are several working plantations with tours that highlight 'the

THE HIGH ART OF JERK

No one escapes the power and spell of jerk when coming to Jamaica. Invented by the Maroons, it has become the signature dish of the island and consequently has evolved into a high art. Jerk essentially is the process and result of creating a tongue-searing marinade for meats and fish, and barbecuing them slowly and deeply in an outdoor pit. The classic jerk pit is an oil drum cut in half, and the meat is best cooked over a fire of pimento wood for its unique flavor.

There is no end to the ingredients that might be found in a jerk marinade. Allspice, a dark berry which tastes like a mixture of cinnamon, clove and nutmeg, is the one essential spice for jerk. Other goodies include Jamaica's famous dark rums, incendiary Scotch bonnet peppers, lime juice, garlic, onions, Worcestershire sauce, maybe a dash of Pickapeppa, fresh ginger, cinnamon and basically anything else growing or lying around the area when you make it.

Jerk is best served hot off the coals wrapped in paper. You normally order by the pound (US$2 to US$5 should fill you up).

NOUVELLE JAMAICAN CUISINE

In recent years Jamaican nouvelle cuisine – also called Caribbean fusion – has heated up. Reinventing traditional dishes and creating a new and distinct cuisine, it fuses traditional Jamaican ingredients and techniques to haute international tastes.

Here are some of the top trendsetting Jamaican restaurants:

- Houseboat Grill, Montego Bay (p195)
- Hungry Lion, Negril (p238)
- Ivan's Bar, Negril (p238)
- Jake's Place, Treasure Beach (p272)
- Mille Fleurs, East of Port Antonio (p136)
- Norma's on the Terrace, Kingston (p90)
- Red Bones Blues Café, Kingston (p89)
- Rockhouse Restaurant & Bar, Negril (p238)
- Strawberry Hill, near Irish Town (p114)

tastes of Jamaica,' including Croydon in the Mountains (p210), Prospec Plantation (p153) and Sun Valley Plantation (p162).

COOKING COURSES

For the finer points of I-tal cuisine, see Laura Osbourne's *The Rasta Cookbook: Vegetarian Cuisine Eaten with the Salt of the Earth.* Excellent on island fruit and vegetables, not to mention fruit drinks and teas.

The best way to learn about Jamaican cooking is to spend time with a coo in his or her home kitchen. Contact the Jamaica Tourist Board to set up a official meeting through the **Meet the People Program** (www.visitjamaica.com), o consider booking the 'Tastes of Jamaica' tour from **Countrystyle Communit Tours** (☎ 962-7758; Astra Country Inn, Mandeville).

EAT YOUR WORDS

bammy – cassava pancake, generally served with fried fish
bellywash – limeade
callaloo – leafy green vegetable, the collard greens of Jamaica; also called Chinese spinach or Indian kale
cassava – starchy tuber also known as yucca or manioc
cho cho – small, pear-shaped gourd; *chayote*
escoveitch – usually fish fried and pickled in local spices
festival – a fried biscuit or dumpling shaped like a sausage
flor de Jamaica – crimson hibiscus flower, often used to flavor teas
Irish moss – health-food drink made with seaweed extract
I-tal – healthy, natural Rastafarian vegetarian fare, using no salt or preservatives
janga – crayfish
jelly – baby coconut meat
jerk – spicy marinade for meat and fish
johnny cakes – fried dumplings
peas – beans, lentils
Pickapeppa – the main condiment of Jamaica, a savory, piquant bottled sauce, the recipe for which is a closely guarded secret
pimento – allspice
roti – flat Indian pan bread
rundown – fish cooked in coconut milk
seapuss – the Jamaican term for octopus, which is generally fried.
Ting – Jamaica's grapefruit soda
yampi – endemic Jamaican yam

Environment

No less a world traveler than Columbus described Jamaica as 'the fairest isle that eyes beheld; mountainous...all full of valleys and fields and plains.' And despite its relatively small size, Jamaica boasts an impressive diversity of terrain and vegetation – although few visitors venture far enough afield to experience it all. The country's primary forest, while dwindling, still harbors an amazing array of birds and plants, and new species are still being discovered in Cockpit Country.

THE LAND

At 11,425 sq km (about equal to the US state of Connecticut, or one-twentieth the size of Great Britain) Jamaica is the third-largest island in the Caribbean and the largest of the English-speaking islands. It is one of the Greater Antilles, which make up the westernmost of the Caribbean islands.

Jamaica is rimmed by a narrow coastal plain except in the south, where broad flatlands cover extensive areas. Mountains form the island's spine, rising gradually from the west and culminating in the tortuous Blue Mountains in the east, which are capped by Blue Mountain Peak at 2256m. The island is cut by about 120 rivers, many of which are bone dry for much of the year but spring to life after heavy rains, causing great flooding.

If you're into caving, refer to Alan Fincham's *Jamaica Underground*, which plumbs the depths of Cockpit Country.

Two-thirds of the island's surface is composed of soft, porous limestone (the compressed skeletons of coral, clams and other sea life), in places several miles thick and covered by thick red-clay soils rich in bauxite (the principal source of aluminum). The interior, dramatically sculpted with deep vales and steep ridges, is highlighted by Cockpit Country, a virtually impenetrable tract in the east full of irregular limestone hummocks, vast sinkholes, underground caves and flat valley bottoms.

Coastal mangrove and wetland preserves, montane cloud forests and other wild places are strewn across Jamaica. Most travelers stick to beach resorts, however. Those who do get close to nature are as yet poorly served by wildlife reserves.

WILDLIFE

Animals

MAMMALS

Jamaica has very few mammal species. Small numbers of wild hogs and feral goats still roam in isolated wilderness areas. The only native land mammal is the endangered Jamaican hutia, or coney, a large brown rodent akin to a guinea pig. Habitat loss now restricts the highly social, nocturnal beast to remote areas of eastern Jamaica.

The mongoose is the animal you are most likely to see, usually scurrying across the road. This weasel-like mammal was introduced from India in the late 19th century to control rats, but it is now considered a destructive pest.

Mongooses were imported from India in 1872 to rid sugarcane fields of rats. Unfortunately they proved more interested in feeding on the snake, a natural predator of the rat. Today the rat and mongoose populations are still going strong, while snake populations are in decline.

AMPHIBIANS & REPTILES

Jamaica harbors plenty of slithery and slimy things. The largest are crocodiles (incorrectly called 'alligators' in Jamaica), found along the south coast, but also in and around Negril's Great Morass and adjacent rivers (see the boxed text on p254). Abundant until biggame hunters appeared around the turn of the century, they are now protected and fewer than a thousand remain.

Jamaica has 24 species of lizard, including the Jamaican iguana, which hangs on to survival in the remote backwaters of the Hellshire Hills.

Geckos can often be seen hanging on the ceiling by their suction-cup feet. Locals attribute a dark side to the harmless critter, from which Jamaicans superstitiously recoil.

Jamaica has five species of snake, none of them poisonous. All are endangered thanks mostly to the ravages of the mongoose, which has entirely disposed of a sixth species – the black snake. The largest is the Jamaican boa, or yellow snake – a boa constrictor (called *nanka* locally) that can grow to 2.5m in length.

The island also harbors 17 frog and one toad species. Uniquely, none of Jamaica's 14 endemic frog species undergoes a tadpole stage; instead, tiny frogs emerge in adult form directly from eggs. All over Jamaica you'll hear whistle frog living up to its name. While it makes a big racket, the frog itself is smaller than a grape.

INSECTS

Jamaica has mosquitoes, bees and wasps, but most bugs are harmless. For example, a brown scarab beetle called the 'newsbug' flies seemingly without control and, when it flies into people, locals consider it a sign of important news to come. Diamond-shaped 'stinky bugs' are exactly that, advertising themselves with an offensive smell.

Lepidopterists should refer to *An Annotated List of Butterflies of Jamaica* by A Avinoff and N Shoumatoff.

Jamaica has 120 butterfly species and countless moth species, of which 21 are endemic. The most spectacular butterfly is the giant swallowtail, *Papilio homerus*, with a 15cm wingspan. It lives only at higher altitudes in the John Crow Mountains and the eastern extent of the Blue Mountains (and in Cockpit Country in smaller numbers).

Fireflies (called 'blinkies' and 'peeny-wallies') flash luminously in the dark.

BIRDS

The island has more than 255 bird species, 26 of which, along with 21 subspecies, are endemic. Many, such as the Jamaican blackbird and ring-tailed pigeon, are endangered.

Bird-watchers should turn to *Birds of Jamaica: A Photographic Field Guide* by Audrey Downer and Robert Sutton. James Bond's classic *Birds of the West Indies*, another reference for serious bird-watchers, was republished as *Peterson Field Guide to Birds of the West Indies*.

Stilt-legged, snowy-white cattle egrets are ubiquitous, as are 'John crows,' or turkey vultures, which are feared in Jamaica and are a subject of several folk songs and proverbs.

Patoo (a West African word) is the Jamaican name for the owl, which many islanders regard as a harbinger of death. Jamaica has two species: the screech owl and the endemic brown owl. There are also four endemic species of flycatcher, a woodpecker and many rare species of dove.

Bird-watchers can also spot herons, gallinules and countless other waterfowl in the swamps. Pelicans can be seen diving for fish, while magnificent frigate birds soar high above like juvenile pterodactyls.

Jamaica has four of the 16 Caribbean species of hummingbird. The crown jewel of West Indian hummingbirds is the streamertail, the national bird, which is indigenous to Jamaica. This beauty boasts shimmering emerald feathers, a velvety black crown with purple crest and long, slender, curved tail-feathers. It is known locally as the 'doctorbird,' apparently for its long bill, which resembles a 19th-century surgical lancet. The red-billed streamertail inhabits the west, while the black-billed lives in the east. Its image adorns the Jamaican two-dollar bill and the logo of Air Jamaica.

MARINE LIFE

Coral reefs lie along the north shore, where the reef is almost continuous and much of it is within a few hundred meters of shore.

DEBT-FOR-NATURE

Nearly a quarter of Jamaica is still covered by deep, verdant rain forest. The forest that runs along the spine of Jamaica's mountains, known to biologists as the Spinal Forest, is home to much of the island's wildlife and most of its plant species. The Spinal Forest also comprises some of the most significant bird habitat in the Caribbean, with 26 species that exist nowhere else.

Jamaica's nascent environmental-protection programs have been focused primarily on addressing the steady degradation of its coral reefs and beaches, natural assets that are integral to the tourism economy. In the meantime, the interior forest has been steadily decimated, the victim of expanding agricultural development, population growth and mining.

In a welcome development, in late 2004 the governments of the US and Jamaica, with substantial support from the **Nature Conservancy** (☎ 703-841-4878, 800-628-6860; www.nature.org; 4245 N Fairfax Dr, Arlington, VA 222203, USA), agreed to a 'debt-for-nature' swap. Under the provisions of the agreement, nearly US$16 million of Jamaica's debt to the US has been canceled.

In exchange, the Jamaican government has pledged to invest the equivalent of almost US$16 million over a 20-year period to create a trust fund that will provide long-term funding to protect and manage the island's national parks and forest reserves. The debt-swap funding has allowed the Jamaican government and a network of local, established conservation organizations to have a reliable source of money for important conservation projects such as conducting research and biological surveys, preparing and planning for new national parks and forest reserves, planting trees, restoring damaged ecosystems and conducting public-education and community-outreach activities.

Leaflike orange gorgonians spread their fingers up toward the light. There are contorted sheets of purple staghorn and lacy outcrops of tubipora resembling delicately woven Spanish mantillas, sinuous boulder-like brain corals and soft flowering corals that sway to the rhythms of the currents.

Flowering Plants of Jamaica by C Dennis Adams has detailed descriptions of individual species, accompanied by illustrations.

Over 700 species of fish zip in and out of the exquisite reefs and swarm through the coral canyons: wrasses, parrotfish, snappers, bonito, kingfish, jewelfish and scores of others. The smaller fry are preyed upon by barracuda, giant groupers and tarpon. Sharks, of course, are frequently seen, though most of these are harmless nurse sharks. Further out, the cobalt deeps are run by sailfish, marlin and manta rays.

Three species of endangered marine turtle – the green, hawksbill and loggerhead – lay eggs at the few remaining undeveloped sandy beaches.

About 100 of the endangered West Indian manatee – a shy, gentle creature once common around the island – survive in Jamaican waters, most numerously in the swamps of Long Bay on the south coast.

Plants

Jamaica boasts 3582 plant species (including 237 orchids), of which at least 912 are endemic. Jamaica also boasts some 60 bromeliad species and 550 species of fern.

For the latest dope on Jamaica's most notorious crop, click on www.cannabisnews.com.

Anthuriums, heliconias and gingers are all common, as are hibiscus and periwinkle. Impatiens color roadsides at cooler heights.

Introduced exotics include the bougainvillea, brought from London's Kew Gardens in 1858. Ackee, the staple of Jamaican breakfasts, was brought from West Africa in 1778. The first mango tree arrived in 1782 from Mauritius, and Captain William Bligh arrived in Jamaica in 1779 bearing 700 breadfruit. Cocoa and cashew are native to Central America and the West Indies, as is cassava. A native pineapple from Jamaica was the progenitor of Hawaii's pineapples (the fruit even appears on the Jamaican coat of arms).

Needless to say, ganja is grown beneath tall plants in remote areas to evade the probing helicopters of the Jamaica Defense Force. The harvest season runs from late August through October.

TREE SPECIES

The national flower is the dark-blue bloom of the lignum vitae tree. Its timber is much in demand by carvers. The national tree is blue mahoe, which derives its name from the blue-green streaks in its beautiful wood. Another dramatic flowering tree is the vermilion 'flame of the forest' (also called the 'African tulip tree').

Logwood, introduced to the island in 1715, grows wild in dry areas and produces a dark blue dye, for which it was grown commercially during the 19th century. Native mahogany and ebony have been logged and decimated during the past two centuries. Other native trees include the massive silk cotton, said to be a favored habitat of 'duppies' (ghosts).

Palms are everywhere, except at the highest reaches of the Blue Mountains. There are many species, including the stately royal palm (a Cuban import), which grows to over 30m.

Much of Jamaica's coast is fringed by mangroves.

To visit Cockpit Country in an ecologically responsible manner, check out the Southern Trelawny Environmental Agency's website www.stea.net.

NATIONAL PARKS

Jamaica's embryonic park system comprises four national parks: Blue Mountains-John Crow National Park, Montego Bay Marine Park, Port Antonio Marine Park and Negril Marine Park.

The 780-sq-km Blue Mountains-John Crow National Park (Jamaica's largest) includes the forest reserves of the Blue and John Crow mountain ranges. Both marine parks are situated around resort areas and were developed to preserve and manage coral reefs, mangroves and offshore marine resources.

There is also a fistful of other wilderness areas with varying degrees of protection, such as the Portland Bight Protected Area (p103).

Additional national parks are being conceptualized and have been touted for years. (See the map, p50, for proposed sites.) Proposals to turn Cockpit Country into a national park have been met with stiff resistance from the Maroons who live there and fear increased gov-

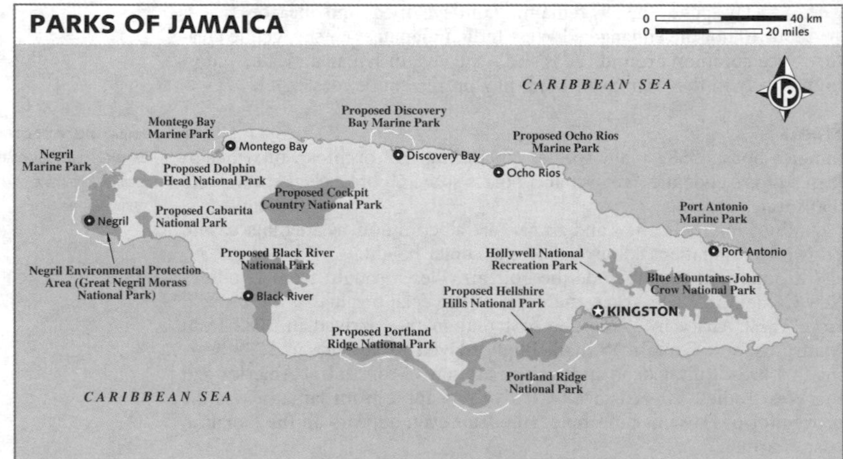

TIPS FOR TRAVELERS

- Take only photographs, leave only footprints. Don't litter, and if you see it, pick it up.
- Support recycling programs.
- Never take 'souvenirs' such as shells, plants or artifacts from historical sites or natural areas. Treat shells, sea urchins, coral and other marine life as sacred.
- Don't buy products made from endangered species. Buying products made of tortoiseshell, coral or bird feathers contributes to the decimation of wildlife.
- Keep to the footpaths. When hiking, always follow designated trails. Natural habitats are often quickly eroded, and animals and plants are disturbed by walkers who stray from the beaten path.
- Don't touch or stand on coral. Coral is extremely sensitive and is easily killed by snorkelers and divers who make contact. Likewise, boaters should never anchor on coral – use mooring buoys. (For further guidelines on protecting the coral, see p228.)
- Try to patronize hotels, tour companies and merchants that act in an environmentally sound manner. Consider their impact on waste generation, noise levels, energy consumption and the local culture.
- Support community tourism. Many local communities derive little benefit from Jamaica's huge tourism revenues. Educate yourself on community tourism and ways you can participate (see the boxed text, p263). Use local tour guides wherever possible.
- Respect the community. Learn about the customs of the region and support local efforts to preserve the environment and traditional culture.
- Tell others. Politely intervene when you observe other travelers behaving in an environmentally or socially detrimental manner.

ernmental authority will infringe on their hard-won autonomy. In the meantime, the Jamaica Environment Trust is working hard to get the region closed to mining and in 2007 succeeded in getting all prospecting licenses suspended.

ENVIRONMENTAL ISSUES

Today, the island the Arawak people called Xaymaca (or 'Land of Wood and Water') is in dire environmental straits. In the mid-1990s, Jamaica had the highest rate of deforestation (5% per year) of any country in the world and, although there is now greater awareness of the problem, it is still a threat. Many of Jamaica's endemic wildlife species are endangered or gone forever, and according to the World Conservation Union, Jamaica ranks among the top 10 countries in the world for numbers of both endangered amphibians and endangered plant species. Legislation has been largely ineffectual: authorities are underfunded and fines are absurdly low. For more information, contact the **Rainforest Trust** (☎ 305-669-8955; rft@rainforesttrust.com; 6001 SW 63rd Ave, Miami, FL 33143, USA).

Over the last decade, deforestation has led to the deterioration of more than a third of Jamaica's watersheds.

Bauxite mining – the island's second most lucrative industry after tourism – is considered to be the single largest cause of deforestation in Jamaica. Bauxite can only be extracted by opencast mining, which requires the wholesale destruction of forests and topsoil. The access roads cut by mining concerns are then used by loggers, coal burners and yam-stick traders to get to trees in and around designated mining areas, extending the deforestation.

Deforestation has also ravaged the Blue Mountains, where farmers felled trees to clear land to grow lucrative coffee plants. When the dwindling tree population caused migratory birds to shun the area, in turn leaving it to insects that ravaged the crop, some farmers began to work with conservationists and park officials planting trees (see p117).

Indeed, the past decade has seen a stirring of eco-awareness. The **National Resources Conservation Authority** (NRCA; ☎ 754-7540; www.nrca.org; c/o Natural Environment & Planning Agency, 10 Caledonia Ave, Kingston 5) is entrusted with responsibility for promoting ecological consciousness among Jamaicans and management of the national parks and protected areas under the Protected Areas Resource Conservation Project (PARC).

The Nature Conservancy (www.nature.org/wherewework/caribbean/jamaica) has been instrumental in protecting the Blue Mountains-John Crow National Park.

The following organizations are also taking the lead in bringing attention to ecological issues:

Jamaica Conservation & Development Trust (☎ 960-2848; www.greenjamaica.org; 95 Dumbarton Ave, Kingston 10)

Jamaica Environment Trust (☎ 960-3693; www.jamentrust.org; 58 Half Way Tree Rd, Kingston 10)

Jamaica Sustainable Development Networking Programme (☎ 968-0323; www.jsdnp.org.jm; 115 Hope Rd, Kingston 6)

National Environmental Societies Trust (☎ 960-3316; www.jsdnp.org.jm/nestjamaica; 95 Dumbarton Ave, Kingston 10)

Jamaica Outdoors

Jamaica's a wily seductress. Luring vacationers by the millions with visions of sugary sand and limitless sun, she soon rouses them from the poolside bar or beach towel with an enticing array of outdoor activities. Indeed, some of the most rewarding items on Jamaica's tourist menu are to be found exploring her caves, reefs, rivers and mountains. Even the most comatose beach-bum is going to wonder just what else is out there after a while.

SCUBA DIVING & SNORKELING

Jamaica's shores are as beautiful below the surface as they are above. This is especially true on the north coast from Negril to Ocho Rios, where conditions for diving are exceptional. Waters offer tremendous visibility and temperatures of around 27°C year-round. Treasures range from shallow reefs, caverns and trenches to walls and drop-offs just a few hundred meters offshore.

'Jamaica's shores are as beautiful below the surface as they are above.'

By law, all dives in Jamaican waters must be guided, and dives are restricted to a depth of 30m. (See the boxed text, p228, on guidelines for protecting the reef.) If you spend enough time in the water, you're practically guaranteed to see parrotfish, angelfish, turtles, eels and the odd barracuda.

Most diving occurs in and around the Montego Bay and Negril marine parks, in proximity to a wide range of licensed dive operators offering rental equipment and group dives. The main draws around Montego Bay are the Point, a dive wall renowned for its dense corals and fish, sharks and rays, and Airport Reef boasting masses of coral canyons, caves and tunnels, and even a DC-3 wreck.

In Negril the caves off the West End have tunnels and the occasional hawksbill turtle. Among the area's highlights are The Throne, a cave with sponges, plentiful corals, nurse sharks, octopi, barracuda and stingrays; Deep Plane, which holds the remains of a Cessna airplane lying at 21m underwater and Sands Club Reef, which lies in 10m of water in the middle of Long Bay.

In Montego Bay try **Resort Divers** (☎ 953-9699), **Fun Divers** (☎ 953-3268; Wyndham Rose Hall Hotel, Rose Hall) or **Jamaica Scuba Divers** (G66; Half Moon Hotel, Ironshore).

In Negril, most all-inclusive resorts have scuba facilities. **Negril Scuba Centre** has locations at **Mariner's Negril Beach Club** (☎ 957-4425, 957-9641), **Negril Escape Resort & Spa** (☎ 957-0392) and **Sunset @ the Palms** (☎ 383-9533), and offers PADI certification and introductory 'resort courses'.

Dives cost around US$50/70 for one-/two-tank dives. A snorkeling excursion, which generally includes equipment and a boat trip, costs US$25 to US$50. 'Resort courses' for beginners (also called 'Discover Scuba') are offered at most major resorts (about US$90), which also offer PADI or NAUI certification courses (US$350 to US$400) and advanced courses.

RAFTING

It was no less than Errol Flynn, a true convert to the Jamaican way of life, who first saw the fun of coasting down the river on a raft of bamboo poles lashed together. The sybaritic actor got the idea watching the banana loads being transported in that manner down the Rio Grande, and before long he'd popularized rafting for pleasure.

Today, you sit on a raised seat with padded cushions, while a 'captain' poles you through the washboard shallows and small cataracts. It's a marvelous experience and gives you a sample of outback Jamaica. Take a hat and sunscreen to guard against the sun.

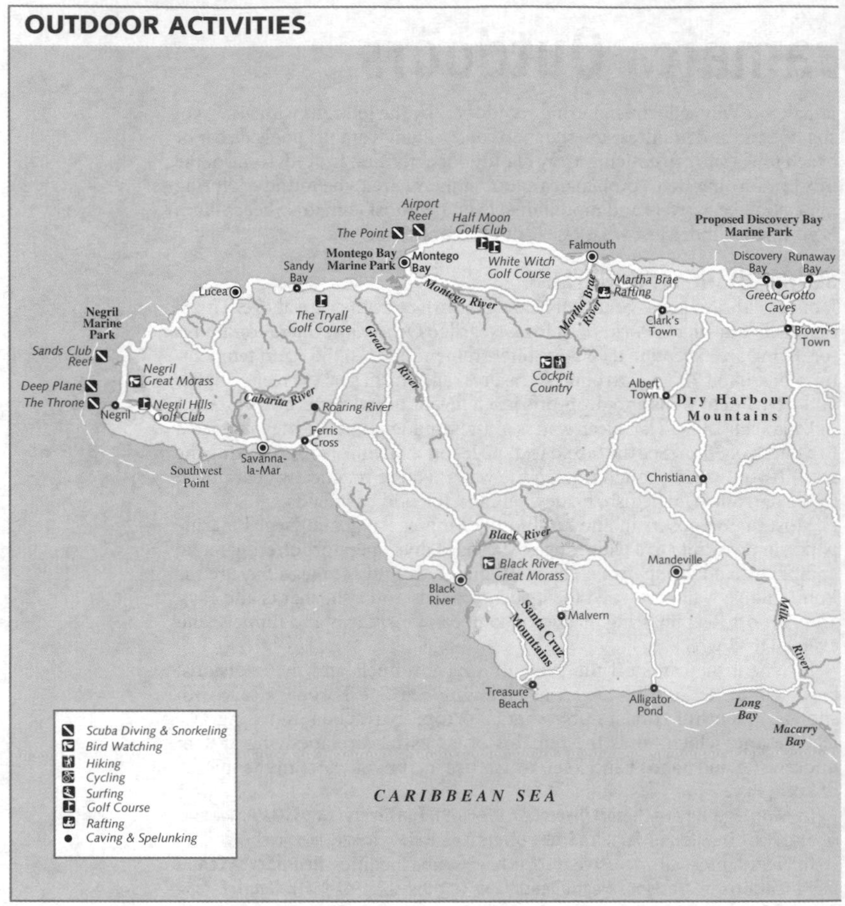

Jamaica's rivers are among the island's true revelations, and trips are offered on along the majestic bends of the Rio Grande as well as the Great and Martha Brae rivers (single companies hold a monopoly at each).

Mountain Valley Rafting (☎ 956-4920; Lethe Estate; per passenger US$40) For trips along the Great River.

Rio Grande Experience (☎ 913-5434, 993-5778; Berridale; per raft US$60, full-moon ride US$120) For trips along Rio Grande.

River Raft Ltd (☎ 952-0889, 940-6398; 66 Claude Clarke Ave, Montego Bay; 1 or 2 persons per raft US$45, with hotel transfer US$50) For trips along Martha Brae.

HIKING

Jamaica's embryonic organized trail system is restricted to the Blue Mountains-John Crow National Park, where a Blue Mountain Ridge Trail – akin to the Appalachian Trail of the eastern USA – is still being developed. The most popular trail leads directly to the summit of Blue Mountain Peak, and reaching it at sunrise is one of the Caribbean's most exhilarating experiences. The view out over the entire island (and as far

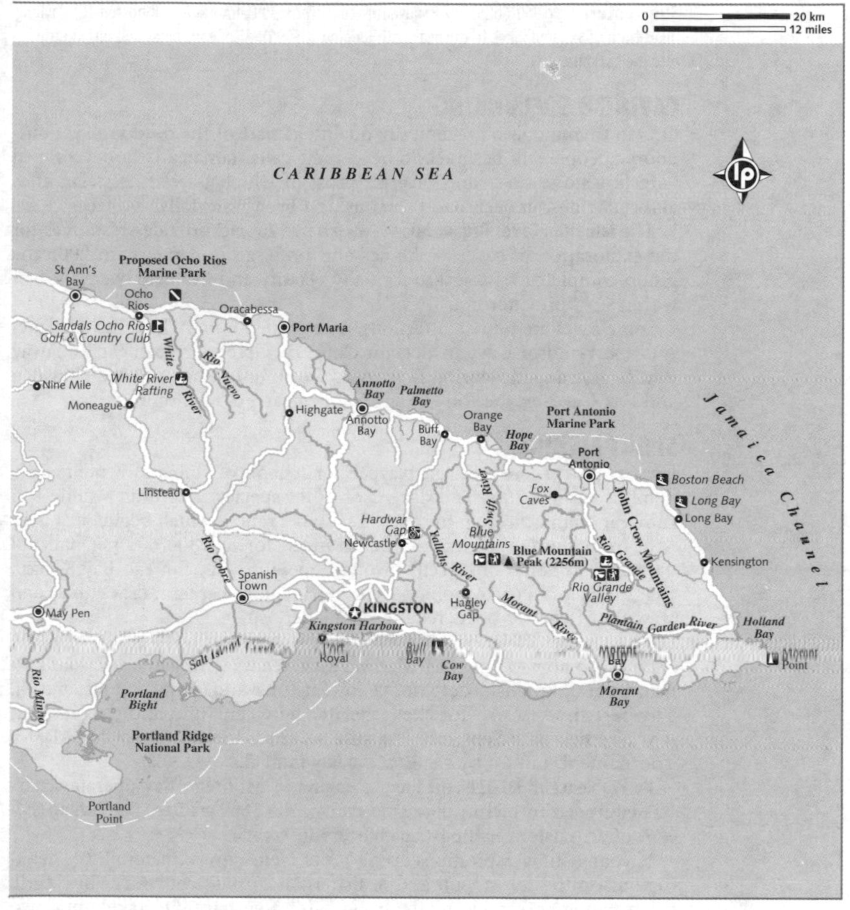

as Cuba if the day's clear) more than compensates for having got up at an inhuman hour.

The second most-developed area for hiking is the Rio Grande Valley in Portland parish, where tour guides offer one- to three-day hikes, some of which venture into the Blue and John Crow Mountains. The remote Cockpit Country also attracts hikers with its otherworldly sylvan limestone hills and sumptuous vistas.

Wherever your walk carries you, always be sure to stay on the established trails: the mountainous terrain in Jamaica is too treacherous to go wandering off the track, as thick vegetation hides sinkholes and crevasses. You should always seek advice from locals about trail conditions before setting out, and take a good guide even if you think you know the route. Here are some suggested tour-guide operators:

Grand Valley Tours (☎ 993-4116, 858-7338; valleytours@cwjamaica.com; 12 West St, Port Antonio) Specializes in hiking trips in the Rio Grande Valley.

Strawberry Hill (☎ 944-8400; www.strawberryhillresort.com; Irish Town) Short tours and longer hikes from US$40.

Sun Venture (☎ 960-6685; www.sunventuretours.com; 30 Balmoral Ave, Kingston 10) Daylong hikes from US$75 and hikes to the peak with lodging (US$95). Also leads hikes and birding trips into the Cockpits.

CAVING & SPELUNKING

OK, so caving doesn't technically qualify as part of the outdoors, yet outdoorsy people will be quick to heed their calls. Jamaica is honeycombed with limestone caves and caverns, most of which boast fine stalagmites and stalactites, underground streams and even waterfalls.

The **Jamaican Caves Organization** (www.jamaicancaves.org) provides resources for the exploration of caves, sinkholes and underground rivers. In 2005 the group completed a project to formally classify and evaluate over 70 caves within Cockpit Country.

Some caves are tourist attractions, with guided tours. These include labyrinthine Windsor Cave in Cockpit Country, Green Grotto near Runaway Bay, large, vaulted Roaring River near Savanna-la-Mar, and the Nonsuch and Fox Caves in the Rio Grande Valley near Port Antonio.

SPORT FISHING

Jamaica's waters are a pelagic playpen for schools of blue-and-white marlin, dolphin, wahoo, tuna and dozens of other species. Deepwater game-fish run year-round through the deep Cayman Trench, which begins just over 3km from shore. Charters can be arranged for US$400/600 per half/full day through hotels or directly through operators in Montego Bay, Negril, Ocho Rios and Port Antonio. A charter includes captain, tackle, bait and crew. Most charter boats require a 50% deposit.

The waters off Jamaica's north coast are particularly good for game fishing. An abyss known as 'Marlin Alley' teems with game fish like sailfish, wahoo, kingfish, dolphin, yellowfin tuna and, yes, the blue marlin. The best time to fish for the latter are between June and August, but if you're here late September be sure to enter the Montego Bay Marlin Tournament, put on by the **Montego Bay Yacht Club** (979-8038).

No Problem (☎ 381-3229) on Pier 1 Marina in Montego Bay operates charters equipped to reel in big-game fish, while **Stanley's Deep Sea Fishing** (957-0667) offers custom fishing-trip charters in Negril.

If your fishing aspirations aren't quite Hemingway material, try heading out on the water with a local fisherman to test your luck. In Negril, fisherman congregating by the bridge are often happy to take you down the South Negril River, and Frenchman's Bay on the southeast coast has plenty of fishermen willing to take you along for a fee.

'There's a lot to be said for your beach lacking tranquility: surf's up!'

SURFING

Sure, the east coast lacks the west's fabled sunsets and more celebrated beaches, but the waves rushing in from the Atlantic have been attracting surfers. There's a lot to be said for your beach lacking tranquility: surf's up!

Boston Beach, 14km east of Port Antonio, is the best-known spot. A narrow bay whose waves roll in with occasional ferocity, it contains a small beachside shack from which you can rent boards cheaply. Long Bay, 16km further south, was badly hit by Hurricane Dean in 2007, but the beach itself has recovered, and it's possible to rent boards here as well.

The **Surfing Association of Jamaica/Jamnesia Surf Club** (☎ 750-0103; PO Box 167, Kingston 2) provides general information about surfing in Jamaica and operates a surf camp at Bull Bay, 13km east of Kingston.

Try **Jah Mek Yah** (☎ 435-8806, in the USA ☎ 954-594-9619; www.theliquidaddiction.com/jaspots.html; Morant Bay, St Thomas), a surf lodge in Jamaica's unspoiled eastern corner, offering relaxed, rootsy surf packages.

CYCLING

Although cycling is not terribly common in Jamaica – in no small part due to the perils of island traffic – one of the island's greatest thrills can be had on a bike: the downhill tour from Hardwar Gap in the Blue Mountains. From Ocho Rios or Kingston, **Blue Mountain Bicycle Tours** (☎ 974-7075; www.bmtoursja.com) will pick you by bus and take you to that peak, 1700m above sea level, put you on a mountain bike and send you down.

'one of the island's greatest thrills can be had on a bike: the downhill tour from Hardwar Gap in the Blue Mountains.'

For more sedate cycling, you can hire bicycles at most of the major resorts. Anything more serious, and you should consider bringing your own mountain or multipurpose bike (you will need sturdy wheels to handle the potholed roads). Check requirements with the airline well in advance, preferably before you pay for your ticket.

Jamaica Mountain Bike Association (Jamba; ☎ 957-0155; rustynegril@hotmail.com; PO Box 104, Negril) A good information source.

Manfred's Jamaican Mountain Bike Tours (in Canada ☎ 705-745-8210; www.nexicom.net/~manfred/; tour US$795) Based in Canada, offering bicycling tours of the south coast.

Rusty's X-Cellent Adventures (☎ 957-0155; rustynegril@hotmail.com; PO Box 104, Negril; tours per person US$50) Offers exciting tours in the hills near Negril.

BIRD-WATCHING

A birder's haven, Jamaica is home to over 250 species of bird, the most common of which are snow-white cattle egrets and the ominous 'John crows,' or turkey vultures. Jamaica boasts four of the Caribbean's 16 species of hummingbird. The crown jewel of West Indian hummingbirds is the streamertail, the national bird, which is indigenous to Jamaica and known as the 'doctorbird.' You are sure to see them – if only because it adorns the Jamaican two-dollar bill.

Birders will also spot herons, gallinules and countless other waterfowl in the swamps. Pelicans can be seen diving for fish, while magnificent frigate birds soar high above like juvenile pterodactyls.

Good spots include the Blue Mountains, Cockpit Country, the Black River Great Morass, the Negril Great Morass and the Rio Grande Valley. All you need in the field are a good pair of binoculars and a guide to the birds of the island. **Windsor Great House** (☎ 997-3832; www.cockpitcountry.com; Windsor) organizes a bird-banding effort on the last weekend of each month.

For birding tours and support, try the following:

Ann & Robert Sutton (☎ 904-5454; asutton@cwjamaica.com; per day US$200) Based in Mandeville, they've been leading major bird tours in Jamaica for more than 30 years.

Fritz Beckford (☎ 952-2009; per 3hr US$20) At Rocklands Bird Sanctuary, near Montego Bay.

Grand Valley Tours (☎ 993-4116, 858-7338; www.portantoniojamaica.com/gvt.html; 12 West St, Port Antonio) Offers birding trips in the Rio Grande Valley.

Jamaica Explorations (☎ 993-7267; mockbrd@cwjamaica.com; Hotel Mockingbird Hill, Port Antonio) Bird-watching tours in Portland parish and the Blue Mountains.

Strawberry Hill (☎ 944-8400; www.strawberryhillresort.com) Birding trips in the Blue Mountains.

GOLF

Jamaica has 12 championship golf courses – more than any other Caribbean island. All courses rent out clubs and have carts. Most require that you hire a caddy – an extremely wise investment, as they know the layout of the course intimately.

The two most famous Jamaican courses can be found near Montego Bay. The **Tryall Golf Course** (☎ 956-5660) and the **White Witch Golf Course** (☎ 953-2800) at the Ritz-Carlton Rose Hall are world-class links that lure golf enthusiasts from all over the world. The less advanced or simply curious can also get in a few swings, though Tryall is sometimes closed to nonmembers in high season.

'should your ball land in the water, best leave it as a souvenir for one of the resident crocodiles.'

For those enticed by scenic links, **Sandals Ocho Rios Golf & Country Club** (☎ 975-0119) six km southeast of Ocho Rios is widely regarded as the most beautiful of Jamaica's links, while golfers in Negril can try the **Negril Hills Golf Club** (☎ 957-4638) with a delightful setting by the Great Morass swampland. And should your ball land in the water, best leave it as a souvenir for one of the resident crocodiles.

For more information on the island's links, contact the **Jamaica Golf Association** (☎ 925-2325; www.jamaicagolfassociation.com; Constant Spring Golf Club, PO Box 743, Kingston 8).

Contemporary Jamaican Music

Each year, Jamaica inspires pilgrims seeking sun, beaches and rum (or a potent cocktail of all three), yet it was the reggae revolution from the late 1960s to the early 1980s that put Jamaican music on the map and made it inexorably distinct from other Caribbean hotspots. Yet while that revolution's legacies can still be heard on the world's stages from great reggae ambassadors such as Jimmy Cliff, Burning Spear and Bunny Wailer, they are no longer the voices of Jamaican youth. There are new faces on the scene and new beats in the air – and no beat is louder than the sound of the dancehall.

Reggae Explosion: The Story of Jamaican Music, by Chris Salewcz and Adrian Boot, traces the evolution of Jamaican music in words and (amazing) photographs.

Today it is dancehall music not roots reggae that is Jamaica's pulse. By day, it comes at you from streetside cassette vendors, passing minibuses and the corner bar where people gather to play dominoes. At night the hard-driving bass rhythms of megawatt mobile discos, known as sound systems, call from the distance. Jamaicans come from miles away to these makeshift dancehalls to hear the 'champion' sound systems, seeking musical medicine to ease the harsh pressures of daily life. They are rarely disappointed. Outside the dancehall, people linger in the shadows of kerosene lanterns. Vendors and card sharks hustle and groove while the disc jockeys tempt youths to buy a ticket and join the show. In the heat of the dance, the sound systems engage in a 'sound clash,' dueling with custom records to win the crowd's favor and boost their reputation. Dancehall divas model their latest bare-as-you-dare outfits, chiseled young men decked out in bright tops and gold chains crowd around the sound systems to study the DJ's every move and, in the shadows, lovers rock in sensual embraces.

It is impossible to summarize the vast historical terrain of Jamaican music with all of its complexity and cultural nuance in a few short pages. What we hope to do is give you an appreciation of the profound importance of music in Jamaican life, a sense of the richness of this creative expression and some practical advice about how you can get first-hand experience of the music scene while visiting.

JAMAICAN SYNCRETISM

It is somewhat misleading to think of the history of Jamaican music as a neat linear chronology, as the marching of one distinct genre into the other, or the passing of the torch from one musician to another.

Most historical overviews of Jamaican music present an orderly progression from mento (Jamaican folk music; 1930s and '40s) to Jamaican R&B ('50s) to ska (its first popular music; early '60s), rocksteady (a short intermediate step; mid-'60s), reggae (the apex of its achievements; late '60s to late '70s) and finally dancehall (the opposite of everything reggae stood for; post-1981). But this view of Jamaican music is oversimplified and obscures much more than it illuminates. The music of different eras, genres and cultures influence each other rather than remaining pure streams that never intersect. The key concept here is the beautiful fusion (anthropologists call it syncretism) of different cultural elements to create something new. This syncretism is the magic of Jamaican music.

Jahworks (www.jahworks.org) is an online zine dedicated to Caribbean (mostly Jamaican) music and culture. The writing is intelligent, informed and entertaining.

Several musical genres are part of the mix of today's music scene. In the 1960s and '70s, Jamaica experienced a golden age of popular music, with the emergence within 10 years of the holy trinity of ska, rocksteady and reggae, but we should not be nostalgic for the past glories; they are very much alive today. The continuing evolution of ska music is an excellent case in point. In Jamaica, ska's popularity peaked in the early '60s with the rise of its most famous band, the Skatalites, and waned by the mid-'60s. Yet a decade later it would be revived in Britain as ska's 'second wave' by the children of Black Jamaican migrants and White English working-class kids who grew up together in London and Birmingham. In turn, these 'two tone' bands (The Beat, Madness, The Specials) would inspire youth in the US to create a 'third wave' of ska in the '80s and '90s (Fishbone, Sublime, Mighty Mighty Bosstones, The Mad Caddies) – and many of their fans have no idea the music originated in Jamaica.

Solid Foundation: An Oral History of Reggae is an intensely readable study of Jamaican music in the words of the people who created it.

Other classic Jamaican genres such as roots reggae, lovers rock and dub have similarly influenced musicians and fans around the world, and now-local variants of these sounds can be found in nearly every corner of the earth from Kauai to Kathmandu. While the wave of popularity may subside in its birthplace, the music nevertheless lives on and keeps changing in ways that its originators could never have anticipated.

MARLEY'S LEGACY: THE STONE THAT THE BUILDER REFUSED

Bob Marley, in his song 'Trenchtown,' asked if anything good could ever come out of Trenchtown. Posing this rhetorical question, one he must have heard a thousand times from members of the Jamaican upper classes, Marley challenged the very ideological foundation that Jamaican society was built on – the notion that one set of people (ie the poor masses of African descent) would be denied their freedom and sense of human worth by a small minority of Jamaica's ruling elite. In one of the song's next verses, Marley exhorts us to 'pay tribute to Trenchtown,' defiantly demanding respect for his hometown, spitting the old paternalism back in the face of his oppressors while at the same time encouraging the ghetto to escape the shackles of 'mental slavery.'

King Jammy's by Beth Lesser covers a period of transition from roots reggae to dancehall. Lesser focuses on King Jammy, the producer and chief architect of the new dancehall sound.

'The stone that the builder refused shall become the head corner stone' (Psalm 118:22) is a line that Bob Marley employed in more than one song. The moral of this parable is that of redemption, the rejected coming back to be the exalted one – the last shall be first. Marley's essential message to the masses was to take pride in where they were from and to realize what they were capable of: greatness, and perhaps even kinship with the divine, Jah Rastafari. This message would resonate around the globe, among people of all walks of life, changing the course of music history forever.

Robert Nesta Marley emerged from a very unlikely place to become one of the truly great musical figures of the 20th century, simultaneously an artistic, political and religious figure of worldwide significance. Acknowledging his singular place in the history of the last century, the international media have given him a number of posthumous honors: in 1999, *Time Magazine* named his album *Exodus* 'album of the century,' while the BBC rated his 'One Love' the song of the millennium. High praise indeed.

Yet as central as Bob Marley was to the development and popularization of Jamaican music and culture, he is only the tip of the iceberg when it comes to understanding the impact of Jamaican music on Jamaica and the world. Over the past 50 years Jamaican music has had a massive effect on global culture disproportionate to the country's size and population. Somehow the poorest and most disenfranchised citizens of one small nation have developed institutions and art forms that have influenced the music of countries around the world. How could this be possible? Perhaps a Jamaican proverb gives the best answer: 'Mi likkle but mi talawah' (I may be little, but I am very powerful).

JAMAICAN MUSICAL GENRES

Ska

The birth of ska occurred in Jamaica's recording studios in the early 1960s when musicians altered the American R&B sound with indigenous musical elements drawn from mento, Rastafarian drumming known as *nyahbinghi*, and other Afro-Jamaican religious music. This largely horn-driven sound was created by many of Jamaica's leading jazz musicians, who went on to form ska's most important band, the Skatalites.

Rocksteady

Rocksteady enjoyed wide popularity for only two years after first emerging in 1966. Generally slower and more refined than ska, rocksteady placed more emphasis on the syncopation of the drum and bass, with the horn section taking a back seat. Patterned to a large extent on the US soul singers, rocksteady was an era of great vocal stylists such as Alton Ellis, Ken Booth, John Holt, Slim Smith and Leroy Sibbles, and great harmony groups (The Paragons, The Techniques, the Wailers and the Heptones).

Reggae

While the term is often used to refer to all of Jamaican popular music, reggae first crystallized as a distinct musical genre in 1968. Reggae's leading stars (Desmond Dekker, Jimmy Cliff, Toots and Maytals, Bob Marley and the Wailers, to name just a few) exploded on the international scene in the 1970s. Reggae is most often associated with roots – that is Rastafari-inspired – reggae. However, there are various subgenres of reggae including lovers rock, rockers and dancehall style.

Mento

Mento, a folk song-and-dance form based on a mix of European and African stylistic elements, was Jamaica's first popular music. It was played on a variety of instruments including the banjo, guitar, fiddle, fife and rhumba box. Often confused with Trinidadian calypso, mento was the first Jamaican music released on record.

Lovers Rock

This is a style of reggae created in the UK with a strong emphasis on romantic themes. A high percentage of lovers rock tunes are cover versions of US soul ballads done over a reggae rhythm. These tunes are often part of the 'early warm' part of a dancehall session before the selectors start spinning the hardcore DJ tunes.

Dub

A genre that's based on the studio remix of previously recorded reggae songs, dub rose to popularity in the early 1970s. Often referred to as 'X-ray' music, dub music is known for its bare-bones drum-and-bass rhythm tracks, spacey studio effects like echo and reverb, and the haunting use of vocal snippets. To check it out, look for records from Lee 'Scratch' Perry, King Tubby and the Mad Professor.

Dancehall

Often referred to as ragga in the UK, the genre of dancehall became the dominant form of Jamaican music after Bob Marley's death in 1981. Dancehall was initially seen as a rejection of everything Marley stood for (Rastafari 'culture,' equal rights and justice, acoustic instruments and vocal harmonies), and it has since been stereotyped as a music based primarily on slackness (raw sexuality) and gun lyrics, the glorification of materialism, digital 'riddims' and DJs (rappers). Since the early 1990s, however, dancehall has experienced an on-again-off-again Rasta renaissance with the return of 'conscious' lyricists such as Garnett Silk, Tony Rebel, Luciano, Sizzla and Anthony B.

THE ELEPHANT IN THE ROOM: HOMOPHOBIA IN DANCEHALL MUSIC

Since the turn of the millennium, dancehall has ridden a wave of international success, surpassing its first wave of crossover success in the early '90s with Shabba Ranks, Cobra, Super Cat and Patra. But is the music able to sustain this latest flash of worldwide popularity?

One of the biggest obstacles is the controversy over homophobia in dancehall lyrics. Some Jamaican artists (including Buju Banton, Beenie Man, Sizzla and Capleton) have become targets of protests from gay-rights groups, particularly in the UK, where activists, asserting homophobic song lyrics are incitement to murder, have led boycotts of record labels and initiated criminal proceedings.

For the most part, Jamaicans have defended the attitudes expressed against gays and lesbians in dancehall lyrics as a matter of cultural and national sovereignty, while activists both inside and outside Jamaica (including Human Rights Watch) have argued that dancehall promotes violence against homosexuals.

In 2005 a 'ceasefire' was brokered in London between gay-rights organizations, dancehall artists and the record companies that represent them. Under the terms of this agreement groups such as Outrage! would stop protesting against dancehall artists as long they refrained from performing material that could be seen as inciting violence against gays and lesbians. How long this agreement holds or what it means back home in Jamaica, where the rights of homosexuals are not guaranteed by law, remains to be seen.

DANCEHALL CULTURE

Many music critics, writers of guidebooks and compilers of CD box sets have decided that Jamaican music declined after Marley's death – that the 'dancehall era' of the past 25 years is of little merit in comparison to the reggae era of the 1970s. Nothing could be further from the truth.

Nevertheless, many observers of the Jamaican music scene seem to feel that dancehall changed everything. Some consider dancehall to be a degeneration from 'classical' reggae or a mere borrowing from American rap. However, this is to misunderstand the evolution of Jamaican music. Rather than tread ing the same old paths that have served them well, Jamaican musicians are moving boldly into new terrain, continuously innovating to make a mark in a competitive field.

The Maytals' 1968 song 'Do the Reggay' was the first record to use the term 'reggae'. Prior to this the music was known as rocksteady.

Remarkably, not even the recent explosion of Jamaican dancehall artists like Shabba Ranks, Shaggy, Beenie Man and Sean Paul onto the world stage has brought dancehall culture itself into focus outside Jamaica. Whether it started in the late 1970s (with the rise of DJs such as The Lone Ranger, Yellowman and Josey Wales) or the mid-1980s (with the advent of digital production techniques and the famous Sleng Teng rhythm) is a matter of some debate. However, as a cultural space where social dances were held, dancehall's roots go back to the slavery era. According to Hedley Jones, former president of the Jamaica Federation of Musicians and sound-system pioneer: 'Dancehall has always been with us, because we have always had our clubs, our market places, our booths...where our dances were kept. And these were known as dancehalls.' For example, it was in the dancehall of the 19th century that mento, Jamaica's first popular music, was born. Dancehall is not the decimation of Jamaica's roots music but the roots of the music itself.

For an outstanding biography of Bob Marley that captures the Jamaica of his times, check out Timothy White's *Catch a Fire*.

Over the past two centuries the power of dancehall has not only endured but grown. It has been the birthing ground for many styles of Jamaican recorded music, including ska, reggae and dub, and has provided a springboard for the careers of the island's aspiring musical artists. After WWII it gave rise to the sound systems, which came to replace live bands as the primary means of musical entertainment for the black, poor Jamaican masses. In turn, the sound systems have been the driving force behind several developments in

Jamaican popular music such as the rise of a local recording industry and the emergence of DJ (Jamaican rap) music. Jamaican sound-system DJs had much to do with the rise of hip-hop in the US and electronic dance music (such as drum and bass) in the UK. Since the 1960s dancehall has been a particularly important vehicle in Jamaica for the people to express, debate and assert their deepest aspirations.

Dancehall is visible and audible in every aspect of daily life in Jamaica: from roadside cassette vendors and bars and taverns blasting Irie FM, to the nightly news and political rallies. The merits and morality of dancehall are the subject of national debate, and the prime minister has felt the need to defend himself against perceived attacks by dancehall lyricists (such as Anthony B in 'Fire Pon Rome') on more than one occasion.

David Katz's *People Funny Boy: The Genius of Lee 'Scratch' Perry* is the first detailed work on the legendary reggae producer and dub maestro who shaped not only reggae but also global pop music.

EXPERIENCING JAMAICAN MUSIC

> 'I want you to relate to my life, welcome to my country, welcome to my world. This is my music, get involved with it. This song that I sing that you can relate to, so you can be introduced to my world, this is your invitation card. You're welcome to the party.'
>
> *Beenie Man, 2001 Grammy winner for reggae*

As Beenie Man suggests, there is no better way to get to know Jamaica than through its music. And, not surprisingly, many visitors to the country come with a desire to experience some of the greatest music in the world in its place of origin. Sadly, many go home frustrated, having only heard reggae CDs played at the hotel bar or danced to a hotel band playing watered-down Jamaican classics and American cover tunes. Ironically, it may be easier for you to experience live Jamaican music in your hometown than while on vacation in Jamaica.

International superstar Shaggy got his nickname from the character from *Scooby Doo*...His album *Hotshot* sold 10 million copies worldwide.

There are many reasons why visitors find it hard to find 'the party.' For one, the heart of Jamaica's music scene is in Kingston, which all but the most adventurous tourists avoid. The Jamaican tourist industry does not push Kingston as a tourist destination and thus the city lacks the visitor-friendly infrastructure (like good public transportation and pedestrian-friendly

HOW TO FIND A STAGE SHOW OR DANCEHALL SESSION

- Listen to the radio to figure out what's going on. IRIE FM (105.1, 107.7) is a good place to start.
- Check the message boards on www.dancehallreggae.com.
- Ask locals where you can find a dancehall session or stage show. Word of mouth is the primary way locals find out 'wha gwaan.'
- Look for posters around town. They may be for sessions two months in the future or past, but they are worth checking out if your timing is just right.
- Once you've found a show, head out late. Sessions rarely get into swing until well past midnight. Take a nap during the day or tank up on some Blue Mountain coffee.
- An alternative to authentic dancehall sessions is to go to nightclub events. Nightclub entertainment features the latest dancehall music and is usually sort of a hybrid between a dancehall dance and a typical North American or European dance-club event. Hot nightclubs include the Asylum and the Quad (p91) in Kingston, or Pier 1 (p196) in Montego Bay.
- Spend some time in Negril: the hotels that dot Seven Mile Beach here frequently have live reggae shows or sound-system events (see p239).

TOP FIVE JAMAICAN MUSIC FAVORITES

Box Sets

- *This is Reggae Music: Golden Era 1960–1975* (Trojan US, 2004)
- *Ska Bonanza: The Studio One Ska Years* (Heartbeat, 1991)
- *Songs of Freedom, Bob Marley* (Island, 1992)
- *Arkology*, Lee 'Scratch' Perry (Island, 1997)
- *The Biggest Dancehall Anthems, 1979-82: The Birth of Dancehall* (Greensleeves, 2002)

Classic Reggae Albums

- *The Harder They Come* soundtrack (Island 1972)
- *King Tubbys Meets Rockers Uptown* (Shanachie, 1976)
- *Blackheart Man*, Bunny Wailer (Island, 1976)
- *Marcus Garvey*, Burning Spear (Island, 1975)
- *The Promised Land*, Dennis Brown (Blood & Fire Records, 2003)

Dancehall Albums

- *'Til Shiloh*, Buju Banton (Island, 1995)
- *Da Real Thing*, Sizzla (VP Records, 2002)
- *Where There Is Life*, Luciano (Island, 1995)
- *Still Blazin'*, Capleton (2002)
- *Many Moods of Moses*, Beenie Man (VP Records, 1997)

Films about Jamaican Music

- *The Harder They Come* (1973)
- *Classic Albums: Bob Marley and the Wailers – Catch a Fire* (2000)
- *Rockers* (1978)
- *Dancehall Queen* (1996)
- *Stepping Razor Red X: Peter Tosh Story* (1992)

streets) that would encourage the traveler wanting to get a taste of the music culture. Aside from the Bob Marley Museum (which rarely offers live music), Kingston itself has no equivalent of Beale Street in Memphis or Bourbon Street in New Orleans – and neither does Montego Bay or Negril.

Second, Jamaica has few venues that offer live music on a nightly or weekly basis. Rather than being held at fixed venues, such as nightclubs, most performances are at open-air festivals and one-off stage shows. Again these are hit and miss, so it's best to check with the Jamaica Tourist Board (JTB; p283) to time your trip if you really want to see one of these festivals (such as Reggae Sumfest; p18). For the most part, live band music is for export, because Jamaican performers can make more money overseas. This situation unfortunately mirrors one of the fundamental contradictions of a neoplantation economy: local products are made for export and items for local consumption are imported.

www.dancehallreggae.com has the latest word on the scene and is a great source of info on the next sound-system party.

Third, local demand for music is high, but the local taste for musical performances is very different from what most tourists have in mind. Rather than live band shows that most foreigners have come to associate with reggae music, dancehall events are the most popular type of musical performances in Jamaica. Dancehall 'sessions' are based on sound systems, sophisticated megawatt mobile discos, rather than live bands. In these vibrant, intense performances, the disc jockeys known as 'selectors' are the stars of the scene, like their counterparts in the electronic dance-music scene.

Here's what you need to know: to begin with, dancehall sessions are not held in halls at all, but in open-air spaces that are created when one or more sound systems are set up for a dance. Some of these are permanent with cement walls, but many are just open spaces that are fenced in for the night in schoolyards, beaches and fields. These events are for local fans of the scene, primarily young and poor, and are avoided and even scorned by the Jamaican middle and upper classes. Until recently, the most popular form of dancehall events were sound clashes, head-to-head musical wars between two or more sound systems playing for the bigger crowd reaction. Since the late '90s, 'juggling' dances have become the rage because they have put the focus back on the dancers themselves rather than the antics of the selectors.

Seven-inch 45 rpm records (the ones with the big hole) are the primary product of Jamaica's record plants and the mainstay of the sound-system dances.

You have to have a spirit of adventure if you want to find your way to a sound-system dance. If you are hell-bent on seeing a dancehall, it's recommended that you go in a group and with a 'guide,' a local who you can trust and who knows the dancehall scene. Street dances in Kingston are the most vibrant (and off the hook), but you go at your own risk. Visitors (except for hardcore Japanese fans) are rare and, while on the whole peaceful, sound-systems are not policed events; pickpockets, stabbings and police raids do occasionally occur. For advice on the Kingston sound-system scene, see the 'Block-Rockin' Beats' box on p92.

Whaddat (www.whaddat.com) covers the Jamaican entertainment scene from a local perspective. Check out the latest dancehall happenings, interviews with current stars, fashions and photographs.

If you're looking for a stage show or country dance outside Kingston, it's not going to be easy to track down information. There's no *Time Out* guide for dancehalls in Jamaica, and newspapers rarely have ads for upcoming dances. The radio is a good source of information, as are the colorful posters plastered on any vertical surface along Jamaica's roadways. Perhaps the best source of information is to ask locals such as those who work at the hotels where you are staying. The entrance fees to dancehalls are reasonable (between US$5 and US$10) while stage shows can range between US$10 and US$30. Leave your valuables at home. Most venues don't have bathrooms, have little in the way of security, and can be hard to reach – it's difficult to get public transportation late at night.

Kingston & Around

As Jamaica's one true city, Kingston is something of an island within the island. Its pace and pulse are alien to the rest of Jamaica, for which it's the governmental, commercial and cultural hub. Most Jamaicans avoid it unless they absolutely have to come here; visitors plotting their island vacation generally give it a pass unless they happen to be flying in.

Give the capital more than a once over, however, and you're likely to be hooked. Despite its seemingly intractable social problems and sometimes intimidating street culture, Kingston sucks you in. Justly proud for having been the launching pad for some of the world's most electrifying music, the city by no means trades on its past reputation; its spirited clubs, bustling record stores and riotous street-system parties attest to the fact that the beat is still alive and bumping. The capital's cosmopolitan make-up ensures its galleries and restaurants pass muster with world travelers.

From Kingston, it's an easy journey to Port Royal, the ruined former pirate stronghold once known for its 'wickedness.' In the days before sugar was king, Jamaica's fortunes hinged on the seafaring adventures of Port Royal's residents. It all came crashing down in 1692 when a massive earthquake caused most of the town to sink into the sea.

Heading west, St Catherine and Clarendon parishes were once the island's wealthiest, and sugar remains the mainstay. The least visited part of Jamaica, it warrants a day trip for its historic importance as the locus of its first capital, St Jago de la Vega, now called Spanish Town.

HIGHLIGHTS

- **Bob Marley Museum** Delve into the life of Jamaica's most revered contemporary hero at his former home and studio (p79)
- **National Gallery** Appreciate the singular vision of Jamaican artists at this internationally acclaimed museum (p72)
- **Weddy Weddy** Get into the groove at this riotous sound-system party, which rattles the windows of Burlington Ave every Wednesday (p92)
- **Port Royal** Retrace the steps of Blackbeard and Henry Morgan at the former pirate capital of the world (p97)
- **Hellshire Beach** Chill out at this atmospheric collection of seaside shacks, where fried fish has been elevated to the status of haute cuisine (p103)

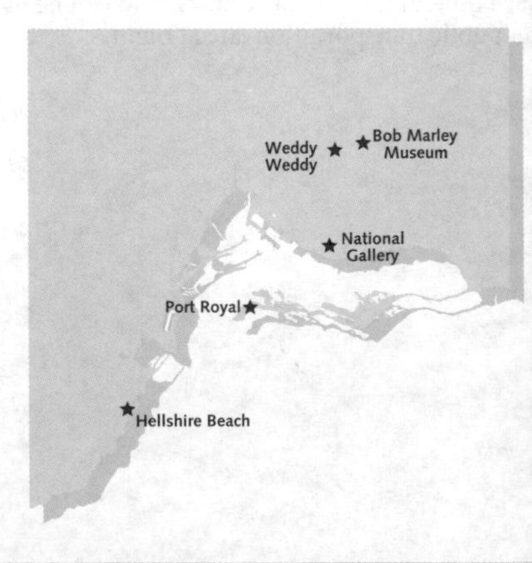

- AREA: 750 SQ KM
- KINGSTON DEC AVERAGE HIGH TEMPERATURE: 31°C

KINGSTON

pop 750,000

Its reputation preceding it like a police siren, Kingston deters most visitors. The crime, traffic, crowds and shantytowns of the capital are simply too volatile to mix into the average vacationer's dream Jamaican cocktail. Few have the time (or inclination) to explore the city long enough to disprove the image.

To be sure, Kingston can be squalid, intimidating and, in places, extremely dangerous, but with some street smarts and an open mind, any visitor will be rewarded with a firm acquaintance of a city as unbridled and unique to the island as it is to the Caribbean and indeed the world. Ground zero for the reggae for which the island made its mark, the capital is about as far from the brochures for pampered resort life as it gets.

Kingston divides neatly into downtown and uptown, and outsiders will find it easy to plan their days by taking their pick of each. Having taken the hit from the 1907 earthquake, downtown is in a state of decay that almost screams 'perpetual.' Yet it still manages to boast a scenic waterfront, Jamaica's greatest art museum and most of Kingston's historic buildings, complemented by a frenetic street-life – most notably on King St or the Parade around William Grant Park, where street preachers and mixtape hawkers vie for the attentions of a bustling humanity.

Not 6km (yet a world) away, uptown holds the city's hotels, restaurants and nightlife, largely confined to the pocket of New Kingston. In addition to two of the city's most essential sights, the Bob Marley Museum and Devon House, the capital's diplomatic and commercial status assures uptown a definite cosmopolitan suaveness – not to mention security.

Sadly, security *does* require mention – the threat of crime in Kingston can never be dismissed. Pockets of the west Kingston shantytowns are as dangerous as any place on the planet, and their volatility can spill over onto the downtown streets after dark. Be sure to follow safety directives (p71), ask your hotel for guidance and keep your wits about you. If you do, a week spent in Kingston repays the curious mind the way few legs of a Jamaican trip can.

HISTORY

On May 10, 1655, an English fleet bearing 7000 men sailed into Kingston Harbour and, after desultory resistance from the Spanish defenders at Passage Fort, captured Jamaica for Oliver Cromwell. For several decades the site of the future city was used for rearing pigs. When an earthquake leveled Port Royal in 1692 (p98), survivors struggled across the bay and pitched camp with the swine. A town plan was drawn up on a grid pattern, centered on an open square.

Though it was devastated repeatedly by earthquakes and hurricanes, the port city prospered throughout the 18th century, becoming one of the most important trading centers in the Western Hemisphere and an important transshipment point for slaves destined for the Spanish colonies.

As the city expanded, the wealthier merchants moved up to the cooler heights of Liguanea, where they built more expansive homes. In 1755, Governor Admiral Charles Knowles bowed to political pressure and transferred his government's offices to Kingston. His successor revoked the act, however, and it wasn't until 1872 that the capital was officially transferred.

In 1907 a violent earthquake leveled much of the city, killing 800 people and rendering tens of thousands homeless. The aftermath witnessed a transformation – modern buildings replaced the ruins and damaged edifices were given new life. This urban evolution reached its zenith in the 1960s, when the Urban Development Corporation reclaimed the waterfront, and several historic landmarks, including Victoria Market, were razed to make way for a complex of gleaming new structures, including the Bank of Jamaica and the Jamaica Conference Centre.

About this time, Kingston's nascent music industry was beginning to gather steam, lending international stature and fame to the city. This, in turn, fostered the growth of New Kingston, an uptown area of multistory office blocks and banks, restaurants, shops and hotels developed in the 1960s on the site of the Knutsford Park racecourse.

The boom years of the 1960s lured the rural poor, swelling the slums and shantytowns that had arisen in the preceding years. Unemployment soared, and with it came crime. The fractious 1970s spawned politically sponsored criminal enterprises whose trigger-happy networks still plague the city. Commerce began to leave downtown for New Kingston, and the middle class began to edge away as well. That exodus began a period of decline from which the downtown has yet to recover.

Despite ongoing inner-city strife, hoteliers and the Jamaica Tourist Board are pushing to dispel the city's negative image and to resurrect its tourist industry. They have long talked up plans to bring cruise ships and tourists back to Kingston. Development of a free port has been proposed, as has a restoration of the historic downtown and Port Royal. Meanwhile, efforts to beautify uptown have flowered with the 2003 opening of Emancipation Park (p77), a welcoming and spacious public swath of green that immediately became a daily gathering place for visitors and residents alike.

ORIENTATION

Overlooking the seventh-largest natural harbor in the world (and the largest in the Caribbean), the capital fans out from the waterfront and rises gently toward the foothills of the Blue Mountains.

The wooded, steep-faced ridge of Long Mountain rises up to the east, with Dallas Mountain, a spur of the Blue Mountains, rising further east, parallel and higher. The city of Kingston is hemmed in to the northeast by Jack's Hill, to the north by Stony Hill and bound to the northwest by Red Hills.

The historic downtown just north of the waterfront forms the city center. Ocean Blvd, Port Royal St and Harbour St parallel the waterfront. King St, the main thoroughfare, leads north from the waterfront to the Parade, surrounding a bustling square at the heart of the historic district.

From here, E Queen St runs east to the Norman Manley International Airport and Port Royal. W Queen St runs west for four blocks, then diverges and becomes Spanish Town Rd, which cuts northwest (toward Spanish Town) through Tivoli Gardens and the industrial estates of southwest Kingston, an altogether depressing drive lined with slums and shantytowns.

A dual carriageway east of the junction of Port Royal St and South Camp Rd runs past the General Penitentiary, and links downtown with the Palisadoes and Norman Manley International Airport.

Both Marescaux Rd and Slipe Rd lead north from downtown to uptown. The two arteries meet at Cross Roads, which is a major junction forming the unofficial boundary with the neighborhood of New Kingston, uptown's heart, immediately to the north. Knutsford Blvd, the main north-to-south artery, bisects New Kingston. Half Way Tree Rd leads northwest from Cross Roads, turning into Constant Spring Rd, which leads to Manor Park and Stony Hill.

Northeast of New Kingston, the middle-class residential area of Liguanea lies up Hope Rd from Half Way Tree Rd. Hope Rd ascends gradually past Mona Heights to Papine, the gateway to the Blue Mountains and the University of West Indies campus at Mona.

Maps

You can get free copies of the JTB's *Discover Jamaica* map from the JTB headquarters (p71). It features a detailed 1:34,000 scale street map of Kingston.

INFORMATION

The following information covers the main outlets for traveler services (such as banks, post offices and telephone centers). The websites **Go Kingston** (www.go-kingston.com) and **Jamaica Travel Guide** (http://jamaicatravelpages.com/kingston-travel-guide) are good starting points for general information.

Bookstores

The following city bookstores are relatively well stocked:

Bookland (Map pp80-1; ☎ 926-4035; 53 Knutsford Blvd) Stock includes a strong selection of titles on Jamaica and the Caribbean, including guidebooks.

Kingston Bookshop (☎ 978-0615; Liguanea Post Mall, 115 Hope Rd) Offers a reasonable selection of general interest and foreign books.

Sangsters Downtown (Map pp74-5; ☎ 967-1930; 33 King St); Uptown (Map pp80-1; ☎ 978-3518; shop 20, Sovereign Centre, 106 Hope Rd) Literature, general interest and reference books.

Cultural Centers

British Council (Map pp80-1; ☎ 929-6915; 28 Trafalgar Rd) Promotes everything British and hosts soirées and cultural events.

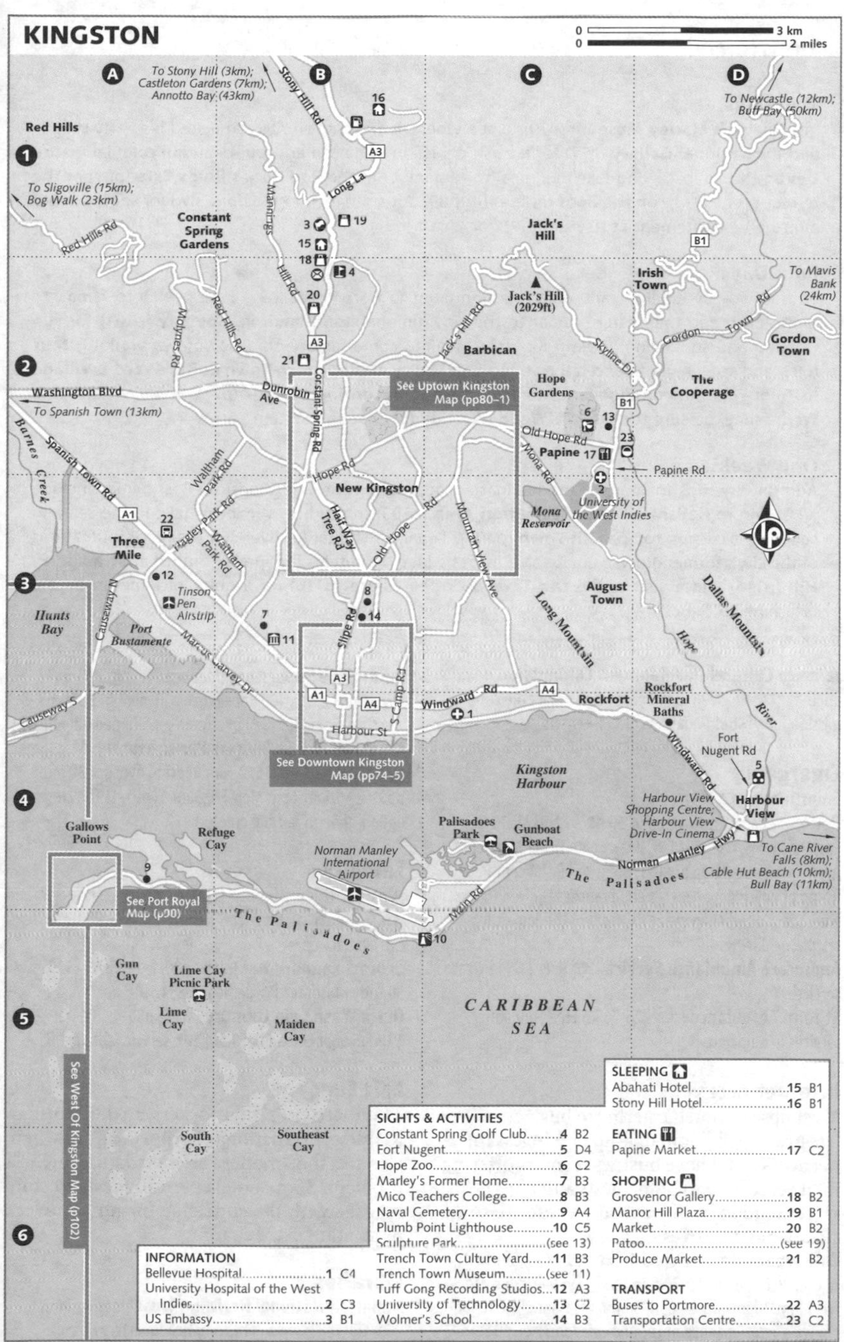
KINGSTON
0 3 km
0 2 miles
To Stony Hill (3km); Castleton Gardens (7km); Annotto Bay (43km)
To Newcastle (12km); Buff Bay (50km)
Red Hills
To Sligoville (15km); Bog Walk (23km)
Stony Hill Rd
Long La
Mannings Hill Rd
Red Hills Rd
Constant Spring Gardens
Jack's Hill
Irish Town
To Mavis Bank (24km)
Jack's Hill (2029ft)
Jack's Hill Rd
Gordon Town Rd
Gordon Town
Molynes Rd
Barbican
Skyline Dr
The Cooperage
Hope Gardens
Washington Blvd
To Spanish Town (13km)
Dunrobin Ave
Constant Spring Rd
See Uptown Kingston Map (pp80–1)
Old Hope Rd
Papine
Papine Rd
Mona Rd
Barnes Creek
Spanish Town Rd
Waltham Park Rd
Hope Rd
New Kingston
University of the West Indies
Mona Reservoir
Hagley Park Rd
Half Way Tree Rd
Old Hope Rd
Mountain View Ave
Three Mile
Tinson Pen Airstrip
August Town
Long Mountain
Dallas Mountains
Hope River
Hunts Bay
Causeway N
Port Bustamente
Marcus Garvey Dr
Slipe Rd
S Camp Rd
Windward Rd
Rockfort
Rockfort Mineral Baths
Causeway S
Harbour St
See Downtown Kingston Map (pp74–5)
Fort Nugent Rd
Windward Rd
Kingston Harbour
Harbour View Shopping Centre; Harbour View Drive-In Cinema
Harbour View
To Cane River Falls (8km); Cable Hut Beach (10km); Bull Bay (11km)
Gallows Point
Refuge Cay
Palisadoes Park
Gunboat Beach
Norman Manley International Airport
Norman Manley Hwy
The Palisadoes
See Port Royal Map (p90)
Main Rd
Gun Cay
Lime Cay Picnic Park
Lime Cay
Maiden Cay
CARIBBEAN SEA
See West Of Kingston Map (p102)
South Cay
Southeast Cay
SLEEPING
Abahati Hotel 15 B1
Stony Hill Hotel 16 B1
SIGHTS & ACTIVITIES
Constant Spring Golf Club 4 B2
Fort Nugent 5 D4
Hope Zoo 6 C2
Marley's Former Home 7 B3
Mico Teachers College 8 B3
Naval Cemetery 9 A4
Plumb Point Lighthouse 10 C5
Sculpture Park (see 13)
Trench Town Culture Yard 11 B3
Trench Town Museum (see 11)
Tuff Gong Recording Studios 12 A3
University of Technology 13 C2
Wolmer's School 14 B3
EATING
Papine Market 17 C2
SHOPPING
Grosvenor Gallery 18 B2
Manor Hill Plaza 19 B1
Market 20 B2
Patoo (see 19)
Produce Market 21 B2
TRANSPORT
Buses to Portmore 22 A3
Transportation Centre 23 C2
INFORMATION
Bellevue Hospital 1 C4
University Hospital of the West Indies 2 C3
US Embassy 3 B1

KINGSTON IN...

Two Days

Visit the **Bob Marley Museum** (p79) to see where Jamaica's favorite son rested his natty dreads and the **National Gallery** (p72) for a crash course in Jamaican art; tour beautiful colonial manse **Devon House** (p78); and take in a meal to remember at the **Red Bones Blues Café** (p89) or the terrace scene at **Up on the Roof** restaurant (p89). After a nap, hit Knutsford Blvd for some sweaty after-hours excitement at **Asylum** (p91) or **Quad** (p91).

Four Days

To the two-day itinerary, add on a morning jaunt to **Port Royal** (p97) for a peek into Jamaica's pirate past, and then catch a boat to the tiny, uninhabited island of **Lime Cay** (p101) for sun worship and snorkeling. Back in Kingston, soak in some history on a downtown **walking tour** (p82) and see what influenced the young Bob Marley at the **Trench Town Culture Yard & Village** (p76) or what his son Ziggy's up to at **Tuff Gong Recording Studios** (p77). If you're here on a Wednesday, be sure to take in a **Weddy Weddy** (p92) sound-system party.

One Week

Add on day trips to some of the fascinating destinations around Kingston. Possibilities include an outing to **Hellshire Beach Recreation Area** (p103) to see how the locals take in the sea and sand; an excursion to **Spanish Town** (p103), Jamaica's capital for over 300 years, for intimations of the city's former glory; a quick spree into the Blue Mountains for Sunday brunch at **Strawberry Hill** (p114) and a visit to the **Old Tavern Coffee Estate** (p116) for a quick pick-me-up before returning to the city.

Jamaica Cultural Development Commission (Map pp80-1; ☎ 926-5726; 3 Phoenix Ave) Contact the commission for a list of Jamaican cultural centers.

Emergency

Emergency (☎ 119)
Police Headquarters (Map pp74-5; ☎ 922-9321; 11 East Queen St); Half Way Tree (Map pp80-1; 142 Maxfield Ave); Cross Roads (Map pp80-1; Brentford Rd) A complete listing of police departments and branches is given in the emergency numbers page at the front of the Jamaican telephone directory.
Ambucare Ambulance Service (☎ 978-2327) Private service.
St John Ambulance (☎ 926-7656) Free ambulance services in Kingston.

Internet Access

Most upscale hotels catering to business travelers provide in-room dial-up or wireless internet access, and have business centers offering internet service to both guests and nonguests; prices tend to be outrageous. These are some cheaper alternatives:

Café What's On (Map pp80-1; ☎ 929-4490; Devon House, 26 Hope Rd; per 30 min US$2; 🕑 9am-9pm Mon-Fri, 11am-10pm Sat, 4-10pm Sun) A pleasant place to log on, with occasional live music and café food (see p91).
Innovative Superstore (Map pp80-1; ☎ 978-3512; Sovereign Centre, 106 Hope Rd; per 30 min US$2.50; 🕑 9am-5pm Mon-Sat) Overly air-conditioned but efficient.
Kingston and St Andrew Parish Library (Map pp80-1; ☎ 926-3315; 2 Tom Redcam Ave; per 30 min US$1; 🕑 9am-6pm Mon-Fri, 9am-5pm Sat) The cheapest option, though not the quietest.

Laundry

Any hotel will wash laundry but the prices may clean out your wallet. Do-it-yourselfers can head to:

Express Laundromat (Map pp80-1; ☎ 978-4319; 30 Lady Musgrave Rd; per load US$1.50)
Quick Wash Coin Laundry (Map pp80-1; ☎ 920-2713; 1 Union Sq; per load US$1.50) Self-service laundry.

Left Luggage

There are no rental lockers at the Norman Manley International Airport, or anywhere else for that matter, as theft is too great a problem. Some hotels permit guests to store luggage with the concierge for up to a week or so at no extra charge.

Libraries

Jamaican National Heritage Trust (Map pp74-5; ☎ 922-1287; www.jnht.com; Headquarters House,

79 Duke St) Maintains archives on the island's architectural history.

Kingston and St Andrew Parish Library (Map pp80-1; ☎ 926-3315; 2 Tom Redcam Ave; 🕑 9am-6pm Mon-Fri, to 5pm Sat) Also here is the headquarters of the Jamaica Library Service (☎ 926-3310).

National Library of Jamaica (Map pp74-5; ☎ 967-1526; Institute of Jamaica, 12 East St; 🕑 9am-5pm Mon-Thu, to 4pm Fri) Incorporates the Caribbean's largest repository of audiovisual aids, books, maps, charts, paintings and documents on West Indian history.

Media

Daily Gleaner (www.jamaica-gleaner.com) Jamaica's dominant newspaper since 1834.

Jamaica Observer (www.jamaicaobserver.com) A boisterous alternative.

Medical Services

Bellevue Hospital (Map p69; ☎ 759-4081; 161 Windward Rd) Public hospital, 24-hour emergency ward.

Harport Pharmacy (Map pp74-5; ☎ 922-7720; 144 Harbour St)

Kingston Public Hospital (Map pp74-5; ☎ 922-0210; North St) Public hospital with emergency department.

Moodies Pharmacy (Map pp80-1; ☎ 926-4174; New Kingston Shopping Centre, 30 Dominica Dr)

University Hospital of the West Indies (Map p69; ☎ 927-1620; UWI campus, Mona) The best, most up-to-date public hospital with 24-hour emergency department.

Woman's Centre of Jamaica (Map pp80-1; ☎ 929-9038, 929-2997; 42 Trafalgar Rd) Offers crisis counseling for women.

Money

Uptown, you'll find more than a dozen banks along Knutsford Blvd, and there are dozens more elsewhere. Most have foreign-exchange counters as well as 24-hour ATMs. Banking hours are 9am to 2pm Monday to Thursday, and 9am to noon and 3pm to 5pm Friday.

National Commercial Bank (Map pp74-5; ☎ 922-3940; 54 King St) A centralized foreign-exchange department; see the yellow pages in the telephone directory for branches throughout Kingston.

Scotiabank (Map pp74-5; ☎ 922-1000; cnr Duke & Port Royal Sts) Its main foreign-exchange center, immediately east of the Jamaica Conference Centre.

Western Union (Map pp80-1; ☎ 926-2454, 888-991-2056; 7 Hillcrest Ave) Has about 20 agencies throughout Kingston.

Post

FedEx (Map pp80-1; ☎ 920-1186; 75 Knutsford Blvd; 🕑 8:30am-5pm Mon-Fri) Has offices throughout Kingston.

DHL (Map pp80-1; ☎ 920-0010; 60 Knutsford Blvd; 🕑 8:30am-5pm Mon-Fri, 8:30am-1pm Sat)

Half Way Tree Post Office (Map pp80-1; ☎ 926-6803; 90 Half Way Tree Rd; 🕑 8am-5pm Mon-Thu, 9am-4pm Fri, 8am-1pm Sat) A better option than the main post office.

Main post office (Map pp74-5; ☎ 922-2120; 13 King St; 🕑 8am-5pm Mon-Thu, 9am-4pm Fri, 8am-1pm Sat) Gets crowded. There's a speedier option in the Liguanea Post Mall at 115 Hope Rd (same hours).

Telephone

You can make international calls and send faxes from most hotels. You'll find plenty of public call centers around town. International call centers are located off the Half Way Tree roundabout. Alternatively, you can use a Cable & Wireless World Talk card from any call box or your hotel room.

In the past, Cable & Wireless ran call centers throughout Jamaica, but most have closed in recent years.

Toilets

Public restrooms in Kingston, including these, are unsavory places, best avoided.

Kingston Mall (Map pp74-5; Orange St, US$0.35) Near the harbor.

Nelson Mandela Park (Map pp80–1; Constant Spring Rd, Half Way Tree)

Tourist Information

Jamaica Information Service (Map pp80-1; ☎ 926-3740; 58A Half Way Tree Rd) Offers statistical, governmental and general information on the island.

Jamaica Tourist Board Uptown (Map pp80-1; JTB; ☎ 929-9200; fax 929-9375; 64 Knutsford Blvd); Norman Manley International Airport (Map p69; ☎ 924-8024; arrivals hall) This uptown office offers maps, brochures and advice for accommodations, much of which is within walking distance.

Travel Agencies

Grace Kennedy Travel (Map pp80-1; ☎ 929-6290; fax 968-8418; 1 St Lucia Ave)

Praise Travel (Map pp80-1; ☎ 929-0215; 9 Cecelio Ave)

DANGERS & ANNOYANCES

Owing to internationally publicized periods of social strife that engulf Kingston every now and again, the city has a reputation as a dangerous destination. In truth, visitors to the city can enjoy its sights and sounds in reasonable safety as long as a few commonsense guidelines are followed.

It's true that Kingston has a notoriously high murder rate, but most take place in the ghettoes and are drug related or the product of violence between politically affiliated gangs. New Kingston and upscale residential areas such as Liguanea and Mona are generally safe for walking, as are most main roads and downtown (though it's certainly *not* an area to be wandering alone at night).

Avoid Kingston entirely during periods of tension, such as elections, when localized violence can spontaneously erupt. If you're in the town when street violence erupts, absolutely avoid downtown and adhere to any curfews that police may impose.

Stick to the main streets – if in doubt ask your hotel concierge or manager to point out the trouble areas. Have the front desk call you a taxi from a service known to them, rather than flagging down the first driver to pass. Avoid West Kingston (especially Trench Town, Jones Town, Greenwich Town and Tivoli), particularly west of the Parade, downtown.

Foreigners, especially white tourists, will stand out from the crowd. Fortunately, visitors to Kingston are not hassled by hustlers and touts to anywhere near the degree they are in the north-coast resorts.

SIGHTS

Downtown

NATIONAL GALLERY OF JAMAICA

The superlative collection of Jamaican art housed by the **National Gallery** (Map pp74-5; ☎ 922-1561, www.galleryjamaica.com; Roy West Bldg, 12 Ocean Blvd; admission US$1.50; 🕑 10am-4:30pm Tue-Thu, to 4pm Fri, to 3pm Sat) is quite simply the finest on the island and should on no account be missed. In addition to offering an intrinsically Jamaican take on international artistic trends, the collection attests to the vitality of the country's artistic heritage as well as its present.

The core of the permanent collection is presented on the 1st floor in 10 galleries representing the Jamaican School, organized chronologically spanning the years 1922 to the present. The first rooms are mainly devoted to the sculptures of Edna Manley and the spectacularly vibrant 'intuitive' paintings (p40), notably the dark landscapes of John Dunkley, the poignant portraiture of Albert Huie and the village life scenes of David Pottinger. Later galleries chart the course of 'Jamaican art for Jamaicans' up to the recent past, including abstract religious works by Carl Abrahams, decidedly surrealist exercises by Colin Garland, ethereal assemblages by David Boxer, Barrington Watson's realist forays and many other works that animate various aspects of Jamaica's national culture.

Elsewhere, the various collections and the presentation spaces of the gallery include the AD Scott Collection of Jamaican art, the Cecil Baugh gallery of ceramics, the Edna Manley Memorial Collection, and the imminently enjoyable Larry Wirth Collection, a unique and cohesive assemblage of works by visionary artist, revivalist bishop and community leader Mallica 'Kapo' Reynolds.

Excellent **guided tours** (☎ reservations 922-1561; admission US$13) are offered, providing illuminating background to the works on show; advance reservations are suggested. An annual National Exhibition is held from December through to spring as a showcase for the best of recent Jamaican art.

AFRICAN-CARIBBEAN HERITAGE CENTRE

Presided over by the Institute of Jamaica, the **Heritage Centre** (Map pp74-5; ☎ 922-4793; www.instituteofjamaica.org.jm; Orange St; 🕑 8:30am-4:30pm Mon-Thu, to 3:30pm Fri) houses a library and a small yet informative gallery that is dedicated to the history of the Middle Passage and a sociocultural exploration of the African diaspora. It is also home to the Memory Bank, an engrossing oral-history archive created to preserve Jamaica's rich folkloric traditions. The center also stages cultural events from lectures and symposia to readings and dance performance.

THE PARADE

The streets surrounding William Grant Park at the bustling heart of the downtown mayhem are known as the **Parade**. The gleaming white edifice facing the park's southeast corner is **Kingston Parish Church** (Map pp74-5; South Pde), today serving a much reduced congregation of true Kingstonians – those 'born under the clock' (within earshot of its bell). The original church was destroyed in the 1907 earthquake and was replaced (in concrete) by the existing building. Note the tomb dating to 1699, the year the original church was built. Admiral Benbow, the commander of the Royal Navy in the West Indies at the turn of the 18th century, lies beneath a tombstone near the High Altar. Marble plaques commemorate soldiers of the West Indian regiments who died of fever or other hardships during colonial wars.

The **South Parade**, packed with street vendors' stalls, is known as 'Ben Dung Plaza' because passersby have to bend down to buy from hawkers whose goods are displayed on the ground. The place is clamorous, and stores blast reggae music loud enough to drive away even the most determined visitor (locals seem inured).

At the northwest corner of William Grant Park – where public hangings took place in colonial days – the structure with a pink, turreted facade is **Bramwell Booth Memorial Hall** (Map pp74-5; North Pde), the headquarters of the Salvation Army, built in 1933. At the time of writing, the 1911 **Ward Theatre** (Map pp74-5; ☎ 922-0453; North Pde) was undergoing renovation, and tours of its interior were expected once it is restored. For now, you can admire the sky-blue facade with white trim.

Coke Memorial Hall (Map pp74-5; East Pde) faces the eastern side of William Grant Park. This crenellated building has an austere redbrick facade in the dour Methodist tradition. The structure dates from 1840, but was remodeled in 1907 after sustaining severe damage in the earthquake.

WILLIAM GRANT PARK

Betwixt North and South Pde is **William Grant Park**, which originally hosted a fortress erected in 1694 with guns pointing down King St toward the harbor. The fort was torn down and a garden, Victoria Park, laid out in 1870, with a life-size statue of Queen Victoria at its center. She has since been replaced by a bust of Sir Alexander Bustamante; Her Majesty's statue now stands on the east side of the park. The park was renamed in 1977 to honor Black Nationalist and labor leader Sir William Grant (1894–1977), who preached his Garveyite message of African redemption here. At the center of the park is a whimsical four-tiered fountain.

HEADQUARTERS HOUSE

This trim little **townhouse-turned-museum** (Map pp74-5; 79 Duke St; admission free; 🕒 8:30am-4:30pm Mon-Fri) is one block north and two east of North Pde. The brick-and-timber house was originally known as Hibbert House, named after Thomas Hibbert, reportedly one of four members of the Assembly who in 1755 engaged in a bet to build the finest house and thereby win the attention of a much-sought-after beauty. It seems he lost the bet. In 1872, when the capital was moved from Spanish Town to Kingston, the house became the seat of the Jamaican legislature and remained so until 1960, when Gordon House was built across the street.

Since 1983, Headquarters House has hosted the **Jamaican National Heritage Trust** (☎ 922-1287; admission free), which has its offices in the former bedrooms and in an extension. Visitors are welcome to roam the rest of the building, including the former debating chamber on the ground floor, holding portraits of Jamaica's national heroes. Upstairs is a lookout tower of the type commonly built by the wealthy merchants of yesteryear to spy incoming vessels. The basement is an Aladdin's cave brimful with art and offbeat relics.

GORDON HOUSE

Jamaica's parliament meets at **Gordon House** (Map pp74-5; ☎ 922-0200; cnr Duke & Beeston Sts; admission to public galleries free), immediately north of Headquarters House. The rather plain brick-and-concrete building was constructed in 1960 and named after national hero the Right Excellent George William Gordon (1820–65); see the boxed text, p29.

You can visit Gordon House by prior arrangement to watch how the Jamaican parliament conducts business. The legislature has a single chamber, where the House of Representatives and the Senate meet at different times – the former at 2pm on Tuesday (and sometimes, during pressing business, on Wednesday at the same hour), and the latter at 10am on Friday. When the legislature is not in session, the marshal sometimes lets visitors in at his discretion.

JEWISH SYNAGOGUE

Jamaica's only **synagogue** (Map pp74-5; ☎ 922-5931; cnr Duke & Charles Sts), home to the United Congregation of the Israelites, is an attractive building dating from 1912 (its predecessor was toppled by the 1907 earthquake).

The place is worth a visit for its fine mahogany staircase and gallery. Sand muffles your footsteps as you roam – a symbolic memorial to the days of the Inquisition, when Jews fleeing persecution in Spain were forced to practice their faith in Jamaica in secret. The synagogue is usually locked, though if you call in advance you can often arrange

DOWNTOWN KINGSTON
To New Kingston (3.5km)
To Wolmer's School (350m); Mico Teacher's College (400m); New Kingston (3.5km)
National Heroes Park
National Heroes Cl
Ministry of Education
North Ave
New North St
Slipe Rd
Slipe Pen Rd
Orange St
Marescaux Rd
Trench Town
Upper Mark La
Lockett Ave
Dumfries St
Upper Johns La
Regent St
Blount St
Upper Rose La
Chestnut Lane
North St
Gleaner Building
Bond St
Pink La
Oxford St
Rose La
Duke St
East St
To Washington Blvd (6km); Spanish Town (23km)
Charles St
Jones Town
Beeston St
Spanish Town Rd
Chancery La
Upper King St
Love La
Church St
Tivoli Gardens
Heywood St
N Parade
Sutton Rd
Old Way
Salt La
Young St
W Queen St
W Parade
William Grant Park
E Parade
E Queen St
Wildman St
Smith La
S Parade
Beckford St
Laws St
Darling St
Marcus Garvey Ave
Pechon St
West St
Matthews La
Princess St
Luke La
Peters La
King St
Temple La
Mark La
Johns La
Georges La
Hanover St
Rum La
Rosemary La
Maiden La
Gold St
Woolworth's; Western Union
Barry St
To Tinson Pen Airport (3km); Causeway (6km); Portmore (10km)
Tower St
Water La
Water St
Harbour St
Port Royal St
Nethersole Pl
Ocean Blvd
Ferry Terminal
Kingston Harbour
Derelict Wharves

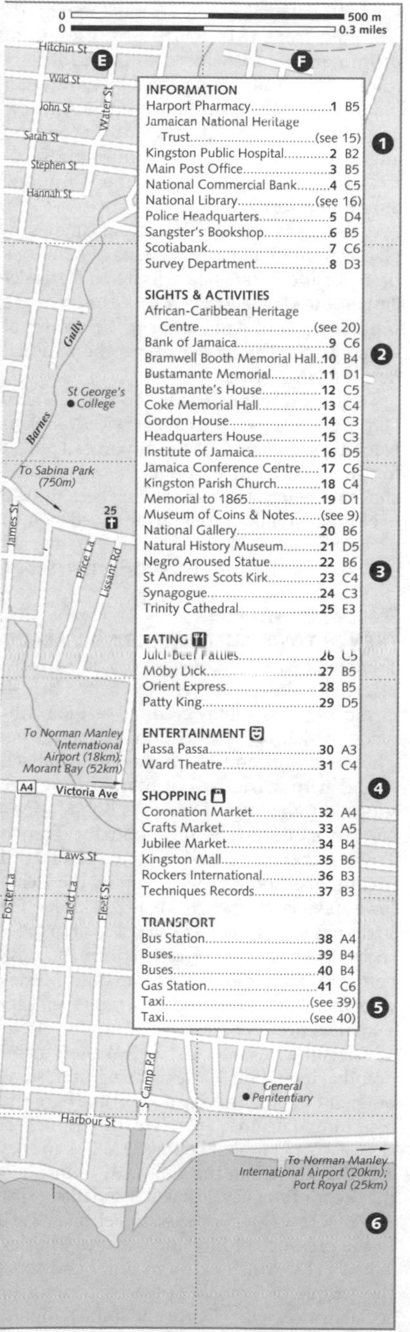

for the caretaker to open up on request for a small donation.

INSTITUTE OF JAMAICA

Toward the south end of East St, the **Institute of Jamaica** (Map pp74-5; ☎ 922-0620; fax 922-1147; www.instituteofjamaica.org.jm; 10-16 East St; adult/child US$2/1; 9:30am-4:30pm Mon-Thu, to 3:30pm Fri) is the nation's small-scale equivalent of the British Museum or Smithsonian. The institute hosts permanent and visiting exhibitions, and features a lecture hall, plus the **National Library** with Jamaican newspapers and texts dating back more than two centuries.

Also here is a **Natural History Museum** (admission US$0.30), accessed by a separate entrance around the corner on Tower St. The dowdy collection offers an array of stuffed birds and a herbarium, rounded out by an eclectic miscellany playing a historical note.

NATIONAL HEROES PARK

The 30-hectare oval-shaped **National Heroes Park** (Map pp74-5; East St) was the Kingston Racecourse. Today its north end is a forlorn wasteland grazed by goats. At the park's southern end, however, National Heroes Circle contains some intriguing statues and memorials. The **tomb of Sir Alexander Bustamante** is a flat marble slab beneath an arch. More interesting is the **Memorial to 1865**, commemorating the Morant Bay Rebellion with a rock on a pedestal flanked by bronze busts of Abraham Lincoln and a black slave with a sword.

Marcus Garvey is also buried here, as is ex-premier Norman Manley, whose body was flown here from England in 1964 and reinterred with state honors. The **Manley Monument**, honoring his son Michael, was dedicated here in March 2002. Nearby is the final resting place of the beloved 'Crown Prince of Reggae,' Dennis Brown, who died in 1999.

National Heroes Park was a dangerous destination in the recent past, but a squad of armed soldiers and a couple of Jamaica Defense Force sentries in full ceremonial dress have made the site safe.

WOLMER'S SCHOOL & MICO TEACHERS COLLEGE

At the northern end of National Heroes Park you'll find **Wolmer's School** (Map p69; ☎ 922-5316; National Heroes Circle), a venerable educational establishment founded in 1729 at the bequest of a Swiss-German goldsmith. It has produced many notable figures, including prime ministers and governor generals.

The impressive wooden colonial structures north of Wolmer's School house one of the oldest teacher-training colleges in the world, **Mico Teachers College** (Map p69; ☎ 929-5260; 1 Marescaux Rd). The original funds to establish the institution were bequest in a bizarre set of circumstances. In 1670, a nephew of Lady Mico refused at the eleventh hour to marry one of her six nieces. The unused dowry was invested, with a portion being set aside as ransom to liberate Christian captives from Barbary pirates. A century and a half later, as piracy waned, the considerable accumulated assets were used to establish the Mico Colleges with a mission to educate former slaves after emancipation. The impressive main building dates from 1909. There's a **museum** (admission US$1.75; 8:30am-4:30pm Mon-Fri) chronicling the history of the institution.

OTHER SIGHTS

The **Bank of Jamaica** (Map pp74-5; Nethersole Pl), the national mint and treasury at the east end of Ocean Blvd, is fronted by a tall concrete statue of Noel 'Crab' Nethersole (minister of finance from 1955 to 1969). Inside the bank building you'll find a small **Museum of Coins and Notes** (☎ 922-0750; www.boj.org.jm; admission free; 9am-4pm Mon-Fri) displaying Jamaican currency through the centuries.

The **Jamaica Conference Centre** (Map pp74-5; ☎ 922-9160; 14-20 Duke St; 9am-4pm Mon-Fri) was built in 1982 as the venue for meetings of the UN International Seabed Authority. It's worth popping inside for a free guided tour, not least to admire the intriguing wicker-basket and bamboo ceilings and walls.

The **Negro Aroused statue** (Map pp74-5; King St) is actually a replica; the original is in the National Gallery. This bronze statue depicting a crouched black man breaking free from bondage is the work of Jamaica's foremost sculptor, the late Edna Manley.

King St retains many of its beautiful old buildings, with wide sidewalks shaded by colonnades. Note the decorative carvings and long Corinthian columns at the **National Commercial Bank building** (Map pp74-5; cnr King & Harbour Sts).

The octagonal Georgian brick structure of **St Andrew's Scots Kirk** (Map pp74-5; ☎ 922-1818; 43A Duke St, entrance on Mark's Lane) serves the United Church of Jamaica and Grand Cayman. It was built from 1813 to 1819 by a group of prominent Scottish merchants and is surrounded by a gallery supported by Corinthian pillars. Note the white-on-blue St Andrew cross in the stained-glass window. You'll be amply rewarded if you visit during a service, when its acclaimed choir, the St Andrew Singers, performs.

Although you can't go inside and there's no plaque to mark it, hardcore fans of Jamaica's first president can pay tribute to **Alexander Bustamante's House** (Map pp74-5; 1A Duke St), at the southern end of Duke St near the corner of Water Lane. This is the site of the national hero's former office.

Trinity Cathedral (Map pp74-5; ☎ 922-3335; 1 George Eddy Dr) Open only for services (5:30am weekdays, 8:30am Sun) or if you call ahead for the caretaker to let you in, this dilapidated church is noted largely for having been the site of Norman Manley's funeral (attended by such dignitaries as Fidel Castro) as well as a small wall of mosaics dating back to Spanish times.

West of Downtown

TRENCH TOWN CULTURE YARD & VILLAGE

Trench Town, which began life as a much-prized housing project erected by the British in the 1930s, is widely credited as the birthplace of ska, rocksteady and reggae music. The neighborhood has been immortalized in the gritty narratives of numerous reggae songs, not the least of which is Bob Marley's *No Woman No Cry*, the poignant Trench Town anthem penned by Vincent 'Tata' Ford in a tiny bedroom at what is now the **Trench Town Museum** (Map p69; ☎ 948-1455; 6-10 Lower First St; entrance US$10 to the yard & museum, with a guided neighborhood tour US$15; no set hr). In the days before superstardom, Bob and Rita Marley were frequent visitors and for a time even kept a small bedroom here.

The museum is stocked with Wailers memorabilia, including Marley's first guitar, some poignant photographs from his time here and nyahbinghi drums. There's a rusted-out carcass of a VW bus that belonged to Bob Marley and the Wailers in the 1960s. Also on site is the **Trench Town Development Association** (TTDA; ☎ 757-6739, 922-8462), opened in February 1999 in the presence of England's Prince Charles. The TTDA, which exists to unify and serve the people of Trench Town by promoting social justice, self-reliance and human dignity

THE YARDS

The ghetto areas of West Kingston are still, as Bob Marley observed during his song of that name, concrete jungles. Acre upon acre of these festering tenements spread out west from the Parade, where much of the city's population growth in recent decades has been concentrated. These areas include Trench Town, Jones Town and sterile housing projects – or 'yards' – such as Majesty Pen and Tivoli Gardens, which were conceived as 'model communities' by ex-premier Edward Seaga while he was minister of welfare and development in the 1960s.

The region was once a calm residential zone. Alas, during the strife of the 1970s the middle classes debunked and moved to the safety of the suburbs. The poor masses filled the void, and conditions rapidly deteriorated, drawing hoodlums, cutthroats and other predatory elements, called 'yardies.' The situation was exacerbated by opposing political parties currying favor among the ghetto constituencies by patronizing gang leaders or 'dons,' who in turn encouraged their gangs to recruit voters and intimidate political opponents at election time.

It's easy to tell which party rules behind the stockades. Upfront, no-nonsense wall murals act as territorial markers that tell the tale of a city at war with itself.

The ghettoes are no-go zones for out-of-towners (even people from neighboring areas dare not enter the 'opposition's' turf).

The **People's Action for Community Transformation** (Map pp80-1; PACT; ☎ 920-0334; fax 960-7208; www.jamaica-kidz.com/pact/; 2-6 Grenada Cres) is a coalition of 26 community-based nongovernmental organizations (NGOs) that work to improve life and community relationships in Kingston's inner city. The organization welcomes donations and will be happy to recommend guides.

through community-based development, is singularly responsible for transforming Bob Marley's former home into a community-based heritage site. The **Culture Yard**, which features a large mural of the man, is one block off Marcus Garvey Dr. It is safe to visit, but don't go wandering elsewhere around Trench Town on your own. To visit, contact the Trench Town Development Association.

Marley's former home (Map p69; 19 Second St) is in a depressing slum 'yard,' nearby, but only visit with a guide from the TTDA.

TUFF GONG RECORDING STUDIOS

Tuff Gong Records – named for its founder, Bob 'Tuff Gong' Marley – is one of the Caribbean's largest and most influential **studios** (Map p69; ☎ 937-4216; admission US$2; www.tuffgong.com; 220 Marcus Garvey Dr). Initially established on Orange St, the enterprise then took up residence at 56 Hope Rd at what is now the Bob Marley Museum before returning to downtown Kingston at its present site. Bob Marley's early mixing board traveled with the studio and is still in use today as the studio continues to turn out hit records, not the least of which are those by his son Ziggy, the studio's current chief. It's a commercial venture with a remastering plant and remixing studio, but visitors are welcome to a 45-minute tour provided you call first to make sure the studio are not in use. A gift store sells CDs and singles, plus T-shirts, tapes, crafts and a miscellany of Marley mementos.

Uptown

EMANCIPATION PARK

Finally unveiled in 2002 after decades of planning, the spacious **Emancipation Park** (Map pp80-1; Knutsford Blvd) has become the pride of New Kingston. This wide open space, carved from the dense urban jungle, has a jogging track, stately fountains and, winningly, reggae music emanating from tiny speakers hidden in the grass. It's a grand place for a promenade, particularly at sunset when the walkways fill with cheerful Kingstonians just liberated from their workplaces.

A controversial focal point – and one that is of great interest to children – is the US$4.5 million statue *Redemption Song*, by Laura Facey Cooper. Depicting a couple of nude, 3m-tall slaves gazing to the heavens, the epic work sometimes elicits prurient comments by passersby due to certain larger-than-life physical attributes of the figures.

At the north edge of the park is **Putt 'n' Play Mini-Golf Park** (Map pp80-1; ☎ 906-4814; 78 Knutsford Blvd; adult/child US$4.25/2.50; 🕔 5-11pm Mon-Thu, to midnight Fri, 11am-midnight Sat & Sun), an 18-hole

MARLEY'S GHOST

Although Bob Marley (1945–1981) was born and buried in Nine Mile (p175) in St Ann's Parish, it was from Kingston that Jamaica's most famous son made his indelible mark on the global music scene. In many ways, the city still bears his footprint as much as reggae does.

Migrating to the capital in 1955, Bob and his mother (his father, a white superintendent of the crown's lands, had abandoned the family) moved into a 'government yard in Trench Town' similar to the one he would later sing of in *No Woman, No Cry.* Not yet the gang-war zone it would become in the 1970s, Trench Town was a desirable neighborhood as well as fertile soil for the emerging music scene. Bob met Bunny Livingston and Peter Tosh here, and in 1963 they formed the Wailin' Wailers and received tutelage from fabled Trench Town vocalist Joe Higgs. The band's first single, *Simmer Down,* reached number one on Jamaica's radio charts.

Success was slow, however, and it wasn't really until the band signed with Island Records in the early '70s (and became Bob Marley and the Wailers) that it began to receive international acclaim with the 1973 albums *Burnin'* and *Catch a Fire.* Unsurprisingly, fame made living in increasingly volatile Trench Town impossible, and in 1975 Marley moved into the house at 56 Hope Rd that is now his museum. The move uptown alienated many back in Trench Town – and also disturbed his affluent new neighbors, who were unused to the trail of Rastafarian visitors and the football matches in the front yard.

Nothing could have prepared them for the night in 1976, when a gang, likely siding with the conservative Jamaica Labour Party, crashed the gates of the Hope Rd home and shot Bob, his wife Rita, and his manager just before a major concert sponsored by the socialist-leaning People's National Party. Remarkably, everyone survived, and Marley even played at the concert, his wounds wrapped in a sling. After the concert, Bob and Rita left the country.

In 1978, Marley made his legendary homecoming at a moment when messages of peace and unity were being all but drowned out by open street warfare. On April 22, a ceasefire was declared between the PNP and the JLP in honor of the One Love Peace concert at the national stadium. With 100,000 people in attendance, including the PNP's Michael Manley and the JLP's Edward Seaga seated in the front row, Marley took to the stage around midnight. During *One Love,* he invited the feuding Manley and Seaga onstage and performed the near-impossible feat of joining their hands together, with his own, in a gesture of unity that probably saved Jamaica from a bloody civil war.

The transformation was not permanent. Before the elections of 1980, almost 800 people were killed when Kingston erupted again in violence, and political gang clashes continue to this day. But Marley's message will never be forgotten.

miniature golf course complete with miniature waterfalls, meandering streams, ponds, sand traps and natural obstacles.

HALF WAY TREE

This neighborhood (Map pp80–1), road junction and major bus terminal is named for a venerable silk cotton (kapok) tree that stood here until the 1870s; its shaded base became the site of both a tavern and market. Today, the spot is marked by a **clock tower** sure to tell the correct time every 12 hours. It was erected in 1813 as a memorial to King Edward VII, whose bust sits on the south side of the tower at the junction of Hope, Hagley Park, Constant Spring and Half Way Tree Rds.

Visitors should avoid lingering in and around Nelson Mandela Park, a small landscaped park on the northeast side of Half Way Tree.

ST ANDREW PARISH CHURCH

This brick **church** (Map pp80-1; ☎ 968-9366; cnr Hagley Park & Eastwood Park Rds; 🕑 Anglican services 6:30am, 7:30am, 9:45am & 6pm Sun, 9am Tue, 6:30am & 9am Wed) is more popularly known as the 'Half Way Tree Church.' The foundations of the existing church were laid in 1692. The exterior is austere and unremarkable, but the stained-glass windows and organ are definitely worth a peek. Outside, there's a very atmospheric graveyard.

DEVON HOUSE

This **restored home** (Map pp80-1; ☎ 929-7029; 26 Hope Rd; admission US$5; 🕑 9am-5pm Tue-Sat) nestles in landscaped grounds on the northwest side of Hope Rd at its junction with Waterloo Rd. A beautiful ochre-and-white house, it was built in 1881 by George Stiebel, a Jamaican wheelwright who hit paydirt in the gold mines of Venezuela. The millionaire rose to become the first black custos of St Andrew. The government bought and restored the building in 1967 to house the National Gallery of Jamaica, which has since moved to its present location downtown.

Antique lovers will enjoy the visit, whose highlights include some very ornate porcelain chandeliers. Note the *trompe l'oeil* of palms in the entrance foyer. Stiebel even incorporated a game room with whist and cribbage tables, a sewing room, and a gambling room discreetly tucked away in the attic. Admission includes a mandatory guided tour.

The tree-shaded lawns attract couples on weekends. The former carriage house and courtyard are home to two of Jamaica's more famous restaurants, Grog Shoppe (p89) and Norma's on the Terrace (p90), and a few quality shops (see p92).

For Emancipation Day, August 1, Devon House puts on a rousing celebration complete with roots plays, a maypole ritual and, naturally, a booming sound system.

JAMAICA HOUSE

About half a kilometer further up Hope Rd from Devon House on the left, **Jamaica House** (Map pp80–1) is faced by a columned portico and fronted by expansive lawns. Initially built in 1960 as the residence of the prime minister, the building today houses the **prime minister's office**. Visitors are restricted to peering through the fence.

KING'S HOUSE

Hidden amid trees behind Jamaica House is the official residence of the governor-general. It lies at the end of a driveway that begins at the junction of E King's House Rd and Hope Rd.

King's House (Map pp80-1; ☎ 927-6424; admission free; 🕑 by appointment 9am-5pm Mon-Sat) was initially the home of the Lord Bishop of Jamaica. The original house was badly damaged in the 1907 earthquake. Today's visitors explore the remake, built in 1909 to a new design in reinforced concrete. The dining room contains two particularly impressive full-length portraits of King George III and Queen Charlotte by Sir Joshua Reynolds.

BOB MARLEY MUSEUM

For many, Jamaica means reggae, and reggae means Bob Marley. If this sounds like you, a visit to Kingston definitely means a visit to the reggae superstar's **former home and studio** (Map pp80-1; ☎ 927-9152; www.bobmarley-foundation.com/museum.html; 56 Hope Rd; adult/child/student US$8.50/3.50/6.75; 🕑 9:30am-4pm Mon-Sat). The creaky wooden house on Hope Rd where Marley once lived and recorded is the city's most-visited site. Today the house functions as a tourist attraction, museum and shrine, but much remains as it was during Marley's day.

The house is guarded by a sentry of faithful Rasta brethren and sisters and shielded by a vibrantly painted wall festooned with Rastafarian murals. Dominating the forecourt is a gaily colored statue of the musical legend. Some of the guides are overly solemn (focusing with eerie earnestness on the room where Marley survived assassination), but the hour-long tour provides fascinating insights into the life he led after moving uptown. His gold and platinum records (*Exodus*, 1977, *Uprising*, 1980; and *Legend*, 1984) are there on the walls, alongside Rastafarian religious cloaks, Marley's favorite denim stage shirt and the Order of Merit presented by the Jamaican government. One room upstairs is decorated with media clippings about the superstar. Another contains a replica of Marley's original record shop, Wail'n Soul'm. Perhaps most powerfully, Marley's simple bedroom has been left as it was, with his star-shaped guitar by the bedside.

The former recording studio out back is now an exhibition hall and theater, where the tour closes with a fascinating film of his final days. A recently upgraded shopping court offers 'official' Marley products including Bob's Honey, produced by a hive of bees that's been buzzing on the site since the musician adopted them in the mid-1970s.

No cameras or tape recorders are permitted inside.

NATIONAL STADIUM & CELEBRITY PARK

The **stadium** (Map pp80-1; ☎ 929-4970; Arthur Wint Dr), built in 1962 when Jamaica hosted the Commonwealth Games, is the venue for most of Jamaica's sporting events of importance. There's a so-called Celebrity Park on the north

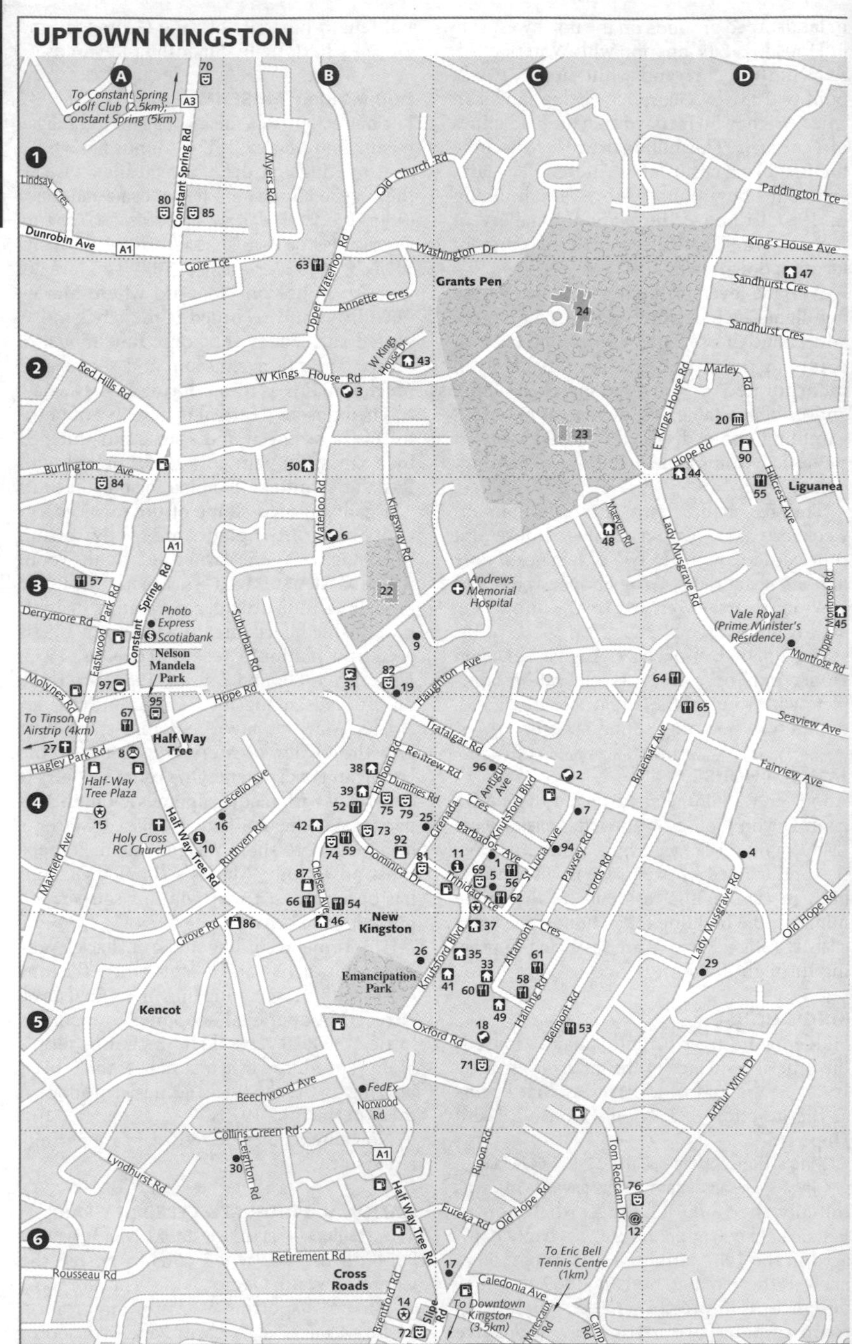

UPTOWN KINGSTON
To Constant Spring Golf Club (2.5km); Constant Spring (5km)
Grants Pen
Liguanea
Andrews Memorial Hospital
Vale Royal (Prime Minister's Residence)
Photo Express
Scotiabank
Nelson Mandela Park
Half Way Tree
To Tinson Pen Airstrip (4km)
Half-Way Tree Plaza
Holy Cross RC Church
New Kingston
Emancipation Park
Kencot
FedEx
Cross Roads
To Eric Bell Tennis Centre (1km)
To Downtown Kingston (3.5km)
Constant Spring Rd
Dunrobin Ave
Lindsay Cres
Gore Tce
Myers Rd
Old Church Rd
Upper Waterloo Rd
Washington Dr
Annette Cres
Paddington Tce
King's House Ave
Sandhurst Cres
W Kings House Rd
W Kings House Dr
Red Hills Rd
E Kings House Rd
Marley Rd
Hope Rd
Hillcrest Ave
Burlington Ave
Waterloo Rd
Kingsway Rd
Maeven Rd
Lady Musgrave Rd
Derrymore Rd
Eastwood Park Rd
Suburban Rd
Molynes Rd
Haughton Ave
Upper Montrose Rd
Montrose Rd
Seaview Ave
Trafalgar Rd
Hagley Park Rd
Holborn Rd
Renfrew Rd
Fairview Ave
Dumfries Rd
Antigua Ave
Knutsford Blvd
Braemar Ave
Cecelio Ave
Ruthven Rd
Half Way Tree Rd
Maxfield Ave
Grenada Cres
Barbados Ave
St Lucia Ave
Pawsey Rd
Lords Rd
Dominica Dr
Trinidad Tce
Chelsea Ave
Old Hope Rd
Grove Rd
Altamont Cres
Haining Rd
Belmont Rd
Oxford Rd
Arthur Wint Dr
Beechwood Ave
Norwood Rd
Collins Green Rd
Leighton Rd
Lyndhurst Rd
Ripon Rd
Tom Redcam Dr
Eureka Rd
Retirement Rd
Rousseau Rd
Caledonia Ave
Brentford Rd
Slipe Rd
Marescaux Rd
Camp Rd
A1
A3
A
B
C
D
1
2
3
4
5
6

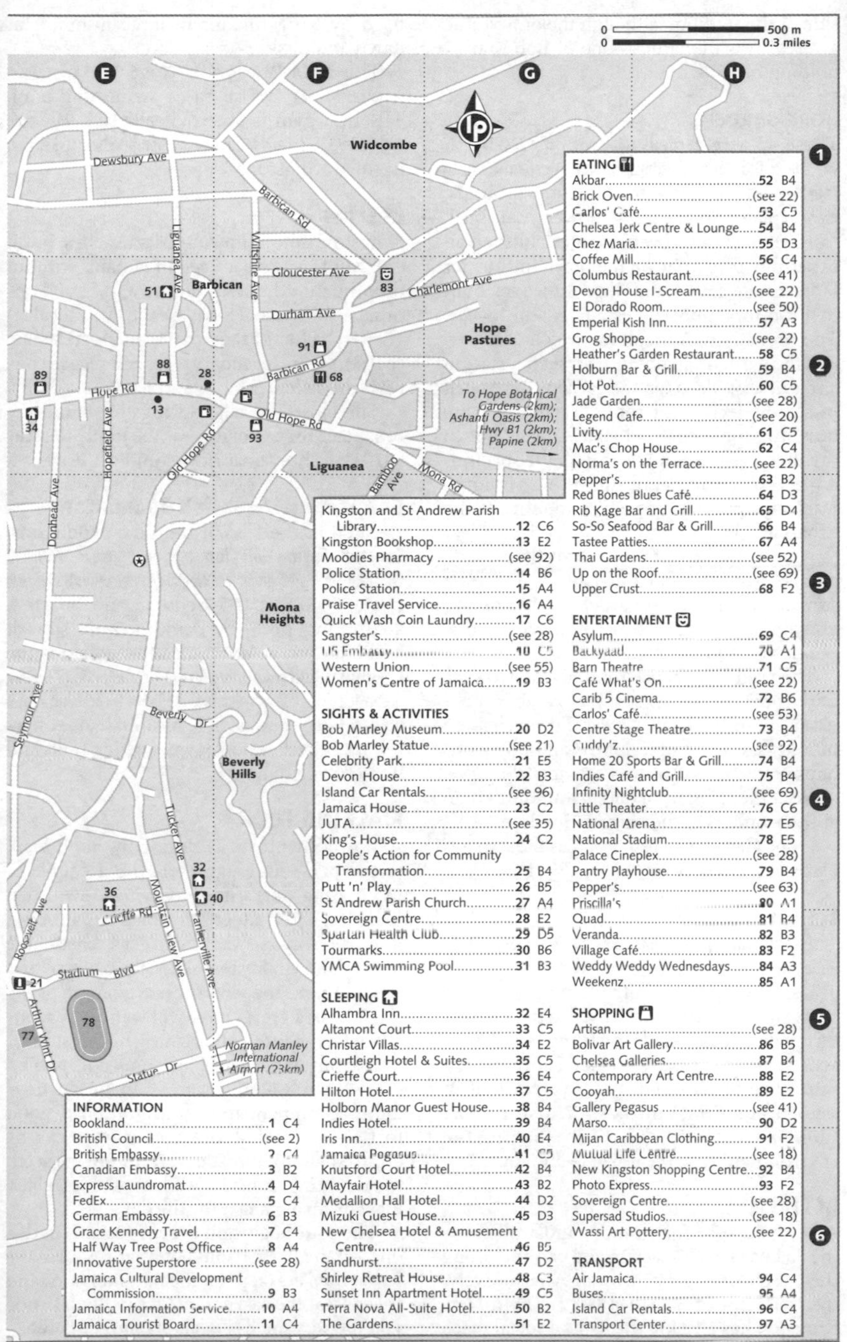
0 500 m
0 0.3 miles
E
F
G
H
1
2
3
4
5
6
Widcombe
Dewsbury Ave
Barbican Rd
Liguanea Ave
Wiltshire Ave
Gloucester Ave
Charlemont Ave
Barbican
Durham Ave
Hope Pastures
Barbican Rd
Hope Rd
Old Hope Rd
Old Hope Rd
Hopefield Ave
Liguanea
Bamboo Ave
Mona Rd
To Hope Botanical Gardens (2km); Ashanti Oasis (2km); Hwy B1 (2km); Papine (2km)
Donhead Ave
Mona Heights
Seymour Ave
Beverly Dr
Beverly Hills
Tucker Ave
Mountain View Ave
Tankerville Ave
Crieffe Rd
Roosevelt Ave
Stadium Blvd
Arthur Wint Dr
Statue Dr
Norman Manley International Airport (23km)
INFORMATION
Bookland....1 C4
British Council....(see 2)
British Embassy....2 C4
Canadian Embassy....3 B2
Express Laundromat....4 D4
FedEx....5 C4
German Embassy....6 B3
Grace Kennedy Travel....7 C4
Half Way Tree Post Office....8 A4
Innovative Superstore....(see 28)
Jamaica Cultural Development Commission....9 B3
Jamaica Information Service....10 A4
Jamaica Tourist Board....11 C4
Kingston and St Andrew Parish Library....12 C6
Kingston Bookshop....13 E2
Moodies Pharmacy....(see 92)
Police Station....14 B6
Police Station....15 A4
Praise Travel Service....16 A4
Quick Wash Coin Laundry....17 C6
Sangster's....(see 28)
US Embassy....18 C5
Western Union....(see 55)
Women's Centre of Jamaica....19 B3
SIGHTS & ACTIVITIES
Bob Marley Museum....20 D2
Bob Marley Statue....(see 21)
Celebrity Park....21 E5
Devon House....22 B3
Island Car Rentals....(see 96)
Jamaica House....23 C2
JUTA....(see 35)
King's House....24 C2
People's Action for Community Transformation....25 B4
Putt 'n' Play....26 B5
St Andrew Parish Church....27 A4
Sovereign Centre....28 E2
Spartan Health Club....29 D5
Tourmarks....30 B6
YMCA Swimming Pool....31 B3
SLEEPING
Alhambra Inn....32 E4
Altamont Court....33 C5
Christar Villas....34 E2
Courtleigh Hotel & Suites....35 C5
Crieffe Court....36 E4
Hilton Hotel....37 C5
Holborn Manor Guest House....38 B4
Indies Hotel....39 B4
Iris Inn....40 E4
Jamaica Pegasus....41 C5
Knutsford Court Hotel....42 B4
Mayfair Hotel....43 B2
Medallion Hall Hotel....44 D2
Mizuki Guest House....45 D3
New Chelsea Hotel & Amusement Centre....46 B5
Sandhurst....47 D2
Shirley Retreat House....48 C3
Sunset Inn Apartment Hotel....49 C5
Terra Nova All-Suite Hotel....50 B2
The Gardens....51 E2
EATING
Akbar....52 B4
Brick Oven....(see 22)
Carlos' Café....53 C5
Chelsea Jerk Centre & Lounge....54 B4
Chez Maria....55 D3
Coffee Mill....56 C4
Columbus Restaurant....(see 41)
Devon House I-Scream....(see 22)
El Dorado Room....(see 50)
Emperial Kish Inn....57 A3
Grog Shoppe....(see 22)
Heather's Garden Restaurant....58 C5
Holburn Bar & Grill....59 B4
Hot Pot....60 C5
Jade Garden....(see 28)
Legend Cafe....(see 20)
Livity....61 C5
Mac's Chop House....62 C4
Norma's on the Terrace....(see 22)
Pepper's....63 B2
Red Bones Blues Café....64 D3
Rib Kage Bar and Grill....65 D4
So-So Seafood Bar & Grill....66 B4
Tastee Patties....67 A4
Thai Gardens....(see 52)
Up on the Roof....(see 69)
Upper Crust....68 F2
ENTERTAINMENT
Asylum....69 C4
Backyaad....70 A1
Barn Theatre....71 C5
Café What's On....(see 22)
Carib 5 Cinema....72 B6
Carlos' Café....(see 53)
Centre Stage Theatre....73 B4
Cuddy'z....(see 92)
Home 20 Sports Bar & Grill....74 B4
Indies Café and Grill....75 B4
Infinity Nightclub....(see 69)
Little Theater....76 C6
National Arena....77 E5
National Stadium....78 E5
Palace Cineplex....(see 28)
Pantry Playhouse....79 B4
Pepper's....(see 63)
Priscilla's....80 A1
Quad....81 B4
Veranda....82 B3
Village Café....83 F2
Weddy Weddy Wednesdays....84 A3
Weekenz....85 A1
SHOPPING
Artisan....(see 28)
Bolivar Art Gallery....86 B5
Chelsea Galleries....87 B4
Contemporary Art Centre....88 E2
Cooyah....89 E2
Gallery Pegasus....(see 41)
Marso....90 D2
Mijan Caribbean Clothing....91 F2
Mutual Life Centre....(see 18)
New Kingston Shopping Centre....92 B4
Photo Express....93 F2
Sovereign Centre....(see 28)
Supersad Studios....(see 18)
Wassi Art Pottery....(see 22)
TRANSPORT
Air Jamaica....94 C4
Buses....95 A4
Island Car Rentals....96 C4
Transport Center....97 A3

side of the stadium, although the only statue at present is the famous one of Bob Marley holding his guitar.

HOPE GARDENS

These 45-acre **gardens** (Map p69; ☎ 927-1257; fax 977-4853; Old Hope Rd; admission free; ⏰ 6am-6pm, to 7pm May-Aug), replete with manicured grounds, exotic plants and beautiful flowers, date back to 1881 when the government established an experimental garden on the site of the former Hope Estate. Part of the Hope Aqueduct, built in 1758 to supply the estate, is still in use. The Ministry of Agriculture, which administers the gardens, maintains a research station and nursery, although the gardens have been in steady decline for some decades and are now in a somewhat sad state. This is not to say that a visit is not rewarding; the spacious lawns, towering palms and flower-scented walkways provide a lovely respite from the urban jungle.

Among the attractions are cycads, or 'sago palms,' from the antediluvian era. There's a sunken garden, forest garden, orchid house, greenhouses, a small aquarium, ornamental ponds and a privet-hedge maze.

The frankly pathetic, ironically named **Hope Zoo** (Map p69; ☎ 927-1085; admission US$0.50; ⏰ 10am-5pm) is home to a motley crew of disenchanted monkeys, lions, tropical birds and other unhappy creatures. Visitors are apt to marvel more at the sad state of the surroundings than at the wonders of the animal kingdom.

Hope Gardens is also home to the Ashanti Oasis vegetarian restaurant (pp80–1).

SCULPTURE PARK

This **sculpture garden** (Map p69; ☎ 927-1680; 237 Old Hope Rd), on the grounds of the University of Technology, just north of the University of the West Indies campus, was unveiled in 2000 featuring nine sculptures by acclaimed Caribbean artists. Notable figures include Laura Facey's sculpture of a woman's torso stretched in a yoga position, and Basil Watson's *The Compass,* depicting humanity shaping the environment with the use of technology.

ACTIVITIES

A favorite spot for runners and walkers is the **Palisadoes** (p95), where you can run along the beach or the main road. Alternatively, the well-kept **Emancipation Park** (p77) in New Kingston has a 1.6km track; it's a social place used by Kingstonians in large numbers at dawn and dusk.

The **YMCA** (Map pp80-1; ☎ 926-0801; kymca@cwjamaica.com; 21 Hope Rd) has a swimming pool. The best gym is **Spartan Health Club** (Map p69; ☎ 927-7575; 9 Lady Musgrave Rd; nonmembers US$15) in uptown Kingston.

Beaches

Kingston is not known for its beaches, but if you can't imagine a week in Jamaica without dipping into the sea there are a few good options. Southwest of town are the lively local favorites, **Hellshire Beach** (p103) and **Fort Clarence** (p103), where legendary weekend reggae concerts are held.

The closest beach to Kingston – and the best place for a cookout – is the lovely **Lime Cay** (p101), a short boat ride from Port Royal.

Golf, Tennis, Squash & Badminton

Located at the foot of the Blue Mountains, **Constant Spring Golf Club** (Map p69; ☎ 924-1610; 152 Constant Spring Rd; green fees weekdays/weekends US$35/41) has a 5665m, par-70 course and boasts a swimming pool, bar, and tennis, squash and badminton courts. Further afield is the **Caymanas Golf & Country Club** (see p106; ☎ 922-3386; green fees weekdays/weekends US$36/44, cart/club rental US$22/44), 10km west of Kingston. It also offers tennis, squash, a pool, gym, jogging trails and horseback riding.

WALKING TOUR

A walk downtown is decidedly *not* a walk in the park (although there *are* a couple of fascinating parks here). Giving downtown Kingston a pass altogether would be a mistake, however. Anyone wanting to get a sense of the history and vitality that shape the country, and see firsthand the vital presence of one of the Caribbean's great cities, will want to personally take the pulse of downtown Kingston.

In our experience, an unaccompanied downtown walking tour – in broad daylight, accompanied by commonsense, good fortune and a dash of street savvy – can be enjoyed without incident. If the streets seem too daunting, consider walking with a trusted local or hiring a taxi for the day.

The tour begins on breezy Ocean Blvd, a once-grand harborfront boulevard. Start at the **Bank of Jamaica** (**1**; p76), the national mint and treasury at the east end of Ocean Blvd. Inside you'll find a small **Museum of Coins and Notes**.

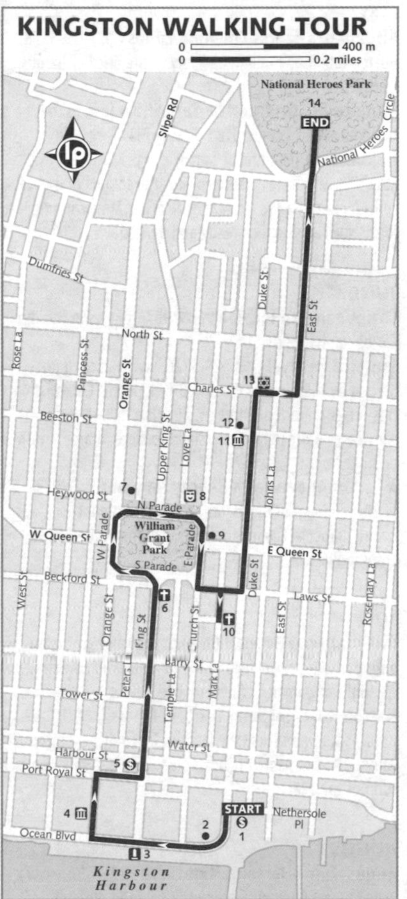

WALK FACTS

Start Ocean Blvd
Finish National Heroes Park
Distance 4km
Duration Two to four hours

Go west half a block along Ocean Blvd to get to the **Jamaica Conference Centre** (**2**; p76). Continue west past the **Negro Aroused statue** (**3**; p76) at the foot of King St.

Turn right (north) on Orange St to get to the **National Gallery** (**4**; p72) and the adjacent **African Caribbean Heritage Centre** (p72).

Continue north half a block on Orange St, then east on Port Royal St to reach King St, the main thoroughfare leading from Victoria Pier to the Parade. Along the way you'll pass by the **National Commercial Bank building** (**5**; p76).

Half a mile up King St you reach the **Parade** (p72) and **Kingston Parish Church** (**6**; p72). Proceed half a block north on Orange St. At the northwestern corner of the park is **Bramwell Booth Memorial Hall** (**7**; p73), the headquarters of the Salvation Army.

The impressive sky-blue facade at the park's northeast corner belongs to the **Ward Theatre** (**8**; p91), dating from 1911. **Coke Memorial Hall** (**9**; p73) faces the eastern side of William Grant Park.

From the park's southeast corner, Laws St heads east one block to Mark Lane, leading one block south to **St Andrew's Scots Kirk** (**10**; p76).

Heading north, follow Duke St, paralleling Mark Lane one block further east, to the corner of Beeston St, where you'll encounter **Headquarters House** (**11**; p73) and **Gordon House** (**12**; p73). At Duke and Charles Sts is the gleaming white **Synagogue** (**13**; p73). Continue east to East St, which leads north to **National Heroes Park** (**14**; p75).

TOURS

Island Car Rentals (Map pp80-1; ☎ 926-8861, 929-5875; fax 929-6787; 17 Antigue Ave) offers three popular excursions into the heart of Kingston. Three of the most popular are the Bob Marley Tour (US$48), which visits landmarks connected to the reggae great; an outing to one-time pirate capital Port Royal (US$54); and a Jamaica Heritage tour of Kingston cultural and historical landmarks (US$58). You will be picked up at your hotel. A minimum of two people are required for a tour.

Other tour providers:

JUTA (Map pp80-1; ☎ 926-1537; 85 Knutsford Blvd) Tours to Port Royal, Devon House and Spanish Town.

Tourmarks (Map pp80–1; ☎ 929-8708; 7 Leighton Rd) Kingston and Port Royal tours, Kingston highlights, and a Hellshire Beach excursion on Sunday.

FESTIVALS & EVENTS

Carnival

The weeklong Kingston **carnival** (www.jamaicacarnival.com, www.bacchanaljamaica.com), held over Easter, is a highlight of the year, although it's lackluster compared to the carnivals of Trinidad or Brazil. It's a big blowout for the Jamaican masses; thousands of costumed revelers take to the streets, with flags waving and bodies painted. There's live reggae and calypso, of course, but soca is king.

Two carnival camps command the scene: Jamaica Carnival and Bacchanal Jamaica, both of which put on their own gigs. A highlight is **J'Ouvert**, an epic party that begins late at night and continues past dawn. Carnival ends the following Sunday with the **Road March**, when the two camps parade through the streets of New Kingston in carnival costume. The route is long and varies from year to year, but both major carnival groups invariably pass through Half Way Tree at some point. Park yourself anywhere along Waterloo Rd between Hope and South Rds and your vantage point should serve you well. Take some grungy clothes and shoes, as the revelers like to throw paint – and rum – over folks. For both events, don't carry anything you can't afford to lose. This includes mobile phones and expensive wigs.

Other Events

Befitting a Caribbean capital city, Kingston is the site of engaging festivals and events year-round. The events calendar (p17) provides information on the major happenings in Jamaica. Other noteworthy Kingston festivals and events are listed below.

JANUARY

Jamaica School of Dance Concert Season (☎ 926-6129, 922-5988) Features creative, Caribbean-themed dancing at the Little Theater.

FEBRUARY

Carib Cement International Marathon (☎ 928-6231) Attracts top national and international athletes in mid-February.

University of West Indies (UWI) Carnival (☎ 927-1660) Lasting a week in mid-February, it is staged by university students from throughout the Caribbean.

MARCH

Jamaica Music Industry (JAMI) Awards (☎ 960-1320) In the first week of March. Features guest performers from reggae to classical.

Miss Universe Jamaica Beauty Pageant Determines who represents the island in the Miss Universe contest. Held mid-March.

APRIL

Devon House Craft Fair (☎ 929-7029) Quality arts and crafts displays, and Jamaican foods.

MAY

All-Jamaica Tennis Championships (☎ 929-5878) Hosted late May through mid-July at the Eric Bell Tennis Centre.

Jamaica Horticultural Society Show Held in the National Arena; contact JTB offices (p71).

Rukumbine (Institute of Jamaica, ☎ 922-0620) In late May, this annual festival celebrates the sounds of mento, considered to be the forerunner to other Jamaican music forms such as ska, rocksteady and dancehall.

JUNE

Caribbean Fashionweek (☎ 967-1089) Showcasing Caribbean haute couture.

Jamaica Festival (☎ 929-5726; www.jcdc.org.jm) Staged by the Jamaica Cultural Development Commission, this series of performances culminating in early June showcases a broad range of island folklore, drama, music and dance.

Miss Commonwealth Beauty Pageant (☎ 953-9020) Held late in the month, this international beauty pageant is open to the 54 nations of the British Commonwealth.

JULY

International Reggae Day (☎ 929-0693) This on-air, online media festival held in the first week in July shines a spotlight on Jamaica's finest reggae artists.

National Gospel Song Contest Finals (☎ 936-5726; www.jcdc.org.jm) Held the last week of July, a spirited competition to name the most outstanding original gospel song of the year.

AUGUST

Augus' Fair & Jamaica Night (☎ 929-5726; www.jcdc.org.jm) An annual appreciation of the pleasures of traditional food, crafts and storytelling, held in the first week of August.

Independence Day Festival & Street Parade (☎ 926-5726; www.jcdc.org.jm) Also in the first week of August. Features music festivals and a traditional Jonkanoo street parade, live music and modern dances.

Independence Day Parade Civic Ceremony (☎ 929-5726; www.jcdc.org.jm) An extravagant dress parade held at historic King's House, full of pomp and pageantry befitting the nation's birthday (August 6).

OCTOBER

Caribbean Heritagefest (☎ 929-5726; www.jcdc.org.jm) A two-day event in mid-October at the Jamworld Entertainment Complex at Portmore, southwest of Kingston. It features food and crafts fairs, folk theater, traditional dance and drumming, and musical performances.

DECEMBER

Devon House Christmas Fair (☎ 929-7029) Promotes a colorful display of arts, crafts and culinary delights in the week before Christmas.

Jonkanoo Food Festival (☎ 929-5726; www.jcdc.org.jm) A lavish Christmas brunch attended by the likes of Pitchy-Patchy, House Boy, Devil, Policeman, Jack-in-the-green and other usual suspects of the traditional Jonkunnu pageant.

SLEEPING

Unlike the tourism boomtowns of the north coast, Kingston's hotels don't pander to tourists. Most lodging options cater instead to the business set with a range of service-oriented options run with crisp efficiency. Most hotels are in uptown, with the classier ones all situated in New Kingston. Pickings are virtually nonexistent downtown; there are a few guesthouses on the edge of downtown, but some might call them, well, hovels. No option in downtown Kingston is listed here.

Uptown

BUDGET

Crieffe Court (Map pp80-1; ☎ 927-8033; crieffe@cwjamaica.com; 10 Crieffe Rd; r US$34, studio US$38-46, 1-/2-bedroom ste US$55/83; P) This well-kept hotel offers an assortment of spotless, spacious rooms with basic decor, studios with kitchens, and a number of suites. All options have fans and air-con, TV and hot water; upstairs rooms have a balcony. The largest suite includes two bedrooms and 10 bunks, making it a great bargain for larger groups. Potted plants abound, and the small restaurant has a tree growing through the floor.

Sandhurst (Map pp80-1; ☎ 927-8244; 70 Sandhurst Cres; s US$40, d US$45-50; P) In a quiet residential neighborhood in Liguanea, this is a favorite option in this price bracket. It verges on the eccentric. The 43 spotlessly kept pale-blue rooms with their black-and-white tile floors, utility furniture and plastic flowers conjure images of Miami in the 1960s. Some have TV and telephone and private veranda. A large dining terrace shaded by mango trees affords views toward the Blue Mountains.

Holborn Manor Guest House (Map pp80-1; ☎ 929-3070; holbornmanor@cwjamaica.com; 3 Holborn Rd; s/d/tr US$55/70/85;) Next door to Indies Hotel, this friendly guesthouse offers 12 rooms with fans, TV and phones but modest, dowdy furnishings and cold water only. There are a few rooms with air-con, for which you will pay an additional US$5. The TV lounge is decked out with crimson crushed-velvet sofas. Rates include a Jamaican breakfast.

New Chelsea Hotel & Amusement Centre (Map pp80-1; ☎ 926-5803; chelseahotelja@yahoo.com, chelseahotelja@hotmail.com; 5 Chelsea Ave; r US$60; P) It's a stretch to call this basic option amusing, but it does provide an economical stay in the heart of the action of New Kingston. Older rooms are dark; modern rooms in an annex are slightly better. All feature air-con, hot water and cable TV. A fifth night is free. It has a pool hall and amusement center, plus disco and rooftop bar.

Mayfair Hotel (Map pp80-1; ☎ 926-1610; www.ja-direct.com/mayfair; 4 W Kings House Close; r US$58-70, ste s/d US$88/128; P) A popular option with Jamaican travelers, this hotel sports a columned portico entrance that hints at grandeur within, but the 32 rooms in eight individual houses are fairly basic, with utility furniture and phone, though all are clean and well lit. Its best feature is the view toward the Blue Mountains. A buffet is hosted poolside on Wednesday and Saturday nights.

MIDRANGE

Indies Hotel (Map pp80-1; ☎ 926-2952, 926-0989; www.indieshotel.com; 5 Holborn Rd; s/d/tr US$65/70/81;) Providing perhaps the best value in Kingston, this well-run operation is highly rated for its cheerful ambience and accommodating atmosphere. The 15 spacious rooms each have TV and phone and overlook a garden patio complete with fishpond; take an upstairs room for sunlight. A quality small restaurant serves economical Jamaican and English-style cuisine (here's your chance for great fish and chips).

Shirley Retreat House (Map pp80-1; ☎ 927-9208, 946-2678; 7 Maeven Rd; r US$65-75;) Operated by the United Church of Jamaica, this option has four simply furnished, well-lit rooms with hardwood floors, pleasant fabrics, fans and private bathrooms with hot water. There's a TV in the lounge (two rooms have small TVs, and one has air-con). Meals are cooked on request.

Sunset Inn Apartment Hotel (Map pp80-1; ☎ 929-7283; 1A Altamont Cres; studio US$62-67, r US$71-79; P) It enjoys an advantageous location in the heart of New Kingston, but, alas, the 11 rooms are dowdy with little light. The studios are small and lack a kitchenette, but the one-bedroom units make amends with small kitchens and large bathrooms. All have TVs, phones and fans. Take an upper-story room for the breeze.

Medallion Hall Hotel (Map pp80-1; ☎ 927-5721; medallionhall@cwjamaica.com; 53 Hope Rd; s/d/tr/q US$71/73/84/97;) A well-run option close to the Bob Marley Museum, this midrange favorite offers 14 varied rooms with adequate furnishing and cable TV. Hardwoods abound. There's a modest restaurant and English pub. Ask for a top-floor room to catch the breeze.

our pick Mikuzi Guest House (Map pp80-1; ☎ 978-4859, 813-0098; www.mikuzijamaica.com; 5 Upper Montrose Rd; r/ste US$80/125;) Not far from the Bob Marley Museum, this welcoming guesthouse offers 11 comfortable rooms, several with kitchenettes, in a handsome home. All but one basic room (US$35) have hot water and air-con. The two highest-priced suites are decked out with art and antiques and are more like small apartments. Few restaurants are nearby, however, so if you lack wheels you'll have to hoof it at mealtime.

Iris Inn (Map pp80-1; ☎ 978-2909; www.iris-inn.com.jm; 26 Tankerville Ave; 1-/2-bedroom US$80/150;) Lurking between the Beverly Hills and the National Stadium, this excellent hotel manages to be off the beaten New Kingston path without straying too far. The one- and two-bedroom options are spacious, with leather couches, cable TV and small kitchens.

Alhambra Inn (Map pp80-1; ☎ 978-9072; 1 Tucker Ave; r US$85-105;) Across from the National Stadium, this is an attractive, two-story property with 20 air-con rooms in Spanish style. It's designed to lure convention business and offers gracious furnishings, cable TV, phones and spacious bathrooms. Upstairs rooms have lofty ceilings and king-size beds. Rates include taxes. Facilities include a restaurant, two bars and a pool in the courtyard.

Christar Villas (Map pp80-1; ☎ 978-3933; www.christarvillashotel.com; 99A Hope Rd; r US$93, studio US$125, 2-bedroom ste US$180-275;) Just east of the Bob Marley Museum, this is the pick of the self-catering options. You can choose from modern, pleasantly furnished studio apartments and one- and two-bedroom suites with satellite TVs, full kitchens and comfy beds. Rates include tax. Upper-story suites tend to get hot. You can cool off in the pool, and there is also a self-service laundry, restaurant and gym. Airport transfer is available on request.

Altamont Court (Map pp80-1; ☎ 929-4497, 929-5931; www.altamontcourt.com; 1 Altamont Cres; r US$128, ste US$160;) A rather soulless though centrally located mid-size hotel with 55 modern, clean one-bedroom studios and suites – each equipped with phone, cable TV, safe, and basic furnishings. Facilities include the Mango Tree, an attractive restaurant offering complimentary breakfast for guests, and a small pool with bar.

TOP END

Knutsford Court Hotel (Map pp80-1; ☎ 929-1000; www.knutsfordcourt.com; 16 Chelsea Ave; s US$105-135, d US$115-145, ste US$155-205, townhouse US$350-360;) This agreeable, newly refurbished hotel has a garden setting and an understated elegance. The 180 rooms – some with private balconies and work desks – are clean and well appointed, each with phone, in-room safe and cable TV. Rates include continental breakfast, served in the lobby. The Melting Pot Restaurant provides exemplary fare and room service.

Courtleigh Hotel & Suites (Map pp80-1; ☎ 929-9000; www.courtleigh.com; 85 Knutsford Blvd; s/d US$115/125, ste US$190-200, office ste US$190, penthouse US$145-435;) Next door to the Hilton, this is a splendid contemporary option with deluxe rooms and one-bedroom suites featuring four-poster beds and tasteful mahogany furnishings, plus cable TV, direct-dial phone, hair dryer and a work desk. The suites have kitchenettes. In addition to the 'executive suite' with full office, there's a state-of-the-art business center, a respected restaurant and the Mingles bar. There's a pool bar with live music on Friday, a small gym and a coin-operated laundry. Rates include continental breakfast.

Hilton Hotel (Map pp80-1; ☎ 926-5430, in the USA & Canada 800-445-8667, in the UK 0845-7581-595; www.hilton.com; 77 Knutsford Blvd; r US$150-245, ste US$255-300;) Strongly oriented toward the business traveler, and boasting contemporary architecture and furnishings and a full complement of facilities, the Hilton has 303 rooms, including 13 suites. The spacious rooms are elegantly furnished and have a small work desk, direct-dial phones, satellite TV and internet access. Other features include a fitness center, boutique, two tennis courts, a cyber center and the Jonkanoo Lounge for night owls.

Terra Nova All-Suite Hotel (Map pp80-1; ☎ 926-2211, 926-9334, in North America 800-526-2422; 17 Waterloo Rd; ste US$207-580;) It's an intimate, all-suite hotel with among the most beautiful and sophisticated rooms in town. Though the colonial mansion was built in 1924, the 35 spacious junior suites in three two-story wings have a contemporary feel, with tropically vibrant fabrics. King-size beds and cable TV are standard – and thumbs up for the marble bathrooms, some of which have Jacuzzis. Facilities include a 24-hour business center and fitness center. The El Dorado dining room (p89) is supremely elegant, plus there's a patio restaurant and La Fresca poolside bar and grill. Rates include taxes and service charge and breakfast.

Jamaica Pegasus (Map pp80-1; ☎ 926-3690; www.jamaicapegasus.com; 81 Knutsford Blvd; s/d US$280/300, ste US$300-800; P ⊠ ✱ 💻 🏊) This glitzy 17-story property has 300 nicely appointed rooms, including 16 suites and three luxury suites. It also offers a panoply of facilities and a selection of restaurants. These include the elegant Columbus for Italian dishes, and a 24-hour Café Deli, where you can get your cup of Blue Mountain coffee during the wee hours. It has a slight edge over the Hilton with its full-service business center and the Royal Club – a more exclusive enclave of rooms and suites catering to business folk. For an unparalleled view, ask for a room facing the mountains.

Around Uptown

BUDGET

Abahati Hotel (Map p69; ☎/fax 924-2082; 7 Grosvenor Tce; r US$40; ✱ 🏊) In a reclusive upscale neighborhood in Constant Spring at the base of Stony Hill, the Abahati offers a cool location at 200m elevation. The 12 rooms are carpeted and clean, with lots of light but tired furniture. Some have air-con. Spacious gardens offer a chance to relax. The hotel's highlight is a pleasing restaurant, Pearl's Café.

Stony Hill Hotel (Map p69; ☎ 942-2357; r US$55-75; ✱ 🏊) Behind the Model-T Ford standing sentry in the forecourt, this rambling, slate-roofed hotel in the hills 8km north of Half Way Tree on the A3, boasts fabulous views over Kingston. An old-world charmer, it has 35 rooms, all with bathrooms with hot water, large windows with views, and an intriguing blend of homey 1960s decor and modern art. Some rooms have air-con and cable TV. There's a bar that's a 1950s time warp. Note: the turnoff is on a dangerous hairpin bend by the Texaco gas station.

MIDRANGE

The Gardens (Map p69; ☎ 927-8275; 23 Liguanea Ave; s/d US$85/160 P 💻 🏊) In a quiet, leafy neighborhood north of the Bob Marley Museum, this wonderful hotel is composed of seven stately townhouses offset by well-tended gardens. The townhouses, which feature large, airy living rooms, can be reserved as double en-suite rooms or shared doubles. One of Kingston's best hotel options.

EATING

As in other matters, Kingston is Jamaica's capital of food; it is here that the national cuisine was born and it is here that it continues to thrive and evolve. Let your taste buds run free!

Most of the notable eateries are found in uptown Kingston, where the culinary adventurer is spoiled for choice. Many offer alfresco dining in the cool evening air and terrific spreads for brunch on Sunday.

Budget

Brick Oven (Map pp80-1; ☎ 968-2153; 26 Hope Rd; patties US$1; 🕑 lunch & dinner) While nearby Norma's and the Grogg Shoppe get all the raves, those in the know swear by the patties served up in this small bakery located just behind Devon House. Pastries and juices are also available at this excellent option for a picnic on the grounds.

Coffee Mill (Map pp80-1; ☎ 929-2227; 17 Barbados Ave; pastries US $1-1.50, sandwiches US $4-5; 🕑 breakfast, lunch & dinner Mon-Fri, 10am-6pm Sat) Sip the best cappuccinos and espressos in Kingston at this intimate café with a small counter and several tables. Pastries and sandwiches are also on offer here.

Livity (Map pp80-1; ☎ 906-5618; 30 Haining Rd; mains US$2-6; 🕑 lunch & dinner) The best vegetarian option in New Kingston, Livity serves up an array of veggie fajitas, soups, salads and tofu dishes. Service can be a little slow, but if you order one of the outstanding fruit juices – try the mango pineapple or the lemonade – and get an outdoor seat, the wait's easy to bear.

Orient Express (Map pp74-5; ☎ 967-2198; 135 Harbour St; mains US$2-6; 🕑 lunch Mon-Sat) One of the precious few options for a decent meal downtown, this joint offers a reasonably good Chinese menu.

our pick **Ashanti Oasis** (☎ 970-2079; Hope Gardens; mains $2-7; 🕑 lunch & dinner) If an oasis within a garden is hard to envision, check out this serene spot centered on a small fountain. You'll be rewarded with excellent vegetarian food from a changing I-tal menu featuring hearty soups (the pumpkin is absolutely divine), veggie burgers and combo platters anchored by a variety of tofu offerings. Fresh juices or a glass of the homemade aloe wine are a must.

Emperial Kish Inn (Map pp80-1; ☎ 920-0541; 2 Hillview Ave, off Eastwood Park Rd; mains US$3-9; ⏰ breakfast, lunch & dinner) The sign over the bar reading 'Love the Animals' immediately reveals where the place is coming from. The only flesh here – yourself notwithstanding – is that which is pressed in the local greeting, the Jamaican 'yardie' handshake, where friends push their fists together while swiping thumbs. On the menu is gluten brownstew, curry tofu, roast yams and an ongoing dialogue about the intricacies of Rastafari.

Chelsea Jerk Centre (Map pp80-1; ☎ 926-6322; 7 Chelsea Ave; mains US$3-10; ⏰ 11am-midnight) Legendary for its mouth-searing jerk pork and chicken, this congenial jerk emporium draws the after-work crowd as well as uptown-based visitors grateful for a chance to get off the main drag. The festival dumplings are especially good.

Holburn Bar & Grill (Map pp80-1; ☎ 754-7963; cnr Chelsea Ave & Dominica Dr; mains US$3.50-8; ⏰ lunch & dinner) This breezy 2nd-floor restaurant is a casual affair with a pool table and delicious 'fish in foil' – a whole snapper steamed with veggies and spices.

Legend Café (Map pp80-1; Bob Marley Museum, 56 Hope Rd; mains US$4-16; ⏰ breakfast & lunch) Offering sustenance to visitors to Bob's former home, this café serves up hearty I-tal stew or curried fish. The fruit juices are the star here – including Bob's favorite, carrot and beetroot.

Hot Pot (Map pp80-1; ☎ 929-3906; 2 Altamont Tce; mains US$5-12; ⏰ breakfast, lunch & dinner Mon-Sat, dinner Sun) A casual, economical haunt with a small back patio that attracts workers from the nearby hotels, Hot Pot serves unfussy, indisputably delicious Jamaican home-style cooking with dishes such as ackee and saltfish, escoveitched fish and garlic chicken. Wash it down with a fresh tamarind juice, coconut water or a Red Stripe.

Moby Dick (Map pp74-5; ☎ 922-4468; 3 Orange St; mains US$6-14; ⏰ breakfast, lunch & dinner Mon-Sat) A terrific option for a pre- or post-National Gallery visit, this former sailors' hangout has been popular for its curries and rotis for nearly a century. The curried goat is truly outstanding, as is the conch version when available. Fortify yourself with one of the fresh juices.

Devon House I-Scream (Map pp80-1; ☎ 929-7086; Devon House, 26 Hope Rd; ⏰ 10am-10pm Mon-Sat, 11am-10pm Sun & holidays) Behind Devon House, it sells excellent ice cream.

Lots of places sell patties for less than US$1. **Patty King** (Map pp74-5; cnr Harbour & East Sts) and **Juici-Beef Patties** (Map pp74-5; cnr Harbour & King Sts) charge about US$0.50 for patties. Uptown, try **Tastee Patties** (Map pp80-1; ☎ 926-2834; cnr Constant Spring & Hagley Park Rds).

For something quick, there are dozens of fast-food joints around town. Some of the major shopping centers, such as **Sovereign Centre** (Map pp80-1; 106 Hope Rd), have food courts – whole floors dedicated to fast-food outlets. For produce, head to Papine Market at the top end of Hope Rd, where ultrafresh vegetables are trucked in straight from the Blue Mountains, or to the market north of uptown on Constant Spring Rd.

Midrange

Upper Crust (Map pp80-1; ☎ 977-5130; 20 Barbican Rd; pastries US$1-5, mains US$10-20; ⏰ lunch & dinner) This open-air pastry shop in Liguanea also serves up an ambitious Jamaican-fusion menu, highlighted by the scrumptious jerk chicken lasagna.

Jade Garden (Map pp80-1; ☎ 978-3476; Sovereign Centre, 106 Hope Rd; dim sum US$3-14, Sunday brunch US$18; ⏰ noon-10pm) You'll forget you're eating in a mall once you step into this elegant spot – particularly if you can grab a table with a view of the mountains. Highlighting the à la carte menu are the deep-fried prawns and a sizzling meat combo platter called Subgum War Bar, but the Sunday dim-sum brunch is really the big draw here.

So-So Seafood Bar & Grill (Map pp80-1; ☎ 968-2397; 4 Chelsea Ave; mains US$5-12; ⏰ lunch & dinner) A casual place, known for its mellow after-work scene, which settles around the bar and two TV sets or sprawls into its outdoor patio. The seafood menu, divided into conch, shrimp, lobster and fish sections, belies the modesty of the name.

Rib Kage Bar and Grill (☎ 978-6272; 12 Braemer Ave; mains $5-30; ⏰ lunch & dinner) While catching a lot of the spillover from ever-popular Red Bones Blues Café across the street, Rib Kage attracts its own following with its succulent baby-back ribs and an array of southern US soul food, served in a relaxed, wood-accented setting. Burgers and a selection of fish entrees are also available. The original branch, at 149 Constant Spring Rd, offers outdoor seating.

Pepper's (Map pp80-1; ☎ 969-2421; 31 Upper Waterloo Rd; mains US$6-14; ⏰ 4pm-late) This friendly open-air eatery is a highly popular after-work hangout among Kingstonians. It has picnic tables, plenty of Red Stripe, and seriously good jerk dishes and seafood favorites including grilled lobster and garlic crab. The two bars (p90) are open late.

Thai Gardens (Map pp80-1; 11 Holborn Rd; dishes US$8-22; ⏰ lunch & dinner) This Thai restaurant shares space with Akbar and offers an extensive menu of pad thai and curries that's a little hit-or-miss.

Akbar (Map pp80-1; ☎ 926-3480; 11 Holborn Rd; mains US$8-24; ⏰ lunch & dinner) Kingston's best Indian restaurant draws crowds for its gracious service, garden graced by a fountain and reasonably priced menu that includes tandoori and vegetarian dishes, complemented by excellent Indian breads. Be sure to insist on extra spiciness, if fire's what you crave. Akbar offers a buffet lunch special (US$15).

El Dorado Room (Map pp80-1; ☎ 926-2211; Terra Nova All-Suite Hotel, 17 Waterloo Rd; mains US$8-24; ⏰ lunch & dinner) The European menu has hints of the Caribbean as well as Jamaican favorites such as pepperpot soup and grilled snapper. Bring a sweater for the frigid air-conditioning. The hotel also has a less expensive outdoor restaurant that serves continental fare. A seafood buffet is offered for Wednesday lunch and dinner. A Jamaican buffet lunch is offered weekdays, and a Sunday brunch buffet (US$21) draws the well-heeled, hungry locals.

Grog Shoppe (Map pp80-1; ☎ 968-2098; 26 Hope Rd; mains US$8-28; ⏰ noon-midnight Mon-Fri, 10am-2pm Sun) Lodged in an expansive brick building that used to be the servants' quarters for Devon House, this atmospheric choice has the look and feel of a colonial pub. The menu features classic pub lunches, such as corned tongue, and tinkered-with Jamaica favorites such as ackee crepes, baked crab backs and roast suckling pig with rice and peas. It's known for its Sunday brunch (US$17). There's live music Tuesday to Saturday evenings.

Chez Maria (Map pp80-1; ☎ 927-8078; 7 Hillcrest Ave; mains US$9-18; ⏰ lunch & dinner) Whether you sit in the garden beneath the mango tree or grab a table on the front terrace, you'll be treated to fine Lebanese cuisine. The mezes, notably the hummus, are excellent and are complimented by homemade pita bread. A host of shawarmas and kebabs awaits if you still have an appetite.

Carlos' Café (Map pp80-1; ☎ 926-4186; 22 Belmont Rd; meals US$9-18; ⏰ 11am-2am) A pleasant, spacious bar (p90) with pasta, surf 'n' turf and stuffed crab backs on offer. Food is served until late.

Heather's Garden Restaurant (Map pp80-1; ☎ 926-2826, 960-7739; 9 Haining Rd; mains US$9-24; ⏰ lunch & dinner Mon-Sat) Grab a table near the immense mango tree stretching through a hole in the roof and savor moderately priced fare ranging from Jamaican crab backs and Cajun-style blackened fish to cottage pie, charbroiled lamb chops, kebabs and seafood. The bar scene gets increasingly raucous with singles as the evening progresses.

our pick **Up on the Roof** (☎ 929-8033; 73 Knutsford Blvd; mains US$9-36; ⏰ lunch & dinner Mon-Thu, dinner Sat) Above the bustle of New Kingston's main drag, this atmospheric rooftop terrace is popular with locals and a terrific starting point before a night on the town. The marlin salad and shrimp with garlic jerk mayo stand out in a menu of Jamaican standards. There's a sporadic calendar of jazz events and poetry readings; on Saturday, the bar mixes cocktails until the last patron leaves.

Columbus Restaurant (Map pp80-1; ☎ 926-3690; Jamaica Pegasus Hotel, 81 Knutsford Blvd; mains US$12-20; ⏰ breakfast, lunch & dinner Mon-Sat) Superlative Italian fare is lovingly prepared in this swanky restaurant popular with business travelers and fashionable Kingstonians. The chefs have a way with pasta – which is to be expected for the price tag – and the gnocchi with wild mushrooms is to die for, but the amaretto cheesecake suggests genius.

Top End

our pick **Red Bones Blues Café** (Map pp80-1; ☎ 978-8262; 21 Braemar Ave; mains US$20-40; ⏰ 11am-1am Mon-Fri, from 7pm Sat) The in-crowd is in at this former colonial house, now a beehive of cultural and culinary activity. Inside, the *shukka-shukka* of martini shakers keeps time with the music, and the walls are beguilingly bedecked with photographs of jazz and blues legends. The food? Stellar dishes include chicken breast stuffed with callaloo and jerked cheddar in a white wine sauce, or the seafood trio of shrimp, mussels and salmon sautéed in a spicy coconut sauce served on a bed of pasta. Opt for patio dining overlooking the gardens or the handsome bar. Call ahead to snag a table – they're in high demand.

Mac's Chop House (☎ 960-6328; 24-22 Trinidad Tce; mains US $22-50; ⏰ dinner Mon-Sat) Perhaps Mac should pay more attention to the chops heralded by its name, as the steaks at this sleek yet intimate spot next door to the Quad nightclub do not justify the New York prices. Nevertheless, the appetizers (notably an unforgettable smoked marlin 'trilogy') and the fish dishes are excellent. The wine list is one of the widest-ranging on the island. Reservations essential.

Norma's on the Terrace (Map pp80-1; ☎ 968-5488; 26 Hope Rd; mains US$22-55; ⏰ 10am-10pm Mon-Sat, closed public holidays) Although its popularity seems to be on the wane outside the expense-account class, this lovechild of Jamaica's leading food emissary Norma Shirley is Kingston's most celebrated restaurant. The seasonal menu explores Caribbean-fusion food with great finesse. Recent gems include the smoked pork loin in teriyaki sauce, red snapper encrusted in herbs in a thyme-and-caper sauce and an exquisite seafood lasagna. Creative salads and desserts (try the English trifle) are not to be missed. Even if a meal is beyond your budget, it's well worth having a drink on the candlelit terrace.

ENTERTAINMENT

Kingston is the best town in Jamaica for bar-hopping and clubbing. From copasetic watering holes to throbbing nightclubs – with a couple of all-night sound-system street jams thrown into the mix – you'll never want for after-hours action in this town.

Many bars, discos and nightclubs feature regularly scheduled events and theme nights, making it possible to get a groove going every night of the week. Those who dig Latin music – or just need a break from dancehall or reggae – are spoiled for choice, as a number of venues crank out the salsa and merengue throughout the week. Similarly, on Friday evening there are a number of after-work parties where Kingstonians unwind and get their groove going in preparation for a long night of dancing.

If dancehall floats your boat, Kingston comes alive on Wednesday night as Weddy Weddy and Passa Passa fire up the sound systems in two consecutive events that together span 12 hours. Definitely not for the meek or mild-mannered! (See opposite.)

For listings, check **What's On Jamaica** (www.whatsonjamaica.com), which also publishes listings in the Friday *Observer*.

Bars

Red Bones Blues Café (Map pp80-1; ☎ 978-8262; 21 Braemar Ave; ⏰ 11-1am Mon-Fri, 7pm-1am Sat) This could easily become your favorite spot in town – it's a hip bar with cool ambience, good conversation and great music. The last Wednesday of the month there's poetry with musical accompaniment, and on Friday there's quality live blues and jazz. An art gallery, open evenings, shows well-chosen local and international talent. And this says nothing of the food (p89).

Indies Café and Grill (Map pp80-1; ☎ 920-5913; 8 Holborn Rd) Dark yet lively sports bar, patronized by young professionals with an enormous screen behind the bar, that gets rambunctious as the night progresses. Karaoke takes over on Thursday. Ignore the food on offer here as the kitchen pays it scant attention.

Cuddy'z (Map pp80-1; ☎ 926-0273; New Kingston Shopping Centre) Perhaps the best sports bar in Jamaica, this hip establishment is the creation of the 'Big Man Inna Cricket,' Courtney Walsh. TVs in each booth and a lively bleachers section with an oversized screen make this a great place to watch a cricket match. The Heineken Wednesdays are very popular.

Home 20 Sports Bar & Grill (Map pp80-1; no phone; 20 Holborn Rd) Amusingly perched atop a functioning car wash, this welcoming outdoor joint is great for an early drink before heading out for the evening. A small kitchen serves passable fish 'n' chips.

Pepper's (Map pp80-1; ☎ 969-2421; 31 Upper Waterloo Rd) You'll feel like a local after a night at this rousing spot, which gets going early for the after-work crowd and continues hopping well past midnight. On Tuesday night there's wine, cheese and live country music, on Thursday it's karaoke and on Sunday, oldies night.

Carlos' Café (Map pp80-1; ☎ 926-4186; 22 Belmont Rd; ⏰ 11am-2am) A pleasant, open-air bar with lively tropical decor, several pool tables, and martini specials on Monday and karaoke on Friday. In the evenings, the softly lit patio is a romantic place.

Veranda (☎ 906-3601; 38 Trafalgar Rd) Small joint with outdoor seating that draws an after-work crowd. They enjoy the large screen TVs, cheap drinks and easy camaraderie.

Priscilla's (Map pp80-1; ☎ 969-9638; 103 Constant Spring Rd) This quiet spot sustains a laid-back vibe and, on special occasions, live music. A great place to meet local Kingstonians.

Backyaad (Map pp80-1; ☎ 755-0132; 126 Constant Spring Rd) Drawing a younger crowd, this nightspot has a *really* loud sound system, fierce dominoes competitions and occasional comedy jams.

Café What's On (Map pp80-1; ☎ 929-4490; Devon House, 26 Hope Rd) This intimate bar at Devon House has occasional live music and art exhibitions.

Nightclubs

Asylum (Map pp80-1; ☎ 929-4386; 69 Knutsford Blvd) Still *the* happening scene, Asylum packs in the crowds from Tuesday through Sunday. Tuesday is ladies night, with free admission until 11pm, and on Thursday the inimitable Stone Love sets up its legendary sound system.

Quad (Map pp80-1; ☎ 754-7823; 20-22 Trinidad Tce; admission US$10) This complex comprises four clubs, each with its own distinct personality. On the main floor is Christopher's Jazz Club, a tasteful jazz bar where the city's movers and shakers gather on a nightly basis. In the basement is Taboo, a so-called 'naughty gentleman's' club with 'exotic' dancers. Every Wednesday, Friday and Saturday, two clubs open up on the top floor: the Voodoo Lounge, which tends to draw an older, more urbane crowd, and Oxygen, which attracts a twenty-something set always ready to get sweaty until 4am. The US$10 admission will give you entry into Christopher's, Voodoo Lounge and Oxygen; Note that Taboo charges a separate US$10 admission.

Infinity Nightclub (Map pp80-1; ☎ 926-2285; 61 Knutsford Blvd) Around the corner from Asylum is Infinity, another happening dance club with theme nights.

Weekenz (Map pp80-1; ☎ 755-4415; 80 Constant Spring Rd) This popular hipster haunt has variable moods, poetry on Tuesday, live reggae on Wednesday, dancehall on Thursday, oldies night on Saturday – and always a thriving after-work scene.

Village Cafe (Map pp80-1; ☎ 970-4861; 20 Barbican Rd) Another popular favorite. Thursday evenings feature a fashion show, but the place really gets rocking on Saturday night, when the locally famous DJs mix up a healthy dose of wicked vibes.

Cinema

First-run Hollywood movies can be seen at the five-screen **Carib 5 Cinema** (Map pp80-1; ☎ 926-6106; cnr Slipe & Half Way Tree Rds), the two-screen **Palace Cineplex** (Map pp80-1; ☎ 978-3522; Sovereign Centre, 106 Hope Rd) and the single-screen **Island Cinema** (Map pp80-1; ☎ 920 7964; Island Life Shopping Centre, 6 St Lucia Ave).

Red Bones Blue Café (Map pp80-1; ☎ 978-8262; 21 Braemar Ave) screens occasional art films in its garden.

Theater

Little Theater (Map pp80-1; ☎ 926-6129; 4 Tom Redcam Dr) Puts on plays, folk concerts and modern dance throughout the year. The main season is July through August. From December through April, producer Basil Dawkins presents a 'mini-season' of smaller productions.

Ward Theatre (Map pp74-5; ☎ 922-0453; North Pde; admission US$3-8) Home to the National Dance Theater Company, known for its rich repertory combining Caribbean, African and Western dance styles. The Jamaica Folk Singers and the Little Theater's annual pantomime – a riotous, irreverent social satire – are also staged here.

Pantry Playhouse (Map pp80-1; ☎ 960-9845; 2 Dumfries Rd) Presents comedies and dramas at a New Kingston playhouse year-round.

Watch out for performances by the **University Singers** (☎ 702-3518), who are acclaimed for their repertoire of Caribbean folk and popular music, choral performances, madrigals, jazz, African songs and pantomime. Don't miss the Cari-Folk Singers, who are dedicated to preserving the Jamaican folk genre.

Also look for listings for **Barn Theatre** (Map pp80-1; ☎ 926-6469; 5 Oxford Rd) and **Centre Stage Theatre** (Map pp80-1; ☎ 968-7529; 18 Dominica Dr).

Stage Shows

Kingston has frequent live stage shows, which are announced on streetside billboards. Top-name artists often perform at the **National Arena** (Map pp80-1; ☎ 929-4970; Arthur Wint Dr).

Sports

Renovated for the 2007 Cricket World Cup **Sabina Park** (Map pp74-5; ☎ 967-0322; South Camp Rd) is *the* place for cricket in Jamaica. The 30,000-seat arena hosted its first test match in 1929 and has been a focal point for the sport ever

BLOCK-ROCKIN' BEATS

Without question, the highpoint of Kingston's nightlife is its free outdoor sound-system parties. A raucous combination of block party, dance club, fashion show and all-out stereo war, sound-system parties can be heard blocks away and go well into the night. Certainly not for the fainthearted or anyone who dislikes dancehall, sound-system dances are, nevertheless, unforgettable cultural experiences and should not be missed.

The best opportunity for visitors to check out a party, and the focus of Kingston's thronging sound-system aficionados, is **Weddy Weddy Wednesdays** (Map pp80-1), presided over by the biggest name in sound-system productions, DJ Stone Love in Burlington Ave in uptown. Generally, the action doesn't start until a little after midnight and once it subsides most of the crowd troops off to the **Passa Passa** sound-system, at the intersection of Spanish Town Rd and Beeston St, which blasts until sunrise. Another popular party is **Uptown Mondays** in Savannah Plaza, which begins around midnight.

Given Kingston's (not altogether unfounded) reputation for crime, sound systems are refreshingly safe events provided you take common-sense precautions and don't flash money or jewelry and leave the cameras at home. The crowd at Weddy Weddy is particularly welcoming, and most Jamaicans are happy to see tourists enjoying so quintessentially Jamaican an experience. Bear in mind, however, that the area around Passa Passa can be rather dodgy, especially if you go home early and leave the crowd behind.

For once-off sound-system parties, look for posters by Stone Love. Another good source is the **Tuff Gong Studios** (p69; ☎ 923-9383, 923-5814; 220 Marcus Garvey Dr).

since. Attending a match – particularly an international test – is a must whether or not you are a fan.

The **National Stadium** (Map pp80-1; ☎ 929-4970; Arthur Wint Dr) hosts track-and-field events and matches by the Reggae Boyz, Jamaica's football (soccer) team that surprised the world by reaching the World Cup finals in 1998.

Kingston hosts the annual **Carib Cement International Marathon** (☎ 928-6231), held every February.

For information about horse racing near Kingston, see p103.

SHOPPING

From glitzy, modern shopping malls to the enclosed chaos of urban markets, Kingston rewards shoppers of all budgets and inclinations. Everything from colonial antiques to goats is for sale (but generally not from the same vendor).

Downtown, everywhere you turn are street vendors trying to hawk anything they can think of while keeping a wary eye out for officials bent on cracking down on unlicensed peddling. In contrast, several modern shopping malls are concentrated on Constant Spring and Hope Rds, where more-prosperous Kingstonians relish the city's burgeoning consumer culture.

Two of the largest shopping centers are **Sovereign Centre** (Map pp80-1; 106 Hope Rd) and **New Kingston Shopping Mall** (Map pp80-1; Dominica Dr).

Art Galleries

Wassi Art Pottery (Map pp80-1; ☎ 906-5016; Devon House, 26 Hope Rd) This pottery sells marvelous vases, planters, plates, bowls and so on, each hand-painted and signed by the artist.

Bolivar Art Gallery (Map pp80-1; ☎ 926-8799; 1D Grove Rd) Works by Jamaica's leading artists are on offer here, but there's also fine books, antiques and maps.

Artisan (Map pp80-1; ☎ 978-3514; Sovereign Centre, 106 Hope Rd) The best of Jamaican creative talent is on sale at Artisan.

Patoo (Map p69; ☎ 924-1552; Manor Hill Plaza, 184 Constant Spring Rd) You'll find local treasures (Tortuga puddings laced with rum, Busha Brown sauces, potpourri baskets, ceramic tableware, decorative ornaments and batik sarongs) at Patoo to tempt you.

In addition, the following galleries feature contemporary Jamaican art:

Chelsea Galleries (Map pp80-1; ☎ 929-0045; Island Life Centre, 12 Chelsea Ave)

Contemporary Art Centre (Map pp80-1; ☎ 927-9958; 1 Liguanea Ave)

Gallery Pegasus (Map pp80-1; ☎ 926-3690, basement, Jamaica Pegasus hotel, 81 Knutsford Blvd)

Grosvenor Gallery (Map p69; ☎ 924-6684; 1 Grosvenor Tce)
Mutual Life Gallery (Map pp80-1; ☎ 929-4302; Mutual Life Centre, 2 Oxford Rd)
Marso (Map pp80-1; ☎ 978-9720; 90 Hope Rd)
Supersad Studios (Map pp80-1; ☎ 740-1632; Mutual Life Centre, 2 Oxford Rd)

Clothing

Mijan Caribbean Clothing (Map pp80-1; ☎ 977-5133; 20 Barbican Rd) Mijan sells quality Jamaican designs.

Cooyah (Map pp80-1; ☎ 978-9215; cooyahdesign@jamweb.net; 96 Hope Rd) This is the place to go for licensed reggae T-shirts and assorted tops and dresses. Cooyah means 'look here' in patois; you should.

Photographic

Photo Express (Map pp80-1; ☎ 977-2679; 130 Old Hope Rd) Fully stocked with film and photography equipment, Photo Express has several branches.

Record Stores

Orange St in downtown Kingston is the best place in all Jamaica to shop for reggae cassettes and CDs. Many of the stores are offshoots of recording studios and pressing plants, so you know that the grooves are still warm. To get you started, check out these:

Rockers International (Map pp74–5; ☎ 922-8015; 135 Orange St)
Techniques Records (Map pp74–5; ☎ 967-4367; 99 Orange St)
Tuff Gong Recording Studios (Map p69; ☎ 923-9383; Marcus Garvey Dr) See p77 for details.

Street Markets & Crafts Stalls

Although it was razed by fire in 2003, the covered **Jubilee Market** (Map pp74–5), which verges on the western end of the Parade, has been rebuilt. Named in honor of Queen Victoria's Jubilee, it's an extremely lively market where seemingly everything's for sale. Be very wary of pickpockets. A bit further west, in the exhilarating pandemonium of **Coronation Market** (Map pp74-5; 🕒 Mon-Sat), shoppers come face to face with the dynamic – and sometimes daunting – aspects of life in downtown Kingston. Stall after stall is stocked with every manner of bric-a-brac, from handmade tools to sound-system speakers. In negotiating with the vendors you'll need to penetrate their artful patois. Coronation Market's proximity to the unpredictable Tivoli Gardens district means that you'll need to choose your friends carefully; many visitors feel more comfortable arriving with a local companion who knows the territory. *Don't* go wandering any further west downtown without a guide who's respected locally. Leave valuables and all but a minimum of money in your hotel safe – and be alert.

Considerably more sedate, the waterfront **Crafts Market** (Map pp74-5; cnr Pechon & Port Royal Sts; 🕒 Mon-Sat) resides in an old iron building where you'll find dozens of stalls selling wickerwork, carvings, batiks, straw hats and other crafts – at prices somewhat lower than elsewhere on the island.

Pickpockets have long been known to work the crowds at Kingston's public markets. Watch your wallet!

GETTING THERE & AWAY

Air

Norman Manley International Airport (Map p69; ☎ 924-8452, 888-247-7678), 27km southeast of downtown, handles international flights; see p285 for more details on international services. Domestic flights depart and land at **Tinson Pen Airstrip** (Map p69; Marcus Garvey Dr) in west Kingston; see p292 for details.

Air Jamaica (Map pp80-1; ☎ 800-359-2475; 4 St Lucia Ave) has its headquarters uptown. Air Jamaica and Air Jamaica Express offer daily service to and from Montego Bay and Ocho Rios from Norman Manley International Airport; the latter airline flies also from Tinson Pen. See p292 for more information.

TimAir (☎ 952-2516, 979-1114) provides air taxi services connecting Kingston with Montego Bay, Negril, Ocho Rios, Port Antonio and Mandeville. See also p292.

Car

From the north coast, the main artery leading into Kingston is the busy A3 road, which wends its way into town through the outlying communities of Stony Hill and Constant Springs. Alternatively, the winding, narrow B1 connects Kingston to the north from Buff Bay to Papine, but know in advance that the challenging road scales and plummets from the heights of the Blue Mountains. (Moreover, during the rainy season, landslides often close the road temporarily.)

From the west, Spanish Town Rd enters Kingston at the Six Miles junction. For uptown Kingston, veer left on Washington Blvd, which changes names to Dunrobin Ave and eventually joins Constant Springs Rd for a straight shot into uptown.

From the east, Windward Rd passes the turnoff for Port Royal and the airport; for New Kingston turn right on Mountain View Ave or South Camp Rd (the latter has helpful 'follow the hummingbird' signs directing the way).

Public Transportation

Buses, minibuses and route taxis run between Kingston and every point on the island. They arrive and depart primarily from the **downtown terminal** (Map pp74-5; Beckford & Pechon Sts) five blocks west of the Parade. Exercise caution, for the terminal adjoins the occasionally volatile district of Trench Town.

A smaller number of buses arrive and depart from the preferable **Half Way Tree junction** (Map pp80–1), where it's a snap to jump a local bus into New Kingston. If you're traveling to Kingston, find out where you will be dropped before boarding a bus. (See p292 for information about Jamaica's bus system.)

GETTING AROUND

To/From the Airport

Norman Manley International Airport is located midway along the Palisadoes, 27km southeast of downtown Kingston. The bus stop is opposite the arrivals hall. Bus 98 operates about every 30 minutes between the airport and downtown to West Pde (US$1). Route taxis operate between the airport and West Pde (US$1.75).

Disembarking from a bus downtown with luggage can be extremely intimidating. If this is your first visit to Kingston, it's much more sensible to grab a **taxi** (JUTA; ☎ 927-4534, 926-1537) between the airport and New Kingston; this will cost about US$20. From **Tinson Pen Airstrip** (Map p69; Marcus Garvey Dr) a taxi costs about US$8 to New Kingston, and a bus to the Parade in downtown is about US$0.25.

Island Car Rentals (Map p69; ☎ 929-5875; www.islandcarrentals.com; 17 Antigua Ave) has chauffeured transfers on offer.

Car

Most car-hire companies offer free airport shuttles. Jamaica's largest and most reputable company, **Island Car Rentals** (Map p69; ☎ 929-5875, in the USA 866-978-5335, in Canada 416-628-8885; www.islandcarrentals.com; 17 Antigua Ave) has its main office in New Kingston, plus an outlet at **Norman Manley International Airport** (Map p69; ☎ 924-8075).

Other companies with offices at Manley airport:

Avis (☎ 924-8293; www.avis.com)
Budget (☎ 759-1793; www.budget.com)
Hertz (☎ 924-8028; www.hertz.com)

Public Transportation

Buses, minibuses and route taxis arrive and depart from the North and South Pdes in downtown, Half Way Tree junction in uptown, and from Papine, at the eastern edge of town off Old Hope Rd.

Kingston's **bus system** (Jamaica Urban Transport Co Ltd; ☎ 749-3196; fares US$0.35-.50; ⏰ 5am-10pm) operates a fleet of Mercedes-Benz and Volvo buses, including buses for the disabled. Buses stop only at official stops. For a current schedule, you can telephone the **JUTC** (☎ 888-588-2287).

Taxi

Taxis are numerous in Kingston except when it rains, when demand skyrockets. Use licensed cabs only (they have red PPV license plates). It's best to get your hotel call for a trusted driver, otherwise taxi companies are listed in the yellow pages. Fares from New Kingston to downtown are about US$10.

AROUND KINGSTON

Whether it's downtown's perpetual slope toward the harbor or the Blue Mountains beckoning from high above uptown, there's something about Kingston's topography that's always tempting the visitor to take a break from its cultural highpoints and nocturnal hotspots. When the pull becomes irresistible, a variety of day trips offer fine counterpoints to your stay in the capital.

BUSES FROM KINGSTON

Destination	Cost (one way)	Distance	Duration	Frequency
Montego Bay	US$8	191km	5hr	6 daily
Ocho Rios	US$4	87km	3hr	8 daily
Port Antonio	US$4	9km	3hr	6 daily

Most popular is a visit to Port Royal, a former pirate den of iniquity cut down by an earthquake in 1692, easily combined with a visit to Lime Cay, the best (and closest) swimming spot in the area. Other good seaside options include Hellshire Beach, celebrated for its fish shacks, and Bull Bay, a rapidly growing surfing community. If it's greenery you crave, Castleton Gardens, a half-hour drive north of Kingston, are the finest botanic gardens in Jamaica. Finally, Jamaica's second city and former capital, Spanish Town, is noted for its Georgian architecture as well as the redbrick splendor of St Jago de la Vega, the oldest Anglican cathedral outside of England.

CASTLETON GARDENS

These **gardens** (off Map p96; ☎ 927-1257; admission free; 🕒 7am-5pm, to 6pm in summer), straddling the A3, 27km north of Half Way Tree, are spread over 12 hectares on the banks of the Wag Water River. Many exotic species introduced to Jamaica were first planted here.

The gardens, which rise up the hillside on the west side of the road, date back to 1860, when 400 specimens from Kew Gardens in London were transplanted on the former sugar plantation owned by Lord Castleton. More than 1000 species of natives and exotics are displayed.

There's a picnic area with cafeteria and toilets. The guides are unpaid (they're not allowed to charge), but tips are welcome.

You can camp on the riverbank here for US$2, and there's a lively little jerk center about 100m north of the gardens.

EAST OF KINGSTON

Watching Long Mountain close in on the sea from downtown Kingston, it's easy to think there's nothing east of Kingston beyond the turnoff to the Palisadoes, home to Norman Manley International Airport and Port Royal. Yet the A4 does manage to squeeze past and make it to St Thomas parish and up into Portland. Before it does, the road brushes through Bull Bay, a gritty town that draws surfers and pilgrims to a fundamentalist Rasta community.

Rockfort Mineral Baths

Providing respite from the urban environment, these **baths** (Map p69; ☎ 938-6551; Windward Rd; public pool adult/child US$2.50/1.50, private pools from US$12; 🕒 7am-5:30pm Tue-Sun), 5km east of downtown Kingston, are fed by a cold spring that made its first appearance following the earthquake of 1907. There's a large public pool – a rarity in Kingston – and 11 private pools of varying sizes, all with whirlpools and wheelchair access. The slightly saline and radioactive water is said to have therapeutic properties. One hour is the maximum allowed in a bath. There's a cafeteria and juice bar, plus changing rooms and lockers. **Massage** (per hr US$30) is offered.

Adjacent to the baths is Rockfort, an English fort with rusty cannons. It was built in 1694 amid rumors of an imminent invasion by the French. The remains of another fort, **Fort Nugent** (Map p69), stand on the hillside about 1.5km east of Rockfort.

Bus 99B operates from the Parade and Half Way Tree in Kingston and travels along Windward Rd (US$0.45). You can also take bus 98, which departs from the Parade and passes Rockfort en route to Port Royal, or bus 97 en route to Bull Bay.

Palisadoes

The **Palisadoes** (Map p69) is a narrow, 16km-long spit that forms a natural breakwater protecting Kingston Harbour. It extends due west from Windward Rd. At the western end, reached via Norman Manley Hwy, lies the historic city of Port Royal, set on a former cay that the Spanish called Cayode Carena, where they careened their ships. The spit earned its name for the defensive palisade that was built across the spit to defend Port Royal from a land-based attack. The Palisadoes is fringed on its harbor side by mangroves that shelter crocodiles and colonies of pelicans and frigate birds.

The 22m-tall, stone-and-cast-iron **Plumb Point Lighthouse** lies midway along the Palisadoes at its elbow. It was built in 1853 and still functions. Despite the lighthouse's presence, in 1997 a freighter ran aground nearby on the windward side of the spit. It is still rusting away.

Bull Bay & Environs

Bull Bay is a small town, 14km east of downtown Kingston, with a reputation for social unrest. The town itself has little to recommend it, but nearby are the pretty, untouristed Cane River Falls, an interesting

AROUND KINGSTON (SOUTHERN PLAINS)

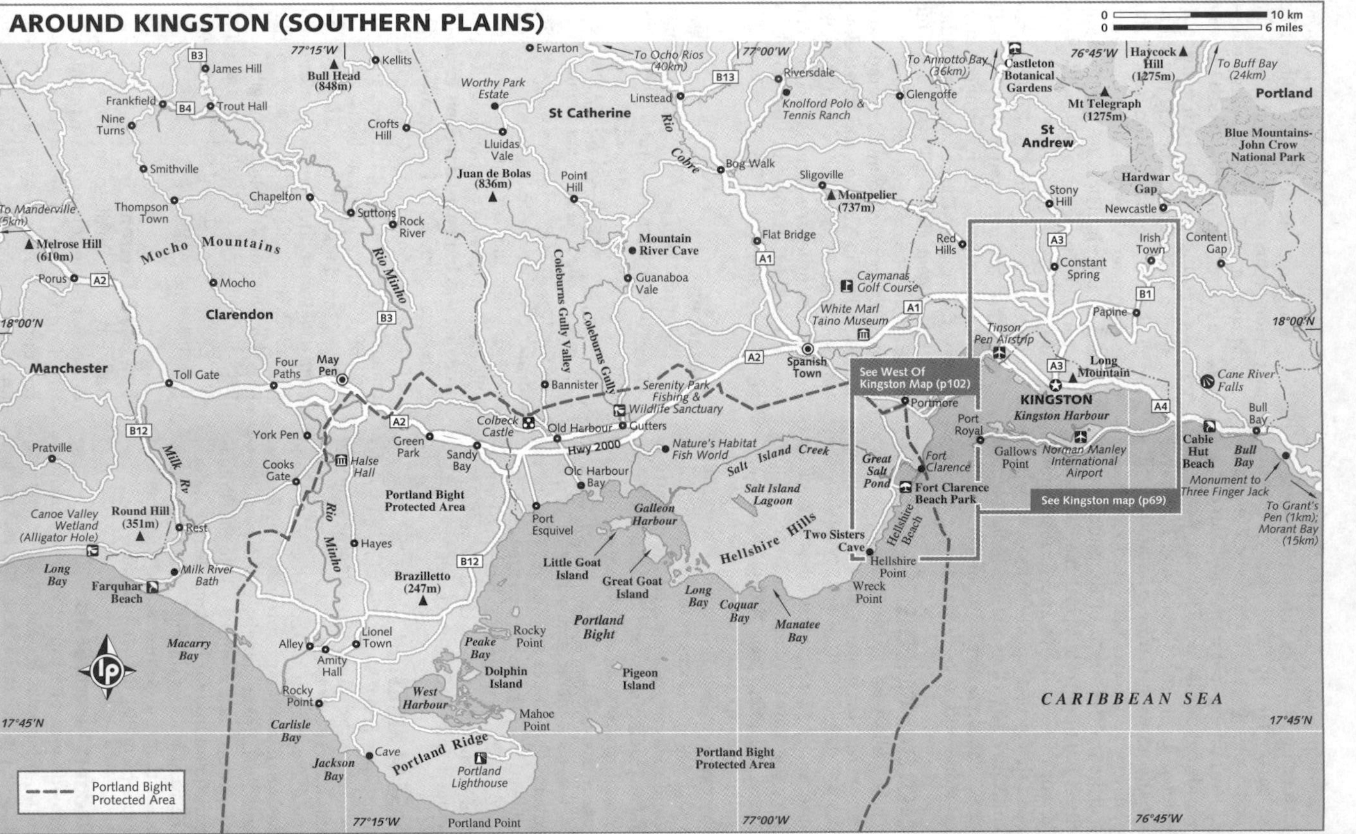

Rastafarian encampment, and Jamaica's most notable surf camp.

To get to Bull Bay from Kingston, take a minibus or route taxi from the Parade, or take bus 97 from Half Way Tree or the Parade (US$0.75).

SIGHTS & ACTIVITIES

Near a site where Maroon warriors mounted ambushes against the British, **Cane River Falls** (Map p96) are a popular bathing spot immortalized by Bob Marley in song. Few tourists show up here; if possible it's best to go with a local companion. The falls are 3km west of Bull Bay; the turnoff from the A4 is at Seven Mile, 3km east of the Harbour View roundabout.

Back on the coast, 1.5km west of Bull Bay is **Cable Hut Beach** (Map p96). It's strewn with litter but surfers rave about the waves that roll into shore here.

Beyond Bull Bay, the main road climbs the scrub-covered hill before making a hairpin descent to Grants Pen and St Thomas parish (see p110). Near the summit you'll pass a **monument to Three Finger Jack** (Map p96), one of Jamaica's most legendary folk heroes. The marker was erected by the National Heritage Trust to recall the deeds of Jack Mansong, who in 1780 and 1781 often single-handedly waged a war of terror against the English soldiers and planters who held the slave territory. Strong, brave, and skilled with machete and musket, his bold exploits were equaled only by his chivalry.

Jamaica is continuing to gain stature as a **surfing** destination and Billy 'Mystic' Wilmot of Jamnesia Surf Camp (see right) remains a focal point in the island for the sport. Jamnesia has a wide array of boards for rent (US$20 per day), from short mini-thrusters to a 2.9m-long board. Individual surfing instruction also is available. The famous 'Board Hut' is packed with boards donated by traveling pros and friends of the burgeoning Jamaican surfing scene.

The **Black Sovereign Ethiopian Embassy** (Ethiopia Africa Black International Congress), painted in the Rasta colors of red, gold and green, is the home of the Bobo Ashantis ('Bobbaheads') and sits on Queensbury Ridge above Bull Bay. About 100 fundamentalist Rastafarians live here and make a living from farming or their skills on the street. The government considers them squatters. Guests with a sincere interest in learning about the sect and its beliefs are welcome as long as they respect 'manners and principles.' When you arrive, you are led to a room festooned with portraits of Haile Selassie. Here you're greeted by the head priest, who will give you a spiel rich in clever metaphor that offers a fascinating insight into Rastafarian philosophy. You are welcome to stay overnight or as long as you wish in simply furnished rooms, but you must contribute 'something' and 'come to salvation' through performing duties on 'campus.' Cameras are welcome.

It's a little more than 1km uphill from the bridge on the A4, 20m east of the Red Lion Pub. You'll need a 4WD. There have been persistent warnings of criminal activity in the area, so to be safe you should present yourself at the Bull Bay police station (on the A4) for an escort up the hill.

SLEEPING

Billy Wilmot, the owner of **Jamnesia Surf Camp** (☎ 750-0103, ☎ 867-2701; Cable Hut Beach; camping per person US$7.50, with provided tent US$10, s/d US$20/30), has done as much as anyone to raise the profile of Jamaican surfing and to introduce the sport to a growing cadre of young hopefuls. The camp offers simple rooms and camping, with shared kitchen facilities and bathrooms. You can pitch your own tent, or use a provided tent that comes with sleeping mat, pillow, linen, night lamp and flashlight. Six-night lodging packages (camping US$179, singles/doubles/triples US$399/721/870) are also offered, including meals and surf shuttle. Jamnesia also offers airport transfers (round-trip US$70).

During the summer months, Jamnesia hosts a learn-to-surf camp for youngsters who want to learn how to shred.

PORT ROYAL

pop 1100

Once the pirate capital of the Caribbean – and for more than 200 years the hub of British naval power in the West Indies – Port Royal today is a dilapidated, ramshackle place of tropical lassitude, replete with important historical buildings collapsing to dust. Today's funky fishing hamlet gives little hint of the town's former flamboyant glory.

The Port Royal Development Project has long touted the tourism potential of Port Royal as a possible marine archaeological attraction, with much lip service given to

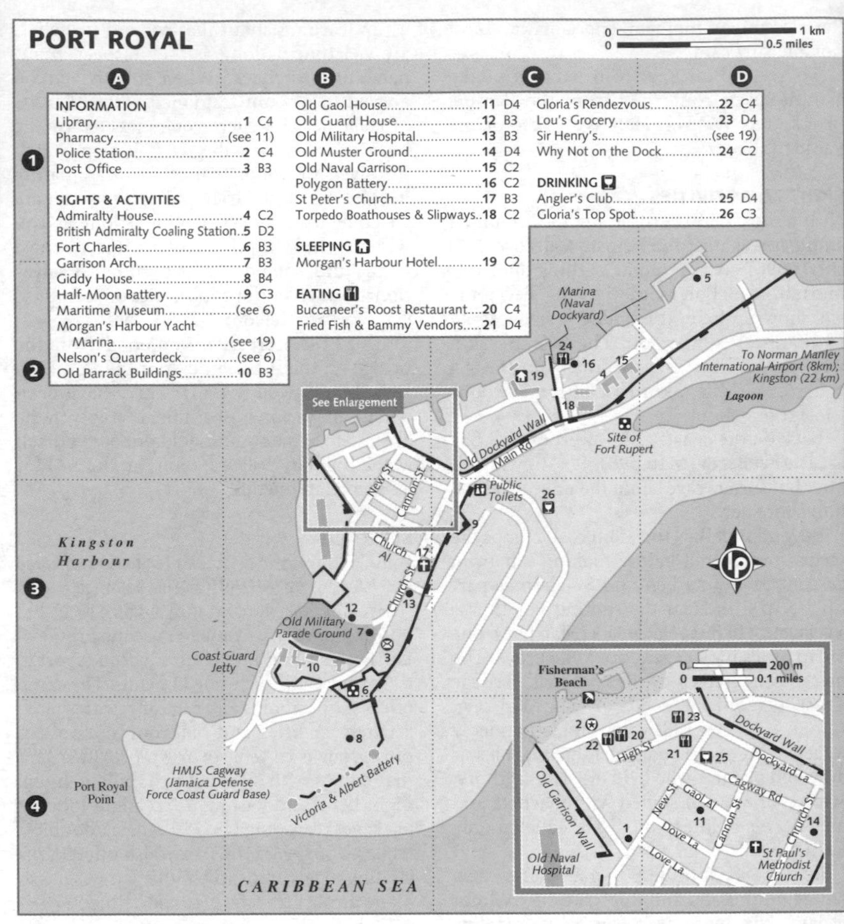

plans for a 32-hectare theme park, cruise-ship pier, entertainment center and arcade, Jamaica music museum, and heritage re-enactments including townsfolk in period costumes. However, the massive project shows no signs of getting off the ground.

Visitors can wander the dusty grounds of Fort Charles, St Peter's Church and the naval cemetery. Most tourist sites are open from 9am to 4pm weekdays and 10am to 5pm weekends.

History

The English settled the isolated cay in 1656. They called it 'Cagway' or 'The Point' and built Fort Cromwell (renamed Fort Charles after the Restoration in 1660). Within two years General William Brayne was able to report that 'there is the faire beginning of a town upon the poynt of this harbor.'

At the time, England sponsored freelance pirates in their raids against Spanish ships and possessions. Almost as soon as the English had captured Jamaica, buccaneers – organized as the Confederacy of the Brethren of the Coast – established their base at Port Royal. They were alternately welcomed and discouraged by the authorities according to the dictates of England's foreign policy (see p26).

Admirals Lord Nelson and Benbow and Edward 'Blackbeard' Teach once lived here, but of all Port Royal's seafaring visitors the best remembered buccaneer is Henry Morgan, whose celebrated exploits included a daring raid on Havana in the 1660s.

The lawless buccaneers were also big spenders. The wealth flowing into Port Royal attracted merchants, rum traders, vintners, prostitutes and others seeking a share of the profits. Townsfolk even invested in the expeditions in exchange for a share of the booty.

By 1682 Port Royal was a town of 8000 people. There were fortresses all around, plus two prisons and, ironically given the number of brothels and alehouses, two Anglican churches, a Presbyterian church, a Roman Catholic chapel, a Jewish synagogue and a Quaker meetinghouse.

At noon on Tuesday, June 7, 1692, a great earthquake shook the island, and Port Royal was destroyed. Two-thirds of the town disappeared underwater, where it remains. The massive quake was followed by a huge tidal wave that washed one ship, the *Swan*, into the center of the town, where it rested on the rooftops, providing shelter for those fortunate enough to scramble aboard. More than 2000 people died, many having fallen into great fissures before being 'squeezed to pulp' when a second tremor closed the gaping holes like pincer jaws. Many of the survivors were claimed by the pestilence that followed, caused by the hundreds of unburied corpses.

Official English policy had changed, and sea rovers who would not give up piracy were hounded and hanged at Gallows Point, a promontory at the harbor mouth of Port Royal. The English government had not written off Port Royal, however. The defensive works were repaired in time to repel a French invasion mounted against Jamaica in 1694. Gradually, Port Royal regained its stature as a merchant town and as a center of the turtling industry.

The near-constant state of war between England and Spain, France and Holland throughout the 18th century marked the beginning of Port Royal's 250-year tenure as headquarters of the Royal Navy in the West Indies.

The advent of peace in 1815 spelled the end of Port Royal's naval glory, and a fire that year consumed much of the town. After being struck by one calamity after another, the old port went into decline. In 1838, Jamaica ceased to be a separate naval command. With the development of steam warships in the early 20th century, Port Royal's demise was sealed. The naval dockyard closed in 1905, and although the defenses were maintained through both world wars, they have since been left to decay.

Orientation & Information

Approaching the town, Norman Manley Hwy runs beside a long brick wall enclosing the old British Admiralty Coaling Station, former Admiralty House, naval garrison quarters and naval dockyard. You enter town through a breach in the old town wall to the main square, or Muster Ground, overlooked by the Half-Moon Battery on the left.

An excellent map, *Port Royal: A Walking Tour*, is included in *Port Royal* by Clinton V Black, which you can buy in the gift store of Morgan's Harbour Hotel (p100).

There are public telephones at Morgan's Harbour Hotel and outside the **police station** (☎ 967-8068; Queen St). The **post office** (🕑 8am-4pm Mon-Fri) is in the old barracks near the fort. There's also a well-stocked **library** (☎ 967-8391; Broad St; 🕑 9am-5pm Mon, Tue & Thu-Sat). There are public toilets on the old Muster Ground.

Sights & Activities

Jamaica's latitude and longitude are measured from the flagstaff of **Fort Charles** (☎ 967-8438; adult/child US$5/2; 🕑 9am-5pm, closed Good Friday, Christmas Day & New Year's Day), a weathered redoubt originally laid in 1655. Among Port Royal's six original forts, only Fort Charles withstood the 1692 earthquake. It was rebuilt in red brick in 1699 and added to several times over the years. It was originally washed by the sea on three sides, but silt gradually built up and it is now firmly landlocked.

At its peak, 104 guns protected the fort. Many cannons still point out from their embrasures.

The marvelous **Maritime Museum** stands in the courtyard and contains a miscellany of things nautical from the heyday of the Royal Navy, plus a fabulous model of the *Jamaica Producer* cargo ship. Nelson lived in the small 'cockpit' while stationed here, and his quarters are replicated. Also of interest is a platform known as Nelson's Quarterdeck. It was here that the young Horatio Nelson was said to keep watch for enemy ships, and once you climb to the top you'll agree that it does offer a splendid vantage point. A plaque on the wall of the King's Battery, to the right of the main entrance of the museum, commemorates his time here.

A small brick hut, the **Giddy House** (so known because it produces a sense of disorientation to people who enter) sits alone amid scrub-covered, wind-blown sand 100m to the southwest of Fort Charles. The red-brick structure was built in 1888 to house the artillery store. The 1907 earthquake, however, briefly turned the spit to quicksand and one end of the building sank, leaving the store at a lopsided angle.

Next to the Giddy House is a massive gun emplacement and equally mammoth cannon – part of the easternmost casement of the **Victoria & Albert Battery** that lined the shore, linked by tunnels. The cannon keeled over in the 1907 earthquake.

OLD GAOL HOUSE

The only fully restored historical structure in town is the sturdy **Old Gaol House**, made of cut stone on Gaol Alley. It predates the 1692 earthquake, when it served as a women's jail. Today it houses a pharmacy.

ST PETER'S CHURCH

Built in 1725 of red brick, this **church** is handsome within, despite its faux-brick facade of cement. Note the floor paved with original black-and white tiles, and the beautifully decorated wooden organ loft built in 1743 and shipped to England in 1996 for restoration. The place is replete with memorial plaques. The communion plate kept in the vestry is said to have been donated by Henry Morgan, though experts date it to later times.

Most intriguing is a churchyard tomb of Lewis Galdye, a Frenchman who, according to his tombstone, '…was swallowed up in the Great Earth-quake in the Year 1692 & By the Providence of God was by another Shock thrown into the Sea & Miraculously saved by swimming until a Boat took him up.'

NAVAL DOCKYARD

The old **naval dockyard** lies to the east of Morgan's Harbour Hotel (right). Its perimeter walls still stand, as does the Polygon Battery and torpedo slipways, though most of the buildings within are gone. The old coaling station lies immediately to the east. Most of the famous ships of the Royal Navy – from the 18th century to the age of steam – berthed here.

NAVAL CEMETERY

Less than 1km east of the dockyard, also enclosed by a brick wall, is the intriguing **naval cemetery**, where sailors lie buried beneath shady palms. Alas, the cemetery's most ancient quarter, which contained the grave of the famous buccaneer Sir Henry Morgan, sank beneath the sea in 1692.

DEEP SEA FISHING

Morgan's Harbour Yacht Marina (VHF channel 68, radio call 'Morgan's Harbour') is a full-service facility that rents boats and yachts and offers **deep-sea fishing** (4-/8-hr trip US$400/650). Fishing trips are also offered from **Why Not On The Dock** (☎ 967-8448; per hr US$115), nearby to the northwest.

Tours

Tour operators in Kingston offer guided tours to Port Royal for about US$50; see p83.

Festivals & Events

The **Port Royal Seafood Festival**, held each year on National Heroes Day, the third Monday in October, is a rollicking good time with scores of vendors selling fried fish, bammy and fish or conch soup, and live on-stage entertainment.

Sleeping & Eating

Morgan's Harbour Hotel (☎ 967-8030; www.morgansharbour.com; s/d US$130/142, ste US$197-206; ✱ 🅿) This atmospheric if overpriced hotel stands within the grounds of the old naval dockyard. Sporting the largest marina in the Kingston area and an atmospheric bar, the hotel is a favorite haunt of sea salts, moneyed and otherwise. It has 50 spacious rooms with terracotta tile floors and French doors opening onto balconies. Cable TV is standard, as are firm king-size beds. Facilities include a gift store and restaurant, and a handsome outside bar.

Buccaneer's Roost Restaurant (☎ 967-8053; Queen St) This down-to-earth eatery, serving seafood for under US$4, is popular with Kingstonians, who spill out onto the street on weekends.

Sir Henry's (Morgan's Harbour Hotel; meals US$7-25) Offering gratifying panoramic views of Kingston Bay and top-notch seafood, this is Port Royal's most pleasant – and most respectable – restaurant. Lobster dishes figure prominently on the menu, as do Jamaican specialties, salads and sandwiches.

Why Not on the Dock (☎ 967-8448; meals US$2-7; 🕑 10am-8pm Mon-Fri, 9am-1am Sat & Sun) On a large deck over the water, this spot serves conch soup, sandwiches and grilled chicken, shrimp and lobster on Friday and Sunday.

On the main square are several economical options serving justifiably famous fried, steamed and escoveitched fish with bammy or rice. The most celebrated is **Gloria's Rendezvous** (5 Queen St; mains US$7.50-9; lunch & dinner), serving tremendously delicious local fare and seafood from an open-air kitchen.

Lou's Grocery (High St) has a minimal stock of groceries for a picnic on the waterfront.

Entertainment

Gloria's Top Spot (☎ 967-8220; 15 Foreshore Rd) Around 100m east of the muster ground, this is *the* place to be on a Friday or Saturday night, when local men of all ages – from youths in the latest hip-hop fashion to geezers in yesterday's duds – filter in and warm up at the bar to await the arrival of the women – from young and attired in spandex 'batty riders' to grannies in more conservative garb. By midnight, everyone is dancing to the latest sounds.

Why Not on the Dock (☎ 967-8448) This place draws a younger, more refined crowd on weekends for drinking and dancing.

Gloria's Rendezvous (5 Queen St) A well-loved oldies party is staged here on Sunday night.

Angler's Club (☎ 967-8101; 40 New St) AKA the Fisherman's Tavern, this is a funky watering hole drawing locals who wash in and out, overindulge in white rum, and pick fights while bartenders boogie at the bar. 'There are a few scalawags, but mostly it's harmless stuff,' one bartender said. It has tremendous character on Friday night when a mountain of speakers is built 7m high in the square and ska music reverberates across the harbor.

Morgan's Harbour Hotel (☎ 967-8030; www.morganshar bour.com) Morgan's sometimes has live bands and dancing, and it offers karaoke on Friday night.

Getting There & Away

Bus 98 runs to Port Royal from the Parade in downtown Kingston several times daily (US$1.25).

A route taxi from the Parade in Kingston costs about US$1.50; a licensed taxi costs about US$35 one way. Airport transfers are about US$15 for the 15-minute taxi ride.

AROUND PORT ROYAL

Lime Cay & Environs

The idyllic Lime Cay is one of half a dozen or so uninhabited, sand-rimmed coral cays sprinkled about 3km offshore from Port Royal. It's the perfect spot for sunbathing and snorkeling. Kingstonians flock here on weekends for picnics.

Maiden Cay is a smaller, shadeless option nearby; it's popular with nudists.

En route to Lime Cay, you'll pass what little remains of **Rackham's Cay** (it's rapidly disappearing beneath the waves); it was named for the infamous Jack Rackham, one of scores of pirates hanged here in metal casings after execution. Nearby is **Gun Cay**, named for the cannons that can still be seen, legacies of a British fortification.

You can catch a ride to Lime Cay on motorized boats (called 'canoes') from fishermen in Port Royal (about US$15 round-trip) and from **Why Not on the Dock** (adult/child US$8.50/4.25 Mon-Fri, US$6.50/4.25 Sat & Sun, 4-person minimum).

Morgan's Harbour Yacht Marina offers customers a two-hour tour of the cays (US$20).

Harbor Mangroves

Bird and nature lovers won't want to miss a visit to the lovely, breeze-swept **mangroves** near Port Royal, providing breeding grounds for pelicans, egrets, frigates and other water-loving seabirds. En route and on request your boatman will pass by Maiden Cay and Lime Cay and within sight of Gun Cay. Voyeurs will want to plan a visit between January and April during the pelican mating season. The trip can be arranged at Morgan's Harbour Yacht Marina or at Why Not on the Dock in Port Royal, and costs about US$20 per person.

WEST OF KINGSTON

Moving west of the capital, you leave behind the spectacular backdrop of the Blue Mountains for the staggered tedium of commuter traffic. The Nelson Mandela Hwy (A1) connects Kingston to Spanish Town, Jamaica's second largest city, before becoming the A2 and soldiering on to May Pen, the capital of Clarendon Parish and home to Halse Hall, a former plantation. From here, it's a mere 20-minute drive to Milk River Bath, the island's most celebrated mineral spa.

Much closer, a 'Causeway' as well as a controversial six-lane bridge completed in 2006 connect Kingston with the drab commuter

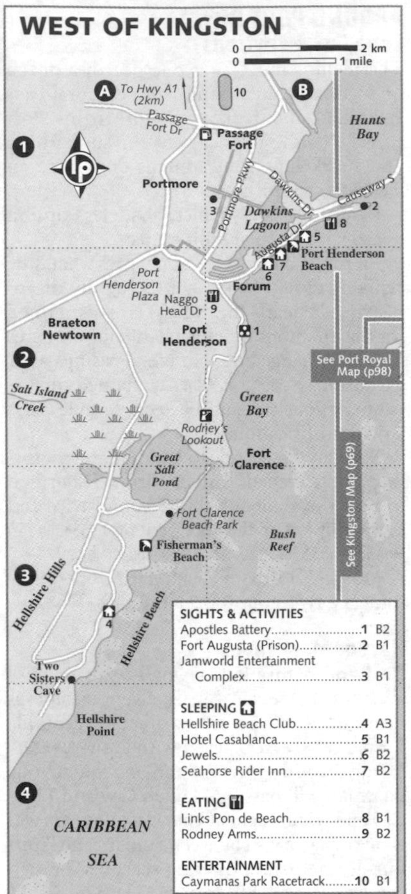

city of Portmore, from which you can reach Hellshire Beach. The J$60 toll (Jamaican dollars only) for crossing the harbor (via a bridge built at no small cost to the taxpayer) aroused vociferous protests. So unmoved were the authorities that, as of February 2008, there was even talk of increasing the toll.

Portmore

pop 150,000

A sprawling residential suburb, Portmore stretches across the plains west of Kingston. Shopping malls, entertainment centers and fast-food joints add color to an otherwise drab environment. The suburb is linked to the capital by the Portmore–Kingston Causeway.

Augusta Dr runs along the breeze-blown harbor shoreline parallel to Port Henderson Beach – the thin strip of sand is terribly littered. At its eastern end is **Fort Augusta**, dating from 1740. The original fort was destroyed when lightning struck the magazine holding 3000 barrels of gunpowder, killing 300 people. The huge crater was filled in and the fort rebuilt. Much decayed, the fort is now a prison.

The **Caribbean Heritagefest** (p84) is held here in mid-October.

SIGHTS & ACTIVITIES

At the west end of the beach (at the southeast corner of Portmore) is **Port Henderson**, a fishing hamlet backed by some fine examples of 18th- and 19th-century architecture, notably **Rodney Arms** (☎ 988-1063; Old Water Police Station, Port Henderson Rd), a restaurant and pub.

About 200m uphill from the Rodney Arms are the ruins of a semicircular gun emplacement replete with cannon, and an old fort and battery – the **Apostles Battery**. It is worth the visit for the views across the harbor, especially at sunset, when Kingston glistens like hammered gold.

SLEEPING

Augusta Dr is lined with hotels that also operate as 'short-time' motels, renting rooms for coital convenience (a four-hour minimum usually applies).

Jewels (☎ 988-6785; Port Henderson; r with fan US$35, r with air-con US$38-52;) This is a gleaming-white hotel with 25 rooms aired by the breezes that channel down the corridors. Rooms are nicely if simply decorated with bright tropical fabrics; upstairs rooms have lofty wooden ceilings.

Hotel Casablanca (☎ 939-6999; 2-4 Port Henderson Rd; r incl breakfast US$43-55;) A modern, castlelike structure with 36 rooms with cable TV and phone. It has a restaurant and bar.

EATING

Rodney Arms (☎ 988-1063; Old Water Police Station, Port Henderson Rd; meals US$12-23; 10am-midnight Mon-Thu, to 1am Fri-Sun) Housed in a beautifully restored Georgian limestone building that was once the Old Water Police Station – where pirates and miscreant marines were detained – this excellent seafood haunt offers crab, a seafood platter, garlic shrimp and other local dishes.

Links Pon De Beach, a beach park at the east end of Port Henderson Beach, serves snack foods and Jamaican fare.

ENTERTAINMENT

Caymanas Park (☎ 939-0848, 988-7258; www.caymanaspark.com; Caymanas Dr; admission US$0.75-1.25) has horse racing each Wednesday and Saturday as well as public holidays.

GETTING THERE & AWAY

Portmore and Port Henderson are reached via the **Causeway** (closed to westbound traffic 6:30-9am Mon-Fri, closed to eastbound traffic 4:30-7pm Mon-Fri), which begins in Kingston at the southern end of Hagley Park Rd at its junction with Marcus Garvey Dr.

Buses to Portmore (US$0.75) operate from Half Way Tree, the Parade and Three Mile (at the junction of Hagley Park and Spanish Town Rds). Alternatively, take a minibus or route taxi from the Parade.

Hellshire Beach Recreation Area

White-sand beaches (owned and operated by the Urban Development Council) fringe the eastern Hellshire Hills and are reached via a road that leads south from Portmore via Braeton Newtown to Hellshire Point, 13km south of Braeton.

The road meets the coast at **Great Salt Pond**, a circular bay lined with briny mangrove swamps where snook, mullet, stingrays and crocodiles ('alligators') can be seen.

At the southeasternmost point of Great Salt Pond is **Fort Clarence Beach Park** (adult/child US$3/1.50; 10am-6pm Fri-Tue), popular with Kingstonians on weekends. It hosts beauty contests and live reggae concerts. It has showers and toilets plus secure parking. A restaurant and bar are open weekends only.

A road to the left of the second, more southerly roundabout leads east to the main beach, called **Fisherman's Beach**, which is the setting of a funky fishing and Rasta 'village' with dozens of gaily painted huts and stalls selling beer, jerk, and fried fish and 'festival' (fried biscuit or dumpling). It's a boisterous, party-hearty place on weekends. In the morning, fishing pirogues come in with their catch. On any day of the week, though, it's a fascinating visit, a slice of the 'real' Jamaica up close. There are toilets and changing rooms.

Hellshire Beach Club (☎ 989-8306; r US$48;) is a modern, handsome, two-story complex with 60 rooms, all with TV, bathrooms and showers. It has a bar and restaurant. It's popular with beachgoers making out…hence the mirrored ceilings.

The best place to eat is **Prendy's on the Beach**, where you can select your fish or lobster (in season) and instruct them how you want it cooked.

From Kingston, buses go to Hellshire Beach from Half Way Tree and the Parade (US$0.75, 30 minutes). Minibuses and route taxis (US$2) run from the Parade.

Portland Bight Protected Area

Created in 1999, this 1876-sq-km **protected area** (PBPA; www.portlandbight.com.jm) comprises Jamaica's largest natural reserve with 210 sq km of dry limestone forest and 83 sq km of wetlands, as well as precious coral reefs (two-thirds of the protected area lies offshore). Its convoluted boundaries extend westward from Kingston Harbour across St Catherine and Clarendon parishes as far as Canoe Valley Wetland (p109), on the border with Manchester parish.

This vital habitat for birds, iguanas, crocodiles, manatees, marine turtles and fish – and 50,000 human beings – is managed by the **Caribbean Coastal Area Management** (CCAM; ☎ 986-3344; pespeut@infochan.com) and **Natural Resources Conservation Authority** (NRCA; ☎ 754-7546; 10 Caledonia Ave).

The CCAM is moving forward with 'community tourism' programs that utilize local fishermen to lead guided boat tours and hikes. An Eco-Heritage Trail beginning at the Hellshire beach and ending at Canoe Valley Wetland was in development at last visit, as was a visitor center to be part of a Biodiversity Conservation Centre and botanical garden (with trails) in the Hellshire Hills, where native plants will be propagated.

SPANISH TOWN

pop 130,000

Spanish Town, Jamaica's capital for more than 300 years, was once considered to boast exemplary town planning. Today, for visitors traveling from Kingston through the city's blighted outlying ghettoes, it's somewhat of a stretch to envisage the former capital's erstwhile grandeur. However, this changes the moment one arrives at the evocative historic center, where you'll find the Caribbean's most extensive assortment of Georgian architecture

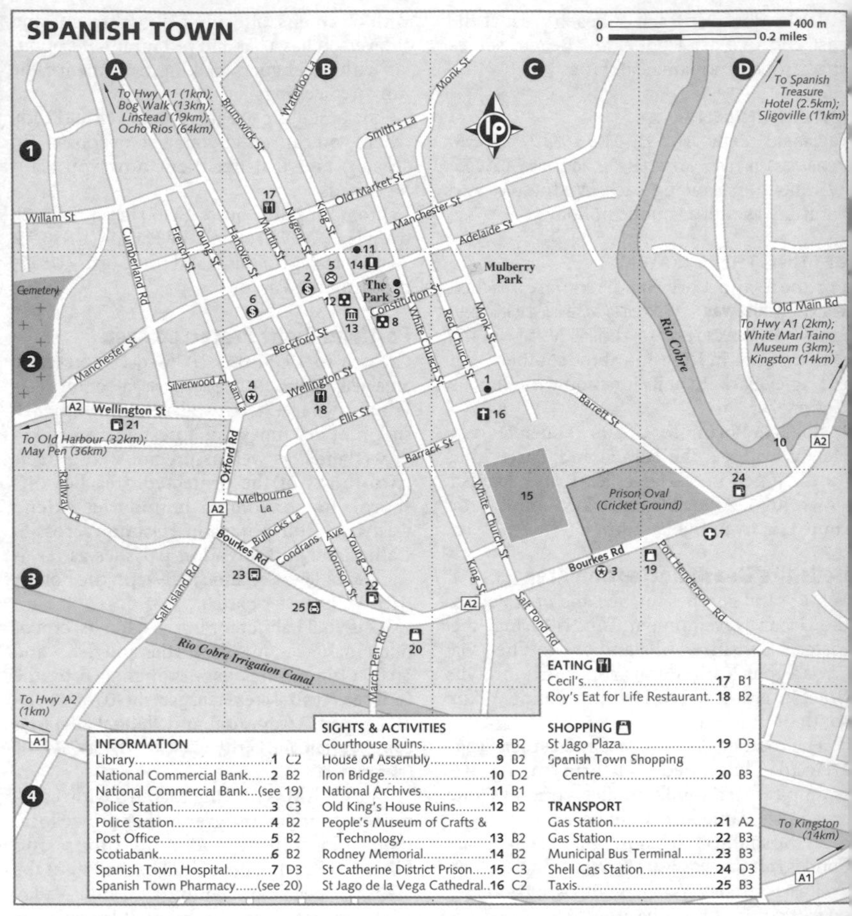

and its greatest cathedral (albeit in a sad state of repair). Few other places in Jamaica bring to life the historic sweep of centuries like Spanish Town.

The island's second-largest urban center and the capital of St Catherine parish, Spanish Town is frequently the locus of Jamaica's most wrenching urban strife. Few tourists spend the night, and those who do must contend with a paucity of safe lodging and services. By all means visit, but consider a day trip from Kingston.

History

After the settlement at Sevilla la Nueva failed in 1534, the Spanish established a new capital at Villa de la Vega – 'the Town on the Plain' – atop foundations that had been lain down earlier by Christopher Columbus' son, Diego. The town grew modestly as the administrative capital, helped along by a silk-spinning industry. However, Villa de la Vega (later renamed St Jago de la Vega) languished, and at its peak had a population of only about 500 people.

The town was poorly defended and was ransacked several times by English pirates. Eventually, in 1655, an English invasion fleet landed and captured the city. The English destroyed much of the town, then they renamed it 'Spanish Town' and made it *their* capital.

For the next 217 years, the town prospered as Jamaica's administrative capital. The menacing Victorian prison and gallows were here. So, too, was a slave market, Jewish synagogues and theaters. Taverns served planters and their families and entourages, who flocked to Spanish Town from all over the island during the 'dead season' (October to December) on the sugar estates, when the legislature was also in session.

Eventually, Spanish Town was outpaced by Kingston, the mercantile capital, and decline set in. When novelist Anthony Trollope called on the governor in the 1850s, he described Spanish Town as 'stricken with eternal death.' Kingston was officially named the capital in 1872, and Spanish Town sank into a century of sloth.

The past decade has seen the establishment of light industrial factories on the outskirts of town, lending a certain commercial vitality.

Orientation

The town sits on the west bank of the Rio Cobre. At its center is the Georgian town square, the Park (formerly called the Parade), between King and White Church Sts, and Adelaide and Constitution Sts. The Spanish laid out the town on a quadrangular grid around the plaza (although it is easy to become confused and lose your sense of direction in the tight, convoluted one-way system).

Information

Spanish Town has no tourist information office.

National Commercial Bank (☎ 984-3017; 14 Nugent St) Has a couple of branches, including one at St Jago Plaza.
Police Town center (☎ 984-2775; cnr Oxford Rd & Wellington St); Highway (☎ 984-1683; 3 Bourkes Rd)
Post office (☎ 984-2409; cnr King & Adelaide Sts)
Public library (☎ 984-2356; 1 Red Church St) Opposite the cathedral.
Scotiabank (☎ 984-3024; 27 Adelaide St)
Spanish Town Hospital (☎ 984-3031; Bourkes Rd) Has a 24-hour emergency department.
Spanish Town Pharmacy (☎ 984-1314; Spanish Town Shopping Centre, 17 Bourkes Rd)

Dangers & Annoyances

Spanish Town is a very hard-edged city; as in Kingston, political gangs hold sway over parts of the city. You should be cautious, especially of petty theft and definitely avoid exploring away from main downtown streets. Also avoid driving near the market (at the western end of Adelaide St), where whole streets are blocked by stalls and piles of rotting, stinking garbage – a stomach-turning sight – and the higglers are surly toward vehicles and foreigners.

Spanish Town is definitely a day trip.

Sights

THE PARK

Spanish Town's finest old buildings enfold **Parade Square**, the town square established by the Spanish as the center of Jamaica's capital city in 1534. Dominating the square on the north side is the elaborate **Rodney Memorial**, built in honor of Admiral George Rodney, who crowned his four-year service as commander-in-chief of the West Indian Naval Station in 1782 when he saved Jamaica from a combined French and Spanish invasion fleet at the Battle of the Saints. He stands within a cupola temple, with sculpted panel reliefs showing the battle scenes. The monument is fronted by two brass cannons from the French flagship.

The building behind the memorial is the **National Archives** (☎ 984-2581; admission free; 9:30am-3:30pm Mon-Fri), with national documents dating back centuries.

On the eastern side of the plaza is the redbrick **House of Assembly**, erected in 1762 and today housing the offices of the St Catherine Parish Council. It has a beautiful wooden upper story with a pillar-lined balcony. The Assembly and Supreme Court sat here in colonial days, when it was the setting for violent squabbles among feuding parliamentarians.

Moving to the south side of the square, you pass the fenced-off **Courthouse Ruins**, destroyed in 1986 by fire. The Georgian building dates from 1819, when it was used as a chapel and armory, with the town hall upstairs.

On the west side of the plaza is the porticoed Georgian redbrick facade of the ruins of the **Old King's House**, a once-grandiose building erected in 1762 as the official residence of Jamaica's governors. The building was destroyed by fire in 1925, leaving only the restored facade. Today the stables, to the rear, house the **People's Museum of Crafts & Technology** (☎ 922-0620; adult/child US$1.75/0.75; 9:30am-4:30pm Mon-Thu, to 3:30pm Fri). A reconstructed smith's shop and an eclectic array of artifacts – from Indian corn grinders to coffee-making machinery – provide an entry point to early Jamaican culture. A model shows how Old King's House once looked.

ST JAGO DE LA VEGA CATHEDRAL

From the town square, take White Church St south for three blocks to **St Jago de la Vega Cathedral**, the oldest Anglican cathedral in the former British colonies. It's also one of the prettiest churches in Jamaica, boasting wooden fluted pillars, an impressive beamed ceiling, a magnificent stained-glass window behind the altar, and a large organ dating to 1849. The church stands on the site of one of the first Spanish cathedrals in the New World: the Franciscan Chapel of the Red Cross, built in 1525. English soldiers destroyed the Catholic church and used the original materials to build their cathedral. The current structure dates from 1714. Note the handsome octagonal steeple with faux-Corinthian columns, and gargoyles with African features, considered unique in the world, above the south window.

Many leading local personalities are buried within its precincts. The oldest tomb dates to 1662 and is inset in the black-and-white transept aisle laid by the Spanish.

ST CATHERINE DISTRICT PRISON

Walking southeast along Barrett St from the church, you'll pass behind the **St Catherine District Prison**. Hangings have been carried out here since 1714. Today, many prisoners are on death row in narrow cells that date back almost three centuries. Conditions in the prison, Jamaica's largest, were condemned in 1994 by the UN Human Rights Committee, and a British Member of Parliament described it during a recent visit as 'like something out of a nightmare.'

IRON BRIDGE

At the bottom of Barrett St, turn left onto Bourkes Rd and follow it east to the narrow **Iron Bridge** spanning the Rio Cobre. The span was made of cast iron prefabricated at Colebrookdale, England, and was erected in 1801 on a cut-stone foundation that dates to 1675. The only surviving bridge of its kind in the Americas, it is still used by pedestrians, if barely. A portion of the neglected structure finally collapsed in 2001.

WHITE MARL TAINO MUSEUM

Jamaica owes much to the influence of the Arawak Indians, whose history is on display at this meager **museum** (☎ 922-1287; admission US$1.75; 🕑 8:30am-5pm Mon-Thu, to 4pm Fri) atop a large pre-Columbian settlement. Archaeological research has been ongoing here since the 1940s. Hunting and agricultural implements, jewelry and carvings are featured. A reconstructed Arawak village is up the hill behind the museum. The museum is 200m north of the A1, about 3km east of Spanish Town. The museum is 200m north of the A1 on the Kingston-bound side of the highway, about 3km east of Spanish Town. Don't try to walk there; instead drive or take a taxi from the taxi stand east of Spanish Town's bus terminal.

Sleeping & Eating

Spanish Town has no hotels or guesthouses downtown, save for a few flophouses that are best avoided. The only decent choice is the motel-style **Spanish Treasure Hotel** (☎ 984-2474; Sligoville Rd; d US$45, ste US$67;), 2.5km northeast of town, with 60 basic but clean rooms. It has a Jacuzzi, a restaurant and bar, and a pool area with nightly music. Also on the premises is a skating rink (per person US$3).

Near the town center, you'll find several decent Jamaican restaurants serving local fare. **Cecil's** (☎ 984-1927; 35 Martin St; meals US$3.50-8; 🕑 breakfast, lunch & dinner), near the corner of Old Market St, is one of the nicer places to eat, serving brown stew, callaloo, oxtail, curried goat and steam fish. Another good option is **Roy's Eat for Life Restaurant** (☎ 984-0551; 12 Wellington St; mains US$2.50-7.50; 🕑 lunch & dinner), a vegetarian restaurant and health-food store selling I-tal foods and juices.

Getting There & Away

In Kingston, buses depart frequently for Spanish Town from both the Parade and Half Way Tree (about US$0.50). In Spanish Town, buses, minibuses and route taxis leave from the **municipal bus terminal** (Bourkes Rd).

A taxi ride between Kingston and Spanish Town will cost about US$20. Taxis depart from the taxi stand to the east of the bus terminal on Bourkes Rd. By car from Kingston, take Washington Blvd from uptown or Marcus Garvey Blvd to Spanish Town Rd from downtown; both join the A1 for a straight shot.

AROUND SPANISH TOWN

Caymanas Golf & Country Club

This **club** (☎ 922-3386; play@caymanasgolfclub.com; green fees weekdays/weekends US$45/60, cart/club rental US$22/15), 10km west of Kingston in the hills north of Spanish Town Rd, is a 6295m, par-70,

18-hole course. Facilities include a pool, gym, squash and tennis courts, jogging trails, horseback riding and a restaurant.

Sligoville

This peaceful village sits on the upper story of Montpelier Mountain (737m), 8km east of Bog Walk at a junction with roads for Kingston (via Red Hills) and Spanish Town.

During the colonial era the area was a popular summer retreat for white society, and the second Marquis of Sligo, the pro-emancipation governor of Jamaica from 1834 to 1836, had a home here. The house, **Highgate Park** (☎ 749-1845), has been recently restored by the National Heritage Trust with the help of US Peace Corps volunteers, who have stayed on to run an **environmental center** (🕑 11am-4pm Mon-Fri) and a **hostel** (dm US$20) from its impressive halls. Meals and a communal kitchen are available.

Bog Walk Gorge

About 11km north of Spanish Town the A1 cuts through an impressive limestone canyon – **Bog Walk Gorge** – carved by the slow-moving Rio Cobre. You drop into the gorge and cross the river via the Flat Bridge, an 18th-century stone bridge.

Every rainy season, landslides block the road, disrupting traffic and adding to the damming effect of the narrow gorge. Flat Bridge is frequently under water after heavy rains; the high-water mark of August 16, 1933, when the river rose 8m above the bridge, is shown on the rock face.

Coleburns Gully

This off-the-beaten-track valley extends northwest from Spanish Town into the central highlands. The road via Guanaboa Vale leads 8km north to **Mountain River Cave**, a National Trust site of archaeological importance, 3km above Guanaboa Vale. Guides will lead you down 1.5km and across the river, where the cave entrance is barred by a grill gate; the steep track is sweaty going, but there's a good spot for swimming in a small river with a waterfall. Inside, you'll discover Arawak petroglyphs painted in black on the walls and ceiling. Many date back up to 1300 years.

Contact Lloyd Wright at the **Jamaica National Heritage Trust** (☎ 922-1287; 79 Duke St, Kingston) to arrange guided tours.

Old Harbour

This otherwise nondescript town is famous for its iron **clock tower** in the town square. The Victorian tower is marvelously preserved, as is the clock, which was installed shortly after the English invasion in 1655 and, amazingly, still keeps good time. Other points of interest are the **Church of St Dorothy**, one of the oldest on the island.

The ruins of the **Colbeck Castle great house** stand amid scrubby grounds 2.5km northwest of Old Harbour; to reach them, follow the road north from the clock tower.

Old Harbour Bay

This large fishing village, facing Portland Bight (p103), 3km south of Old Harbour, is the site of the south coast's largest fish market. Fishermen land their catch midmorning, and it makes a photogenic sight with the nets laid out and the colorful pirogues drawn up on the otherwise ugly shore. The village is a squalid place of tin and wood shacks and is prone to flooding in the rainy season.

The **Cockpit Salt Marsh**, an estuary near the mouth of the Bowers River, is good for bird-watching and spotting crocodiles. The CCAM (p103) offers nature trips by rowboat. Similar trips are offered to Salt Island and Black Creeks, navigable for several kilometers, and to the marsh and the Goat Islands.

You can catch a bus to the marsh from Old Harbour. From the Parade in Kingston, there's a daily bus to Old Harbour.

MAY PEN & AROUND

The A2 continues westward from Old Harbour to May Pen and continues across the flatlands of the Clarendon Plains to Toll Gate, marking the beginning of a 610m, 14.5km ascent of Melrose Hill en route to Mandeville (p260).

The B12 runs south from Toll Gate to several sites of modest interest.

May Pen

pop 48,000

The capital of Clarendon parish, 58km west of Kingston midway between Spanish Town and Mandeville, is a teeming market and agricultural town. It's bypassed by the A2 (Sir Alexander Bustamante Hwy), which runs about 1.5km south of town. If you venture into town, expect a degree of pandemonium, especially on Friday and Saturday when the market is held south of the main square.

Be prepared for terrible congestion, honking horns and pushy drivers who add to the general mayhem.

The annual **Denbigh Agricultural Show** is held on the Denbigh Showground, 3km west of town, on Independence weekend in early August. Farmers from each parish display the fruits of their labors, from yams to livestock. Live entertainment and food vendors round out the bill. For information, contact the **Jamaica Agricultural Society** (☎ 922-0610, 967-4094; 67 Church St, Kingston).

There's really little to detain you after seeing Halse Hall.

INFORMATION

CIBC (☎ 986-2578; 50 Main St) You can exchange money and travelers checks here.
May Pen Hospital (☎ 986-2528; Muirhead Ave) Three kilometers west of the town center.
Police station (☎ 986-2208; Main St) Around 100m west of the main square.
Post office (☎ 986-2443) It's 100m northeast of the square.
Scotiabank (☎ 986-2212; 36 Main St)

SIGHTS

Halse Hall

This is a handsome **great house** (☎ 986-2561; tours by arrangement), on the B12, 5km south of May Pen, situated up on a hillock with commanding views. After the English invasion in 1655, the land was granted to Major Thomas Halse, who built the house on an old Spanish foundation and whose grave is behind the house in a small cemetery. For a time the house was occupied by Sir Hans Sloane, the famous doctor and botanist, whose collection of Jamaican flora and fauna formed the nucleus of what later became the Natural History Museum in London. Today, it is owned by the bauxite concern, Alcoa Minerals, which uses it for conferences and social functions. To take a tour call and ask for Mrs Chambers.

SLEEPING & EATING

Hotel Versalles (☎ 986-2775; contact@jamaicahotelversalles.com; 42 Longbridge Ave; r US$74, ste US$81;) Over 1km southwest of town, it's the only accommodation of any worth. This expansive, modern hotel sports lush lawns nibbled by Shetland ponies. It has 27 modestly furnished rooms as well as 17 suites, six studios and eight apartments with phone and bathrooms. The Versalles Disco has karaoke on Thursday, Latin music on Saturday and oldies night on Sunday.

Hot Pot (☎ 986-2586; 18A Manchester Ave; meals US$2-6) is the place for inexpensive Jamaican fare.

There are plenty of fast-food joints and simple restaurants on Main St.

GETTING THERE & AROUND

The transportation center is on Main St, 200m southeast of the main square. You can catch buses, minibuses and route taxis here to Christiana, Spanish Town, Kingston, Ocho Rios, Mandeville, Negril, Milk River and most other destinations in the region.

Milk River Bath

This well-known **spa** (☎ 902-6902; fax 902-4974; adult/child per bath US$1.75/0.85, free for hotel guests; 7am-9pm), 23km southwest of May Pen, is fed from a saline mineral hot spring that bubbles up at the foot of Round Hill, 3km from the sea. The waters are a near-constant 33°C (92°F). Immersion is said to cure an array of ailments ranging from gout and lumbago to rheumatism and nervous conditions.

The spa, which is attached to the Milk River Hotel, is owned by the government. The six timeworn public mineral baths and three private baths are cracked and chipped, though clean.

These are the most radioactive spa waters in the world; they're 50 times more so than Vichy in France and three times those of Karlsbad in Austria. Hence, bathers are limited to only 15 minutes, though you are allowed three baths a day. Imbibing the waters is also recommended by the spa staff as a stirring tonic. Kingstonians flock on weekends seeking treatments. Indulge yourself with the **Massages** (US$35 per hour) on offer.

About 200m north of the spa is the **Milk River Spa Mineral Pool** (c/o Ministry of Tourism ☎ 920-4929; 10am-6pm Sat, Sun & holidays), an open-air swimming pool.

Beyond Milk River Bath, a dirt road lined with tall cacti leads 2.5km to **Farquhar Beach**, a funky fishing village at the river mouth. You can watch fishermen tending their nets and pirogues, and you can hire a boat and guide to take you to the mouth of the Alligator Hole River in search of crocodiles and elusive, endangered manatees.

A bus operates from May Pen three times daily.

SLEEPING & EATING

Milk River Hotel (☎ 902-4657; fax 986-4974; Clarendon; d without/with bathroom US$110/117) A rambling, homey, white-porched hotel with shady verandas, louvered windows, etched wooden motifs above the doors, well-worn pine floors and 20 modestly furnished, pleasant rooms. Guests are not charged for using the mineral spa. Meals are served in a cozy dining room, where the menu includes Jamaican favorites such as mutton stew and stewed fish. Breakfasts include a health-food special for US$8.

Diana's Seafood Bar (Farquhar Beach) A sky-blue shack serving steamed fish (US$4) and basic Jamaican fare. Diana is a pleasant lady who also has Diana's Guest House; its one room has a double bed and an outside bathroom and toilet, but no electricity (it's lit by a kerosene lamp). Rates here are negotiable.

Canoe Valley Wetland

This is a government-owned **wildlife reserve** (☎ 377-8264; admission free; ⏰ Mon-Sat), also known as Alligator Hole. It's notable for its family of three manatees (all females) that inhabits the diamond-clear water, in which crocodiles (called 'alligators' locally) also hover. They live amid dense, 1m-tall reeds in jade-blue pools fed by waters that emerge at the base of limestone cliffs. Herons, grebes, jacanas, gallinules and other waterfowl are abundant.

There's a small visitor center. You can take an hour-long trip by canoe with a guide. Don't forget to tip the guides. The turnoff is signed 1.5km north of Milk River Bath on the B12.

Blue Mountains & Southeast Coast

Kissing the sky over the eastern half of Jamaica, the majestic Blue Mountains throw the rest of the island into sharp relief. Barely an hour's drive from Kingston, their slopes, crags and fern forests seem light years from the capital's gritty streetscape. Some 2000m above sea level, the ruggedness of the mountains forms the perfect counterpoint to beachside hedonism.

Hiking in the Blue Mountains is the best way to get to know them. Climbing Blue Mountain Peak rewards with striking panoramas (weather permitting) across the entire island; less arduous treks to Cinchona Gardens or through the Holywell Recreation Area offer wonderful samples of the region's plantlife. Sixty-five distinct species of orchid are among the more than 200 endemic plants that grace the mountains. The bird-watching here is equally stunning – look out for the yellow-billed parrot and the streamertail hummingbird (also known as the doctor bird). If you're really lucky, you may catch sight of the endangered giant swallowtail butterfly, the second largest butterfly on earth.

As for human life, you'll find the residents of the area west of the peak preoccupied with growing one of Jamaica's most famous crops: coffee. Several working plantations reveal the nuances of the cultivation process, culminating in a cup or two of Blue Mountain Coffee – which tastes even more heavenly when you can smell the beans from a nearby field.

Largely ignored by tourists, the parish of St Thomas lies in the shadow of the Blue Mountains. Site of the 1865 Morant Bay Rebellion, it is home to the ramshackle old spa town of Bath. If you have time for exploration, you should definitely try to make it through the mangrove fields to the lighthouse at Morant Point, the island's easternmost tip.

HIGHLIGHTS

- **Strawberry Hill** Reward yourself with a meal, spa treatment or night of romance at one of Jamaica's best hotels (p114)
- **Blue Mountain Peak** Set out before dawn for the greatest high in Jamaica (p119)
- **Old Tavern Estate** See how a red berry is transformed into the world's best coffee bean (p116)
- **Cycling from Hardwar Gap** Quicken your pulse with a rip-roaring descent from the high mountains, through coffee plantations and villages (p113)
- **Morant Point Lighthouse** Find your way to this remote beacon providing a privileged view of coast and mountains (p122)

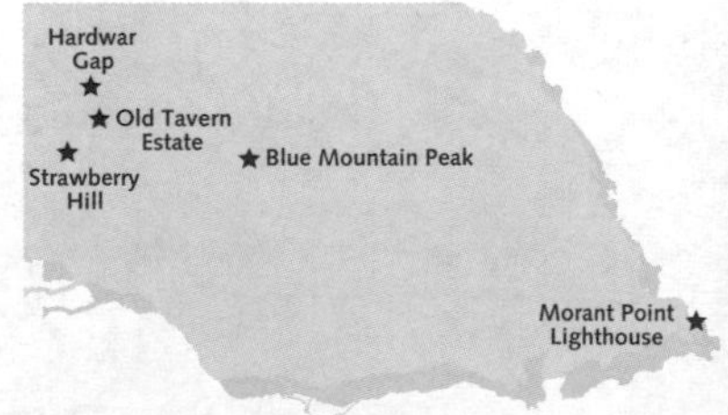

- AREA: 750 SQ KM
- STRAWBERRY HILL DEC AVERAGE HIGH TEMPERATURE: 23.3°C

HISTORY

With their dense primary forests and forbidding topography, the prospect of life in the Blue Mountains has discouraged all but the most determined settlers over the centuries. During the 17th and 18th centuries, these same formidable qualities made the territory the perfect hideout for the Windward Maroons, who from their remote stronghold at Nanny Town resisted enslavement and British colonialism for more than 100 years. But this region's primary claim to fame has always been coffee cultivation; it has been a mainstay since the very first coffee factories were erected around Clydesdale in the mid-18th century. Meanwhile, back down at sea level, the southeast coast of St Thomas parish is notable for its long history of protest and rebellion, and the independent spirit of the region has kept it at odds with the government even up to this day.

CLIMATE

Moisture-laden trade winds blowing in from the northeast spill much of their accumulation on the Blue Mountains, which forms a rain shadow over Kingston and the southern parishes. The temperature drops 1°C to 2°C for every 300m rise in elevation (indeed, it can freeze in the early morning above 1700m). From June through to September you'll experience the best weather for exploring.

St Thomas parish, like Kingston, lies in the rain shadow and there's far less precipitation than up in the Blue Mountains.

GETTING THERE & AROUND

The Blue Mountains are best explored by private car. From Kingston's eastern fringe, public transportation runs from Papine, but service is disorganized and delays and cancellations are frequent. Public transportation is far more predictable on the southeast coast along the A4 road.

BLUE MOUNTAINS

Deriving their name from the azure haze that settles lazily around their peaks, this 45km-long mountain range looms high above the eastern parishes of St Andrew, St Thomas, Portland and St Mary. The Blue Mountains were formed during the Cretaceous Period (somewhere between 144 and 65 million years ago) and are the island's oldest feature. Highest of the highlights, **Blue Mountain Peak** reaches 2256m above sea level, and no visit to the area should neglect a predawn hike to its summit for a sunrise view.

Unsurprisingly, the Blue Mountains' largely unspoiled character owes much to the difficulty in navigating around the area. Roads are narrow and – as often as not – dirt tracks that are utterly impossible to pass without 4WD, especially after heavy rains. If you are spending time in the area, contacting a tour guide or making arrangements with your hotel are highly advisable.

Activities

HIKING

The Blue Mountains are a hiker's dream, and dozens of trails lace the hills. Many are overgrown, but others remain the mainstay of communication for locals.

By far the most popular route is to 'The Peak,' which in Jamaica always means Blue Mountain Peak. The steep and exhilarating trail is well maintained.

These trails (called 'tracks' locally) are rarely marked. When asking for directions from locals, remember that 'a few chains' can mean several kilometers, while 'jus a likkle way' may in fact be a few hours of hiking. Within the Blue Mountains-John Crow National Park, hiking trails are categorized as guided, nonguided and wilderness.

A Hiker's Guide to the Blue Mountains, by Bill Wilcox, is an indispensable guide for serious hikers.

Guided Hikes

Guides can be hired from most hotels in the area for about US$35 for a half day, and US$45 for a full day. Freelance guides hire themselves out at Penlyne Castle, Hagley Gap and Mavis Bank. On overnight trips you're expected to pay for the guide's food and accommodations.

In addition to others, the following offer guided hikes:

Forres Park Guest House & Farm (www.forrespark.com; Kingston ☎ 927-5957; Mavis Bank ☎ 927-8275) A good option for custom hiking trips. See p118.

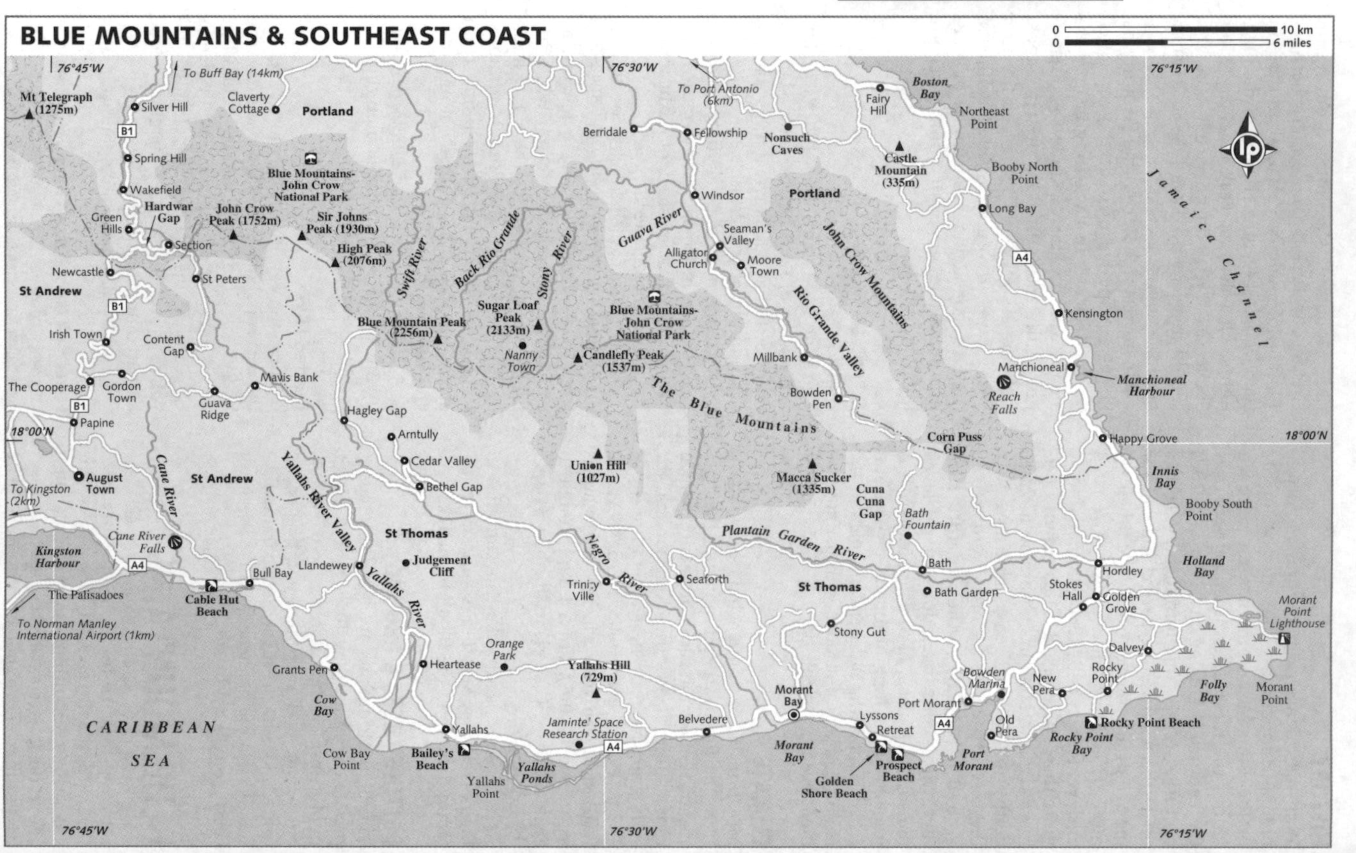
BLUE MOUNTAINS & SOUTHEAST COAST
0 10 km
0 6 miles
76°45'W
76°30'W
76°15'W
18°00'N
Jamaica Channel
CARIBBEAN SEA
Mt Telegraph (1275m)
To Buff Bay (14km)
Silver Hill
Spring Hill
Wakefield
Hardwar Gap
Green Hills
Section
Newcastle
Claverty Cottage
Portland
Blue Mountains-John Crow National Park
John Crow Peak (1752m)
Sir Johns Peak (1930m)
High Peak (2076m)
St Peters
St Andrew
Irish Town
The Cooperage
Gordon Town
Content Gap
Guava Ridge
Mavis Bank
Papine
August Town
To Kingston (2km)
Kingston Harbour
The Palisadoes
To Norman Manley International Airport (1km)
Cane River Falls
Cane River
Cable Hut Beach
Bull Bay
Llandewey
Yallahs River Valley
Yallahs River
Hagley Gap
Arntully
Cedar Valley
Bethel Gap
St Thomas
Judgement Cliff
Blue Mountain Peak (2256m)
Swift River
Back Rio Grande
Sugar Loaf Peak (2133m)
Nanny Town
Stony River
Candlefly Peak (1537m)
Union Hill (1027m)
Grants Pen
Cow Bay
Cow Bay Point
Heartease
Yallahs
Bailey's Beach
Yallahs Point
Yallahs Ponds
Orange Park
Jaminte' Space Research Station
Yallahs Hill (729m)
Trinity Ville
Negro River
Berridale
To Port Antonio (6km)
Fellowship
Windsor
Guava River
Alligator Church
Seaman's Valley
Moore Town
Nonsuch Caves
Portland
John Crow Mountains
Rio Grande Valley
Millbank
Bowden Pen
The Blue Mountains
Macca Sucker (1335m)
Cuna Cuna Gap
Plantain Garden River
Seaforth
Belvedere
Morant Bay
St Thomas
Stony Gut
Lyssons
Retreat
Golden Shore Beach
Prospect Beach
Port Morant
Bowden Marina
Old Pera
New Pera
Rocky Point
Rocky Point Bay
Rocky Point Beach
Dalvey
Folly Bay
Morant Point
Morant Point Lighthouse
Holland Bay
Booby South Point
Innis Bay
Golden Grove
Hordley
Stokes Hall
Bath
Bath Garden
Bath Fountain
Corn Puss Gap
Reach Falls
Manchioneal
Manchioneal Harbour
Kensington
Happy Grove
Long Bay
Booby North Point
Northeast Point
Boston Bay
Fairy Hill
Castle Mountain (335m)
A4
B1

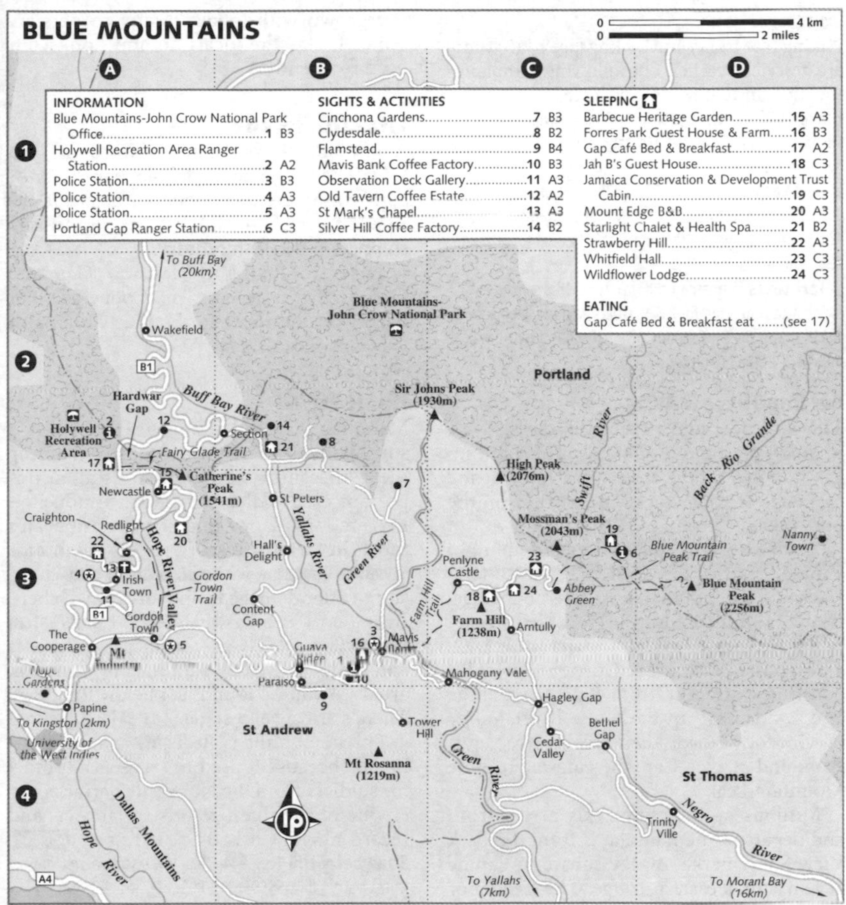

Mount Edge B&B (☎ 944-8151, 351-5083; jamaica eu@kasnet.com; Newcastle) Offers trips to the peak (US$60) and cycling tours (US$45). See p115.

Strawberry Hill (☎ 944-8400; www.strawberryhill resort.com; Irish Town) Short tours and hikes from US$40. See p114 for more details on Strawberry Hill.

Sun Venture (☎ 960-6685; www.sunventuretours.com; 30 Balmoral Ave, Kingston 10) Daylong hikes from US$75 and hikes to the peak with lodging (US$95).

Maps

If you're hiking alone buy the 1:50,000 or 1:12,500 Ordnance Survey topographic map series, available from the **Survey Department** (☎ 922-6630; www.nla.gov.jm; 23½ Charles St, Kingston). Four different sheets – numbers 13, 14, 18 and 19 – cover the area around Blue Mountain Peak; you may need to buy all four (US$5 each).

CYCLING

An exhilarating way to see the Blue Mountains is by mountain bike – the sturdier the better as the going can be steep and arduous.

If you're not traveling with a bicycle, join a tour. **Blue Mountain Bicycle Tours** (☎ 974-7075; www.bmtoursja.com; 121 Main St, Ocho Rios; tour adult/child US$93/65) will pick you up in Kingston or Ocho Rios and take you by bus to the Hardware Gap at 1700m up in the mountains. The downhill cycling tour then begins, and stops along the way include a coffee-roasting facility. You may be sharing the road with 40 other cyclists.

Mount Edge B&B (p115) offers a similar tour (US$45) with smaller groups, also from Hardwar Gap, but the bikes are a mixed bag. Check the brakes before setting out!

Tours

Hiking (see p111) and cycling (see p113) tours are described earlier. The following companies mostly conduct tours in vehicles.

Barrett Adventures (☎ 382-6384; www.barrett adventures.com; Rose Hall, Montego Bay) Customized tours by minivan.

Island Car Rentals (☎ 929-5875, in Canada 416-628-8885, in USA 866-978-5335; www.islandcarrentals.com; 17 Antigua Ave, Kingston) Personally chauffeured tours of the Blue Mountains.

Safari Tours Jamaica (☎ /fax 795-0482; safari@cwjamaica.com; Mammee Bay) Offers daylong 'jeep safaris' (US$75) into the Blue Mountains. It also has a two-day mule ride and a hiking tour.

Getting There & Away

Traveling by your own vehicle is the best way to enjoy the Blue Mountains. There are no gas stations; fill up on gas in Papine at the east edge of Kingston or in Buff Bay on the north coast.

From Kingston, follow Hope Rd uphill to Papine, from where Gordon Town Rd (B1) leads into the mountains. At The Cooperage, the B1 (Mammee River Rd) forks left steeply uphill for Strawberry Hill resort (near Irish Town) and Newcastle. Gordon Town Rd continues straight from The Cooperage and winds east up the Hope River Valley to Gordon Town, then steeply to Mavis Bank and Hagley Gap, the gateway to Blue Mountain Peak.

Minibuses and route taxis arrive from and depart to the mountains from the Park View Supermarket on the square in Papine at Kingston's eastern fringe. The frequency of service changes from day to day depending on demand. For the two main routes, you can generally expect at least one morning run and one in the afternoon, but exact departure times are impossible to predict.

Destinations include Mavis Bank (one way US$3, 15km, 1½ hours) and Newcastle (US$3, 23km, 1¼ hours).

From the north coast, the B1 heads into the mountains from Buff Bay. During the rainy season, the road often closes following landslides, but it's always good to check its status before departing. When the road is open, there is no regular bus service from Buff Bay up the B1, and route-taxi service is infrequent at best.

The roads hug the mountainside in endless switchbacks and are narrow and often overgrown with foliage. Many corners are blind. Do as the locals do and honk your horn frequently.

THE COOPERAGE

About 3km above Papine via Gordon Town Rd is The Cooperage, a hamlet named for its community of Irish coopers who made the wooden barrels in which coffee beans were shipped in the 19th century.

Buses to Redlight, Hardwar Gap and Gordon Town all pass The Cooperage. For details on the route to the Blue Mountains via Gordon Town, see p118.

IRISH TOWN

Mammee River Rd climbs to Irish Town, a small hamlet where the coopers lived during the 19th century. Potatoes are still an important crop, reflecting the Irish influence. Largely famous for one of the Caribbean's most luxurious resorts, it also contains **St Mark's Chapel**, a white clapboard church restored after damage from Hurricane Gilbert. Irish Town also has the pleasant **Observation Deck Gallery** (☎ 944-8592), which features arts and crafts as well as paintings by Jamaican artists; it can be found just below the town. There's also a **police station** (☎ 944-8242).

Further uphill is **Redlight**, a hamlet so-named because it used to serve as a brothel for soldiers from the Newcastle barracks.

One of the finest resorts in Jamaica, and record mogul Chris Blackwell's pet, **our pick** **Strawberry Hill** (☎ 944-8400; www.strawberryhillresort.com; r/ste/villa US$595/695/895; P ✖ 💻) is a luxury retreat just north of Irish Town. Gaze at Kingston and the harbor 950m below from a deckchair by the infinity-edge pool, check out the small display of Blackwell's gold and platinum records, or roam the bougainvillea-draped grounds. The Caribbean-style cottages range from well-appointed mahogany-accented studio suites, each with canopied four-poster beds, to a four-bedroom, two-story house built into the hillside. A sumptuous breakfast is included in the rates, as are transfers. Bird-watching, hiking and other tours are available and Strawberry Hill also hosts a calendar of special events throughout the year. If you're having trouble relaxing, Strawberry Hill's renowned spa offers an 'elemental nature consultation' to determine your customized treatment based on five elements (earth, air, fire, water and infinity). No children are allowed.

Many Kingstonians make the tortuous drive to Strawberry Hill for some of the finest nouvelle Jamaican cuisine on the island (dinners US$18 to US$45). Reservations are advised.

In order to get to Irish Town, you can take a bus (US$0.30) or route taxi (about US$1) from Papine.

NEWCASTLE

Newcastle hangs invitingly on the mountainside high above Irish Town. The road climbs to 1220m where, 21km from Kingston, you suddenly emerge on a wide parade ground guarded by a small cannon. The military encampment clambers up the slope above the square. Newcastle was founded in 1841 as a training site and convalescent center for British soldiers. Since 1962 the camp has been used by the Jamaica Defense Force.

With good fortune you may even arrive to watch recruits being drilled. Note the insignia (which dates back to 1884) on the whitewashed stone wall, commemorating those regiments stationed at Newcastle. Visitors are allowed only around the canteen, shop, roadways and parade ground.

Three kilometers above Newcastle you reach **Hardwar Gap**, at the crest of the Grand Ridge. See p113 for information about the thrilling cycling in this area.

Activities

HIKING

Just across from the Gap Café Bed & Breakfast, you can pick up the Fairy Glade trail, which leads to Catherine's Peak 150m above the town. Green Hills Trail, Fern Walk Trail and Woodcutter's Trail also begin north of Newcastle.

Sleeping & Eating

Mount Edge B&B (☎ 944-8151, 351-5083; d bunk US$25, r with shared bath US$30-50, with bath US$40, weekly US$100-250; P 🖳) This is a good budget option, especially for longer stays. The all-wood house has three rooms, including one with a four-poster king-sized bed. The spacious, no-frills lounge has a kitchen and wide glass windows on all sides. Meal packages are offered. The place is an official bird-watching station and organizes hiking and cycling tours.

Barbecue Heritage Garden (☎ 944-8411; cottage US$65) Set 400m east of Newcastle parade ground, this is a simple yet exquisite two-bedroom wooden cottage (with live-in caretakers) set in a coffee estate (circa 1750) with views toward Kingston. The bathroom has a claw-foot tub and hot water, and there's a kitchen and a TV lounge with sofa bed and phone. The old coffee-drying barbecues are now laid out as gardens.

Gap Café Bed & Breakfast (☎ 997-3032, 923-7078; r US$70) On the hillside at 1280m near Hardwar Gap, just below the entrance to Holywell Recreation Area, the Gap Café Bed & Breakfast has a cozy Hansel-and-Gretel-style, one-bedroom, self-catering cottage with a veranda. Walkways lead through the beautiful gardens. The Full Moon Frolics (US$70) are hosted here, drawing locals for festive get-togethers with music, dance, and fine dining. The café here (open 10am to 5pm Monday to Friday, 10am to 6pm Saturday and Sunday) is a fabulous place to rest and take in the vistas over a soda or cappuccino. It offers dining either indoors or alfresco on a wooden terrace. A 'Jamaican special' breakfast costs US$12, and afternoon high tea is also served (US$25). The eclectic lunch menu includes curried Caribbean shrimp, smoked pork chops, curry goat and sandwiches. Dinner is by reservation only.

The army camp store – the Tuck Shop – sells snacks.

BLUE MOUNTAINS-JOHN CROW NATIONAL PARK

The Blue Mountains-John Crow National Park protects 78,210 hectares and is managed by the Natural Resources Conservation Authority (NRCA). The park includes the forest reserves of the Blue and John Crow Mountain Ranges and spans the parishes of St Andrew, St Thomas, Portland and St Mary. Ecotourism is being promoted and locals are being trained as guides.

Camping is not permitted except at designated sites, listed on p116. Camping 'wild' is not advised.

See also p119 for details on Blue Mountain Peak.

Route taxis making the run from Papine to Newcastle (US$3) can be persuaded to continue the extra 4km to drop you at the national park entrance in Holywell. Return transport from the park, however, is not assured; you may wish to negotiate with the route-taxi driver to be picked up.

Information

There are ranger stations at Holywell Recreation Area and Portland Gap (near Blue Mountain Peak), and at Millbank in the Upper Rio Grande Valley (p141). Entry to the park is free, except for Holywell Recreation Area. Here are other contacts:

Blue Mountains-John Crow National Park Office (☎ 977-8044; Mavis Bank; 🕑 10am-4pm Mon-Fri) Rangers are on hand to provide information on weather and trails; survey maps are on display.

Jamaica Conservation & Development Trust (☎ 920-8278; www.greenjamaica.org.jm; 29 Dumbarton Ave, Kingston 10) Provides management and supervision of the national park.

Sights & Activities

Holywell Recreation Area (adult/child US$5; 🕑 10am-5pm Mon-Fri), spanning Hardwar Gap, protects 120 hectares of remnant woodland, lush with dozens of fern species, epiphytes, impatiens, violets, nasturtiums, wild strawberries and raspberries. The mist-shrouded uppermost slopes are densely forested with rare primary montane forest. Pine trees dominate. The **bird-watching** is fabulous. The ranger station is a short distance beyond the entrance. An orientation center hosts occasional live entertainment such as traditional music and dance, plus outdoor games, storytelling and a treasure hunt for the kids (contact the national park office for information). There are viewpoints and picnic spots.

Hiking trails lead off in all directions through the ferny dells, cloud forest and elfin woodland. The 1.2km **Oatley Mountain Trail**, which requires a guide (US$10), has educational signs leading to a river good for bathing; the 2km **Waterfall Trail** leads down along a stream to a small falls.

Here, **camping** (per person US$1.50) is allowed. There are water faucets and toilets. You can rent rustic **cabins** (2-/4-bed cabin US$55/78) with twin beds (reportedly damp) and basic kitchens; bring your own bedding and food (there's a gas ring and fridge). Advance reservations are essential via the Blue Mountains-John Crow Park Office or the Jamaica Conservation & Development Trust (above). Book holiday/weekend stays several weeks in advance. There's a security guard at the ranger station.

SECTION

Heading northeast from Holywell, the road drops steeply toward the hamlet of Section and then curls its way down to Buff Bay, 29km north. As soon as you crest the ridge, the vegetation on the north-facing slope is noticeably more lush. You'll pass several cottages with colorful gardens.

A turnoff to the right at Section leads 1.5km to the ridge crest, where the main road loops south and drops to Content Gap, eventually linking up with the road from Gordon Town to Mavis Bank. A steep and muddy dirt road to the left drops to the simple **Silver Hill Coffee Factory**, where tours are offered; 4WD is recommended.

Sights

OLD TAVERN COFFEE ESTATE

About 1.5km southwest of Section and some 1200m above sea level, there's a small, anonymous **cottage** (☎/fax 924-2785; www.exportjamaica.org/oldtavern; 🕑 Sat-Thu) that you would surely pass by if you didn't know that its occupants, Alex and Dorothy Twyman, produce the best of the best of Blue Mountain coffee. Alex immigrated to Jamaica from England in 1958 and started growing coffee a decade later. Dorothy oversees the roasting, meticulously performing quality control by taste. The environmentally conscious Twymans keep their use of chemical pesticides and fertilizers to a bare minimum and compost all by-products before returning them to the soil.

Although the Twymans' coffee is widely acclaimed as the best on the island, until 1997 they weren't allowed to sell an ounce due to Kafkaesque government regulations. Finally, the Twymans were granted an exclusive license to grow, process, roast and sell a 'single estate coffee' under an estate label – the only estate on the island permitted to do so.

The Twymans welcome visitors by prior arrangement, except Friday. Visitors can sample the coffee and homemade mead, honey and coffee liqueur.

Contact either Strawberry Hill (p114) or Barrett Adventures (p114) to arrange a tour to the Old Tavern Coffee Estate. You can also call from Kingston to arrange a visit.

Sleeping & Eating

Starlight Chalet & Health Spa (☎ 968-3116; www.starlightchalet.com; s/d US$80/90, ste US$85-285) A rejuvenating sanctuary that makes a fantastic base for hiking and bird-watching. It's in the lee of the mountain divide at the turn-off for the Silver Hill Coffee Factory. Set amid a flower-filled hillside garden with dramatic alpine vistas, the

HALLOWED GROUNDS

Since coffee grows best on well-watered, well-drained slopes in cooler yet tropical climates, it is no surprise that it thrives in Jamaica's Blue Mountains. The region's distinctly flavored coffee is acclaimed by connoisseurs as among the world's best. To be designated 'Blue Mountain,' it must be grown – and roasted – in a prescribed area.

In 1728 at Temple Hall Estate, near the village of Castleton north of Kingston, governor Sir Nicholas Lawes introduced coffee to Jamaica and other planters followed suit, prompted by the growing demand in Europe. During the peak years, from 1800 to 1840, production rose to 17,000 tons a year and Jamaica became the world's largest exporter.

Emancipation in 1838 brought an end to many of the plantations. Many slaves left the estates and planted their own coffee. As steeper slopes were planted, coffee quality began to decline. The end of Britain's preferential tariffs for Jamaican coffee further damaged the industry at a time when high-quality coffee from Brazil was beginning to sap Jamaica's market share. By the close of WWII, Jamaica's coffee industry was on its last legs.

There has been a resurgence in the popularity of Blue Mountain coffee in the last decade, largely thanks to interest from Japan, where Blue Mountain coffee is a treasured commodity and sells for US$130 or more per kilogram. More than 90% of Blue Mountain coffee is sold to Japan at a preferential rate, which means that the beans that make it to North America and Europe can be quite expensive, while much of the coffee you get in Jamaica is of inferior quality.

Sadly, the high prices the beans get abroad only encouraged deforestation at home. Tearing down trees brought coffee farmers more valuable land, but also chased away migratory bird populations – some of whom (ironically) prey on borer beetles and caterpillars that infest the coffee crop. Since 2006 wildlife experts from Humboldt State University in California have been working with park officials to convince farmers that the lack of trees ultimately makes coffee farming unsustainable.

modern, three-story plantation-style hotel has carpeted, modestly furnished rooms and oversized two- and three-bedroom suites. There's a small bar and restaurant where filling home-style meals are served by gracious staff. The no-frills spa has a sauna and massage rooms, and offers full treatments (US$45 to US$75). Nature walks and special-interest excursions are offered, as are yoga programs.

AROUND SECTION

Clydesdale

This is a derelict old coffee plantation and a popular spot for budget accommodations. The much-battered waterwheel and coffee mill machinery are partially intact. It has picnic spots and a small waterfall where you can skinny-dip. The **Morces Gap Trail** begins here.

By prior arrangement with the Forestry Department of Jamaica, you can **camp** (☎ 924-2667; www.forestry.gov.jm; Forestry Dept, 173 Constant Spring Rd, Kingston; camping US$5). There is safe drinking water and a natural pool in the Clyde River.

From Section take the horrendously potholed 'main' road toward Guava Ridge; the turnoff for Clydesdale is about 1km above the hamlet of St Peters. Then you will cross over the Chestervale Bridge above the Brook's River and immediately reach a Y-fork. Take the left, steeply uphill road for Clydesdale and Cinchona Gardens. It's a terribly rocky drive, suited for a 4WD only.

Cinchona Gardens

Not the ubiquitous coffee plant, but the cultivation of Assam tea and cinchona (whose quinine – extracted from the bark – was used to fight malaria) led to the founding of **Cinchona** (☎ 927-1257; admission free, tip to caretaker/guide expected) in 1868. The grounds were later turned into a garden to supply Kingston with flowers. In 1903 the Jamaican government leased Cinchona to the New York Botanical Gardens and, later, to the Smithsonian Institute.

Today, the gardens are a little run down, but it's really the fabulous views that lure you up the 1370m. To the north stand the peaks, but you can also peer down into the valleys of the Clyde, Green and Yallahs Rivers. A dilapidated old house full of weathered antiques sits atop the 2.5-hectare gardens, fronted by lawns and exquisite floral beds. The **Panorama Walk** begins to the east of the gardens, leading through a glade of towering bamboo and opening to staggering views. Half a dozen other tracks snake off into the nether reaches of the mountains, including the 16km **Vinegar Hill Trail**, which winds its way to Buff Bay.

If you've come with a sleeping bag, you can spend the night (US$8): claim a spot on the floor in the main house or set up camp on the grounds.

Finding Cinchona is difficult and highly unadvisable without a guide. From Clydesdale continue uphill along the muddy dirt track for about 3km. There are several unmarked junctions; you'll undoubtedly take some wrong turns and need to backtrack. Ask at every opportunity. Don't underestimate the awful road conditions, with ruts deep enough to hang up your chassis and leave your wheels spinning in thin air. *A 4WD with low-gear option is absolutely essential.* Far easier is a more direct and populated route via Mavis Bank; you'll still need to ask directions.

Both Strawberry Hill (p114) and Barrett Adventures (p114) offer great excursions to Cinchona Gardens.

GORDON TOWN

Gordon Town, at 370m, is a hamlet centered on a wide square with a **police station** (☎ 927-2805), post office and tiny courthouse. It began life as a staging post for Newcastle in the days before the Mammee River Rd was cut from The Cooperage. To reach Cinchona, Mavis Bank and the trail to Blue Mountain Peak, turn right at the square and cross the narrow bridge.

The **Gordon Town Trail** begins in Gordon Town and follows the Hope River Valley via Mt Industry and Redlight. Another 21km trail leads from Gordon Town to Sugar Loaf (2133m) via Content Gap, Top Mountain and Cinchona, and a third 16km track leads via the Flamstead coffee plantation and Orchard to Mavis Bank.

There is nowhere to stay in Gordon Town, and the only eating options are a few simple rum shops and stalls.

Buses and minibuses operate from the Parade, Half Way Tree and Papine in Kingston (US$0.30).

GUAVA RIDGE

This is the site of a ridge-crest junction for Content Gap and sights to the north, while Mavis Bank and Blue Mountain Peak are straight ahead.

A road to the right, signed for 'Bellevue House' 50m east of Guava Ridge, leads 6km through pine and eucalyptus forests to the coffee plantation of **Flamstead** (☎ 960-0204; peterking@flamstead.com; visits by prior appointment). This former great house of Governor Edward Eyre (see p30) was a lookout from which Horatio Nelson and other British naval officers surveyed the Port Royal base. Views over the Palisadoes and Kingston Harbour are fabulous.

MAVIS BANK

Mavis Bank, around a one-hour drive from Kingston, is a tidy little village in the midst of coffee country.

In the village center you'll find the **police station** (☎ 977-8004), a post office, a public telephone and the **People's Cooperative Bank** (☎ 977-8010; 9am-3pm Mon-Fri), which represents Western Union.

The **Mavis Bank Coffee Factory** (☎ 977-8015; tour US$8; 9-11am & 1-3pm Mon-Fri), 1km southwest of Mavis Bank, is a working factory that has been producing Blue Mountain coffee for over a century. Ask the chief 'cupper' to demonstrate 'cupping' (tasting), the technique to identify quality coffee. You can tour the factory to see the coffee beans drying (in season) and being processed. At the end of the tour you can purchase roasted beans at bargain prices. For more on Blue Mountain coffee see the boxed text on p117.

The **Farm Hill Trail** begins at Churchyard Rd and leads uphill for 8km to Penlyne Castle and on to Blue Mountain Peak.

As you enter the village, you'll see **Forres Park Guest House & Farm** (www.forrespark.com; Forres Park ☎ 927-8275; Kingston ☎ 927-5957; cabin US$75, r US$75), a working coffee farm with an enviable hillside setting, amid lush gardens and tiers of coffee bushes flowing downhill like folds of green silk. It rents six rooms (with balconies) in the main lodge and three basic wooden cottages with red concrete floors and pine furniture. Meals are cooked by request. You can rent mountain bikes. Bird-watching tours are offered by appointment, as are guided hikes (US$40 to US$65) to Mavis Bank, Cinchona Gardens and Blue Mountain Peak.

Getting There & Away

A bus runs here twice daily from Papine via Gordon Town (US$1). Route taxis operate more frequently (US$2.50). A tourist taxi from Kingston costs about US$25.

HAGLEY GAP & PENLYNE CASTLE

The ramshackle village of Hagley Gap sits abreast a hill east of Mavis Bank and is the gateway to the Blue Mountain Peak. The road forks in the village, where a horrendously denuded dirt road to Penlyne Castle begins a precipitous ascent.

Penlyne Castle is the base for 12km hikes to and from Blue Mountain Peak. Most hikers stay overnight at one of three simple lodges near Penlyne Castle before tackling the hike in the wee hours.

Bring warm clothing. One minute you're in sun-kissed mountains, the next, clouds swirl in and the temperature plunges.

Sleeping & Eating

Wildflower Lodge (☎ 929-5395; r without/with bath US$13/33, cottage US$55) About 400m east of the ridge crest at Penlyne Castle, this hardwood structure has 36 bunks in basic rooms with communal bathrooms with solar-heated water, plus three appealing private rooms with private bathrooms downstairs. A two-bedroom cottage at the bottom of the garden sleeps up to six. An atmospheric dining room has hammocks on the veranda and faces southeast down the mountain. Breakfasts cost about US$5; lunch and dinner cost US$6.50. You have use of a large but basic kitchen. The lodge offers horseback rides and guides for the climb.

Whitfield Hall (☎ 927-0986, 926-6612; www.whitfieldhall.com; camping per tent US$8, dm adult/child US$15/12, s/d US$25/40, 4-person cottage US$60) About 400m uphill from Wildflower Lodge, nestled amid pine trees, this former plantation dating from 1776 is a more basic option and has bunks for up to 40 people, with four to eight bunks per room. The dark, gloomy lounge has a huge fireplace (there's a US$5 firewood charge) and smoke-stained ceiling. Gas lamps provide illumination. Guests share two basic bathrooms with toilets and tubs (cold water only), plus a small kitchen. If the hostel is full, camping is allowed on a wide lawn beneath eucalyptus trees. There are picnic tables, benches and a barbecue pit, as well as water and toilets. Locals will cook on request. You can hire guides (US$40 to the peak).

Jah B's Guest House (☎ 377-5206; farmhillcoffee@yahoo.com; dm/r US$14/30) This friendly place run by a family of Bobo Rastas has a basic but cozy wooden guest house, on the left 400m below Wildflower Lodge. It has several rooms with four bunks apiece, plus a shared shower and flush toilet; there are also four private rooms. Jah B himself cooks I-tal meals (about US$8) amid a cloud of ganja smoke and a nonstop volley of friendly banter. His son Alex now runs the outfit and offers transfers from Kingston in his beat-up 4WD and will guide you up Blue Mountain Peak for US$55.

Getting There & Away

From Papine in Kingston minibuses and route taxis run regularly to Mavis Bank, but less frequently to Hagley Gap via Gordon Town. Avoid starting out on Sunday.

Most hotels (including Whitfield Hall and Wildflower Lodge) in the Blue Mountains offer 4WD transfers to Penlyne Castle from Mavis Bank (from US$20 per vehicle) or Kingston (from US$40). The Wildflower and Whitfield transfers are untrustworthy in late evening, when drivers often don't show up (or refuse to continue), stranding people in Mavis Bank. Be sure to arrange a transfer for no later than mid afternoon.

If driving, continue through Mavis Bank to Mahogany Vale and cross the Yallahs River.

Penlyne Castle is reached via a 5km dirt road that ascends precipitously from Hagley Gap. Only 4WD vehicles with low-gear option can make the journey, which is dauntingly narrow and rugged.

BLUE MOUNTAIN PEAK

From Penlyne Castle to the summit of Blue Mountain Peak (2256m) is a 950m ascent and a three- or four-hour hike one way. It's not a serious challenge, but you need to be reasonably fit.

Don't litter, and *stay on the path*!

Most hikers set off from Penlyne Castle in the wee hours to reach the peak for sunrise. Your guide will rouse you at about 2am. Fortified with a breakfast of coffee and cereal, you set out single file in the pitch black along the 12km round-trip trail (you'll need a flashlight and a spare set of batteries, just in case). Midway, at Portland Gap, there's a ranger station and cabin (see p120).

As you hike, reggae music can be heard far, far below, competing with the chirps of crickets and katydids singing to attract mates. Myriad blinkies and peeny-wallies will be doing the same, signaling with their phosphorescent semaphore.

You should arrive at the peak around 5:30am, while it is still dark. Your stage is gradually revealed: a flat-topped hump, marked by a scaffolding pyramid and trig point (in the cloud it is easy to mistake the real summit for a smaller hump to the left of the hut near the summit).

If the weather's clear, Cuba, 144km away, can be seen from the peak, which casts a distinct shadow over the land below. After a brief celebratory drink and snacks, you'll set off back down the mountain, arriving at your accommodations in time for brunch.

By setting out for the summit a few hours later, say 5am, you may still make the top before the mists roll in, and you'll have the benefit of enjoying the changing vegetation and scenery with greater anticipation for what lies ahead (and above). You pass through several distinct ecosystems, including an area of bamboo and primordial giant tree ferns. Further up is cloud forest, dripping with filaments of hanging lichens and festooned with epiphytes and moss. Near the top is stunted dwarf or elfin forest, with trees like hirsute soapwood and rodwood no more than 2.5m high – an adaptation to the cold.

Don't hike without a guide at night. Numerous spur trails lead off the main trails and it is easy to get lost. These mountains are not kind to those who lose their way.

Although hiking boots or tough walking shoes are best, sneakers will suffice, though your feet will likely get wet. At the top it can be icy with the wind blowing, and temperatures can approach freezing before sunrise, so wear plenty of layers. Rain gear is also essential, as the weather can change rapidly. Clouds usually begin to form in the early morning, followed by a cold breeze.

Guides can be hired locally at Hagley Gap or Penlyne Castle, or through most local hotels, for US$30/40 per half/full day. For organized hikes, see p111.

Sleeping

Jamaica Conservation & Development Trust Cabin (☎ 960-2848/9, 920-8278/9; www.greenjamaica.org.jm; 29 Dumbarton Avenue, Kingston 10; beds US$5) The Jamaica Conservation & Development Trust maintains a dimly lit cabin halfway up the trail at Portland Gap (4km above Abbey Green). You can camp (US$5) outside, where there's a cooking area and water from a pipe; you'll need to bring your own tent. The terribly run-down hut has a fireplace, but holes in the roof can douse the fire (a waterproof cover for your sleeping bag is a good idea). You need to reserve with the Jamaica Conversation & Development Trust.

SOUTHEAST COAST

Jamaica's southeast corner is the island's ugly duckling, viewed only in passing by most visitors as they hurtle from Kingston to Portland. Its narrow scrub-covered coastal plain has only unappealing gray-sand beaches and limited tourist infrastructure. Life revolves mostly around small fishing villages where the work is still performed by canoe and net. Surfers, however, rave about more than a dozen prime surf spots. (For specifics, contact the Surfing Association of Jamaica; see p56.)

YALLAHS & AROUND

Southeast of Bull Bay and the parish boundary between St Andrew and St Thomas, the A4 from Kingston makes a hairpin descent to Grants Pen, then winds through scrub-covered country until it reaches the coast at Yallahs, 16km east of Bull Bay. If you are traveling between Kingston and Portland parish, the jerk stands of Yallahs' Main St are a cheerful place to rest and regroup. Past Yallahs, a series of long, dark-gray beaches, with colorful pirogues drawn up, extends eastward to **Morant Bay**.

The wide gully of the Yallahs River, 3km west of town, begins 1370m up in the Blue Mountains. The boulders along the lower riverbed attest to the power and threat of flash floods.

Sights

YALLAHS RIVER VALLEY

A road leads north from Yallahs through the rugged Yallahs River Valley. About 5km northwest of town, you cross the river near Heartease, where it is said you can witness Revivalist spirit-cult meetings occasionally held on the eastern riverbank near the old bridge.

At the village of Llandewey, 11km northwest of Yallahs, you can gain a fine view of **Judgement Cliff**, which looms up a sheer 300m. It was formed by a 1692 earthquake that caused the mountainside to collapse.

The deteriorating road then claws its way up into the Blue Mountains, ascending sharply beyond the hamlet of Bethel Gap to Hagley Gap and Mavis Bank; you'll need a 4WD.

YALLAHS PONDS

Two large lakes east of Yallahs, the **ponds** are enclosed by a narrow, bow-shaped spit of sand. The ponds are exceedingly briny due to evaporation. Algae flourish and often turn the ponds a deep pink, accompanied by a powerful smell of hydrogen sulfide ('bad egg gas').

You can still see the remains of an old stone **signal tower** built on the sand spit in the 1770s by the English to communicate with Port Royal. It is listed as a national monument.

On the hillside just beyond Yallahs Ponds is the **Jamintel space research station**, linking Jamaica to the international satellite network.

MORANT BAY

pop 9900

Morant Bay, the only town of importance along the south coast, squats on a hill behind the coast road. Most of the town's early colonial-era buildings were burned in the Morant Bay Rebellion of 1865, led by the town's national hero, Paul Bogle (see p30), but a couple of gems remain.

October 11 is **Paul Bogle Day**, when a party is held in the town square and a 10km road race sets out from Stony Gut.

Information

Police station (☎ 982-2233; 7 South St) Next to the old courthouse.

Post office (☎ 982-2294; Queen St)

Scotiabank (☎ 982-1577; 23 Queen St) Opposite the Texaco gas station, with an ATM and currency exchange.

Sights

The **Paul Bogle statue** stands in front of the courthouse. By noted sculptor Edna Manley, it depicts Bogle standing grimly, hands clasped over the hilt of a machete. The **courthouse** was rebuilt in limestone and red brick after being destroyed in the 1865 rebellion. Bogle is buried beside the courthouse alongside a mass grave holding the remains of many slaves who lost their lives in the rebellion. The spot is marked by a moving memorial dedicated to 'those who love freedom.'

Diagonally across from the courthouse is a handsome, ochre-colored **Anglican church** dating to 1881.

The **Stony Gut Monument**, commemorating Bogle, stands opposite his **chapel**, 14km inland at the village of Stony Gut.

Sleeping & Eating

Morant Villas Hotel (☎ 982-2418; morantvillasja.com; 1 Wharf Rd; r US$45-75, studio/ste US$48/62) Sitting amid lawns and tall palms atop a bluff on the coast road just east of town, this hotel has 22 simple yet clean rooms with fans and private bath with hot water. There are also 10 studios with kitchens, plus suites. A restaurant and bar serves seafood for US$6 to US$12.

Getting There & Away

Minibuses and route taxis to Kingston (US$2 to US$3, two hours, three daily) and Port Antonio (US$2.50 to US$4, 2½ hours, two daily) arrive and depart from beside the Shell gas station on the A4 at the west end of town.

RETREAT

A small beachside residential community about 5km east of Morant Bay, Retreat draws Kingstonians on the weekends. It sits between two of the few pleasant beaches along Jamaica's southern coast. The aptly named **Golden Shore Beach** is hidden from view from the road. Watch for the hand-painted sign. Further east is **Prospect Beach**, a 'public bathing beach.'

Golden Shore Beach Resort (☎ /fax 982-9657; www.goldenshorehotel.com; downstairs r US$47-62, ste US$70; P ✱ 🖳) Located at Golden Shore Beach, this is a well-run hotel that offers 27 rooms in three categories in a condo-style unit amid landscaped grounds. The rooms are clean and boast refreshing, contemporary furnishings. The resort's gracious restaurant opens onto lawns fronting a beach.

Whispering Bamboo Cove (☎ 982-2912; www.discoverjamaica.com/whisper.html; 105 Crystal Dr; r US$50-75, ste US$90) A comfortable, contemporary villa-style hotel facing the beach in Retreat, it offers 10 airy, spacious and tastefully furnished rooms with tropical fabrics and antique reproductions.

BATH

This village, 10km north of Port Morant, lies on the bank of the Plantain Garden River, amid sugarcane and banana plantations. The town owes its existence to the discovery of hot mineral springs in the hills behind the present town in the late 17th century. A spa was developed, and socialites flocked. Today its relative poverty attests to the pitiful wages paid to plantation workers.

The one-street hamlet has a post office, **police station** (☎ 982-2115) and Shell gas station.

A bus (US$1) runs daily from the Parade in Kingston, as do minibuses and route taxis (US$3.50).

Sights & Activities

BATH GARDEN

At the east end of town is an old limestone church shaded by royal palms that flank the entrance to a **horticultural garden** (🕑 dawn-dusk) established by the government in 1779. Many exotics introduced to Jamaica were first planted here: bougainvillea, cinnamon, mango, jackfruit, jacaranda and the famous breadfruit brought from the South Pacific by Captain William Bligh aboard HMS *Providence*. The garden has seen better days, but there's no admission charge.

BATH FOUNTAIN

Local legend says that in the 1690s a runaway slave discovered hot springs that cured the injuries he received while escaping. He was so impressed by this miracle that he returned to tell his master. In 1699 the government bought the spring and an adjoining 460 hectares; they created the Bath of St Thomas the Apostle, and then formed a corporation that would administer mineral baths for the sick and infirm. The waters have therapeutic value for skin ailments and rheumatic problems.

Two springs issue from beneath the **bath house** (20min bath for 1/2 persons US$2.50/4.50; 🕑 8am-9:30pm Tue-Sun). The water here can be scorching (it varies from 46°C to 53°C). You soak in a deep, ceramic-tiled pool. The homey spa also offers a variety of massages. Arrive early on weekends, before the crowds arrive. To get there, turn up the road opposite the church in Bath and follow the road 3km uphill.

Pay no attention to the touts attempting to 'guide' you to the springs, offer 'massage' (to females only) or sell you dead swallowtail butterflies.

HIKING

A trail, for experienced hikers only, leads from Bath Fountain up over **Cuna Cuna Gap** to the Rio Grande Valley. Obtain Sheet 19 (showing St Thomas parish) and Sheet 14 (Portland parish) of the Ordnance Survey 1:12,500 map series from the **Survey Department** (☎ 922-6630; www.nla.gov.jm; 23½ Charles St, Kingston) for more detailed information.

Sleeping & Eating

Bath Fountain Hotel & Spa (☎ 703-4345; r without/with bath US$30/40, deluxe US$50) is your only option. It's a recently renovated, pink colonial hotel that dates to 1747 and contains the spa baths on the ground floor. The clinically white bedrooms are modestly furnished, lacking air-con and TVs. It has a small restaurant (breakfast US$2.50 to US$5, lunch and dinner US$7.50 to US$11).

GOLDEN GROVE

Golden Grove is 10km northeast of Port Morant (and 11km east of Bath). It's a desperately poor hamlet of corrugated-tin and wood huts on stilts, dominated by the plantations of Tropicana Sugar Estates, east of the road, and the banana plantations of Fyffes to the west.

On the A4 west of Golden Grove, a side road loops eastward via New Pera and Old Pera, and eventually deposits you at **Rocky Point Beach**, where fishing pirogues are drawn up. Locals pour in on any weekend to splash in the shallows and jive to ear-shattering reggae and rap.

MORANT POINT

Golden Grove is the gateway to Morant Point, a peninsula that juts into the Caribbean Sea. Erected in 1841, the 30m-tall, red-and-white-striped **Morant Point Lighthouse** (admission free) marks Morant Point, the easternmost tip of Jamaica. If he's in, ask the lighthouse keeper to show you the way to the top. The powerful view and the windy silence make for a profound experience as you look out over rippling sugarcane fields toward the cloud-haunted Blue Mountains.

The lighthouse is best reached by car; there's a turnoff at the gas station on the A4 in Golden Grove. It's a labyrinthine course, however, and completely unsigned. You'll absolutely need a guide to lead you; ask at the gas station. A 4WD is recommended during the rainy season.

Port Antonio & Northeast Coast

Sleepy Portland parish is the least developed resort area in Jamaica, and the most rugged and scenic. Forested mountains with deep gorges and rushing rivers beckon hikers. Along the coast, the surf rolls into perfect beach-lined coves. Pocket-sized beaches line the shore.

The beauty of Portland cannot be overstated. But the parish, long considered 'the next big thing' in Jamaican tourism, struggles to attract its rightful share of tourists. Several of the area's attractions have closed for want of visitors; others have been put on hold, awaiting 'redevelopment.' A new cruise-ship marina is underused. However, Portland remains a forward-thinking place. It's the first parish in Jamaica to adopt the Green Globe 21 program (www.greenglobe21.com) principles, which mandate sustainable environmental and social practices. The parish council will be first to tell you that, in Portland, the future is green.

The only town of any size is Port Antonio. With a lively market and an interesting collection of Georgian buildings mixed with tin-roofed shacks, 'Portie' is lively by day and peaceful by night. Inland are lush expanses of tropical rain forest and the Rio Grande Valley, one of Jamaica's best territories for hiking, bird-watching and other outdoor pursuits.

Hugging the coast to the southeast of Port Antonio is a succession of appealing communities: Fairy Hill is famous for its gentle beaches, Boston Bay for its burgeoning surf scene and famous jerk cuisine. Long Bay, with its dramatic setting and mellow vibe, has a countercultural appeal, making it irresistible for navelgazers and stargazers alike. Further off the beaten track you'll find unspoiled fishing villages where travelers can ease into a laid-back local lifestyle.

HIGHLIGHTS

- **Port Antonio** Wander the streets in Jamaica's most picturesque town (p124)
- **Frenchman's Cove** Watch an afternoon disappear on a sublime white-sand beach next to a freshwater stream (p133)
- **Rio Grande Valley** Drift merrily merrily merrily merrily on a raft down the Rio Grande past the former banana plantations in this verdant valley (p139)
- **Kwaaman and Tacky Waterfalls** Contemplate these wonderful primordial falls from the pools below (p143)
- **Boston Bay** Stuff your face with fine Jamaican jerk and shred some waves with local surfers (p137)

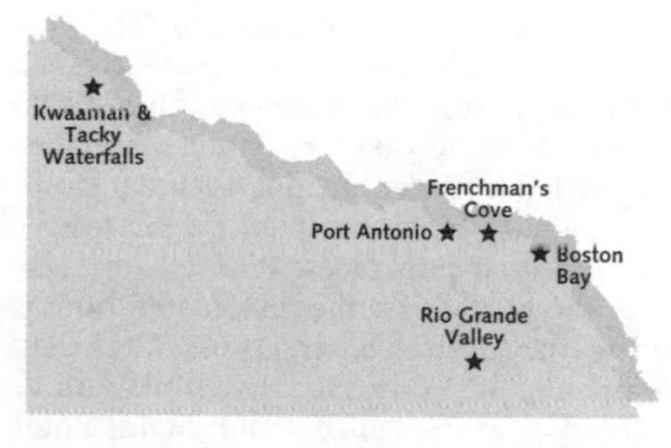

- AREA: 820 SQ KM
- PORT ANTONIO DEC AVERAGE HIGH TEMPERATURE: 28°C

HISTORY

The last of Jamaica's lands to be officially settled, Portland parish was the last great stronghold of the Windward Maroons, who survive to this day in the Rio Grande Valley with many African-based traditions intact. In the late 19th century Portland's economy enjoyed a precipitous spike thanks to the United States' newfound appetite for the banana. The fruit cargo ships that sailed to and from Port Antonio served double duty as transport for some of Jamaica's first tourists, making 'Portie' the island's first destination resort. In recent years, Portland parish has led the nation in establishing 'green' tourism practices.

CLIMATE

Port Antonio enjoys a tropical climate with relatively high rainfall. The temperature hits an average of 33°C in summer and 28°C in winter. The evenings are cooled by wonderful breezes floating in off the mountains. The rainiest times are May/June and October/November.

GETTING THERE & AWAY

The Ken Jones Aerodrome, located about half an hour west of Port Antonio, receives charter flights but international passengers must rely on the airports in Montego Bay or Kingston. Minibus and route-taxi traffic is high in and out of Port Antonio, where it's a simple matter to find local transport to Ocho Rios, Kingston and beyond.

PORT ANTONIO

pop 13,000

Cupping an unruffled bay while backing into the sleepy Rio Grande Valley, Port Antonio is the perfect capital for Portland. The parish's only sizable town is largely untarnished by the duty-free, tourist orientation of Ocho Rios or Montego Bay, its streets, squares, quayside and market inviting leisurely strolls – invitations freely accepted by the town's dog and goat populaces. Wandering away from the bustle past the dilapidated houses lining the potholed streets of Titchfield Peninsula, it's very easy to think you've roamed onto the set of some quaint colonial ghost town.

Ironic, then, that the tentacles of Jamaican tourism first found purchase in Port Antonio. The town came to prominence as the island's major banana port, and its prosperity began luring visitors at the turn of the 20th century. Celebrity visitors, led by cinematic and real-life swashbuckler Errol Flynn (p130), descended on the town in the 1930s. And when the tourist attentions moved on to the west of the island, Port Antonio went back to bananas.

Rumors of the town's development are rife. In 2004 a state-of-the-art marina was built with the aim of luring cruise ships, and while they have yet to appear, hope has not been abandoned. Plans for Navy Island, former home and playground of Flynn and his Hollywood guests, range from an ecological theme park to a casino, but nothing's made it to the blueprint stage. Talk of enlarging Ken Jones Aerodrome to receive international flights remains just that.

All of which will suit you just fine if you seek a low-key Jamaican port town and an ideal base for setting out to discover some of Portland's hidden treasures.

HISTORY

The Spanish christened the bay 'Puerto Anton' in the 16th century, but made no serious effort to settle. In 1723 the British laid out a rudimentary town on the peninsula and named it Titchfield; a fort was added in 1729. But rampant fevers in the swampy coastlands and constant raids by marauding Maroons deterred all but a few settlers.

Following peace with the Maroons in 1739, Titchfield expanded. Many settlers grew sustenance crops, including bananas. Enter the Yankee skipper Captain Lorenzo Dow Baker (1840–1908), a fruit-shipping magnate, who arrived here in 1871 and established the banana trade that created a boomtown overnight. Baker and his Boston Fruit Company went on to own 40 banana plantations from Port Antonio to Buff Bay, making Port Antonio the 'banana capital of the world.' Port Antonio grew so wealthy that, it is said, planters would light their cigars with US$5 bills.

In the 1890s Baker began shipping tourists from the cold US northeast in his empty banana boats. Although Portland's banana bonanza was doomed in the 1930s by the onset of Panama disease, the arrival of movie star Errol Flynn and, later, numerous bluebloods and Hollywood stars, gave new cachet to Port Antonio as a tourist resort.

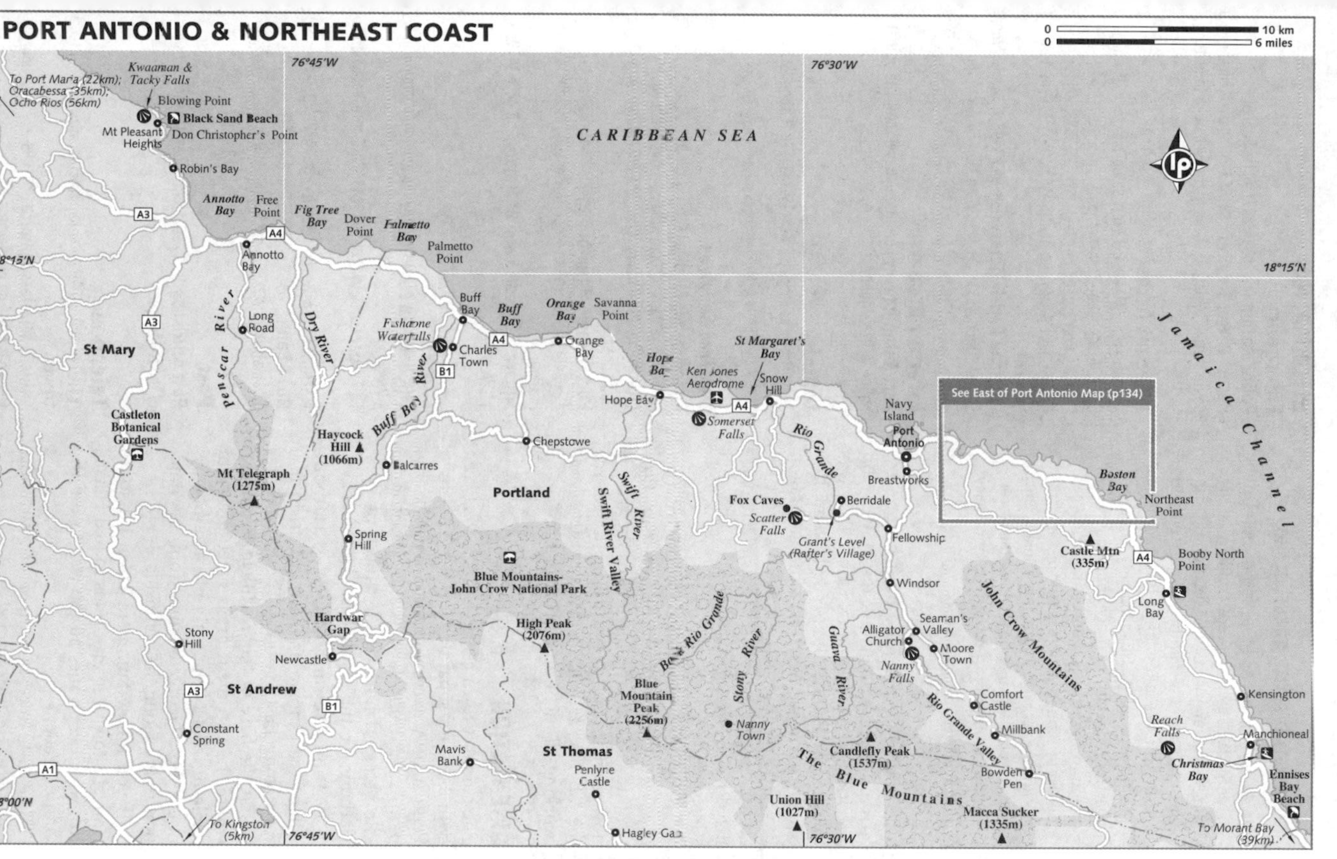
PORT ANTONIO & NORTHEAST COAST
0 10 km
0 6 miles
76°45'W
76°30'W
18°15'N
18°00'N
To Port Maria (22km); Oracabessa (35km); Ocho Rios (56km)
Kwaaman & Tacky Falls
Blowing Point
Black Sand Beach
Mt Pleasant Heights
Don Christopher's Point
Robin's Bay
CARIBBEAN SEA
Annotto Bay
Free Point
Fig Tree Bay
Dover Point
Palmetto Bay
Palmetto Point
Buff Bay
Orange Bay
Savanna Point
St Margaret's Bay
Ken Jones Aerodrome
Snow Hill
Hope Bay
Somerset Falls
Navy Island
Port Antonio
Breastworks
See East of Port Antonio Map (p134)
Boston Bay
Northeast Point
Jamaica Channel
Castle Mtn (335m)
Booby North Point
Long Bay
Kensington
Manchioneal
Reach Falls
Christmas Bay
Ennises Bay Beach
To Morant Bay (39km)
St Mary
Long Road
Pencar River
Dry River
Castleton Botanical Gardens
Mt Telegraph (1275m)
Haycock Hill (1066m)
Buff Bay River
Charles Town
Balcarres
Chepstowe
Portland
Spring Hill
Blue Mountains-John Crow National Park
Swift River
Swift River Valley
Rio Grande
Fox Caves
Scatter Falls
Berridale
Grant's Level (Rafter's Village)
Fellowship
Windsor
John Crow Mountains
Seaman's Valley
Alligator Church
Moore Town
Nanny Falls
Comfort Castle
Rio Grande Valley
Millbank
Bowden Pen
Macca Sucker (1335m)
Hardwar Gap
Newcastle
Stony Hill
St Andrew
High Peak (2076m)
Back Rio Grande
Stony River
Guava River
Blue Mountain Peak (2256m)
Nanny Town
Candlefly Peak (1537m)
The Blue Mountains
Union Hill (1027m)
Constant Spring
Mavis Bank
St Thomas
Penlyre Castle
Hagley Gap
To Kingston (5km)
A1
A3
A4
B1

PORTLAND & THE GREEN GLOBE

In adopting the Agenda 21 principles of Green Globe (which were codified at the Rio Earth Summit of 1992), Portland parish has undertaken a number of measures to ensure the greenness of its future. Among the projects of its 'sustainability strategy' are the reduction of greenhouse gases by planting more trees, conserving resources by using biodegradable pesticides and recycling paper, and improving drinking and surface water quality by instituting a water-control monitoring program. It's not easy being green.

In the 1960s a second brief heyday occurred when a luxurious resort went up overlooking Frenchman's Cove. This was followed by Prince Alfonso de Hohenlohe's equally exclusive Marbella Club at Dragon Bay. The regal resorts attracted the jet set crowd, and the coves east of town were colonized by the very rich, setting a trend that still continues.

Today, as in the past, all of the bananas exported from Jamaica depart from Port Antonio's dock. The loading of the fruit is now mechanized, so you will no longer see the tallyman tallying bananas or stevedores 'working all night on a drink of rum.'

ORIENTATION

The compact town center is nestled between twin harbors separated by the Titchfield Peninsula. A narrow channel separates the peninsula from Navy Island, less than a kilometer offshore, at the mouth of West Harbour. To the east is East Harbour bay.

W Palm Ave runs along West Harbour. Allan Ave (known as 'Folly Rd' to locals) runs along East Harbour. The town center lies at the base of the Titchfield Peninsula, where the two main drags meet at a right angle in front of the main plaza and courthouse. Fort George St runs from this junction uphill along the peninsula.

If you follow Summers Town Rd south from the town center it leads to Red Hassell Rd, which continues all the way to the Rio Grande Valley.

The clock tower in front of the courthouse has a city directory painted on it.

INFORMATION

Emergency

Police station (☎ 993-2527/46; Harbour St)
Resort Patrol Services (☎ 993-7482) Based in the police station, it patrols to guard the welfare of tourists.

Internet Access

D-Tech (☎ 993-4184; 3 West St, upstairs; per 30min US$1.25; 9am-7pm Mon-Sat)
Don J's Computer Centre (☎ 715-5559; Village of St George, Fort George St; per hr US$2.50; 10am-4pm Mon-Fri)
Portland Parish Library (☎ 993-2793; 1 Fort George St; per 30min US$1; 9am-6pm Mon-Fri, 9am-1pm Sat)

Internet Resources

Port Antonio (www.portantoniotravel.com) The official online visitor's guide.

Laundry

Ever Brite Laundry (☎ 715-1851; 20 Harbour St) Drop-off laundry service.

Medical Services

Agape Family Medical Clinic (☎ 993-2338; 32 Harbour St; 9am-4:30pm Mon-Sat) Has emergency service.
City Plaza Pharmacy (☎ 993-2620; City Centre Plaza, Harbour St)
Port Antonio Hospital (☎ 993-2646; Nuttall Rd; 24hr) Above the town on Naylor's Hill, south of West Harbour.
Square Gift Centre and Pharmacy (☎ 993-3629; 11 West St)

Money

CIBC Jamaica Banking Centre (☎ 993-2708; 3 West St)
FX Trader Cambio (☎ 993 3617; City Centre Plaza, Harbour St)
National Commercial Bank (☎ 993-9822; 5 West St)
RBTT Bank (☎ 993-9755; 28 Harbour St)
Scotiabank (☎ 993-2523; 3 Harbour St)

Post

Post office (☎ 993-2651; Harbour St) On the east side of the town square.

Telephone

There are public telephones near the clock tower.

Cable & Wireless Jamaica (☎ 993-2775; Harbour St) Overseas calls and phonecards.

Tourist Information

Jamaica Tourist Board (JTB; ☎ 993-3051; 2nd fl, City Centre Plaza, Harbour St; 8:30am-4:30pm Mon-Fri) Offers only a paucity of information.

Travel Agencies

Travel Experts (☎ 993-2645; City Centre Plaza, Harbour St)

DANGERS & ANNOYANCES

Note that a few locals try to eke out a living by scamming tourists. Watch out for a scam involving a local DJ or musician offering for sale recorded discs containing original music – most often these are blank.

Guard your valuables when browsing Musgrave Market, and stick to the main streets if walking at night.

SIGHTS

Port Antonio's heart is the **town square**, at the corner of West St and Harbour St. It's centered on a clock tower and backed by a handsome red-brick Georgian courthouse topped by a cupola. About 50m down West St is the junction of William St, where the smaller **Port Antonio Square** has a **cenotaph** honoring Jamaicans who gave their lives in the two world wars.

On the west side is the clamorous and colorful **Musgrave Market**, supported by thick limestone columns. Following William St south to Harbour St, you can turn left to peek inside **Christ Church**, a red-brick Anglican building built in neo-Romanesque style around 1840 (much of the structure dates from 1903). The singular item of note is the brass lectern donated by Captain Lorenzo Dow Baker. Further down Harbour St is the **historic police station**.

On the north side of the town square is the imposing façade of the **Village of St George**, a beautiful three-story complex with an exquisitely frescoed exterior in Dutch style.

Along the hilly Titchfield Peninsula – known locally as 'the Hill' – are several dozen Victorian-style gingerbread houses, notably **DeMontevin Lodge** (21 Fort George St), an ornate rust-red mansion, which is now a hotel. Many of the finest homes line King St, which runs down the center of the peninsula (parallel to Queen and Fort George Sts). The peninsula is now a National Heritage Trust Site and is slated to receive a restoration.

Further north at the tip of the peninsula are the **Fort George ruins**, dating from 1729. The parade ground and former barracks today house **Titchfield School**, not open to the public. Beyond the school, several George III–era cannons can still be seen mounted in their embrasures in 3m-thick walls.

Navy Island

This lushly vegetated 25-hectare island is popular with local day-trippers on weekends…or it was when the ferries ran.

In colonial days the British Navy used it to careen ships for repair and it built a small battery, plus jetties and warehouses. Nothing remains of the navy's presence. In the mid-20th century Errol Flynn bought the island. His former home became a hotel, which later fell into decay. In early 2002 the Port Authority and the Urban Development Corporation (UDC) jointly took over the island with a view to developing the jaded property as an upscale resort and ecological theme park.

Folly

This two-story, 60-room mansion on the peninsula east of East Harbour was built entirely of concrete in pseudo-Grecian style by a North American millionaire. It was in private use until 1936, when the roof collapsed. Sea water had been used in the construction, causing the iron reinforcing rods to rust.

Today the shell of the structure remains, held aloft by limestone columns. It makes a perfectly peculiar locale for a picnic.

Nearby stands the bright-orange **Folly Point Lighthouse**, built in 1888.

ACTIVITIES

You can charter sport-fishing boats such as **La Nadine** (☎ 909-9552; caribbecapt@aol.com; half day US$550-750, full day US$800-1200) from Errol Flynn Marina in Port Antonio. *La Nadine* also does harbor tours (US$25 per person, minimum of four people).

Located at the new marina, **Lady G'Diver** (☎ 844-8711, 995-0246; www.ladygdiver.com; 2-/4-dive package US$84/152; Errol Flynn Marina) is a full-service dive shop; dive boats leave at 11am and 2pm daily. It has a retail store, PADI instruction and equipment rentals.

TOURS

Port Antonio makes an excellent base from which to take excursions into the verdant forests of the Rio Grande Valley and into the Maroon country towns of Moore Town and Nanny Town.

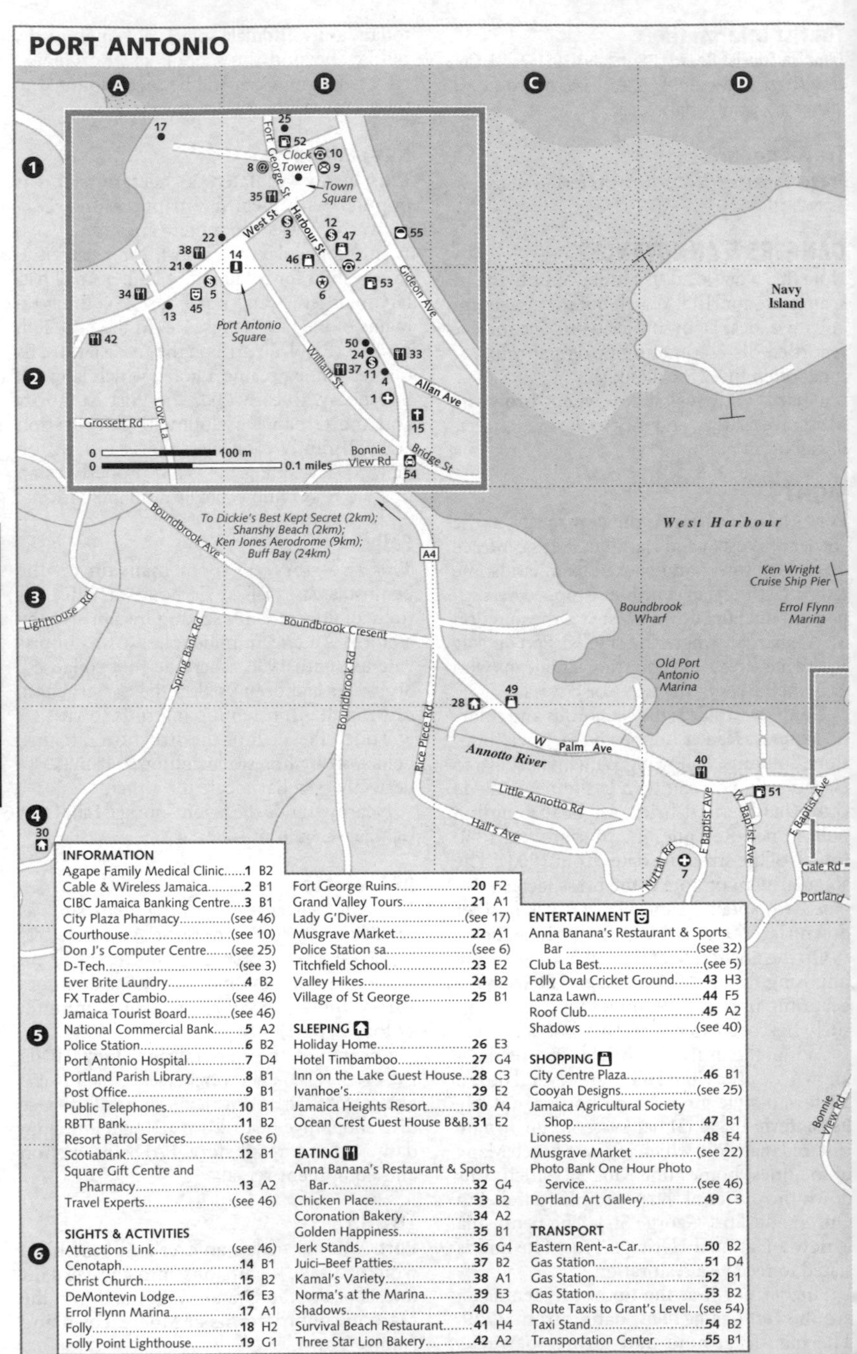

PORT ANTONIO
A
B
C
D
1
2
3
4
5
6
Fort George St
Clock Tower
Town Square
West St
Harbour St
Gideon Ave
Port Antonio Square
William St
Allan Ave
Love La
Grossett Rd
Bonnie View Rd
Bridge St
0 100 m
0 0.1 miles
Navy Island
West Harbour
To Dickie's Best Kept Secret (2km); Shanshy Beach (2km); Ken Jones Aerodrome (9km); Buff Bay (24km)
Boundbrook Ave
A4
Ken Wright Cruise Ship Pier
Errol Flynn Marina
Boundbrook Wharf
Lighthouse Rd
Boundbrook Cresent
Spring Bank Rd
Boundbrook Rd
Rice Piece Rd
Old Port Antonio Marina
W Palm Ave
Annotto River
Little Annotto Rd
Hall's Ave
E Baptist Ave
W Baptist Ave
Nuttall Rd
Gale Rd
Portland
Bonnie View Rd
INFORMATION
Agape Family Medical Clinic......1 B2
Cable & Wireless Jamaica..........2 B1
CIBC Jamaica Banking Centre.....3 B1
City Plaza Pharmacy..............(see 46)
Courthouse..........................(see 10)
Don J's Computer Centre.......(see 25)
D-Tech..................................(see 3)
Ever Brite Laundry....................4 B2
FX Trader Cambio.................(see 46)
Jamaica Tourist Board...........(see 46)
National Commercial Bank........5 A2
Police Station...........................6 B2
Port Antonio Hospital...............7 D4
Portland Parish Library..............8 B1
Post Office................................9 B1
Public Telephones....................10 B1
RBTT Bank...............................11 B2
Resort Patrol Services.............(see 6)
Scotiabank...............................12 B1
Square Gift Centre and Pharmacy............................13 A2
Travel Experts......................(see 46)
SIGHTS & ACTIVITIES
Attractions Link....................(see 46)
Cenotaph..................................14 B1
Christ Church............................15 B2
DeMontevin Lodge....................16 E3
Errol Flynn Marina....................17 A1
Folly...18 H2
Folly Point Lighthouse..............19 G1
Fort George Ruins....................20 F2
Grand Valley Tours...................21 A1
Lady G'Diver.........................(see 17)
Musgrave Market......................22 A1
Police Station sa......................(see 6)
Titchfield School.......................23 E2
Valley Hikes..............................24 B2
Village of St George..................25 B1
SLEEPING
Holiday Home...........................26 E3
Hotel Timbamboo......................27 G4
Inn on the Lake Guest House....28 C3
Ivanhoe's..................................29 E2
Jamaica Heights Resort............30 A4
Ocean Crest Guest House B&B.31 E2
EATING
Anna Banana's Restaurant & Sports Bar.......................................32 G4
Chicken Place...........................33 B2
Coronation Bakery....................34 A2
Golden Happiness.....................35 B1
Jerk Stands...............................36 G4
Juici–Beef Patties.....................37 B2
Kamal's Variety.........................38 A1
Norma's at the Marina..............39 E3
Shadows...................................40 D4
Survival Beach Restaurant........41 H4
Three Star Lion Bakery.............42 A2
ENTERTAINMENT
Anna Banana's Restaurant & Sports Bar..................................(see 32)
Club La Best............................(see 5)
Folly Oval Cricket Ground........43 H3
Lanza Lawn..............................44 F5
Roof Club.................................45 A2
Shadows ....(see 40)
SHOPPING
City Centre Plaza......................46 B1
Cooyah Designs....................(see 25)
Jamaica Agricultural Society Shop...47 B1
Lioness......................................48 E4
Musgrave Market..................(see 22)
Photo Bank One Hour Photo Service................................(see 46)
Portland Art Gallery..................49 C3
TRANSPORT
Eastern Rent-a-Car....................50 B2
Gas Station...............................51 D4
Gas Station...............................52 B1
Gas Station...............................53 B2
Route Taxis to Grant's Level...(see 54)
Taxi Stand................................54 B2
Transportation Center...............55 B1

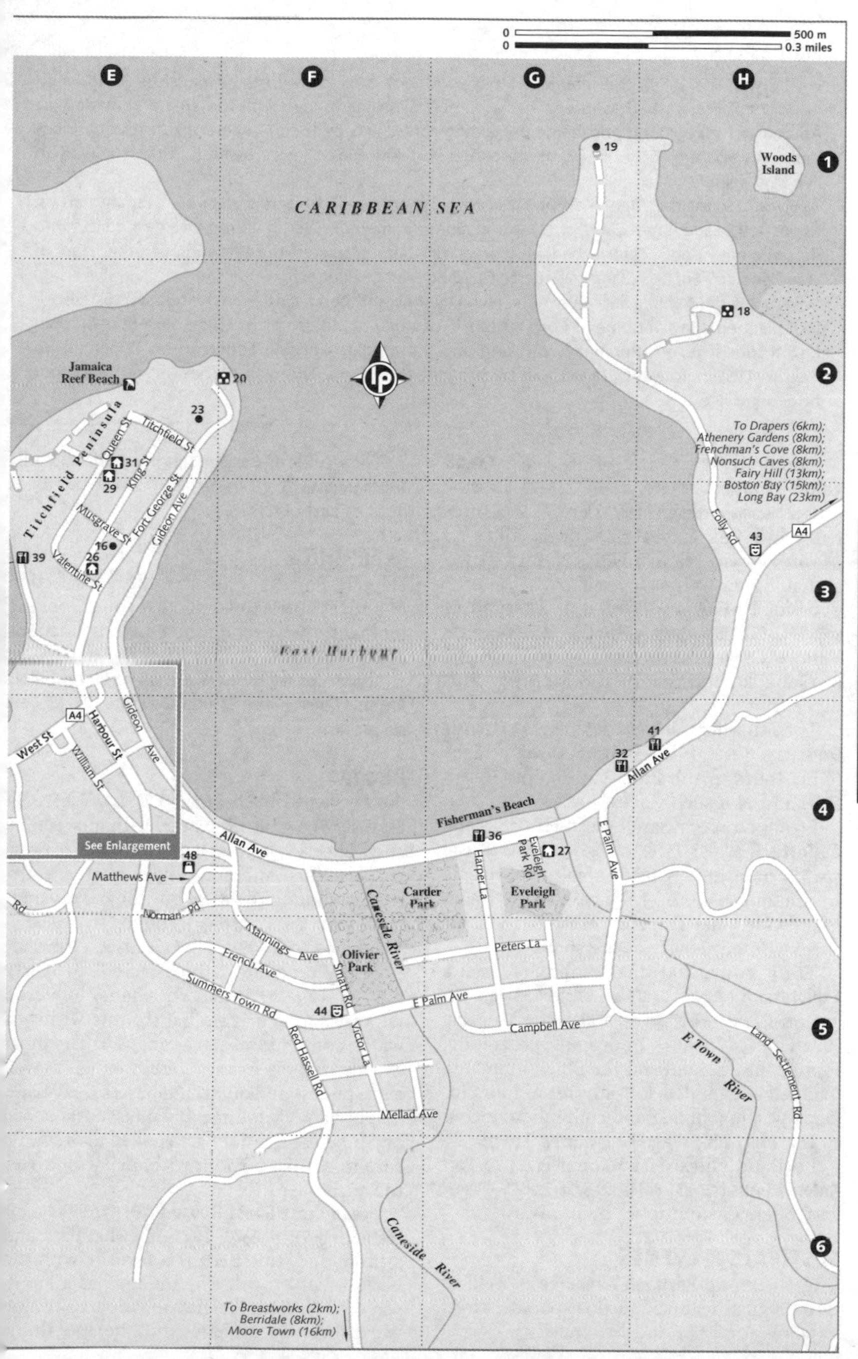

0 500 m
0 0.3 miles
E
F
G
H
1
2
3
4
5
6
19
Woods Island
CARIBBEAN SEA
18
Jamaica Reef Beach
20
23
Titchfield Peninsula
Titchfield St
Queen St
31
29
King St
Fort George St
Gideon Ave
Musgrave St
16
39
26
Valentine St
To Drapers (6km); Athenery Gardens (8km); Frenchman's Cove (8km); Nonsuch Caves (8km); Fairy Hill (13km); Boston Bay (15km); Long Bay (23km)
Folly Rd
43
A4
East Harbour
A4
West St
Harbour St
Gideon Ave
William St
See Enlargement
41
32
Allan Ave
Fisherman's Beach
36
Allan Ave
48
Matthews Ave
Harper La
Eveleigh Park Rd
27
E Palm Ave
Carder Park
Eveleigh Park
Caneside River
Norman Rd
Mannings Ave
Olivier Park
Peters La
French Ave
Smatt Rd
Summers Town Rd
44
E Palm Ave
Campbell Ave
Victor La
Red Hassell Rd
E Town River
Land Settlement Rd
Mellad Ave
Caneside River
To Breastworks (2km); Berridale (8km); Moore Town (16km)

ERROL FLYNN

Errol Flynn (1909–59), the infamous Hollywood idol, arrived in Portland parish in 1946 when his yacht *Zacca* washed ashore in bad weather. Flynn fell in love with the area and made Port Antonio his playground and home (his acting career was by then washed up). In his autobiography, *My Wicked, Wicked Ways,* he described Port Antonio as 'more beautiful than any woman I've ever seen.'

Flynn bought the Titchfield Hotel and Navy Island, where he threw wild, extravagant parties. Locals tell exaggerated tales of Flynn's exploits: 'Remember de day 'im drove de Cadillac into de swimming pool?' Flynn's beguiling ways inevitably attracted the attention of other stars of stage and screen, like Clara Bow, Bette Davis and Ginger Rogers.

With his third wife, Patrice Wymore, Flynn later established a cattle ranch at Boston Estate. He also planned a lavish home at Comfort Castle and had grandiose plans to develop Port Antonio into a tourist resort. But heavy drinking and a profligate lifestyle added to his ill-health. He died in 1959 before his plans could be brought to fruition. The wild parties are no more, but his legend lives on.

Excellent trips are offered by **Grand Valley Tours** (☎ 993-4116, 858-7338; www.portantoniojamaica.com/gvt.html; 12 West St) to Scatter Falls and Fox Caves as well as hikes to Moore Town, Nanny Falls, Nanny Town and along the White River Trail.

Guided hikes are offered by **Valley Hikes** (☎ 993-3881; 26 Harbour St) in the Rio Grande Valley, as well as Maroon culture tours, horseback riding, bird-watching and other trips.

The **Attractions Link** (☎ 993-2102, 394-3320; City Centre Plaza, Harbour St) offers Port Antonio highlights tours to the Blue Mountains, Reach Falls and Nonsuch Caves.

From Drapers San Guest House, **Carla Gullotta** (☎ 993-7118; carla-51@cwjamaica.com) (p135) occasionally leads small contingents by minibus to some of the best reggae shows islandwide. She arranges tickets and will act as your intermediary at the show.

Tour coordination company **Jamaica Explorations** (☎ 993-7267; www.hotelmockingbirdhill.com/english/portantonio/hiking.php) at Hotel Mocking Bird Hill (p136) aims to promote ecocultural tourism in Portland and the Blue Mountains. Tailor-made guided soft-adventure tours include walking, hiking and cultural excursions to the Maroon village of Charles Town.

Portland enthusiast Joanna Hart of **Port Antonio Tours** (☎ 831-8434, 859-3758; joahart@hotmail.com) offers custom tours by minivan.

FESTIVALS & EVENTS

The weeklong **Portland Jamboree** is held in mid-August, featuring a float parade, street dancing, food fair and live music.

The weeklong **Port Antonio International Marlin Tournament** (☎ 927-0145; rondq@mail.infochan.com) is held in early October.

SLEEPING

Happily, Port Antonio offers the best selection of budget hotels in Jamaica. If you're looking for luxury, however, the best accommodations are east of town.

Guest-house owners are served by the **Port Antonio Guest House Association** (☎ 993-7118; www.go-jam.com).

Budget

Holiday Home (☎ 993-2425, 993-2882; 12 King St; s/d/t US$35/40/55) A charming hotel with nine rooms and a cheery communal lounge. They're basic yet spacious, and some have shared bathrooms with cold water, but they're all spic-and-span. Breakfasts are cooked to order.

Ivanhoe's (☎ 993-3043; 9 Queen St; r US$30-60) Recently renovated, this gracious property has 12 well-lit rooms with fans, louvered windows and private bathrooms with hot water; some rooms have cable TV. The most expensive room has air-conditioning. It's well run, spotless and quiet, and has a breezy patio and homey TV lounge. Breakfast costs US$5, and lunch and dinner are cooked to order. Be sure to ask for a room with a view out over the harbor.

Ocean Crest Guest House B&B (☎ 993-4024; 7 Queen St; r US$35, d US$70;) Somewhat dark and a little loud, this B&B is a favorite with the backpacker crowd. The lounge has a large-screen TV. Four bright new deluxe rooms were recently unveiled on the top floor the balconies have a stunning view of Port Antonio and its picturesque bay.

Inn on the Lake Guest House (☎ 993-3468; onthe lake@cybervale.com; 17A W Palm Ave; r with/without air-con US$55/50, cottage US$120; P) No it's not on a lake, but this welcoming guesthouse offers six cozy rooms, each with its own outside entrance and cable TV, radio and hot water. There's also a two-bedroom cottage with kitchen.

Midrange

Jamaica Heights Resort (☎ 993-3305; www.jamaica heights.net; Spring Bank Rd; d US$75-125, cottage US$175; P) This is a splendid hilltop plantation home set amid lush gardens with incredible views of the town and bay. The columned verandas, whitewashed walls, dark hardwood floors, louvered windows, French doors and cool white-and-blue color scheme combine to provide a gracious environment. The six rooms and two cottages are tastefully furnished with white wicker and antiques, plus four-poster beds. A spa offers massage and treatments, and there's a beautiful plunge pool plus a nature trail.

Hotel Timbamboo (☎ 993-2049; hoteltimbamboo .com; 5 Everleigh Park Rd; s US$50-70, 1-/2-/3-bedroom ste US$85/150/200; P) Offering rare comfort for a Port Antonio hotel so centrally located, the Timbamboo has spacious, sunny rooms with modern furniture, carpeted floors and cable TV. Suites have sizable kitchens, while some rooms have balconies with views of the Blue Mountains. The hotel's sun deck is a great place to unwind.

Top End

Port Antonio has no top-end hotels, but to the east in nearby Fairy Hill are several exceptional choices – see p135.

The Port Antonio area has many luxurious villas, situated both on the water or in the hills with soaring views, where couples, families and small groups can spend a few days or more in style. Contact the **Jamaican Association of Villas & Apartments** (JAVA; ☎ 974-2508; www .villasinjamaica.com; PO Box 298, Ocho Rios).

EATING

Port Antonio has more than its share of cheap eateries offering economical Jamaican fare. On Allan Ave (Folly Rd), along the waterfront east of downtown, are a number of beachside jerk stands and simple eateries serving roasted fish and seafood. For a more upscale experience, head to the new marina.

Budget

Golden Happiness (☎ 993-4524; cnr Fort George & West Sts; mains US$4-6; lunch & dinner) Here you'll find reasonable quality Chinese food, including a vast menu of chop sueys and sweet-and-sour dishes. The dining room is spartan, but it's a good place to take in the hustle and bustle of West St – or to order take-out.

Survival Beach Restaurant (☎ 384-4730; 24 Allan Ave; mains US$5-10; breakfast, lunch & dinner) In addition to the usual local fare, natural juices and the best jelly coconut in town, this choice shack serves a tasty dish made with coconut milk, pumpkin, Irish potato, garlic, scallion, thyme, okra, string beans and three kinds of peas, served with sides of cabbage and callaloo. Just ask for the vital I-tal stew (US$5). Tip from Oliver the owner: call in advance.

Shadows (☎ 993-3823; 40 W Palm Ave; mains US$6-24; breakfast, lunch & dinner) With tables surrounding a comfortable outdoor bar set back from the street, this casual place serves good Jamaican and Chinese. The seafood specials are always a hit.

Juici-Beef Patties Chicken Place Coronation Bakery (William St) is a good spot for cheap patties. (☎ 993-4984; 29 Harbour St; mains US$3-5; lunch & dinner) serves good for fried chicken. (☎ 993-2710; 18 West St) is known for its doughnutlike pastries called 'holey bulla' and other desserts. For fresh, oven-baked bread, try **Three Star Lion Bakery** (☎ 993-3007; 27 West St).

If self-catering, **Kamal's Variety** (☎ 993-2756; 12 West St) is a well-stocked grocery store with a currency exchange desk offering competitive rates.

Midrange & Top End

Anna Banana's Restaurant & Sports Bar (☎ 715-6533; 7 Allan Ave; breakfast US$4, seafood dinners US$12-16; breakfast, lunch & dinner) Overlooking a small beach on the southern lip of the harbor, this breezy restaurant-bar specializes in hearty Jamaican breakfasts, jerk or barbecued chicken and pork and, for dinner, large plates of conch and lobster prepared the local way. The curried goat is particularly good. There are two pool tables, darts and friendly, accommodating service.

our pick **Dickie's Best Kept Secret** (☎ 809-6276; breakfast/dinner US$12/25; breakfast & dinner) Almost too well kept a secret for its own good, Dickie's

PORT ANTONIO & NORTHEAST COAST

is an unsigned hut on the A4, less than 2km west of Port Antonio that offers enormous five-course meals in two small rooms perched over the sea. Dickie and his wife Joy promise to cook anything you want (provided they can get the ingredients). Invariably, the meal begins with a palate-cleansing fruit plate followed by soup and a callaloo omelette. Just when you think you can't eat another bite, the main course – typically garlic lobster or fresh fish – arrives. Dickie's has only a few tables, so reservations are essential. The owners serve no alcohol, but you may bring your own.

Norma's at the Marina (☎ 993-9510; Ken Wright Cruise Ship Pier; mains $11-20; ⏰ lunch & dinner) Fronting a lovely white-sand beach, this quality restaurant can be a forlorn place – but some might find the solitude blissfully peaceful. Steaks, chops and fish prepared in the continental style are served at outdoor tables overlooking the Errol Flynn Marina.

ENTERTAINMENT

Roof Club (11 West St; weekend entry US$5; ⏰ late Thu-Sun) This is Port Antonio's infamous hang-loose, rough-around-the-edges reggae bar. Young men and women move from partner to partner. You're fair game for any stranger who wants to try to extract a drink from you. It's relatively dead midweek, when entry is free. But on weekends it hops with Crazy Saturdays, as well as on Thursday – 'Ladies Nite.'

Club La Best (5 West St; ⏰ 9:30-till the last person leaves) The newest, liveliest spot in Port Antonio, La Best assumes a different identity depending on the evening. Fridays are dancehall and ladies' nights, Sundays groove to a mellow blend of reggae and old-school R&B, and periodic live shows occur Saturdays.

Shanshy Beach (☎ 815-7411; general admission free, events US$3; ⏰ 8am-2am) This pretty but badly maintained stretch of sand 2km west of Port Antonio has a big, bad sound system. An area DJ collective called Big Bad Trouble International spins for theme nights including the After Work Jam on Friday featuring dancehall music; Cranked Saturdays with hip-hop, R&B and reggae; and Talent Explosion Sundays featuring local flair. Signs reading 'No Gun Salute' forbid the carrying of concealed weapons. There's a restaurant and bar.

Shadows (☎ 993-3823; 40 W Palm Ave) A less rowdy option than most, this place plays vintage music on Tuesday and Sunday. Other nights it can verge on comatose.

Anna Banana's Restaurant & Sports Bar (☎ 715-6533; 7 Allan Ave) This beachside bar is the place to go for darts, pool and a rum punch. Friday heats up with the help of local DJs.

Lanza Lawn (cnr Smatt & Summers Town Rds; admission US$5; ⏰ Tue, Thu & Fri) This popular venue goes nuts on Crazy Fridays as local DJs trade grooves and pass the mic. Sister P (see below) invites the public to nyahbinghi drumming sessions here on Tuesday and Thursday nights.

You can watch cricket at the **Folly Oval Cricket Ground** (Allan Ave), on the east side of East Harbour.

SHOPPING

Musgrave Market (West St) This has a craft market on its north side. Look for a stand called 'Rock Bottom' selling well-made crafts and reggae-inspired duds.

Portland Art Gallery (☎ 882-7732; 2 West Palm Ave) A simple gallery and studio staffed by Hopeton Cargill, a Port Antonio realist painter. He's delighted to act as an ambassador for the local art scene.

Cooyah Designs (☎ 993-4207; 2nd fl, Village of St George, Fort George St) This shop specializes in 'roots wear' clothing with original designs.

Lioness (☎ 715-3529; 10 Matthews Ave) A small shop that sells clothing, drumming CDs, crafts and art. It's run by Sister P, a woman regarded by many to be the heart and soul of the community. Sister P also organizes the Fi Wi Sinting festival (p142).

Jamaica Agricultural Society shop (☎ 993-3743; 11 Harbour St; ⏰ 9am-5pm Mon-Fri) This organization has been championing the cause of the small farmer in Jamaica since 1895. Here you can buy local honey, spices and Blue Mountain coffee at a fair price.

The **City Centre Plaza** (Harbour St) has a number of shops including **Photo Bank One Hour Photo Service** (☎ 993-2716; City Centre Plaza, Harbour St).

GETTING THERE & AROUND

Air

Ken Jones Aerodrome (☎ 913-3173), 9km west of Port Antonio, was no longer receiving flights from Air Jamaica Express at last visit. These days the only incoming flights are private planes and chartered flights of International Airlink and TimAir (see p197).

Most upscale hotels offer free transfers to and from the Ken Jones Aerodrome for guests. There's no shuttle-bus service, although you can flag down any minibus or route taxi passing along the A4. A tourist taxi will cost about US$10.

Boat
The **Errol Flynn Marina at Port Antonio** (☎ 993-3209, 715-6044; www.themarinaatportantonio.com) offers customs clearance for private vessels.

Car
There's an office in town for **Eastern Rent-a-Car** (☎ 993-3624; 16 Harbour St) and gas stations on W Palm Ave, Fort George St and Harbour St.

Public Transportation
There's a **transportation center** (Gideon Ave) that extends along the waterfront. Buses, minibuses and route taxis leave regularly for Annotto Bay, Port Maria (where you change for Ocho Rios) and Kingston.

Taxi
Taxi transfers from the Montego Bay and Kingston airports, are offered by **JUTA** (Port Antonio ☎ 993-2684; Kingston ☎ 979-0778; Montego Bay ☎ 952-0813) and **Island Car Rentals** (Kingston ☎ 926-8861; Norman Manley International Airport ☎ 924-8075; Donald Sangster International Airport ☎ 952-5771).

For licensed taxis, call **JUTA/Port Antonio Cab Drivers' Co-op** (☎ 993-2684). Taxis hang out by hotels. They can also be found pretty easily in town, notably along Gideon Ave and the intersection of Bridge St and Summers Town Rd. Licensed taxis to Port Antonio cost about US$100 from Kingston and US$230 from Montego Bay.

EAST OF PORT ANTONIO

PORT ANTONIO TO FAIRY HILL
Beyond the turnoff for Folly the A4 meanders east of Port Antonio through the coastal villages of Drapers, Frenchman's Cove and Fairy Hill. This is where most visitors to Port Antonio, and indeed to Portland, will find accommodations and explore the nearby Rio Grande Valley, Nonsuch Caves, Blue Lagoon as well as the luxuriate sands of Frenchman's Cove, San San Beach and Winnifred Beach.

While the hotels and restaurants of Drapers, Frenchman's Cove and Fairy Hill will accommodate most budgets and tastes, be sure to venture into the local communities, small as they are. Portlanders are among the most gracious of all Jamaicans, and their acquaintance enhances any visit to their parish.

Information
In the little hamlet of Drapers is a small **post office** (Hwy A4; 8am-4pm Mon-Fri, 8am-noon Sat), and a **police station** (☎ 993-7315) just east of Frenchman's Cove.

Sights
TRIDENT CASTLE
Just 3km east of Port Antonio, the road circles around the deep Turtle Crawle Bay. Squatting atop the western headland is a magnificent gleaming-white castle built in the 1980s by Baroness Elisabeth Siglindy Stephan von Stephanie Thyssen. This is Trident Castle, part of the Trident Hotel & Villas resort. The architect, Earl Levy, eventually took over the property after a tiff with the baroness.

At the time of writing the castle was for sale.

FRENCHMAN'S COVE
This small cove, just east of Drapers, 8km from Port Antonio, boasts one of the prettiest **beaches** (admission US$5; Wed-Mon) for miles. A stream winds lazily to a white-sand beach that shelves steeply into the water. Bring insect repellent. There's a snack bar serving jerk chicken and fish (US$7 to US$9), alfresco showers, bathrooms and a secure parking lot.

SAN SAN BEACH
San San (☎ 993-7300; entrance US$5; 10am-4pm) is a private beach used by residents of the villas on Alligator Head, and by guests of Goblin Hill, Fern Hill and Jamaica Palace hotels. Passersby, however, can gain access. It has a bar and restaurant, snorkeling equipment (US$10 per day) and kayaks (US$25 per hour).

BLUE LAGOON
The waters that launched Brooke Shields' movie career (and the site of a less-famous Jacques Cousteau dive), the Blue Lagoon is by any measure one of the most beautiful spots in Jamaica. The 55m-deep 'Blue Hole' (as it is known locally) opens to the sea through a narrow funnel, but is fed by freshwater springs that come in at about 40m deep. Its

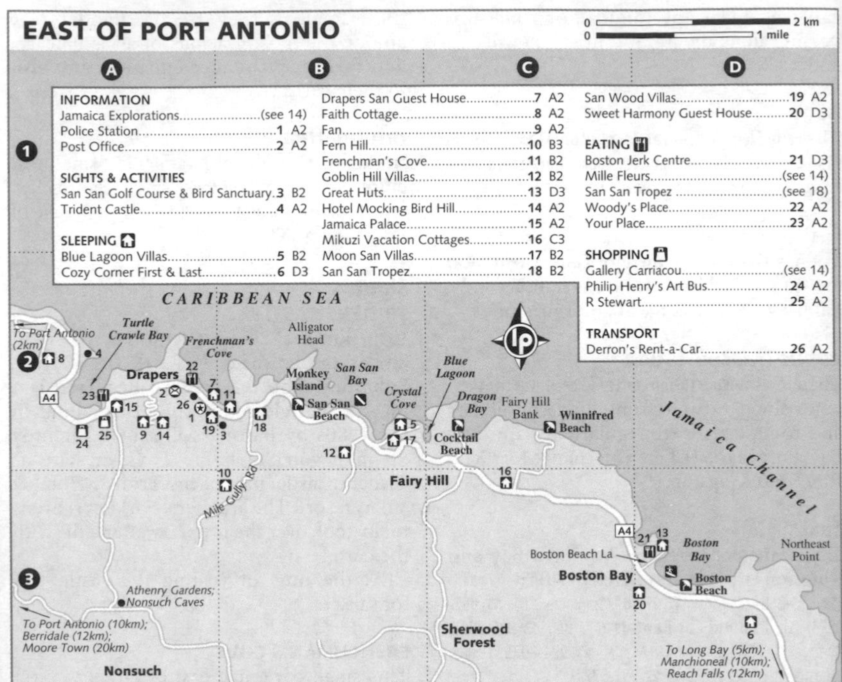

color changes through every shade of jade and emerald during the day, and you're welcome to take a dip.

Here you'll also encounter boat operators eager to take you on a short boat ride (US$15) to nearby **Cocktail Beach** (where parts of the Tom Cruise vehicle *Cocktail* was filmed) and lovely, undeveloped Monkey Island, a short distance away.

The lagoon is public property and accessible from the road. Tours may demand an entrance 'donation,' but J$200 (about US$3) should assuage them. At last visit the restaurant adjacent to the lagoon, which had closed following Hurricane Ivan, was under construction, and its completion is expected late 2008.

FAIRY HILL & WINNIFRED BEACH

Thirteen kilometers east of Port Antonio, Fairy Hill is a small clifftop hamlet. A dirt road from here leads steeply downhill to Winnifred Beach – up until recently a great place to hang with 'real' Jamaicans.

At last visit, the vendors who had long done once-brisk business at Winnifred Beach, had been evicted by the UDC and fence posts had been set up around the property. The UDC reportedly intends to develop the beach as an eco-attraction, but many local residents who have always enjoyed free access are wary of the plan. In February 2008 the government agreed to hear the lawsuit between local activists fighting to keep it accessible to local community, but at the time of writing there had been no resolution to the dispute.

Activities

Good **scuba diving** abounds: the shoreline east of Port Antonio boasts 13km of interconnected coral reefs and walls at an average of 100m to 300m offshore. Alligator Head is known for big sponge formations and black corals. Hammerhead sharks are common at Fairy Hill Bank.

For dive tours, instruction and equipment, contact **Lady G'Diver** (p127) at the Errol Flynn Marina.

San San Golf Course & Bird Sanctuary (☎ 993-7645; 9/18 holes US$50/70; 8am-5pm) is an 18-hole course laid out along valleys surrounded by rain forest. The bird sanctuary comprises primary forest and is not developed for tourism.

Sleeping

Some of Jamaica's most pleasant hotels, villas and guest houses are found along this stretch of coast.

BUDGET

our pick **Drapers San Guest House** (☎/fax 993-7118; www.go-jam.com/drapersan-e.html; Hwy A4, Drapers; s $27, d US$48-52) Run by Carla Gullotta, an activist who is culturally and politically 'plugged in,' this rambling yet cozy little house comprises two cottages with five doubles and one single room (two share a bathroom), all with fans, louvered windows and hot water. One unit is two-story, with a thick wooden staircase and a kitchen. There's a small beach with snorkeling just a few meters from the house. It's all very family-oriented, and there's a comfy lounge and communal kitchen. Rates include breakfast; dinner can be served by arrangement.

Mikuzi Vacation Cottages (☎ 978-4859; www.mikuzijamaica.com; Hwy A4, Fairy Hill; r US$35-65, cottages US$100) This economical place, set in pleasingly landscaped grounds, provides a perfect hideaway. Two tastefully appointed cottages and a small house are presided over by a warm and attentive caretaker. The cheaper garden cottage lacks a kitchen. Discounts are given for longer stays.

MIDRANGE

Faith Cottage (☎ 993-3703; www.go-jam.com/faith-e.html; Dolphin Bay; s/d US$60/75; P) Inland from Dolphin Bay, this is a gracious, pink-painted hotel with turrets and gables. It has nine spacious rooms with small TVs, fans and modern, modest decor. There's a small pool and the owner takes loving care of her guests. Meals on request.

Fan (☎ 993-7259; Drapers; villa incl breakfast US$100) In the hills behind Drapers overlooking the harbor is this beautiful villa rental with gingerbread trim, a large living room and a separate dining room in the guest apartment. Meals can be provided on request. It's a bargain! Reservations are made through the Port Antonio Guest House Association (p130).

Fern Hill (☎ 993-7375, 993-7531; www.fernhillclubhotel.com; Mile Gully Rd, San San; r/ste US$80/115, 1-/2-bedroom villas US$147/265; P) On a breezy hilltop at San San, up Mile Gully Rd, the 16 spacious though slightly jaded twin-level units are spread across the hillside, and each has a balcony beyond French doors. Suites have mezzanine bedrooms and their own hot tubs; most have gratifying views of the sea. When there's a full house, a mento band entertains on weekends.

San San Tropez (☎ 993-7213; www.sansantropez.com; Hwy A4, San San Bay; s/d US$99/140, 2-bedroom ste $195; P) This Italian-run hotel offers gracious, well-lit, cross-ventilated, air-con rooms and suites. The furnishings are modern and graced by bright tropical decor. There's a sun deck. Meal plans are offered in a restaurant affording splendid views. It gives passes to San San Beach.

Frenchman's Cove (☎ 933-7270; www.frenchmanscove.com; Hwy A4, Frenchman's Cove; r/ste US$120/135, 1-/2-/3-bedroom cottages US$160/225/295; P) An old great house with 10 rooms and two suites, plus 18 one-, two- and three-bedroom stone cottages amid the broad green swathe. Facilities are minimal, but ready access to one of Jamaica's prettiest beaches makes amends.

Moon San Villas (☎ 993-7600; www.moonsanvilla.com; Hwy A4, Fairy Hill; 1-/2-/3-bedroom US$155/310/460; P) Sitting above Blue Lagoon, this is a tastefully decorated three-level house with a TV/VCR lounge and four bedrooms, all with wide windows, fans and their own utterly romantic decor. Two rooms have king-sized beds. The bargain rates include a gourmet breakfast and passes to San San Beach. French-inspired meals are offered on request.

TOP END

Goblin Hill Villas (☎ 993-7443; www.goblinhillvillas.com; Goblin Hill Rd; 1-bedroom villa US$140-215, 2-bedroom villa US$225-295; P) Popular with families, this 5-hectare hilltop estate above San San Beach offers 16 two-bedroom and 12 one-bedroom villas, fully equipped and surrounded by lawns and forest. Most have views down to San San Bay. A meandering nature trail encircles the property. The villas are huge and have massive open windows and wide verandas. Each comes with its own private maid and butler (optional), but has neither telephone nor TV. The resort has a TV lounge and reading room, two tennis courts and the Tree Bar built around a massive fig tree.

Jamaica Palace (☎ 993-7720; www.jamaica-palacehotel.com; Hwy A4; r deluxe/superior US$178/198, ste US$240; P) A somewhat aloof neoclassical property overlooking Turtle Crawle Bay. Artworks dot the property, while the cavernous 24 rooms and 55 suites boast king-sized beds, crystal chandeliers, period antiques and Georgian bay windows. In the landscaped grounds is a 35m-long pool shaped like the island of Jamaica. Rates include tax and service charge.

Hotel Mocking Bird Hill (☎ 993-7267; www.hotelmockingbirdhill.com; Mocking Bird Hill Rd; r US$165-255, ste US$305-450;) The trek up a winding dirt road to this romantic, 'eco-chic' 10-room property in the hills above Frenchman's Cove is well worth it. All rooms are lovingly appointed with well-chosen fabrics and modern art and appliances. Most boast ocean views from private balconies. Facilities include a Caribbean-bright lounge and a bar, the Gallery Carriacou plus a variety of health and wellness services, including massage. Meals at Mille Fleurs are sublime. Trails lead through the lush hillside gardens…fabulous for bird-watching!

San Wood Villas (☎ 995-5788, 993-7302; rose@geejam.com; off Hwy A4, San San Bay; d without/with meals US$400/600; P) Home of Gee Jam recording studios, this sprawling, well-conceived 'rock-and-roll hotel' offers classy cabins, suites in a fabulously decorated house, and a large studio with a kitchenette that resembles a Caribbean-styled New York City loft. Lodging is offered intermittently for much of the year, when the place is not occupied by visiting luminaries like No Doubt, Keith Richards and India.Arie. Of course there's an attractive pool, exercise room and hot tub, as well as spa services and yoga. Meals are served as part of a meal plan. The owner, Jon Baker, is a music industry veteran with a taste for hip-hop and reggae. He is choosy about accepting guests, preferring 'characters' with a 'good story.' Advance reservations required.

Blue Lagoon Villas (☎ 993-8491, in the USA 800-237-3237; www.bluelagoonvillas.com; Hwy A4; 2/3 bedroom villas per week US$7500/8500, 4-bedroom villa US$9500-12,500; P) Immediately west of Blue Lagoon and facing Monkey Island, these oft-photographed, flamboyantly priced villas provide a stunning setting and real luxury. Each two- to four-bedroom villa is exquisitely furnished and staffed with a housekeeper/cook and houseman. Sea kayaks are provided. They are rented solely by the week, and rates include airport transfers.

Eating & Drinking

This stretch of road has many accommodations but few independent restaurants. Most folks eat at their hotels – which generally have restaurants open to nonguests – or are catered to by the staff of their villa.

Your Place (Hwy A4, Drapers; mains US$2-7; lunch & dinner) This roadside newcomer has a small indoor dining area and an outdoor patio, both of which are great for enjoying its chicken (barbecue or stewed) or fish dishes. Be sure to order a side of festival (a fried biscuit shaped like a sausage), which is particularly good here.

Woody's Place (☎ 993-7888; Hwy A4, Drapers; mains US$3-9; lunch & dinner) This pleasant spot – with an outdoor patio and an indoor counter that doubles as a local meeting place – prepares tremendous hotdogs and burgers, grilled cheese and Jamaican dinners to order. Vegetarians are catered for by a veggie burger heaped with stewed callaloo.

our pick **Mille Fleurs** (☎ 993-7267; Hotel Mocking Bird Hill; Mocking Bird Hill Rd; 3-course dinner US$45; 7am-10pm) Come for a rum punch at the bar whose balcony offers great views of Port Antonio across the bay, then go downstairs to this candlelit gourmet restaurant for one of the best meals on the island. Nouvelle-Jamaican specialties from a changing menu invariably including a homemade pasta dish. A three-course dinner, which has a vegetarian option, ends with a trolley of regional liqueurs. The special Mille Fleurs continental breakfast costs US$18.50. Reservations required.

San San Tropez (☎ 993-7213; Hwy A4, San San Bay; mains US$12-25; breakfast, lunch & dinner) This is the place to go for great Italian seafood and pizzas. The menu is vast, and there's a large wine list.

Shopping

Gallery Carriacou (☎ 993-7267; Hotel Mocking Bird Hill; 10am-5pm Thu-Tue) boasts a fabulous array of paintings, ceramics, sculptures and other quality works of fine art by local artists. It also hosts workshops and cultural events. En route, you might call in at **Philip Henry's Art Bus** (☎ 993-3162; Hwy A4), roadside at Turtle Crawle Bay, to check out his array of woodcarving and assorted crafts.

In Drapers you'll find the roadside gallery of renowned self-taught artist **R Stewart** (Hwy A4), who more than likely will be working on his latest canvas at the edge of the road. His whimsical, masterful depictions of Jamaican life regularly inspire impulse buys from passersby.

Getting There & Away

Buses run infrequently between Port Antonio and Boston Bay and to other points beyond. Minibuses and route taxis (US$1 to US$2.50) run more frequent services.

Derron's Rent-a-Car (☎ 993-7111; Hwy A4) has an outlet in Drapers.

BOSTON BAY

Boston Bay, 2.5km east of Fairy Hill, is a pocket-sized beach shelving into jewellike turquoise waters. High surf rolls into the bay and locals spend much of their time surfing (you can rent boards on the beach). Few dispute its reputation as the best surfing spot in Jamaica.

Alongside its surfing hot spot status, Boston is equally as famous for the highly spiced jerk chicken and pork sizzling on many smoky barbecue pits along the roadside. Today, jerk has garnered a worldwide fan base but until the 1950s was virtually unknown outside this area. The practice of marinating meat with jerk seasoning was first developed centuries ago not far from here by the Maroons, and the modest shacks at Boston Bay were among the first to invite attention.

Sweet Harmony Guest House (☎ 993-8779; fax 993-3178; Hwy A4; r US$50-60) offers three clean rooms with double beds and mosquito nets, wall fans and shower-baths with cold water only. There's a pleasant sunny veranda, where guests while away the hours and days. Meals are available by arrangement. You'll find it about 400m inland from the A4, just east of the beach.

our pick **Great Huts** (☎ 993-8888; www.greathuts.com; Boston Beach Lane; African-style tent per person US$60-139, tree house US$157) This is a notable exception to the general rule that accommodations in Boston Bay are simple. Perched on a scenic crag overlooking Boston Bay, it has nine tents or huts, each decorated with distinctive and imaginative Afrocentric design, and two spacious 'tree houses.' These two-story open-air structures have verandas, bamboo-walled bedrooms, Jacuzzi baths and kitchenettes. Alfresco showers are enhanced by the squawking of a small aviary of parrots. If you can tear yourself from your room, the Cliff Bar, featuring excellent pizzas and superlative views of the sea, and the hotel's own beach on the rocks below will demand attention.

Cozy Corner First & Last (☎ 993-8450; Hwy A4; d US$20) is a quiet private home with two simple but nicely appointed rooms with fans, TV and hot water. It's just south of Boston Bay, on the roadside about 200m from the shore. There's a small bar, but for food you're on your own.

our pick **Boston Jerk Centre** (Boston Beach Lane; 200g chicken US$4) is the best place to get jerked. A series of open-air stalls, the jerk center is popular with locals as well as tour groups. Get there early, as food tends to be sold out by mid-afternoon. (For more information about jerk, see p45).

A frequent habitué of the beach is the Maroon Prophet, a roots bush doctor selling his handmade tonic and blood cleanser made from roots and 'bush' according to tradition. Other roots tonic specialists sell their bitter brews here as well.

Boston Bay is 15km east of Port Antonio; buses (about US$1) and minibuses and route taxis (US$2.50) will get you there or back.

LONG BAY

Heading east from Boston, the road hugs the coast and passes through 8km of striking scenery. Waves chew at rocky headlands as magnificent frigate birds circle overhead like juvenile pterodactyls. Your destination is Long Bay, in one of the most dramatic settings in all of Jamaica. The 1.5km-wide bay has rose-colored sand, deep turquoise waters and breezes pushing the waves forcefully ashore. Canoes are drawn up on the beach, with fishing nets drying beside them.

Long Bay appeals to budget travelers as well as surfers, and has drawn a large number of expats who have put down roots and opened guesthouses. The lifestyle here is laid-back and rootsy, something like Negril felt 30 years ago.

There's a dangerous undertow, so avoid swimming, but surfers love the waves. Surfboards are often available for rent on the beach (per half-day US$10), as are boogie boards (US$2.50).

The **public library** (☎ 913-7957; Hwy A4; per 30min US$1; 🕒 Mon-Sat) offers internet access.

Sleeping

Likkle Paradise (☎ 913-7702; r US$30) Up an unnamed lane just south of the library, this friendly place offers two clean rooms with

HURRICANE DEAN

On August 20, 2007, Hurricane Dean slammed its way through the Caribbean, the eye passing the southern coast of Jamaica without causing any of the havoc that was feared. Yet though the storm essentially passed Jamaica by, its winds stirred the sea to pound the east coast, and Long Bay was badly hit.

Comparatively speaking, the damage wasn't that bad. The palms on Long Bay beach were toppled, and at last visit a small forest of stumps lined the sands. But they should grow back quickly. Similarly, many of the hotels and cafés were forced to close and took the opportunity to upgrade with a new coat of paint.

As Jamaicans are fond of saying: 'an' so it go.' Translation: it goes with the territory.

private bathrooms and a quiet patio overlooking a small lawn and garden. Guests enjoy full kitchen privileges; the owner lives upstairs.

Rose Garden Guest House (☎ 913-7311, 382-3277; Rose Garden Rd; r US$30-40, 4-bed apt US$50) Located at the southern end of town, this simple guest house provides good value, particularly for groups. On the top floor, from which guests enjoy a bird's-eye view of the sea, there are two tiny bedrooms, a loft and a kitchenette. There's an additional bedroom with two beds and communal kitchen downstairs, and a kid-sized dunk pool in the garden.

Yahimba (☎ 382-6384, 402-4101; www.yahimba.com; Hwy A4; cabana US$75) Situated right on the beach next to Cool Runnings Beach Bar & Grill, these brightly painted African-style cabanas were badly hit by the hurricane. After being temporarily out of commission, the hotel is finally up and running. The location, smack bang in the middle of the public beach, may not afford a lot of privacy – or, for that matter, security – but those mesmerized by the waves pouring in may not notice.

Rose Hill Cottage (☎ 913-7452; Rose Garden Rd; cottage US$40-90) This private cottage is offered by Peter-Paul Zahl, a seasoned German author who has long called Jamaica home. Perched above the main road and affording tremendous views of the beach, the self-contained cottage has a small bedroom, sleeping loft, living area and kitchen. There are plenty of German-language books lying about. Your host, who inhabits a house a stone's throw away, has an insouciant air and the gift of the gab. The cottage is self-catering, but a delicious Caribbean dinner is offered nightly.

Villa Seascape (☎ 913-7762; Hwy A4; d/villa US$60/120; P) At this well-maintained guesthouse the sea licks the walls of the veranda. Two adjacent buildings contain three modest, nicely furnished rooms with fans. In each, two rooms share a bathroom. Breakfast is included; other meals are prepared to order.

Hotel Jamaican Colors (☎ 913-7716, 893-5185; www.hoteljamaicancolors.com; Hwy A4; 1-/2-/3-bedroom cottage US$59/65/95, house US$100-195; P) This spiffy hotel located on the cliffs 2km south of Long Bay offers 12 comfortable and immaculate cottages. Each has a modern bathroom and comfortable double bed draped with mosquito netting. Also on the premises is a family-friendly house with two bedrooms, loft and kitchenette. There's an open-air restaurant featuring the proprietor's astonishing sand collection, displayed on the wall in labeled test tubes. The hotel has an inviting pool and large Jacuzzi bath. The French hosts also arrange excursions to area attractions and dispense information of interest to surfers.

Eating

The following restaurants are all located on the beach.

Sweet Daddy's (☎ 913-7475; meals US$3.50-12) A local favorite serving fresh fish, lobster and hearty breakfasts. The cook and proprietor says that she 'takes good care of vegetarians.'

Cool Runnings Beach Bar & Grill (☎ 387-9305; meals US$4-7; lunch & dinner) This beach bar and restaurant is a good first stop; the proprietor represents local guest houses and can help you find accommodations. The food is well prepared and tasty – everything is made from scratch, including a wickedly rich mayonnaise. One of the signature dishes is a lovely coconut cream fish (US$8). On Saturday night there's a beach party playing old roots reggae and R&B.

Chill-Out (☎ 913-7171; meals US$4-10; lunch & dinner) Just down the beach from Cool Runnings, this is another popular thatched beachfront eatery and bar. Try the steamed fish and vegetables liberally seasoned with allspice (US$9). Sound-system parties are frequently held in the evenings.

Numerous rustic beachside shacks sell inexpensive Jamaican fare (US$2 to US$6) and double as no-frills 'rum shops' with music at night.

Getting There & Away

Minibuses and route taxis run between Port Antonio and Long Bay (US$2.50).

MANCHIONEAL

pop 2200

A sleepy fishing village 11km southeast of Long Bay, Manchioneal is set in a deep, scalloped bay with calm turquoise waters and a wide, shallow beach where colorful pirogues are drawn up. It's a center for lobster fishing and the surf is killer – July is said to be the best month.

Just as Boston Bay is famous for its jerk pork and chicken, Manchioneal is a culinary destination for roast fish or conch in foil, which you can purchase from small shacks on the beach. There are plenty of jerk stalls and rum shops, some serving steamed fish, fish tea, roast conch and so on.

Three kilometers southeast of Manchioneal, **Ennises Bay Beach** is a great place to spend a lost afternoon shooting the breeze with local Rastafarians. There's a refreshment stand and lovely views of the John Crow Mountains.

Three kilometers north of Manchioneal, **Christmas River Heartical Roots Corner** (☎ 993-6138, 437-3742; r US$30), is celebrated by surfers who come to set up camp in a thatched, no-frills Arawak-style octagonal cabin with two beds. Sizable waves pour into Christmas Bay, serving to beguile and occasionally thrill those traveling with a board (the proprietor may be persuaded to loan one). There's an outdoor bathroom and shower, and a second small cottage with a single bed. Bring mosquito repellent! The owners' pals – full of bravura – hang at a bar serving simple meals to order.

our pick Zion Country (☎ 993-0435; www.zioncountry.com; s/d US$40/50) Hit hard by Hurricane Dean, this place atop the shoreline cliffs, about 2km south of the Hwy A4 turnoff for Reach Falls, has bounced back admirably. An excellent backpacker and ecotourist haven, it holds four appealing hillside log-and-bamboo cottages sharing two bathrooms, with hammocks on the veranda and three showers. There is a bar and small restaurant set in a lush garden. A private beach, which has been replanted after the hurricane, receives year-round visits from manatees.

Zion Country offers some excellent tours, including a good-value three-day excursion into the Blue Mountains, including an ascent of the peak (US$270 for two people). There's a Kingston highlights tour (US$170 for two people), and van transfers are offered to Kingston (US$110 one way) and Montego Bay (US$220 one way).

Bryan's Restaurant (☎ 993-6518; Main St; meals US$2-5) This rooftop eatery offers simple but delicious Jamaican fare, served on a sunny veranda. Pay for your meal at the B&L Supermarket on the 1st floor before heading up the stairs.

For masks and other fine woodwork, Winsome Shaw operates a **crafts' stall** (☎ 335-6057) on the road to Reach Falls.

REACH FALLS

All of Jamaica's tumbling cascades are refreshing, but this waterfall is downright rejuvenating. This peaceful spot is surrounded by virgin rain forest, and features a series of cascades tumbling over limestone tiers from one hollowed, jade-colored pool to another.

Unfortunately Jamaica's UDC took over the **falls** (🕒 8:30am-4:30pm Wed-Sun; adult/child US$10/5) and while the ensuing clean-up makes it more tourist-friendly than before, the prices are prohibitive for the community and the guides are not the locals who used to earn their living from tours. At last visit the Mandingo Cave, the crown jewel of the falls, was off limits while it got the clean-up treatment from the UDC.

To get here, you can catch any of the minibuses and route taxis that run between Kingston and Port Antonio via Morant Bay, get off in Manchioneal, then walk or hitchhike 3km uphill to Reach Falls (the turnoff is signed, 1km south of Manchioneal). A charter taxi from Port Antonio costs about US$50 roundtrip.

RIO GRANDE VALLEY

The Rio Grande rushes down from 900m in the Blue Mountains and has carved a huge gorge that forms a deep V-shaped wedge between the Blue Mountains to the west and the John Crow Mountains to the east.

Red Hassell Rd runs south from Port Antonio and enters the Rio Grande Valley at Fellowship.

Activities

HIKING

Popular hikes include those to White Valley, known for its large population of giant swallowtail butterflies; to Dry River Falls; and to Scatter Falls and Fox Caves.

Other hikes are demanding, with muddy, overgrown trails and small rivers that require fording. Don't attempt to hike off the beaten path without a guide. The Corn Puss Gap trail is particularly difficult, as is the wild path from Windsor to Nanny Town.

Scatter Falls & Fox Caves

An excellent and easy hike takes you to Scatter Falls and Fox Caves, reached by crossing the Rio Grande on a bamboo raft at Berridale, then hiking for 30 minutes through a series of hamlets and banana groves. The falls tumble through a curtain of ferns into a pool where you can take a refreshing dip. There are changing rooms nearby as well as toilets, a campground, a bamboo-and-thatch bar, and a kitchen that serves a hot lunch – though this must be ordered in advance through Grand Valley Tours (see p130).

A steep, 15-minute hike from the falls leads to the caves, which have some intriguing formations, some of which resemble Rasta dreads. The roof is pitted with hollows in which tiny bats dangle, and you can see where the falls emanate from the caves.

As the path is unsigned and you'll be passing through private property, it's imperative that you visit accompanied by a guide.

Nanny Town

This former village stronghold belonging to the Windward Maroons is perched on the brink of a precipitous spur on the northeastern flank of Blue Mountain Peak, about 16km southwest of Moore Town as the crow flies. It is named for an 18th-century Ashanti warrior priestess and Maroon leader, now a national hero (see opposite). In 1734 English troops captured and destroyed Nanny Town.

It's a tough 16km hike from Windsor, 5km north of Moore Town. Grand Valley Tours has a three-day guided hike. There are numerous side trails, and it's easy to get lost if you attempt to hike on your own.

Organized Hikes

Grand Valley Tours (p130) offers a series of guided hikes that include simple walks to places like Scatter Falls and Fox Caves (US$35 to US$40), challenging hikes, such as the trip to Nanny Town (US$200), and overnight hikes, where you sleep either in a tent or in rustic lodgings with bunk beds. Prices depend on the number of people. Grande Valley also offers 'bush' camping, mountain-biking tours (US$45) and horseback rides (US$40). At the end of each excursion, you'll be well fed, often with local cuisine prepared in a private home.

Valley Hikes (p130) is also recommended for guided hikes into the Rio Grande Valley, plus Maroon culture tours, horseback riding, bird-watching and other trips.

RAFTING

Errol Flynn supposedly initiated rafting on the Rio Grande during the 1940s, when moonlight raft trips were considered the ultimate activity among the fashionable.

Today paying passengers make the 11km journey of one to three hours (depending on water level) from Grant's Level (Rafter's Village), about 2km south of Berridale, to Rafter's Rest at St Margaret's Bay. When the moon is full, unforgettable moonlight trips are offered. These are less regimented; your guide will be happy to pull over on a moon-drenched riverbank so that you can canoodle with your sweetie or just open the ice chests to release the beer.

Reserve at **Rio Grande Experience Ltd** (☎ 913-5434, 993-5778; Berridale; per raft US$60, double for full-moon rides; 🕑 8:30am-4pm). You can buy tickets at Rafter's Village at Grant's Level if you don't have reservations.

Hotel pickups are offered, or you can have your car driven to Rafter's Rest to await your return (US$15). The drivers are insured, but make clear to them that you expect them to drive slowly and safely.

A route taxi from Port Antonio to Grant's Level costs about US$2; they depart from the corner of Bridge St and Summers Town Rd. Licensed taxis cost about US$20 roundtrip.

ATHENRY GARDENS & NONSUCH CAVES

Athenry Gardens, high in the hills southeast of Port Antonio, is a former coconut plantation and agricultural research center, now a lush garden that boasts many exotic and native species. The highlight is bat-filled **Nonsuch Caves** (☎ 919-6656, 779-7144; admission US$7.50; 9am-4pm), 14 separate chambers full of stalagmites and stalactites.

The caves and garden are about 11km southeast of Port Antonio via Red Hassell Rd. After 3km along Red Hassell Rd there's a Y-fork at Breastworks. The right fork leads to Berridale and the Rio Grande; take the left for Nonsuch.

You can also reach Nonsuch Caves from Drapers via the same road that circles back to Port Antonio.

MOORE TOWN

This one-street village, 16km south of Port Antonio, stretches uphill for several hundred meters along the Wildcane River. Today it looks like any other Jamaican village, but is important as the former base of the Windward Maroons. The village was founded in 1739 following the signing of a peace treaty granting the Maroons their independence. Moore Town is still run semi-autonomously by a council of 24 elected members headed by a 'colonel.' The locals attempt to keep alive their lore and legends, and still bring out their *abengs* (goat horns) and talking drums on occasion.

Visitors expressing interest in the fascinating history of the Windward Maroons will be warmly welcomed. On arrival, it's considered polite to pay respects to Colonel Wallace Sterling (☎ 898-5714). If he's not about, you may be approached by one of his emissaries and asked for a small donation. Trails lead from Moore Town, including one to **Nanny Falls**, about 45 minutes away.

Grand Valley Tours (p130) leads trips, including a 'Moonlight at Moore Town' community tour that aims to connect visitors to the spirit of the Maroons.

Moore Town's sole site of interest is **Bump Grave**, at the southern, uppermost end of town. Topped by a flagpole flying the Maroon and Jamaican flags, the oblong stone and plaque mark the grave of national hero Nanny of the Maroons. There's a gate around the grave, but it can be opened for a small donation.

Moore Town is unsigned and lies in a hollow to the left of a Y-junction at Seaman's Valley; the road to the right continues via Alligator Church through the Upper Rio Grande Valley. In Moore Town the road dead-ends in the village.

Minibuses and route taxis operate to Moore Town from Port Antonio (about US$1.50 each way). A minibus from Port Antonio runs in early morning and again in early afternoon (US$1).

UPPER RIO GRANDE VALLEY

The road to the right of the Y-junction at Seaman's Valley leads via Alligator Church to Bowden Pen, 16km or so up the river valley. The paved road ends at Alligator Church. Beyond here, the dirt road is extremely rough and narrow and you'll need a 4WD.

The ranger station for Blue Mountains-John Crow National Park is at **Millbank**, 3km before Bowden Pen, near the summit ridge of the John Crow Mountains, which parallels the valley like a great castle wall. A trail leads to the **White River Falls**, a series of seven cascades. It's a tough trek through the rain forest.

A short distance above Bowden Pen the track begins rising more precipitously and the vegetation closes in. Don't push too far, for there is nowhere to turn your vehicle back. You can continue on foot across the Corn Puss Gap.

Valley Hikes (p130) and Grand Valley Tours (p130) offer tours; the latter operates a campsite just beyond Millbank. You must arrange with the company in advance. Both companies can also arrange lodging in private homes in the area.

A minibus from Port Antonio goes as far as Millbank, as do route taxis (US$2).

WEST OF PORT ANTONIO

PORT ANTONIO TO HOPE BAY

There's nothing inspirational about Hope Bay, which has a somewhat sad, gray beach. A loop drive, however, can be made from here up the Swift River Valley, where plantations grow cacao.

Both route taxis (US$1.50) and minibuses (US$1) pass Somerset Falls and Hope Bay between Annotto Bay and Port Antonio.

Sights

Somerset Falls (☎ 993-3115, 995-3354; Hwy A4; adult/child US$7/3; 9am-5pm), 14km west of Port Antonio, is hidden in a deep gorge about 3km east of Hope Bay. The Daniels River cascades down through a lush garden of ferns, heliconias, lilies and crotons. Visitors have to negotiate some steep, twisty steps.

The recently renovated site has a restaurant, bar, jerk pit, ice-cream shop and massage therapy space. Yet further in the falls themselves are mercifully unspoiled. They're also less touristy than those at Dunn's River given Portland's more low key tourist status.

The entrance fee includes a guided tour through a grotto by boat to the Hidden Fall which tumbles 10m into a jade-colored grotto. Bring a swimsuit to enjoy a large swimming area.

Sleeping & Eating

Rio Vista Resort & Villas (☎ 993-5444; fax 993-5445; www.riovistajamaica.com; Rafter's Rest; r US$65-95, ste US$70-105, 1-/2-bedroom villa US$135/175; P) Atop a ridge near the turnoff for Rafter's Rest on the Rio Grande, 6km west of Port Antonio, this is a superb option. This handsome modern house, built into the remains of an old plantation home, has an enviable setting high above the Rio Grande, with mountains behind – you'll find it hard to concentrate on breakfast from the patio. Five genteel villas have lofty ceilings and polished wood floors; three have two bedrooms and kitchen plus TV lounge. All units feature a kitchen, cable TV, ceiling fans and a housekeeper. Airport transfers and car rentals are available.

Buccaneers Room (☎ 993-5444; Rio Vista Resort & Villas; breakfast US$5-10, dinner US$12-28) This acclaimed restaurant serves beautifully conceived Jamaican fare prepared with handpicked herbs and produce from the capacious grounds of the Rio Vista Resort. The coffee that's served here is also grown on-site.

Shopping

Sundial (☎ /fax 913-0443; sundial@aol.com; Main St, Hope Bay) A colorful store that strives to bring you 'natural and traditional healing remedies from the laboratory of the Most High for what might be ailing you.' On the shelves you'll find booklets, videos and tonics produced from old Maroon recipes with ingredients including African eyebright, woodroot, manback and koromantee.

ORANGE BAY

The road between Hope Bay and Orange Bay takes an inland route and is wonderfully scenic with dense jungle foliage, open forests of towering palms and hillsides covered with tropical plants boasting leaves the size of elephant ears. You'll pass by huge stands of bamboo up on the ridge and expansive plantations of banana. Along the way there are simple roadside stands that sell produce, pepper shrimp and simple fare. You'll also pass **Pon Di Corner**, an excellent jerk center and rest stop covered with vivid mural paintings.

At Orange Bay the road rejoins the coast. Of interest is the picturesque old **rail station** that served the Kingston–Annotto Bay line until it ceased operation in 1983. The building now houses a video store as well as the daughter of the former stationmaster. Across the street is **Marsha's Pub**, which hosts sound-system parties in the evenings, rattling windows for miles around.

Almond Lodge (☎ 385-4139, 372-7929; d US$30-40; P), a roadside lodge with plenty of personality, offers several simple but clean fan-cooled rooms and bathrooms with no hot water, each containing one double bed. There's a pebble and black-sand beach which you are likely to have all to yourself, and a small restaurant and bar with pool table. The bar occasionally hosts parties.

BUFF BAY

pop 11,000

This is a small, neatly laid-out town in the midst of a major banana-producing area, with several colonial-era buildings of modest interest, centered on the Anglican church.

The post office is 100m east of the church. Buff Bay also has a small **hospital** (☎ 996-1478), and the **police station** (☎ 996-1497) is at the east end of town.

Fishdone Waterfalls is a beautiful spot on a private coffee plantation near Buff Bay. The falls are surrounded by rain forest, and there are trails for hiking.

Growing in popularity and importance is the annual culture festival **Fi Wi Sinting** (☎ 715-3529; www.fiwisinting.com; admission US$5) which celebrates the African heritage of Jamaican music, dance, song, storytelling and food. It's held the third weekend of February at **Nature's Way**, 5km east of Buff Bay. An African marketplace offers robes, batiks and jewelry, and performances are staged throughout the day. In a moving ritual, the official celebration comes to a close when libation is poured in remembrance of those who survived the 'middle passage,' a term designating the passage of slaves to Jamaica from Africa. A boat covered in flowers is released into the sea. The festival provides a rare opportunity to witness Kumina drumming, a tradition with direct ties to Africa, believed to be a form of communication with the dead. A Kumina drum circle keeps a sizable crowd dancing deep into the night.

For a snack or meal, head to **Kildare Villa Great House** (☎ 996-1240; Main St), at the eastern end of town. It's a colonial structure operating a well-stocked gift store selling patties and desserts. The Jamaican seafood restaurant upstairs offers patio dining and serves such fare as ackee, saltfish and brown stew chicken (US$7), and staples such as fried chicken and curried goat (US$4 to US$12). There's a grocery store attached.

Located on the coastal side of the raod to Orange Bay, **Blueberry Hill Jerk Centre** (US$2-7) has developed a well-deserved reputation for its pork and chicken, drenched in a punishing jerk sauce

BUFF BAY RIVER VALLEY

The B1 heads south from the town center and climbs 32km through the valley of the Buff Bay River to Hardwar Gap, at an elevation of 1370m, before dropping down to Kingston. Note that during the rainy season, the road is sometimes put out of commission by landslides, so check conditions before setting out.

ANNOTTO BAY

This erstwhile banana port is a downtrodden one-street town that springs to life for the Saturday market. Depressing shanties line the waterfront. The paltry remains of **Fort George**, and some gingerbread colonial-era structures with columned walkways, stand on Main St. The most intriguing is the venerable yellow-and-red brick **Baptist chapel**, built in 'village baroque' style in 1894, with cut-glass windows and curious biblical exhortations engraved at cornice height.

Three kilometers west of town is the junction of the A4 with the A3.

The town has a small **hospital** (☎ 996-2222), a **police station** (☎ 996-9169; Main St) and a **National Commercial Bank** (☎ 996-2213; Main St). The **Annotto Bay Branch Library** (☎ 996-2508; Hwy A4; per 30min US$1.25) offers internet access.

Nestled on the banks of the Penscar River at Long Road, **River Edge** (☎ 944-2673; riveredge99@hotmail.com; camping per person US$7, dm/apt per person US$20/35), about 13km inland from Annotto Bay. Primarily a campsite, it also has basically furnished dorm rooms and one simple studio apartment with kitchenette and private bathroom with hot water. You can camp on the lawns (tents are rented). Meals are by request.

The best place to eat in Annotto Bay is the **Human Service Station** (US$2-5), at the side of the road to Buff Bay as you're leaving town. It serves fish stews as well as chicken, many of whom can be seen roaming around the yard.

ROBIN'S BAY

Midway to Port Maria from Annotto Bay, on the A3, you'll pass a turnoff to the north that hugs a lonesome shoreline with gray-sand beaches backed by lagoons. After 4km you'll emerge in **Mt Pleasant Heights**, a fishing village nestled atop Don Christopher's Point, named for the Spanish guerrilla leader Don Cristobal Arnaldo de Ysassi, who led the resistance against the 1655 British invasion, culminating in the Battle of Rio Nuevo (see p160).

The paved road ends at Robin's Bay (known as Strawberry Fields in the 1970s, when it was a free-love haven for American hippies). There are persistent rumors about pirate's treasure still hidden away in the area's sea caves.

You can also reach Robin's Bay from Port Maria by a hiking trail that leads along one of the few stretches of Jamaican coastline that remains pristine. Locals can lead you to remote **Black Sand Beach**, and the **Kwaaman and Tacky Waterfalls**. In refreshing contrast to Jamaica's more famous – and thus more visited – waterfalls, Kwaaman and Tacky are so pristine and isolated that, if you stumbled across them wandering up the coast from Robin's Bay, you might be tempted to claim them as your own. Kwaaman Waterfall is a 32m cascade that tumbles into a clear pool you can swim in. Gazing up from the water at the contorted rockface behind the falls, you'll be able to make out what appears to be dreadlocks formed in the rock by the continual flow of water over centuries. Tacky Falls lacks the dreads but is equally worth the visit, particularly if the weather's calm and you can take a boat ride from Robin's Bay.

Creating an eyesore at the far end of Robin's Bay, the chintzy, ostentatious **Robin's Bay Village & Beach Resort** (☎ 361-2144, 361-2188; fax 968-0958;

s US$60-70, d US$65-75, cottage s/d US$85/95, 3-bedroom ste US$430; P) is a large, recently built hotel in want of guests. There are 43 rooms with standard amenities including phone and satellite TV; most are fan-cooled, but those in the superior category have air-conditioning. The huge two-story penthouse suites have polished-wood floors and full kitchen with formal dining room.

our pick **River Lodge** (☎ 995-3003, in Germany 089-74-999-797; www.river-lodge.com; s/d US$50/80, d cottages US$90-100) is a truly atmospheric option that has sprouted up from the ruins of a centuries-old Spanish pirate fort, established by longtime Jamaica resident Brigitta Fuchslocher. The rooms – which probably once were barracks for buccaneers – have white bleached-stone walls and blood-red floors, and are lit by skylights. The bathrooms (cold water only) are festooned with climbing ivy; the bathroom in the upstairs 'tower' room is alfresco. Meals are a social affair, served in a small thatched restaurant; rates include breakfast and dinner.

Also offered are two splendid cottages with privileged sea views, located less than 1km from the lodge. One is an octagonal bamboo hut with private bathroom and fridge, the other is a Moorish-style cottage with kitchenette and a delightful hearth on the patio, perfect for roasting fish. There's a romantic rooftop veranda.

River Lodge also coordinates local excursions, including a boat trip with local fishermen (US$20). The complex is now complemented by the aptly named Natural Vibes bar. Overlooking the sea it offers a menu largely devoted to seafood and there's a nightly bonfire and several hammocks.

Any one of the public vehicles that travel between Ocho Rios and Annotto Bay or Port Antonio will let you off at the junction to Robin's Bay on the A3. It's then a 6km walk to Robin's Bay. With good timing, you can connect with bus JR16A, which operates between Kingston and Robin's Bay, or with the few route taxis that run to Robin's Bay from the A3.

Ocho Rios & North Coast

Five hundred years after Christopher Columbus dropped anchor on the north-central coast, the region is booming with tourists. Ocho Rios, the main town in the area, is the island's second-busiest cruise-ship berth, disgorging almost half a million visitors each year to shop and catch glimpses of Dunn's River Falls (Jamaica's highest-grossing tourist attraction) and Dolphin Cove.

However, it's very easy to shake the pre-fab commercialism and enjoy some of the island's most enduring attractions. The town itself, backed by green hills and fronted by a wide, scalloped beach and a reef-sheltered harbor, boasts an excellent reggae museum, several fine botanic gardens looking out over the bay and an exuberant nightlife.

It's also a good base for exploring the area. Zigzagging inland through Fern Gully beneath a canopy of trees, you'll soon realize why St Ann's is known as 'the garden parish.' The bucolic, hilly terrain offers excellent vistas to pilgrims on the way to Nine Mile, the birthplace of Bob Marley, or foodies seeking Walkerswood and the mysteries of jerk sauce.

East of Ocho Rios, the quaint town of Oracabessa is home to Goldeneye, Ian Fleming's former home and now one of Jamaica's most elegant hotels. Further along the coast brings you to Firefly, Noel Coward's former home. Along the way, you can take in a working plantation, or enjoy some of Jamaica's best snorkeling and diving. West of Ocho Rios, along the well-paved road to Montego Bay, lies a succession of historic coastal towns like Runaway Bay, Discovery Bay and St Ann's Bay, where Columbus decamped.

HIGHLIGHTS

- **Dunn's River Falls** Come early to avoid the teeming masses and climb one of the world's most famous waterfalls (p152)
- **Walkerswood** Discover the mysteries of jerk at this world-renowned producer of sauces, marinades and chutneys (p166).
- **Canopy tour** Make like Tarzan and zip from platform to platform in the Cranbrook Flower Forest (p171).
- **Firefly** Savor the jaw-dropping view from author Noel Coward's well-preserved former home (p163).
- **Reggae Xplosion** If you can't pay homage to Bob Marley's final resting place at Nine Mile, this excellent museum captures reggae in all its vitality (p149).

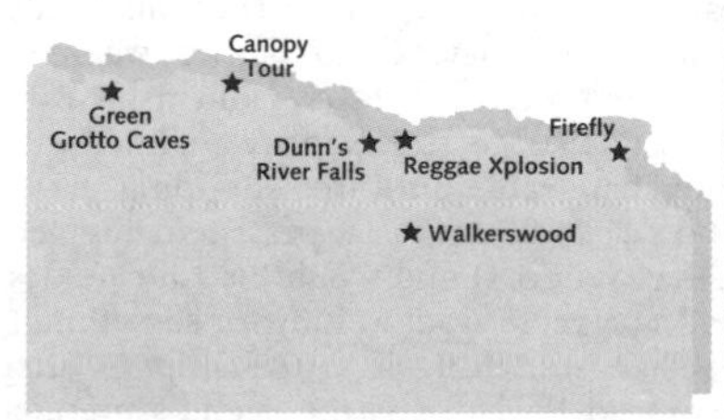

- AREA: 1834 SQ KM
- OCHO RIOS DEC DAILY HIGH TEMPERATURE: 26°C

HISTORY

The name Ocho Rios is a corruption of the Spanish term *chorreros,* which means, roughly, 'swift water.' The area was one of the last strongholds of Spanish dominion over the island, and the site of Spain's last stand in Jamaica can be found at Rio Nuevo, east of modern-day Ocho Rios. It was here that the British instituted huge sugar and pimento (allspice) plantations, crops that defined the region until the mid-20th century, when bauxite mining and tourism took over.

CLIMATE

The north central coast has some of the island's most predictable weather – that is, predictably hot and humid. Temperatures stay within a 16° to 30°C range throughout the year. The rainiest periods occur in May to June and September to October.

GETTING THERE & AWAY

The majority of international air travelers fly into Donald Sangster International Airport in Montego Bay, while domestic charter passengers fly into Boscobel Aerodrome, 16km east of town. Ocho Rios is also Jamaica's second-busiest cruise-ship port. With its central-north-coast location, land travelers have no trouble finding transport to and from town via minibus or route taxi.

OCHO RIOS

pop 16,500

Wrapped around a small bay with postcard-worthy snugness, Ocho Rios is a former fishing village that the Jamaica Tourist Board earmarked for tourism in the mid-1980s. Whatever character Ocho Rios lost when the local nets were redirected from fish to the tourist dollar, its streets today are lined with interchangeable duty-free shopping plazas and fast-food emporia, persistent higglers (street vendors) and would-be tour guides, and a palpable air of waiting for something.

That something is cruise ships – after Montego Bay, this is the island's premier port of packaged call. Yet 'Ochi's' beaches lack the splendor of MoBay's, it has nothing approaching the latter's downtown historic center, and the disembarkation dock here is so centrally located as to command the town's focus. When the floating resorts pull in, their human cargo streams into town to meet the local traffic in souvenirs untainted by memories; the full frontal hustle is on.

Note, however, that the cruise ships are generally gone by nightfall and seldom dock on weekends. The hordes can be avoided with a little planning, and if you're looking for a good base for exploring the north coast and the scenic interior of St Ann's Parrish, this is it. A terrific reggae museum, a lively nightlife scene, a trio of serene hillside gardens and an abundance of fine hotels and guesthouses make Ochi a good place to pause.

HISTORY

Although plantations developed during colonial times, Ocho Rios never evolved as a fruit-shipping port of any consequence. Things began to change in the 1940s when Reynolds Jamaica Mines built the deep-water Reynolds Pier west of town. An overhead conveyor belt still carries bauxite ore 10km from the Reynolds open-cast mines at Lydford, in the hills south of town.

Nonetheless, Ocho Rios was still just a quiet village in the 1960s when the Jamaican government formed the St Ann Development Council and then launched a systematic development. It dredged the harbor and built a small marina, reclaimed the shore, brought in sand for Turtle Beach, and built shopping complexes and housing schemes. By the early 1980s, Ocho Rios' character had been established: a meld of American-style fast-food franchises, nondescript shopping malls, an enclave of mediocre hotels in town, and more tasteful, upscale English-style hotels a discrete distance east. The construction of Island Village, a major shopping and entertainment complex (see p149) has spruced up 'Ochi.'

ORIENTATION

Greater Ocho Rios extends for 6km between Dunn's River Falls, 3km to the west of the town center, and Harmony Hall, 6km to the east.

The main coastal road, the A3, passes just south of the town center via a two-lane highway. West of a roundabout (traffic circle) at Milford Rd the A3 becomes DaCosta Dr; east of the roundabout it is known officially as the Ocho Rios Redevelopment Rd. South of the roundabout, Milford Rd is a trunk of the A3 that leads to Fern Gully and, eventually,

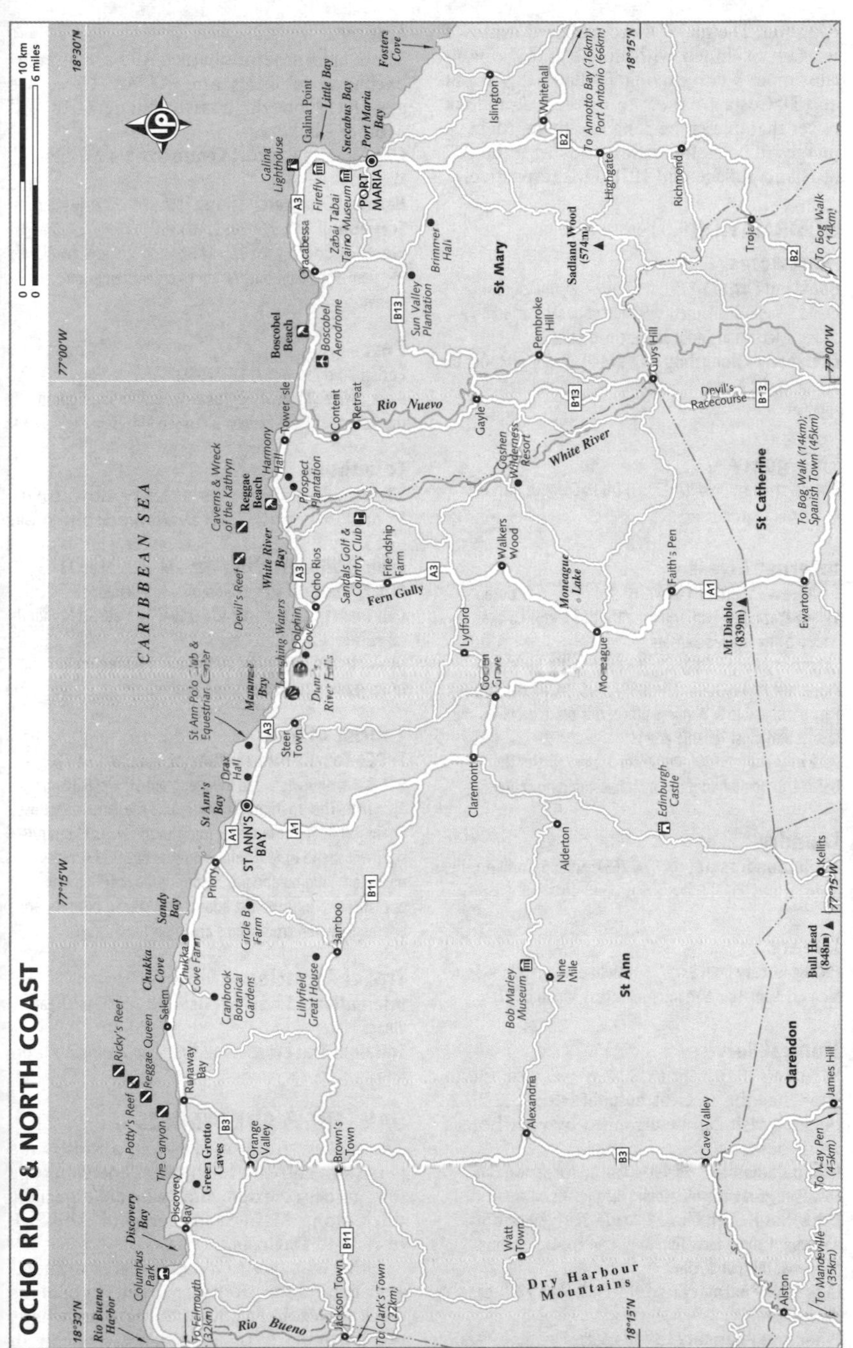

OCHO RIOS & NORTH COAST

Kingston. The major thoroughfare downtown is Main St. Lined with hotels and shops, it runs in an S-curve along Turtle Bay. Main St and DaCosta Dr meet to the east at a clock tower that marks the center of town. Main St merges to its east and west ends with the A3, at Island Village and IRIE FM, respectively.

INFORMATION

Bookstores

Bookland (☎ 675-8791; novtraco@cwjamaica.com; Island Village) The largest selection of books, including a strong selection of Caribbean-themed titles.

Everybody's Bookshop (☎ 974-2932; Shop 44, Ocean Village Plaza) A smaller inventory of titles and stationary supplies.

Emergency

Police station (☎ 974-2533) Off DaCosta Dr, just east of the clock tower.

Internet Access

EZ Access Internet Café (☎ 974-7038; 67B Ocean Village Plaza; per 15min/30min/1hr US$2/4/6) Located within a store called Sensations.

Internet Jungle (☎ 974-9906; Shop 13-15, Island Plaza; per 15min/30min/1hr US$2.50/5/10, all day US$20) Part of the Cable & Wireless office, this place provides the fastest and most reliable access.

Jerkin'@Taj (☎ 795-0862; per 15min/30min/1hr US$2/4/8) You'll find it in Taj Mahal shopping center.

Laundry

Carib Laundromat (☎ 974-7631; Shop 6, Carib Arcade, Main St; load US$5) Offers a wash-and-dry service.

Library

Public library (☎ 974-2588; Milford Rd; 🕒 9am-5pm Mon-Fri, 9am-1pm Sat; internet access 30min US$1)

Medical Services

St Ann's Bay, about 11km west of Ocho Rios, has the nearest **hospital** (☎ 972-2272). A doctor's visit can be arranged by your hotel's front desk.

Island Radiology (☎ 790-0150; Evelyn St near One Love Park) X-ray and ultrasound diagnostics.

Ocho Rios Health Clinic (☎ 974-2691; Graham St; 🕒 8am-4:30pm Mon-Thu, 8am-4pm Fri) Expect long queues at this public clinic.

Ocho Rios Pharmacy (☎ 974-2398; Shop 27, Ocean Village Plaza)

Pinegrove Pharmacy (☎ 974-5586; Pinegrove Plaza)

Money

There are numerous banks. All have foreign-exchange facilities and ATMs. There are also ATM booths next to Island Grill and Mother's bakery.

CIBC Jamaica Banking Centre (☎ 974-2824; 29 Main St)

National Commercial Bank (☎ 974-2522; 40 Main St)

Scotiabank (☎ 974-2081; Main St)

Western Union (☎ 926-2454; Shop 3, Pier View Plaza; 🕒 9am-5pm Mon-Sat) Arranges urgent remittance of money.

Post

FedEx (☎ 795-3723; 17 Main St)

Post office (Main St; 🕒 8am-5pm Mon-Sat) Opposite the Ocho Rios Craft Park; you can send faxes and telegrams.

Telephone

There are payphones aplenty downtown. WorldTalk cards are available from most gift shops.

Cable & Wireless office (☎ 974-9906; Shop 13-15, Island Plaza) For faxes, telegrams and telephone service.

Call Direct Centre (☎ 974-7594; 74 Main St) Economical calls overseas.

Digicell (☎ 795-4974; 70 Main St) East of the clock tower, selling cell phones and phonecards.

Tourist Offices

TPDCo Tourist Information (TPDCo; ☎ 974-7705, 974-3866; Shop 3, Ocean Village, Main St; 🕒 8:30am-5pm Mon-Thu, to 4pm Fri) Represents the Jamaica Tourist Board. While it doesn't offer much in the way of literature, staff will spend time helping you suss out Ochi's transportation, lodging and attractions options. TPDCo also operates two information booths on Main St, but they are open only when cruise ships are in port.

Travel Agencies

International Travel Service (☎ 974-9246; Ocean Village Plaza)

Trafalgar Travel (☎ 974-5108; Shop 2, cnr DaCosta Dr & Graham St)

DANGERS & ANNOYANCES

The biggest annoyance in Ocho Rios is the persistent entreaties of hustlers and would-be tour guides (see opposite), who are especially thick along Main St and around the clock tower and DaCosta Dr.

Otherwise, try to avoid the area immediately behind the produce market, south of the clock tower. Use caution at night anywhere, but particularly on James Ave, a poorly lit street with several nightspots and a hang-out strip of ill repute.

SIGHTS

Beaches

The main beach of Ocho Rios is the long crescent of **Turtle Beach** (adult/child US$1/0.50; 6am-6pm), stretching east from the Turtle Towers condominiums to the Renaissance Jamaica Grande Resort. There are changing rooms, and palms for shade.

Island Village Beach (admission US$3; 6am-6pm), located at the west end of Main St, is a peaceful, smaller beach that offers lockers (US$5), towels (US$5) and beach chairs and umbrellas (US$5 apiece).

Both beaches offer a complete range of water sports (see p153).

Immediately west of Island Village Beach is **Columbus Foot**, a tiny fishermen's beach with colorful pirogues (fishing boats) and nets festooning shade trees.

Mahogany Beach, 1km east of the town center, is a small and charming beach.

Turtle River Park

Near Island Village on Main St, this welcome new **green space** (8am-6pm) in the middle of downtown represents a positive new trend in Jamaica's approach to urban development. The lushly gardened park with manicured lawns also provides a zone free from the hustle of the main drag.

Island Village

Since its 2002 opening, this self-contained **entertainment park** (974-8353/4/5/6; www.islandjamaica.com; 9am-midnight), at the junction of Main St and DaCosta Dr, has changed the face of Ocho Rios. The 2-hectare development, brainchild of resort and media visionary Chris Blackwell, claims to resemble a 'Jamaican coastal village.' It doesn't. Quibbles aside, you will find a peaceful beach, upscale craft shops, a cinema, Jimmy Buffett's Margaritaville and Blue Runnings (both with bars and restaurants), a videocasino, Reggae Xplosion (see right) and a village green and amphitheater for live performances. The fences around the place reveal that this is not a public space, but rather a kind of daycare center for skittish, newly arrived cruise-ship passengers who lack the will – or the confidence – to explore the streets of Ocho Rios. Admission to the village is free, but you will be charged to use the beach or visit Reggae Xplosion, and for some special events.

Reggae Xplosion

This impressive **museum** (675-8895; Island Village; admission US$7; 9am-5pm Mon-Fri, 10am-5pm Sat) provides an excellent presentation of the grand lineage of Jamaican music, from ancient African drumming to the futuristic digital rhythms of dancehall. The self-billed 'interactive reggae experience' is divided into mento, ska, reggae, dancehall and other sections, including one commemorating Bob Marley. It features posters, photographs and videos. Headphones let you listen to sounds of each era. There's even a makeshift artists' recording studio with Lee 'Scratch' Perry's original sound-gear. The entrance fee includes a guided tour.

Gardens

With walk-ways and trails leading through lush gardens with streams, cascades and pools filled with carp, crayfish and turtles, **Coyaba River Garden** is a paradise. *Coyaba* is an Arawak word for 'heaven' or 'paradise.' The **Coyaba Museum** (974-6235; www.coyabagardens.com; Shaw Park Rd; admission US$5; 8am-6pm) traces Jamaica's heritage from early Arawak days to independence. There's a gift store, vegetarian restaurant, waterfall and art gallery. Coyaba is just shy of 2km west of St John's Church (on the A3), not far from Shaw Park Gardens; follow the signs. Admission includes a 30-minute guided tour.

The **Shaw Park Gardens** (974-2723; shawparkbchhtl@cwjamaica.com; Shaw Park Rd; admission US$10; 8am-5pm) is a tropical fantasia of ferns and bromeliads, palms and exotic shrubs, spread out over 11 hectares centered on an 18th-century great house. Trails and wooden steps lead past waterfalls that tumble in terraces down the hillside. A viewing platform offers a bird's-eye vantage over Ocho Rios. There's a bar and restaurant. The gardens are signed from opposite the public library on the A3.

The 8-hectare **Enchanted Gardens** (795-2750; Eden Bower Rd; admission US$12; 8am-5pm) are an Edenlike setting featuring a lush landscaped park with 14 waterfalls, huge pools, a fruit orchard and separate fern, spice, cactus and lily gardens. It also has a walk-in aviary. Guided tours are offered.

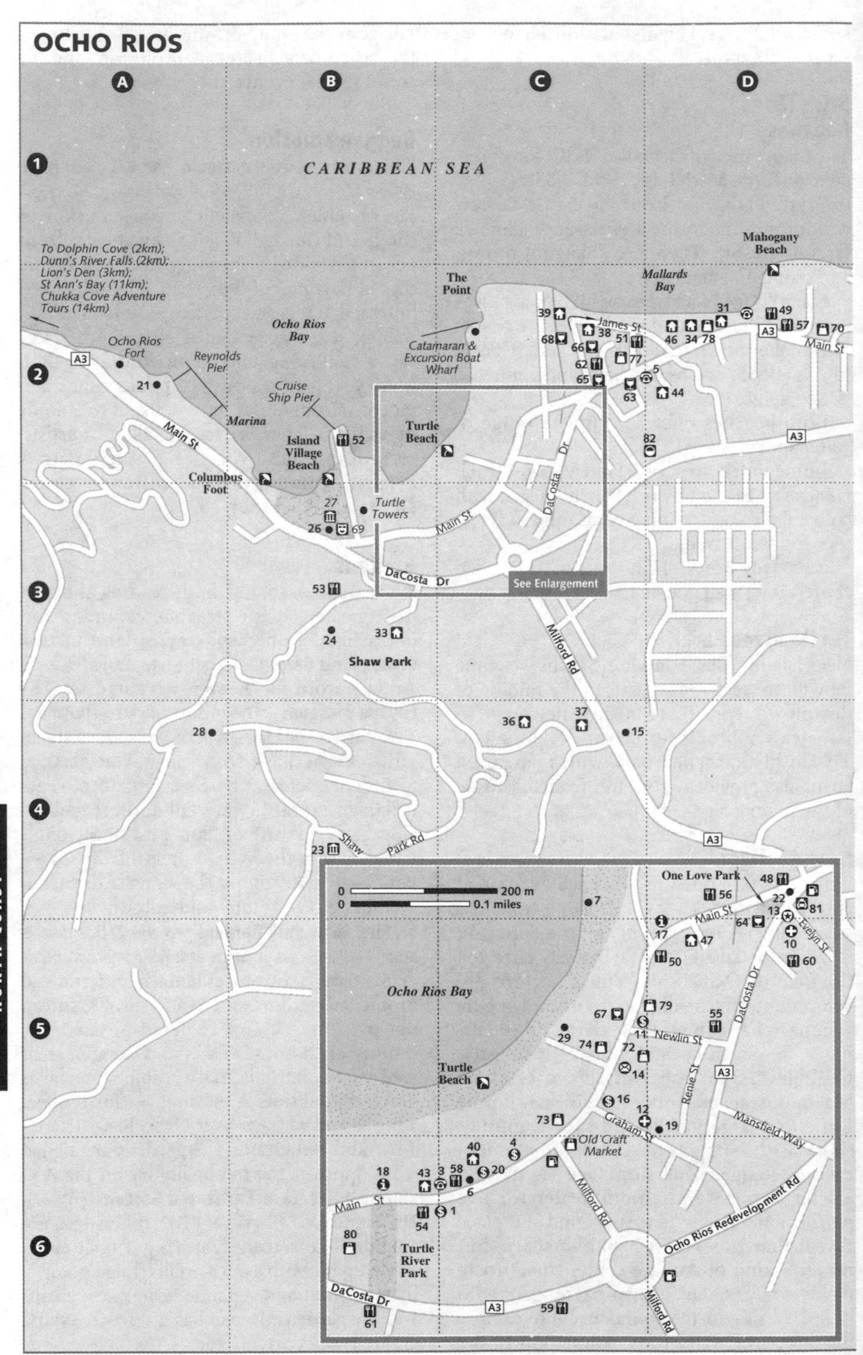
OCHO RIOS
CARIBBEAN SEA
To Dolphin Cove (2km); Dunn's River Falls (2km); Lion's Den (3km); St Ann's Bay (11km); Chukka Cove Adventure Tours (14km)
Ocho Rios Fort
Reynolds Pier
Ocho Rios Bay
Marina
Cruise Ship Pier
The Point
Catamaran & Excursion Boat Wharf
Mallards Bay
Mahogany Beach
James St
Main St
Island Village Beach
Columbus Foot
Turtle Beach
Turtle Towers
DaCosta Dr
See Enlargement
Shaw Park
Milford Rd
Shaw Park Rd
200 m
0.1 miles
One Love Park
Evelyn St
Newlin St
Renie St
Graham St
Mansfield Way
Old Craft Market
Turtle River Park
Ocho Rios Redevelopment Rd
A3

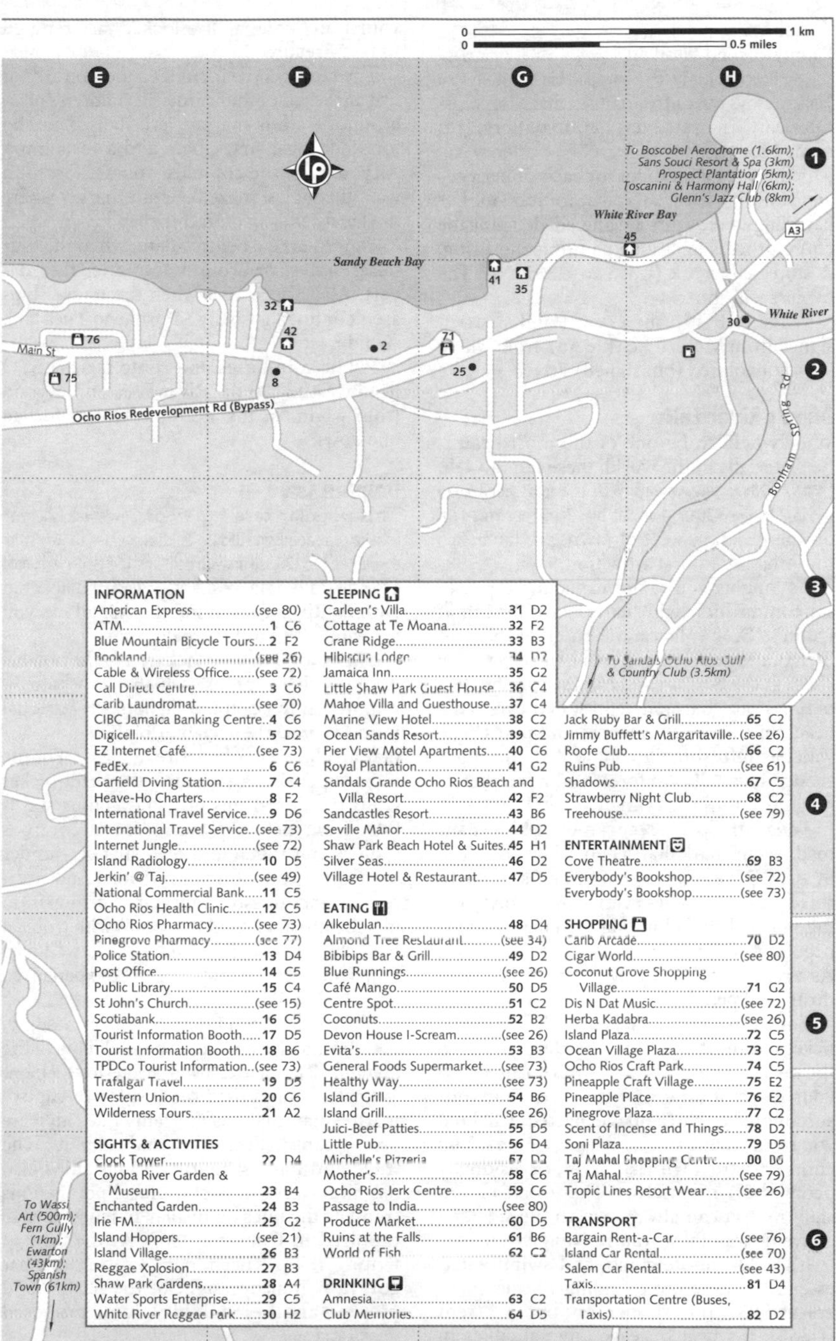
0 — 1 km
0 — 0.5 miles
E
F
G
H
1
2
3
4
5
6
To Boscobel Aerodrome (1.6km); Sans Souci Resort & Spa (3km); Prospect Plantation (5km); Toscanini & Harmony Hall (6km); Glenn's Jazz Club (8km)
White River Bay
A3
Sandy Beach Bay
White River
Main St
Ocho Rios Redevelopment Rd (Bypass)
Bonham Spring Rd
To Sandals Ocho Rios Golf & Country Club (3.5km)
To Wassi Art (500m); Fern Gully (1km); Ewarton (43km); Spanish Town (61km)
INFORMATION
American Express....(see 80)
ATM....1 C6
Blue Mountain Bicycle Tours....2 F2
Bookland....(see 26)
Cable & Wireless Office....(see 72)
Call Direct Centre....3 C6
Carib Laundromat....(see 70)
CIBC Jamaica Banking Centre..4 C6
Digicell....5 D2
EZ Internet Café....(see 73)
FedEx....6 C6
Garfield Diving Station....7 C4
Heave-Ho Charters....8 F2
International Travel Service....9 D6
International Travel Service..(see 73)
Internet Jungle....(see 72)
Island Radiology....10 D5
Jerkin' @ Taj....(see 49)
National Commercial Bank....11 C5
Ocho Rios Health Clinic....12 C5
Ocho Rios Pharmacy....(see 73)
Pinegrove Pharmacy....(see 77)
Police Station....13 D4
Post Office....14 C5
Public Library....15 C4
St John's Church....(see 15)
Scotiabank....16 C5
Tourist Information Booth....17 D5
Tourist Information Booth....18 B6
TPDCo Tourist Information..(see 73)
Trafalgar Travel....19 D5
Western Union....20 C6
Wilderness Tours....21 A2
SIGHTS & ACTIVITIES
Clock Tower....22 D4
Coyoba River Garden & Museum....23 B4
Enchanted Garden....24 B3
Irie FM....25 G2
Island Hoppers....(see 21)
Island Village....26 B3
Reggae Xplosion....27 B3
Shaw Park Gardens....28 A4
Water Sports Enterprise....29 C5
White River Reggae Park....30 H2
SLEEPING
Carleen's Villa....31 D2
Cottage at Te Moana....32 F2
Crane Ridge....33 B3
Hibiscus Lodge....34 D2
Jamaica Inn....35 G2
Little Shaw Park Guest House....36 C4
Mahoe Villa and Guesthouse....37 C4
Marine View Hotel....38 C2
Ocean Sands Resort....39 C2
Pier View Motel Apartments....40 C6
Royal Plantation....41 G2
Sandals Grande Ocho Rios Beach and Villa Resort....42 F2
Sandcastles Resort....43 B6
Seville Manor....44 D2
Shaw Park Beach Hotel & Suites..45 H1
Silver Seas....46 D2
Village Hotel & Restaurant....47 D5
EATING
Alkebulan....48 D4
Almond Tree Restaurant....(see 34)
Bibibips Bar & Grill....49 D2
Blue Runnings....(see 26)
Café Mango....50 D5
Centre Spot....51 C2
Coconuts....52 B2
Devon House I-Scream....(see 26)
Evita's....53 B3
General Foods Supermarket....(see 73)
Healthy Way....(see 73)
Island Grill....54 B6
Island Grill....(see 26)
Juici-Beef Patties....55 D5
Little Pub....56 D4
Michelle's Pizzeria....57 D2
Mother's....58 C6
Ocho Rios Jerk Centre....59 C6
Passage to India....(see 80)
Produce Market....60 D5
Ruins at the Falls....61 B6
World of Fish....62 C2
DRINKING
Amnesia....63 C2
Club Memories....64 D5
Jack Ruby Bar & Grill....65 C2
Jimmy Buffett's Margaritaville..(see 26)
Roofe Club....66 C2
Ruins Pub....(see 61)
Shadows....67 C5
Strawberry Night Club....68 C2
Treehouse....(see 79)
ENTERTAINMENT
Cove Theatre....69 B3
Everybody's Bookshop....(see 72)
Everybody's Bookshop....(see 73)
SHOPPING
Carib Arcade....70 D2
Cigar World....(see 80)
Coconut Grove Shopping Village....71 G2
Dis N Dat Music....(see 72)
Herba Kadabra....(see 26)
Island Plaza....72 C5
Ocean Village Plaza....73 C5
Ocho Rios Craft Park....74 C5
Pineapple Craft Village....75 E2
Pineapple Place....76 E2
Pinegrove Plaza....77 C2
Scent of Incense and Things....78 D2
Soni Plaza....79 D5
Taj Mahal Shopping Centre....80 D6
Taj Mahal....(see 79)
Tropic Lines Resort Wear....(see 26)
TRANSPORT
Bargain Rent-a-Car....(see 76)
Island Car Rental....(see 70)
Salem Car Rental....(see 43)
Taxis....81 D4
Transportation Centre (Buses, Taxis)....82 D2

Wassi Art

Family-owned **Wassi Art** (☎ 974-5044; www.wassiart.com; Bougainvillea Dr; ⏲ 9am-5pm Mon-Sat, 10am-4pm Sun) employs over fifty artists to make its colorful, richly decorated terra-cotta pottery. It is named for the 'wassi' wasp, or potter wasp, which makes a mud pot for each of her eggs and stuffs it with a caterpillar for food for her hatchlings. Free tours are offered, detailing the entire process including painting and firing. A store sells work (US$5 to US$5000). The owners will ship.

Wassi Art is in the Great Pond District, signed from Milford Rd (the A3), from where it's a convoluted (but signed) drive.

Dunn's River Falls

Widely held to be one of the most beautiful waterfalls in the world, these famous **falls** (☎ 974-2857; www.dunnsriverfallsja.com; adult/child US$15/12; ⏲ 8:30am-4pm Sat-Tue, 7am-5pm Wed-Fri), on the A3, 3km west of town, are Jamaica's top-grossing tourist attraction.

As long as you're not expecting a peaceful communion with nature, a morning at Dunn's River Falls can be an enjoyable and invigorating experience. Join hands in a daisy chain at the bottom and clamber up the tiers of limestone that stairstep 180m down to the beach in a series of cascades and pools. The water is refreshingly cool and the falls are shaded by a tall rain forest and a number of magnificent tree specimens.

Today, the place seems more like a man-made theme park than a natural wonder. The St Ann Development Company sees fit to spike the entrance fee every year or so, knowing full well that climbing the falls is a non-negotiable item on many visitors' to-do lists. As a result, you are likely to encounter great throngs of people.

You must buy a ticket at the roadside ticket booth, then follow the stairs down to the beach. The powerful current can sweep your feet from the slippery rocks, but your sure-footed guide (a tip is expected) will hold you by the hand and carry your camera. You climb at your own risk – yes, occasionally people hurt themselves. There's a first-aid station. You can always exit to the side at a convenient point if your nerves give out.

It's a 30-minute climb, and swimwear is essential. There are changing rooms, lockers (US$5) and rubber booties for rent (US$5). It's best to leave any valuables in your hotel safe, as the lockers are reputed to be unsecure.

The facility now includes a mento yard for live music, an orchid garden, a children's playground, a crafts market, jerk stalls, a gazebo for weddings, snack bars and a restaurant. As you leave the complex, you are forced to walk through a mazelike craft market where the hard sell is laid on thick.

Plan to arrive before 10am, when the tour buses arrive, or around 4pm after they depart. Also try to visit when the cruise ships aren't in town (usually Saturday to Tuesday). Avoid Easter.

Public minibuses and route taxis (US$1) head west to Dunns River Falls and beyond from Main St; it's a simple matter to flag one down.

Dolphin Cove

This popular **cove** (☎ 974-5335; www.dolphincovejamaica.com; admission US$45, 'touch encounter' US$67, 'swim encounter' US$129, 'swim with dolphins' US$195, 'swim, hold & feed the sharks' $119; ⏲ 8:30am-5:30pm), adjacent to Dunn's River Falls along the A3, allows you to swim with bottlenose dolphins.

Three dolphin packages are offered, notably 'Swim with Dolphins,' which grants you 30 minutes in the dolphin lagoon. Professional trainers direct the sociable dolphins, who display an almost goofy desire to please. For the most expensive experience, the thrill-seeker grabs the dorsal fins of two dolphins and is lifted from the water. Even more adventurous visitors can touch and feed sharks – under the Cove's watchful supervision. And if direct contact doesn't appeal, basic admission includes an aquarium and pools with tropical fish, sharks, stingrays and eels, as well as a mini zoo with exotic species to be experienced on a 'Jungle Trail.'

If the prices don't deter you from visiting, you should also consider the wellbeing of the dolphins. The **Jamaica Environmental Trust** (JET; www.jamentrust.org) opposes the display of captive marine mammals, as mortality rates increase during capture, transport and captivity. The trade and harvesting of wild dolphins also has an adverse impact on local populations (most of the ones on display in Jamaica were captured in Cuban waters). At the time of writing, JET has been trying to ensure proper governmental oversight of the facility and prevent another dolphinarium, proposed near Lucea.

Reservations are advisable in winter. Bring a towel and leave your jewelry at the hotel.

Prospect Plantation

If you've been wondering why St Ann is called 'the garden parish,' you'll find your answer at this beautiful old hilltop great house and 405-hectare working **plantation** (☎ 994-1058; A3; tours US$32; 🕑 tours 10:30am, 2pm & 3:30pm Mon-Sat), 5km east of town. On a pleasant, educational tour you'll travel by tractor-powered jitney through scenic grounds among banana, cassava, cocoa, coconut, coffee, pineapple and pimento. Three horseback tours are also offered (US$58) through a gorgeous working plantation with excellent views of the sea and countryside. For US$89, you can take the tour on a camel.

Both Minibuses and route taxis (US$1 to US$2) head east on the A3 toward Prospect Plantation from the Ocho Rios transportation center, south of the clock tower.

Harmony Hall

A beautiful great house by the A3 about 6km east of town, **Harmony Hall** (☎ 974-2870; www.harmonyhall.com; 🕑 10am-6pm, Tue-Sun) dates to 1886 when it was a Methodist manse that adjoined a pimento estate. The restored structure is made of cut stone, with a wooden upper story trimmed with gingerbread fretwork and a green shingled roof with a spire. Reborn as an arts-and-crafts showcase, it holds shows in the Front Gallery throughout the year; an exhibition season runs mid-November to Easter. The Back Gallery features fine arts and crafts. An acclaimed restaurant on the ground floor serves outstanding Italian fare (see p157).

ACTIVITIES

Golf

Tee up at **Sandals Golf & Country Club** (☎ 975-0119; Bonham Spring Rd; green fees US$100; 🕑 7am-5pm), in the hills, 6km southeast of town and signed off the A3. One of the most scenic in Jamaica, this is a 6035m, par-71 course with a driving range, putting green, and clubhouse. Caddies (9/18 holes US$12/17) are mandatory, and cart rental (9/18 holes US$25/40) is recommended. Club rental (US$25 to US$45) and lessons (per hour US$40) are also offered.

Water Sports

Virtually the entire shoreline east of Ocho Rios to Galina Point is fringed by a reef, and it's great for **snorkeling** and **scuba diving.** One of the best sections is Devil's Reef, a pinnacle that drops more than 60m. Nurse sharks are abundant at Caverns, a shallow reef about 1km east of the White River estuary; it has many tunnels plus an ex-minesweeper, the *Kathryn*. You can arrange dives and snorkeling at the **Garfield Diving Station** (☎ 395-7023; 50 Main St, Turtle Beach; 1-tank dive US$50, snorkeling tour US$35). Most resorts have their own scuba facilities.

For an extensive range of water sports and touring opportunities, **Water Sports Enterprise** (☎ 974-2244; 50 Main St, Turtle Beach) offers activities including glass-bottom boat rides (US$30), snorkeling at Marine Garden (US$25) or Paradise Reef (US$30), windsurfing (US$30), sunfish sailing (US$80), jet ski (US$60/100 per half/full hour), scuba diving (1-/2-/4-tank dives US$45/70/140) or lessons (US$20), and parasailing (single/tandem US$50/100). Beach chairs, umbrellas and lockers are available to rent (US$5 each).

At **Island Village Beach** you can rent snorkeling gear (US$10 per day), kayaks (single/double US$8.50/10 per hour), windsurfing gear (US$40 for 30 minutes) and Hobie-cats (US$30 for 30 minutes).

Upscale hotels also offer water sports.

Sport-fishing boats are available for charter from the marina. For a chartered sunset cruise, try **Heave-Ho Charters** (☎ 974-5376; Main St; per person US$40).

TOURS

The Ocho Rios area offers more organized outdoor adventure tours than any other Jamaican resort area. Most tours include transportation from area hotels.

There are several options for **horseback riding** tours. Prospect Plantation (left) offers guided tours (US$58) through a gorgeous working plantation. **Hooves** (☎ 972-0905; www.hoovesjamaica.com; 61 Windsor Rd, St Ann's Bay; US$55-125) offers guided horseback tours in three categories: beach, mountain and rain-forest trails. Reservations are required. The 'rainforest honeymoon ride,' for experienced riders, is the most expensive (recent matrimony not required).

The most popular horseback adventure company, **Chukka Caribbean Adventure Tours** (☎ 972-2506; www.chukkacaribbean.com/jamaica; US$76) offers a three-hour horseback tour that passes through several old sugar plantations and finishes up on a private beach. The tour culminates with a bareback ride into the sea. Chukka Caribbean also operates a number of other recommended tours (p170).

These tour providers offer hotel transfers:

Blue Mountain Bicycle Tours (☎ 974-7075; www.bmtoursja.com; bicycle tour adult/child US$93/60; 121 Main St) Offers a downhill cycling tour in the Blue Mountains.

Calypso Rafting (☎ 974-2527; www.calypsorafting.com; PO Box 54, Ocho Rios; per raft US$50, inner tube per person US$20) Bamboo raft/inner tubing on the White River.

Island Hoppers (☎ 974-1285; helicopter@mail.infochan.com; 120 Main St; tours per person 20/30/60min US$75/115/225, minimum 3 paid seats; charters per hr US$720) Aerial tours by helicopter.

Wilderness Tours (☎ 969-6653; www.wildernessatvtours.com; Reynolds Pier, Main St; tours per person US$59-80) All-terrain vehicle tours into the mountains and through the forest.

FESTIVALS & EVENTS

Jamaican Carnival (www.jamaicacarnival.com, www.bacchanaljamaica.com), held island-wide over Easter, is celebrated in a big way in Ocho Rios. At Chukka Cove (p170) a riotous all-night party featuring soca music called Bacchanal is held; other venues throughout the area also stage events. See p83 for more information.

The **Ocho Rios Jazz Festival** takes place in June. Check out p17 of the Events Calendar for more information.

The **Harmony Hall Anniversary Crafts Fair** is held every November. See p153 for details on Harmony Hall.

SLEEPING

Lodging options in and around Ocho Rios include simple guest houses, a smattering of good midrange options and a large number of resorts. Options also include self-catering condominium resorts and fully staffed villas. If you choose one of the options on James Ave, exercise caution at night.

The accommodations below extend westward to Dunn's River Falls and eastward to Harmony Hall.

Villas of varying ranges of opulence are represented by **Sun Villas** (in the USA ☎ 888-625-6007; www.sunvillas.com) and **Jamaican Association of Villas & Apartments** (JAVA; ☎ 974-2508; www.villasinjamaica.com). See p277 for more information on renting villas.

Budget

Mahoe Villa and Guesthouse (☎ 974-6613; 11 Shaw Park Rd; r without bath US$20-30, r with bath US$40, r with bath & Jacuzzi US$75; Ⓟ) If you've been looking high and low for a decent US$20 room, this is it. On the road to Shaw Park Gardens is this brilliantly priced guest house with 11 spic-and-span, fan-cooled rooms of varying size. The large house has polished wood floors and is replete with original works of art. There's a communal kitchen, cable TV, and several hammocks strung up in the yard.

Marine View Hotel (☎ 974-5753; www.marineviewhotel.com; 9 James Ave; s/d US$30/70;) This no-frills place has 25 nondescript rooms. And while there's not much ambience, its central location makes amends for this. Top-floor rooms offer a glimpse (barely) of the sea. Superior rooms have air-con; deluxe rooms also have TV. There's a good-value restaurant, a game room and an outdoor pool.

Carleen's Villa (☎ 974-5431; 85A Main St; r US$40; Ⓟ) A serviceable budget option, popular with European backpackers, located east of the town center toward Mahogany Beach. Rooms, some of which are a tad gloomy, are fan-cooled and have cable TV. A stairway leads to a communal terrace overlooking the sea, perfect for a spontaneous frolic; there are terrific snorkeling opportunities a short swim away. Food is prepared for groups.

Little Shaw Park Guest House (☎ 974-2177; www.littleshawparkguesthouse.com; 21 Shaw Park Rd; r US$50, apt US$60; Ⓟ) Providing a restful retreat, this trim place is set among 0.6 hectares of beautifully tended lawns, bougainvillea, and has a gazebo and hammocks. There's a room in the owner's house and seven spacious (though dark) cabins with homey decor. Also on offer are well-lit studio apartments with kitchens, cable TV and hot water. Meals are available by request. This is also your only opportunity for camping (US$20) in Ocho Rios.

Ocean Sands Resort (☎ 974-2605; oceansands@yahoo.com; 14 James Ave; s/d US$50/70;) This attractive property offers an oceanfront setting and its own pocket-size beach, with coral, at your doorstep. A tiny restaurant sits at the end of a wooden wharf. The 35 pleasant rooms have French doors that open onto private balconies. Rates include breakfast.

Pier View Motel Apartments (☎ 974-2607; 19 Main St; d US$60-75, apt US$80, ste US$99; Ⓟ) Also centrally located, this budget option offers studios and a range of modestly furnished rooms and apartments, all with fans, refrigerator and cable TV; there are also suites with air-con – lacking kitchen – that sleep up to four.

Midrange

Village Hotel & Restaurant (☎ 974-9193; www.geocities.com/villagehotel; 54 Main St; r US$81, apt US$95, with balcony/Jacuzzi US$100/135, ste US$140-220;) This modern charmer offers four carpeted rooms featuring contemporary decor, cable TVs, and phones. It also has one- and three-bedroom suites with kitchenettes. A courtyard restaurant serves complementary breakfast to guests and also does Jamaican dishes. There's a spa and gym.

Silver Seas (☎ 974-2755; 66 James Ave; r US$100;) A bit worn around the edges, but atmospheric. The rooms are clean and well kept, and each has a large, private patio with a stellar ocean view. You'll find it hidden away behind Pengrove Plaza.

Crane Ridge (☎ 974-8050, 866-277-6374; www.craneridge.net; 17 DaCosta Dr; ste US$110, deluxe 1-/2-bedroom ste US$168/240;) Offering a breezy hilltop location on the west side of town, this modern, all-suite resort features 119 suites in six three-story structures. Some rooms have loft bedrooms. An airy restaurant on stilts looms over a large pool. There's a shuttle service to the hotel's private beach and to Shaw Park Gardens and Dunn's River Falls.

our pick **Cottage at Te Moana** (☎ 974-2870; www.harmonyhall.com; cabin US$120;) With its small clifftop garden overhanging a reef, this exquisite reclusive rental offers a delightful alternative to Ochi's resort hotels. The clifftop bedroom is reached via an external staircase and has a king-size bed and ceiling fan, and a magnificent artist's aesthetic. It has a fully equipped kitchen and separate living area, plus a veranda with hammock chairs. Steps lead down to a coral cove good for snorkeling, and kayaks are available. There's a three-night stay minimum.

Hibiscus Lodge (☎ 974-2676; www.hibiscusjamaica.com; 83 Main St; r US$140-152;) A good-value option close to the town center that overlooks a coral reef, where the snorkeling is superb. A stairway descends alongside a cliff overhang, past a large coop of cooing doves, and down to a private sunning deck, perfect for a spontaneous jump in the sea day or night. A small gallery of contemporary Jamaican art complements the main building nicely. The rooms are all modestly furnished; the deluxe ones are worth the extra expense for their large private balconies; ones near the street can be quite loud, however. There's also a breezy bar and the Almond Tree (p157), a fine restaurant.

Sandcastles Resort (☎ 974-5626; www.sandcastlesochorios.com; 120 Main St; r/ste US$149/230;) Large centrally located option that's a beach ball's throw from Turtle Beach, this well-refurbished resort has bright studios and one- and two-bedroom suites in various configurations. All have cable TV, plus modern furnishings. It has a sports bar.

Seville Manor (☎ 795-2901; 84 Main St; r US$55, apt US$64) This small charmer tucked off Main St has 28 rooms with rich, modern furnishings and a cozy ambience. It has a restaurant and bar.

Top End

Jamaica Inn (☎ 974-2514, 877-470-6975; www.jamaicainn.com; ste/cottages US$550-860/1340-1760;) Winston Churchill's favorite hotel, this exquisite family-run 'inn', tucked in a private cove, exudes patrician refinement. The 45 suites are a soothing combination of whites and Wedgwood blues, with mahogany beds, Edwardian furnishings and colonial-theme prints. The West Wing veranda suites hang over the sea (East Wing rooms nudge up to the beach). There's a croquet lawn, game room, library and a bar with a warm clubby feel. Men are required to wear jackets for dinner (plus a tie in winter) and women's dress code is in accordance. Water sports include scuba diving, and guests have access to the facilities at Shaw Park Beach Hotel (p156). Rates include breakfast and dinner; children under 14 are not admitted.

Royal Plantation (☎ 974-5601; www.royalplantation.com; ste US$605-1245;) While luxury can be found across Jamaica, its lap is surely on this 8-acre spot nestled around two private beaches. From the neoclassical lobby decked in Victorian furnishings to the C Bar (Jamaica's only caviar and champagne bar) to the orchids that grace the garden areas to the pillow menu for your room, the Royal Plantation goes the extra mile. All 74 rooms face the sea and feature marble bathrooms, and there are three gourmet restaurants, notably Le Papillon, an intimate French boîte with a dress code. An array of water sports is on offer, while the cigar-rolling displays and an artist in residency program help make this one of the most unique hotels on the island.

All-Inclusives

Please see p275 for general information about all-inclusive resorts in Jamaica. The following prices are all for three nights, all-inclusive.

Shaw Park Beach Hotel & Suites (☎ 974-2552-4, 800-377-1126; www.shawparkbeachhotel.com; Cutlass Bay; d US$846-939, ste US$1860;) This old favorite reopened in 2005 as an adults-only all-inclusive resort. Its thatch-roofed oceanfront units are spread along a wide golden-sand beach in a private cove. Choose from 33 standard, 60 superior and 12 two-bedroom suites, all with cable TV, and private balcony or terrace (ask for a tiled room; they're cooler). Features include an oval pool, two tennis courts, game room and disco, plus water sports and floor shows.

Sans Souci Resort & Spa (☎ 994-1544, in North America ☎ 800-448-7702; www.couples.com; d US$1500-2250; P) On the A3 east of town, this sophisticated resort has a sublime setting in a secluded cove backed by lime-green lawns. All 148 suites feature king-size beds, CD player, cable TV, direct-dial phones and 24-hour room service. Some have Jacuzzis. One of the two beaches is for nude bathing. The resort has a volleyball court, jogging track and fitness center plus full-service spa. A huge range of water sports are offered, including scuba lessons, as are tennis and activities that include reggae dance classes.

Sandals Grande Ocho Rios Beach & Villa Resort (☎ 974-1027, in North America ☎ 877-726-3257; www.sandals.com/main/ochorios; d US$1650-3900; P) This newly renovated confection, the result of a recent merging of Sandals Ocho Rios and Beaches Grande Sport Villa Golf Resort & Spa, is conceived as an all-inclusive 'Garden of Eden' for couples (including those of the same-sex variety). With 17 categories encompassing 529 rooms, suites and villas, this resort offers a mind-boggling array of accommodations. There are one-bedroom suites overlooking the ocean, private villas nestled in the hillside, and secluded cottages. If money is no object, the suites at the highest level include a personal butler. Rates include all meals, transfers and use of the Sandals Golf & Country Club (p153). Children are not permitted.

EATING

Ocho Rios has a good range of international cuisine and several economical Jamaican restaurants; many places are open late. After dark, you'll find many smoking oil-drum barbecues along the roadside, particularly in the area surrounding the clock tower.

Budget

Centre Spot (☎ 323-0042; 75E Main St; meals US$2.50-4; lunch & dinner) This unassuming hole-in-the-wall place whips up local favorites such as curried goat; specials include the ever-popular cow head (no explanation supplied). For breakfast, if you're hungry consider the porridge – a cup of the cornmeal or peanut variety really sticks to your ribs.

Island Grill (☎ 974-3160; Main St, Island Village; US$2-8; 8am-11pm) Branch of the ubiquitous chain is good for take-out jerk dishes.

Alkebulan (☎ 375-7939; 63 Main St; meals US$3-7; 7am-10pm Mon-Sat) A healthy choice for vegetarians and Rastafarians, this eatery near the clock tower serves I-tal food such as peanut porridge, curry beans, veggie-ball stew and a range of roots tonics and juices.

World of Fish (☎ 974-1863; 3 James Ave; US$3-8; 11am-1am) Popular with locals, this casual and economical eatery serves fresh seafood, including lobster and shrimp. In keeping with the Jamaican capacity for making juice from just about anything that grows, sweet nectars of June plum, ginger and soursop are served.

Healthy Way (☎ 974-9229; Ocean Village Plaza; meals US$4-6; breakfast & lunch Mon-Sat) A vegetarian kitchen and health-food store selling herbs, teas, juices and supplements, plus hearty chow such as a delicious tofu cheeseburger, stew peas and large fruit plates to go.

Lion's Den (☎ 848-4413; A3; meals US$4-9; breakfast, lunch & dinner) West of town between Dolphin Cove and Dunn's River Falls, this place looks like a tourist trap but it is worth a stop for the excellent, well-priced Jamaican fare and unique, artistic decor. The dining room resembles a Rastafarian chapel with hand-carved columns and wicker 'tree limbs' reaching to the ceiling. Outside on the patio, under a shady canopy of trees, you can spy on the goings-on at Dolphin Cove (bring binoculars). The menu boasts local specialties such as roast fish (US$6).

Scotchie's (☎ 794-9457; Jack's Hall Fair Ground; US$4-10; lunch & dinner) This roadside offshoot of the superlative jerk center in Montego Bay lies adjacent to an Epping Gas station just west of Dunn's River Falls, where its pork, chicken and sausage water the mouths of locals and visitors alike.

Michelle's Pizzeria (☎ 974-4322; in the Pineapple Hotel, Main St; US$6-8; ⏲ lunch & dinner) In addition to four styles of pizza (including a 'Hawaiian' with pineapple), this causal spot serves an array of pastas and hero sandwiches to be eaten on a small patio.

Ocho Rios Jerk Centre (☎ 974-2549; DaCosta Dr; US$3-7; ⏲ lunch & dinner) Good for sizzling jerk chicken and pork. Fish is also available.

Mother's (Main St; ⏲ 24hr), with several outlets, and **Juici-Beef Patties** (1 Newlin St) are fast-food eateries serving patties and pastries (US$1).

For ice cream, head to **Devon House I-Scream** (Island Village; per scoop US$1.25).

There's a **General Foods Supermarket** (☎ 974-2510; Ocean Village Plaza) and smaller grocery stores scattered along Main St. You can buy fresh produce at the produce market on the south side of DaCosta Dr near the clock tower.

Midrange

Café Mango (☎ 974-7416; 12 Main St; mains US$5-15; ⏲ 9am-10pm) This place offers airy dining and a large menu offering spicy hot chicken wings, other finger foods, burgers and pizzas.

Blue Runnings (☎ 675-8794; Island Village; mains US$6-14; ⏲ 8am-7pm Mon-Sat, from 11am Sun) On the periphery of Island Village is this pleasant place with a shady, peaceful patio. Jamaican fare such as jerk pork or chicken, steamed fish and a wholesome vegetarian platter (US$6) is served by day; in the evening the darkened, candlelit tables make for a romantic place to imbibe the local poison.

Bibibips Bar & Grill (☎ 974-8759; 93 Main St; mains US$6-28; ⏲ 10am-midnight) This popular, touristy oceanfront bar and restaurant with a porch overlooking Mahogany Beach serves up a range of seafood, burgers, jerk and barbecue dishes that don't quite live up to their pricing.

our pick **Coconuts** (☎ 795-0064; Fisherman's Point; US$7-25; ⏲ breakfast, lunch & dinner) Whether you stop in for a 'ménage à trios' plate (coconut shrimp, conch and chicken samosas), have a jerk chicken quesadilla or dig into a steak, the terrace at Coconuts invariably keeps you here longer than you intended. And why not? The view of the bay is stellar, and the drink specials ease you into the evening, when Coconuts becomes a lively bar (see p158).

Little Pub (☎ 795-1831; 59 Main St; mains US$8-14; ⏲ 8am-midnight) Totally touristy yet enjoyable, Little Pub serves good American breakfasts. An eclectic lunch and dinner menu is strong on steak and seafood at modest prices. It has an all-you-can-eat-and-drink buffet on Friday nights (US$20).

Ruins at the Falls (☎ 974-8888; 17 DaCosta Dr; lunch buffet US$14, mains US$9-24; ⏲ breakfast & lunch) Set amid a tropical garden with a lovely bridal-veil waterfall and pools, this Jamaican-Chinese restaurant has one-of-a-kind ambience. The all-inclusive lunchtime buffet features beverages, live entertainment and a garden tour.

Top End

Almond Tree Restaurant (☎ 974-2813; Hibiscus Lodge, 83 Main St; mains US$8-25; ⏲ breakfast, lunch & dinner) Providing a splendid perch for a sunset dinner, this clifftop spot features a dining pavilion stairstepping down the cliffside. Candlelit dinners are served alfresco. The menu ranges from seafood and continental fare to steadfast Jamaican dishes.

Passage to India (☎ 795-3182; Soni's Plaza, 50 Main St; US$9-25; ⏲ lunch & dinner Tue-Sun, lunch Mon) On the rooftop of a duty-free shopping center, Passage to India offers respite from the crowds below in addition to very good northern Indian fare. The naan is crisp, the curries sharp, and the menu divided into extensive chicken, mutton, seafood and vegetarian sections. Tandoori options are also on offer.

our pick **Toscanini** (☎ 975-4785; Harmony Hall; mains US$10-24; ⏲ lunch & dinner Tue-Sun) One of the finest restaurants on the island, this roadside spot is run by two gracious Italians who mix local ingredients into recipes from the motherland. The daily menu ranges widely, encompassing such appetizers as prosciutto with papaya or marinated marlin and mains like lobster pasta, or shrimp sautéed with garlic and Appleton rum. Leave room for desserts such as strawberry tart or apple and plum strudel. Treat yourself!

Evita's (☎ 974-2333; Eden Bower Rd; mains US$12-18; ⏲ lunch & dinner) This charmer sits high above Ochi in a romantically decorated 1860s house. It is an airy setting with exquisite views. The Italian-Jamaican menu includes jerk spaghetti and the trademark 'Lasagna Rastafari.' Recommended are the smoked marlin carpaccio and wickedly good herb-crusted lamb chops. If you're lucky the gregarious proprietor Eva will stop by your table and give your shoulder a squeeze.

ENTERTAINMENT

There's a healthy bar scene and a decent choice of nightspots, but in general Ochi after hours lacks the verve of Negril or the authenticity of Kingston. Nonetheless, it's not hard to find a good party atmosphere *somewhere* on any night of the week.

Island Village (right) has a range of entertainment options on offer in the one spot, and includes the raucous Margaritaville. Many all-inclusive resorts sell night passes permitting full access to meals, drinks and entertainment.

Bars

Coconuts (☎ 795-0064; Fisherman's Point) The potent cocktails and omnipotent US$20 all-you-can drink hard liquor special make the terrace here an excellent vantage point for watching the cruise ships pull out from the dock across the street.

Jimmy Buffett's Margaritaville (☎ 675-8800; Island Village; admission charged for special events; 🕑 10am-10pm) This corporate franchise has turned getting drunk into big business. As with its counterparts in Montego Bay and Negril, the music is too loud and the drinks are too expensive, but some people find the orchestrated good-time vibe to be irresistible. The menu aims for the lowest common denominator with selections including the artery-clogging 'Cheeseburger in Paradise' and Caesar salads, pizzas and sandwiches.

James Ave, dubbed 'Reggae Strip,' has several discos and 'entertainment centers.' Use caution around here at night.

Here are some other places that are worth checking out:

Jack Ruby Bar & Grill (☎ 795-0768; 1 Main St) Live bands and sound-system parties in the rear courtyard.

Treehouse (in Soni's Plaza, 50 Main St) Cocktail bar located in a shopping center that tends to fill with tourists.

Ruins Pub (☎ 974-9712; 17 DaCosta Dr) This is a classy, peaceful environment, perfect for enjoying a quiet drink.

Nightclubs

Amnesia (☎ 974-2633; 70 Main St; admission US$5; 🕑 Wed-Sun) A classic Jamaican dancehall, this remains the happening scene. Theme nights include an oldies jam on Sunday, ladies night on Thursday and an after-work party on Friday. This is all leading up to Saturday's dress-to-impress all-night dance marathon.

Strawberry Night Club (James Ave; admission US$5) Attempting to compete with Amnesia is this somewhat subdued local haunt featuring video slots and a pool table downstairs. The scene is hit-or-miss.

Club Memories (☎ 974-2667; cnr DaCosta Dr & Main St) Whatever its memories, the club various from night to night based on the evening's theme. Thursday is 'Ladies Nite,' and Sunday is oldies night. Happy hour is from 7pm to 9pm Friday. There's a dress code.

Roofe Club (☎ 974-1042; 7 James Ave; admission US$3) The gritty Roofe sends earth-shattering music across the roofs of town; it's the place to get down and dirty with the latest dancehall moves. It can get rough.

Cinemas

For the latest Hollywood releases try **Cove Theatre** (☎ 675-8886; Island Village; admission US$7).

Live Music

The touristy venue **Little Pub** (☎ 795-1831; 59 Main St) is an old favorite, replete with sports TV and the occasional eclectic floor show to amuse you while you sit at the bar. A resident band plays here six nights per week. The live-entertainment schedule changes night by night, and includes an Afro-Caribbean musical, karaoke, and a weekly cabaret on Friday.

Near Tower Isle, **Glenn's Jazz Club** (☎ 975-4360; Tower Cloisters Condominium Hotel), on the A3 east of town, features live (albeit wan and listless) jazz.

Also on the A3 east of town, the **White River Reggae Park** (☎ 929-4089) infrequently hosts sound systems. Also look for posters around town advertising live music or sound systems at Reggae Beach (p160)

At Island Village, the **Village Green** (Island Village) hosts two live shows each week for the tourist crowds.

Little Pub and most top-end hotels have live music and cabaret shows.

SHOPPING

Excellent pottery and ceramics are available at Wassi Art (see p152), where you can watch it being made.

The **Island Village** (cnr Main St & DaCosta Dr) has over a dozen pleasant stores with carefully chosen merchandise. These include several beachwear shops, duty-free stores, an outlet for film and photography needs, and some upscale outlets for quality paintings, carvings and crafts. Shops include Herba Kadabra for spices, healing herbs and potions; Rum, Roast & Royal, which specializes in rums, coffees and cigars; and Tropic Lines Resort Wear – get that tacky flower-print shirt you've been admiring.

For incense, oils and a variety of herbs, try out **Scent of Incense and Things** (☎ 795-0047; 79 Main St). **Island Plaza** (Main St) is a good place to shop for cell phones and assorted gizmos.

Six kilometers east of town, **Harmony Hall** (☎ 975-4222; www.harmonyhall.com; Tue-Sun) has the best quality art. It's renowned for its Christmas, Easter and mid-November craft fairs, and regular exhibitions.

For Cuban cigars, try **Cigar World** (☎ 974-6317; 25 Taj Mahal Shopping Centre).

For craft stalls, **Ocho Rios Craft Park** (Main St) and **Dunn's River Craft Park** (Dunn's River Falls) both have dozens, as do **Pineapple Place** (Main St), to the east of town, and **Coconut Grove Shopping Village** (Main St), which is opposite Beaches Royal Plantation Golf Resort & Spa. Fern Gully (p166), to the south of Ocho Rios, is lined with stalls where artists sell their paintings and carvings at prices marginally lower than you'll find elsewhere.

Soni Plaza and Ocean Village Plaza, both on Main St, host duty-free stores, including **Taj Mahal** (☎ 974-6455), which offers a vast array of watches and jewelry.

For music tapes and CDs, try **Dis N Dat Music** (☎ 795-2775; Island Plaza) and **Vibes Music Shack** (Ocean Village Plaza). The latter has more obscure sounds.

GETTING THERE & AWAY

Air

Boscobel Aerodrome (☎ 975-3101) is at Boscobel, about 16km east of town. No international services land here.

Air Jamaica Express (☎ 726-1344, 888-359-2475) serves Ocho Rios with scheduled flights to and from Montego Bay (US$66) and Tinson Pen Aerodrome (US$64) in Kingston.

Boscobel Aerodrome is also served by two air-charter companies. **International Air Link** (☎ 940-6660, 940-0195; www.intlairlink.com) serves Montego Bay (seat/charter US$87/244), Negril (US$122/364) and Kingston (US$180/554). **TimAir** (☎ 952-2516; www.timair.net) flies on demand to Montego Bay (US$133/364).

Public Transportation

Buses, minibuses and route taxis arrive and depart Ocho Rios at the **transportation centre** (Evelyn St). If you are coming from the east, you will be deposited at the taxi stand near One Love Park, up the hill from the harbor.

Buses operate throughout the day between Ocho Rios and Montego Bay (US$4), plus Kingston (US$4) and smaller towns along the way. Minibuses and route taxis are almost as cheap and more comfortable. It's a two-hour ride from either Montego Bay or Kingston.

If you are heading to Port Antonio by bus, you will have to change buses at St Mary (US$1.50).

Taxi

JUTA (☎ 974-2292) is the main taxi agency catering to tourists. A licensed taxi will cost about US$90 between Ocho Rios and Montego Bay, and about US$80 between Ocho Rios and Kingston (US$100 to the international airport at Kingston).

Island Car Rentals (☎ 974-2666, 888-991-4255; www.islandcarrentals.com; Shop 2, Carib Arcade) offers chauffeured transfers to and from Kingston or Montego Bay.

GETTING AROUND

There is no shuttle service from the airport to downtown. Local buses (US$0.75) and minibuses and route taxis (US$1.50) pass by. A tourist taxi will cost about US$20.

Ocho Rios has no bus service within town. Minibuses and route taxis ply Main St and the coast road (US$1 for short hauls; US$4 to Boscobel or Mammee Bay).

Car-rental rates are cheaper in Ocho Rios than elsewhere on the island, averaging US$50/300 for the day/week.

Island Car Rentals (see above) is the most reputable company. Also try, **Budget** (☎ 974-1288; 15 Milford Rd), **Bargain Rent-a-Car** (☎ 974-8047; Shop 1A Pineapple Place Shopping Center, Main St) or **Salem Car Rental** (☎ 974-0786; www.salemcarrentals.com; Shop 7, Sandcastles Resort).

Government-established taxi fares from downtown are Dunn's River Falls US$25, Firefly US$65, Prospect Plantation US$32, Sandals Golf & Country Club US$28 and Shaw Park Gardens US$22.

EAST OF OCHO RIOS

While the signal of **IRIE FM** (Hwy A3) carries all over the island, the limits of Ocho Rios are immediately apparent once you pass the radio station's studios at the town's eastern edge. The seaside resorts quickly give way to isolated villas and fishing villages like Port Maria as the coastal road winds its way east along cliffs and bluffs. The sense of leaving tourist Jamaica behind is enhanced by the drop-off in road quality. At last visit, intermittent repairs slowed the road between Oracabessa and Port Antonio.

Drawn by the coastal beauty and unspoiled character, two of Jamaica's most famous visitors, author Noel Coward and James Bond creator Ian Fleming, made their homes in the area. While Coward settled in Firefly, with its spectacular view down on the coastline, Fleming found refuge at Goldeneye, now one of the island's most elegant hotels.

REGGAE BEACH TO BOSCOBEL BEACH

East of Ocho Rios, habitations begin thinning out along the A3. Several beaches lie hidden below the cliffs; notable among them is Tower Isle, 8km east of Ocho Rios.

Jamaica Beach, between Tower Isle and Rio Nuevo, is renowned for its dive sites offshore.

Reggae Beach

Located east of Harmony Hall on the A3, this vibe-filled yellow **sand beach** (admission US$5; 9am-5pm) is popular with locals and savvy travelers alike. It's the perfect place to while away an afternoon imbibing roots tonic under shady almond trees. Kayaks are available for rent, and jerk chicken and fish are readily available. Raucous sound-system parties are held here now and then; you'll see posters plastered all over Ocho Rios.

Tower Isle & Rio Nuevo

The Rio Nuevo meets the ocean about 8km east of Ocho Rios. In 1658, the bluff west of the river's mouth was the site where English forces fought their decisive battle against the Spanish, sending them scampering off to Cuba with their collective tail between their legs. A plaque placed here records the events:

> On this ground on June 17, 1658, was fought the battle of Rio Nuevo to decide whether Jamaica would be Spanish or English. On one side were the Jamaicans of both black and white races, whose ancestors had come to Jamaica from Africa and Spain 150 years before. The Spanish forces lost the battle and the island. The Spanish whites fled to Cuba but the black people took to the mountains and fought a long and bloody guerrilla war against the English. This site is dedicated to them all.

Tower Isle, on the coast about 1km from Rio Nuevo, is notable mainly for the ostentatious presence of the all-inclusive resort, Couples Ocho Rios.

Boscobel Beach

This beach, 6km east of Rio Nuevo, is a hamlet dominated by Boscobel Beach Spa Resort & Golf Club. The Boscobel airstrip is located here.

Further east find fishing hamlets nestled in turquoise lagoons protected by coral reefs.

Sleeping

Skip's Place (☎ 975-7010, cell 467-4319; Stewart Town; d US$25-50, 2-bedroom cottage US$100, cottage sleeping 6 US$150) One kilometer west of Boscobel Beach, this friendly haven for budget travelers offers 16 modest rooms of varying sizes, cooled by cross-ventilation and featuring basic furnishings. Owners Skip and Patricia Walters also rent out a three-bedroom flat with kitchen. Skip, an avid fisherman, offers boat rides and fishing excursions; your daily catch will likely end up on the dinner table that night. Meals are served to order in a small restaurant. There's no sign on the road. The turnoff is just west of Breezes at the bottom of a small hill; look for the shack decorated with a portrait of Haile Selassie.

Hunter's Rest (☎ 975-5490; www.aileensgardenweddings.com; Tower Isle; s/d US$55/75; P) On the main road, just across from the Rio Nuevo battle site, is this small, welcoming guesthouse offering six simple, clean rooms with cable TV and kitchenettes with fridges. There's an unheralded beach a five-minute walk away.

Crisanns Beach Resort (☎ 975-4467; www.chrisannsresort.com; Tower Isle; studio US$105, r US$115-120,

1-/2-/3-bedroom ste US$147/170/260;) Also in Tower Isle is this well-run resort, offering pleasant suites with full kitchens, cable TV and room safes. The economical rates charged for multiple-bedroom suites make this a great value for groups, but the property is a mite small and can get crowded. There's a tiny beach and swimming cove.

Sea Palms (975-4400; www.seapalms-jamaica.com; 1-/2-/3-/4-bedroom apt per week US$1000/1800/2800/3900;) At Tower Isle, these handsomely appointed, spacious waterfront apartments have fully equipped kitchens, cable TV and private patios or balconies as well as personal maid and cook service. You can rent by the week. There's a small cove for swimming and an attractive pool set among manicured lawns.

This stretch of coast also features two all-inclusive resorts:

Beaches Boscobel Resort & Golf Club (974-7777, in North America 888-232-2437; www.beaches.com; 3 nights all-inclusive d US$1725-1975;) The Sandals chain recently spent US$18 million to create one of the best family-friendly resorts in Jamaica. Kids will find plenty to do: there's a state of the art video games center, a pool with a gigantic water slide, a fully equipped and staffed day-care center, a teen disco and even a petting zoo. Accommodations range from suites designed for families to honeymoon-style beach sanctuaries. There are adults-only areas, plus five bars, four tennis courts, a gym, volleyball, water sports and Olympic-size pool, plus complimentary golf at Sandals Golf & Country Club (p153).

Couples Ocho Rios (975-4271, in the USA 800-268-7537, in the UK 1582 794 420; www.couples.com; Tower Isle; 3 nights all-inclusive d US$1900-2050;) This all-inclusive, upscale resort is strictly for couples. The 212 rooms were refurbished in chic contemporary vogue – classy! – and have four-poster king-size beds, satellite TV, CD players and balconies. Suites feature oversize Jacuzzis. A complete array of sports and water sports are offered. There are four restaurants. A small island is reserved for nude bathing and weddings.

Eating

Skip's Place (975-7010; dishes from US$5; breakfast, lunch & dinner) Enjoying a breezy clifftop setting, 1km west of Boscobel Beach, this unassuming joint serves just-caught seafood and lovingly prepared Jamaican dishes.

Cliff View (975-4417; Tower Isle; mains US$6-17; breakfast, lunch & dinner) Just west of the Rio Nuevo is this popular upscale restaurant serving seafood, continental, and Jamaican dishes.

Colette's Café (btwn Tower Isle & Rio Nuevo) is a twee little roadside shop where Colette and her mom serve simple Jamaican fare, patties, ice cream and bottled coconut water.

Getting There & Away

Minibuses and route taxis traveling between Ocho Rios and Oracabessa serve Rio Nuevo and Tower Isle.

ORACABESSA

pop 10,000

Taking its name from the Spanish *oro cabeza* (golden head) Oracabessa, 21km east of Ocho Rios, is a small one-street, one-storey village with a vague aura of a Wild West town. The street itself is lined with Caribbean vernacular architecture, its wooden houses trimmed with fretwork. This was a major port for shipping bananas in the 19th-century, yet while the boom era has passed, the town itself is far from derelict.

Below Oracabessa is the marina (formerly a banana-loading port), in the lee of a tombolo on whose western flank pirogues and fishing boats bob at anchor.

Information

A **Scotiabank** (975-3203; Main St) with ATM is in the town center, as is the **post office** (Main St). The private **Oracabessa Medical Centre** (975-3304; Vermont Ave; 7:30am-2:30pm Mon & Tue, 7am-12:30pm Wed-Sat) is opposite the Esso gas station at the east end of town; and the **Oracabessa Health Centre** (726-1625; Main St; 8:30-4:30pm Mon-Fri) is opposite the police station. The **Oracabessa Pharmacy** (975-3241; Main St) is in Edwards Plaza.

Get online at **Jee's Business Centre** (726-0686; Nix-Nax Plaza; per hr US$3.50) or at the **library** (975-3293, Main St; per hr US$1.65).

The **James Bond Oracabessa Fishing Tournament** (975-3663) is held in October.

Sights

BEACHES

James Bond Beach (975-3665; jbb@islandjamaica.com; adult/child US$5/3; 9am-6pm Tue-Sun) is today the setting for concerts and special events.

FLEMING...IAN FLEMING

Ian Fleming, inventor of legendary superspy James Bond, first came to Jamaica in 1942 while serving for British Naval Intelligence. In 1946 he bought a house on the shore at Oracabessa and named it 'Goldeneye,' and he wintered here every year until his death in 1964.

It was here that Fleming conceived his secret agent 007, the creation of whom the author attributes to living in Jamaica. 'Would these books have been born if I had not been living in the gorgeous vacuum of a Jamaican holiday? I doubt it,' he wrote in *Ian Fleming Introduces Jamaica*. All 14 of Fleming's James Bond novels were written here, and five were set in Jamaica.

In the same book, he related, 'I was looking for a name for my hero – nothing like Peregrine Carruthers or Standfast Maltravers – and I found it, on the cover of one of my Jamaican bibles, *Birds of the West Indies* by James Bond, an ornithological classic.'

The house is now part of Goldeneye hotel and can be rented (see opposite).

It has toilets, showers and changing rooms, and water sports that include jet-ski safaris (US$55) and glass-bottom boat rides (US$25). The beach provides an excellent setting for infrequent music events; if one is on the horizon you'll see posters plastered about. A small bar and restaurant provides refreshment.

Adjacent to the Bond beach is **Fisherman's Beach**, a rootsy alternative where one can enjoy simple I-tal and seafood fare and the occasional sound-system party.

SUN VALLEY PLANTATION

This working **plantation** (☎ 995-3075, 446-2026; tour incl snack US$12; ⏲ 9am-2pm) and botanical farm is at Crescent on the B13, some 5km south of Oracabessa and 8km west of Port Maria. Owners Lorna and Nolly Binns offer enjoyable garden tours in a plantation setting beside the Crescent River. You can opt to visit the groves of coconuts and other tropical fruits and medicinal herbs.

Sleeping

Nix-Nax (☎ 975-3364; dm US$10-25) Located to the northeast of the town center at the school crossing, this inimitable hostelry offers dorm-style beds, private rooms with shared bath, and one cheerful top-floor room with veranda and private bath. There's no hot water, phones or TV; self-catered meals can be prepared in the two communal kitchens. Also on the site is a Montessori-style preschool (making for lively afternoons when school is in session), and a holistic healing center. Your host, Domenica, a Harlem transplant who has run the guesthouse for more than 20 years, prides herself on flexible arrangements for travelers, saying that it's 'good place for the broke and busted.'

Paradise Jamaica (☎ 792-4386, 975-3428; paradisejamaica.com; Gibraltar; r US$27.50-37.50; Ⓟ 💻 🏊) This attractive colonial-style guesthouse, located on the main road in Gibraltar 3km west of Oracabessa, offers simple, bargain-priced rooms in an old house affording grand sea views. Breakfast is included in the rates; dinner is by arrangement. Self-catered meals can be prepared in a communal kitchen or on an outdoor barbecue.

Tamarind Great House (☎ 995-3252; Crescent Estate; d US$65-85; Ⓟ 🏊) This place is a gem, and a bargain to boot. Nestled atop a hill 6km south of Oracabessa, this 'plantation guesthouse' is run by delightful English hosts Gillian and Barry Chambers. The setting is sublime, with lush valleys and mountains all around. At night the surrounding hills resonate with the sounds of innumerable birds and insects: a welcome change from the sound systems rattling the windows everywhere else. The house boasts gleaming wood floors cut from a single tree and offbeat antiques including a mysterious iron lung. The 10 large bedrooms, reached by a wide staircase, each open to a vast veranda. There's a TV lounge and an elegant dining room. The excellent restaurant serves stick-to-your-ribs breakfasts (US$12) and full-course dinners (US$35) on the veranda.

Tamarind is 1.5km south of Sun Valley Plantation. From the minibus and taxi stand at Oracabessa, take Jack's River Rd. It's a long 6km from the main road. Keep a keen eye out for the directional signs along the way. The road is rough. The proprietors appreciate advance reservations.

Golden Seas Beach Resort (☎ 975-3251; www.goldenseas.com; s US$94-121, d US$110-137, studio US$136-152, ste US$160-175; Ⓟ ⊠ ❄ 🏊) On the A3, 1km west of Oracabessa, is this attractive hotel of cut stone, with 79 comfortable if uninspired rooms with cable TVs, phones and patios that overlook a pool with swim-up bar. The hotel offers water sports, tennis clinics, a spa and gym, cabaret shows and an excellent resident band. Meals are provided both à la carte and through an all-inclusive plan (per person per day US$50).

our pick **Goldeneye** (☎ 975-3354, 800-688-7678, in the UK ☎ 020-7440-4360; www.goldeneyehotel.com; 1-/2-bedroom villa US$895/1095, entire complex US$6000-8500) If this looks like the type of place James Bond might have retired to, it's possibly because his creator Ian Fleming used to live here. There are eight villas, including Fleming's abode (spectacular decor, highlighted by Balinese fabrics), sprinkled across expansive grounds on a quaint cove. Additional waterfront cottages, built of wood and stone and painted in autumnal colors, have ceiling fans, a kitchen, a TV room and pampering yet discreet stewards. There's a communal entertainment room where 007 movies are shown, but the coup de grâce is the hotel's secluded, private island with its own beach and water sports. Organized excursions, a tennis court and swimming pool seem a little banal after that. Located on the A3 immediately east of Oracabessa.

Eating & Drinking

Jah Willy's Calabash Inn (☎ 369-3617; lunch & dinner) Off Waterfront Rd, this is a cool place to hang for a game of dominoes or volleyball with the locals. Willy serves seafood and jerk for US$2 and less.

Dor's Fish Pot (☎ 726-0372; Racecourse; lunch & dinner) On the A3, 1km east of town, is this lively yet rustic jerk and seafood eatery atop the breezy cliffs.

Tamarind Great House (☎ 995-3252; tamarind@go-jamaica.com; Crescent Estate; 3-course meal US$40; dinner) This is the place to head for a full-course English-style gourmet meal. Reservations are required.

La Shanka Tavern (Main St) Opposite the market, this lively rum shop is good for a spirited game of dominoes.

Getting There & Away

Minibuses and route taxis pass through en route between Ocho Rios and Port Antonio, and between Ocho Rios and Kingston.

FIREFLY

Set amid wide lawns high atop a hill 5km east of Oracabessa and 5km west of Port Maria, **Firefly** (☎ 997-7201, 994-0920; admission US$10; 9am-5pm Mon-Fri) was the home of Sir Noel Coward, the English playwright, songwriter, actor and wit (see the boxed text, p164). When he died in 1973, Coward left the estate to his partner Graham Payn, who gifted it to the nation. Today the house is a museum, looking just as it did on Sunday, February 28, 1965, the day the Queen Mother visited.

Your guide will lead you to Coward's art studio, where he was schooled in oil painting by Winston Churchill. The studio displays Coward's original paintings and photographs of himself and a coterie of famous friends. The upper lounge features a glassless window that offers one of the most stunning coastal vistas in all Jamaica. The view takes in Port Maria Bay and the coastline further west. Contrary to popular opinion, Coward didn't write his famous song *A Room with a View* here (it was written in Hawaii in 1928). His bedroom features his mahogany four-poster bed and closets still stuffed with his Hawaiian shirts and silk PJs.

Coward lies buried beneath a plain white marble slab on the wide lawns where he entertained many illustrious stars of stage and screen. A statue of the man gazing out at his favorite view graces the lawn and a stone hut that once served as a lookout for the pirate Henry Morgan is now a gift store, bar and restaurant. Musical and theatrical performances are hosted and a Moonlick party with live jazz band is held on weekends closest to the full moon.

Firefly is well signed along three different routes from the A3.

GALINA POINT & LITTLE BAY

Five kilometers east of Oracabessa, the A3 winds around the promontory of Galina Point. A 12m-high concrete lighthouse marks the headland. South of Galina you'll pass Noël Coward's first house, **Blue Harbour** (p164) squatting atop 'the double bend,' where the road and shoreline take a 90-degree turn and open to a view of Cabarita Island. The road drops steeply from Blue Harbour to Cocomo Beach in Little Bay.

The beach is unappealing, despite being popular in the '50s and '60s with Coward and co, but the snorkeling is good about

NOEL COWARD'S PEENY-WALLY

The multitalented Sir Noel Coward first visited Jamaica in 1944 on a two-week holiday. He found peace of mind here and dubbed his dream island 'Dr Jamaica.' Four years later he rented Ian Fleming's estate, Goldeneye, at Oracabessa, while he hunted for a site to build his own home. He found an incredible view over Little Bay near Galina, 6km east of Oracabessa.

In 1948 Coward bought the eight-acre estate and set to work building Coward's Folly, a three-story villa with two guest cottages. He named his home Blue Harbour. He had a swimming pool built at the sea's edge and invited his many notable friends, a virtual 'Who's Who' of the rich and famous.

The swarm of visitors, however, eventually drove Coward to find another retreat.

While painting with his lover Graham Payn at a place called Lookout (so-named because the pirate Henry Morgan had a stone hut built atop the hill to keep an eye out for Spanish galleons), Coward was struck by the impressive solitude and incredible view. The duo lingered until nightfall, when fireflies (or 'peeny-wallies' in the Jamaican dialect) appeared. Within two weeks Coward had bought the land, and eight years later he had a house built, big enough for only himself. He named it Firefly.

Coward lived a remarkably modest lifestyle in Jamaica; he set up the now-defunct Designs for Living shop in Port Maria, the profits from which went to train local children in arts and crafts. Coward himself recorded his love of the island and islanders on canvas, in bright, splashy colors.

Coward had spent 30 years in Jamaica when he suffered a heart attack at the age of 73. He is buried on the lawns of Firefly beneath a marble slab that reads simply: 'Sir Noel Coward/Born 16 December 1899/Died 26 March 1973.'

50m out (check with locals about current swimming conditions).

The **Zabai Tabai Taino Museum** (☎ 994-9391; 12 Hudson St; admission free), on the main road, is an offbeat museum celebrating the Taino culture. Many of the artifacts were dug up on the owner's property, which has a cave with what are purportedly Taino paintings that glow translucent in winter. The museum has no set hours.

Minibuses and route taxis pass through en route between Ocho Rios and Port Antonio, and between Ocho Rios and Kingston.

Sleeping & Eating

Belretiro Inn (☎ 994-0035; r US$13-35;) Signed off the A3, this inn has 12 modestly furnished rooms with private baths and cold water. It has a seawater swimming pool and a bar.

Little Bay Inn (☎ 994-2721, 373-5871; r US$20-25; P) On the main road just at the turnoff for Firefly, this modest new hotel offers 10 simple, fan-cooled rooms with double beds and private bath. There's a small restaurant and jerk center.

Caribbean Pearl (☎ 994-2731; caribbeanpearl@cwjamaica.com; r US$45-75; P) On the A3, this attractive place rests on a breezy hilltop at the southern end of Little Bay. It is run to an excellent standard. The elegant, intimate villa-style hotel has eight rooms that are furnished with hardwoods and white wicker. Mosquito nets drape over the beds. Wide windows open to shady verandas where you can relax.

Hotel Casa Maria (☎ 725-0156, in North America ☎ 509-547-7065; nwas@cwt.com; r US$50-60; P) Next to the Caribbean Pearl, this is an option if all else fails. The 20-room hotel has lost its panache since Noel Coward and his celebrated guests frequented the bar in the 1950s and 1960s. The fan-cooled rooms are pleasantly, though modestly, furnished. Cheaper rooms have garden views; superior rooms have private balconies with ocean views.

Tradewinds Resort (☎ 994-0420; r incl breakfast US$55-65; P) Further along from Hotel Casa Maria is this modern, motel-style resort, cascading down the windswept cliffs to a rocky shore. It has 14 modestly furnished rooms and a cottage suite, all with their own splendid views, white tiles, small TVs, phones and remote-control air-con. There's a small lap pool and a restaurant.

Blue Harbour (☎ 725-0289, in the USA ☎ 505-586-1244; www.blueharb.com; r per person US$100; P) Once owned by Noel Coward and visited by Marlene Dietrich, Katherine Hepburn,

Errol Flynn and Winston Churchill, this is a rather offbeat hotel offering delicious seclusion. Villa Grande, the main building, has four upstairs bedrooms with a combination of antiques and dowdy utility furniture, plus cable TV. Meals are served on a wide veranda with bay views. Villa Rose has four spacious rooms with basic furnishings and decor. Villa Chica is where Marlene Dietrich went to be left alone; it's smaller and very private, with more pleasing, tropical decor. Blue Harbour comes fully staffed with cook and housekeeper. There's a saltwater pool. Rates include three meals.

Mystic Cliff Villas (☎ 994-0135; www.mystic-cliff.com; d US$250; P) Nine years in the making, this dramatic property is the lovechild of Everton and Cecilia McKenzie; at last visit they were proudly putting the finishing touches on their singular creation in anticipation of welcoming the first guests. On a craggy clifftop, the McKenzies have created a striking environment featuring dramatic terraces, elevated walkways, a secluded swimming cove, several small sea caves, the On the Rocks gazebo bar and a saltwater 'infinity' pool.

On offer are six villas spread between the three tastefully appointed cottages and the commanding main house. Each has an ocean view plus large bedroom and bathroom and private patio or balcony. Also offered are jeep tours and rentals. You'll find the villas on the small road adjacent to the western edge of the Tradewinds Resort. Rates include airport transfers, maid and cook service and full breakfast.

PORT MARIA

pop 8000

Gazing down from the lawn at Firefly, you might think Port Maria is a quaint fishing village nestled around a deep turquoise and aquamarine bay with mountains rising behind. When you arrive, it's soon apparent that there's nothing particularly alluring about this capital St Mary parish.

Fishing pirogues can be seen on **Pagee Beach**, lining the shore. You can hire a guide and boat to go fishing or to take you to Cabarita Island. The beach is safe for swimming. It is also the most westerly spot for surfing along the north coast, with long peelers. The rocks are sharp, however; local surfers advise surfing in front of the point closest to town. The action is best in the morning before the trade winds kick in.

St Mary's Parish Church, at the extreme west end of town, was built in 1861 in quintessential English style. Facing it is the **old courthouse**, destroyed in 1988 by fire but since partially restored and today housing a **Civic Centre**. A monument in front commemorates 'Tacky of the Easter Rebellion,' in honor of the hero of that 1760 revolt.

Remains of **Fort Haldane** can be seen on a bluff beside the A3, 1km north of town.

You can get online at **St Mary Parish Library** (☎ 994-2213; Claude Stuart Park; per 30min US$1.15).

The best place to spend the night in downtown Port Maria is **Sunrise Apartments** (☎ 871-3960; 37 Warners St; r US$50; P), offering four clean and comfortable fan-cooled apartments with kitchenettes and dining areas. There's a laundry room and secure parking.

For a good meal, head to **Almond Tree Club & Restaurant** (☎ 994-2379; 56 Warners St; mains US$3.50-5; breakfast, lunch & dinner), offering typical authentic Jamaican dishes, fried chicken, chop suey and, for breakfast, a selection of porridges. For a quick snack, **Juici Beef Patties** (Stennet St; patties US$0.40), on the southeast side of the town square, sells beef and veggie patties. Wash them down with bottled coconut water.

You can catch buses or minibuses to Port Maria from Ocho Rios and Kingston.

BRIMMER HALL

This 2000-acre working **plantation** (☎ 994-2309; tours US$18; 9am-4pm Mon-Fri, tours 11:30am, 1:30pm & 3pm), near Bailey's Vale, 10km southwest of Port Maria, grows bananas, coconuts, sugarcane, pineapple and citrus for export. It's centered on a wooden great house with an impressive interior furnished with oriental rugs and antique furniture, and even an original suit of armor. One-hour plantation tours by canopied jitney cost US$15. It is signed from the A3.

SOUTH OF OCHO RIOS

The A3 winds through sweeping pastoral country on its way south. At Moneague, the road meets up with the A1 from St Ann's Bay, continues over Mt Diablo and drops dramatically to Kingston.

FERN GULLY

Passing through this lush **gorge** is one of the prime attractions of Ocho Rios. Milford Rd (the A3) zigzags uphill through the 5km canyon of an old watercourse that was planted with hundreds of different fern species around 1880. Today, the trees form a canopy overhead, filtering subaqueous light, while crafts vendors ply their wares at the side of the road. Over the years, exhaust from traffic has harmed the ferns, and there's been talk of closing the gully altogether and making it a national park.

WALKERSWOOD

As you climb from Fern Gully on the A3, the forest canopy opens up at this village up in the cool hills of St Ann parish. Its main claim to fame is the tongue-searing **Walkerswood** jerk sauce, now available all over the world. Nobody with even a passing interest in the art of jerk should pass up the opportunity to visit the plant (☎ 917-2318; www.walkerwood.com; 8am-4:30pm Mon-Sat; adult/child US$15/7.50), where its marinades and seasonings are produced. Walkerswood began as a local farmer's co-op dedicated to providing irrigation and jobs for the community. Today, close to 200 people work full-time at the environmentally conscious plant.

After a complimentary drink, the tour takes you through a herb garden complete with Mother Thyme, who explains all the spices that go in to making jerk. The history of jerking, a process the Maroons discovered in the 17th century, is revealed. A quick tour of the factory and a sampling of Walkerswood's various products, from the blazing scotch bonnet pepper sauce to the tangy sorrel chutney to the savory guava jam, round out the tour. There's a small restaurant and gift shop on the premises.

In the cooler hills near Lydford, **Murphy Hill** (☎ 927-1003, 469-4968; Spring Mountain Rd; r US$25-30), 5km west of Walkerswood, has a relaxing, quiet guesthouse with clean rooms and genuine antiques. There's a small restaurant. The **grounds** (admission US$2; 🕓 10am-7pm) are also open to the public, with a swimming pool popular with Jamaicans escaping the heat of the lowlands. It has fabulous views.

The craft shop **Art Beat** (☎ 917-2154) is owned by Nancy Burke, alias Inanci. She sells jewelry, carnival and *duppy* (ghost) masks, painted rocks, and other intriguing creations. Her shop is on the main square in Walkerswood, facing the post office.

GOSHEN WILDERNESS RESORT

A sign outside this lakeside '**wilderness resort**' (☎ 974-4613, 974-5189; Goshen; adult/child US$3/2; 🕓 10am-5pm Tue-Sun), 6km east of Walkerswood, happily proclaims: 'You catch it, we cook it.' Its prime attraction is 42 large ponds stocked with tilapia just waiting for you to yank them out of the water.

Attractions include an aviary, a petting zoo, volleyball, paddleboats and kayaks, nature trails and horseback rides (per hour US$40). A one-hour ATV tour of the plantation and nearby hills costs US$45; there's a longer tour to Spanish Bridge and a lovely swimming spot on the White River (US$80). A fishing package (adult/child US$21/14) includes a drink, tackle and a guide. The chef will prepare your fish with bammy (pancake-shaped cassava bread) and festival (a fried biscuit shaped like a sausage), but burgers, hot dogs and jerk dishes are also available at the thatched restaurant and bar.

To get here from Ocho Rios, take the turnoff from the A3 at the White River estuary. Eventually you'll reach a three-way road junction called Goshen. Turn east (left when coming from Ocho Rios) down the deteriorated road. The Wilderness Resort is 1km beyond the gates for Goshen great house – marked 'Goshen.' If you don't have a car, ask at the transportation center in Ocho Rios for minibuses heading to Goshen.

MONEAGUE

This small crossroads town, at the junction of the A3 and the A1, 19km south of Ochi, was favored during the 19th century as a hill resort, and before that as a staging post on the journey between Spanish Town and the north coast. The Moneague Training Camp of the Jamaica Defense Force is here, with two **Saracen armored cars** at the gateway.

Café Aubergine (☎ 973-0527; mains US$12-28; 🕓 lunch & dinner Wed-Sun) Also called Moneague Tavern, this restaurant is in a 250-year-old tavern 1km south of town. Tasteful art, china and real silverware abound. The menu is written on parchment and consists of Mediterranean-influenced Jamaican nouvelle cuisine, such as crayfish Provençal, chicken in coconut curry sauce, and roast lamb Provençal. Leave room for the chocolate gateau. The café hosts an Oktoberfest Party with German fare. Reservations are required.

FAITH'S PEN

South of Moneague, the A1 climbs steadily to Faith's Pen, 27km south of Ocho Rios. It's a destination for the taste buds, a place where competitive roadside cooks try to outdo each other with good-natured culinary bravado. The road is lined with stalls selling citrus fruits and dozens of stands where you can sample jerk and try oddities such as cow-cod soup, a concoction made of bull's testes – reputed to be an aphrodisiac – best washed down with 'roots' wine. If this sounds a tad unappetizing, there's plenty of equally remarkable fare to choose from.

The road continues up the pine-forested slopes of Mt Diablo (839m). At 686m the A1 crests the mountain chain and begins its steep, winding descent to Ewarton and the lush Rosser Valley, beautiful when seen from these heights. The summit of Mt Diablo marks the boundary between the parishes of St Ann to the north and St Catherine to the south.

WEST OF OCHO RIOS

Sadly, the best of the many beaches along this stretch of coast have been snapped up by resorts both ritzy and gaudy. The Dry Harbour Mountains, rising steeply inland, offer recommended scenic drives.

MAMMEE BAY

A favorite with Jamaican beachgoers, Mammee Bay – 5.5km west of Ocho Rios and 4km east of St Ann's Bay – has several little beaches, some hidden away. Much of the beachfront is a private residential estate, but access is offered to the public beaches. Locals flock to Fisherman's Beach, where jet skis can be rented.

At **Laughing Waters** – also called Roaring River – 1km east of Mammee Bay and 1km west of Dunn's River Falls, a river appears from rocks amid a shallow ravine about 3km from the sea and spills to a charming little beach. This is where Ursula Andress famously appeared, dripping with brine, in the James Bond movie *Dr No* (the beach is known as 'James Bond Beach'). Look for the large fenced-in electrical power structure beside the A3. Follow the river to the beach. Public access to the falls is by foot.

The **St Ann Polo Club & Equestrian Centre** (☎ 972-2762; Mammee Bay; lessons per hr US$15) offers horseback lessons, and hosts the **Hi-Pro Family Polo Tournament & International Horse Show** in August.

Sleeping

Rose Garden Hotel (☎ 972-2825; r US$80, r for 4 people US$100;) About 500m east of the Sandals resort, this small hotel has 24 studio suites with kitchenette, private bathroom with hot water, TV and balcony. The rooms are modestly furnished and uninspiring, but they're clean and have lots of light. There's a sundeck, plus a dining room. The rates include breakfast.

Cannon Villas & Silver Palms (☎ 927-1852; www.silvercannon.com; villas & cottages US$360, studio $US210, 1-/2-/3-bedroom apt US$210/240/360;) At Old Fort Bay, on the east side of Mammee Bay, this secluded property is a good choice for groups and families. There are villas and apartments, each with a living and dining area, satellite TV, fully equipped kitchen and a patio. It also has modern three-bedroom townhouses (Silver Palms), plus one- and two-bedroom apartments fronting a pool and Jacuzzi. A housekeeper is provided.

Sandals Dunn's River Golf Resort & Spa (☎ 972-1610; in North America ☎ 877-726-3257; 3 nights all-inclusive d US$1135-1725, ste US$2160-2495;) A popular, upscale, all-inclusive couples-only resort. A dramatic curving staircase and gleaming marble columns in the lobby recreate the opulence of an Italian palazzo, reflected in the ritzy Roman-style full-service spa. The 250 rooms come in eight categories, all in Sandals' plantation style. The resort boasts a huge swimming pool with cascading waterfall, plus a second pool, three Jacuzzis (two are big enough for 40 people each), a pitch'n'putt course, a tour desk, four specialty restaurants, a video-game room, a billiards room and a theater and disco.

Villas of varying ranges of opulence are represented by **Sun Villas** (in North America ☎ 888-625-6007; www.sunvillas.com) and **Jamaican Association of Villas & Apartments** (JAVA; ☎ 974-2508; www.villasinjamaica.com; PO Box 298, Ocho Rios).

ST ANN'S BAY

pop 12,000

This small market town and parish capital, 11km west of Ocho Rios, rises up the hillside above the bay. Check out the several well-preserved old buildings in Caribbean vernacular style, especially along Braco St.

Christopher Columbus landed here in 1494 during his second voyage to the Americas and christened the bay Santa Gloria. He might well have considered renaming it something less pleasant when, during his fateful fourth and final voyage in 1503, he was forced to abandon his ships in the bay. Columbus and his crew were stranded for more than a year before finally being rescued (see the boxed text, p170).

In 1509 the Spaniards built the first Spanish settlement on the island about 700m west of St Ann's Bay, at Sevilla la Nueva. The site was abandoned within four decades and it was later developed as a sugar estate by a British planter. Other planters established sugar estates nearby, and the town grew and prospered as a bustling seaport with forts on opposite sides of the bay.

Marcus Garvey, founder of the Black Nationalist movement, was born here and is honored each August 17 with a parade.

Shoppers can browse the arts and crafts market, beside the A1 opposite Braco St.

Buses, minibuses and route taxis travel between Montego Bay and Ocho Rios and call at St Ann's.

Information

Cable & Wireless office (☎ 972-9701; 11 King St; ⏲ 8am-4pm Mon-Fri) International calls and faxes.

Library (☎ 972-2660; 2 King St; internet access per 30 min US$1) One hundred meters east of Braco St.

National Commercial Bank (☎ 972-0722; 19 Main St) Has a 24-hour ATM.

Pine Grove Pharmacy (☎ 972-0334; 55 Main St)

Police station (☎ 972-2211; cnr Main & Braco Sts)

Post office (☎ 972-2307; Main St) Just east of Braco St.

Quick Stop Laundromat (Wharf St)

St Ann's Bay Public General Hospital (☎ 972-2272) At the far west end of Main St, with an emergency clinic. Several doctors' clinics are concentrated west of the town center on Main St.

Scotiabank (☎ 972-2531; 18 Braco St) 24-hour ATM.

Votech Educational Centre (☎ 794-8812; Main St; internet access per 30min US$1) International calls and faxes, and internet services.

Sights

MAIMA SEVILLE GREAT HOUSE & HERITAGE PARK

This historical **park**, less than 1km west of present-day St Ann's, marks the site of the first Spanish capital on the island – Sevilla la Nueva – and one of the first Spanish settlements in the New World. Traces of the original Spanish buildings, including a church and a **sugar mill**, are visible, accessed via a grassy track leading to the ocean from the A1

This was also the site of an Arawak village. In 1982 Sevilla la Nueva was declared a Site of the Americas by the Organization of American States, which funds ongoing excavations by the Jamaica National Heritage Trust.

When the English captured Jamaica from the Spanish, the land on which Sevilla la Nueva had been built was granted to Richard Hemming, an officer in Oliver Cromwell's army. Hemming's descendants developed the property as a sugar estate that's now owned by the Jamaica National Trust Commission. The property is dominated by the Seville Great House, built in 1745 by Hemming's grandson. Explore the decrepit 'English Industrial Works' that include the ruins of a sugar mill, copra kiln, waterwheel and boiling house, plus the Hemming tombs.

The original great house, duly restored, contains a **museum** (☎ 972-2191; www.jnht.com/st_ann/seville_grthse.htm; admission adults/children US$5/2; ⏲ 9am-5pm) depicting the history of the site from Arawak times through the era of slavery and the colonial period.

More Spanish **ruins** stand by the shore just east of the mouth of the Church River.

There are **horseback tours** (US$70 inc lunch; 9am & 2pm) from on the property that end with a jaunt into the sea. A nature tour with a local bush doctor will enlighten you about tropical fruits.

OTHER SIGHTS

The grassy forecourt of the parish library on King St is dominated by the **Marcus Garvey Statue**, with the hero portrayed larger than life in gray bronze (see the boxed text, p32).

Westward along Main St you'll pass the **courthouse**, at the corner of Market St. It was erected in elegant cut limestone and red brick in 1866 with a pedimented porch bearing the scales of justice. Visitors are welcome to observe the court when it's in session. Across the way is the **market**, topped by a clock tower, which gets busy on Fridays and Saturdays. One hundred meters further west lies quaint **St Ann's Bay Baptist Church** (☎ 972-0408).

Nearby, on Hospital Rd just off Main St, is the warehouse of **Seville Pottery** (☎ 972-9517), which makes superb ceramics, including exquisite blue-glazed bottles.

At the west end of Main St stands the **Columbus Monument**, topped by a bronze figure of the explorer dolled up as a Spanish grandee.

One hundred meters up the hill from the Columbus Monument is the exquisite church **Our Lady of Perpetual Help**, built in contemporary Spanish design by an Irish priest in 1939, with stones recovered from the ruins of Sevilla la Nueva. Inside, great beams support the organ loft. This is one of the few Catholic churches in all of Jamaica.

Festivals & Events

A festival of traditional music and dance, **Jamaica Night**, is held at Maima Seville Great House in April. An **emancipation celebration** is held on the grounds every July 29 to August 1, and a **National Mento Yard** celebrates the Jamaican heritage in October.

The **St Ann Family Fun Day and Kite Festival** (☎ 972-9607) is held each Easter Monday at Drax Hall, on the A3 immediately east of St Ann's Bay.

Sleeping & Eating

Motel 64 (☎ 972-2308; Main St; r US$18) This very basic downtown motel offers 14 small rooms with only minimal furnishings, but they are clean and have fans and private showers.

our pick **High Hope Estate** (☎ 972-2277; www.highhopeestate.com; all-inclusive d per person per day/week US$110-180; P 💻 ⊠ 🏊) Set amid 16 hectares of manicured gardens, lawns and woodland high in the hills above St Ann's Bay, this quirky yet chic Venetian-style villa built in 1961 resembles a location from a Fellini film. Each of its seven rooms, decorated with antiques, has a minibar and mini-library of books; three have wonderful ocean views and verandas. There's a well-stocked library, and you're welcome to peruse and play the original owners' collection of vinyl records. A pool is inset in a sundeck. Rates include breakfast and afternoon 'high tea.' Other meals, lovingly prepared with ingredients hand-picked from the property's fruit trees and garden, are available on request. To get here, take

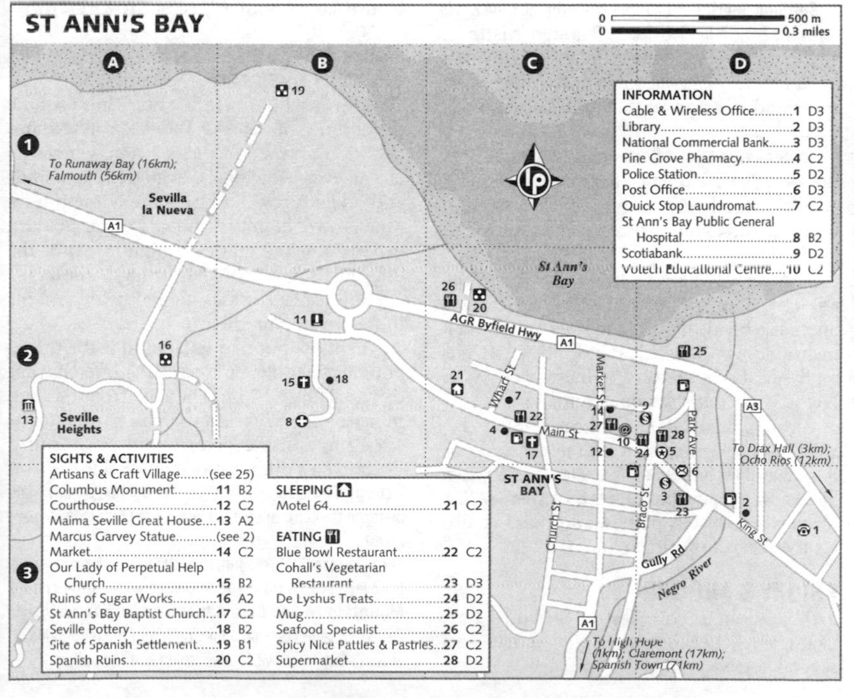

COLUMBUS MAROONED

As any experienced island traveler will tell you, in Jamaica the best-laid plans can veer wildly astray. Such was the case with Jamaica's first European tourist, Christopher Columbus. In 1503, on his fourth voyage to the New World – and his second trip to Jamaica – the explorer's two remaining ships were pummeled by a storm. Leaking badly, the ships managed to make land on Jamaica's north-central coast near modern-day St Ann's Bay. With one of his worm-eaten ships nearly submerged and all the rigging gone, Columbus and his downtrodden crew dug in and tried to make friendly with the locals.

Fortunately they were able to come to agreeable terms with the Arawaks living nearby in a village called Aguacadiba. Diego Mendez, the de facto operations manager for Columbus, wrote of the welcome hospitality they had received. And so began the short-lived honeymoon between the European interlopers and Jamaica's indigenous people.

Now that they could depend on all-inclusive service, Columbus turned to other matters. He sent Mendez off in a canoe to Hispaniola to fetch help – that's another story! – and sank dejectedly into a period of idleness. Predictably, his Arawak friends soon tired of their obligation to the moody explorer, who was derelict in paying his bills.

To frighten them back into submission, Columbus performed a disingenuous parlor trick by consulting his trusty almanac and 'predicting' that their vengeful God would express his consternation with a sign of anger in the sky. When night fell, a lunar eclipse caused the moon to have an eerie 'bloody' quality and the Arawaks fell into a panic. The next morning room service resumed, and Columbus and his men survived for 12 more months until help arrived from Santo Domingo.

Church St south (uphill) three blocks from downtown St Ann's and continue uphill for about 1.5km.

Seafood Specialist (☎ 794-8870; cnr Jail Lane & A1; mains US$2-6; lunch & dinner) Though rustic, it serves wholesome local fare such as brown stew, plus excellent steamed or fried fish with yams and rice and peas, washed down with natural juices.

Cohall's Vegetarian Restaurant (☎ 794-8537; 18 Musgrave St; mains US$2-6; breakfast, lunch & dinner) A health-food restaurant and store selling soups, patties, gluten, beans, carrot juice and fruit drinks.

Mug (☎ 972-1018; mains US$4-12; lunch & dinner) The Mug is 300m east of the Seafood Specialist, beside the A1, and it serves seafood, including fish-and-chips and lobster. It has a popular barbecue on Wednesdays – 'Mug Night' – when it stays open until 1am.

Clean, modern **De Lyshus Treats** (☎ 972-2317; Main St) serves inexpensive Jamaican fare, as does **Blue Bowl Restaurant & Lounge** (Main St), two blocks west. **Spicy Nice Patties & Pastries** (22 Main St; patties US$0.30) sells patties, and there is also a supermarket on Braco St.

PRIORY & AROUND

Priory, about 1.5km west of St Ann's Bay, has a small beach with water sports and several hotels.

You can turn inland and head into the hills for views down the coast. Here you'll find **Lillyfield Coffee Museum**, at Lillyfield Great House, about 5 miles east of Brown's Town.

Sights & Activities

CHUKKA COVE FARM

This former polo field west of Priory is now the home of **Chukka Caribbean Adventures** (☎ 972-2506; www.chukkacaribbean.com), which offers an ever-growing list of guided excursions and adventures. The trips are sometimes a mite crowded, but the quality of service and expertise of the guides is high. Most of the offerings can be booked through a hotel including transfer; rates quoted below are for those arriving on their own steam.

The most popular excursion is the three-hour **Horseback Ride 'n Swim** (US$76), offered twice daily at 9am and 2pm. The waterfront ride culminates with an exciting bareback trot into the sea. Bring sunscreen, towel and a swimsuit.

Chukka's other tours include these ones:

Canopy Tour (2hrs; US$88) Sail through the canopy from platform to platform on a zip line in the Cranbrook Flower Forest.

Jeep Safari (3½hrs; adult/child US$66/53) A tour by jeep to Coyaba River Garden and through mountain scenery.

Mountain to Sea Bike Adventure (3hours; adult/child US$60/48) An exceptional bike ride from the mountains of St Ann's Bay to a cove for swimming and snorkeling.

River Tubing Safari (1½hrs; adult/child US$66/48) A family-friendly float three miles down the White River.
River Kayak Safari (1¼ hr; adult/child US$66/48) Paddle down the White River.
Zion Bus Line (5hrs; US$73) This is the easiest way to visit Nine Mile, the birthplace and final resting place of Bob Marley.

The farm also hosts a popular Easter Sunday carnival, when crowds flock from as far afield as Kingston.

CIRCLE B FARM

This working **plantation** (913-4511; tours US$12, with lunch US$25; 10am-5pm), at Lewis, near Richmond Hill, about 1.5km south of the A1, has tours that demonstrate the raising of avocados, bananas, coconuts and vegetables. The farm is reached via a turnoff 1km west of Sevilla la Nueva at Priory, 3km west of St Ann's Bay. Also on site is a guest house; see below.

CRANBROOK FLOWER FOREST

This 130-acre **botanical garden** (995-3097; www.cranbrookff.com; adult/child US$10/5; 9am-sunset) is a treat, crafted in the lush valley that carves up into the hills south of Laughlands, about 5km west of Priory; it's signed off the A1, a kilometer and a half west of Chukka Cove. The garden is built around a colonial-era building and includes theme gardens, a hothouse orchid display, pools, and lush lawns (with croquet) fringed by banks of anthuriums and other tropical flowers.

Guided nature walks (about 90 minutes) lead to the river, reflecting giant tree ferns, spectacular torch ginger, heliconia and other exotic species. Volleyball, river tubing and horseback rides are available.

Sleeping

Circle B Farm Guest House (913-4511; dm US$20, r US$50) In the middle of the Circle B Plantation is this simple backpacker's lodge offering several dorm-style rooms, each with three single beds. There's a communal kitchen and lounge and one private room with kitchenette. Meals are not offered; if you lack wheels you may want to consider bringing food to prepare.

H'Evans Scent (427-4866; www.hevansscent.com; Free Hill; r per person US$80;) In the tiny hill town of Free Hill, 10km south of Priory, this evolving ecotourism experiment is the brainchild of Derek Evans, better known in the UK as fitness celebrity Mr Motivator. The sprawling hilltop property is lavishly gardened and has many nooks and crannies designed specifically for blissful repose. Rooms are brightly painted in lime green, yellow and orange, and each has two twin beds, a CD player and mosquito nets, and there's also a one-bedroom suite with a lounge and fridge. On the property are diversions such as zip wire rides, and, blessedly far away, an ATV track. Meals are provided in the extensively decorated main house. Be sure to visit the herb garden and learn from the bush doctor all the health-giving benefits of the local plants.

Seacrest Beach Hotel (972-1594; www.seacrestresorts.com; 12 Richmond Estate; r US$85-110, ste US$120, 2-bedroom villa US$170;) Off the A1 in Priory – look for a giant rusty anchor next to picturesque ruins – is this compact and friendly property. Bougainvillea spills over whitewashed walls onto a tiled sundeck, giving the place a distinctly Mediterranean feel. Rooms have TV, phone and private balcony overlooking a beach. Car-rental discounts are offered with your room.

Columbus Beach Cottages (972-1516, 972-1847; Richmond Estate; 1-/2-bedroom apt US$60/100;) Just down the road from the Seacrest is this seaside lodging that doubles as a marine laboratory for Hofstra University in New York. It's a pleasant place conjuring up memories of summer camp. Students mill about, and there's a resident marine biologist. Guests have opportunities to get involved in the research. The apartments sleep three and have no frills; most are fan-cooled but a couple have air-con. Each is equipped with a serviceable kitchen. As for swimming, some visitors are put off by the seaweed growing along the rocky shore, but others are undaunted. There's a gazebo over the ocean, perfect for sunset reflection.

RUNAWAY BAY

This bay (16km west of St Ann's) has a modicum of hotels and tourist facilities, though the place is far from sophisticated. Divers, however, find much to celebrate. This one-street village stretches along the A1 for 3km, merging with Salem to the east. Several small beaches are supposedly public, although most are the backyards for a few all-inclusive resorts. If you're hankering for a dip in the big blue, head to the white-sand **Cardiff Hall Public Beach** (admission free; 7am-sunset), opposite the gas station. There is also a somewhat twee **fisherman's beach** in Salem, east of Runaway Bay, where the occasional sound-system party is staged on the weekend.

Information

Dr Patrick Wheatle (☎ 973-7761; Main St, Salem) Medical clinic.
Johnny's Pharmacy (☎ 973-6071; Main St, Salem) Next door to Dr Patrick Wheatle.
Nu Innovations (☎ 973-6775; Northern Shopping Complex, Salem; per 30min US$1.25) Internet access.
Police (☎ 110, 973-3433)
Post office (☎ 973-2477) On the main road in Runaway Bay.
Runaway Self-Service Launderette (☎ 973-6535; Rose Plaza, Salem)
Scotiabank (Main St, Salem) ATM outlet.

Activities

SCUBA DIVING & WATER SPORTS

Runaway Bay has excellent diving. There's a wreck in shallow water in front of Club Ambiance, plus two cars and a plane offshore from Club Caribbean. A reef complex called Ricky's Reef is renowned for its sponges. More experienced divers might try the eponymous Canyon. Here, too, is the Reggae Queen, a 30m-long sunken tugboat. Potty Reef will have you flush with excitement; divers can't resist having their photo taken sitting on, er, King Neptune's throne.

Diving company **Reef Divers** (☎ 973-4400; Club Ambiance, Main Rd, Runaway Bay) offers one/two tank dives (US$42/75) and certification programs (from US$120).

OTHER ACTIVITIES

The 6294m course at **Breezes Golf Club** (☎ 973-7319; day pass US$80; 🕑 6:30am-9pm) is par-72, with several elevated tees and a putting green. There's a pro shop and, upstairs, a classy restaurant and sports bar. Caddies are mandatory (US$15 for 18 holes, or US$10 for nine holes). Guests staying at Breezes and Hedonism III play for free.

South of Runaway Bay, **Dover Raceway** (☎ 975-2127) is the setting for auto and motorcycle races. Races are held once every other month, April to December.

Sleeping

HOTELS

Salem Resort (☎ 973-4256; r with fan/air-con/kitchen US$35/45/55; P ✲ 🏊) This family-run resort in Salem offers 24 rooms, each modestly furnished with queen-sized beds, satellite TVs and phones. There are two bars and a restaurant.

Tamarind Tree Resort Hotel (☎ 973-2628; tamarindtree@cwjamaica.com; r US$40-45, 3-bedroom cottage US$135; P ✲ 🏊) A 25-room hotel on the A1, 100m from the beach. All the rooms have phone and cable TV and are pleasantly furnished; most have small balconies. The bar next door makes a racket late into the night. The hotel also offers three large and pleasing cottages, and a simple restaurant.

Piper's Cove Resort (☎ 973-7156; www.piperscoveresort.com; r US$95; P ✲ 🏊) This exceedingly attractive and well-run hotel offers a peaceful environment and personal, thoughtful service that you could never get at an all-inclusive resort. There are 14 spacious one-bedroom suites with kitchens spread between four Spanish-style villas with gracious plantation-style rattan furnishings, cable TV and private balconies. Meals – provided on request – can be had on an airy poolside pavilion. Childcare and laundry services are available.

Runaway Bay Heart Hotel (☎ 973-6671; www.runawayheart.com.jm; d US$90-95, tr US$110-115, 2-bedroom ste US$180; P ✲ 🏊) With a breezy hillside setting, this plantation-style manor has 56 spacious, tropically furnished, well-lit rooms with satellite TVs and coastal vistas. The service is excellent, as well it should be: next door is the hotel training school. The hotel overlooks the SuperClubs Golf Club, to which hotel guests enjoy special rates. A shuttle runs to Cardiff Hall Beach. Amenities include a fitness center and an elegant restaurant.

VILLAS

The **Jamaica Association of Villas & Apartments** (JAVA; ☎ 974-2508, 800-845-5276; www.villasinjamaica.com) offers fully-staffed beachside and hilltop villas, including **Hummingbird Hill** (per week US$7000; P ⊠ ✲ 🏊), a five-bedroom mansion situated on spacious, beautifully landscaped grounds and **Bean Bird Cottage** (per week US$1436), a cozy love-nest set at the water's edge.

ALL-INCLUSIVES

Royal Decameron Club Caribbean (☎ 973-4802; www.decameron.com; 3 nights all-inclusive s cottage US$375-465, d US$570-750, ste US$390-510; P ⊠ ✲ 💻 🏊) In Salem, this good-value all-inclusive has 20 rooms and 20 one-bedroom suites on 12 acres. The highlights are the pleasingly austere 135 conical, African-style thatched-roof cottage rooms. Some have lofts that are much enjoyed by the kiddies. The rooms are spacious, with king-size beds and wooden cathedral ceilings. There's plenty of activity at the disco and three bars. The Beach Jetty bar has swings and a singing bartender. There's a well-kept 300m-long beach. Activities include a full range of water sports, a PADI dive center and party cruises.

Breezes Runaway Bay (☎ 973-4820, in the USA ☎ 800-467-8737, in the UK ☎ 01749-677200; www.superclubs.com; Runaway Bay; 3 nights all-inclusive d US$505-627; P ⊠ ⁘ 🖳) This is the only place in Jamaica – so far – to offer an underwater wedding. The 238-room, 27-acre all-inclusive resort run by SuperClubs fronts the best beach in Runaway Bay and appeals to a mass market. Bedrooms overlook lush gardens and pool. A nude section has its own Jacuzzi (one of three on site). Facilities include scuba diving and a trapeze, plus well-stocked stores, a nightclub and disco, and a choice of restaurants. The price includes golf at the golf club.

Hedonism III (☎ 973-4100, in the USA ☎ 800-467-8737, in the UK ☎ 01749-677200; www.superclubs.com; 3 nights all-inclusive US$1100-2000; P ⊠ ⁘ 🖳) SuperClubs' latest all-inclusive resort for uninhibited adults is a bootylicious 10-acre property with 225 rooms, some of them 'swim-up.' Each boasts king-size beds, cable TVs (with adult viewing), lively tropical fabrics and large Jacuzzi tubs. As the porter might explain with a well-practiced wink, the mirrored ceilings 'make things look bigger.' The two beaches, alas, are unimpressive. Activity centers on three pools, including a nude pool-and-Jacuzzi where X-rated antics regularly occur. A see-through waterslide coils down from the Octopussy disco. The complex is segregated into 'nude' and 'prude' sections with separate but equal facilities; in the nude division being naked is obligatory. There are far more single men than women guests; a third female in a group stays free ('a threesome is a freesome').

Franklyn D Resort (☎ 973-4592, in North America ☎ 800-337-5437, in the UK ☎ 020-8795-1718; www.fdrholidays.com; 3 nights all-inclusive d US$1800-2100, child 6-15 US$30, child less than 6 free; ⁘ 🖳) This Spanish hacienda-style, all-inclusive family resort has 67 smartly decorated suites, including some two- and three-bedroom apartments. Children find plenty to do in the several kid-friendly facilities. A 'Girl Friday' is assigned to each suite to look after the kids. The resort has three restaurants and a bar, plus an ocean-front spa and waterslide, and a state-of-the-art computer/business center.

Eating

Nana Kofi Vegetarian Restaurant (☎ 973-4266; mains US$2-6; breakfast, lunch & dinner Mon-Sat) About 100m west of the gas station, it specializes in health food and vegetarian cuisine. Typical dishes include chick-pea soup, vegetarian patties and veggie burgers.

Tek It Easy (A1; mains US$3-7; lunch & dinner) At this economical rooftop haunt, Jamaican fare – primarily chicken and fish – competes for attention alongside the freely flowing overproof rum. There's karaoke every Tuesday night.

Blue Pearl (☎ 973-1678; A1; mains US$3-8; lunch & dinner) Serving Jamaican favorites such as curried goat and escoveitched fish in a clifftop garden, this casual eatery is a good place to sample local fare prepared with gusto.

Seafood Giant (☎ 973-4801; mains US$3-16; breakfast, lunch & dinner) At the west end of Runaway Bay, it serves such dishes as jackfish with spinach roasted in foil or fried with bammy, plantain, rice and peas; otherwise order curried, creole or braised garlic shrimp. The filling meals are excellent value. However, if you pick your own fish, you'll be charged 'according to size.'

Cardiff Hall Restaurant (☎ 973-2671; Runaway Bay Heart Hotel; mains US$7-17; breakfast, lunch & dinner) This cheerful restaurant serves well-made Jamaican and continental fare. Reservations are essential.

Rising Sun (☎ 973-7908; mains US$6-18; lunch & dinner Tue-Sun) Next to the gas station, this Swiss-run eatery is recommended for smoked marlin appetizer, pizzas and curried shrimp.

In Salem, there's a **Devon House I-Scream** (A1) and **L&M Grocery** (☎ 973-7292; Main St).

Entertainment

Most fun-hungry visitors make the short journey to Ocho Rios for their after-hours kicks or settle for what's on at their resort; subsequently, local entertainment options are few. The usual charmless go-go clubs include the **19th Hole Club** (☎ 973-5766; Salem Plaza), which also has pool tables and live music. Also here is Club Encore, one of the nicer bars among the less-than-inspiring options, and Slick's Tappa Top 8 Ball Sports Bar, with pool tables.

For a more touristy option, try the shows at Club Caribbean or the **Safari Disco** (Club Ambiance, Main Rd), which has special attractions on weekends. You can buy a night pass to many area resorts (US$45 to US$75) granting unlimited booze, food and entertainment.

Getting There & Around

Buses, minibuses and route taxis traveling the A1 between Montego Bay (1½ hours; US$2 to US$3) and Ocho Rios (40 minutes; US$1 to US$1.50) stop in Runaway Bay. Public transport arrives and departs from the square in front of Patty Place, catercorner to the post office.

In Salem, **Salem Car Rentals** (☎ 973-4167; www.salemcarrentals.com) and **Caribbean Car Rentals** (☎ 973-3539) are located on the main road.

DISCOVERY BAY

This wide flask-shaped bay, 8km west of Runaway Bay and 8km east of Rio Bueno, is a popular resort spot for locals drawn to its Puerto Seco Beach. The town itself has only marginal appeal.

Resembling a kind of giant nipple, the Kaiser Bauxite Company's Port Rhoades bauxite-loading facility dominates the town (it was used for the headquarters of Dr No – Crab Cay – in the James Bond movie, *Dr No*). Large freighters are fed by conveyor belts from a huge storage dome that looks like a rusty pumpkin. You can follow the road signed 'Port Rhoades' uphill 1km to a lookout point offering fantastic views over the bay (there is a pair of high-power, pay-per-view binoculars). Note the metal likeness of Anancy, the folkloric spider, in the playground of the Kaiser's Sports Club, en route.

Locals believe this to be the location where Christopher Columbus first landed on Jamaican soil in 1494, though others say it was at Rio Bueno (p207).

Information

There's a cambio and supermarket at Columbus Plaza, on Discovery Bay Rd, which heads south from the A1 at the Texaco station.

D/Bay Laundromat (☎ 670-0381; Discovery Bay Rd) Opposite Columbus Plaza.
Judrich Pharmacy (☎ 973-9073; Main St) On the A1 in the center of town.
Kaiser Medical Clinic (☎ 973-3568; 🕑 8am-4:30pm Mon-Fri) Just off the A1, immediately east of Port Rhoades Rd; it's signed at the turnoff for Kaiser, west of town.
National Commercial Bank (A1) Operates an ATM in the shopping complex next to the Texaco on the A1.
Pow Wow's (☎ 973-9866; Columbus Plaza) Offers currency exchange.

Sights

PUERTO SECO BEACH

The eastern side of the bay is rimmed with white-sand beaches. With its soft sand and limpid waters, **Puerto Seco Beach** (☎ 973-2660; adult/child US$4/2; 🕑 8am-5pm), in the center of town, is a real charmer. Open to the public, it sports rustic eateries and bars and a fun park with a waterslide for kids not interested in sun-tanning. On weekends and holidays the beach is teeming, but during the week the place is often deserted. You can rent fishing boats, sea bikes and jet skis.

COLUMBUS PARK

This open-air roadside **museum** (admission free) sits atop the bluff on the west side of the bay. Highlighted by a mural depicting Columbus's arrival in Jamaica, the eclectic museum features such memorabilia as anchors, cannons, nautical bells, sugar-boiling coppers and an old waterwheel in working condition that creaks and clanks as it turns. There's also a diminutive locomotive formerly used to haul sugar at Innswood Estate.

GREEN GROTTO CAVES

This impressive system of **caves and tunnels** (☎ 973-2841; www.greengrottocavesja.com; adult/child US$20/10; 🕑 9am-4pm), 3km east of Discovery Bay, extends for about 16km. The steps lead down into the impressive chambers, where statuesque dripstone formations are illuminated by floodlights. Pre-Columbian Arawaks left their artwork on the walls. Much later, the caves were used as a hideout by the Spanish during the English takeover of the island in 1655. Runaway slaves in the 18th century also took refuge here, and between the two world wars, the caves were used by smugglers running arms to Cuba. The highlight is Green Grotto, a glistening subterranean lake 36m down. The entrance fee includes fruit punch and a guided one-hour tour. Your guide will attempt to amaze you by tapping stalactites to produce eerie sounds.

Sleeping & Eating

Accommodationer (☎ 973-2559, 973-2499; Main St; d/tr US$30/42;) This somewhat scruffy place in the center of town needs a coat of paint but is otherwise a decent choice for budget travelers. Rooms are equipped with fridges and cable TV and king-size beds. There's a communal kitchen and shady patio.

On the east side of town, two open-air jerk centers compete for customers. **Mackie's Jerk Centre & Bar** (☎ 973-9450; mains US$2-8; lunch & dinner) serves particularly good pork and chicken and stages an entertaining dominoes tournament on Tuesday nights. **Ultimate Jerk Centre** (☎ 973-2054; mains US$2-8; lunch & dinner), opposite Green Grotto Caves, is another old favorite. The curried goat stew is particularly good.

Cheap eats can also be had at the roadside stalls lining Main St, selling jerk chicken, bammy and more.

Getting There & Around

Buses, minibuses and route taxis ply the A1 between Montego Bay and Ocho Rios and stop in Discovery Bay, notably at the junction of the A1 and the road to Brown's Town.

DRY HARBOUR MOUNTAINS

Paved roads lead south from Discovery Bay, Runaway Bay and St Ann's Bay and ascend into the Dry Harbour Mountains. In this off-the-beaten-track area, the badly potholed roads twist and turn through scenic countryside as they rise to the island's backbone.

Only two main roads run east–west. The lower, the 'Great Interior Rd' (the B11), parallels the coast about 11km inland. It begins at Rock, 2km east of Falmouth, and weaves east to Claremont.

BROWN'S TOWN

pop 8000

Brown's Town is a lively market town 11km south of Runaway Bay. Many noble houses on the hillsides hint at its relative prosperity. The town is at its most bustling during market days (Wednesday, Friday and Saturday), when the cast-iron **Victoria Market** (cnr Main St & Brown's Town Rd) overflows with higglers (street vendors).

Irish estate-owner Hamilton Brown (1776–1843) financed the building of **St Mark's Anglican Church** (☎ 975-2641; cnr Main St & Brown's Town Rd) in Victorian Gothic style (allegedly, he also arranged for the Baptist church to be burned down so that blacks would have nowhere to worship). Note the fine cut-stone **courthouse** (Brown's Town Rd) with neoclassical columned portico; and **St Hilda's School** (☎ 975-2218; St Christopher's Rd), a grand Teutonic Anglican-run structure on the hill immediately east of town; the girls wear lavender uniforms.

You can buy patties and pastries at **Spicy's Patties & Pastries** (☎ 975-2544; Top Rd), on the north side of the Victoria Market, which sells fresh produce at stalls that also spill along Main St. Several modest restaurants along the commercial corridor sell hearty Jamaican fare for US$2 to US$8.

Public transport arrives and departs from the east end of Top Rd, a block off Main St. Minibuses and route taxis (US$3) operate between Brown's Town and Kingston via Claremont and Moneague, and more than a dozen ply the Ocho Rios route via Discovery Bay and Runaway Bay.

NINE MILE

The small community where the 'King of Reggae' was born on February 6, 1945, is set dramatically in the midst of the Cockpits. Despite its isolated location 60km south of Ocho Rios, the village of Nine Mile is decidedly on beaten path for pilgrimages to Bob Marley's birth site and resting place. At the **Nine Mile Museum** (☎ 999-7003; ninemilejamaica.com; admission US$15; 9am-5pm), Rastafarian guides given to impromptu singing of Marley's songs lead pilgrims to the hut – now festooned with devotional graffiti – where the reggae god spent his early years before moving to Kingston and where you'll see the single bed he sang of in 'Is This Love.' Another highlight is the Rasta colored 'rock pillow' on which lay his head when seeking inspiration. Marley's body lies buried along with his guitar in a 2.5m-tall oblong marble mausoleum inside a tiny church of traditional Ethiopian design.

Each year on February 6, this place has traditionally been the site of Bob Marley's birthday celebration, when fans from around the world make the trek to play and hear music throughout the night. (In 2005, the celebration was held in Ethiopia in honor of the 60th anniversary of Marley's birth.) Bob's widow, Rita, periodically expresses disdain at how her husband's legacy has been turned into a tourism 'product,' and though she has spoken of exhuming him for burial in Africa, the prospect grows increasingly unlikely each year.

The **museum restaurant** (US$5-7) serves I-tal dishes in a rootsy bar. Club Marcus, opposite the museum, is a lively bar serving snacks.

The museum shop sells Marley paraphernalia of every description. The guides and abundant hangers-on have an annoying habit of hitting you up for extra money. Give them a J$100 (about US$1.60) bill and you're likely to receive a contemptuous stare for being a skinflint! Don't be suckered.

Getting to Nine Mile is no simple matter. It's extremely secluded, but cab drivers in Ocho Rios know the route (haggle hard for a reasonable fare; US$75 is common). Minibuses and route taxis operate between Brown's Town, Alexandria and Claremont, stopping in Nine Mile. An easier way to visit is via the 'Zion Bus Line' tour offered by **Chukka Caribbean Adventures** (☎ 972-2506; www.chukkacaribbean.com; US$65), which departs from Ocho Rios.

If you are driving, be sure to pull up right outside the museum compound and honk your horn so that they can open the gate. The alternative is to park on the street and pay any number of locals to watch the vehicle.

CAVE VALLEY

This tiny village sits on the border of St Ann and Clarendon parishes, 13km south of Alexandria, at the north end of Vera Ma Hollis Savanna, a 11km-long valley. During the early years of the British occupation in the late 17th century, the region was a center for the Maroons. The British built a barracks here during the First Maroon War in the 1730s.

The Cave River rises in the mountains near Coleyville, 16km west of Cave Valley, where in the dry season you can see the **Cave River Sinks**, two holes into which the river disappears to reemerge 21km north near Stewart Town.

The road through the Cave River Valley eventually reaches Spaldings, Christiana and Mandeville.

Route taxis running between Brown's Town and May Pen pass through.

Montego Bay & Northwest Coast

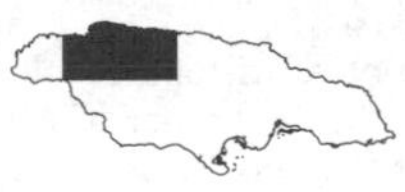

Gateway to Jamaica for the vast majority of its visitors, Montego Bay forms most first impressions of the island. For some, the vision is celestial, and they embrace 'MoBay' from the catered comfort of an all-inclusive beachside resort. For others, it's simply a tourist trap en route to the 'real Jamaica;' and they flee as soon as they get their bearings.

In truth, the attractions of Montego Bay and the surrounding northwest coast offer enough variety to repay deeper exploration. In addition to its celebrated beaches, MoBay's 'Hip Strip' boasts enough fine restaurants for a pleasurable tour de fork followed by some of the most pulsating nightlife on the island. Pockets of downtown will pique interest in St James Parrish's vibrant (and violent) past, a historical thirst that can be slaked with visits to the great estates of Greenwood and Rose Hall, or to the fading Georgian marvel of Falmouth.

Some of Jamaica's most remarkable nature spots are within easy striking distance. The snorkeling and scuba diving in the limpid waters of the Montego Bay Marine Park are world class, and the rafting on the Great and Martha Brae Rivers is truly unforgettable. And barely an hour from the resorts – though truly a world away – rolls the eerie hillscape of Cockpit country, Jamaica's most unspoilt (and often impenetrable) region, where the hiking and caving are terrific, and you can take exhilarating horseback rides straight into the sea.

HIGHLIGHTS

- **Reggae Sumfest** Dance until dawn to Jamaica's most renowned musicians at this world-class midsummer reggae festival (p189)
- **Sunset sailing trips** Party hearty on a cocktail-propelled jaunt across the bay and toast the sun as it plops into the sea (p188)
- **Falmouth** Lose yourself among the faded Georgian splendor of this compelling historic market town (p202)
- **Greenwood Great House** Explore the exquisite period furnishings of this well-preserved great house with a remarkable view of the sea (p201)
- **Rafting the Martha Brae** Serenade your beloved or splash your pal as you glide down one of Jamaica's loveliest rivers on a bamboo raft (p205)
- **Windsor Caves** See what Cockpit Country looks like from down below in one of the island's most expansive and accessible caves (p214)

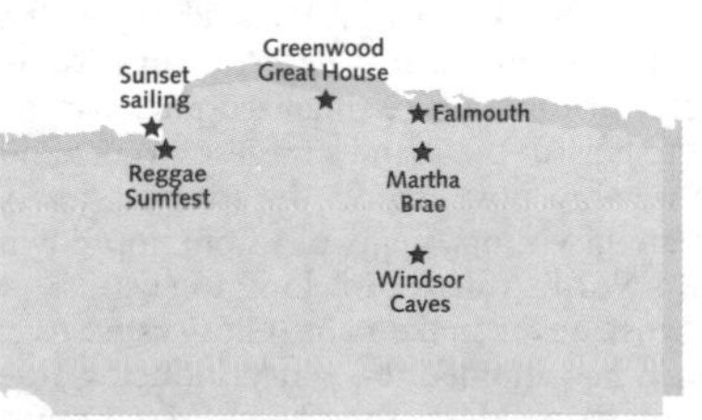

- AREA: 1480 SQ KM
- MONTEGO BAY DEC AVERAGE HIGH TEMPERATURE: 28.3°C

HISTORY

In 1494 Christopher Columbus dropped anchor in the harbor of what is today known as Montego Bay. The Spanish put down roots here in 1510, and the English took control in 1655, transforming the town into an affluent sugar-production and trading center. The plantation culture came crashing down in the 1831 slave revolts, when nearly all of the plantations and estates were razed. Post-emancipation, Montego Bay languished until the early 20th century, when it took its place as Jamaica's most popular tourist destination. For more details of the region's history, see right.

CLIMATE

MoBay's balmy weather is world famous. The most pleasant months are December to February, when the temperature hovers between 22° and 28°C and the coast enjoys the cooling effects of the northeasterly trade winds. October is the wettest month with average rainfall of 188mm; winter is generally the driest season.

GETTING THERE & AWAY

Montego Bay is home to Jamaica's busiest airport and cruise-ship port. Buses, minibuses and route taxis arrive and depart from the busy transportation station off Barnett St, downtown.

MONTEGO BAY

pop 110,000

A bustling town with a turbulent history, a thriving port and a hopping 'hip strip,' Montego Bay is Jamaica's most charged city. While spring-breakers descend on MoBay each year for bouts of ritualized raucousness, being host to the island's busiest airport and cruise-ship port assures the town a steady stream of visitors, many of whom pop down from North America for long weekends.

Most never make it off Gloucester Ave, which has attained the wince-inducing title of 'hip strip.' Most of the hotels, restaurants, bars and souvenir emporia line this parade, which runs parallel to the beach; everything is here – and a loose confederacy of hustlers patrols the strip ready to offer guidance (and other services) should you find it all overwhelming. Despite its gaudiness, the strip boasts some of the best eating options on the island.

Streetlife of another, more genuine, order courses through downtown. Centered on pedestrian Sam Sharpe Sq, the town fans out over a grid, its streets lilting to the beats pulsing from competing storefronts while push-cart peddlers lurch in and out of routes they alone know. Downtown features a selection of decaying Georgian buildings that hint at earlier prosperity and the excellent Museum of St James, which bears poignant testament to the city's brutal slave history.

Montego Bay is also a major port city, based on the container-shipping trade at the Montego Freeport. The town spreads tentacles of light industry west as far as Reading, 6km away. An equal distance to the east, Ironshore (p198) marks the beginning of a series of swanky all-inclusive resorts.

HISTORY

Columbus anchored in Montego Bay in 1494 and called it Gulf of Good Weather. In 1655 a settlement appeared on Spanish maps: Manterias, after the Spanish word *manteca,* or lard, from the days when the Spanish shipped 'pig's butter' derived from the herds of wild hogs that flourished in the nearby hills. Following the British takeover that year, the parish of St James was established. As sugar was planted, Montego Bay took on new importance, and St James became the most important sugar-producing parish on the island. Wealthy planters and merchants erected lavish townhouses and a parish church. Many original buildings perished in fires and hurricanes, which also destroyed valuable records in the western part of the island, obscuring this early history.

Montego Bay and its hinterland were the setting for the slave rebellion of Christmas 1831, when estates throughout St James were put to the torch. Militia and regular troops stationed in Montego Bay quickly quelled the revolt, and the courthouse became a center for savage retribution (see the boxed text, p188).

After emancipation in 1834 the sugar trade slipped into decline. The city once again languished until it was revived by the development of the banana trade, and by the tourist trade that developed in the late 1880s when Dr Alexander G McCatty founded a sanitarium at what is today Doctor's Cave Beach. Rich Americans and Britons flocked

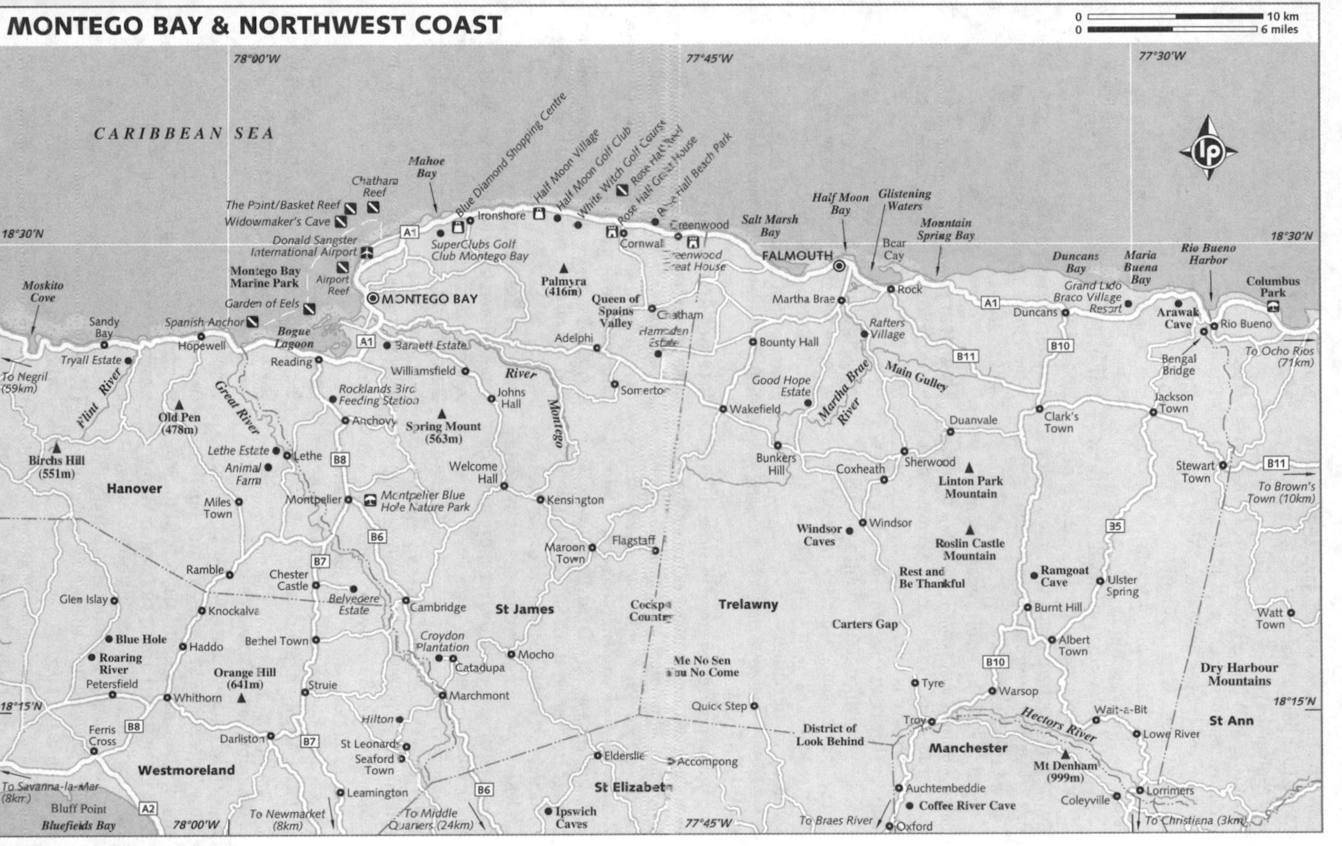
MONTEGO BAY & NORTHWEST COAST
0 10 km
0 6 miles
78°00'W
77°45'W
77°30'W
18°30'N
18°15'N
CARIBBEAN SEA
Mahoe Bay
Chatham Reef
The Point/Basket Reef
Widowmaker's Cave
Blue Diamond Shopping Centre
Half Moon Village
Half Moon Golf Club
White Witch Golf Course
Rose Hall Great House
Rose Hall Beach Park
Ironshore
SuperClubs Golf Club Montego Bay
Donald Sangster International Airport
Montego Bay Marine Park
Airport Reef
Garden of Eels
MONTEGO BAY
Moskito Cove
Sandy Bay
Spanish Anchor
Hopewell
Bogue Lagoon
A1
Barnett Estate
Tryall Estate
To Negril (59km)
Flint River
Reading
Williamsfield
Rocklands Bird Feeding Station
Anchovy
Spring Mount (563m)
Johns Hall
Montego River
Old Pen (478m)
Great River
Birchs Hill (551m)
Lethe Estate
Lethe
Animal Farm
B8
Welcome Hall
Hanover
Miles Town
Montpelier
Montpelier Blue Hole Nature Park
Kensington
B6
B7
Palmyra (416m)
Queen of Spains Valley
Cornwall
Greenwood
Greenwood Great House
Chatham
Hampden Estate
Adelphi
Sorrento
Salt Marsh Bay
FALMOUTH
Half Moon Bay
Glistening Waters
Bear Cay
Mountain Spring Bay
Martha Brae
Rock
Bounty Hall
Rafters Village
B11
Good Hope Estate
Martha Brae River
Main Gulley
Wakefield
Duanvale
Bunkers Hill
Coxheath
Sherwood
Linton Park Mountain
Windsor Caves
Windsor
Roslin Castle Mountain
Duncans Bay
Maria Buena Bay
Rio Bueno Harbor
Columbus Park
Grand Lido Braco Village Resort
Duncans
Arawak Cave
Rio Bueno
B10
Bengal Bridge
To Ocho Rios (71km)
Clark's Town
Jackson Town
Stewart Town
To Brown's Town (10km)
35
Maroon Town
Flagstaff
Ramble
Chester Castle
Belvedere Estate
Cambridge
St James
Cockpit Country
Trelawny
Rest and Be Thankful
Ramgoat Cave
Ulster Spring
Burnt Hill
Watt Town
Glen Islay
Knockalva
Blue Hole
Haddo
Bethel Town
Croydon Plantation
Mocho
Catadupa
Carters Gap
Albert Town
Me No Sen You No Come
Roaring River
Orange Hill (641m)
Struie
Marchmont
Tyre
Warsop
Dry Harbour Mountains
Petersfield
Whithorn
Quick Step
Hectors River
Wait-a-Bit
Hilton
Troy
District of Look Behind
St Ann
Lowe River
Ferris Cross
Darliston
St Leonards
Seaford Town
Elderslie
Accompong
Manchester
Mt Denham (999m)
Westmoreland
To Savanna-la-Mar (8km)
Leamington
St Elizabeth
Auchtembeddie
Lorrimers
Bluff Point
A2
Coffee River Cave
Coleyville
Bluefields Bay
To Newmarket (8km)
To Middle Quarters (24km)
Ipswich Caves
To Braes River
Oxford
To Christiana (3km)

onto the banana boats to 'take the waters.' Many later bought homes here, adding luster to Montego Bay.

During WWII the US Air Force built an airstrip east of town, which in the postwar years served to open up Montego Bay to tourism on a larger scale. Round Hill and Tryall resorts were built west of town, cementing MoBay's chic reputation.

In the late 1960s the bay was dredged, and Montego Freeport was constructed (the port is now a center of light industry). Later, a separate cruise-ship terminal appeared, launching a new breed of visitor.

In the 1990s the resort became somewhat jaded, but in recent years it has been revived and spruced up with a discernible makeover. Gloucester Ave is safer than ever, the cruise ships are back en masse, and even downtown has been revivified to the point where timid cruise-ship passengers dare to walk off their sea legs while taking in some of the splendid Georgian architecture.

ORIENTATION

The tourist quarter, north of the town center, arcs along Gloucester Ave, a narrow shoreline strip lined with hotels, restaurants and public beaches. Northward, Gloucester Ave becomes Kent Ave, which stretches for about a kilometer and ends at tiny Dead-End Beach. The airport is accessed from Sunset Blvd, which stretches east from the junction of Gloucester and Kent Aves and continues east, beyond the airport, as the A1 to Ironshore and the north coast.

Queen's Dr traverses the steep Miranda Hill, which rises behind the tourist strip, linking the airport with the southern end of Gloucester Ave, forming a roundabout. The town center lies south of this junction and is accessed by Fort St, a bustling thoroughfare that leads to the vibrant heart of MoBay, Sam Sharpe Sq.

The compact historic center is laid out as a rough grid of narrow and chaotically crowded streets. St James St, the bustling main street, runs south from Sam Sharpe Sq and ends at Barnett St, which is one-way heading into town but becomes two-way after its intersection with Cottage Rd. Barnett St turns into the A1 heading west to Reading and Negril.

Howard Cooke Dr begins at the Gloucester Ave roundabout and runs south along the bayfront, linking the A1 with Montego Freeport.

Maps

The *Discover Jamaica* map published by the Jamaica Tourist Board (JTB) includes a detailed map of Montego Bay. You can get a free copy at any JTB office (see opposite).

INFORMATION

Bookstores

Sangster's Bookshop (Map pp186-7; ☎ 952-0319; 2 St James St) The largest bookstore in town, but it's only modestly stocked.

Emergency

Police stations Barnett St (Map pp186-7; ☎ 952-2333, 952-1557; 14 Barnett St); Union St (Map pp186-7; ☎ 940-3500; 49 Union St); Church St (Map pp186-7; ☎ 952-4396, 952-5310; 29 Church St); Catherine Hall (Map pp182-3; ☎ 952-4997, 953-6309; cnr Southern Cross Rd & Howard Cooke Dr)

Police Tourism Liaison Unit (Map pp182-3; ☎ 952-1540; Summit Police Station, Sunset Blvd)

Internet Access

Cyber Shores (Map pp182-3; ☎ 971-8907; Gloucester Ave; per 15 min/1 hr US$2/7.50; 8am-8:30pm) At Doctor's Cave Beach, with a wi-fi network serving the beach.

Internet Place (Map pp186-7; ☎ 979-2460; Shop 8, A&B's Complex, 11 Market St; per 30 min/1 hr US$1.70/3.40) A downtown option with attractive rates.

Internet Resources

Official Visitors Guide (www.montego-bay-jamaica.com) An up-to-date online resource to MoBay and environs.

Mobay Tourist (mobaytourist.com) The official visitors guide to Montego Bay.

What's On Jamaica (www.whatsonjamaica.com) Entertainment and culture listings.

Laundry

Brown's Laundromat (Map pp186-7; ☎ 971-9224; 36 Church St; per load US$1) Coin-operated machines.

Fabricare Centre (Map pp186-7; ☎ 952-6897; 4 Corner Lane; per load US$1.25) Offers one-hour dry cleaning plus laundry and drop-off service.

Wonder Wash (Map pp182-3; ☎ 971-4739; Westgate Shopping Centre; per load US$1) On the A1, south of downtown.

Library

Parish library (Map pp186-7; ☎ 952-4185; North St) An impressive collection of books on Jamaica, but the building itself is in a state of disrepair.

Medical Services

Downtown, you'll find plenty of pharmacies.

Cornwall Medical Centre (Map pp186-7; ☎ 979-6107; 19 Orange St) Private clinic.

Cornwall Regional Hospital (Map pp182-3; ☎ 952-5100; Mt Salem Rd) Has a 24-hour emergency ward.

Doctor's Hospital (Map pp182-3; ☎ 952-1616; Fairfield Rd) Private hospital southeast of town.

Fontana Pharmacy (Map pp182-3; ☎ 952-3860; Fairview Shopping Centre) The best-stocked and largest pharmacy in town.

Montego Bay Dental Clinic (Map pp186-7; ☎ 952-2338; 11 Dome St)

Money

There's a 24-hour money-exchange bureau and a branch of **National Commercial Bank** (Map pp182-3; ☎ 952-2354) in the arrivals hall at Donald Sangster International Airport. You'll need local currency to take the bus into town, but taxis accept US dollars.

Money-exchange bureaus on the main strip include **FX Trader** (Map p186-7; ☎ 952-3171; 37 Gloucester Ave; 🕑 9am-5pm Mon-Sat) upstairs at the Pelican restaurant, and **Cambio King** (Map p184; ☎ 971-5260; Gloucester Ave) at the northern end. Downtown, several bureaus can be found on St James St; look for 'cambio' signs.

Banks on Gloucester Ave include a branch of **First Global Bank** (Map p184; ☎ 971-5260; 53 Gloucester Ave), and flanking the Doctor's Cave Beach Club are ATMs operated by National Commercial Bank and Scotiabank.

Downtown, banks on Sam Sharpe Sq and in the Bay West Centre all have 24-hour ATMs. The cruise-ship terminal is served by a branch of **National Commercial Bank** (Map pp182-3; ☎ 979-8060) in the Montego Freeport Shopping Centre.

Western Union (☎ 926-2454) has branches at the Pelican restaurant on Gloucester Ave (Map p184); at 19 Church St (Map pp186–7); and in Shop 9, Overton Plaza (Map pp186–7), at the top of Dome St.

Post

FedEx (Map pp182-3; ☎ 952-0411, 888-991-9081; Chatwick Plaza, 10 Queen's Dr)

DHL (☎ 979-0543; 34 Queens Dr)

Post office Fort St (Map pp186-7; ☎ 952-7016); White Sands Beach (Map p184; ☎ 979-5137; Gloucester Ave)

Telephone

Most hotels offer international call service.

Cable & Wireless Telecommunications (C&W; Map pp186-7; ☎ 952-5440, 888-952-9700; 20 Church St) Has public phones outside its offices downtown, on either side of Church St.

Tourist Information

Jamaica Tourist Board booth (Map pp182-3; ☎ 952-3009; 🕑 concurrent with flight arrivals) In the arrivals hall at Donald Sangster International Airport.

Jamaica Tourist Board office (Map p184; ☎ 952-4425; fax 952-3587; 🕑 8:30am-4:30pm Mon-Fri, 9am-1pm Sat) Off Gloucester Ave, opposite the entrance to the now-closed Cornwall Beach.

TPDCo information booth (Map pp186-7; ☎ 979-7987; 🕑 9am-5pm) At the downtown craft market.

Travel Agencies

Many of the larger hotels operate travel offices. Downtown, some reputable agencies include the following:

Trafalgar Travel (Map pp186-7; ☎ 979-1556; Sam Sharpe Sq)

Tropical Travel Service (Map pp186-7; ☎ 952-5822; 7 Church St)

DANGERS & ANNOYANCES

Things have dramatically improved along Gloucester Ave in recent years, although harassment of tourists by hustlers remains an annoyance. By day, visitors get up close and personal with street-level entrepreneurs offering ganja, transportation and even services of a decidedly more intimate nature. A common approach is for a hustler to claim he knows you from your hotel, and many visitors just off the plane are not savvy enough to see through it. As always it's best to respond with a polite but firm 'no thanks' and keep moving; simply ignoring them only aggravates hustlers – and makes them more aggravating.

Keeping the hustlers (mostly) in line are the beat-walking men and women of the Montego Bay Resort Patrol wearing trim bulletproof vests.

Downtown is not patrolled; it's safe to walk in the historic center during daylight hours but stick to the main streets and stay alert. At night downtown is not the best place for a solo stroll. Avoid the dangerous Flankers area across the highway from the airport.

Beware traffic! Cars are often driven at a breakneck pace; don't expect the driver to give way. Even 'tourist-friendly' Gloucester Ave can be a hazard. Use caution when crossing streets and watch for deep gutters and potholes.

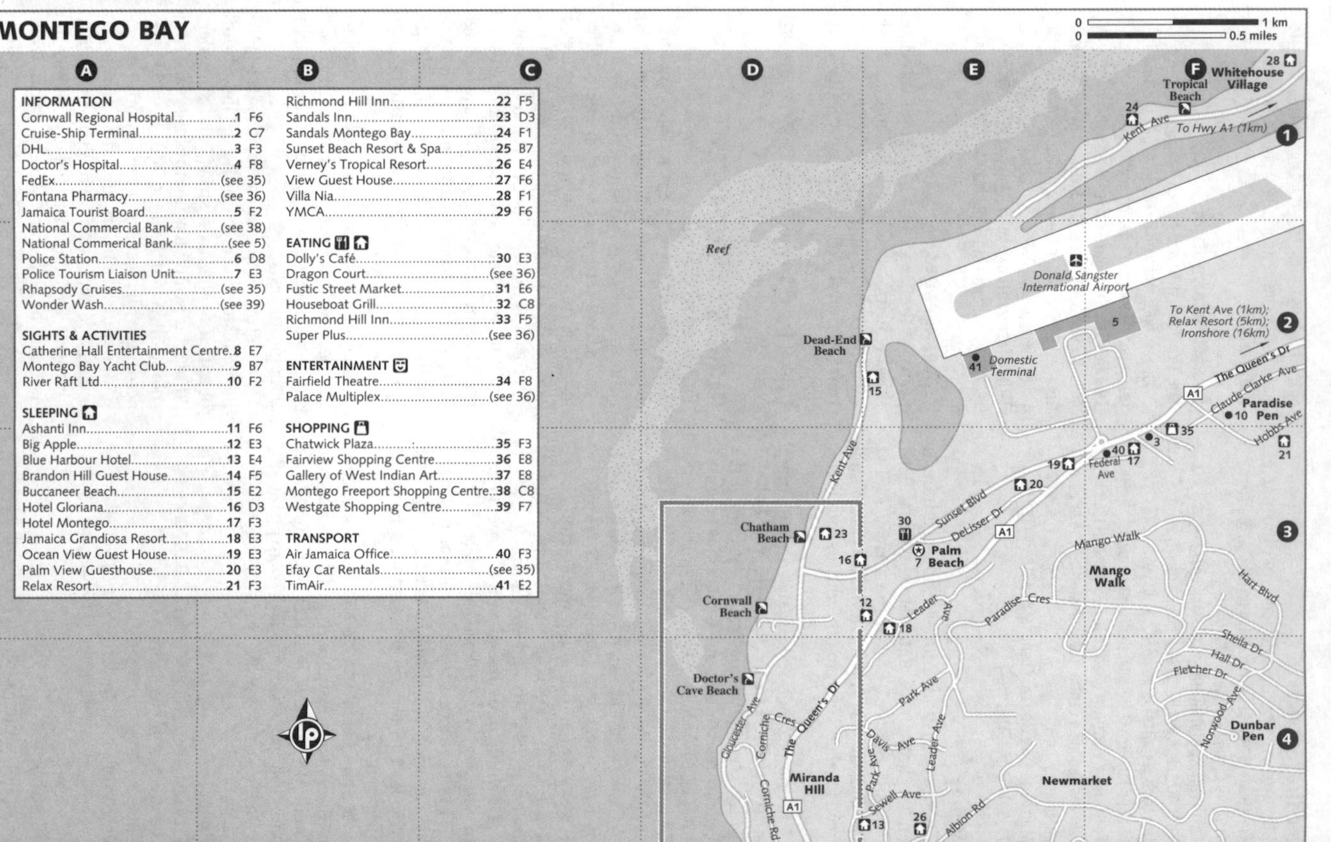
MONTEGO BAY
0 1 km
0 0.5 miles
A
B
C
D
E
F
1
2
3
4
INFORMATION
Cornwall Regional Hospital 1 F6
Cruise-Ship Terminal 2 C7
DHL 3 F3
Doctor's Hospital 4 F8
FedEx (see 35)
Fontana Pharmacy (see 36)
Jamaica Tourist Board 5 F2
National Commercial Bank (see 38)
National Commerical Bank (see 5)
Police Station 6 D8
Police Tourism Liaison Unit 7 E3
Rhapsody Cruises (see 35)
Wonder Wash (see 39)
SIGHTS & ACTIVITIES
Catherine Hall Entertainment Centre 8 E7
Montego Bay Yacht Club 9 B7
River Raft Ltd 10 F2
SLEEPING
Ashanti Inn 11 F6
Big Apple 12 E3
Blue Harbour Hotel 13 E4
Brandon Hill Guest House 14 F5
Buccaneer Beach 15 E2
Hotel Gloriana 16 D3
Hotel Montego 17 F3
Jamaica Grandiosa Resort 18 E3
Ocean View Guest House 19 E3
Palm View Guesthouse 20 E3
Relax Resort 21 F3
Richmond Hill Inn 22 F5
Sandals Inn 23 D3
Sandals Montego Bay 24 F1
Sunset Beach Resort & Spa 25 B7
Verney's Tropical Resort 26 E4
View Guest House 27 F6
Villa Nia 28 F1
YMCA 29 F6
EATING
Dolly's Café 30 E3
Dragon Court (see 36)
Fustic Street Market 31 E6
Houseboat Grill 32 C8
Richmond Hill Inn 33 F5
Super Plus (see 36)
ENTERTAINMENT
Fairfield Theatre 34 F8
Palace Multiplex (see 36)
SHOPPING
Chatwick Plaza 35 F3
Fairview Shopping Centre 36 E8
Gallery of West Indian Art 37 E8
Montego Freeport Shopping Centre 38 C8
Westgate Shopping Centre 39 F7
TRANSPORT
Air Jamaica Office 40 F3
Efay Car Rentals (see 35)
TimAir 41 E2
Whitehouse Village
Tropical Beach
Kent Ave
To Hwy A1 (1km)
Reef
Donald Sangster International Airport
Domestic Terminal
To Kent Ave (1km); Relax Resort (5km); Ironshore (16km)
The Queen's Dr
Claude Clarke Ave
Paradise Pen
Hobbs Ave
Dead-End Beach
Federal Ave
Sunset Blvd
DeLisser Dr
A1
Chatham Beach
Palm Beach
Mango Walk
Hart Blvd
Cornwall Beach
Leader Ave
Paradise Cres
Sheila Dr
Hall Dr
Fletcher Dr
Norwood Ave
Doctor's Cave Beach
Park Ave
Davis Ave
Gloucester Ave
Corniche Cres
Dunbar Pen
Miranda Hill
Sewell Ave
Corniche Rd
Albion Rd
Newmarket

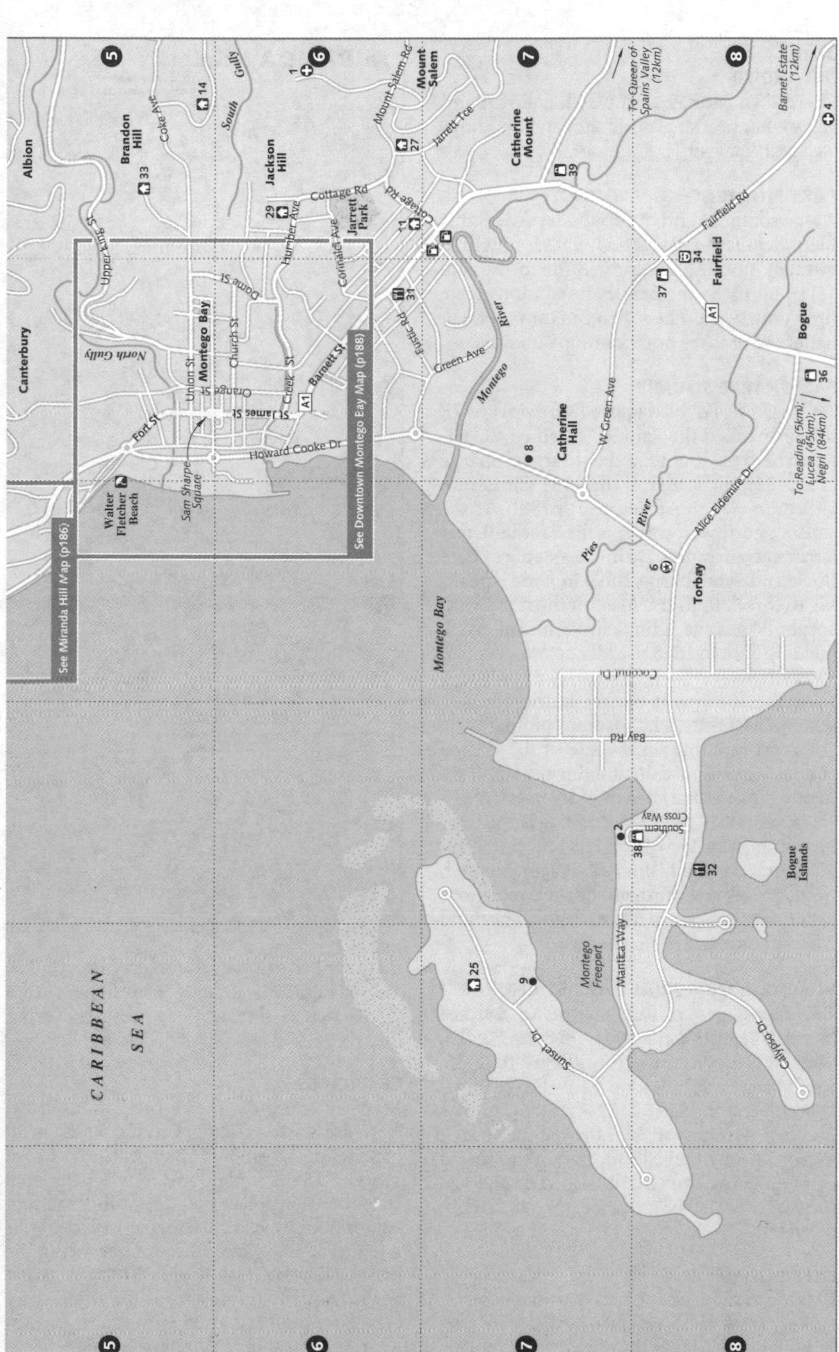

CARIBBEAN SEA
Montego Bay
See Miranda Hill Map (p186)
See Downtown Montego Bay Map (p188)
Albion
Canterbury
Brandon Hill
Jackson Hill
Mount Salem
Catherine Mount
Catherine Hall
Jarrett Park
Fairfield
Bogue
Torbay
Bogue Islands
Montego Freeport
Walter Fletcher Beach
Sam Sharpe Square
Montego Bay
Upper King St
Coke Ave
Fort St
Union St
Orange St
St James St
Church St
Dome St
Creek St
Barnett St
Humber Ave
Cottage Rd
Connaught Ave
Mount Salem Rd
Jarrett Tce
Fustic Rd
Green Ave
Howard Cooke Dr
W Green Ave
Alice Eldemire Dr
Fairfield Rd
Coconut Dr
Bay Rd
Southern Cross Way
Mantica Way
Sunset Dr
Calypso Dr
North Gully
South Gully
Montego River
Pies River
A1
To Queen of Spains Valley (12km)
Barnet Estate (12km)
To Reading (5km); Lucea (45km); Negril (84km)

SIGHTS

Downtown

Downtown MoBay – crowded, colorful and gritty – has several historic sites and buildings well worth a visit.

FORT MONTEGO

At the southern end of Gloucester Ave is this inauspicious **fort** (Map pp186-7; Fort St), of which virtually nothing remains. Built in the late 18th century by the British, its cannons were fired only twice. The sole remnant is a small battery with three brass cannons on rails.

SAM SHARPE SQUARE

This bustling cobbled **square** (Map pp186–7), formerly called the Parade, is named for national hero the Right Excellent Samuel Sharpe (1801–32), the leader of the 1831 Christmas Rebellion (see the boxed text, p188). At the square's northwest corner is the **National Heroes Monument**, an impressive bronze statue of Paul Bogle and Sam Sharpe, Bible in hand, speaking to three admirers. Also on the northwest corner is the **Cage**, a tiny cut-stone and brick building built in 1806 as a lockup, now a small souvenir shop.

At the southwest corner is the copper-domed **Civic Centre**, a handsome colonial-style cut-stone building on the site of the ruined colonial courthouse. It contains the small yet highly informative **Museum of St James** (☎ 971-9417; admission US$3; 9:30am-4:30pm Tue-Thu, to 3:30pm Fri, 10:30am-2:30pm Sat) with relics and other exhibits tracing the history of St James parish from Arawak days through the slave rebellions to the more recent past. An art gallery and 200-seat theater are also here.

BURCHELL MEMORIAL BAPTIST CHURCH

Two blocks east of Sam Sharpe Sq, **Burchell Memorial Baptist Church** (Map pp186-7; ☎ 952-6351; Market St) is a brick structure dating to 1835. Sam Sharpe was a deacon here. The original church was founded in 1824 by Rev Thomas Burchell. An angry mob destroyed the church in reprisal for Burchell's support of the emancipation cause, but the missionary escaped to sea. Sam Sharpe's remains are buried in the vault.

CREEK DOME

Lurking at the end of Creek St is the bizarre-looking **Creek Dome** (Map pp186-7; cnr Dome St & Creek St), built in 1837 above the underground spring

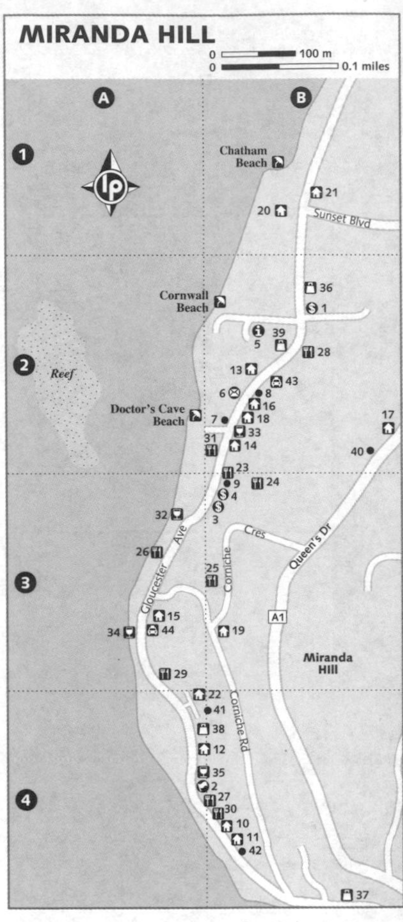

that supplied drinking water for Montego Bay. The structure is actually a hexagon with a crenellated castle turret in which the 'Keeper of the Creek' lived and collected a toll.

CHURCH ST

Many of the most interesting buildings in town are clustered along Church St, the most picturesque street in MoBay. At the corner of Water Lane is a plantation-style octagonal structure that today houses a police station. About 50m west, at the corner of King St, is a redbrick Georgian building harboring the **National Housing Trust** (Map pp186-7; ☎ 952-0063; 1 King St). Equally impressive is the three-story Georgian building at 25 Church St – headquarters of Cable & Wireless Jamaica.

The highlight, however, is **St James Parish Church** (Map pp186-7; ☎ 952-2775; Church St), regarded as the finest church on the island. The current church was built between 1775 and 1782 in the shape of a Greek cross, but was so damaged by the earthquake of March 1, 1957, that it had to be rebuilt.

With luck, the tall church doors will be open and you can view the beautiful interior, which contains among other things a stunning stained-glass window behind the altar. Note the marble monuments, including some fine works by John Bacon, the foremost English sculptor of the late 18th century. One is a memorial to Anne May Palmer, whose virtuous life was up-ended in literature to create the legend of the White Witch of Rose Hall. Look carefully at her neck and you'll detect faint purple marks. Locals consider this proof of the fable that the 'witch' was strangled.

Facing the church is the **Town House** (Map pp186-7; ☎ 952-2660; 16 Church St), with a handsome redbrick frontage buried under a cascade of bougainvillea and laburnum. It dates from 1765, when it was the home of a wealthy merchant. It has since served as a church manse and later as a townhouse for the mistress of the Earl of Hereford, Governor of Jamaica. In the years that followed it was used as a hotel, warehouse, Masonic lodge, lawyer's office and synagogue. Its current incarnation is a clothes store.

Further Afield

BARNETT ESTATE

The sea of sugarcane south of Montego Bay is part of the **Barnett Estate** (Fairfield Rd), a plantation owned and operated since 1755 by the Kerr-Jarretts, one of Jamaica's preeminent families; their holdings once included most of the Montego Bay area. Today the family (now in its 11th generation) holds the land in trust for the government and manages it accordingly.

The **Bellfield Great House** (☎ 952-2382; lunch tour adult/child US$40/20, as part of hotel-sponsored tour US$60/30, basic tour without lunch US$20; 9am-5pm Mon-Sat), built in 1735, has been restored and is now a showcase of 18th-century colonial living. The former plantation manager's house doubles as a museum charting the development of the area since the day that Colonel Nicholas Jarrett arrived with Cromwell's invasion army in 1655.

The estate is about 800m to the east of Doctor's Hospital. It's poorly signed: take the right turn at the Y-fork marked for Day-O Plantation, then the signed right turn at Granville Police Station.

MONTEGO BAY MARINE PARK & BOGUE LAGOON

The waters of Montego Bay are gorgeous to behold both above and below the surface, but they have long been compromised by the effects of fishing, water sports and pollution. With the creation in 1991 of the **Montego Bay**

MONTEGO BAY & NORTHWEST COAST

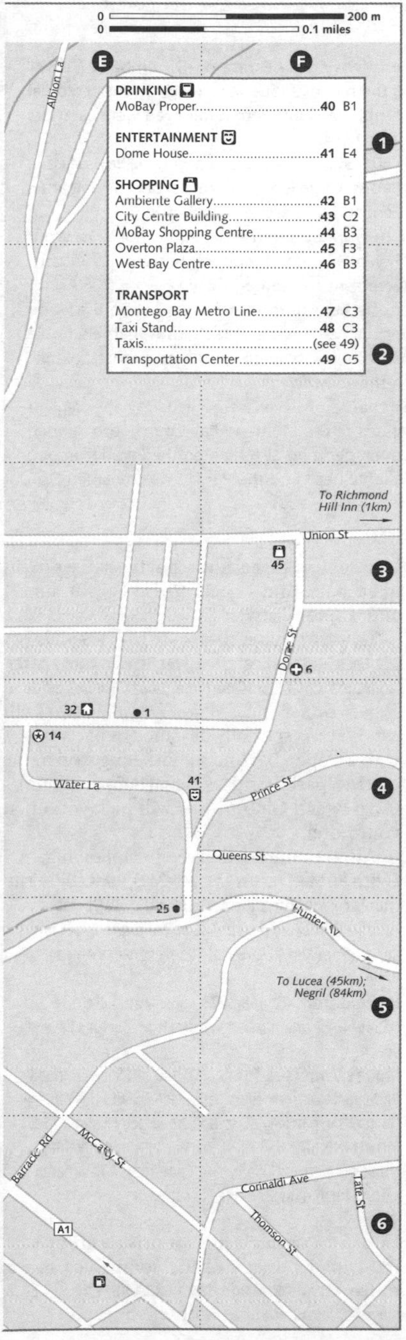

Marine Park, Jamaica's first national park, environmental regulations at last began to be strictly enforced to protect the area's coral reefs, rich flora and fauna, and shoreline mangroves. The park extends from the eastern end of the airport westward (almost 10km) to the Great River, encompassing the mangroves of **Bogue Lagoon**.

You can hire canoes or set out with a guide to spot herons, egrets, pelicans and waterfowl, while swimming and crawling below are barracudas, tarpon, snapper, crabs and lobsters. Request a guide two days in advance; there's no charge but donations are gladly accepted. Authority is vested in the **Montego Bay Marine Park Trust** (MBMPT; Map pp186-7; ☎ 971-8082; www.mbmp.org; Pier 1, off Howard Cooke Dr). MBMPT maintains a meager **resource centre** (🕑 9am-5pm Mon-Fri) with a library on the vital ecosystem.

ACTIVITIES

MoBay boasts two public beaches, each offering **water sports**. Some of the resort hotels have private beaches and many have their own water-sports operators.

If you want to play **golf**, the area offers three championship courses east of Montego Bay (see p199). A fourth course at Tryall is a 30-minute journey west (p208).

For **tennis**, there are courts at Walter Fletcher Beach, and some resort hotels have courts for guests.

Beaches

Visiting Montego Bay without parking yourself for an hour or a day on a stunning white-sand beach would just be *wrong*. Know in advance that these are not places to enjoy solitude, however, but rather to celebrate the fun-loving throng.

Private **Cornwall Beach** has been closed for renovation for several years now, but the two main beaches remain open, with facilities that include changing rooms, snack bars and water-sports providers.

DOCTOR'S CAVE BEACH

Founded as a bathing club in 1906, this world famous stretch of sand with a perpetual party vibe is now owned by **Doctor's Cave Beach Club** (Map pp182-3; ☎ 952-2566; www.doctorscavebathingclub.com; adult/child US$5/2.50; 🕑 8:30am-6pm). It can get ridiculously crowded during the winter months, so if you're going to make a day of it, arrive early to stake out your turf. Facilities

PREACHING RESISTANCE

The weeklong Christmas Rebellion, which began on Kensington Estate on December 27, 1831 and engulfed much of the Montego Bay region, was the most serious slave revolt to rock colonial Jamaica. Its impact and the public outcry over the terrible retribution that followed were catalysts for the British parliament passing the Abolition Act in 1834.

The instigator of the revolt was Samuel Sharpe (1801–32), the slave of a Montego Bay solicitor. Sharpe acted as a deacon of Montego Bay's Burchell Baptist Church and became a 'daddy,' or leader, of the church. Sharpe used his pulpit as a forum to encourage passive rebellion.

In 1831 Sharpe counseled fellow slaves to refuse to work during the Christmas holidays. Word of the secret, passive rebellion spread throughout St James and neighboring parishes. Inevitably, word leaked out and war ships and extra troops were sent to Montego Bay.

The rebellion turned into a violent conflict when the Kensington Estate was set on fire. Soon plantations and great houses throughout northwest Jamaica were ablaze, and Sharpe's noble plan was usurped by wholesale violence. Fourteen colonialists were murdered before colonial authorities suppressed the revolt. Swift and cruel retribution followed.

As part of the coloniolists' retribution, more than a thousand slaves were killed. Day after day for six weeks following the revolt's suppression, magistrates of the Montego Bay Courthouse handed down death sentences to scores of slaves, who were hanged two at a time on the Parade, among them 'Daddy' Sam Sharpe. He was later named a national hero and the Parade was renamed Sam Sharp Sq.

include a food court, grill bar, internet café and water sports, plus changing rooms. You can rent shade umbrellas and inflatable air mattresses (lilos) for US$5, snorkel gear for US$5 and chairs for US$4.

WALTER FLETCHER BEACH

An attraction for both locals and tourists alike, this beach is a long sliver of white sand down at the south end of Gloucester Ave, and the venue for the **Aquasol Theme Park** (Map pp186-7; ☎ 940-1344; www.aquasoljamaica.com; adult/child US$5/3; 🕑 9am-10pm), which offers netball, volleyball, tennis courts, water sports, the MoBay 500 go-cart track and Voyage Sports Bar & Grill. You can rent lockers, beach mats, chairs and umbrellas.

DEAD END BEACH

Aligning Kent Rd just north of Gloucester Rd, this narrow strip, also known as Buccaneer Beach, is popular with locals. There are no facilities here (beyond those at a few hotels over the road), but the lack of crowds seems to make the sunsets over the bay all the more gorgeous.

Sailing & Cruising

Several yachts and cruise boats run party cruises. Most companies charge US$45 to US$60 for three-hour party cruises with open bars, and US$35 to US$45 for sunset and dinner cruises.

Rhapsody Cruises (Map pp182-3; ☎ 979-0102; Shop 204, Chatwick Plaza) offers a **'wet 'n' wild cruise party'** (admission US$60; 🕑 10am-1pm & 3-6pm Mon-Sat) aboard *Day Dreamer* and *Tropical Dreamer*, two swift catamarans specially designed as party boats, with an open bar and a snorkeling stop in the marine park. Cruises depart from Doctor's Cave Beach Club. A bus will pick you up at your hotel.

Also recommended are the following:

Calico Pirate Cruises (☎ 940-2493; www.calicopiratecruises.com; party cruise per person US$60) Operates *Calico*, a 55ft ketch resembling an old pirate ship. Cruises depart from Pier 1 Marina at 10am every day except Wednesday.

Intimidator (☎ 468-5773; sunset/snorkel cruise US$48/40) A catamaran departing from Doctor's Cave beach.

Mobay Undersea Tours (☎ 940-4465; www.mobayunderseatours.com; tours per person US$60) Has tours over the reeds in partially glass-bottomed 'semi-submarines'.

Montrose (☎ 852-6884; party cruise or snorkeling cruise per person US$45; 🕑 10am-1pm) A catamaran setting forth daily from Pier 1 Marina.

You can charter yachts for private group sailing trips from any of the companies above, or from the **Montego Bay Yacht Club** (☎ 979-8038; mbyc@cwjamaica.com) at Montego Freeport.

Scuba Diving

MoBay offers first-rate dive sites. Most are close to shore and range from teeming patch reefs to awe-inspiring walls that begin in as little as 10m of water.

For advanced divers, **The Point** north of the airport is considered 'the ultimate wall dive,' due to the dense corals and fish, sharks and rays that are fed by crystal-clear waters scoured by currents. The wall here starts at 20m and drops to at least 90m. **Airport Reef**, off the southwestern edge of the airport, is considered by many to be the best site on the island, with masses of coral canyons, caves and tunnels, and even a DC-3 wreck.

Most companies providing diving also offer snorkeling trips. Resort Divers (p198) offers dives and certification courses and rents equipment.

Northeast of Montego Bay, recommended companies are Dive Seaworld (p198), **Fun Divers** (☎ 953-3268; Wyndham Rose Hall Hotel, Rose Hall) and **Jamaica Scuba Divers** (G66; Half Moon Hotel, Ironshore).

Sport Fishing

The waters off Jamaica's north coast offer spectacular game fishing. Deep-water game fish like blue marlin, sailfish, wahoo, king fish, dolphin and yellowfin tuna use the abyss known as 'Marlin Alley' as a migratory freeway (June and August are peak months for marlin). The **Montego Bay Marlin Tournament** is held in late September; contact the **Montego Bay Yacht Club** (☎ 979-8038; mbyc@cwjamaica.com).

Half- and full-day charters can be booked through hotels, from the company **No Problem** (☎ 381-3229; Pier 1 Marina; half-/full-day charter US$360/690), which is equipped to reel in big-game fish.

TOURS

Barrett Adventures (☎ 382-6384; www.barrettadventures.com; Rose Hall) organizes customized minivan tours around Montego Bay as well as islandwide.

Johns Hall Adventure Tours (☎ 971-7776; www.johnshalladventuretour.com; 26 Hobbs Ave) picks you up from your hotel and offers a variety of local historical plantation tours (US$50 including lunch) as well as a tour of its own Bird Sanctuary (US$50 including lunch).

Tropical Tours (Map p184; ☎ 952-0400; www.tropicaltours-ja.com; 49 Gloucester Ave) offers a guided tour (US$40) of Montego Bay and environs, including visits to Rose Hall Great House, a working sugar plantation, the Bob Marley Experience and a blessedly brief stop at a craft market.

Sunflower Travel & Tours (Map p184; ☎ 952-1418; www.sunflowertoursja.com; fax 979-6771; Montego Bay Club Resort, Gloucester Ave) provides a full-day 'Black River Special' tour (US$95 per person) to the Appleton Rum Estate and YS Falls, which includes a brief incursion by boat into the Black River wetlands. Other offerings include Dunn's River Falls (US$45), Blue Mountains via Kingston (US$110), Nine Mile (US$85) and Rose Hall Great House ($US60). All tours include transportation.

Caribic Vacations (Map p184; ☎ 953-9896; www.caribicvacations.com; 69 Gloucester Ave) runs a wide range of tours islandwide, including a package tour to Appleton Rum Estate, Black River and YS Falls every Tuesday and Wednesday (US$95). It specializes in excursions to Cuba.

Irie Tours (Map p184; ☎ 971-5886; irietoursltd@cwjamaica.com; 33 Gloucester Ave) is Caribic's affiliate and also has a broad range of island tours, including a jeep safari (US$75) and a Montego Bay highlight tour on Monday and Friday (US$35).

All Nations Carriage Tours (Map pp186-7; ☎ 979-2514; 10 Fort St) offers 40-minute, horse-drawn carriage tours to many MoBay historic sites spread between Gloucester Ave and the old town (US$15/25/35 per child/adult/couple). You can even arrange to have a carriage pick you up at the airport. If you don't have a reservation, you can find the carriages parked by the Fantasy Craft Market on the 'hip strip,' or across from Sandals Inn.

Maroon Attraction Tours (Map pp186-7; ☎ 971-3900, 700-8805; 32 Church St) runs a cultural, educational and historic **tour** (US$60; 🕑 8am-3:30pm Tue, Thu & Sat) to Maroon Town (p211). This excellent educational excursion, which includes breakfast and lunch, takes visitors to historical sites, into private homes and to a local school. The intricacies of community, history and folklore are engagingly presented by an authoritative guide. By arrangement, you can also hire a guide to take you to Accompong (p257).

Other tour agencies post advertisements around town.

FESTIVALS & EVENTS

Montego Bay's most celebrated annual events are its two high-profile music festivals, the Air Jamaica Jazz and Blues Festival, held in late January and Reggae Sumfest, held in July. See the events calendar on p17 for information on those festivals.

The Pineapple Cup Montego Bay Race (p17) is another notable Montego Bay celebration.

Contact the Montego Bay Yacht Club (p188), which also hosts an **Easter Regatta**, or Jamaica Sailing Week, each March or April. It also sponsors the **Jam-Am Yacht Race** (☎ 979-8262) in December.

SLEEPING

Montego Bay boasts 40% of the hotels in Jamaica, most of them are clustered along Gloucester Ave; deluxe resorts nestle on their own beaches east of town around Ironshore (p198).

Properties listed under the Miranda Hill heading are accessed from Queens Dr, the Gloucester Ave bypass road, and are generally removed from the beaches.

If you arrive without reservations the Jamaica Tourist Board information booth in the arrivals hall at Donald Sangster International Airport can assist.

Montego Bay is the birthplace of the all-inclusive resort concept and the area offers several options for those seeking a hassle-free vacation. Prices quoted here are for the high season (December 15 to April 15); low-season rates can be considerably lower. Rates presented are guidelines; they vary considerably depending on source of booking, season and current specials. See p275 for general information about all-inclusive resorts in Jamaica.

Downtown

Linkage Guest House (Map pp186-7; ☎ 952-4546, 979-0308; 32 Church St; s US$18-25, d US$25) Providing somewhat of an adventure, a night in this backpackers' haunt will give you a flavor of life in downtown Jamaica. Here you'll find 15 rooms in an old wooden house; they're simple and serviceably clean, with fans, louvered windows and hot water in the shared bathrooms. The doors lack reliable locks, however, so secure your belongings.

YMCA (Map pp182-3; ☎ 952-5368, 832-8017; 28 Humber Ave; s/d US$20/30) On the south side of town at the east end of Humber Ave, this bare-bones hostel has 15 basic rooms with shared cold-water bathrooms and fans. There's a TV lounge, plus ping-pong.

Ashanti Inn (Map pp182-3; ☎ 952-7300; 50 Thompson St, cnr Cottage Rd; r US$25-50; ❄) On the east side of town, this pleasant small inn is well kept with tasteful albeit modest furnishings. It has 15 rooms with cable TV and phones, opening to shaded patios. There's a small, quality restaurant serving local favorites, and a veranda providing a privileged view of bustling downtown.

Gloucester Ave

BUDGET

Hotel Gloriana (Map pp182-3; ☎ 970-0669; www.hotelgloriana.com; 1-2 Sunset Ave; s US$40-55, d US$45-60, ste US$60-99; P ❄ 🏊) Just east of the end of Gloucester Ave en route to the airport, this large family-run option has well-worn, somewhat dark rooms with cable TV for a fair price. There's a large pool and no-nonsense restaurant, but for meals you'll fare better at Dolly's Café next door.

Caribic House (Map p184; ☎ 979-6073; fax 979-0322; 69 Gloucester Ave; standard s US$45-59, d US$51-69; ❄) This compact, no-frills option across the street from Doctor's Cave Beach (and right above the Jamaica Bobsled Café) is a favorite of the budget-minded. It has 17 basic rooms with fridges and large bathrooms, including one 'superior' room with kitchen, dining room and three beds.

MIDRANGE

our pick **Knightwick House** (Map p184; ☎ 952-2988; tapas 45@hotmail.com; Corniche Rd; s US$45, d US$65-70; P ❄) Behind and above the Coral Cliff Hotel, this wonderful B&B is close to the action without being submerged by it. Run by a charming couple, Jean and Stanley Magnus, the colonial structure – boasting terra-cotta floors, wrought-iron railings and abundant artwork – has three modest yet appealingly furnished bedrooms with one, two and three beds. All are well lit and airy, and each has a balcony.

Bayshore Inn (Map p184; ☎ 952-1046; theporkpit@hotmail.com; 27 Gloucester Ave; r US$60; P ❄) Attached to the Pork Pit restaurant and facing Walter Fletcher Beach, this is a pleasant, modern place with 15 modestly furnished rooms with fans, air-con and cable TV.

Buccaneer Beach (Map pp182-3; ☎ 952-6489; fax 979-2580; 7 Kent Ave; s/d US$69/89; P ❄ 🏊) A small, modest property with a homey feel. Rooms have tile floors, phone, cable TV and safety box, plus large balconies. There's a plunge pool in each of the front and back courtyards, plus a piano bar with large-screen TV. Its reclusive location at the end of Kent Ave is a five-minute walk from Gloucester Ave.

Beach View Apartments (Map Map p184; ☎ 952-8784, 997-2342; www.marzouca.com/villa_hsp.html; 39 Gloucester Ave; d/tr apt US$69/120; P) Not a bad option, with spacious if dark apartments equipped with microwaves and fridges. Apartments have one or two bedrooms with a total of three or four beds; additional guests are charged US$15. When the sounds of the traffic on Gloucester Ave subside, a well-populated coop of white-wing doves provides cooing ambience.

Toby Resorts (Map p184; ☎ 952-4370; fax 952-6591; www.tobyresorts.com; cnr Gloucester Ave & Sunset Blvd; s US$80-100, d US$90-110; P) This pleasant favorite offers 72 air-conditioned rooms in two-story units surrounding a pool and sundeck with bar. Rooms are nicely furnished with faux-marble floors and pine and rattan furniture, plus phones. Most have small verandas. Facilities include a gameroom, Toby's Good Eats restaurant, a pool bar, and elevated bar with a lounge and large-screen TV. When there's demand, the hotel offers yoga classes.

Altamont West (Map p184; ☎ 952-9087; www.altamontwesthotel.com; 33 Gloucester Ave; s/d US$90/120, ste US$280-420; P) For guests who can't rouse themselves to cross the street for Walter Fletcher Beach, this MoBay newcomer offers a sundeck as well as an outdoor pool. Rooms are modern and gold-accented and come with cable TV, radio and hairdryers. Children under 12 stay for free.

Montego Bay Club Resort (Map p184; ☎ 952-4310, 212-840-6636, in the USA ☎ 800-223-9815; Queen's Dr; s/d from US$100/125; P) A good option for self-caterers, this 14-story highrise condominium complex is above Gloucester Ave. The rental units are clean, spacious and clinically white, with kitchenettes and balconies with good views. There's a restaurant. An elevator provides direct access to Gloucester Ave.

Gloustershire Hotel (Map p184; ☎ 952-4420, in North America 877-574-8497, in the UK 0800-169-7103; www.gloustershire.com; Gloucester Ave; s US$110-125, d US$115-130, ste US$125-130; P) A faded, service-oriented 95-room hotel across the street from Doctor's Cave Beach, this MoBay veteran nestled against the cliff offers rooms with direct-dial phones, safes, satellite TV and a pastel décor that could use some attention. Most rooms feature a balcony. It offers a pool deck with Jacuzzi, a restaurant and a helpful tour desk.

Doctor's Cave Beach Hotel (Map p184; ☎ 952-4355; www.doctorscave.com; Gloucester Ave; s US$120-135, d US$125-140, ste US$159; P) If convenient beach access is a priority, this large hotel across the street from the main beach is a fine choice. Its labyrinthine corridors lead to well-appointed rooms and suites decorated in tropical themes. The lush gardens at the back are tight up against the cliff face, where there's a whirlpool. A splendid restaurant opens onto a small swimming pool and has live entertainment. The Grotto Bar here hosts a cocktail party on Tuesday and Saturday (6pm to 7pm).

Coral Cliff Hotel (Map p184; ☎ 952-4130; www.coralcliffjamaica.com; 165 Gloucester Ave; s/d/tr US$110/130/140, ste d/tr US$180/200; P) This 21-room hotel attached to the Coral Cliff Gaming Lounge offers nine centenary rooms with a yesteryear charm, 10 modern rooms furbished with appealing tropical decor, and two suites in elegant plantation style with spacious balconies. All rooms have air-con, cable TV and phones. There's a swimming pool, gym, library and TV lounge, and an atmospheric restaurant plus flamboyant video-slot lounge.

Wexford (Map p184; ☎ 952-2854; www.thewexfordhotel.com; 39 Gloucester Ave; s US$120-125, d US$125-130, apt US$150-175; P) This recently revamped, efficient option offers 60 spacious rooms, modestly furnished, with balconies, telephones and cable TV. One wing has one-bedroom apartments with kitchenettes. A small bar and the Wexford Grill are onsite. The Wexford is convenient for Aquasol Beach, to which guests have free access.

Royal Decameron Montego Beach Resort (Map p184; ☎ 952-4340, 888-790-5264; 2 Gloucester Ave; all-inclusive d US$130; P) This reinvented place (formerly Jack Tar Village) gets high marks in the all-inclusive section. A welcoming low-rise beachfront resort, it has 128 rooms with lively tropical decor and its own private beach overlooked by a competent restaurant. Rooms all have ocean views and balconies. The range of activities includes tennis, golf and water sports.

TOP END

Breezes (Map p184; ☎ 940-1150; fax 940-1160; www.breezes.com/resort_montegobay; all-inclusive d US$254-400; P) This soulless but efficient SuperClubs all-inclusive towers over Doctor's Cave Beach, where guests have free access. It has 124 graciously appointed but cramped rooms and suites around an L-shaped pool that forms the foreground for a high-tech stage at night – a noise problem if you want to sleep. Rooms have satellite TVs, VCRs, CD players, hair dryers and in-room safes. Entertainment includes theme nights. Facilities include two restaurants, beach grill, four bars, rooftop Jacuzzi, gameroom, water sports, beauty salon and massage, a fitness center and a nightclub.

Sandals Inn (Map pp182-3; ☎ 952-4140; www.sandals.com/main/montego; Kent Ave; all-inclusive d US$590-1550; P ⊠ ❄ 💻 🏊) A modest, 52-room couples-only resort, this place is run to exacting standards and offers a range of entertainment, water sports and top-notch cuisine. The public beach across the road is much smaller than the hotel brochure suggests, but guests get free access to Sandals' other two MoBay properties.

Miranda Hill

MIDRANGE

Big Apple (Map pp182-3; ☎ 952-7240; fax 971-8631; 18 Queen's Dr; d/ste US$55/80; P ❄ 🏊) This pleasant hilltop inn has a commanding view and 21 tiled and air-con rooms with satellite TV, most with two double beds and views. Rooms vary. Furnishings are modest and bathrooms are small. Newer rooms are larger. Meals are prepared on request (US$6 to US$8).

Blue Harbour Hotel (Map pp182-3; ☎ 952-5445; http://fly.to/jamaica; 6 Sewell Ave; s/d/tr US$58/68/86; P ❄ 🏊) This intimate 25-room hotel, poised on a hill above the strip, has basic rooms, some with kitchenettes. Rooftop dining in the hotel restaurant is available, as is a meal plan accepted by 10 local restaurants. The hotel also arranges local tours.

Palm View Guesthouse (Map pp182-3; ☎ 952-8321; www.montego-bay-jamaica.com/palmview/; 22 DeLisser Dr; d US$45, 1-/2-/3-bedroom ste US$60/120/170; P ⊠ ❄ 🏊) Lacking in pretension, this secure, well-kept property five minutes from the airport offers rooms and suites with balconies, phones, small TVs and spacious bathrooms. The old furniture just makes the place feel more comfortable.

Verney's Tropical Resort (Map pp182-3; ☎ 952-2875; www.verneyhousehotel.com; fax 979-2944; 3 Leader Ave; d/tr US$63/77; P ❄ 🏊) Popular with Jamaican families, this secluded option offers views over sugarcane fields. The 25 rooms are homey and clean and have cable TV. The open-air bar is pleasant, and there's a restaurant.

Jamaica Grandiosa Resort (Map pp182-3; ☎ 979-3205; jamaicagrandiosa@hotmail.com; 3 Ramparts Close; r US$70; P ❄ 🏊) A newer hilltop property with 38 rooms with modest furnishings, cable TVs and grandiose views. The dining room has a lofty vista. It has a small breeze-swept pool and sundeck, plus a pool table and an undistinguished bar.

TOP END

El Greco Resort (Map p184; ☎ 940-6116, in the USA 888-354-7326, in Canada 800-597-7326; www.elgrecojamaica.com; Queen's Dr; 1-/2-bedroom US$125/184, extra person US$40; P ❄ 💻 🏊) At first glance, the El Greco may seem a tad dated, but happily it turns out to be an impeccable, well-run establishment. Sharing its perch over the strip with Montego Bay Club Resort, it has 96 suites with kitchenettes, satellite TV, tile floors, rattan furniture and floral prints. French doors open to balconies. It has tennis courts. Nanny and laundry services are available. A restaurant serves up good Jamaican cooking (mains US$13 to US$16).

our pick Richmond Hill Inn (Map pp182-3; ☎ 952-3859; www.richmond-hill-inn.com; Union St; s/d US$85/115, ste US$189; P ❄ 🏊) Gazing out over the town and the bay this charming hotel, built of limestone and molasses and chock-full of antiques, is far removed from the MoBay bustle. The rooms have cable TV and modest furnishings. It's noted for its restaurant (see p195), which has attracted many of the great and famous. There's also a six-person penthouse suite (US$450).

Further Afield

BUDGET

View Guest House (Map pp182-3; ☎ 952-3175; fax 979-1740; 56 Jarrett Tce; r with fan/air-con US$30/35; ❄ 🏊) On the southeast edge of town near the airport is this basic option with 14 clean rooms. Home-cooked meals are served, and it has a communal kitchen and bar, plus a view overlooking the city.

Ocean View Guest House (Map pp182-3; ☎ 952-2662; 26 Sunset Blvd; s/d/tr US$35/45/55; ❄) This is the cheapest hotel near the airport and is a bargain at these rates, although rooms are no-frills and the service casual to the extreme. It has a TV lounge.

Brandon Hill Guest House (Map pp182-3; ☎ 952-7054; www.brandonhillguesthouse.com; 28 Peter Pan Ave; s US$40-50, d U$45-55; P ❄ 🏊) This well-run option offers attractive gardens and a nice view, with 16 modestly furnished, well-lit rooms. Breakfast and snacks are prepared to order, but dinner must be had elsewhere.

MIDRANGE

Hotel Montego (Map pp182-3; ☎ 940-6009, 952-3286; www.studentadvtrav.com/jamaica/hotel_montego.html; Federal Ave; r/ste US$64/96; P ❄ 🏊) Convenient to the airport, this student-oriented place is a little past its prime, with 33 rooms and suites with king-size beds, TVs, phones and frumpy decor. There's a breezy veranda pool, plus a bar and restaurant.

Villa Nia (Map pp182-3; ☎ 382-6384; www.carolynscaribbeancottages.com/VillaNia; N Kent Ave; d US$85-95; P 💻) This excellent-value hotel, next to Sandals Montego Bay on the shoreline, flanking the runway of Donald Sangster International Airport, offers five individually rented bedrooms with fans and luxurious private bathrooms in a breezy, fully equipped modern villa with two kitchens. A large sundeck perched out over the sea has cushy lounge chairs and tables shaded by umbrellas. Added bonus: the villa can arrange canoe trips on the sea with local fishermen.

Relax Resort (☎ 979-0656; www.relax-resort.com; 26 Hobbs Ave; r US$78, studio US$93, 1-/2-/3-bedroom ste US$110/69/246; P ❄ 💻 🏊) A breeze-swept property, this agreeable option offers 47 rooms with ocean views, floral prints, tile floors, spacious bathrooms, tiny TVs, and telephones. It has a sumptuous three-bedroom villa, four studio apartments plus two one-bedroom apartments. Tours are offered.

TOP END

Sunset Beach Resort & Spa (Map pp182-3; ☎ 979-8800, 800-888-1199; www.sunsetbeachjamaica.com; Sunset Dr; 3 nights all-inclusive d US$780-960, ste from US$1320; P ❄ 💻 🏊) At the end of the Montego Freeport Peninsula is this 420-room, twin highrise, upscale, all-inclusive resort. Rooms have ocean or bay views, with one king-size or two double four-poster mahogany beds, hair dryer, telephone, cable TV, in-room safe and private balcony. Twelve of the 32 suites have Jacuzzis. It also has four restaurants, five bars, a disco and nightly entertainment, plus tennis courts, pools, gym and spa, business center and three beaches (with a nudist section) with water sports. A Kiddies Club caters to families.

Sandals Montego Bay (Map pp182-3; ☎ 952-5510; www.sandals.com; N Kent Ave; 3 nights all-inclusive d US$2000-3050, ste US$3500-6000; P ⊠ ❄ 💻 🏊) This place takes up 8 hectares of splendid beachfront north of the airport and is a superb all-inclusive, couples-only resort where you and the one you love can seek out that honeymoon sparkle while snorkeling, sailing and sunning to your heart's content. It has 245 rooms and suites in 10 categories, all with lively plantation-style furniture. There are four pools, four whirlpools, five restaurants, four bars and top-notch entertainment. Every kind of water sport is available, including scuba.

EATING

Jamaica's tourism epicenter gives epicureans plenty to celebrate. The steady influx of free-spending vacationers – many of them desperate to escape from the tyranny of the all-inclusive meal plan – means there are plenty of upmarket restaurants representing a good range of international cuisine. If Jamaican food floats your boat, you'll have no trouble finding creative chefs keen to show off the national pride in one of Montego Bay's elegant restaurants. Those on a budget can settle into a cook shop or pick up some street meat at a roadside stand for fare that's economical and anything but pedestrian. Self-caterers are served by well-stocked modern supermarkets, but the smartest among them also seek out local fishermen to haggle over a fresh lobster or a choice specimen from the morning catch. You'll find them in Whitehouse Village at the northern edge of town.

You can buy fresh produce downtown at the **Gully Market** (Map pp186-7; Orange St) between Union and William Sts, and **Fustic Street Market** (Map pp182-3; Barnett St).

For ice cream, head to **Devon House I-Scream** (Map pp186-7; ☎ 940-4060; Bay West Centre, Howard Cook Dr) or **Calypso Gelato** (Map p184; ☎ 979-5172; 75 Gloucester Ave).

Downtown supermarkets include those at **MoBay Shopping Centre** (Map pp186-7; cnr Howard Cooke Dr & Market St) and **Westgate Shopping Centre** (Map pp182-3; Barnett St) on the A1 south of town, but the largest and most modern is the new **Super Plus** (Map pp182-3; ☎ 953-6980; Fairview Shopping Centre, Alice Eldemire Dr).

Downtown

BUDGET

Adwa (Map pp186-7; ☎ 940-7618; City Centre Mall; mains US$2-5; 🕑 breakfast & lunch) In the unlikely setting of the second floor of a shopping mall, this small vegetarian eatery with a changing menu doles out salads and excellent, filling dishes like curried tofu in addition to fresh fruit juices and smoothies. Grab a vegetable or soy patty to go.

Nyam 'n' Jam (Map pp186-7; ☎ 952-1922; 17 Harbour St; mains US$5-9; breakfast, lunch & dinner) This local fave, adjoining the downtown craft market, has real-deal Jamaican fare and daily specials including standards like jerked meat, and callaloo and saltfish – but also more adventurous choices like cow mouth, cow foot and oxtail.

Pier One (Map pp186-7; ☎ 952-2452; Howard Cooke Dr; mains US$5-15; lunch & dinner) Although primarily known for being a nightclub, the waterfront setting away from the strip makes this a relaxing place to come for sandwiches, burgers or Jamaican seafood dishes like jerked conch with papaya.

Butterflake Pastries (Map pp186-7; ☎ 952-0070; 2 Union St; breakfast, lunch & dinner) and nearby **Juici Patties** (Map pp186-7; ☎ 979-3733; 36 St James St; breakfast, lunch & dinner) are good for cheap meat and vegetable patties.

For bakeries, try the **Viennese Bakery** (Map pp186-7; ☎ 952-3711; 43 St James St) or **Hilton's Bakery** (Map pp186-7; ☎ 979-3128; 5 Church St).

Gloucester Ave

BUDGET

Raine's Burger Bar (Map p184; St James Plaza; breakfast US$3-8; breakfast, lunch & dinner) This popular breakfast spot serves it up all day, including homemade muffins, omelettes, and ackee and saltfish. Fish and chips and burgers are also available.

Pork Pit (Map p184; ☎ 952-1046; 27 Gloucester Ave; mains US$4-8; 11am-11pm) Searing tongues for decades, this jumping jerk joint is MoBay's best. Eat at open-air picnic tables shaded by a gargantuan silk-cotton tree that the chef reckons to be 300 years old. Finger-lickin' jerk chicken, pork, fish and shrimp are ordered by the pound, with yams, 'festival' and sweet potatoes as sides.

Hillside Restaurant & Lounge (Map p184; ☎ 328-0147; Corniche Rd; mains US$4-13; breakfast, lunch & dinner) This small, friendly eatery tucked behind the Coral Cliff Hotel serves daily specials like curried conch and oxtail stew, all made to order, hot and fresh. On most afternoons and evenings there is a fierce dominoes competition on the small terrace.

Dolly's Café (Map pp182-3; ☎ 979-0045; Hotel Gloriana Plaza, 1 Sunset Blvd; mains US$6-20; breakfast, lunch & dinner) This cozy pub-style dining room is the place for *real* Jamaican cooking. The menu features time-honored favorites like pepperpot soup, roast pumpkin and a unique, delectable snack that you'll want to take along for the ride: baked coconut chips. You can't do much better than Dolly's hearty Jamaican breakfasts; standout selections include 'steam fish and bananas' and 'mackerel rundown' (salted fish stewed in coconut milk).

MIDRANGE

Pelican (Map p184; ☎ 952-3171; Gloucester Ave; mains US$6-12; 7am-11:30pm; ☒) Don't be mistaken by the roadside diner appearance of this good-value local favorite. Its menu of Jamaican dishes is outstanding, highlighted by red snapper in parchment paper, cooked in wine and béchamel sauce. Other dishes include stew peas with rice and stuffed conch with rice and peas, but the Pelican also serves sirloin steaks and seafood. Sunday buffet is US$12.

Groovy Grouper (Map p184; ☎ 952-3680; mains US$6-14; 9am-1:30am) Location is the attraction of this spot on Doctor's Cave Beach. The food – from burgers to lobster – is average, but on a beautiful breezy evening you may not notice.

El Campay Gallo (Map p184; ☎ 531-0637; 47 Gloucester Ave; mains US$7-14; lunch & dinner) You'll be warmly welcomed as if you're one of the family. This exuberant family-run place serves traditional Cuban dishes like *empanadillas* (meat-filled pastry) and potent cocktails. If you're lucky, the owner will display his considerable talent as a jazz violinist.

Toby's Good Eats (Map p184; ☎ 952-4370; Toby Resorts, cnr Gloucester Ave & Sunset Blvd; mains US$8-12; breakfast, lunch & dinner) This casual hotel eatery is a good place for a decent meal followed by a game of pool. The menu features red snapper prepared the local way – steamed in foil with Jamaican veggies and spices – and vegetable dishes plus pasta.

Brewery (Map p184; ☎ 979-2613; Miranda Ridge Plaza; mains US$8-16; 11am-2am) Grab a seat in the roomy dining room or out on the patio overlooking the strip and sample the large portions of Jamaican, Mexican and American dishes that lure visitors and locals, many of whom stick around as the bar takes over. Wednesday has a lobster special.

our pick **Native Restaurant & Bar** (Map p184; ☎ 979-2769; mains US$8-25; 29 Gloucester Ave; breakfast, lunch & dinner) An excellent place to learn about Jamaican cuisine, this modest yet engaging spot features an extensive menu and open-air veranda. Try 'goat in a boat' (curried goat in a pineapple half) or 'yard man fish' (whole fish escoveitched or steamed). If you're really hungry, consider the 'Boonoonoonoos' sampler (composed of ackee and saltfish, jerk chicken, curried goat, escoveitched fish, plantains and pineapple) – it's like taking a crash course in Jamaican food.

Guangzhou Restaurant (Map p184; ☎ 952-6200; Miranda Ridge Plaza, 39 Gloucester Ave; meals US$9-21; noon-10pm Mon-Sat, 5-10pm Sun) With an impressive view of the bay and a menu strong on seafood, this old favorite serves up a huge variety of Chinese, Thai and Mongolian dishes. Sample the scrumptious curried squid (US$12).

TOP END

Marguerite's (Map p184; ☎ 952-4777; Gloucester Ave; mains US$12-33; 6-10:30pm) Adjoining Margaritaville, this celebrated restaurant provides a lovely setting from which to watch the sunset while drinking cocktails, followed by dinner on the elegant clifftop patio. The pricey menu edges toward nouvelle Jamaican and fresh seafood, but also includes sirloin steak and inventive pasta dishes. The chef displays his culinary chops at a central flambé grill.

Ma Lou's (Map p184; ☎ 952-4130; Coral Cliff Casino, 165 Gloucester Ave; mains US$14-31; dinner) With African-themed decor and exciting nouvelle-Jamaican cuisine, this small place tucked away in the Coral Cliff Casino is one of the nicest restaurants in town. The adventurous menu features delicacies such as roasted Peking chicken, curry with coconut and fried plantain, and specialty jerks. A nice touch is the large window open to the kitchen by the front door, where you can chew the fat with the garrulous chef.

Town House by the Sea (Map p184; ☎ 952-2660; Gloucester Ave; mains US$14-35; lunch & dinner) This elegant dining room overlooking the beach takes food seriously, so come seriously hungry. If you've been craving snails – and who hasn't? – you'll find escargot with a Jamaican twist. Equally rich is the stuffed lobster, red snapper or the filet mignon. If you're merely peckish, choose from the pasta, curry and Jamaican dishes. The smoked marlin is one of the best on the island.

Richmond Hill (Map pp182-3; ☎ 952-3859; Richmond Hill Inn, Union St; mains US$20-45; lunch & dinner) The terrace restaurant 150m above town offers amazing views of the bay, as well as an upscale selection of seafood and steaks. Lunch is a lighter affair, with sandwiches and fish 'n' chips. Worth the trek uphill, even if only for a drink.

Nikkita's (Map p184; ☎ 979-6473; Gloucester Ave; mains US$28-50; dinner) Outstanding French–Caribbean fare that lives up to its expensiveness. In an elegant if dark dining room with marble floors and wrought-iron chairs, you can feast on mouthwatering mahi-mahi, broiled or baked lobster and an array of steak dishes. The perfect spot for a last-night-in-Jamaica send-off bash.

Further Afield

TOP END

Dragon Court (Map pp182-3; ☎ 979-8822; Fairview Shopping Centre, Alice Eldemire Dr; meals US$8-26; lunch & dinner) This is the best fine-dining option for Chinese cuisine in MoBay, located in the modern Fairview Shopping Centre. The menu is replete with Chinese standards with a few standouts including the tempting crispy duckling with plum sauce and 'reggae fish,' with pimentos and other Jamaican spices.

our pick **Houseboat Grill** (Map pp182-3; ☎ 979-8845; mains US$15-30; Southern Cross Blvd; 6-10pm Tue-Sun) Moored in Bogue Bay at Montego Bay Freeport, this converted houseboat is one of Jamaica's top-notch restaurants. The changing menu offers eclectic Caribbean fusion cuisine such as spicy conch fritters with a rémoulade dipping sauce, or honey-soy-glazed, grilled tenderloin of beef with Chinese oyster sauce, and homemade ice cream. You can dine inside, or reclusively out on the moondeck. The bar draws the local middle class and is open until the last guest goes home. Reservations are strongly recommended on weekends.

DRINKING & ENTERTAINMENT

Compared to Negril, Montego Bay has a surprisingly lethargic nightlife. Upscale hotels mostly have lackluster live bands, carnival-style floor shows and yawn-inducing limbo contests. Those staying at all-inclusive resorts or upmarket hotels may never be tempted to prowl outside the compound at night. The others can make do with a decent selection of lively bars and the always engaging street theater.

Details of opening and closing hours for bars and clubs are hard to pin down. Most venues insist that they don't close until the last person leaves, and you're welcome to text that claim.

For listings, check **What's On Jamaica** (www.whatsonjamaica.com).

MoBay Proper (Map pp186-7; ☎ 940-1233; Fort St) Attracting a young local crowd, this exuberant bar serves libations on the terrace and has decent Jamaican cooking. Beneath a 'chandelier' of Heineken bottles, the pool table generates considerable heat, while dominoes are the rage with an older crowd out on the patio. On Friday night there's a fish fry and vintage reggae, and live jazz rings in each new month on the first Sunday.

Jamaican Bobsled Café (Map p184; ☎ 952-1448; 69 Gloucester Ave; 🕑 10am-2am) This watering hole makes a good-natured attempt to capitalize on everybody's favorite fish-out-of-water story – the Jamaican bobsled team immortalized in the film *Cool Runnings*, which is in a perpetual loop on a corner screen. It's a good spot for grabbing one of the many rum-based concoctions and watching the hullabaloo along the strip, a sight more engaging than watching John Candy.

El Campay Gallo (Map p184; ☎ 531-0637; 47 Gloucester Ave; 🕑 closes 3am) This Cuban restaurant is also perhaps the friendliest bar in town…so much so that the bartender, who makes a truly fine mojito, will often join you for a drink.

Jimmy Buffett's Margaritaville (Map p184; ☎ 952-4777; Gloucester Ave; cover after 10pm US$5) This popular place claims to have 'put the hip into the Hip Strip'. Who would have thought that anything to do with Jimmy Buffett could obtain a cachet of cool? Ignoring the sleeping patterns of the strip's many hotel guests, outrageously loud music is pumped into the air until the moment before dawn. Four open-air bars, 15 big-screen TVs and dance floors on decks that overhang the water offer plenty of diversion until the wee hours. If that's not enough excitement, there's a waterslide to carry revelers through the plumbing to flush them ignominiously into the ocean near a floating trampoline.

Rose's Bar (Map p184; ☎ 952-9391; 39 Gloucester Ave) This two-story joint has a low-key bar with a pool table and a patio on the bottom floor. Upstairs is a disco that plays 'all styles' every night of the week.

Blue Beat Jazz & Blues Bar (Map p184; ☎ 952-4777; Gloucester Ave; 🕑 closes 2am) Located next to Marguerite's restaurant, Montego Bay's first jazz and blues martini bar offers live music nightly and Asian–Caribbean fusion cuisine.

Groovy Grouper (Map p184; ☎ 952-3680; Doctor's Cave Beach Club) Its stunning beachside location is its best feature, but the cocktails cost a small fortune.

Montego Bay Yacht Club (Map pp182-3; ☎ 979-8038; Montego Bay Freeport) This rum-happy haunt attracts an eclectic crowd that includes crusty old sea-salts and expats eager to talk about their new boats. Nonmembers must be signed in as guests.

Rum Jungle (Map p184; ☎ 952-4130; Coral Cliff Gaming Lounge) The atmospheric bar boasts imaginative African decor…great if you don't mind the constant background noise of slot machines. There's a nightly cabaret.

Voyage Sports Bar & Grill (Map pp186-7; Aquasol Theme Park, Walter Fletcher Beach) Overlooking the sea, with large-screen TVs, well-crafted margaritas and DJs on Tuesday night.

Brewery (Map p184; ☎ 979-2613; Miranda Ridge Plaza) This is a popular sports bar with fiercely competitive karaoke on Thursday and talented DJs on the weekends.

Beach Parties & Stage Shows

The **Bob Marley Entertainment Centre** (Map pp182-3; Howard Cooke Dr), sometimes called the Catherine Hall Entertainment Centre, occasionally hosts sound systems in addition to being the main venue for Reggae Sumfest.

Live reggae shows are infrequently staged on the beaches; events are publicized on posters placed around town and on IRIE FM (107.7 on your radio dial).

Nightclubs

Pier One (Map pp186-7; ☎ 952-2452; Howard Cooke Dr; admission US$5, 'ladies free') throws a big dance party on Friday night. Jimmy Buffet's Margaritaville competes with World Beat Night on Friday and DJs most other nights. The Brewery has well-known DJs who rock the house on Friday and Saturday nights, while Aquasol Theme Park occasionally stages big-name DJs; check local listings.

Other Venues

Coral Cliff Gaming Lounge (p184; ☎ 952-4130; Gloucester Ave; 🕑 24hr) Over 100 video slot machines, plus a big-screen TV and free drinks, with nightly floor shows, cabarets and/or live jazz.

Dome House (Map pp186-7; ☎ 952-2571; Dome St) Dance and theater performances.

Fairfield Theatre (Map pp182-3; ☎ 952-0182; Fairfield Rd) The home stage of MoBay's Little Theatre Company.

Palace Multiplex (Map pp182-3; ☎ 979-8359; Fairview Shopping Centre, Alice Eldemire Dr) First-run Hollywood flicks.

SHOPPING

Cashing in on the droves of tourists intent on taking home a souvenir, Gloucester Ave is lined with shops containing indistinguishable inventories of rum, cigars, T-shirts and the like. There are three craft markets offering the usual choices as well as a few buried treasures. Duty-free shopping is also big business, offering bargains on consumer items such as jewelry, perfume and leather goods.

Some of the shopping centers around town include Chatwick Plaza, Fairview Shopping Centre and Westgate Shopping Centre (all on Map pp182–3); the West Bay Centre, MoBay Shopping Centre and Overton Plaza (Map pp186–7); and Miranda Ridge Plaza and St James Plaza (Map p184). For good arts and crafts, visit the Gallery of West Indian Art (see below).

Galleries

Gallery of West Indian Art (Map pp182-3; ☎ 952-4547; www.galleryofwestindianart.com; 11 Fairfield Rd) In the suburb of Catherine Hall, this is a quality gallery that sells arts and crafts from around the Caribbean including Cuban canvases, hand-painted wooden animals, masks and handmade jewelry. Most of the work here is for sale.

Ambiente Gallery (Map pp186-7; ☎ 952-7747; 10 Fort St) Fine-art prints by regional artists.

Craft Markets

For the largest selection head to the **Harbour Street Craft Market** (Map pp186-7; Harbour St; 7am-7pm), which extends for three blocks between Barnett and Market Sts. **Fort Montego Craft Market** (Map p184; 8am-7pm), behind the fort, and **Fantasy Craft Market** (Map p184; 8am-7pm), at the southern end of Gloucester Ave, offer less variety and quality.

Duty-Free Goods

City Centre Building (Map pp186–7) – a shopping plaza opposite the library on Fort St – has several duty-free shops including **Bijoux** (☎ 952-2630), **Chulani** (☎ 952-2158) and **Casa de Oro** (☎ 952-3502), all with jewelry, ceramics and so on. Most duty-free stores open at 10am.

Record Stores

Clapper's Music (Map pp182-3; ☎ 979-5836; 27 Gloucester Ave) Located behind the Pork Pit, this place is the best-stocked reggae music shop in town.

GETTING THERE & AWAY

Air

Air Jamaica (Map p184; ☎ 922-4661, 888-359-2475, in the USA 800-523-5585; www.airjamaica.com; 9 Queen's Dr; 8:30am-4:30pm Mon-Fri) operates jet and prop-plane services between MoBay's Donald Sangster International Airport and Kingston's Norman Manley International Airport and Tinson Pen (US$60 each way, several flights daily). Get tickets at the Montego Bay office or at the airport.

TimAir (Map pp182-3; ☎ 952-2516, 979-1114; www.timair.net; domestic terminal, Donald Sangster International Airport), an 'air taxi' service, offers charter flights to Negril (US$179), Ocho Rios (US$362), Port Antonio (US$599) and Kingston (US$483).

See p292 for more details on domestic charter service. See p285 for information about international air service.

Boat

Cruise ships berth at the Montego Free-port, about 3km south of town. Taxis to downtown MoBay cost US$10. See p290 for details on cruise companies serving Montego Bay.

Montego Bay Yacht Club (Map pp182-3; ☎ 979-8038; fax 979-8262; Montego Freeport) has hookups, gasoline and diesel.

Car

Avis (☎ 952-0762), **Budget** (☎ 952-3838), **Hertz** (☎ 979-0438) and **Island Rental Car** (☎ 952-5771) all have offices at Donald Sangster International Airport.

Companies with offices in Montego Bay include **Efay Car Rentals** (Map pp182-3; ☎ 952-8280; Shop 6, Chatwick Plaza) and **Sunbird Car Rentals** (Map p184; ☎ 952-4975; 19 Gloucester Ave).

Public Transportation

Buses, minibuses and route taxis arrive and depart from the transportation station off Barnett St at the south end of St James St. There's an **inspector's office** (7am-6pm) inside the gate where you can ask for the departure point of the bus you're seeking.

The following approximate fares apply for minibuses and route taxis:

Destination	Duration	Cost
Duncans	1hr	US$2
Falmouth	30min	US$2
Kingston	3½hr	US$7.50
Lucea	1¼hr	US$1.50
Negril (transfer at Lucea)	1½hr	US$3
Ocho Rios	2hr	US$3.50

Montego Bay Metro Line (Map pp186-7; ☎ 952-5500; 19A Union St) bus service was introduced in 2001, linking MoBay with the suburbs and outlying towns (a flat fare of US$0.35 applies).

Taxi

Jamaica Union of Travelers Association (JUTA; ☎ 952-0813) has taxi stands on Gloucester Ave at the Gloucestershire and Coral Cliff hotels and at Doctor's Cave Beach Hotel, downtown at the junction of Market and Strand Sts, and by the bus station. Identify JUTA members by the red plates and JTB decal emblazoned on their vehicles.

A list of official JUTA fares from Montego Bay is posted at the airport. At last visit, certified fares from the airport for up to four passengers were US$40 to Falmouth, US$100 to Negril, US$100 to Ocho Rios, US$200 to Kingston and US$250 to Port Antonio.

GETTING AROUND

You can walk between any place along Gloucester Ave and downtown (it's about 2.5km from Kent Ave to Sam Sharpe Sq). You'll need a vehicle for anywhere further.

To/From the Airport

You'll find taxis waiting outside the arrivals lounge at the airport. There is an official taxi booth immediately outside customs. Your taxi driver will probably call for a porter…who'll expect a tip for taking your luggage the 10m to your car! A tourist taxi to Gloucester Ave costs US$8. Alternatively, you can catch a minibus or route taxi from the gas station at the entrance to the airport (US$0.50).

Scooter & Bicycle

Sun Cruise Bike Rental (Map pp182-3; ☎ 979-0614; 32 Gloucester Ave) is next to the Wexford hotel. Here you can rent bicycles for US$20 per day with a US$200 credit-card slip deposit. Scooters cost US$40 to US$45 with a US$1000 deposit.

Public Transportation

There is no in-town bus service. Montego Bay Metro Line buses (p197) operate to the suburbs, as do minibuses and route taxis. All depart and arrive at the transportation station near the junction of St James and Barnett Sts.

Taxi

Licensed JUTA taxis cruise Gloucester Ave; they charge a steep US$8 minimum. See left for a list of taxi stands. Published fares from Gloucester Ave are US$8 to the airport, US$20 to Greenwood, US$10 to Ironshore, US$10 to Montego Freeport and US$10 to Rose Hall.

THE EAST COAST TOWARD RIO BUENO

East of Montego Bay the A1 hugs the coast, which here is not particularly scenic, all the way to Falmouth, 37km away.

IRONSHORE

This residential suburb about 8km east of Montego Bay is a center for deluxe resorts and villas, several of which line the shoreline of the scintillating Mahoe Bay.

The Blue Diamond Shopping Centre, near the highway at Ironshore, has a **Scotiabank** (☎ 953-8451), as well as **Diamond Drugs Pharmacy** (☎ 953-9184), **Express Laundromat** (☎ 953-8918) and **Shopper's Fair** (☎ 953-3926), a well-stocked supermarket.

In the midst of all the resorts east of Ironshore, the Half Moon Village shopping center has a National Commercial Bank and the **MoBay Hope Medical Center** (☎ 953-3649; 24hr emergency).

Activities

Most all-inclusive resorts have scuba facilities and snorkeling gear for guests. The most established provider on the north coast is **Resort Divers** (☎ 953-9699, 940-1183; www.resortdivers.com; Holiday Inn Sunspree, Rose Hall Rd; 4-/5-dive package US$140/180, certification US$395, 'discover scuba' package US$90; single dive with own equipment US$40; dives 9am, 11am, 1:30pm), which offers dives, certification courses and rental equipment.

Dive Seaworld (☎ 953-2180; diveseaworld.com; Cariblue Beach Resort; 1-tank dive US$45; dives 9am, 11am, 12:30pm, 2pm, 6pm) also offers scuba diving and rents snorkeling gear (day use US$30).

For horseback trail rides, you can't do better than **Rocky Point Stables** (☎ 953-2286; www.horsebackridingjamaica.com) just west of Half Moon Village. This full-blown equestrian center leads **excursions** (US$60; 10am) into the mountains rising from the Rose Hall

Estate and a classic bareback **beach ride** (US$60; 7am & 4pm) during which you and your horse splash straight into the turquoise sea. For the kiddies there's also a **pony ride** (US$15; 10:30am & 3:30pm). Riding lessons cost US$50 per 45 minutes. Transportation from your hotel can be arranged.

Rocky Point Stables also offers a **mountain-biking tour** (US$40; 9:30am) on the Mount Zion trail through scenic countryside.

GOLF

The alluring **White Witch Golf Course** (953-2800; Ritz-Carlton Rose Hall; green fees Ritz-Carlton guests/visitors US$189/209, US$109 2.30-4.30pm), a 6143m par-71 championship course, is perhaps the most splendid option. Green fees cover caddy and cart. A well-situated restaurant serves lunch and dinner.

Also noteworthy is **Half Moon Golf Club** (953-2560, 953-3105), about 5km east of Ironshore; this Robert Trent Jones–designed, 6506m, par-72 course (green fees US$150, plus US$35 for cart rental and US$20 for a caddy). The **David Leadbetter Golf Academy** (953-9767; fax 953-9369) is here; private lessons are offered (hour/half-day/full day US$125/275/525).

SuperClubs Golf Club Montego Bay at Ironshore (953-2800; green fees guests/visitors US$189/209, US$109 after 2pm) is a links-type course (6065m and par 72) known for its blind-shot holes. Green fees cover cart and caddy.

Sleeping

Cocomo's Guest House (953-9437, 831-7584; cocomos1@aol.com; Coral Gardens; r US$50;) A no-frills place on the A1 with seven rooms with cable TV and well-worn furniture. Some share a toilet and shower. There's also a communal kitchen. Meals are prepared on request.

Cariblue Beach Resort (953-2022; www.caribluehotel.com; Rose Hall; s US$65-95, d US$95-110;) This fading resort on the A1 offers 22 spacious though meagerly furnished rooms with phones and TVs. Most have a balcony. It has a restaurant, the Dive Seaworld dive shop (opposite) and a wide range of water sports.

All Seasons Beach Resort (953-1440; allseasons68@hotmail.com; St James; townhouse US$122-180;) A quiet seafront property offering spacious two- and three-bedroom townhouses priced attractively for families and groups traveling en masse. Each unit has a well-equipped kitchen and cable TV. The Furnishings are a tad chintzy but overall the buildings and grounds are attractive and well kept. Equipment for sea kayaking and snorkeling is available.

Coyaba Beach Resort & Club (953-9150, 800-237-3237; www.coyabajamaica.com; r US$320-400;) At Mahoe Bay, this tranquil family-run resort offers contemporary elegance. It has 50 recently refurbished luxurious rooms and junior suites furnished 'plantation style' with hand-carved beds, floral drapes and rich mahogany reproduction antiques. Some rooms have direct beach access but all feature in-room safe, telephone, satellite TV/VCR and marble bathrooms. Water sports are offered, and there's a sundeck. The elegant Vineyard Restaurant offers splendid nouvelle-Jamaican cuisine. The resort also has an ocean-side bar and grill and a second bar with a warm, clubby feel. The full-service SpaSerenity (open 9am to 6pm Monday to Saturday and by appointment Sunday) is here.

Half Moon (953-2211, in the USA 800-626-0592; www.halfmoon-resort.com; s US$355-425, d US$400-470, ste US$425-725, villas US$1520-1650;) One of the great Caribbean resorts, the Half Moon is an exclusive colonial-style affair named for its private, 1.5km-long crescent beach, behind which are 160 hectares of beautifully landscaped gardens containing an 8-hectare nature reserve. With a staff of 750, the place feels more like a utopian village than a resort. It has 420 rooms and suites with Georgian plantation-era decor, and villas that have hosted the likes of the Queen of England and Prince Ranier. Facilities include gourmet restaurants, squash courts, 13 tennis courts, equestrian center, full-service spa, conference center, championship golf course (left) and the Half Moon Village. Unlike some other Jamaican resorts, Half Moon takes its environmental responsibilities seriously; a new state-of-the-art US$1.6 million water-treatment plant earned it the 'Green Hotel of the Year' award given by the Caribbean Hotel Association.

Ritz-Carlton Rose Hall (953-2800, in North America 800-241-3333; www.ritzcarlton.com/resorts/rose_hall_jamaica; 1 Ritz-Carlton Dr, Rose Hall; d US$309-509, ste US$519-2500;) With nearly half a kilometer of prime beachfront and 427 resplendent rooms and sumptuous suites, this luxury resort mixes up-to-the-minute amenities with refined old-world charm. Rich fabrics and mahogany abound, tastefully blended with fresh tropical colors. Each unit is equipped with cable TV, three telephones, safety deposit box, computer hook-up and ritzy marble bathrooms with terry robes. The 51 executive suites and 36 'club rooms' are regal indeed. There are six restaurants and lounges, a tennis center and two courts, a business center, championship golf course, full service spa and fitness center and full convention facilities.

ALL-INCLUSIVES

Holiday Inn Sunspree (☎ 953-2485, in North America 800-465-4329; Rose Hall; 3 nights all-inclusive d US$1050-1200, ste US$1350; P ⊠ ⁙ ▣ ⛱) Well-run but never exciting, this all-inclusive offers 524 tastefully appointed rooms and 26 family suites in ungainly seven-story buildings around a handsome sundeck and vast free-form pool. It has special facilities for children. Mom and dad are also catered for with a fitness spa, tennis and volleyball courts, miniature golf, glass-bottom boats, a disco, and four restaurants and bars.

Sandals Royal Caribbean (☎ 953-2231; fax 953-2788; 3 nights all-inclusive d US$1800-2250, ste US$2400-2730; P ⊠ ⁙ ▣ ⛱) This remodeled upscale couples-only all-inclusive at Mahoe Bay offers 187 rooms in six categories, all in Sandals' trademark plantation style. Its beach is relatively small but water sports, land sports, entertainment and cuisine are up to par. Highlights include Sandals Cay, with the Royal Thai restaurant (one of four restaurants) and its own swimming pool and Jacuzzi.

Eating & Drinking

Traditionally, most visitors to Ironshore dined at the upscale restaurants in the resorts, but in the last decade, a handful of new arrivals have brought some culinary zest to the area.

our pick **Scotchies** (☎ 953-8041; Hwy A1; ½ pound portion US$5; ⏲ lunch & dinner) Widely regarded as the best jerk shack in Jamaica (hence the world), this roadside yard with thatched-covered tables doles out impeccable portions of chicken, pork and fish accompanied by sides of yams, festival or breadfruit. Cool your tongue off with a Red Stripe…and then go back for more.

Live Bait (☎ 953-8293; Hwy A1; mains US$5-16; ⏲ lunch & dinner) When it opened in 2003, this bright-yellow jazz bar was an instant favorite among local hipsters. Classic jazz posters inform the proceedings, and there's a not-bad selection of wine on offer. Outside, a breezy terrace overlooks the bay. Open late.

Country Style Bar (☎ 953-8791, 883-6214; Hwy A1; mains US$6-15; ⏲ breakfast, lunch & dinner) This brand-new place looks like it's been around for eons. Owner/curator, Ansel Barrett, has filled every available nook and cranny with his delightful collection of bric-a-brac ranging from portraits of Robert Kennedy to preserved insects. The building itself is a casual masterpiece, extensively embellished with tile fragments and an offbeat assemblage of found objects. The main lounge is stylishly comfortable with a collection of vintage easy chairs and tables. A small beach looks out on an island to which you can kayak. The menu includes hearty breakfasts and a typical roster of Jamaican fare. You'll find it just east of Coyaba Beach Resort.

Akbar/Thai Gardens (953-9770; Half Moon Village; mains US$12-26; ⏲ lunch & dinner) Occupying a single dining room, this venue is served by two distinct kitchens. Both are recommended for superb Indian and Thai cuisine, tremendous atmosphere, and a reasonably priced and broad menu including several vegetarian options.

Royal Stocks (☎ 953-9770; Half Moon Village; mains US$12-26; ⏲ lunch & dinner) This pub affects an olde-English feel, serving pricey burgers and steaks, Jamaican favorites and an authentic steak-and-kidney pie (US$12). TVs broadcasting English football enhance the anglophile ambience.

Sugar Mill Restaurant (☎ 953-2228; Half Moon Golf Club; mains US$30-40; ⏲ 11am-11pm) Beautifully situated overlooking the green expanses of a golf course and adjacent to a 200-year-old working watermill, this is a fine restaurant serving seafood, steak and Jamaican specialties that are as superb as the setting. Reservations are required.

Entertainment

Bob Marley Experience (☎ 953-3449; www.reggaeexperience.com; Half Moon Village; admission free) Shows hourly screenings of an engaging documentary on Marley's life in a 68-seat theater.

Blue Diamond Cinema (☎ 953-9020) Screens the latest releases in the Blue Diamond Shopping Centre.

Shopping

The Half Moon Village is an upscale and pleasant shopping center with pristine grounds that has become a destination in itself for guests at area resorts.

THE WHITE WITCH OF ROSE HALL

John Rose Palmer, grandnephew of John Palmer, who built Rose Hall, married Anne May Patterson in 1820. Although the young woman was half English and half Irish, legend has it that she was raised in Haiti, where she learned voodoo. Legend also says that Anne May was a murderous vixen. The lascivious lady allegedly practiced witchcraft, poisoned John Palmer, stabbed a second husband and strangled her third. Her fourth husband escaped, leaving her to dispose of several slave lovers before she was strangled in her bed.

This famous legend is actually based on a series of distorted half-truths. The inspiration for the story, originally told in writing in 1868 by John Costello, editor of the *Falmouth Post*, was Rose Palmer, the initial lady of Rose Hall. She did have four husbands, the last being John Palmer, to whom she was happily wed for 23 years (she died before her husband, at age 72). Anne Palmer, wife of John Rose Palmer, died peacefully in 1846 after a long, loving marriage.

In 1929 novelist HG DeLisser developed the fable into a marvelous suspenseful romance, *The White Witch of Rose Hall*.

You will find that the A1 is lined with makeshift stalls selling wood carvings and crafts.

Getting There & Away

A great number of minibuses and route taxis ply the A1 road, traveling to and from Donald Sangster International Airport and Montego Bay's transportation center, Gloucester Ave and downtown. You'll pay about US$1 to travel from MoBay to Ironshore.

ROSE HALL TO GREENWOOD

East of Ironshore the A1 dips and rises past coastal scrubland, residential estates and several colonial-era great houses.

Sights

ROSE HALL GREAT HOUSE

This **mansion** (☎ 953-2323; rosehall@cwjamaica.com; adult/child under 12 US$20/10; ⏰ 9am-6pm), with its commanding hilltop position 3km east of Ironshore, is the most famous great house in Jamaica.

Construction of the imposing house was begun by George Ashe in the 1750s and was completed in the 1770s by John Palmer, a wealthy plantation owner. Palmer and his wife Rose (after whom the house was named) hosted some of the most elaborate social gatherings on the island. Slaves destroyed the house in the Christmas Rebellion of 1831 and it was left in ruins for over a century. In 1966 the three-story building was restored to haughty grandeur.

Beyond the Palladian portico the house is a bastion of 18th-century style, with a magnificent mahogany staircase and doors, and silk wall fabric that is a reproduction of the original designed for Marie Antoinette during the reign of Louis XVI. *Don't touch!* Many of the antiques are the works of leading English master carpenters of the day.

Much of the attraction is the legend of Annie Palmer, a multiple murderer said to haunt the house (see the boxed text, above). Her bedroom upstairs is decorated in crimson silk brocades. The cellars now house an English-style pub and a well-stocked gift shop. There's also a snack bar.

Tours of the house are mandatory and commence every 15 minutes till 5:15pm.

GREENWOOD GREAT HOUSE

This marvelous **estate** (☎ 953-1077; www.greenwoodgreathouse.com; admission US$14; ⏰ 9am-6pm) sits high on a hill 8km east of Rose Hall, and is a far more intimate property. Construction began on the two-story, stone-and-timber structure in 1780 by the Honorable Richard Barrett, whose family arrived in Jamaica in the 1660s and amassed a fortune from its sugar plantations. (Barrett was a cousin of the famous English poet Elizabeth Barrett Browning.) In an unusual move for his times, Barrett educated his slaves.

Unique among local plantation houses, Greenwood survived unscathed during the slave rebellion of Christmas 1831. The original library is still intact, as are oil paintings, Dresden china, a court jester's chair and plentiful antiques, including a mantrap used for catching runaway slaves. Among the highlights is the rare collection of musical instruments, containing a barrel organ and two polyphones, which the guide is happy to bring to life. The view from the front balcony down to the sea is quite stunning.

After exploring the house you can drink a cold one at the atmospheric **Level Crossing** (☎ 953-1077), a bar situated near the entrance to the house.

Buses traveling between Montego Bay and Falmouth will drop you off anywhere along the A1; ask to be let off across from the Total gas station on the seaside of the road and take the road up the hill. It's a good 20-minute slog to the top.

ROSE HALL BEACH PARK

This private **beach** (☎ 680-0969; adult/child US$6/3; 9am-5pm) 3km east of the Wyndham Rose Hall Resort is a white-sand paradise offering water sports including PADI-certified diving, banana-boat rides, jet-skiing and parasailing. There's a restaurant and bar.

Activities

Wyndham Rose Hall Resort & Country Club (☎ 953-2650) has a 6033m par-72 golf course known for its superb coastal vistas. Green fees are US$135 including cart rental and a caddy.

Sleeping & Eating

Dunn's Villa Resort Hotel (☎ 953-7459, in the USA 718-882-3917; www.dunnsvillaresort.com; Cornwall; d from US$85, incl breakfast US$113; P) In the hills, in the village of Cornwall 3km inland (follow the signs from the highway), this well-kept, homey hotel has 11 rooms with satellite TV and wide balconies. The spacious public areas are minimally but attractively furnished. There's a Jacuzzi on a raised sundeck. The hosts rent mountain bikes (US$8) and offer lunch, dinner and weekend brunch poolside.

Royal Reef Hotel & Restaurant (☎ 953-1700; www.royalreefja.com; r US$75-177; P) On the A1 at Greenwood, this gracious, modern Mediterranean-style hotel has 19 rooms. Its decor includes classical wrought-iron furnishings and exquisite tropical murals. An elevated amoeba-shaped pool is inset in the terra-cotta terrace, which has an outside grill overlooking a tiny beach overgrown by mangroves. The excellent continental cuisine, mostly prepared with Jamaican flavor, is served both alfresco and in an intimate dining room (meals US$20 to US$35).

Wyndham Rose Hall Resort & Country Club (☎ 953-2650, in the USA 800-996-3426, in the UK 020-8367-5175; www.wyndham.com; d US$235-315, 3 nights all-inclusive d US$1330-1450; P) This 488-room resort just west of Rose Hall Great House offers both all-inclusive and traditional pay-as-you-go lodging. Fronted by a beautiful 300m-long beach, the two unsightly highrise buildings contain spacious rooms with one king-size or two queen-size beds. The amenities include six restaurants, four bars, three pools, an impeccable 18-hole golf course and six tennis courts. Services for families include a kid's club (open from 9am to 5pm) and nannies for hire. A major water park – Sugar Mill Falls – has three terraced pools, an 85m waterslide, meandering canals complete with waterfalls, and the obligatory swim-up bar.

White Witch's Hideaway Pub & Grill (☎ 953-2323; Rose Hall Great House; meals US$3-7) An atmospheric dungeonlike pub beneath the Rose Hall Great House that once served as a dungeon of sorts. The barkeeps will tell you all about it in gruesome detail. It serves typical Jamaican meals, plus fish and chips, sandwiches and other snacks.

Getting There & Away

Minibuses and route taxis ply the A1 road. You'll pay about US$2 to travel from MoBay to Rose Hall.

FALMOUTH

pop 9500

Falmouth's early history is one of sugar and slavery. Few other towns in Jamaica have retained their original architecture to quite the same degree as Falmouth, which has a faded Georgian splendor. The city, 37km east of Montego Bay, has been the capital of Trelawny parish since 1790.

To walk among the cut-stone warehouses at the eastern end of town – places where human beings were inventoried, awaiting sale – is a disquieting experience. Plans for a monument and museum devoted to slavery and its legacy continue to inch forward; in the meantime, the spooky old buildings bear silent witness.

There have been several plans to restore the town, but very little effort has been undertaken and many historic buildings are now decrepit. However, several individuals have done fine restoration work, as has the **Georgian Society** (☎ 952-4089; fax 979-8013).

Wednesday and Saturday are market days, when everything from bootleg underpants to fresh ginger to homemade root tonics are up for grabs. Much of Trelawny parish shows up for good deals on produce, baby chick-

CHANGING THE COASTLINE

Formerly ignored by developers, the stretch of coastline between Falmouth and Rio Bueno has caught their rapacious eyes over the past decade. Indeed, as the A1 heads east, there are spots where the sea struggles to peak through the mass of hotels, resorts and villas under construction.

Following the May 2005 ground-breaking for a US$400 million water project on the Martha Brae River, a period of unprecedented development began. East of Falmouth a US$1.2 billion 'resort colony' called Harmony Cove was planned to include six hotels, two golf courses and 200 posh villas. Another behemoth project by a Spanish hotel chain, the Oyster Bay Resort, broke ground to add a whopping 1700 rooms.

Falmouth itself was bound to be affected. In 2008, construction began in the port on a marina for cruise ships, which are expected to begin arriving in the winter of 2009. The influx of cruise-ship day-trippers, disembarking for a few hours of souvenir shopping while en route between Montego Bay and Ocho Rios, will dilute the town's frayed charm. To accommodate them, the development of Hampden Wharf is expected to include, among other things, a concert hall, restaurants and duty-free shopping malls. There's still no word on whether the long-proposed slavery museum will be part of the complex.

Further controversy surrounds the 10,000-seat Greenfield Stadium, which was completed in time to host the opening ceremony for the 2007 Cricket World Cup. Built with a loan from the Chinese government that stipulated only Chinese engineers and workers could be employed on its construction – quite a blow given the scarcity of jobs in the area – it has been largely out of use since the tournament. Perhaps it will be revived for the cruise-shippers.

ens, yam sprouts, coffee beans, bars of soap and…you name it.

History

Falmouth was laid out in 1790 and named for the English birthplace of Sir William Trelawny, then the governor of the island. The streets were planned as a grid and patriotically named after members of the royal family and English heroes. Planters erected their townhouses using Georgian elements adapted to Jamaican conditions.

With its advantageous position, Falmouth became the busiest port on the north coast. Outbound trade consisted mainly of hogsheads (large casks) of wet sugar and puncheons (casks) of rum, while slaves were off-loaded for sale in the slave market.

The town's fortunes degenerated when the sugar industry went into decline during the 19th century and it was dealt a further blow with the advent of steamships, which the harbor was incapable of handling. By 1890 the port was essentially dead. The city has struggled along ever since.

Old-timers still wax poetic about the filming of the Steve McQueen movie *Papillon*, which was shot in Falmouth in 1972. Locals were hired en masse for the production. McQueen is remembered by a de facto tour guide named Moses as 'a nice guy who smoked a lot of cigarettes.'

Orientation & Information

The A1 from Montego Bay runs along Duke St into Water Sq, the town's node. It then zigzags east, continuing to Ocho Rios. Market St, one block west of Water Sq, runs south to Martha Brae and Good Hope.

Ambulance (☎ 954-3250)
Cable & Wireless (☎ 954-5910; 23 Market St; 🕑 8am-4pm Mon-Fri) Telephone and fax services.
Cambio King (☎ 954-4082; cnr Market & Duke Sts) Currency exchange at good rates. Located upstairs from Marguerite's Supermarket.
Falmouth Hospital (☎ 954-3250; Rodney St) Emergency services.
Island Internet (☎ 954-7936; 6 Thorpe St; per 30 min/1 hr US$1.75/2.50; 🕑 10am-7pm Mon-Sat) High-speed internet and overseas calls for US$0.20 per minute.
Library (☎ 954-3306; Rodney St; internet access per 30 min US$1)
National Commercial Bank (☎ 954-3232; Water Sq)
Police station (☎ 119, 954-3222; cnr Rodney St & Market St)
Post office (☎ 954-3050; cnr Cornwall St & Market St)
Scotiabank (☎ 954-3357; cnr Market St & Lower Harbour St) Scotiabank also operates an ATM in the shopping center near the eastern edge of town.
Trewlawny Pharmacy (☎ 954-3189; 19 Market St)

Sights & Activities

The best place to orient yourself is **Water Sq**, at the east end of Duke St. Named for an old circular stone reservoir dating to 1798, the square (actually a triangle) has a fountain topped by an old waterwheel. Today it forms a traffic roundabout.

The market, on the east side of Water Sq, was once the site of slave auctions. The current structure was built in 1894 and named for two of Queen Victoria's grandsons. Today, as the **Albert George Shopping & Historical Centre**, it still functions as a market with craft stores and contains a very small **museum** (admission free; 9am-5pm Mon-Sat) with a motley collection of colonial-era artifacts.

One block east of Walter Sq is Seaboard St and the grandiose Georgian **courthouse** in Palladian style, fronted by a double curling staircase and Doric columns, with cannons to the side. The current building, dating from 1926, is a replica of the original 1815 structure that was destroyed by fire. The town council presides here.

Some 50m east along Seaboard St, **Tharp House** sags from age yet is still one of the best examples of an elegant period townhouse. Today housing the tax office, it was formerly the residence of John Tharp, at one time the largest slaveholder in Jamaica.

Continue along Seaboard St to the **Phoenix Foundry**, built in 1810 at the corner of Tharpe and Lower Harbour Sts, with its strange-looking conical roof. Behind the foundry, guarded by locked gates, is the **Central Wharf** where slaves were brought ashore, to be replaced in the holds by sugar, rum and other victuals born of their back-breaking labor. The crumbling warehouses are on their last legs. The property has been purchased with plans to transform it into a visitors center chronicling the barbarous history of slavery. At the time of writing, there's still no word when the museum might open.

Retrace your steps to Water Sq and cut down Cornwall St. One of the most stately edifices is the restored **Baptist Manse** (cnr Market & Cornwall Sts), formerly the residence of nonconformist Baptist preacher William Knibb, who was instrumental in lobbying for passage of the Abolition Bill that ended slavery. The porticoed **post office** is adjacent.

At the bottom of colonnaded Market St stands the **Methodist Manse**, a stone-and-wood building with wrought-iron balconies and Adam friezes above the doorways. A diversion along Trelawny St leads one block west to **Barrett House**, the handsome restored former home of wealthy planter Edward Barrett.

On Rodney St, which runs west along the shore, is the historic **police station**, constructed in 1814. The prison here once contained a 'treadmill,' a huge wooden cylinder with steps on the outside. Shackled above the mill, slaves had to keep treading the steps as the cylinder turned. If they faltered, the revolving steps battered their bodies and legs. The ancient lockups are still in use.

On July 31, 1838, slaves gathered outside **William Knibb Memorial Church** (cnr King & George Sts) for an all-night vigil, awaiting midnight and then the dawn of full freedom, when slave shackles, a whip and an iron collar were symbolically buried in a coffin. Knibb and his wife are buried in the graveyard, which also holds a memorial to him erected by emancipated slaves.

The oldest extant building in town is **St Peter's Anglican Church**, built in 1785 and enlarged in 1842, lies four blocks west along Duke St. The graveyard tombstones are spookily sun-bleached, like bones.

Sleeping & Eating

Greenside Villa Inn (☎ 954-3127, 865-6894; studios US$34-40, plus each additional person US$6) This inn is about 3km west of Falmouth and features studio apartments. The rooms are simple but spacious and clean and have private bathrooms and ceiling fans. The units with kitchenettes have small gas stoves. Meals are cooked on request.

Falmouth Resort (☎ 954-3391; 22 Newton St; r US$35; P) The only accommodation in the center of town. If you want to get a feel for bustling Jamaican downtown life, this is a good option. It's not really a resort in the classic sense, but it does have 12 clean, modest rooms with private bathrooms and cable TV, and welcoming, helpful staff. Meals are prepared on request. Take an upstairs room for privacy and a view.

Golden Pagoda (☎ 617-5482; 24 Duke St; mains US$3-7; lunch & dinner) On the main road west of Water Sq, Golden Pagoda serves inexpensive Chinese and is a good place for people-watching.

Peter's Highway Bar (☎ 836-8872; mains US$4-6; lunch & dinner) On the A1 heading east out of town, an airy roadside rum dispensary and kitchen that doles out good jerk chicken and pork. Welcoming travelers are the flags of many nations hand-painted on the walls, along with a proverb 'Who God Bless No Man Curse' above the image of Bob Marley.

Irie Life (☎ 454-3094; 2-4 Tharpe St; mains US$4-7; 🕑 8am-6pm Mon-Thu, 7am-4pm Fri) A good choice of vegetarian and seafood dishes as well as natural juices.

de Nest Lounge (☎ 617-5308; Tharpe St; 🕑 4pm-close) An engaging watering hole next to Irie Life, this is a comfortable air-conditioned pub and disco that occasionally stages live acts.

Spicy Nice Bakery (☎ 954-3197; Water Sq) Spice is nice at this bakery, where you can buy fresh baked breads, pastries and spicy meat and vegetable patties.

Getting There & Away

Buses, minibuses and route taxis arrive and depart on opposite sides of Water Sq for Martha Brae (US$.50), Montego Bay (US$1.25) and Ocho Rios (US$2.50).

MARTHA BRAE

Situated on a small hill and nearly encircled by the emerald-green waters of the scenic Martha Brae River, this small village 3km due south of Falmouth is justly famous for rafting. The river rises at Windsor Caves (p214) in the Cockpit Country and spills into the sea at Glistening Waters, east of Falmouth.

Activities

RAFTING

A rafting trip down a 4.8km stretch of the Martha Brae River is a quiet thrill. The journey takes 90 minutes on 9m-long bamboo rafts, each carrying one or two passengers, poled by a skilled guide. The upper reaches tumble at a good pace before slowing further downriver, where you stop at 'Tarzan's Corner' for a swing and swim in a calm pool. At the end, after being plied with rum punch, you'll be driven back to your car or tour bus.

Trips begin from Rafters Village, about 1.5km south of Martha Brae. There you'll find an itinerant mento band and a picnic area, bar, restaurant, swimming pool, bathrooms, changing rooms and a secure parking lot. Your captain will pause on request so that you can take a dip or climb a tree.

You can book your adventure at Rafters Village or with the **River Raft Ltd** (☎ 952-0889, 940-6398; www.jamaicarafting.com; 66 Claude Clarke Ave, Montego Bay; per raft 1-2 people US$60, with hotel transfer per person US$50) office in Montego Bay. You can also book the trip in advance from tour desks at area hotels. Remember to tip your raft guide.

Getting There & Away

From Martha Brae a well-maintained road winds through the river gorge to Sherwood. Another rougher road leads southwest to Good Hope Estate (p213) and links with a rough road that leads west from Sherwood to the Queen of Spains Valley (p211).

Minibuses and route taxis regularly run to Martha Brae from Falmouth (US$0.75).

GLISTENING WATERS

At night, Glistening Waters (also known as Luminous Lagoon), a large bay at Rock about 1.6 km east of Falmouth, boasts a singular charm – it glows an eerie green when the water is disturbed. The green glow is due to the presence of microorganisms that produce photochemical reactions when disturbed. The concentrations of microorganisms is so thick that fish swimming by look like green lanterns.

Half-hour boat trips are offered from **Glistening Waters Marina** (☎ 954-3229, 888-991-9901; per person US$15; 🕑 7-9pm).

Sights & Activities

BEAR CAY & WORLD BEACH

A curlicue spit, **Bear Cay**, hooks around the north side of the bay. **World Beach**, the lonesome 3km-long, white-sand beach on the north side, has long been appreciated by savvy travelers for its good snorkeling, sunbathing and solitude. At the time of research, 75% of Bear Cay remained undeveloped. Hawksbill sea turtles – an endangered species – are regularly sighted coming to shore to lay eggs in the deep, soft sand. The gorgeous beach, lined with casuarina pines, is an unheralded Jamaican treasure that ought to qualify for protected-area status. But change is coming fast to this area. Construction is apparently set to begin on a 1700-room resort, and few here are speculating on the fate of the turtles.

You can access World Beach from Time 'n Place, or you can rent a boat at Glistening Waters Marina or Fisherman's Inn; picnic meals are available.

SPORT FISHING & BOATING

The river mouth in Glistening Waters is one of the few places in Jamaica that still offers good **fishing** for tarpon, known as the 'silver bullet' for its feisty defense on a line. No license is required.

In Rock, next to Herbie's Restaurant (a local favorite for succulent roast fish), you can charter a **fishing excursion** (☎ 422-4439; half-/full-day charter US$250/400, drop-line per hr US$40, minimum 2 hr) with 'Kojak' Mowatt and hit the waters in search of marlin, kingfish and mahi mahi.

Glistening Waters Marina charters spiffy sport-fishing **boats** (half-day from US$380) with captain and crew.

Sleeping

our pick **Time 'n Place** (☎ /fax 954-4371, 843-3625; www.mytimenplace.com; cottages without/with air-con US$75/80; P) This delightful spot has three quaint all-hardwood cottages (each housing up to three people) for rent right on World Beach. The cottages have louvered windows, hot water, coffee makers and radios. The rustic beach bar and restaurant is a truly great place to hang out – it was a setting in the movie *How Stella Got Her Groove Back* and has been the backdrop for many a photo shoot. Owner Tony knows about a secret local cavern – he calls it the 'Bottomless Blue Therapeutic Cave'- where you can swim beneath stalagmites by candlelight. Make friends with him and he just might take you there.

Fisherman's Inn (☎ 954-3427; fax 954-3078; s/d US$120/125;) This well-run, charming hotel at Rock Wharf near Glistening Waters, 2km east of Falmouth, offers 12 spacious and pleasingly furnished rooms with big bathrooms and private patios. There are two restaurants. Water sports and Glistening Waters tours are offered.

ALL-INCLUSIVES

FDR Pebbles (☎ 617-2500, in North America 800-337-5437; www.fdrholidays.com/pebbles; 4 nights all-inclusive family of 4 US$1300-1500; P) A good sense of fun pervades this efficiently run, attractive all-inclusive family resort right on the beach. Walkways lined with frangipani, hibiscus and bougainvillea, course through the grounds, while the pine and cedar two-story units feature 96 suites. Each has a king and day bed, TV, telephone, mini-refrigerator and balcony. Facilities include a full range of water sports, three restaurants, fitness center, tennis, disco and a panoply of facilities and activities for children. A well-trained group of nannies looks after the kids.

Starfish Trelawny Beach & Fun Resort (☎ 954-2450, in North America 800-467-8737; www.superclubs.com/brand_starfish/resort_trelawny; 4 nights all-inclusive family of 4 US$1300-1756, cottage US$1540-1740; P) Also focusing on families but less visually appealing than FDR Pebbles, this highrise, 350-room all-inclusive resort offers predictably appointed rooms, five restaurants, tennis courts, ice-skating rink, gym, rock-climbing wall, circus workshop and a full range of water sports. Kids' facilities include a castle with a moat for a pool.

Eating

Time 'n Place (☎ /fax 954-4371; www.mytimenplace.com; meals US$5-15; breakfast, lunch & dinner) This is a fun and funky beachside hut with tables on the sand, swings and hammocks at the bar, and charming service. Take your pick from burgers with fries to an array of Jamaican dishes, including coconut shrimp and grilled garlic lobster. The proprietor's favorite cocktail – a concoction blended from rum cream, Tía Maria and vodka – is called The Beyond, and that's just where it takes you.

Fisherman's Inn (☎ 954-3427; mains from US$10; 7am-10:30pm) Offers stylish dining indoors or on the terrace overlooking Glistening Waters. The menu ranges from salads, seafood and steaks to Creole specialties such as brown stew.

Glistening Waters Marina Restaurant & Lounge (☎ 954-3229; mains US$11-31; 8am-11pm) A clean, modern place that offers Jamaican and continental fare, from onion rings and steamed fish to lobster and pepper steak. It has killer cocktails in a tall sundae glass. Diners on a budget should consider the jerk center next door.

Getting There & Away

Minibuses and route taxis travel the A1 road to and from Falmouth (US$0.50).

DUNCANS

This small town on a hillside 11km east of Falmouth is centered on an old stone clock tower in the middle of a three-way junction. The new highway now diverts ongoing traffic around the town; keep watch for the turnoff from the A1. Minibuses and route taxis pick up and drop off passengers to/from Duncans at the clock tower in the town center.

Kettering Baptist Church, built in 1893, commemorates William Knibb, a Baptist missionary and a leading abolitionist who founded an emancipation village for freed slaves here in 1840.

During his childhood, singer and activist Harry Belafonte was a frequent visitor to the **Sober Robin** (☎/fax 954-2202; r with fan/air-con US$18/30; P ❄ 🏊), an interesting hotel situated on the old road that enters Duncans from the west. The lobby and lounge are cheerfully atmospheric with framed photos of classic movie stars, a small bar with table tennis and a pool table, and plenty of books lying about. The rooms are a little threadbare but are priced accordingly. Less-expensive rooms have a fan but lack TV and hot water. Breakfast is prepared to order.

The personable Victoria has recently returned to Jamaica from a long furlough in Connecticut to fulfill her dream of constructing a great house in her image **Victoria's Villa B&B** (☎ 954-9353, 805-5092, in the USA 256-782-2787; s incl breakfast & dinner US$60, d incl breakfast & dinner US$80-85; P) This brand-new, imposing house stands out among the as-yet undeveloped lands to the west of the Silver Sands in Duncans Bay. The decor reflects the tastes and personality of the owner. Five large guest rooms with fans have cable TV and balconies but no phone. They can get a little warm. The grounds are peaceful and exuberantly gardened.

Silver Sands Villa Resort (☎ 954-2001, 888-745-7245; www.silversands-jamaica.com; cottage 1/2 bedroom from US$130/230, villas per week US$1300-2500; P ❄ 🏊), 1.5km west of Duncans, has more than 40 upscale one- to five-bedroom villas and cottages spread over 90 hectares. The cottages require a minimum three nights booking. The enclosed estate backs a private 300m-long, white-sand beach. Each unique villa is privately owned and individually decorated, and has a cook, housekeeper and gardener. Most have TVs and their own pools. Weekly rates offer savings and include airport transfers. Facilities include a bar-grill.

Just west of the Silver Sands is the public **Jacob Taylor Beach**, where you'll find a small, mellow craft market and a rum shop.

RIO BUENO

Rio Bueno is a tumbledown fishing village where fishermen still tend their nets and their lobster pots in front of ramshackle Georgian cut-stone buildings. These are featured in the 1964 movie *A High Wind in Jamaica*, which was filmed here.

The town, 52km east of Montego Bay, is set on the west side of a deep, narrow bay that may be the site where Columbus first set foot in Jamaica on May 4, 1494, after anchoring his caravels *Nina*, *San Juan* and *Cardera*.

Sites of interest include the 18th-century ruins of **Fort Dundas**, an **Anglican church** that dates to 1833 and a **Baptist church** erected in 1901 to replace another destroyed in anti-missionary riots of the abolitionist era.

Minibuses and route taxis pick up and drop off passengers along the A1 as it passes through town. The stretch of coastal road from here to Discovery Bay is known as the Queen's Hwy.

Activities

If riding a horse bareback into the sea sounds like your cup of tea, **Braco Stables** (☎ 954-0185; www.bracostables.com; per person with/without transportation US$70/60; 🕑 rides 10:30am & 2:30pm) offers excellent group rides through sugarcane country that culminate in a bareback ride into the turquoise surf. The ride ends with refreshments at the Braco Great House (clothing required). The stables are well signed from the main road.

Sleeping & Eating

Hotel Rio Bueno (☎/fax 954-0048; Main St; s/d/ste US$95/120/250; P ❄) Converted from a Georgian wharfside warehouse, this old place is infused with a unique ambience. The hotel is a museum of Joe James' artwork (and includes a gallery of his exuberant paintings and carvings). It has 20 rooms, most with French doors opening onto balconies that overlook the bay. The huge, atmospheric suite has hardwood floors, open-plan layout and lots of light. Rates for double rooms and the suite include breakfast.

Lobster Bowl Restaurant (☎ 954-0048; Hotel Rio Bueno, Main St; 3-course dinner US$15-35, lunch US$7-19; 🕑 breakfast, lunch & dinner) This spacious restaurant has an old-time nightclub feel and features the artwork of Joe James. As the name suggests, lobster and seafood figure prominently on the menu. The property also includes Joe's Bar, with tons of character.

Rio Brac Rest Stop (☎ 954-0269; Queens Hwy; meals US$5-10; 🕑 from 7am) An upscale roadside restaurant and jerk center about 400m east of Grand Lido Braco Village Resort.

THE WEST COAST TOWARD TRYALL ESTATE

West from Montego Bay the A1 follows the coast, offering little in the way of nice beaches or attractions. Eight kilometers west of town the road crosses the mouth of the Great River, then sweeps past Round Hill Hotel & Villa and, further along the A1, Tryall Estate and the world championship Tryall Golf Course.

HOPEWELL

This small wayside village 15km west of Montego Bay has a bustling daily market; on Saturday the streets are cacophonous with the sounds of higglers from the hills.

If you've got money to burn – or a sky-high limit on your credit card – time spent at the 45-hectare **Round Hill Hotel & Villas** (☎ 956-7050, in the USA 800-972-2159; www.roundhilljamaica.com; d US$550, ste US$600-900, villa US$1200-3700, daily meal plan per person US$90-110; P ⊠ ⁂ 💻 🏊) resort is worth every penny. Having celebrated its 50th anniversary in 2003, this hotel still commands a prestige and allure that few others can match. The 36 rooms are in the beachfront Pineapple House, redesigned by Ralph Lauren. With access to an infiniti pool, each has a kitchen and is exquisitely decorated with antique furniture and stately four-poster bamboo beds. The 28 privately owned villas are furnished to their owners' tastes – Lauren owns one. Many have private pools. Facilities include a gym, tennis courts, water sports (including scuba diving that's open to the public), a beauty salon and a wellness center, which offers all manner of therapies. Live jazz is offered thrice weekly.

Also at Round Hill, **Georgian Dining Pavilion & Almond Tree Terrace** (lunch/dinner from US$12/28) serves continental and Jamaican dishes. Dining on the terrace is a romantic indulgence and worth the splurge for the setting. Afternoon tea is a bargain at US$3. Nonguests should call ahead.

Sports Club Restaurant & Bar (meals US$6-11), beside the entrance to Round Hill, offers Jamaican fare served in modestly elegant surroundings.

TRYALL ESTATE

The **Tryall Water Wheel**, 5km west of Hopewell, stands amid the ruins of the old Tryall sugar plantation. Much of the estate, including the huge wheel (beside the A1) that drove the cane-crushing mill, was destroyed in the slave rebellion of Christmas 1831 (see the boxed text, p188). Restored to working condition in the late 1950s, the wheel is still turned by water carried by a 3km-long aqueduct from the Flint River.

The hilltop great house is today the hub of one of Jamaica's most exclusive resort properties: the Tryall Club, built atop the remains of a small fort that is still guarded by cannons. The great house and 890-hectare resort complex are closed to nonguests.

Activities

The championship, 6328m par-71 **Tryall Golf Course** (☎ 956-5660) is one of the world's finest courses. Green fees for guests cost US$40 in summer, US$65 in winter (nonguests pay US$125 year-round). Caddies cost US$15 and cart rental costs US$27.

Sleeping

Tryall Club (☎ 956-5660, in North America 800-336-4571; www.tryallclub.com; 1-bedroom ste US$400-500, 2-bedroom ste US$675-860, 2-bedroom villa US$860, 7-bedroom villa US$1480-1700; P ⊠ ⁂ 💻 🏊) Magnificently situated amid 890 hectares of lush hillside greenery, this old hilltop great house offers 13 villa suites, each fully staffed and including kitchen, living room, dining room and oversized marble bathroom. A new wing includes 52 gracious junior suites. More than 55 privately owned, sumptuous estate villas are scattered throughout the estate, each uniquely decorated by individual owners and staffed with a cook, housekeeper and gardener. Other facilities include a gourmet restaurant and bar, tennis, water sports and golf.

INLAND: SOUTH OF MONTEGO BAY

The hill country inland of MoBay offers working plantations, great houses, eco-resorts and a village of poor white farmers that is one of Jamaica's strangest anomalies. Most points of interest are reached either via the B8, which winds south from Reading and crosses a broad upland plateau before dropping onto the plains of Westmoreland, or the B6, which leads southeast from Montpelier (10km south of Reading).

The southeast quarter of St James parish culminates in the wild Cockpit Country.

LETHE

This small village is the starting point for raft trips on the Great River. The turnoff for Lethe is 3km south of Reading off the B8; signs show the way. If you pass the sign for Rocklands Bird Feeding Station, you've gone too far. The graceful stone bridge spanning the Great River was built in 1828. The overgrown remains of an old sugar mill stand on the riverbank.

Driving west to Lethe, about 3km from the B8, you'll arrive at a Y-junction. The fork to the left leads to Lethe; the one to the right leads to **Nature Village Farm** (☎ 912-0281; 🕑 10am-11pm Mon-Fri, 11am-11pm Sun), a farm turned family resort and restaurant that offers fishing and other attractions.

Sights & Activities

A perfect spot to take the kids, **Animal Farm** (☎ 953-3583; animalfarm@mailcity.com; adult/child US$4/2.50; 🕑 tours by arrangement Mon-Fri, 10am-5pm Sat & Sun) at Copse, 3km west of Lethe, is dedicated to aviculture and has hundreds of birds. It also has a petting zoo, donkey rides, a playground, hiking and birding.

Rhea's World (☎ 956-4920; lethe@cwjamaica.com), on the west bank of the river on the north side of Lethe, features a water garden and mini-botanical gardens where anthuriums are grown for export. Alas, they're not particularly appealing. A jitney tour (US$6 to US$11) leads into the adjacent banana plantation. More-adventurous souls seeking an authentic bush experience can hire a guide (US$10) and hike into the hills. A restaurant provides hot lunches (US$12).

Mountain Valley Rafting (☎ 956-4920), headquartered at Lethe Estate, offers tranquil one-hour river trips on the Great River from Lethe. You're piloted 3km downstream aboard long, narrow bamboo rafts poled by an expert rafter, who waxes poetic about the birds, flora and fauna as you glide along. Trips cost US$80 for two passengers (children under 12 are half price), including lunch and transfers. For an extra US$15 per person, you'll get lunch, a plantation tour and a fresh piña colada at the end of the excursion. If you show up under your own steam, you'll pay US$40 for the raft trip alone.

Lethe Estate can arrange special river-raft wedding celebrations where the bride, groom and guests are carried down the river in specially decorated rafts to the plantation.

Sleeping

Lethe Estate (☎ 956-4920; letheestate@cwjamaica.com; ste per person US$65; P ✖ ✖) Located on resplendently gardened grounds about 1km from the town center. It's a terrifically relaxing place that offers spacious two- and three-bedroom suites with balconies that overlook the river. The suites are painted in earthy tones, are nicely decorated and come with a fully equipped kitchen and satellite TV. Cooking and nanny services are available.

ROCKLANDS BIRD FEEDING STATION

Rocklands (☎ 952-2009; admission US$10; 🕑 9am-5pm) is a favorite of birders. They have flocked here since 1958, when it was founded by Lisa Salmon, who tamed and trained over 20 bird species to come and feed from your hand (over 140 bird species have been recorded here). Every songbird and hummingbird on the island seems to know about the place. You'll see ground doves, orange and banana quits, the Jamaican woodpecker (a flicker) and oriole, and, of course, hummingbirds, including the deep purple Jamaican mango hummingbird and the ever-popular 'doctorbird.'

The 'station' was also the longtime home of Miss Salmon. She went to bird heaven in 2000 but her replacement, Fritz Beckford, is also a passionate champion of birds. He has a beatific air about him; he'll pour birdseed into your hand or provide you with a sugar-water feeder with which to tempt birds. Guests sit agog as hummingbirds streak in to hover like tiny helicopters before finally perching on their outstretched fingers. Fritz estimates that his feathered friends devour nearly 900kg of seed each year…so much for 'bird-sized' appetites. If you need more bird action, Fritz leads tours from the house into the bush (US$20 per person).

A tremendous way to enjoy the bird feeding station is to spend the night in **Rocklands Bird Sanctuary Cottage** (☎ 952-2009; whole house per night US$120; P ✖), a nicely appointed three-bedroom, two-bathroom home that sleeps up to six people. The house has a fully equipped kitchen and dining area. One of the bedrooms has a Jacuzzi tub.

Just up the road from Rockland's is **Allspice Villa** (☎ 912-3623; www.allspicevilla.com; Rock Pleasant Mt; ste US$400; P), a glorious recent addition to the area's thriving villa rental scene. This reclusive and romantic getaway has it all: jaw-dropping panoramic views, a lovely pool and spacious Jacuzzi on the veranda, a state-of-the-art kitchen and even a pool table. Rates include a full breakfast; other meals are made by arrangement. The owners, who live on the property, require a three-day minimum stay and advance reservations. Airport transfers and island transportation are offered.

By car, Rocklands is a 30-minute drive from Montego Bay. Take the B8 (Long Hill Rd) from Reading toward Anchovy; turn left about 200m south of the signed turnoff for Lethe on Rock Pleasant Rd. The road leading to Rocklands is agonizingly steep and narrow in places.

Alternatively, you can take a bus or route taxi from Montego Bay bound for Savanna-la-Mar or Black River, but be prepared for a tough 30-minute hike to and from your destination. If a taxi sounds better, be prepared to shell out US$50 for the round-trip journey.

MONTPELIER

Passing through Anchovy, you drop south into a broad valley, planted in citrus but formerly an important sugar estate. The great house of the old Montpelier sugar plantation burned down a few years back but **St Mary's Anglican Church** (1847) still stands on a knoll overlooking the remains of the sugar factory.

The B8 splits at a gas station just south of the church. The main road continues southwest. The road to the southeast (the B6) leads toward Seaford Town.

With all Jamaica's roiling waterways, you'd think that white-water rafting would be a staple of tour operators. Not so. **Caliche Rainforest Park & Adventure Tour** (☎ 940-1745; calicheadventuretours@yahoo.com; rain forest/canyon white-water rafting trip per person US$70/80; 9am & 1pm) takes full advantage of the Great River's big water, which grows progressively more tranquil as it approaches the sea. Two 2½-hour trips are offered: one over a quiet stretch of river through a tropical rain forest that is appropriate for small children, and a wet and wild romp through Class III-IV waters with internationally trained and experienced guides. The experience concludes at a waterfall and swimming hole.

Barrett Adventures (☎ 382-6384; www.barrettadventures.com; Rose Hall) offers tours including transfer.

CATADUPA

Twenty years ago locals had a thriving trade selling crafts and making clothing to order for train passengers headed to the Appleton Rum Estate (you were measured en route to Appleton and clothes were finished and ready to pick up on the way back). Today Catadupa, 3km east of the B6 from the hamlet of Marchmont, is a collection of aging buildings around the disused railroad station. Locals eke out a living growing coffee and bananas. The village is named for nearby cascades and reflects the Greek name for the Nile cataracts in Egypt.

Croydon in the Mountains Plantation

Reached via a side road 1.5km from Catadupa, this 54-hectare working **plantation** (☎ 979-8267; www.croydonplantation.com) was also the birthplace of national hero Sam Sharpe. It's a gorgeous place with terraces planted in coffee, citrus and pineapples. A 'see, hear, touch and taste' tour is offered from 10:30am to 3pm Tuesday, Thursday and Friday; the fee is US$65 including lunch and transfers. Advance reservations are required.

Caribic Vacations (p189) and Tropical Tours (p189) offer tours from Montego Bay.

HILTON

Overgrown with thumbergia, the beautiful hilltop plantation home of **Hilton** (☎ 952-3343; hiltonhiday@n5.com.jm) near St Leonards, 3km southwest of Marchmont, is the venue for the all-day **Hilton High Day Tour** (call-in visitors US$56, incl transfers from Montego Bay US$64; Tue, Wed, Fri & Sun). The day begins with a Jamaican breakfast in the house, where antiques abound. You then take a guided walk to Seaford Town (1.5km) and the village of St Leonards. The walk should create an appetite for a roast-suckling-pig luncheon prepared in a brick oven back at Hilton. The meal also features a choice of homemade lemonade, shandy (half lemonade, half beer) or rum punch. For the rest of the afternoon you're free to relax or roam the 40-hectare plantation or lounge around listening to the mento band.

SEAFORD TOWN

This sprawling hillside village of scattered tumbledown cottages has a singular history. It was settled between 1834 and 1838, when more than 1200 Germans arrived in Jamaica; an initial group of 251 settled Seaford. The land was donated by Lord Seaford (the Germans were promised that they would receive title after five years' labor; they toiled for 15 before the land became theirs). The initial community was a mix of Protestants and Catholics but most were converted to Catholicism by Father Tauer, an energetic Austrian priest who settled here in the 1870s.

The farmland turned out to be a tangled wilderness. Few of the settlers were farmers; most were tradespeople or former soldiers. Fortunately, the immigrants received free rations for the first 18 months, but even before the rations ran out the Germans had settled into a life of poverty. Tropical diseases and social isolation soon reduced the population and only a fraction of the original settlers stayed.

Today fewer than 200 Seaford inhabitants claim German ancestry, and white people are only 20% of the population. Still, after 150 years there are relatively few mulattos in evidence. Socially, Seaford remains segregated in key ways. Its white residents remain practicing Catholics and they still observe a few folk customs.

The red, zinc-roofed, old stone **Church of the Sacred Heart** sits atop a rise overlooking Seaford. Its precursor was built by Father Tauer in the late-19th century, but was totally demolished in the hurricane of 1912. Take time to browse the graveyard.

In front of the church is the tiny, somewhat dilapidated **Seaford Town Historical Mini-Museum** (☎ 640-6486, 333-1507; admission US$2), which tells the fascinating tale of Seaford's German origins. There are maps and photographs of the early settlement, plus artifacts spanning 150 years, including such curiosities as cricket bats made from the stems of coconut leaves. There are no set hours; ask around town for the good Mrs Shakes, who keeps the key to the museum.

KNOCKALVA & AROUND

Following the B8 southwest from Montpelier leads to Knockalva, the center of an agricultural-training farm and cattle-breeding center.

The hills to the south of Knockalva are festooned with groves of bamboo. Eight kilometers south of Knockalva you pass through the village of Whithorn. As you round a bend immediately beyond it, the sugarcane plains of Westmoreland are suddenly laid out below.

Mount Tambrin Retreat (☎ 357-6363, 437-4353; www.mountambrin.com; per person incl breakfast US$130, 3-night minimum), at Darliston, about 10km east of Whithorn, is an incredible mountain refuge where American artist Rus Gruhlke has created a fabulous garden and artists' retreat. Sculptures abound. It has six modestly furnished rooms (four with shared bathroom) plus a library-lounge and an architecturally grand gallery-theater. The property grants fabulous views over the southwest coast. Meals are served family style.

QUEEN OF SPAINS VALLEY

About 3km south of Montego Bay the Montego River twists through a narrow, thickly wooded gorge that deposits you at **Adelphi**, 21km east of Montego Bay, at the head of the Queen of Spains Valley. The valley is as flat and green as a billiard table, with sugarcane rippling as far as the eye can see. It runs east as far as Good Hope Estate (p213).

A bus travels through the Queen of Spains Valley via Hampden from Montego Bay (US$1).

MONTEGO BAY TO MAROON TOWN

Few travelers venture into the hills to the southeast of Montego Bay, accessed by Fairfield Rd, 2.5km south of town. The potholed road ascends to the western flanks of Cockpit Country.

The hamlet of **Kensington**, 21km southeast of Montego Bay, is famous as the site where, in 1831, slaves set fire to the ridgetop plantation and initiated the devastating Christmas Rebellion (see the boxed text, p188). A roadside plaque commemorates the event.

Maroon Town lies 5km to the southeast of Kensington, on the edge of the rugged Cockpit Country. Guides will tout themselves to lead you to caves and supposed battle sites from the Maroon Wars, but there's little to see. **Maroon Attraction Tours** (☎ 971-3900, 700-8805; fax 979-0308; 32 Church St) offers a 'cultural, educational, and historic tour' to Maroon Town on Tuesday, Thursday and Saturday (US$55, 8am to 3:30pm).

Johns Hall Plantation (☎ 952-6944; www.johnshall adventuretour.com; tour US$50; 🕑 11am-2pm Mon, Wed & Sat), at Johns Hall about 10km southeast

GOING GREEN IN COCKPIT COUNTRY

A vital watershed and home to several endangered species, including the Jamaican blackbird, the black-billed parrot and the giant swallow-tail butterfly, as well as more than 60 endemic plants, **Cockpit Country** has long been earmarked for national-park status (it is currently a national reserve). Complicating the issue is the staunch opposition of local Maroons, who fear giving the area increased federal protection will infringe on their hard-won autonomy. With the help of the Nature Conservancy, the Jamaica Forestry Department is conducting a landmark biodiversity conservation project in the area and is educating local communities about the benefits of conservation and ecotourism. In another promising development, in 2004 Jamaica and the US signed a US$16 million agreement under a debt-for-nature swap program, aimed at supporting Jamaica's forest-conservation activities.

of Montego Bay, is open for the 'town and country tour' from Montego Bay; a hot Jamaican lunch is included.

NORTH COCKPIT COUNTRY

Jamaica's most rugged quarter is a 1295-sq-km limestone plateau taking up the whole of southwest Trelawny, inland of Falmouth. The area of eroded limestone features is studded with thousands of conical hummocks divided by precipitous ravines. From the air, Cockpit Country resembles a bright-green egg carton.

Conical hummocks? Precipitous ravines? If it sounds daunting, it is. Overgrown with luxuriant greenery, most of the region remains still unexplored and uninhabited. No roads penetrate the region (although a rough dirt road cuts across the eastern edge between Clark's Town and Albert Town) and only a few tracks make even half-hearted forays into its interior.

The nearly impenetrable region proved a perfect hideout for the Maroons who, through their ferocity, maintained an uneasy sovereignty from the English colonialists. The southern section is known as 'District of Look Behind,' an allusion to the Maroon practice of ambushing English soldiers.

Much of the vegetation around the perimeter has been cleared in recent years by charcoal burners, and a few valley bottoms are cultivated by smallholders who grow bananas, yams, corn, manioc and ganja. It's unwise for foreigners to explore here unless accompanied by someone known in the area. You could easily get lost or worse – if you stumble upon a major ganja plot, you're likely to be considered a DEA (Drug Enforcement Agency) agent and the consequences could be serious.

The southern portion of Cockpit Country lies in St Elizabeth parish and is accessed from the south by side roads from the B6. See p255

Information

Nature Conservancy (☎ 978-0766; www.nature.org; Unit 5, 32 Lady Musgrave Rd, Kingston 5) Working with Cockpit Country residents to develop stable long-term protection for the region's fragile ecosystem.

Southern Trelawny Environmental Agency (☎ 610-0818; www.stea.net; 3 Grants Office Complex, Albert Town) Concerns itself with the social aspects of Cockpit Country communities and can arrange private lodging and guides for visitors.

Windsor Research Centre (☎ 997-3832; www.cockpitcountry.com; Windsor Great House) A science-based operation at the Windsor Great House, devoted to monitoring Cockpit Country's fragile environment. The website, replete with up-to-date information about regional ecology, is a joy for nature geeks.

Wildlife

Most of the Cockpits are still clad in primary vegetation that in places includes rare cacti and other endemic species known only in that specific locale. The northern slopes are typically more lush. The hilltops are relatively sparsely vegetated due to soil erosion. The Cockpits are generally covered in tall scrub, including brambles and scratchbush.

Most of Jamaica's 27 endemic bird species are found in the Cockpits, including black- and yellow-billed parrots, todies and the endangered golden swallow. The Jamaican boa and giant swallowtail butterfly are among other rare species, which include 37 of Jamaica's 62 amphibian and reptile species.

Activities

HIKING

A few hunters' tracks lead into and even across the Cockpit Country. Most are faint tracks, often overgrown. Hiking away from these trails can be dangerous going. The rocks are razor sharp and sinkholes are everywhere, often covered by decayed vegetation and ready to crumble underfoot. Never travel alone. There is no one to hear you call for help should you break a leg or fall into a sinkhole. Take lots of water: there is none to be had locally.

Hire a local guide who knows the way. You'll need a machete, stout walking shoes, rain gear and a powerful flashlight in the event of a delay past sunset. Take warm clothing if you plan on overnighting, as nights can get cold.

The easiest – but by no means easy – trail across the Cockpits is an old military trail connecting Windsor (in the north) with Troy (in the south), about 16km as the crow flies. It's an arduous full day's hike with a guide. It is a more difficult hike southbound, leading gradually uphill; an easier option is to begin in Troy (p258) and take the downhill route. For more information, consult www.jamaicancaves.or g/hiking-jamaica.htm.

In Windsor, you can hire Martell or Franklyn (Dango) Taylor as guides (from US$10, depending on distance).

Albert Town, on the east flank of the Cockpits, is evolving as a base for organized hikes. Contact the Southern Trelawny Environmental Agency in Albert Town for recommended guides.

SPELUNKING

The Cockpits are laced with mostly uncharted caves. Guides lead trips into the better-known caverns. Elsewhere, exploring is for experienced and properly outfitted spelunkers only. There is no rescue organization, and you enter caves at your own risk. The most accessible are Windsor Caves at Windsor (p214).

The **Jamaican Caves Organization** (www.jamaicancaves.org/main.htm) provides resources for the exploration of Jamaican caves, sinkholes and underground rivers. In 2005 the group completed a project to formally classify and evaluate over 70 caves within the Cockpit Country.

Jamaica Underground by Alan Fincham is a rare but essential compendium providing the most thorough information available on the island's charted caves.

Tours

Cockpit Country Adventure Tours (☎ 610-0818; www.stea.net/ccat_main.htm; 3 Grants Office Complex, Albert Town; tours US$55-70) Sponsored by the Southern Trelawny Environmental Agency, local guides are used to lead hikes and cave exploration in the rugged Freeman's Hall district. The most arduous visits the Quashie River and the Quashie Cave, featuring a 'cathedral room' and an underground waterfall.

Sun Venture Tours (☎ in Kingston 960-6685, in Ocho Rios 920-8348; www.sunventuretours.com; 30 Balmoral Ave, Kingston 10) Runs guided hikes and birding trips into the Cockpits for US$85.

GOOD HOPE ESTATE

This great house and working plantation is 13km south of Falmouth, at the western end of Queen of Spains Valley. The property is set on the northern edge of Cockpit Country and the views have no rival.

The estate was owned by John Tharp (1744–1804), who became the richest man in Jamaica. At one time he owned more than 4000 hectares and 3000 slaves in Trelawny and St James parishes. The house was built around 1755 and the collection of 18th-century Jamaican Georgian cut-stone buildings includes sugar works and a waterwheel.

The great house first became a hotel in the early 1900s when an American banker came to Jamaica looking for antiques and happened upon Good Hope. Today **Good Hope Country House & River Cottage** (☎ 469-3443; www.goodhopejamaica.com; 10-bedroom house per week US$14,500, 3-bedroom cottage per week US$4400; P ⊠ ✱ ≋) is one of Jamaica's most opulent villa rentals.

The 10-bedroom 'country house,' with spectacular views, is popular for weddings and special events. Here the architecture and mood are fabulous, with high ceilings, gleaming hardwood floors and a two-story cut-stone 'counting house' that is now the honeymoon suite. The house is fully furnished with 18th- and 19th-century antiques and a fine collection of maps and paintings. Meals, cooked to order, average US$50 per person per day.

The three-bedroom river cottage is a restored 19th-century house set in extensive gardens and perched above an idyllic swimming hole. There are three bedrooms with antique four-poster beds and private bathrooms, a full kitchen, a comfortable living room and an enormous shaded veranda.

David Pinto, an acclaimed ceramist, operates a **pottery studio** (☎ 954-4635) open to the public. Pottery workshops are offered through **Anderson Ranch Arts Center** (☎ in the USA 970-923-3181).

WINDSOR

A narrow 3km-long valley southeast of Good Hope Estate is surrounded by towering cliffs. It is most easily accessed from Sherwood at the north end. The paved road through here dead-ends at Windsor near the head of the valley; from here you can hike across the Cockpits to Troy. This is as far as you can go into this wild country without hiking, and here the natural beauty of the wild Cockpit Country interior is on display in its truest form.

Windsor is reached by traveling the road from Falmouth to Martha Brae, then crossing the bridge to the east and turning right to follow the valley south into the hills. Minibuses and route taxis operate between Montego Bay and Brown's Town via Sherwood, from where you can walk or hitchhike the remaining 5km to Windsor.

Sights

WINDSOR GREAT HOUSE

Built in 1705 by John Tharp, **Windsor Great House** now serves as a hostelry and scientific research center. Early evening is the best time to visit. Take insect repellent. It's not marked by a sign; to find it, take a left at the junction at the end of the paved road.

WINDSOR CAVES

These off-the-beaten-track **caverns** were donated to the World Wildlife Fund in 1995 with the proviso that they never be developed. The entrance is a 1km hike from the road, ending with a clamber up a narrow rocky path. Beyond the narrow entrance, you'll pass into a large gallery full of stalactites and a huge chamber with a dramatically arched ceiling. In rainy season you can hear the roar of the Martha Brae River flowing deep underground.

About 50,000 bats inhabit the caves; their egress at dusk is an amazing sight!

You'll need a local guide, who can usually be found at Dango's shop at the end of the road. It's emblazoned with the epitaph 'Jah Love is a Burning Flame'; here you'll likely find cave wardens Martell or Franklyn 'Dango' Taylor. One of them will lead the way with a flashlight or bamboo torch to visit Rat Bat Cave and the Royal Flat Chamber. Depending on how deep into the cave you wish to go and the size of your group, the fee is US$5 to US$20 per person.

For experienced cavers who arrive with spelunking gear, Martell or Franklyn will lead the way on a remarkable four-hour subterranean excursion through Windsor Cave all the way to its 'back door' at Bamboo Batam. You'll need to bring 30m of rope and basic rappelling equipment, and a desire to wade for an extended period with water up to your waist in total darkness. Eventually, you will emerge and make the return journey in the blessed daylight. For this you'll be charged only US$25 per person, but most people are inclined to tack on a substantial tip.

See p56 for general information about spelunking in Jamaica.

Sleeping & Eating

Last Resort (☎ 931-6070, 700-7128; iscapc@cwjamaica.com; per person US$15; P) With Spartan single and double rooms, shared bathrooms and a communal kitchen, this back-to-basics place is the perfect locale from which to enjoy the singular scenery. It's also the current headquarters of the Jamaican Caves Organization. Because farming takes place on the property, delicious fresh produce can often be purchased at a very low price. Look for the sign at the terminus of the incoming road.

Miss Lilly's (☎ 788-1022; Coxheath; r US$30) In Coxheath at the northern entrance to Windsor Valley, and marked by a sign reading 'Lilly's Bar,' is this simple guesthouse run by a welcoming and jovial lady. Two simply appointed rooms share a bathroom (cold water only) and have fans. A small bar and a grocery are attached, and Miss Lily cooks meals.

Windsor Great House (☎ 997-3832; www.cockpitcountry.com; r incl breakfast US$30-40, lunch US$10, dinner US$15) Budget travelers can stay inexpensively at this colonial mansion with several no-frills cut-stone rooms with shared bathroom (cold water only). The place is first and foremost a research center, and resident naturalists Mike Schwartz and Susan Koenig occasionally stage four-course 'Meet the Biologist' dinners (US$25); call for a schedule and reservations.

A bird-banding effort happens the last weekend of each month; to participate you must first become a member (US$20).

A Texan, Patrick Childres, offers two rooms in a **two-story house** (campsites US$10, rooms US$10). You can also camp by the river. The simple place has water from a spring, plus solar panels to power the radio and a battery for lighting. You can cook over a fire or simple stove. Well-known guides Martell and Franklyn 'Dango' Taylor act as caretakers and will provide food and even cook lunch or dinner for US$5. The house is unsigned; look for one of the Taylor brothers at the shop at the crossroads.

ALBERT TOWN

This small market center lies high in the mountains about 24km inland of Rio Bueno. The B5 climbs through the Cockpits with dramatic views en route. Albert Town is a base for guided hikes into the Cockpit Country, immediately to the west (see p213).

The B5 rises southeast from Albert Town to the spine of Jamaica, with vistas of lush, rolling agricultural land interspersed with pine forest. You'll crest the mountains (and the boundary with Manchester parish) just south of Lorrimers, about 14km south of Albert Town. Christiana (p258) is about 3km further south.

West of Albert Town, the B10 climbs along the eastern edge of Cockpit Country and beyond Warsop drops dramatically to Troy (p258), a gateway to the Cockpits.

Every year, on Easter Monday, the wildly entertaining **Trelawny Yam Festival** features such highlights as the yam-balancing races, best-dressed goat and donkey, and crowning of the Yam King and Queen.

The **Southern Trelawny Environmental Agency** (☎ 610-0818; www.stea.net; 3 Grants Office Complex) is on the west side of the town square. If you're looking for lodging, its staff can recommend local B&Bs.

Global Telefax (☎ 610-1853; 🕓 8:30am-4pm) is on the south side of the square.

Buses and minibuses operate between Albert Town and Falmouth, Mandeville, Kingston and Spaldings. There is a gas station in town (closed Sunday).

Negril & West Coast

In the 1970s, Negril lured hippies with its offbeat beach-life to a countercultural Shangri-la where anything goes. To some extent anything still goes here, but the innocence left long ago.

To be sure, the gorgeous 11km-long swath of sand that is Long Beach is still kissed by the serene waters into which the sun melts every evening in a riot of color that will transfix even the most jaded. And the easily accessible coral reefs offer some of the best diving in the Caribbean. At night, rustic beachside music clubs keep the reggae beat going without the watered-down-for-tourist schmaltz that so often mars the hotspots of Montego Bay and Ocho Rios.

Yet these undeniable attractions have done just that – attract. In the last three decades, Negril has exploded as a tourist venue, and today the beach can barely be seen from Norman Manley Blvd for the intervening phalanx of beachside resorts. And with tourism comes the local hustle – you're very likely to watch the sunset in the cloying company of a ganja dealer or an aspiring tour-guide-cum-escort.

The less-developed West End lies on the cliffs slightly to the south of Long Beach. Here smaller, more characterful hotels mingle with intimate jerk shacks and lively bars, and it's much easier to mix with locals without the perpetual sense of just being seen as an extension of your wallet. The sunset's just as magnificent from the cliffs, and you'll probably get a better idea of what Negril was like 40 years ago.

HIGHLIGHTS

- **Long Bay** Hang loose or party hearty on this 11km stretch of beach, whose fiery sunsets never fail to live up to their hype (p238)
- **Abba Jahnehoy's Garden** Take to the hills for some meditation and learn about Rastafarianism at this tranquil retreat and garden (p224)
- **Scuba Diving** Plumb the grottoes and reefs off Negril for some of the best diving on the island (p227)
- **Great Morass** Walk among towering palms through verdant wetlands filled with bird life (p224)
- **Roaring River Park** Disappear into the country at one of Jamaica's most scenic and atmospheric caves (p244)

- AREA: 3217 SQ KM
- NEGRIL DEC AVERAGE HIGH TEMPERATURE: 28°C

HISTORY

The Spanish called Negril's bay and adjacent headland Punta Negrilla (Dark Point), referring to the black conger eels that used to proliferate in the local rivers. During the colonial era pirates favored Negril's two bays to provide safe anchorage during plundering forays. During the War of 1812 between Britain and the US Bloody Bay was the point of assembly and departure for the British naval armada's ill-fated expedition to storm New Orleans. Bloody Bay was also used by 19th-century whalers who butchered their catch here (hence the name). When a road was finally constructed to Negril in 1959, the area slowly began to attract vacationers – as well as a coterie of hippies – but it wasn't until the late 1970s, when the first resorts opened, that Negril began to stake its claim as Jamaica's coolest party destination.

CLIMATE

Negril has Jamaica's lowest rainfall and driest climate. The sun shines strongly 350 days a year on average but there is always the possibility of brief afternoon showers.

GETTING THERE & AWAY

Nearly all international air passengers fly into Donald Sangster International Airport in Montego Bay, 81km from Negril. From there you can arrange for a private minivan or taxi, or take public transportation in the form of a minibus or route taxi.

NEGRIL

pop 4400

Negril, 81km west of Montego Bay, is the vortex around which Jamaica's fun-in-the-sun vacation life whirls. You'll soon find yourself falling in love with Negril's insouciance and its scintillating 11km-long beach sliding gently into calm waters reflecting a palette of light blues and greens. Coral reefs lie just offshore, and you'll want your camera close by to record the consistently peach-colored sunsets that get more applause than the live reggae concerts.

Tourism is Negril's only industry. But despite phenomenal growth in recent decades, Negril can be as laid-back as anywhere else in Jamaica and there's an easygoing rapport between visitors and locals.

Once upon a time – in the mid-1970s, to be exact – Negril was still an off-the-beaten-track nirvana to the budget-minded, beach-loving crowd. It was a 'far-out' setting where you could drool over sunsets of hallucinogenic intensity that had nothing to do with the 'magic' mushrooms that still show up in omelettes and teas.

Negril's innocence is long gone. The red-eyed hippies have been joined by neatly groomed youths who whiz about on rented motor scooters, often with a local lass or dreadlocked 'Rent-a-Rasta' (p284) clinging tightly behind. Today the area is roughly divided into two distinct areas with dissimilar personalities. Long Bay and its extended white-sand beach is brash and touristy while the West End, with its small boutique hotels and counterculture credentials, suggests a former flower child who now carries a laptop and platinum credit card.

In spite of Negril's perhaps predictable evolution from a remote, sensual Eden to a big-money resort, the place remains Jamaica's best destination for Dionysian revelry. Let your hair down, sample the local pleasures and let Jamaica happen around you.

HISTORY

Only in 1959 was a road cut to Negril, launching the development of what was then a tiny fishing village. Electricity and telephones came later. The sleepy beachfront village soon became a popular holiday spot for Jamaicans. About the same time, hippies and backpackers from abroad began to appear. They roomed with local families or slept on the beach, partook of ganja and magic mushrooms, and generally gave Negril its laid-back reputation. In 1977 the first major resort – Negril Beach Village (later renamed Hedonism II) – opened its doors to a relatively affluent crowd seeking an uninhibited Club Med–style vacation. Tales of Hedonism's toga parties and midnight nude volleyball games helped launch Negril to fame. By the mid-1980s Negril was in the throes of a full-scale tourism boom that continues today. (The early days of tourism in Negril are regaled in *Banana Shout,* a humorous novel by local hotelier Mark Conklin concerning the escapades of an American draft dodger who moves to Negril.)

This let-it-all-hang-out tradition still overflows during the March to April spring break when US college kids swarm for wet T-shirt

NEGRIL & WEST COAST

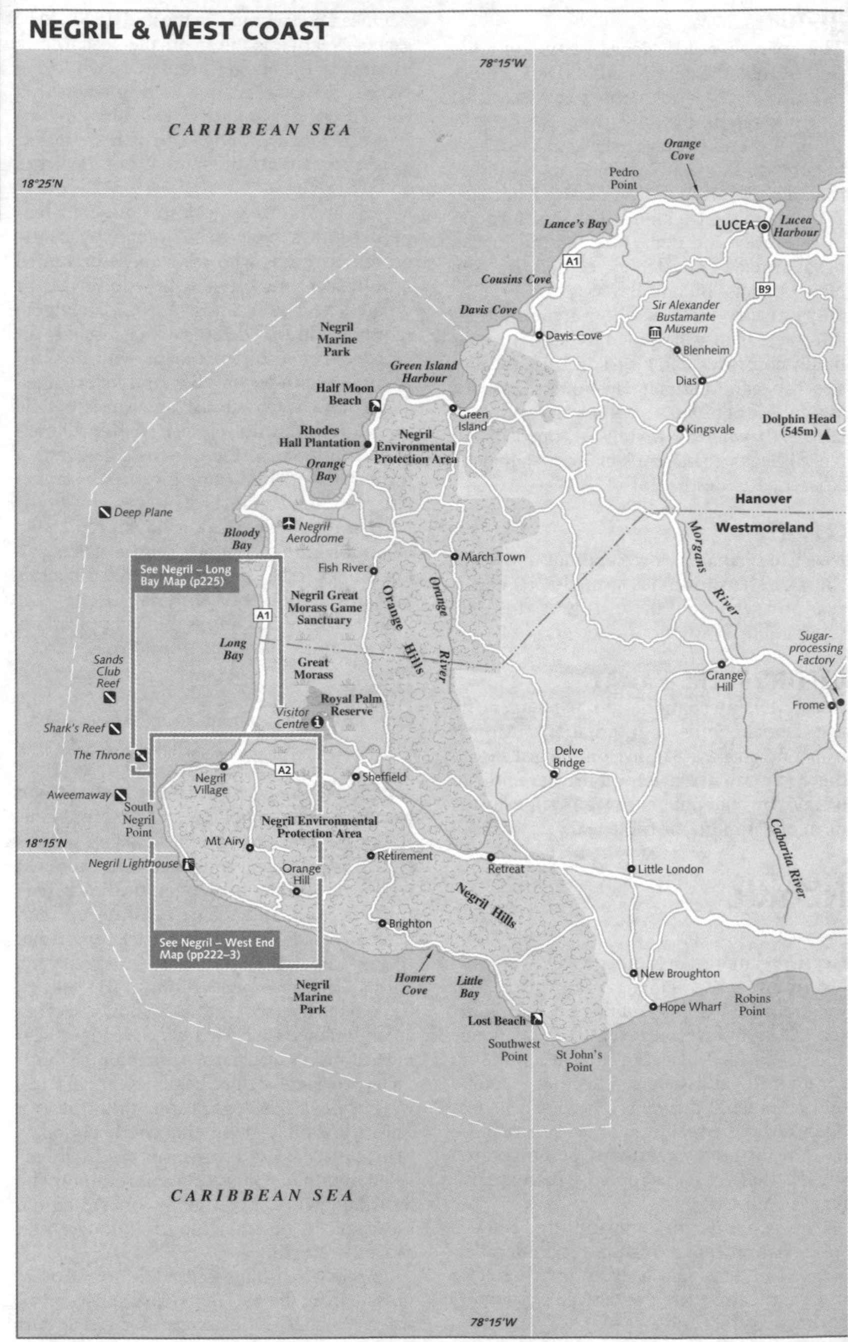

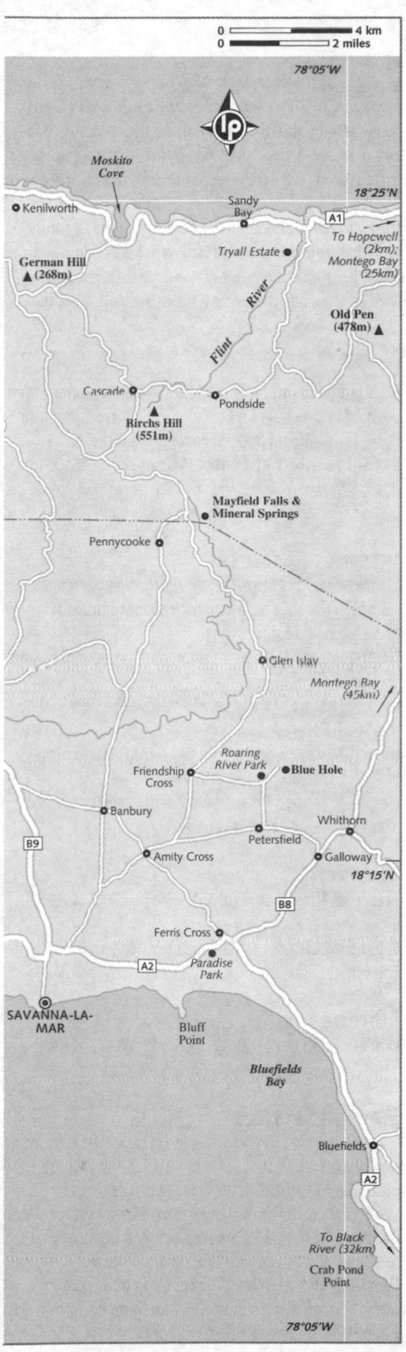

contests, drinking competitions and general party time.

Nonetheless, the resort has developed an active and environmentally conscious spirit under the guidance of expat residents, resulting in the creation of the Negril Marine Park within the Negril Environmental Protection Area. The park encompasses the shoreline, mangroves, offshore waters and coral reefs, and is divided into eight recreational zones. In 2001 the Chamber of Commerce adopted an environmental 'green' standard for hotels to adhere to. Recent projects include a new recycling center – a rarity in Jamaica.

ORIENTATION

Negril is divided in two by the South Negril River, with Long Bay to the north and West End to the south. The apex is Negril Village, which lies immediately south of the river and is centered on a small roundabout from which Norman Manley Blvd leads north, West End Rd leads west, and Sheffield Rd goes east and becomes the A2, leading to Savanna-la-Mar, 30km away.

Long Bay and its blindingly white beach fringed by palms stretches north from the South Negril River. Water-sports concessions line the beach. By night this section comes to life with the blast of reggae from disco bars.

Long Bay is paralleled by Norman Manley Blvd, a two-lane highway about 100m inland from the beach. The road is lined with hotels, restaurants and food shacks for almost its entire length, except for a 1km section toward its northern end that has been set aside as Long Bay Beach Park, popular for nude bathing.

Long Bay is anchored to the north by the low rocky headland of Rutland Point. Beyond is a deeply scalloped cove, Bloody Bay, rimmed by a beautiful beach. Negril's upscale all-inclusive resorts are located here or on the north end of Long Bay.

Negril Village consists of some shopping plazas and a handful of banks and other commercial ventures, plus a few houses and shacks dispersed among the forested hills known as Red Ground.

A rocky limestone plateau rises south of the South Negril River and extends southward for several kilometers. The area is known as the West End or 'the Rock.' The coral clifftop is indented with coves good for swimming in crystal-clear azure waters, providing a dramatic setting for dozens of small hotels and

'CALICO' JACK'S LAST STAND

Before you park yourself on the sand, consider the plight of 'Calico' Jack Rackham, a pirate who dallied a little too long on the beach. In 1720 'Calico' Jack, so named for his fondness for calico underwear, and his buccaneers paused in Bloody Bay after a particularly satisfying plundering spree. He and his band of merry men got a little too merry on the local rum, and in the course of their beach party were taken unaware by the British navy, which overwhelmed them after a struggle worthy of the bay's name.

After the battle, the British were shocked to find that two of 'Calico' Jack's cohorts were actually women: Mary Read and Anne Bonney, who had been his mistress. Rackham was executed and his body suspended in an iron suit on what is now called Rackham Cay, at the harbor entrance at Port Royal, as an example to other pirates. The lives of Read and Bonney were spared because they claimed to be pregnant.

restaurants built atop the rock face. It was the setting for scenes from the movies *20,000 Leagues Under the Sea*, *Papillon* and *Dr No*.

West End Rd snakes south along the cliff top (be careful walking – the road is narrow, with many blind corners and fast-moving vehicles). About 1km south, the road is renamed Lighthouse Rd and leads past Negril Lighthouse, beyond which its name changes again to Ocean Dr. Ocean Dr runs through scrubland for 3km to the junction with William Hogg Blvd, which runs inland over the Negril Hills, meeting up with Whitehall Rd and then dropping down to Sheffield Rd.

INFORMATION

Bookstores

Top Spot (Map pp222-3; ☎ 957-4542; Sunshine Village, West End Rd) Well stocked with international publications.

Emergency

Fire emergency (☎ 110, 957-4242)
Medical emergency (☎ 110)
Police emergency (☎ 119)
Police station (Map pp222-3; ☎ 957-4268; Sheffield Rd)

Internet Access

There are dozens of internet cafés; many also offer internet-based international calls.

Blue Water Internet (Map pp222-3; ☎ 884-6030; West End Rd; per 20min US$1.50; 🕑 8am-11pm) Very hi-tech equipment, this cafe also serves delicious ice cream.

Café Taino (Map p225; ☎ 957-9813; www.cafetaino.com; Norman Manley Blvd; per 30min US$1.75) Internet access and international phone calls.

Easy Rock Internet Café (Map pp222-3; ☎ 957-0816; West End Rd; per hr US$4) Offering an amiable café atmosphere; you can plug in your laptop and make international calls.

Mi Yard (Map pp222-3; ☎ 957-4442; www.miyard.com; West End Rd; per 30min US$1.75; 🕑 24hr) Mi Yard also hosts a lively Negril bulletin board on its website.

Sunshine Internet Center (Map pp222-3; ☎ 957-4236; Sunshine Village, West End Rd; per hr US$4) A businesslike alternative with card readers and disk burning.

Internet Resources

Chamber of Commerce (www.negrilchamberofcommerce.com) Good information about community projects and green initiatives.

Negril (www.negril.com) Commercial site with numerous listings.

Negril Jamaica (www.negriljamaica.com) Operated by the Negril Resort Association.

Negril Today (www.negriltoday.com) Features reviews of hotels, restaurants and activities.

Negril Message Board (www.negril-message-board.com) A popular online meeting place.

Laundry

Fresh 'n' Nice Laundromat (Map pp222-3; ☎ 957-9494; Shop 1, Plaza de Negril)

West End Cleaners (Map pp222-3; ☎ 957-0160) Behind Scotiabank.

Libraries

Library (Map pp222-3; ☎ 957-4917; West End Rd; 🕑 10am-6pm Mon-Wed & Fri, 1-5pm Thu)

Medical Services

The nearest hospitals are in Savanna-la-Mar and Lucea.

Long Bay Medical & Wellness Center (Map p225; ☎ 957-9028; Norman Manley Blvd) General practice. Oya Oezcan (☎ 440-7071) is based here and does physical therapy and massage. She also speaks German.

Negril Beach Medical Center (Map p225; ☎ 957-4888; Norman Manley Blvd; 🕑 9am-5pm, doctors on call 24hr) Has a lab open 9:30am to 2pm Tuesday and Friday.

Negril Health Centre (Map pp222-3; ☎ 957-4926; Sheffield Rd; 🕑 9am-8pm Mon-Fri) Government-operated.

Negril Pharmacy (Map pp222-3; ☎ 957-4076; Plaza de Negril)

Ocean View Pharmacy (Map pp222-3; ☎ 957-9599; King's Plaza, West End Rd)

Money

Banks are open 9am to 2pm Monday to Thursday and 9am to 4pm Friday. There's an ATM on the north side of Plaza de Negril. While many hotels offer currency exchange, you'll get better rates at banks or a private enterprise. Avoid the black-market currency-exchange touts that hang out around Negril Square.

Scotiabank (Map pp222-3; ☎ 957-4236; West End Rd) Northwest of Plaza de Negril; offers currency exchange and ATMs.

Timetrend (Map p225; ☎ 995-3242; Norman Manley Blvd) Private currency-exchange business.

National Commercial Bank (NCB; Map pp222-3; ☎ 957-4117; Sunshine Village, West End Rd)

Western Union (Map pp222-3; Hi Lo Supermarket, Sunshine Village, West End Rd)

Post

Airpak Express (Map p225; ☎ 957-5051; Negril Aerodrome) Handles UPS service.

FedEx (Map p225; ☎ 957-5533; Negril Aerodrome)

Post office (Map pp222-3; ☎ 957-9654; West End Rd) Between A Fi Wi Plaza and King's Plaza.

Telephone

There are public phones at the main craft market and at Plaza de Negril. Several internet cafés now offer internet-based international calls. Hotels charge roughly US$2.50 for three minutes to the USA or Western Europe and US$0.50 per minute locally.

Cable & Wireless office (Map pp222-3; ☎ 888-957-9700; shop 27, Plaza de Negril; 🕑 8am-4pm Mon-Fri, 9am-4pm Sat) Public phones and WorldTalk cards.

Tourist Offices

Jamaica Tourist Board (Map p225; ☎ 957-4803, 957-9314; Times Square Plaza, Norman Manley Blvd; 🕑 9am-5pm Mon-Fri) Dispenses local maps and events information.

Negril Chamber of Commerce (NCC; Map pp222-3; ☎ 957-4067; www.negrilchamberofcommerce.com; Sunshine Village, West End Rd; 🕑 9am-4pm Mon-Fri) Publishes an annual *Negril Guide*. You can pick it up at hotels or at the NCC office west of the post office.

Negril Marine Park Office (Map p225; ☎ 957-3735) Behind the Negril Crafts Market at the south end of Norman Manley Blvd; can provide information on the marine park.

Travel Agencies

Advanced Travel Service (Map pp222-3; ☎ 957-4057; upstairs, Plaza de Negril)

Caribic Vacations (Map p225; ☎ 957-3309; Norman Manley Blvd)

National Travel Service (Map pp222-3; ☎ 957-4343; Sunshine Village, West End Rd)

DANGERS & ANNOYANCES

There are no particular problems in Negril that can't be encountered elsewhere in Jamaica, although in Negril they are multiplied, so a few reminders are in order. For more information on any of the subjects below, see p278.

The hustlers who work the beach for a living will definitely want to establish a relationship with you, and you can expect to be endlessly offered everything from drugs to the hustlers themselves. Usually – but alas not always – you can shake them off with a firm 'not interested' or 'maybe on the way back,' if you know you're not passing back that way. Tourist police now patrol the beach but, by law, all Jamaican beaches must permit public access so the hustlers are free to roam. Some hotels post security guards on the beach but they're not always that effective.

Though ganja is smoked in plain view in Negril, undercover police agents are present and rarely a week goes by without one or more visitors being arrested. Tourists have been reported as suffering harmful side effects from ganja, especially from ganja cakes. This is also true of hallucinogenic wild mushrooms. Apparently drinking alcohol while on mushrooms can induce a 'bad trip' – and the same term may end up describing your vacation.

Prostitution is an established part of the local scene and short-term holiday liaisons are a staple. Female visitors should expect to hear a constant litany of well-honed lines enticing you to sample some 'Jamaican steel.'

Opportunistic theft occurs, especially of items left on the beach, as does burglary in budget and midrange properties. There have even been reports of tourists being robbed at gunpoint in their hotels; never open your hotel door to strangers without first ascertaining their identity. At night take a taxi rather than walk the dimly lit roads.

There are no sidewalks alongside West End Rd, so be careful when walking the road; traffic whips past pell-mell.

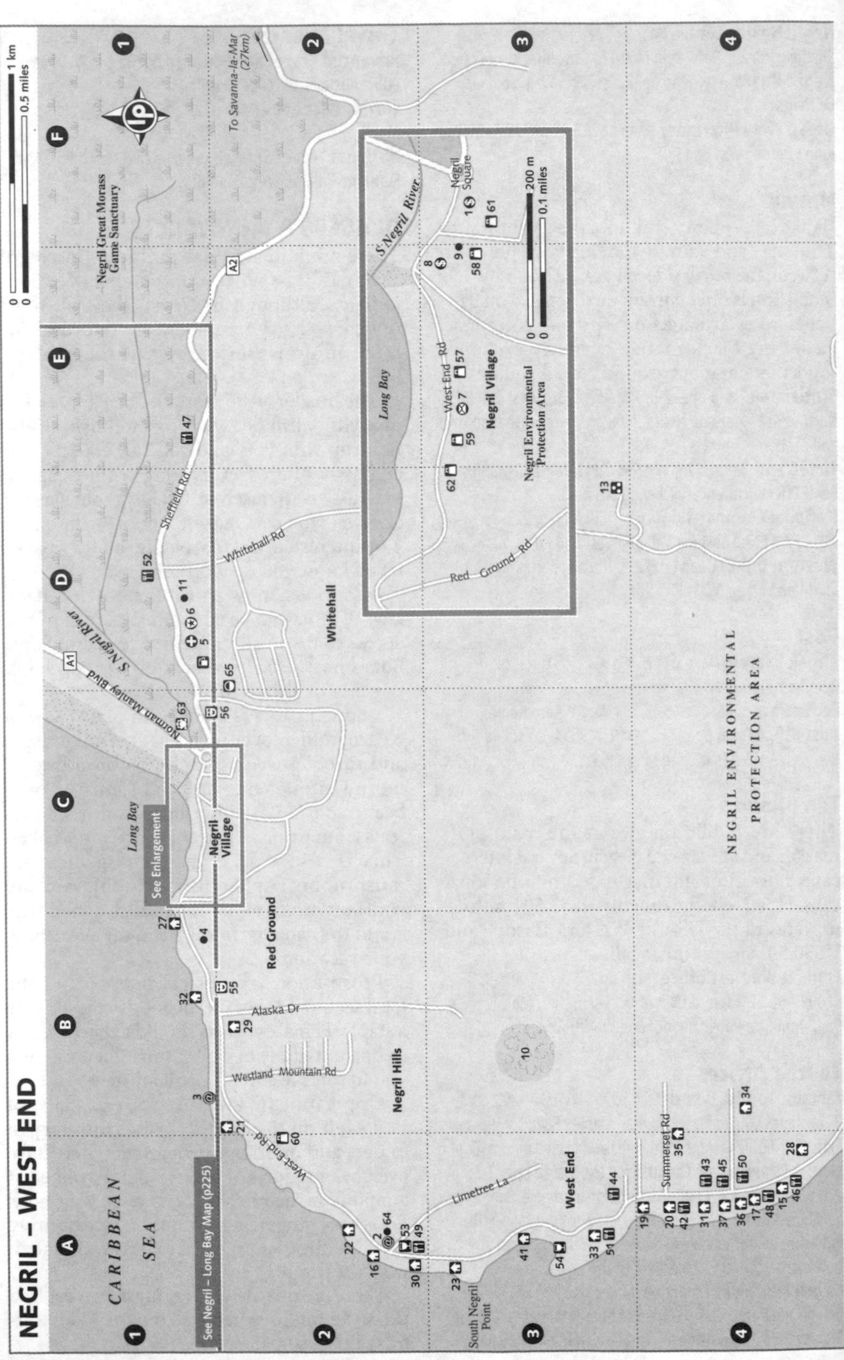
NEGRIL – WEST END
CARIBBEAN SEA
Long Bay
See Enlargement
Negril Village
Red Ground
Negril Hills
Whitehall
West End
South Negril Point
NEGRIL ENVIRONMENTAL PROTECTION AREA
Negril Great Morass Game Sanctuary
S Negril River
Norman Manley Blvd
Sheffield Rd
Whitehall Rd
Alaska Dr
Westland Mountain Rd
West End Rd
Limetree La
Summerset Rd
Red Ground Rd
Negril Square
Negril Environmental Protection Area
To Savanna-la-Mar (27km)
See Negril – Long Bay Map (p225)
1 km
0.5 miles
200 m
0.1 miles

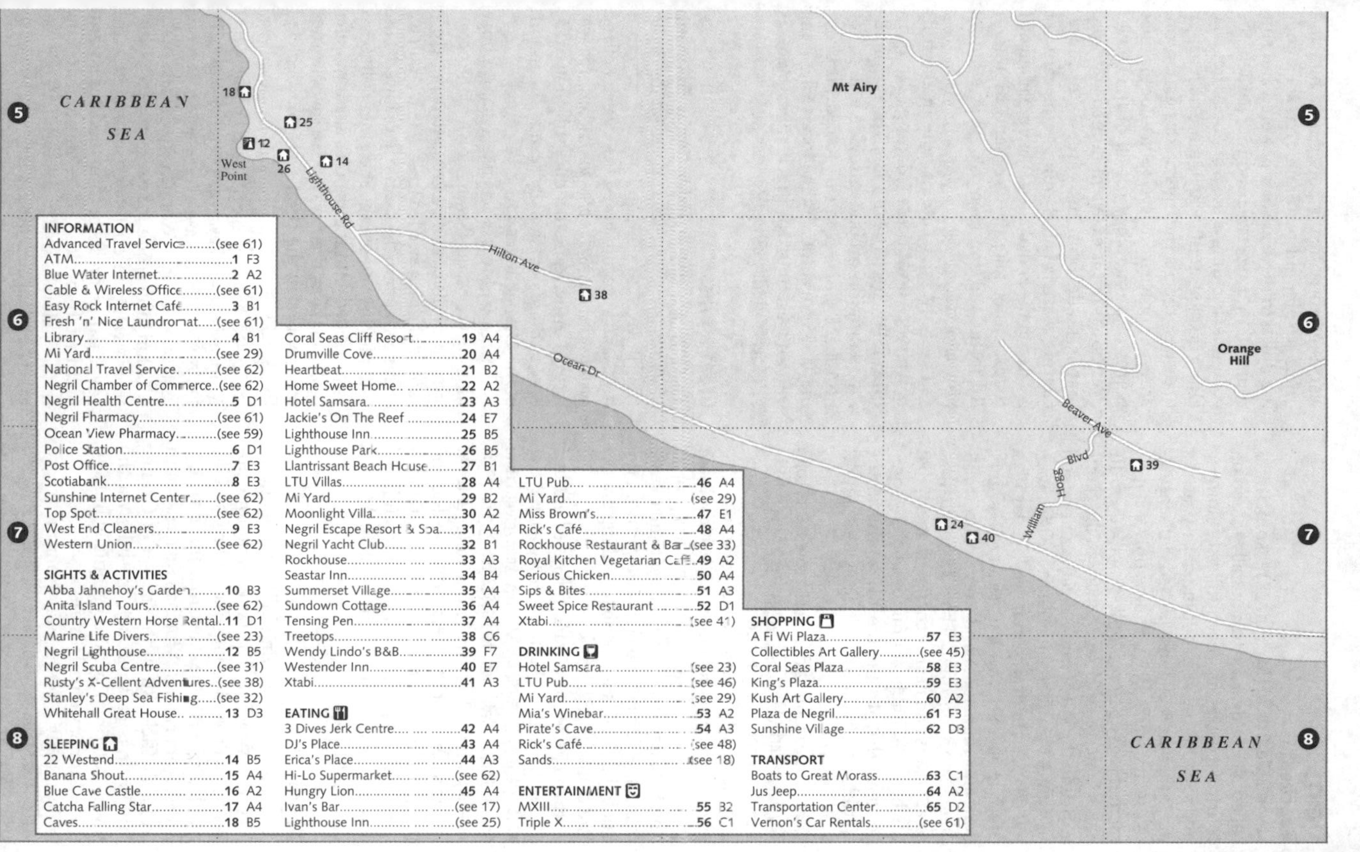
CARIBBEAN SEA
Mt Airy
Orange Hill
West Point
Lighthouse Rd
Hilton Ave
Ocean Dr
Beaver Ave
Hogg Blvd
William
CARIBBEAN SEA
INFORMATION
Advanced Travel Service........(see 61)
ATM.......................................1 F3
Blue Water Internet....................2 A2
Cable & Wireless Office.........(see 61)
Easy Rock Internet Café.............3 B1
Fresh 'n' Nice Laundromat.....(see 61)
Library.....................................4 B1
Mi Yard..................................(see 29)
National Travel Service. ....(see 62)
Negril Chamber of Commerce..(see 62)
Negril Health Centre.... ....5 D1
Negril Pharmacy..........................(see 61)
Ocean View Pharmacy..........(see 59)
Police Station..............................6 D1
Post Office..................................7 E3
Scotiabank..................................8 E3
Sunshine Internet Center.......(see 62)
Top Spot...................................(see 62)
West End Cleaners......................9 E3
Western Union...........................(see 62)
SIGHTS & ACTIVITIES
Abba Jahnehoy's Garden.........10 B3
Anita Island Tours...................(see 62)
Country Western Horse Rental..11 D1
Marine Life Divers...................(see 23)
Negril Lighthouse.....................12 B5
Negril Scuba Centre..................(see 31)
Rusty's X-Cellent Adventures..(see 38)
Stanley's Deep Sea Fishing.....(see 32)
Whitehall Great House.. ....13 D3
SLEEPING
22 Westend..................................14 B5
Banana Shout...............................15 A4
Blue Cave Castle..........................16 A2
Catcha Falling Star.......................17 A4
Caves..18 B5
Coral Seas Cliff Resort..........19 A4
Drumville Cove.........................20 A4
Heartbeat...................................21 B2
Home Sweet Home....................22 A2
Hotel Samsara............................23 A3
Jackie's On The Reef.................24 E7
Lighthouse Inn..........................25 B5
Lighthouse Park.........................26 B5
Llantrissant Beach House.........27 B1
LTU Villas..................................28 A4
Mi Yard......................................29 B2
Moonlight Villa..........................30 A2
Negril Escape Resort & Spa......31 A4
Negril Yacht Club......................32 B1
Rockhouse..................................33 A3
Seastar Inn..................................34 B4
Summerset Village......................35 A4
Sundown Cottage........................36 A4
Tensing Pen................................37 A4
Treetops......................................38 C6
Wendy Lindo's B&B...................39 F7
Westender Inn.............................40 E7
Xtabi...41 A3
EATING
3 Dives Jerk Centre....................42 A4
DJ's Place...................................43 A4
Erica's Place...............................44 A3
Hi-Lo Supermarket...................(see 62)
Hungry Lion................................45 A4
Ivan's Bar..................................(see 17)
Lighthouse Inn..........................(see 25)
LTU Pub......................................46 A4
Mi Yard......................................(see 29)
Miss Brown's..............................47 E1
Rick's Café..................................48 A4
Rockhouse Restaurant & Bar...(see 33)
Royal Kitchen Vegetarian Café..49 A2
Serious Chicken..........................50 A4
Sips & Bites...............................51 A3
Sweet Spice Restaurant...............52 D1
Xtabi..(see 41)
DRINKING
Hotel Samsara..........................(see 23)
LTU Pub...................................(see 46)
Mi Yard....................................(see 29)
Mia's Winebar.............................53 A2
Pirate's Cave...............................54 A3
Rick's Café...............................(see 48)
Sands..(see 18)
ENTERTAINMENT
MXIII..55 B2
Triple X.......................................56 C1
SHOPPING
A Fi Wi Plaza..............................57 E3
Collectibles Art Gallery..........(see 45)
Coral Seas Plaza..........................58 E3
King's Plaza................................59 E3
Kush Art Gallery..........................60 A2
Plaza de Negril............................61 F3
Sunshine Village..........................62 D3
TRANSPORT
Boats to Great Morass..................63 C1
Jus Jeep..64 A2
Transportation Center..................65 D2
Vernon's Car Rentals................(see 61)

SIGHTS

Beaches

Seven Mile Beach (Map p225) – sometimes called Negril Beach – was initially touted on tourism posters as 'seven miles of nothing but you and the sea.' But the once-peaceful place that drew all those blissed-out sensualists in the early 1970s is now only a happy memory. As before, topless sunbathers lie half submerged on lounge chairs in the gentle surf, and the sweet smell of ganja smoke still perfumes the breeze, but otherwise the beach has changed in nearly every way. Today it's a much livelier place with scores of restaurants, bars and nightspots and every conceivable water sport on offer. The swaying palms, clear waters and nearby coral reefs mean that the beach is still beautiful to behold – some contend that it's the most beautiful in the Caribbean – but if you're looking for solitude, look elsewhere.

More peaceful and far less crowded is **Long Bay Beach Park** (Map p225), north of Seven Mile Beach, where you'll find more sugary sand and picnic tables plus changing rooms.

Another splendid option is **Bloody Bay Beach** (Map p225), with no facilities and few people, save for a few savvy travelers and a smattering of locals enjoying some repose away from the hubbub. There's a jerk shack selling snacks and drinks.

If you prefer your water fun doled out in a theme-park, the 2-hectare **Kool Runnings Water Park** (Map p225; ☎ 957-5400; www.koolrunnings.com; Norman Manley Blvd; adult/child US$28/19; 🕑 11am-7pm Tue-Sun) offers 10 different rides, ranging from the 15m drop of the Jamaica Bobsled to the tranquil Rio Bueno Lazy River ride. Food is available at three restaurants, and children can be easily distracted at Captain Mikie's Coconut Island.

Negril Hills

This range of low-lying hills rises inland of Negril's West End. The raised limestone upland is wild and smothered in brush. Tiny hamlets sprinkle the single road that provides access from Negril: Whitehall Rd leads south from Sheffield Rd to the hamlet of Orange Hill, swings east through the hills via the town of Retirement, and eventually links to the A2 for Savanna-la-Mar.

Seemingly a world away from the Negril strip, **Abba Jahnehoy's Garden** (Map pp222-3; ☎ 371-4050, 578-9578) is a three-story meditation and learning center that is poised on a hill, and offers a splendid panoramic view extending down to the sea. Solar powered and surrounded by a vegetable and root garden, the octagonal building is the work of Janhoi Jaja. He's a gracious Rasta who is more than happy to discuss the ins and outs of Rastafarianism, or reggae or Negril's development or the finer points of numerology (or all of the above) over bowls of his excellent homemade soup that is made from his garden's produce. Getting there is half the fun, as the garden's located at the end of a series of unmarked dirt roads: either take the Westland Mountain Rd to the top and then ask, or give Janhoi himself a call.

The only other site of note in the hills is **Whitehall Great House** (Map pp222–3), in ruins following a fire in 1985. The surrounding plantation grounds provide a stage for horseback rides. Don't be fooled into paying US$5 for a tour by the locals who hang out and attempt to attach themselves as self-described 'guides.'

Great Morass

This virtually impenetrable 3km-wide swamp of mangroves stretches 16km from the South Negril River to Orange Bay. The swamp is the island's second-largest freshwater wetland system and forms a refuge for endangered waterfowl. American crocodiles still cling to life here and are occasionally seen at the mouth of the Orange River.

The Great Morass acts like a giant sponge filtering the waters flowing down to the ocean from the hills east of Negril, and is thereby a source of much-needed fresh water. Drainage channels cut into the swamp have lowered the water levels, and sewage and other pollutants have seeped into the region's shallow water table, making their way to sea where they have poisoned the coral reefs and depleted fish stocks.

The easiest way to get a sense of the Great Morass is at the **Royal Palm Reserve** (Map pp218-19; ☎ 957-3115; www.royalpalmreserve.com; adult/child US$10/5; 🕑 9am-6pm). Wooden boardwalks make a 1.5km loop around the reserve. Three distinct swamp forest types are present – the royal palm forest, buttonwood forest and bull thatch forest. They're all home to butterflies galore as well as doctorbirds, herons, egrets, endangered black parakeets, Jamaican woodpeckers and countless other birds. Two

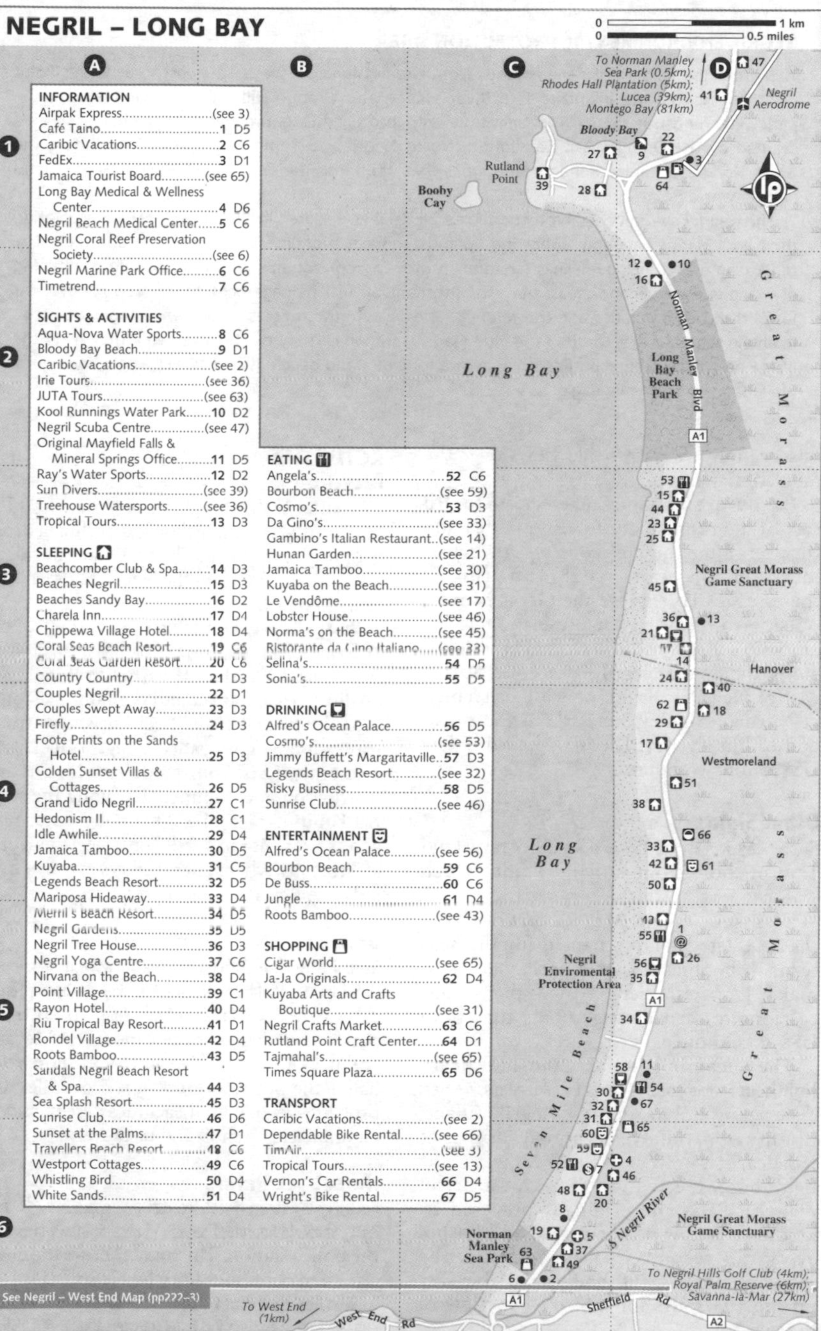
NEGRIL – LONG BAY
0 1 km
0 0.5 miles
A
B
C
D
1
2
3
4
5
6
INFORMATION
Airpak Express........................(see 3)
Café Taino..............................1 D5
Caribic Vacations......................2 C6
FedEx.....................................3 D1
Jamaica Tourist Board...........(see 65)
Long Bay Medical & Wellness Center..............................4 D6
Negril Beach Medical Center......5 C6
Negril Coral Reef Preservation Society...............................(see 6)
Negril Marine Park Office..........6 C6
Timetrend...............................7 C6
SIGHTS & ACTIVITIES
Aqua-Nova Water Sports..........8 C6
Bloody Bay Beach.....................9 D1
Caribic Vacations....................(see 2)
Irie Tours..............................(see 36)
JUTA Tours............................(see 63)
Kool Runnings Water Park.......10 D2
Negril Scuba Centre...............(see 47)
Original Mayfield Falls & Mineral Springs Office.........11 D5
Ray's Water Sports..................12 D2
Sun Divers............................(see 39)
Treehouse Watersports..........(see 36)
Tropical Tours........................13 D3
SLEEPING
Beachcomber Club & Spa.........14 D3
Beaches Negril........................15 D3
Beaches Sandy Bay..................16 D2
Charela Inn.............................17 D4
Chippewa Village Hotel...........18 D4
Coral Seas Beach Resort..........19 C6
Coral Seas Garden Resort........20 C6
Country Country......................21 D3
Couples Negril.........................22 D1
Couples Swept Away...............23 D3
Firefly....................................24 D3
Foote Prints on the Sands Hotel.....................................25 D3
Golden Sunset Villas & Cottages...............................26 D5
Grand Lido Negril....................27 C1
Hedonism II............................28 C1
Idle Awhile.............................29 D4
Jamaica Tamboo.....................30 D5
Kuyaba...................................31 C5
Legends Beach Resort.............32 D5
Mariposa Hideaway................33 D4
Merril's Beach Resort.............34 D5
Negril Gardens........................35 D5
Negril Tree House...................36 D3
Negril Yoga Centre..................37 C6
Nirvana on the Beach..............38 D4
Point Village...........................39 C1
Rayon Hotel............................40 D4
Riu Tropical Bay Resort...........41 D1
Rondel Village.........................42 D4
Roots Bamboo.........................43 D5
Sandals Negril Beach Resort & Spa...................................44 D3
Sea Splash Resort....................45 D3
Sunrise Club...........................46 D6
Sunset at the Palms.................47 D1
Travellers Beach Resort...........48 C6
Westport Cottages...................49 C6
Whistling Bird.........................50 D4
White Sands............................51 D4
EATING
Angela's.................................52 C6
Bourbon Beach......................(see 59)
Cosmo's..................................53 D3
Da Gino's..............................(see 33)
Gambino's Italian Restaurant..(see 14)
Hunan Garden.......................(see 21)
Jamaica Tamboo...................(see 30)
Kuyaba on the Beach............(see 31)
Le Vendôme..........................(see 17)
Lobster House.......................(see 46)
Norma's on the Beach...........(see 45)
Ristorante da Gino Italiano.....(see 33)
Selina's..................................54 D5
Sonia's...................................55 D5
DRINKING
Alfred's Ocean Palace.............56 D5
Cosmo's.................................(see 53)
Jimmy Buffett's Margaritaville..57 D3
Legends Beach Resort...........(see 32)
Risky Business.......................58 D5
Sunrise Club..........................(see 46)
ENTERTAINMENT
Alfred's Ocean Palace...........(see 56)
Bourbon Beach......................59 C6
De Buss.................................60 C6
Jungle....................................61 D4
Roots Bamboo.......................(see 43)
SHOPPING
Cigar World..........................(see 65)
Ja-Ja Originals........................62 D4
Kuyaba Arts and Crafts Boutique..............................(see 31)
Negril Crafts Market...............63 C6
Rutland Point Craft Center......64 D1
Tajmahal's............................(see 65)
Times Square Plaza.................65 D6
TRANSPORT
Caribic Vacations....................(see 2)
Dependable Bike Rental.........(see 66)
TimAir...................................(see 3)
Tropical Tours.......................(see 13)
Vernon's Car Rentals...............66 D4
Wright's Bike Rental................67 D5
To Norman Manley Sea Park (0.5km); Rhodes Hall Plantation (5km); Lucea (39km); Montego Bay (81km)
Negril Aerodrome
Bloody Bay
Rutland Point
Booby Cay
Long Bay
Norman Manley Blvd
Long Bay Beach Park
Great Morass
Negril Great Morass Game Sanctuary
Hanover
Westmoreland
Negril Enviromental Protection Area
Seven Mile Beach
S Negril River
Norman Manley Sea Park
A1
A2
To Negril Hills Golf Club (4km); Royal Palm Reserve (6km); Savanna-la-Mar (27km)
See Negril – West End Map (pp222–3)
To West End (1km)
West End Rd
Sheffield Rd

NEGRIL ENVIRONMENTAL PROTECTION AREA

This protected wilderness zone extends from Green Island on the north coast to St John's Point (south of Negril) and inland to Fish River village and Orange Hills. It also includes a marine park extending out to sea. The intention is to protect the entire Negril watershed (the area drained by the Orange, Fish, Newfound, North Negril and South Negril Rivers), including the Great Morass swampland and all land areas that drain into the Caribbean between Green Island and St John's Point.

The Negril Environmental Protection Area (NEPA) was declared in November 1997, incorporating the Negril Marine Park and embracing uplands, morass, shoreline, offshore lagoon and reefs. The NEPA plan establishes guidelines for tourism growth, moratoriums on further cutting or draining of mangrove or wetland areas, the establishment of 'fish management zones', sewage systems for outlying communities and the reforestation of deforested areas. It also encourages hotels to maintain their beaches through the Blue Flag Award which they can be awarded if they meet the Blue Flag environmental outfit's strict criteria for water and beach quality as well as environmental management (www.blueflag.org).

observation towers provide views over the tangled mangroves.

If you are driving, take Sheffield Rd east of the roundabout for 10 minutes and turn left after the golf course. Otherwise, local tour operators (p228) run trips to the reserve. To explore the Great Morass outside the Royal Palm Reserve, negotiate with villagers who have boats moored along the South Negril River (just northeast of Negril Village), or with fishermen at Norman Manley Sea Park, at the north end of Bloody Bay. It costs approximately US$35 for two hours.

Other Sights

Booby Cay (Map p225) is a small coral island 1km offshore from Rutland Point, which was used as a South Seas setting in the Walt Disney movie *20,000 Leagues Under the Sea.* The island is named for the seabirds – 'boobies' in local parlance – that make their nests here. Water-sports concessionaires can arrange boats for about US$25 roundtrip.

The gleaming white, 20m-tall **Negril Lighthouse** (Map pp222-3; West End Rd; admission free; 9am-sunset), 5km south of Negril Village, illuminates the westernmost point of Jamaica, at 18° 15' north, 78° 23' west. The lighthouse, erected in 1894 with a prism made in Paris and originally powered by kerosene, is now solar powered and flashes every two seconds. Wilson Johnson, the superintendent, will gladly lead the way up the 103 stairs for a bird's-eye view of the coast.

ACTIVITIES

Bicycling

The intense traffic along Norman Manley Blvd and West End Rd makes cycling a dicey proposition in town. The best place to ride is along Ocean Dr or in the Negril Hills, southeast of Negril.

Rusty's X-Cellent Adventures (Map pp222-3; ☎ 957-0155; rustynegril@hotmail.com; Treetops, Hilton Ave; tours per person without/with bike rental US$25/35) offers high-quality two- to four-hour mountain-bike tours into the Negril Hills. Exciting single-track routes follow goat paths to high ridges with awesome views; your guide provides casual instruction and commentary along the way. All equipment – bikes, helmets, water and accessories – is included. Tours begin and end at Treetops, where gnarly bikers can also find lodging. Reservations are required.

Golf

Negril Hills Golf Club (☎ 957-4638; www.negrilhillsgolfclub.com; Sheffield Rd; green fee US$58, club/cart rental US$18/35, caddy US$14; 7:30am-4pm) An 18-hole par-72 course that borders the Great Morass, about 5km east of Negril. If you plop your ball in the water, forget it – the crocodiles will probably get to it first! Facilities here include a clubhouse, pro shop and restaurant.

Horseback Riding

Country Western Horse Rental (Map pp222-3; ☎ 955-7910; Sheffield Rd; rides US$50; 8am-5pm) is next to the police station. The route follows the coast and then continues into the Negril Hills.

Rhodes Hall Plantation (☎ 957-6883; rhodes@cwjamaica.com; 2-hr rides incl hotel transfers US$50-60), 5km north of Negril at Green Island, offers rides through banana plantations and up into the hills; see p241.

Sailing & Cruising

Several companies offer two- and three-hour excursions. Tours can be booked at most hotels. Most trips include snorkeling and plenty of booze, but don't mix the two!

Wild Thing Watersports (☎ 957-9930; www.wildthingwatersportsnegril.com) Day cruises on a 45ft catamaran go to Rhodes Hall (US$85; Monday, Wednesday and Friday) and Half Moon Bay (US$60, Tuesday, Saturday and Sunday). There are also daily sunset cruises to Rick's Café (US$50). You'll find the boat at Chances restaurant on Negril Beach.

Island Charters (☎ 957-6163) Two party boats, *Sunsplash* and *Sunsation*, with adults-only cruises and fun cruises for kids.

Glass-bottom boat rides are a great way to see the fish life and coral if you don't want to get wet. There are several to choose from on Long Bay beach, including **Best Boat Reef Tours** (☎ 957-3357).

Stanley's Deep Sea Fishing (Map pp222-3; ☎ 957-0667; www.stanleysdeepseafishing.com; Negril Yacht Club) offers whale- and dolphin-watching cruises.

Scuba Diving

Negril offers extensive offshore reefs and cliffs with grottoes, shallow reefs perfect for novice divers and mid-depth reefs right off the main beach at Long Bay. Clusters of dwarf tube sponges are a noteworthy feature. The West End offers caves and tunnels; its overhangs are popular for night dives. Hawksbill turtles are still quite common here.

Visibility often exceeds 30m and seas are dependably calm. Most dives are in 10m to 23m of water. (For more general scuba-diving information, see p53.)

There are several sites here that will be of interest for prospective divers. **Aweemaway** is a shallow reef area south of the Throne, and has tame stingrays. **Deep Plane** is the remains of a Cessna airplane lying at 21m underwater. Corals and sponges have taken up residence in and around the plane, attracting an abundance of fish, and nurse sharks hang out at a nearby overhang. **Sands Club Reef** lies in 10m of water in the middle of Long Bay. From here, a drift dive to **Shark's Reef** leads through tunnels and overhangs with huge sponges and gorgonian corals. **The Throne** is a 15m-wide cave with massive sponges, plentiful soft corals, nurse sharks, octopuses, barracuda and stingrays.

Most all-inclusive resorts have scuba facilities. The following are among the companies offering PADI certification and introductory 'resort courses'.

Marine Life Divers (Map pp222-3; ☎ 957-3245; www.mldiversnegril.com; Hotel Samsara, West End Rd; 1-/2-tank dive US$40/70) English- and German-speaking instructors.

Negril Scuba Centre (www.negrilscuba.com; 1-/2-tank dive US$40/70) Mariner's Negril Beach Club (☎ 957-4425, 957-9641; Norman Manley Blvd); Negril Escape Resort & Spa (Map pp222-3; ☎ 957-0392; West End Rd); Sunset at the Palms (Map p225; ☎ 383-9533; Bloody Bay Beach).

Sun Divers (Map p225; ☎ 957-4503; www.sundiversnegril.com; Point Village; 1-/2-tank dive US$40/70) Many trips led by the charismatic Ansel Clarke.

Snorkeling

Snorkeling is especially good at the southern end of Long Bay and off the West End. Expect to pay about US$5 an hour for masks and fins from concession stands on the beach. Most of the scuba-diving providers offer snorkeling tours (about US$25).

Sport Fishing

The waters off Negril – teeming with tuna, blue marlin, wahoo and sailfish – provide some excellent action for sport-fishing enthusiasts. **Stanley's Deep Sea Fishing** (Map pp222-3; ☎ 957-0667; www.stanleysdeepseafishing.com; Negril Yacht Club) offers custom fishing-trip charters (US$400/600/800 per half/three-quarter/full day for up to four people; for additional passengers add US$50/75/100 per head).

For a more offbeat experience, head out into the briny with a local fisherman; ask around by the bridge over South Negril River, or talk to the fishermen near North Negril River.

Water Sports

The waters off Negril are usually mirror-calm – ideal for all kinds of water sports. Numerous concessions along the beach rent jet skis (about US$40 for 30 minutes), plus sea kayaks, sailboards and Sunfish (about US$20 per hour). They also offer waterskiing (US$25 for 30 minutes), glass-bottom boat rides (US$15) and banana-boat rides (using an inflatable banana-shaped raft towed by a speedboat; US$15).

Parasailing on Long Bay is offered by **Ray's Water Sports** (Map p225; ☎ 957-4349; www.rayswatersportsnegril.com) at the north end of Long Bay,

THE FRAGILE CORAL REEFS

Negril's offshore reefs have been severely damaged by the resort boom and human tinkering with the Great Morass. The percentage of live coral cover is now so low that further coral loss could seriously threaten the functioning of the entire ecosystem.

Reef restoration is an important part of the NEPA project (see the boxed text, p226). But nothing can be done to bring back the marine turtles that once favored the beach for nesting.

The **Negril Coral Reef Preservation Society** (NCRPS; ☎ 957-3735; http://negril.com/ncrps), located next to the Negril Crafts Market on Norman Manley Blvd, has established a code of conduct for snorkelers and scuba divers, including the following guidelines:

- Never touch corals; even slight contact can harm them.
- Select points of entry and exit to avoid walking on corals.
- Maintain a comfortable distance from the reef, so as to avoid contact.
- Stay horizontal in the water while you're near or above the reef.
- Move slowly and deliberately in the water – relax as you swim and take your time.
- Take nothing living or dead out of the water, except recent garbage which does not have living organisms on it.
- Never touch, handle or feed marine life except under expert guidance and following locally established guidelines.

Aqua-Nova Water Sports (p225; ☎ 957-4323; www.negrill.com/aquaa; Norman Manley Blvd) at Mariner's Beach Club and **Treehouse Watersports** (Map p225; ☎ 957-4893; Negril Tree House, Norman Manley Blvd).

TOURS

Several tour operators offer a standard fare of excursions to the Black River Morass and Appleton Rum Estate (about US$85) to the east in St Elizabeth parish, Mayfield Falls (US$65) and Roaring River (US$60).

Anita Island Tours (Map pp222-3; ☎ 957-9946; Sunshine Village, West End Rd)

Caribic Vacations (Map p225; ☎ 957-3309; caribicvacations.com; Norman Manley Blvd) The largest operator. Also has tours to the Royal Palm Reserve.

Clive's Transport Service (☎ 956-2615; www.clivestransportservicejamaica.com) Offers reliable, comfortable tours islandwide and airport transfers (one to three people US$50) in a nine-passenger minivan.

Irie Tours (Map p225; ☎ 957-3806; Negril Tree House, Norman Manley Blvd)

JUTA Tours (Map p225; Jamaican Union of Travelers Association; ☎ 957-9197; Negril Crafts Market, Norman Manley Blvd)

Tropical Tours (Map p225; ☎ 957-4110; tropical@cwjamaica.com; Norman Manley Blvd)

FESTIVALS & EVENTS

January

Jamaica Sprint Triathlon (☎ 957-4061) Held at the Couples Swept Away resort's sports complex.

February

Jamaica Beachfest Starting in late February and now spanning six weeks to early April is Negril's famous spring-break celebration, featuring live music and plenty of booze.

Unleash the Tiger (☎ 957-4005; The Jungle) A big concert in observance of Jamaican Carnival.

March & April

Negril Ice Cream and Chocolate Festival (☎ 957-3454) Easter Sunday and Monday.

Negril Music Festival (☎ 968-9356) Three-day reggae and calypso festival in March.

August & September

Epicurean Escape (☎ 518-5006; Grand Lido Negril) Seminars and tastings for foodies, from jerk to champagne.

December

Reggae Marathon & Half-Marathon (☎ 922-8677; www.reggaemarathon.com) Both a full- and a half-marathon with a musical soundtrack staged on Norman Manley Blvd.

SLEEPING

In Negril more than any other resort town in Jamaica, travelers are spoiled for choice when it comes to accommodations. With rooms for all budgets – including a bountiful selection of quality economical choices – your pleasurable task is to pick the one that best suits your sensibilities. The large number of one-of-a-kind independent hotels has some visitors moving from place to place over the course of their vacations, just for the fun of it.

In general beach properties are more expensive than hotels of equivalent standard in the West End. Unless otherwise noted, all 'Long Bay' beach hotels are on Norman Manley Blvd, and all 'West End' hotels are on the coast road, variously called West End Rd, Lighthouse Rd and Ocean Dr.

The hotels recommended here are listed by price range. Rates quoted are for winter (high season) unless otherwise noted. Summer (low season) rates can be 20% to 60% lower.

Long Bay

BUDGET

Westport Cottages (Map p225; ☎ 957-4736, 307-5466; s/d US$15/20) This offbeat place with a communal vibe on the roundabout end of Long Bay is extremely popular with the backpacking crowd. Owner Joseph Mathews says it's approved for 'smoke-friendly heartical people.' Joseph has 17 very rustic, somewhat stuffy huts with mosquito nets and fans. The well-kept bathrooms and cold showers are outside. Newer rooms to the rear are preferable. A communal kitchen is available, and bicycles (US$5 per day) and snorkeling equipment (free!) are provided. Airport transfers are offered at a bargain (US$5).

Roots Bamboo (Map p225; ☎ 957-4479; www.rootsbamboo.com; camping per person US$10, r US$30; d with porch & shower US$55, with air-con US$70;) This is a popular beachside option with 26 well-kept cabins right on the beach. Some have showers; others share a communal shower block with campers. There's a small beachside bar and restaurant with pool tables. If it's peace and solitude you seek, try another place; here there are regularly scheduled live reggae concerts and a perpetual party atmosphere.

Golden Sunset Villas & Cottages (Map p225; ☎ 957-4241, 957-9703; www.thegoldensunset.com; s US$35-75, d US$45-86;) Another longtime favorite of the budget crowd. It has 21 rustic cottages and 'economy' rooms with fan and cold water only, 'standard' rooms with hot water and fan, and 'superior' rooms with air-con and TV. All rooms share kitchenettes.

Negril Yoga Centre (Map p225; ☎ 957-4397; www.negrilyoga.com; d US$46-75;) The eight rustic yet atmospheric rooms and cottages – most with fridges and fans – surround an open-air, wood-floored, thatched yoga center set in a garden. Options range from a two-story, Thai-style wooden cabin to an adobe farmer's cottage; all are pleasingly if modestly furnished. The staff make their own yogurt, cheese and sprouts, and cook meals on request. Naturally, yoga classes are offered (guests/visitors US$10/15), as are massages (US$60). There's a communal kitchen. This is a good option for women traveling alone and families with children.

Travellers Beach Resort (☎ 957-9308; www.travellersresorts.com; s US$51-55, d US$94-127, ste US$190; P) Although overrun during spring break, Travellers is a real bargain the rest of the year. The 60-room family-owned resort features 14 bungalows, two suites and 39 simple rooms. There's a small water grotto and fish tanks in the lobby with a snapping turtle. The bar is lively and the beach restaurant serves excellent jerk chicken.

MIDRANGE

Chippewa Village Hotel (Map p225; ☎ 957-4676; chippewavillageresort.com; cottage d US$55, studio US$80, 1-/2-/3-bedroom US$140/180/200;) This cheerful choice offers three octagonal studio units with screened porches and lofty ceilings and six one- to three-bedroom apartments. They are all rustic, rough-hewn affairs oozing a warm ambience, epitomized by American Southwest decor, throw rugs and tasteful fabrics. A small swimming pool under a shade canopy is inset in a wooden sundeck. There's a small restaurant and bar, with American home cooking (for guests only), plus a Jacuzzi, steam room and a viewing tower overlooking the Great Morass.

Sunrise Club (Map p225; ☎ 957-4293; www.sunriseclub.com; s/d US$70/98, meal plans per person US$22-38; P) Easing back onto the Great Morass, this gracious getaway is enhanced by its intimate aesthetic, with earth colors, natural hardwoods and creative architectural touches in American Southwest style. It has 15 rooms: older rooms to the rear are simply furnished but have neat bathrooms, while newer rooms feature blue mahoe furnishings. All have screened windows, fans and cable TV. It has a hip bar with a cosmopolitan clientele, and its outstanding Lobster House restaurant serves great breakfasts propelled by divine espresso.

Kuyaba (Map p225; ☎ 957-4318; www.kuyaba.com; cottage US$77, r US$97, honeymoon ste US$106) With considerable style, this tasteful family-run hotel offers six quaint rustic wooden cabins with filigree trim, done up in bright Caribbean colors. There are also three deluxe rooms and a suite with king-sized bed upstairs in a handsome stone-and-timber house tastefully decorated with terra-cotta floors. The ecoconscious owners are gourmands and run the splendid Kuyaba on the Beach restaurant, attached to the property. There's also a well-stocked gift store and live music 7pm to 9pm nightly.

White Sands (Map p225; ☎ 957-4291; www.whitesandsjamaica.com; r US$69-108, studio/villa US$138/540;) Providing good bang for the buck, this attractive property offers simple yet elegant one-bedroom octagonal units with varied amenities, and an excellent four-bedroom, four-bathroom villa that sleeps eight people and has its own pool. There's also a pleasant, well-maintained garden and a parrot who recites dub poetry.

Mariposa Hideaway (Map p225; ☎ 957-4918; www.mariposahideaway.com; r US$80-140, 2-bedroom apt US$150; P) This Italian-run hotel is a twee place. In addition to rooms there are excellent studios with kitchenettes, and a family-size apartment, all with cable TV and fridge. A great bonus here is the Ristorante da Gino Italiano, where the grappa starts flowing before noon.

Rayon Hotel (Map p225; ☎ 957-9166; www.rayonhotels.com; r US$100-120, ste US$140; P) This spiffy complex opposite the beach is a well-run operation that covers all the bases. The superior rooms have four-poster beds, cathedral ceilings with fans and private balconies; there are also suites with full kitchens. Facilities include a beauty salon offering massage, a pool bar and a tennis court.

Jamaica Tamboo (Map p225; ☎ 957-4282; www.jamaicatamboonegril.com; r US$95, 1-/2-bedroom cottage US$125; P) Featuring modestly furnished hardwood structures and a happening beachside bar and restaurant, this recently updated option has 22 rooms with balconies, two simple one-bedroom cottages plus a two-bedroom cottage with kitchenette.

Sea Splash Resort (Map p225; ☎ 876-957-4041, 800-254-2786; www.seasplash.com; r US$120-156, ste US$180-204; P) At this elegant resort the suites are tastefully appointed, each with large balcony, fully equipped kitchenette, screened-off bedroom and plenty of amenities. There is a handsome beach bar, and guests gain access to the facilities at the nearby Couples Swept Away resort. Sea Splash is also home to Norma's on the Beach (p236), one of the best restaurants in Negril.

Merril's Beach Resort (Map p225; ☎ 957-4751; www.merrilsbeach.com; per person gardenside tr/d/s US$60/75/90, per person beachside tr/d/s US$ 88/103/124;) A short distance from Negril Gardens, this attractive place has 28 rooms in a two-story unit in lush landscaped grounds. All rooms have verandas. It offers water sports and a beach bar, and is popular with European tour groups. The beach here has been accorded the prestigious Blue Flag award for Merril's attention to the environment.

Coral Seas Beach Resort (Map p225; ☎ 957-9226, in the USA ☎ 800-223-6510; www.coralseasnegril.com; r US$90-120, studio US$125, apt US$95-140;) This well-run option is a sequestered beachside place in a garden of bamboo and hibiscus. You can choose from rooms with verandas, fully equipped apartments, two honeymoon suites or clifftop units. The pool has a bar. Coral Seas Garden Resort, a sister property, is across the street and has rooms of a similar standard and price.

Legends Beach Resort (Map p225; ☎ 957-3834; www.visitnegril.com/legends; d US$110-125, tr US$125-140; P) This beachfront resort offers 49 gleaming white rooms with basic furnishings that include ceiling fans, two double beds and balconies or verandas. Higher-priced rooms face the beach. There are two pools plus a lively restaurant and sports bar; reggae shows are staged on Tuesday and Friday night.

our pick **Rondel Village** (Map p225; ☎ 957-4413; www.rondelvillage.com; d US$95-150, 1-/2-bedroom villa US$210/245;) Highly affable and efficient hotel whose Green Globe Certification attests to its commitment to preserving the environment. Graced by walkways lined with an array of indigenous fruit trees, the family-owned Village offers well-appointed studios and beachfront rooms clustered around a small pool and Jacuzzi. You can also choose octagonal one- and two- bedroom villas that sleep up to six and feature marble floors, French doors, satellite TV, DVD and CD players, fully equipped kitchenettes and Jacuzzi. It has a seafront restaurant and a popular bar, Irie on the Beach.

TOP END

Country Country (Map p225; ☎ 876-957-4273; www.countrynegril.com; cottages US$165-185;) This color-crazy charmer has that mellow Negril vibe down cold. On offer are 14 air-con wooden cottages with gingerbread trim and fretwork; pastels dominate and lend a chic warmth.

Some have king-sized beds and separate sitting areas.

Idle Awhile (Map p225; ☎ 957-9566, 877-243-5352; www.idleawhile.com; r US$190, ste US$230-305; P ✻ 🖳) This exquisite boutique hotel is highly recommended for its eight airy, delightfully appointed rooms and five suites with contemporary vogue and tropical decor. There's a wireless network, and guests are allowed free access to Couples Swept Away's sport complex (p232). Snacks, seafood, Jamaican dishes and fresh juices are served beachside beneath umbrellas.

Firefly (Map p225; ☎ 957-4358; www.jamaicalink.com; studio/cottage US$137/175, ste US$180-200, apt US$176-255; P ✻ 🖳) A refined choice where nudists dwell in style, Firefly offers four handsome, all-hardwood cottages, plus one-bedroom studios, apartments and penthouse suites. Each is different but all have kitchenettes and verandas. There's a Jacuzzi, and guests get free access to Couples Swept Away's facilities.

Beachcomber Club & Spa (Map p225; ☎ 957-4170; www.beachcomberclub.com; r US$150-175, 1-bedroom apt US$220, 2-bedroom apt US$350-375; P ✻ 🖳) Operating with crisp efficiency, this handsome 45-room hotel has an open air beachside restaurant, Gambino's, plus a nightly entertainment schedule, tennis and water sports. All rooms are well furnished, with ceiling fans, telephone and satellite TV; suites and apartments have kitchenettes.

Foote Prints on the Sands Hotel (Map p225; ☎ 957-4300; www.footeprintshotel.com; s US$135-145, d US$165; P ✻ 🖳) This family-run hotel on the beach offers 30 rooms, studios (with kitchenettes) and some two-bedroom apartments with TV, telephone and safe. Some have ceiling fans and most have balconies. Facilities include an onsite restaurant and bar, Jacuzzi, tour desk, water sports and excursions.

Negril Tree House (Map p225; ☎ 957-4287; www.negril-treehouse.com; r US$150-170, ste US$275-350; P ✻ ♿) This unpretentious resort is a favorite for its 16 octagonal bungalows and oceanfront villas nudging pleasingly up to the beach. Each has a TV and a safe. More elegant one- and two-bedroom suites each feature kitchenette, king-sized bed and a Murphy bed in the lounge, which opens onto a wide veranda. The beachside bar is popular. Water sports are offered, and the resort has a tour desk, gift store, masseuse and manicurist.

Charela Inn (Map p225; ☎ 957-4277; www.charela.com; s US$155-186, d US$174-212, tr US$218; P ✻ 🖳 ♿) Run by a Jamaican–French couple, Daniel and Sylvie, this engaging spot resembles a Spanish hacienda and surrounds a courtyard. The 49 rooms feature contemporary decor with lots of hardwood, plus ceiling fans, hair-dryers, telephones and balconies or patios. The onsite Le Vendôme restaurant is one of the finest on Negril.

Nirvana on the Beach (Map p225; ☎ 957-4314, in the USA 716-789-5955; www.nirvananegril.com; d cottage US$190-205, ste US$210-225) The place to stay if you're seeking meditation, with one-, two- and three-bedroom cottages set in Zen-like tropical gardens. Each all-hardwood cabin has a king-sized bed, dining room, kitchen and screened wraparound windows. Meals prepared on request.

Whistling Bird (Map p225; ☎ 957-4403, in the USA 303-442-0722; www.negriljamaica.com/whistlingbird; s/d/tr US$140/210/315, all-inclusive per person per day from US$125; P ✻) Similar to Nirvana, this family-run place has 24 rooms in bungalows and cottages with wood-accented decor and wicker furniture. Each is equipped with phone and cable TV. It's low-key and a great place to relax beneath shady bamboo. It has a restaurant and beach bar.

Negril Gardens (Map p225; ☎ 957-4408, in the USA 305-284-1300, in the UK 0207-259-1840; www.negrilgardens.com; gardenside s/d/tr US$126/142/173, beachside s/d/tr US$147/163/184; ✻ ♿) This conscientious resort proudly displays its Green Globe certification, offering 65 nicely appointed rooms in gaily colored two-story cottages with balconies. Garden-view rooms are situated across the road.

ALL-INCLUSIVES

Prices quoted below are for three nights, all-inclusive double occupancy during the high season (December 15 to April 15); low-season rates can be considerably lower. Rates presented are guidelines; they vary considerably depending on the source of booking, season and current specials. See p275 for general information about all-inclusive resorts in Jamaica.

Point Village (Map p225; ☎ 957-5170; www.pointvillage.com; d US$960-1020 ste US$1110-1380; P ✻ ♿) A family-friendly hotel at Rutland Point, with 175 recently refurbished one- to three-bedroom suites with kitchens in Mediterranean-style limestone villas scattered through 6 hectares. The hotel's wave-pounded shoreline holds pocket-sized beaches (one for nudes) and cooling pools cut into the coral. Water sports, picnic trips to Booby Cay and guided bicycle rides are included.

Sunset at the Palms (Map p225; ☎ 957-5350; www.sunsetatthepalms.com; d US$1500-2100, ste US$1275-1800;) An ecoconscious resort with heaps of jungle atmosphere. It has 86 all-hardwood, Thai-style cabins raised on stilts amid lush grounds full of croaking tree frogs. Interior decor features leather sofas and Chinese rugs. Superior rooms have TV; all rooms have safes. Facilities include a fitness center and tennis court plus games room, Jacuzzi, swim-up bar and romantic restaurant serving top-notch cuisine. A path leads to the beach.

Sandals Negril Beach Resort & Spa (Map p225; ☎ 957-5216; www.sandals.com; d US$1000-1250;) A tasteful couples-only resort, this 8-hectare deluxe property sprawls over wide lawns trimmed to perfection. At its node is a huge pool with swim-up bar abuzz with happy guests. There are 227 rooms in six categories, including exquisite honeymoon suites in gracious cottages with Edwardian decoration, plus villa-suites with loft bedrooms and marble bathrooms.

Hedonism II (Map p225; ☎ 957-5070; www.superclubs.com/brand_hedonism; d US$925-1975;) Famous for its risqué attitude and weekly lingerie parties (and notorious for its sheer tackiness), this adults-only resort has 280 rooms and suites with mirrored ceilings. Sadly, the strange retro decor is somewhat of a turn-off. There are two fine beaches – one for nudes and the other for 'prudes,' a rock-climbing wall, ice-skating rink and, of course, a disco (inset with glass-bottomed Jacuzzi in the roof). Guests include many more single males than females; a third female in a group stays free.

Riu Tropical Bay Resort (Map p225; ☎ 957-5900; www.riu.com; d US$1464-1794;) This 420-room behemoth offers good value for the budget-minded crowd. Room decor is tastefully contemporary, featuring Caribbean pastels. The rooms have satellite TV, in-room safes and minibars. The resort features a nude beach section, a full array of water sports, fitness center and spa, tennis courts, volleyball courts, disco and a selection of restaurants and entertainment.

Couples Swept Away (Map p225; ☎ 957-4061; www.couples.com; d US$1600-2150;) A magnificent all-inclusive, adults-only resort that boasts the island's best-equipped sports and fitness facility. Pathways coil through an 8-hectare botanical rush-hour of ferns and heliconias to the 134 suites, which are housed in 26 two-story villas and boast terra-cotta tile floors, deep-red hardwoods and vast louvered windows. Free golf at Negril Hills Golf Club is included.

Couples Negril (Map p225; ☎ 957-5960; www.couples.com; d US$1550-2950;) This attractive property boasts classy contemporary decor that the company terms 'Negril Chic.' The lobby opens over a wide pool at the heart of the 7-hectare resort. The 216 rooms are pleasingly hip, appointed with richly colored fabrics, iridescent curtains, dark bamboo and oh-so-chic furniture. The suites have a vast bathroom with Jacuzzi and his-and-hers sinks. The beach on Bloody Bay has been accorded the prestigious Blue Flag award for its environmentally sound upkeep.

Beaches Sandy Bay (Map p225; ☎ 957-5100; www.beaches.com; d US$1650-1850;) Another spiffy property, this family-friendly option on about 3 hectares includes 130 attractive rooms in three-story accommodations blocks and villas. On offer are also suites and one-bedroom villas. Children and teens are offered a games room and organized activities, including beach volleyball.

Grand Lido Negril (Map p225; ☎ 957-5010; www.grandlido.com; d US$1780-2900;) Boasting Mediterranean flair, this sprawling property is the flagship of the SuperClubs chain. The 210 spacious, tastefully furnished suites and split-level junior suites (some with whirlpool) with mezzanine bedrooms are spread through 9 hectares of gardens, which feature nine bars, including three 24-hour bars with Jacuzzis. Take your pick of several restaurants. A full range of water sports is offered, as are cruises aboard M/Y *Zien*, a 147ft motor yacht that was a wedding gift to Prince Rainer and Grace Kelly from Aristotle Onassis.

Beaches Negril (Map p225; ☎ 957-9270; www.beaches.com; d US$2000-2750, ste US$2940-6390;) Another impressive Sandals all-inclusive resort, this one caters to families, singles and couples. It loosely resembles a castle, with thick limestone walls, wrought-iron furniture and lanterns. It has 215 rooms, including 39 junior suite buildings in quasi-Spanish hacienda style. It has a gigantic pool and plenty of facilities for kids. Guests get access to Sandals Negril (left).

West End

BUDGET

Treetops (Map pp222-3; ☎ 957-0155, 866-4592; tobynegril@hotmail.com; Hilton Ave; dm US$15, d US$45; P) This special house – some might call it a castle – is the creation of Rusty Jones of Rusty's X-Cellent Adventures, Negril's premier mountain-biking haven. As such, you can expect to find muddy, gnarly bikers and other agreeable sorts bunking here. There are four rooms with double beds and one with bunks; each is fan-cooled and equipped with mosquito netting with screened windows. Hammocks abound. There's a communal kitchen and a truly rad roof deck with sweeping views over the Negril Hills. A housekeeper comes daily and can cook meals on request.

Lighthouse Park (Map pp222-3; ☎ 957-0252; sef@cwjamaica.com; cabins/cottages US$45/120) This old favorite south of the lighthouse suffered a body blow from Hurricane Ivan and all of the bamboo-and-thatch cabins succumbed to the elements. With great resilience, the owners have restored the property with two wood-and-concrete cottages with private bathrooms and verandas. There's also an apartment suite with kitchenette and two rooms. All the accommodations are charming and comfortable, perched on the cliff affording excellent sea views. The place draws rootsy artist types and enjoys frequent repeat customers. Prices are negotiable.

Lighthouse Inn (Map pp222-3; ☎ 957-4052; cottages s/d/q US$35/50/60) Four six-person cottages with kitchenettes, solar-heated water, louvered windows and wicker furniture. It has a free beach shuttle, plus a restaurant offering candlelit dining.

22 Westend (Map pp222-3; ☎ 898-6349; d/tr US$40/55) For a homey experience this friendly and accommodating little guest house near the lighthouse has two bedrooms fan-cooled with cross ventilation, shared bath, alfresco shower and communal kitchen. The live-in owner cooks with organic veggies from the garden. It's good for groups; each room can hold three people.

Mi Yard (Map pp222-3; ☎ 957-4442; www.miyard.com; s/d/tr US$50/60/70; ❄ 💻) With 24/7 internet access and yummy meals served till all hours, this agreeable little place offers four simple, clean, albeit somewhat dark, tiled rooms – two have air-con – and two no-frills yet charming wooden Caribbean-style cottages with balconies.

Negril Yacht Club (Map pp222-3; ☎ 957-9224; www.negrilyacht.com; r US$55-70) Not really a yacht club, this waterfront hotel offers 16 no-frills rooms with fans and cable TV. The open-air bar features the cheapest beer in town. It's a little timeworn, but boasts a semi-private beach, an anomaly on the West End.

Summerset Village (Map pp222-3; ☎ 957-4409; www.summersetvillage.net; Summerset Rd; r US$40-50, 1-/2-bedroom cottage US$40/80, Thatch House US$200; ❄ 🏊) Set about 300m inland on 3 hectares of landscaped grounds, this property offers casual seclusion. In addition to standard rooms, there are 10 air-con 'superior' rooms in a condo-style unit; eight rooms in a 'chateau'; one- and two-bedroom octagonal cottages; and a five-bedroom 'Thatch House' with a suite and kitchen, which can also be rented by the room. Summerset offers a shuttle to the beach. There's a restaurant and bar.

LTU Villas (Map pp222-3; ☎ 957-0382; www.negril.com/ltu/villas; villas with/without air-con US$65/50; P ❄) A tremendous bargain on the West End with 10 spacious, pleasant rooms with fridges, ceiling fans and cable TV. Each is tastefully furnished with two double beds and comfortable wicker couches and chairs. The upstairs rooms with dark wood cathedral ceilings are preferred. Most guests quickly fall into the habit of taking their meals at LTU Pub (p238).

Wendy Lindo's B&B (Map pp222-3; ☎ 804-2600; wendybbja@hotmail.com; Beaver Ave; d incl breakfast US$70) Another terrific bargain, this quaint guest house can be found about 9km south of Negril off William Hogg Blvd. Wendy, an expat from the Isles of Scilly, offers three rooms (two share a bath) in her charming house – a little piece of England built atop a coral outcrop with ocean views. Her cottage is full of antiques, cozy couches and porcelain china. The clean, airy rooms have private patios, ceiling fans, screened windows and hot water. Wendy's husband, John, offers a taxi service and island tours. There is a two-night minimum stay.

MIDRANGE

Heartbeat (Map pp222-3; ☎ 957-4329; www.heartbeatjamaica.com; studio US$44-95, duplex cottage US$55-110, house US$147; P 💻) A peaceful and delightful option on the top of the cliffs with thatched, all-hardwood octagonal cabins on pillars. You can also choose from self-sufficient studio apartments, a house sleeping eight and an attractively priced duplex cottage. They capture lots of light and have terraces. Some of the units have kitchenettes.

our pick **Banana Shout** (Map pp222-3; ☎ 957-0384; www.bananashout.com; 1-/2-/4-person cabins US$80/150/200; P) Occupying a particularly choice bit of clifftop turf, these cheerful green and orange cabins perched over the sea are offbeat and homey. Tastefully decorated with Jamaican and Haitian art, each has a ceiling fan, hammocks and kitchenette. Step outside to a dramatic stairway descending to a sea cave with sundeck and freshwater shower. Two of the cabins include loft bedrooms; one can accommodate up to six people.

Blue Cave Castle (Map pp222-3; ☎ 957-4845; www.bluecavecastle.com; s/d US$75/120; P) Providing perhaps the best view of Long Bay from the West End, this atmospheric, all-stone concoction attracts nudists, travel junkies and freethinkers. The 14 bedrooms are cavelike, but in a good way. Each is equipped with a CD player, ceiling fan and refrigerator; tower rooms open to the sea and superior rooms include air-con and cable TV. Stairs from the castle lead down to a blue cave.

Seastar Inn (Map pp222-3; ☎ 957-0553; www.seastarinn.com; s/d US$69/129; P) This peaceful modern place is run by a charming Canadian–Jamaican couple. It offers deluxe studio apartments with satellite TV, coffeemakers and safes. It has a restaurant and swim-up bar in the lush garden, plus a free beach shuttle and bicycles for rent (US$8/30 per hour/day). Cell phones are provided for guests and rates include breakfast.

Sundown Cottage (Map pp222-3; ☎ 361-1401, 990-9125; cottage US$80) This beguiling cottage adjacent to Tensing Pen is an ideal private spot for the couple seeking to get a groove on. A veritable home away from home, the fan-cooled one-bedroom nest has a kitchenette and sundeck, and a cheerful ambience colored by pastels. Tremendous value.

Moonlight Villa (Map pp222-3; ☎ 957-4838; www.moonlightvilla.com; s/d/tr US$80/100/120; P) This unheralded gem offers bright, spacious, exceedingly pleasant rooms with wide doors opening to glorious sea views. Each has cable TV, coffeemaker, ceiling fan, and a double and single bed. From a wide sunny veranda a stairway descends to the sea.

Xtabi (Map pp222-3; ☎ 957-0120; www.xtabi-negril.com; r US$83-90, cottages US$210, extra person US$25; P) This chic and casual hotel bills itself as 'the meeting place of the gods.' Its clientele is decidedly human, but the setting is truly divine. You can choose from rooms, simple garden cottages or quaint octagonal seafront bungalows perched atop the cliff. They're pleasingly appointed, if nothing fancy. The bar is lively and the restaurant appealing. It has sunning platforms built into the cliff. Children under the age of 15 are free. Massage is offered (US$40 per hour).

Home Sweet Home (Map pp222-3; ☎ 957-4478, in the USA 800-925-7418; www.homesweethomeresort.com; r US$110, ste US$175-$250, penthouse US$225;) Yet another cliffhanger with 12 rooms plus two suites, all with private balconies, fans and private showers. It features a clifftop bar and restaurant, a Jacuzzi and multi-tiered sundecks overhanging the teal-blue waters.

Hotel Samsara (Map pp222-3; ☎ 957-4395; www.negrilhotels.com/samsara; r US$85-95, pillar house US$110;) This popular option offers 50 modestly furnished rooms (some with air-con) and cottages, plus charming huts on stone pillars near the water's edge. A PADI scuba-diving center with multilingual dive masters is also on site (see p227). The bar hosts a daily sunset happy hour and occasional live concerts on the sundeck. An all-inclusive plan is available.

Coral Seas Cliff Resort (Map pp222-3; ☎ 957-3147, www.coralseasnegril.com; s/d US$70/60, studio s/d US$70/80;) These elegant villas with nicely furnished rooms and cable TV have less personality than their West End counterparts, but overall it's a well-run operation offering a high degree of comfort. The airy restaurant and bar are in well-tended grounds.

Drumville Cove (Map pp222-3; ☎ 957-4369; www.negril.com/dcmain; r with/without air-con US$75/65, cabin US$75) Its 14 rooms are cramped but clean and romantic, and the property is dramatically landscaped. There are also three cozy cabins, each with four beds (two in a loft) and a kitchenette. Drumville also boasts two pools, one saltwater.

Westender Inn (Map pp222-3; ☎ 957-4991; www.westenderinn.com; r/ste/villa US$69/99/119; P) Near the junction with William Hogg Blvd this old-timer has been given a welcome refurbishing. It offers 13 clean, well-appointed self-catering units set in handsome grounds. Rooms are adequately appointed and have patios with hammocks. A suite has a kitchenette, TV and Jacuzzi. There's a small beach as well as a bar and restaurant.

TOP END

Catcha Falling Star (Map pp222-3; ☎ 957-0390; www.catchajamaica.com; 1-/2-bedroom cottage US$135/250; P) In the inimitable West End style, these pleasant fan-cooled cottages – including several with two bedrooms – sit on the cliffs. Each is named for an astrological sign and comes with microwave oven, fridge, bar and double beds draped in mosquito netting. Breakfast is delivered to your veranda and is included in the rates; other meals by request. A tiered cliff affords easy access to the sea, where clothing-optional bathing can be enjoyed in a private cove. Popular masseuse Oya Oezcan offers her services here (US$70 per hour).

Rockhouse (Map pp222-3; ☎ 957-4373; www.rockhousehotel.com; r/studio/villa US$150/175/325; P) One of the West End's most beautiful and well-run hotels, with 13 thatched rondavels (two are 'premium villas') of pine and stone, plus 15 studios dramatically clinging to the cliffside above a small cove. Decor is basic yet romantic, with net-draped poster beds and strong Caribbean colors. Each cabin has a ceiling fan, refrigerator, safe, minibar, alfresco shower and wraparound veranda. Catwalks lead over the rocks to an open-sided, multi-level dining pavilion (with one of the best restaurants around; p238) overhanging the ocean. A dramatically designed pool sits atop the cliffs. Spa services, massage (US$70 per hour) and daily yoga classes (US$20) are offered. In the lounge there's a projection screen where Jamaican films are frequently shown.

Negril Escape Resort & Spa (Map pp222-3; ☎ 957-0392; www.negrilescape.com; s US$170-290, d US$180-300, tr US$220-340, ste US$ 490-580; P) The 10 spacious cottages here are named and decorated with a different 'ethnic' theme: Romancing the Kasbah, with its Arabian-style pillows and terra-cotta accents, suggests Morocco; the paper lanterns and bamboo blinds of Oriental Express hint at the Far East; Atlantis features mermaids on its murals. A hopping bar and an onsite branch of the Negril Scuba Centre round out the property.

Tensing Pen (Map pp222-3; ☎ 957-0387; www.tensingpen.com; cottages US$295-539, per week US$960-3060) Among the more acclaimed places is this tranquil, reclusive option with 12 thatched cottages on a hectare of land. Most are 'pillar houses' – an architectural style that has come to be associated with the West End – perched above the coral cliffs in natural gardens. All have exquisite bamboo and hardwood details, though otherwise rooms differ markedly in decor. Each cottage is equipped with a fridge. Guests take meals – perhaps Negril's best cuisine – in an extravagant structure inspired by the architecture of South African hunting lodges. Continental breakfast is included in the rates.

Llantrissant Beach House (Map pp222-3; ☎ 957-4259, 305-321-7458, in the USA 800-331-6951; www.beachcliff.com; 1-11 people US$530-600; P) One of the more charming options, this century-old two-story, four-bedroom home rests on a point near the roundabout. The vintage house – simply yet exquisitely furnished, with ceiling fans and louvered windows – comes fully staffed and includes satellite TV, stereo and fax access. A tennis court and two private beaches enhance the experience. Rates are calculated based on overall occupancy.

Jackie's on the Reef (Map pp222-3; ☎ 957-4997, in the USA 718-469-2785; www.jackiesonthereef.com; r or cottage per person US$175;) This tranquil option is 11km south of the Negril roundabout, just north of the intersection with William Hogg Blvd. It operates as a New Age haven focusing on spiritual renewal. A natural stone 'temple' is divided into four rooms, each with two handmade wooden beds and an outdoor shower and bathroom enclosed within your own private backyard. Massages are given on a veranda, and meditation, tai chi and spa treatments are offered. There's a small cooling pool set in the reef top. The facility is more rustic than the rates might suggest. Rates include breakfast, dinner and exercise class. Day packages (lunch and massage) are offered to nonguests.

our pick Caves (Map pp222-3; ☎ 957-0269, in the USA 800-688-7678, in the UK 0800-688-7681; www.thecavesresort.com; 3 nights all-inclusive cottage US$1995-2085; P) Perhaps the finest boutique hotel in Jamaica, and one beloved of the Hollywood elite (some of whom are helicoptered in), the Caves offers 10 handcrafted, individually styled one- and two-bedroom wood-and-thatch cottages set in lush gardens above the cave-riddled cliffs. Rooms feature exquisite hand-carved furniture, batik fabrics, one-of-a-kind art, CD player with CDs, plus ceiling fans and mosquito nets over the king- or queen-sized beds. Many have exquisite outside showers. Paths wind down to a free-form Jacuzzi studding the rock face, and then to a cave with molded benches where you can meditate to the reverberations of the waves (or have dinner if you order a day in advance). There's also a sauna, plus an Aveda spa. Rates include all meals and self-service bar.

EATING

Negril has more eclectic dining options than anywhere else in Jamaica. A surplus of rustic eateries along Long Bay and on the coast road around West End offer budget snacks and meals. Some food stands have no access to running water – take all commonsense health precautions. Unless otherwise noted, all 'Long Bay' restaurants are on Norman Manley Blvd and all 'West End' eateries are on the coast road, variously West End Rd, Lighthouse Rd and Ocean Dr.

Local delicacies (besides hallucinogenic mushroom omelettes and ganja muffins) include crab pickled in red peppers. Easier to find is pasta, pizza and plenty of good vegetarian (I-tal) fare.

A fully stocked grocery store in Negril Village is the **Hi-Lo Supermarket** (Map pp222-3; ☎ 957-4546), to the rear of Sunshine Village. Small grocery stalls dot Norman Manley Blvd; the best of several small groceries along West End Rd is **DJ's Place** (Map pp222-3; ☎ 957-0943).

Long Bay

BUDGET

Sonia's (Map p225; mains US$4-12; ⌚ 5:30am until 'anytime') Serving Miss Sonia's unique patties with fillings ranging from ackee and veggies to chicken and lobster.

Bourbon Beach (Map p225; ☎ 957-4405; mains US$2-7) Though it's best known for its live reggae concerts, those in the know swear by its jerk chicken. The sauce is thick and paste-like, and well complemented by a Red Stripe as you wait for a show.

Selina's (Map p225; ☎ 957-9519; mains US$5-12; ⌚ breakfast, lunch & dinner) An outstanding breakfast spot that enjoys many repeat customers for the callaloo and cheese omelettes, banana pancakes, killer smoothies and hand-roasted coffee. The lunch menu features salads and burgers, though the *pièce de résistance* is the cheese-and-vegetable quesadilla. Sundays see a jazz band that draws a mixed crowd of locals and visitors.

MIDRANGE

our pick **Lobster House** (Map p225; ☎ 957-4293; Sunrise Club; mains US$8-22; ⌚ breakfast, lunch & dinner) Renowned for its pink gnocchi in a parmesan cream and its signature lobster dishes, this congenial outdoor spot's brick oven has brought it the status of best pizzeria in town – if you need proof, try the Queen Aragosta pizza with lobster tails. Many, however, come for a cup of what is arguably the best espresso on the island, made from the proprietor's vintage 1961 Faema espresso machine.

Cosmo's (Map p225; ☎ 957-4784; mains US$5-18; ⌚ breakfast, lunch & dinner) A steadfast beach favorite with three thatched bars and dining areas near Long Bay Beach Park. Conch is the specialty here, whether steamed, curried or anchoring a hearty soup. Your host, Cosmo Brown, is also universally saluted for the pot of curried goat or oxtail that is perpetually simmering on the back burner.

Jamaica Tamboo (Map p225; ☎ 957-4282; mains US$6-24; ⌚ breakfast, lunch & dinner) Near Kuyaba, this is a bamboo-and-thatch two-story restaurant (lit by brass lanterns at night) with a varied menu that includes a breakfast of 'pigs in a blanket' (pancakes and sausage) and a fruit platter with ice cream. It also has snack foods such as deep-fried lobster niblets, sandwiches and pizzas.

Da Gino's (Map p225; ☎ 957-4918; Mariposa Hideaway mains US$14-15; ⌚ breakfast, lunch & dinner) Host Gino Travaini proudly serves fresh pasta and homemade bread plus delectable Italian fare in a secluded beachside garden setting with four open pavilions. Specialties include seafood linguine, scaloppini and lobster Reservations recommended.

Angela's (Map p225; ☎ 957-9793; Bar-B-Barn Hotel mains US$8-14; ⌚ breakfast, lunch & dinner) This upstairs restaurant with a veranda overlooking a slice of the beach features excellent Italian food from a menu divided into pizza, pasta salad, chicken and fish. Among the highlight are the pollo marsala, jerk salmon and lobste *fra diavolo.*

Hunan Garden (Map p225; ☎ 957-4369; Countr Country; mains US$6-18; ⌚ lunch & dinner) For a filling meal, head to this candlelit option serving a wide selection of Chinese dishes such as sliced duck with ginger and scallion. Cal ahead for takeout.

TOP END

Norma's on the Beach (Map p225; ☎ 957-4041; Sea Splas Resort; mains US$13-28; ⌚ dinner) The Negril branc of Norma Shirley's celebrated Jamaican culinary empire, this Norma's seems to hav escaped the hype surrounding her Kingsto flagship. The 'new world Caribbean' food at this stylish beach restaurant is just as adventurous. Expect to find the likes of lobster, Cornish game hen, jerk chicken and pasta as well as tricolored 'rasta pasta.' Lunches are more burger and tuna-melt oriented.

Le Vendôme (Map p225; ☎ 957-4648; Charela Inn; mains US$30-42; breakfast, lunch & dinner) This formal French restaurant is living proof that gourmet cuisine can also be healthful. Take your table on the terra-cotta terrace with a pleasant garden view and choose from classic French dishes like *duck à l'orange* and escargots Burgundy style, or regional creations like baked snapper, all prepared with locally grown vegetables and spices. There's a daily five-course gourmet dinner (US$26 to US$39) – or curried goat if you prefer Jamaican fare.

Gambino's Italian Restaurant (Map p225; ☎ 957-4170; Beachcomber Club & Spa; mains US$10-25; breakfast, lunch & dinner) This highly ranked restaurant spread across a capacious deck on the sand serves a wide range of pasta and other Italian classics, many seasoned with Jamaican spices. The fettuccine with lobster is good enough to distract you from the noise drifting over from Margaritaville next door.

Kuyaba on the Beach (Map p225; ☎ 957-4318; Kuyaba; mains US$18-30; breakfast, lunch & dinner) The name means 'Celebrate!' in the Arawak language, which is exactly what happens here each evening at sunset. This perennial beach favorite is well loved for its thatched open-air restaurant and heaps of ambience. The lunch menu features burgers, kebabs and gourmet sandwiches, plus superb pepper shrimp. For dinner the changing menu offers a wide range of pasta dishes, a great pepper steak, or the Cuban crab and pumpkin cakes with papaya mustard.

West End

BUDGET

Sweet Spice Restaurant (Map pp222-3; ☎ 957-4621; Sheffield Rd; mains US$3-16; lunch & dinner) This unassuming bright-blue clapboard house is a favorite among several authentic Jamaican restaurants in Sheffield Rd that are frequented by locals. Portions are heaped, prices are inexpensive and the food authentic. The menu includes curried goat and fish, conch steak and pepper steak. No alcohol is served but there are plenty of fruit juices.

Royal Kitchen Vegetarian Café (Map pp222-3; ☎ 775-0386; mains US$4-7; breakfast, lunch & dinner) This welcoming roadside I-tal eatery is popular with local Rastafarians and those who come to collect their pearls of wisdom. The fare – strictly vegetarian – is served on simple tables where you are sure to make friends with inquisitive passersby. The juices are especially good.

Serious Chicken (Map pp222-3; ☎ 464-2720; mains US$2-6; breakfast, lunch & dinner) Aptly named, this friendly roadside spot is devoted to the bird, serving it up in salads, stews, curries and barbecue dishes in a thatched hut. You can't go wrong here, and if you stick around at night you're bound to be invited to join a game of dominoes.

Sips & Bites (Map pp222-3; ☎ 957-0188; mains US$4-20; breakfast, lunch & dinner Sun-Fri) This large, welcoming open-air restaurant serves classic Jamaican fare including oxtail, curried goat, brown stew lobster and conch steaks. Wash it down with the day's special natural juice. Starting bright and early, hearty Jamaican breakfasts are served.

our pick **3 Dives Jerk Centre** (Map pp222-3; ☎ 957-0845; quarter/half chicken US$4/7; noon-midnight) It's no small tribute to 3 Dives that its jerk overshadows its reputation for lengthy waits (sometimes over an hour). Fortunately, the chefs are more than happy to let you peek into the kitchen, where there's bound to be a pile of super-hot Scotch bonnet peppers threatening to spontaneously combust, and you can sip cheap Red Stripe on the cliffs at the end of a small garden. This is also the site of the annual Negril Jerk Festival (p18).

Mi Yard (Map pp222-3; ☎ 957-4442; mains US$2-7; 24hr) This economical choice provides a good breakfast spot with omelettes, ackee and saltfish and other hearty fare. Later in the day – and all night long – the classic Jamaican menu features fish and chips, brown-stewed fish and fried chicken. Dine in the garden or on a shady patio.

Erica's Place (Map pp222-3; ☎ 889-3109; mains US$2.50-15; lunch & dinner) This simple shack noted for its lobster has a long history of serving good, cheap Jamaican fare. The stewed chicken is highly recommended.

Miss Brown's (Map pp222-3; ☎ 957-9217; Sheffield Rd; mains US$4-28; 6:30am-midnight) Two kilometers east of the roundabout, this place serves 'mushroom daiquiris,' mushroom omelettes and mushroom tea. Be warned – *they're hallucinogenic*. It also serves well-priced standard Jamaican dishes.

MIDRANGE

Lighthouse Inn (Map pp222-3; ☎ 957-4052; mains US$10-20; ⏰ lunch & dinner) Aka 'Busha's Place,' this recommended eatery features splendid appetizers such as mozzarella with tomatoes, goat cheese and olives. Meals are prepared with a European touch and include an excellent seafood fondue, lobster in curry, and red snapper stuffed with callaloo. The lively tropical decor is enhanced by candlelight.

LTU Pub (Map pp222-3; ☎ 957-0382; mains US$9-18; ⏰ 7:30am-midnight) Providing a perfect setting for a sunset dinner, this small clifftop open-air bar and restaurant features an eclectic menu with Jamaican dishes, delicious creations like chicken with callaloo and cream, an array of steaks and burgers, and quite possibly the only schnitzel in town. Just south of Rick's Café, it's a favorite haunt of expats and their local friends.

Xtabi (Map pp222-3; ☎ 957-0120; mains US$8-24; ⏰ breakfast, lunch & dinner) Offering a marvelous cliff-face setting that you will want to explore before and after your meal, this well-established restaurant features a varied and reasonably priced menu mixing seafood and Jamaican and continental dishes. Try the lobster Benedict or the conch burger.

Rick's Café (Map pp222-3; ☎ 957-0380; mains US$20-30; ⏰ lunch & dinner) You'll join the touristy throng at this ever-popular West End institution. The somewhat pricey menu features steaks, fresh seafood and Cajun fare. The loud music precludes an intimate meal, but if you're in the mood for a party – or a dip in the pool between courses – this place fits the bill. While you eat, local divers try to outdo each other from the 10m-tall cliffs.

TOP END

Rockhouse Restaurant & Bar (Map pp222-3; ☎ 957-4373; mains US$15-30; ⏰ breakfast, lunch & dinner) Lamplit at night, this pricey yet relaxed spot boasts outstanding nouvelle Jamaican treats such as vegetable tempura with lime and ginger, specialty pastas and daily specials like watermelon spare ribs and blackened mahi-mahi with mango chutney. At the very least, you should stop by for a sinful bananas Foster.

Ivan's Bar (Map pp222-3; ☎ 957-0390; Catcha Falling Star; mains US$10-32; ⏰ lunch & dinner) Although the service can be a little bewildering, there's no doubt about the food at Catcha Falling Star's restaurant overlooking the sea. Papaya Ahoy is an excellent 'boat' of papaya filled with shrimp or snapper drizzled in a coconut sauce. Coconut pimento chicken and Caribbean crabcakes also hit the spot.

our pick **Hungry Lion** (Map pp222-3; ☎ 957-4486; mains US$12-30; ⏰ dinner) Renovated in late 2007, this brightly painted spot serves intricate fare from a changing menu of mostly fish and vegetarian dishes, like a vegetarian shepherd's pie or quesadillas stuffed with shrimp and cheese. The alfresco rooftop dining room is tastefully decorated with earth tones and original art. The music is trancelike, and the bar serves an extensive menu of cocktails and juices.

DRINKING & ENTERTAINMENT

Negril gives Kingston a run for its money when it comes to the after-hours pursuits of cocktails, dancing and, best of all, white-hot live reggae music. There are dozens of bars, one big nightclub and several venues on the beach where live acts keep things throbbing well into the night. Things *really* hop during rabble-rousing spring break.

Bars

The booze starts flowing each evening along Long Bay in time to toast the setting sun, when many bars offer happy-hour incentives to lure you in. In the West End, bars are lively in the early evening before petering out as the beach bars take over.

LONG BAY

Jimmy Buffett's Margaritaville (Map p225; ☎ 957-4467), the most ostentatious of the beach bars, sustains a spring-break vibe all year long. There are big-screen TVs, a basketball court, trampolines in the sea, volleyball, swing hammocks and multiple bars with entertainment. It hosts wet T-shirt contests and the like, and has nightly specials, including karaoke on Sunday.

Most of the bars along the beach are, quite frankly, interchangeable, offering boozers front-row deck chairs for the sunset and barstools for the evening. **Alfred's Ocean Palace** (Map p225; ☎ 967-4735), **Cosmo's** (Map p225; ☎ 957-4330), **Legends Beach Resort** (Map p225; ☎ 957-3834) and **Risky Business** (Map p225; ☎ 957-3918) compete with Margaritaville with satellite TVs, pool tables and beach parties. All the above fence off their beach sections at night and charge a cover for entry.

Sunrise Club (Map p225; ☎ 957-4293), at the hotel of that name, has a cool bar if you want to escape the beach mayhem. All the live-music venues listed below are also terrific bars, even when there are no acts on stage.

WEST END

Rick's Café (Map pp222-3; ☎ 957-0380) A little pricey and the reggae cover band really lays on the schmaltz, yet this two-story restaurant, with sun deck, rope swing and cliff diving platform still has its kitschy charm. To be sure, it *is* shamelessly touristy (it's been a *long* time since the Rolling Stones have stopped by), but the party-hearty vibe makes Rick's the proper spot from which to launch a big night out.

Sands (Map pp222-3) Even if you can't afford to stay at Caves, you can still join sunset cocktails. Sadly, only guests are allowed to stay after 7:30pm.

Pirate's Cave (Map pp222-3; ☎ 957-0925) Another great hot spot for sunset, Pirate's starts off a little more mellow than the nearby hotel bars but attracts more locals and gathers strength as the evening progresses.

LTU Pub (Map pp222-3; ☎ 957-0382) A friendly and comfortable clifftop haunt centered on a small yet lively tiki bar: the perfect place to strike up a conversation at sunset or enjoy a Bloody Mary before noon.

Mi Yard (Map pp222-3; ☎ 957-4442; 🕑 24hr) Popular with locals, this place draws a late-night crowd into the wee hours, when you can swig shots of white rum and slap down dominoes with locals.

Mia's Winebar (Map pp222-3; ☎ 957-0694) This newcomer eschews the local focus on cocktails and beer (of course, you can get those too) and offers free internet access with each glass.

Nightclubs

Jungle (Map p225; ☎ 957-4005; admission US$10; 🕑 Wed-Sun) A happening disco and the only one you'll find outside of an all-inclusive resort. It's not the most urbane place, with its tacky decor, but the DJs *definitely* know what they're doing; during the high season guest talent from Miami and New York regularly takes command of the turntables. The best nights are Thursday, when women enter free before midnight, and Saturday. There's not much action before midnight.

Triple-X (Sheffield Rd; admission US$5; 🕑 daily) is the go-go club of choice in Negril.

Nonguests can obtain passes (US$25-50) for entry to the discos in the following upscale all-inclusive resorts: Sandals Negril, Hedonism II, Couples, Beaches Negril and Grand Lido. Once inside the gates you can booze and party to your heart's content without having to shell out another cent.

Live Music

Negril's reggae concerts are legendary, with live performances every night in peak season, when there's sure to be some big talent in town. Several venues offer weekly jams, with a rotation system so they all get a piece of the action. The really big-name acts usually perform at **MXIII** (Map pp222-3; West End Rd) and **Hotel Samsara** (Map pp222-3; ☎ 957-4395).

You will also find sound-system jams where the DJs ('selectors') play shatteringly loud music – usually dancehall with some Euro-disco – on speakers the size of railroad boxcars. The most popular jams are in the Negril Hills, near Little Bay.

Information about upcoming events is posted on streetside poles.

The following venues stage free reggae concerts.

Bourbon Beach (Map p225; ☎ 957-4405; 🕑 Tue, Fri & Sun) The best spot for live reggae on Long Bay, Bourbon Beach occasionally hosts big name acts. Cover US$5 to US$10.

Alfred's Ocean Palace (Map p225; ☎ 957-4669; 🕑 Tue, Fri & Sun) This Negril institution is one of the oldest beach bars. Shows begin around 10pm and continue deep into the night. Cover US$4.

Roots Bamboo (Map p225; ☎ 957-4479; 🕑 Wed & Sun) With a rotating roster of musicians anchored by a rock-solid 'riddim' section, the house Hurricane Band shows tourists a thing or two about roots music here each Wednesday. Sundays see a free jazz show. Cover US$5 to US$10.

De Buss (Map p225; ☎ 957-4405; 🕑 Mon, Thu & Sat) The house band here is well loved and draws a sizable crowd.

Risky Business (Map p225; ☎ 957-4735; 🕑 Mon, Thu & Sat) This place goes all out during spring break. Occasionally, jazz is featured on Wednesday night. Cover US$12.

SHOPPING

Locals hawk carvings, woven caps, hammocks, jewelry, macramé bikinis, T-shirts and crafts on the beach and along West End Rd. Competition is fierce. Haggling is part of the fun. Don't be hustled into a purchase you don't want.

There are three main crafts centers: **Rutland Point Craft Centre** (Map p225; Norman Manley Blvd) opposite Couples Negril, the **Negril Crafts Market** (Map p225; Norman Manley Blvd) just north of Plaza de Negril and **A Fi Wi Plaza** (Map pp222-3; Negril Village, West End Rd).

Times Square Plaza (Map p225; ☎ 957-9263; Norman Manley Blvd), **Plaza de Negril** (Map pp222-3), **Coral Seas Plaza** (Map pp222-3) and **Sunshine Village** (Map pp222-3; West End Rd) have good souvenir shops. Times Square Plaza has duty-free and jewelry stores, including **Tajmahal's** (Map p225; ☎ 675-4579), and it has **Cigar World** (Map p225; ☎ 957-3299), selling Cuban cigars.

Kush Art Gallery (Map pp222-3; ☎ 957-0728; West End Rd) sells Wassi Art pottery and other quality crafts, as does the **Kuyaba Arts and Crafts Boutique** (Map p225; ☎ 957-4318; Kuyaba, Norman Manley Blvd) at the Kuyaba hotel. **Collectibles Art Gallery** (Map pp222-3; ☎ 957-4486; The Hungry Lion, West End Rd) and **Ja-Ja Originals** (Map p225; ☎ 957-4326; Coco La Palm Hotel, Norman Manley Blvd) are traditional galleries showing original painting and sculpture by noted local artists.

GETTING THERE & AWAY

Negril Aerodrome (☎ 957-5016), at Bloody Bay about 11km north of Negril Village, is served by the domestic charter company **TimAir** (Map p225; ☎ 957-5374; www.timair.net), an 'air taxi' service offering on-demand charter flights for small groups going to Montego Bay, Ocho Rios, Port Antonio and Kingston. Fares start at US$66 per person between Negril and Montego Bay. See p292 for more details on domestic charter service.

Dozens of minibuses and route taxis run between Negril and Montego Bay. The 1½-hour journey costs about US$5, and you may need to change vehicles in Lucea. Minibuses and route taxis also leave for Negril from Donald Sangster International Airport in Montego Bay (the price is negotiable, but expect to pay about US$10). Alternatively, buses operated by tour companies make the run for around US$35.

In Negril, buses bound for Montego Bay (US$3), Savanna-la-Mar (US$3) and Kingston (US$12, about four hours) depart from the **transportation center** (Map pp222-3; Sheffield Rd), 1km east of the roundabout. There's an **inspector's office** (🕑 7am-6pm) inside the gate, where you can ask for the departure point of the bus you're seeking.

The tour companies **Caribic Vacations** (Map p225; ☎ 957-3309) and **Tropical Tours** (Map p225; ☎ 957-4110) offer minibus transfers between Montego Bay airport and Negril (about US$35 each way).

A licensed taxi between Montego Bay and Negril will cost about US$60. In MoBay, call the **Jamaica Union of Travelers Association** (JUTA; ☎ 979-0778).

GETTING AROUND

Negril stretches along more than 16km of shoreline, and it can be a withering walk. At some stage you'll most likely need transportation. Upscale resorts at the north end of Long Bay have shuttles to the village, and several hotels on the West End run shuttles to the beach.

There's no scheduled bus service between the airstrip and hotels. A taxi costs about US$15 for a journey between the airport and Negril Village or to any point in between.

Minibuses and route taxis cruise Norman Manley Blvd and West End Rd. You can flag them down anywhere. The fare between any two points should never be more than US$1 to US$2.

Local car-rental companies include **Jus Jeep** (Map pp222-3; ☎ 957-0094; West End Rd) and **Vernon's Car Rentals** (Plaza de Negril Map pp222-3; ☎ 957-4522; Norman Manley Blvd Map p225; ☎ 957-4354).

More than a dozen places along Norman Manley Blvd and West End Rd rent motorcycles (US$40 to US$50 per day), scooters (US$25 to US$35) and bicycles (US$10). For bicycle rentals, try **Wright's Bike Rental** (Map p225; ☎ 957-4908; Norman Manley Blvd) or **Negril Yacht Club** (Map pp222-3; ☎ 957-9224; West End Rd). The latter also offers scooter rentals, as does **Dependable Bike Rental** (Map p225; Vernon's Car Rentals, Norman Manley Blvd; ☎ 957-4354).

Tourist taxis display a red license plate. Fares are regulated by the government (about US$2 per 3km) but few drivers use meters. Negotiate your fare before stepping into the cab. Your hotel will call a cab for you, or you can order taxis from **JUTA** (☎ 957-9197). There are taxi stands at the Negril Crafts Market and in front of Coral Seas Plaza.

NEGRIL TO TRYALL

Northeast from Negril, the new A1 expressway leads to Tryall and on to Montego Bay. The only town of note is Lucea and the main draw in the area is Mayfield Falls.

GREEN ISLAND HARBOUR

Immediately north of Negril, the A1 swings around a wide expanse of swampland – the Great Morass. After 16km you pass the shores of a deep cove – Green Island Harbour – where pirogues line the thin, gray-sand shore. Minibuses and route taxis going between Negril and Lucea stop in Green Island Harbour.

Half Moon Beach (☎ 957-6467; admission US$1; 8am-10pm) is a beautiful, hassle-free stretch of sand beloved by locals and families. Part of the Negril Marine Park, there are healthy reefs just offshore and no motorized watercraft. Nudism is permitted.

Rhodes Hall Plantation (☎ 957-6334), 3km southwest of Green Island Harbour, is a picturesque, 220-hectare fruit-and-coconut plantation with several thatched bars and a restaurant backing a small but attractive beach where hot mineral springs bubble up. Follow the beach west and you may see crocodiles at the mouth of the river. Horseback riding is offered (US$50/60 per one/two hours).

Sleeping & Eating

Half Moon Beach (☎ 957-6467; camping US$10, cabins from US$50) Offers camping and five simple but spacious wooden cabins with bare-bones furnishings. The thatched restaurant serves sandwiches, burgers and simple Jamaican snacks (mains US$3 to US$5).

Rhodes Hall Plantation (☎ 957-6334; www.rhodesresort.com; 2-person/family cottage US$95/330;) Has two handsome beachfront cottages with private bath with hot water, plus kitchen.

You can eat cheaply at the roadside jerk stalls at Green Island Harbour.

BLENHEIM

This tiny hamlet, 6km inland of Davis Cove, is important as the birthplace of national hero Alexander Bustamante, the island's first prime minister. 'Busta' is honored with a memorial ceremony each August 6. The rustic three-room wooden shack where Bustamante was born has been reconstructed as the **Sir Alexander Bustamante Museum** (☎ 922-1287; admission free; 9am-5pm). It includes memorabilia telling of the hero's life. It has public toilets and a picnic area to the rear.

LUCEA

pop 7500

'Lucy,' as the town is commonly known, is built around a harbor ringed by hills on three sides. Forty kilometers equidistant from Negril and Montego Bay, Lucea is small enough for visitors to walk everywhere.

The once-bustling port abounds in old limestone-and-timber structures in 'Caribbean vernacular' style, with gingerbread wood trim, clapboard frontages and wide verandas. The oldest dates to the mid-1700s. Lucea has appeared in several films, including *Cool Runnings* and *Wide Sargasso Sea*. The **Hanover Historical Society** (☎ 956-2584; Watson Taylor Dr) is active in the town's preservation.

In a yellow house about 100m east of the Texaco gas station in the center of town, the well-known artist Lloyd Hoffstead has a **gallery** (☎ 956-2241; Seaview Dr; 9am-5pm Mon-Fri), which displays his paintings and sculptures.

Information

Hanover Parish Library (☎ 956-2205; Internet access per 30min US$1) West of downtown.

Lucea Hospital (☎ 956-2233, 956-3836) On the headland behind Hanover Parish Church, with an emergency department.

National Commercial Bank (☎ 956-2348; Main St)

Police station (☎ 956-2222; Sir Alexander Bustamante Sq, Watson Taylor Dr)

Scotiabank (☎ 956-2553) Faces the roundabout in the center of town.

Sights

Sir Alexander Bustamante Square is centered on a small fountain fronting the handsome courthouse. Note the vintage 1932 fire engine beside the courthouse.

The town's restored **courthouse** (☎ 956-2280; Watson Taylor Dr) has limestone balustrades and a clapboard upper story topped by a clock tower supported by Corinthian columns. The clock was sent to Lucea in 1817 by mistake – it was actually intended for the Caribbean island of St Lucia. It has supposedly worked without a hitch ever since.

On the east side of the square is **Cleveland Stanhope market**, which bustles on Saturdays. A walk north up the main frontage road curls past some of Lucea's finest historical houses, many in a state of near decrepitude, and deposits you atop the headland with a fine view east over Lucea Harbour. At the hillcrest is **Hanover Parish Church**, established in 1725. It's architecturally uninspired but has several interesting monuments; a Jewish section of the walled cemetery recalls the days when Lucea had a vibrant Jewish community.

A side road that begins 200m west of the church leads to the **Hanover Museum** (☎ 956-2584; admission US$2; 8:30am-5pm Mon-Thu, 8:30am-

4pm Fri), a tiny affair housed in an old police barracks. Exhibits include prisoners' stocks, a wooden bathtub and a miscellany of pots, lead weights and measures. It also has a tiny gift shop, toilets and a snack bar.

On the headland beyond the church is **Rusea High School**, a venerable Georgian-style red-brick building constructed in 1843 as an army barracks. The overgrown remains of **Fort Charlotte** overlook the channel a short distance beyond Rusea High School. It's named after Queen Charlotte, wife of King George III of England. The octagonal fortress still boasts cannons in its embrasures.

Sleeping & Eating

West Palm Hotel (☎ 956-2321; Fort Charlotte St; r with/without air-con US$35/30; ❄) A musty old wooden building behind Hanover Parish Church that has 23 simple rooms with basic furnishings and private bathrooms with hot water. It has a modest bar and restaurant.

Global Villa Guest House (☎ 956-2916; globalvilla@hotmail.com; r US$50-60; ❄) Eight kilometers west of town on the A1, it offers 10 nicely furnished, clean rooms with louvered windows and tiled floors. There's a good restaurant serving hearty Jamaican fare.

Tommy's Restaurant (☎ 956-3106; Main St; mains US$2-10; 🕑 breakfast, lunch & dinner) Between the town square and Hanover Parish Church, this is an ever-popular place that serves healthy natural foods, including tofu dishes, steamed fish and natural juices.

Vital Ital (☎ 956-2218; Seaview Dr; mains US$3-5; 🕑 9am-'whenever') East of town beside the harbor, a vivaciously decorated shack serving 'culture cooked foods' like tofu and gluten, stewed greens and peas and a refreshing tonic of sorrel and ginger.

Getting There & Away

Buses, minibuses and route taxis arrive and depart Lucea from the open ground opposite the market. Lucea is a midway terminus for public vehicles traveling between Montego Bay and Negril, and you may need to change vehicles here. A bus between Lucea and MoBay or Negril costs about US$3. A minibus or route taxi costs about US$5.

MAYFIELD FALLS

The Dolphin Head Mountains rise inland of Moskito Cove and are known for their cascades. The grandest of these are at Mayfield, near Pennycooke, about 16km south of Moskito Cove (6km east of Lucea). Here, a series of 21 falls and pools beckons you to take a refreshing dip in any of the delightful swimming holes, which are shaded by glades of bamboo. You can even swim through a cave.

Original Mayfield Falls & Mineral Springs (☎ 957-4864; www.mayfieldfalls.com; admission US$10, with lunch US$25) is a working tropical farm and tour attraction. To reach the cascades you'll cross a bamboo-and-log bridge then follow the sun-dappled river course, clambering over river stones. You can learn about ackee, breadfruits and other Jamaican fruits, vegetables and flowers, and even join in traditional African music and dance during show time (2:30pm Tuesday and Friday). You can book a tour (per person US$65) at the office in Negril on Norman Manley Blvd, or through many local hotels; the price includes transportation, lunch and refreshment.

Getting There & Away

From the A1, take the road inland from Moskito Cove via Cascade. The route is signed, but there are several turnoffs and the route is quite complex; you should ask your way to be sure. You can also reach Mayfield Falls from Tryall or Hopewell via Pondside, or by turning north at Savanna-la-Mar and taking the Banbury or Amity Cross routes (about 24km) along a road that is deplorably potholed.

Caribic Vacations (in Montego Bay ☎ 953-9896, in Negril 957-3309) offers excursions (US$65).

NEGRIL TO SAVANNA-LA-MAR

Tourism has been slow to develop along the southern shore of Westmoreland, a parish dependent on the sugar industry, with gritty Savanna-la-Mar the only town of any import.

Roads fan out from Savanna-la-Mar through the Westmoreland Plains. This flat, mountain-rimmed area, planted almost entirely in sugarcane, is drained by the Cabarita River, which feeds swamplands at its lower reaches. The fishing is good, and a few crocodiles may still live in more secluded swampy areas, alongside an endemic fish – the 'God-a-me' – that can live out of water in moist, shady spots. The river is navigable by small boat for 19km.

Several beaches with active fishing communities provide an insight into Jamaican life.

LITTLE BAY & AROUND

Southeast of Retirement, a badly eroded side road loops down to **Homers Cove** (locals call it 'Brighton Beach') and, immediately east, Little Bay, with handsome beaches and peaceful bathing. Little Bay is imbued with the kind of laid-back feel that pervaded Negril before the onset of commercialization. It's a great place to commune with Rastas and other Jamaicans who live by a carefree axiom in ramshackle homes, dependent on fishing and their entrepreneurial wits. The area is popular for reggae and dancehall sound systems that lure the local crowd from miles around.

Bob Marley used to hang out here in the 1970s. **Bob Marley's house** still stands beside **Bob Marley's Spring**, where he bathed; it's now a private house.

A mangrove swamp extends east of Little Bay, beyond which lies the fishing community of **Hope Wharf** and a long sliver of white sand called **Lost Beach**. Crocodiles and marine turtles can be found here. Dolphins and humpback whales frequent the waters offshore year-round.

The annual **Uncle Sam's Donkey Derby** is held on Little Bay beach the first Sunday in February.

Sleeping & Eating

Garden Park (☎ 867-2897; per tent US$10, cabin with shared/private bathroom US$20/25) Also known as Uncle Sam's, this little budget heaven on the cliffs of Little Bay offers camping amid shady almond trees as well as rustic cabins and communal showers and toilets. Its atmospheric eatery – a gaily decorated bamboo bar festooned with girlie posters, crab shells and other miscellany – serves 'dapper' soup and other simple fisherfolk fare. Uncle Sam's also puts on sound-system events. Full-moon parties are held in the Bat Cave, when a cavern is lit up with hundreds of candles, the reggae is cranked up and everyone parties down.

Romie's Ocean View (☎ 442-3721; info@RomiesOceanView.com; Homers Cove; cottage US$30) Simple yet charming wooden cottages with verandas and bathrooms with solar-heated water. Bicycle and snorkel-gear rentals are offered, as are guided excursions. Jamaican meals (US$3 to US$5) are served.

Lost Beach Resort (☎ 640-1111, in the USA 800-626-5678; www.lostbeach.com; cabin US$59, 1-bedroom apt US$99-129, 2-bedroom apt US$129-149, 3-bedroom apt US$149-179; P ⊠ 💻 🏊) With a wide, sandy beach, this quiet hotel is good for families who want a more peaceful environment than Negril can offer. The modern hotel features exotic hardwood furnishings in 14 spacious one- to three-bedroom suites with kitchenettes. Two thatch-and-wood beach cabins have loft bedrooms and kitchenettes. There is a large sundeck, kids' playground, Jacuzzi and a huge library with pool table. Rates depend on the season.

FROME

Frome lies at the heart of Jamaica's foremost sugar estate, in the center of a rich alluvial plain. The area is dominated by the Frome **sugar-processing factory** (☎ 955-6080), on the B9 north of Savanna-la-Mar and south of the town of Grange Hill. Constructed in 1938, the factory became the setting for a violent nationwide labor dispute. During the Depression of the 1930s many small factories were bought out by the West Indies Sugar Company. Unemployed workers from all over the island converged here seeking work. Although workers were promised a dollar a day, the men who were hired received only 15 cents a day and women only 10 cents. Workers went on strike for higher pay, passions ran high and violence erupted. When the crowds rioted and set fire to the cane fields, the police responded by firing into the crowd, killing four people. The whole island exploded in violent clashes. The situation was defused when labor activist Alexander Bustamante mediated the dispute. His efforts gave rise to the island's first mass labor unions and the first organized political party, under his leadership (see p31).

A **monument** at a crossroads north of the factory gates reads: 'To Labour leader Alexander Bustamante and the Workers for their courageous fight in 1938. On behalf of the Working People of Jamaica.'

Free tours of the factory can be arranged by reservation.

Frome also boasts two attractive churches, including **St Barnabas Anglican Church**, in a vaguely Teutonic style.

ROARING RIVER & BLUE HOLE

If you're looking for a brief escape from the fun-in-the sun ethos of Negril, spend an hour or two down the caves at **Roaring River Park** (cave tours adult/child US$15/8; 8am-5pm). This natural beauty spot contains mineral waters that gush up from the ground in a meadow full of water hyacinths and water lilies. A stone aqueduct takes off some of the water, which runs turquoise-jade. Steps lead up a cliff face gashed by the mouth of a subterranean passage lit by electric lanterns (you can enter the caves only with guides from the cooperative). Inside, a path with handrails leads down to chambers full of stalagmites and stalactites. Take your swimming gear to sit in the mineral spring that percolates up inside the cave, or in the 'bottomless' blue hole outside the cave. Harmless fruit bats roost in the recesses.

As you arrive an official guide will meet you to show the way to the ticket office, and then around the gardens and cave; ignore the touts who congregate outside posing as tour guides. It has secure parking, a reception lounge, changing rooms, playground and crafts shops. A restaurant serves cheap Jamaican fare, as does Chill Out View, on a hill overlooking the burbling spring.

The lane then continues beyond Roaring River for about 1km uphill through the village to **Blue Hole Gardens** (918-1341; www.jamaicaescapes.com/bluehole; admission US$8), a beautiful sinkhole that is surrounded by a landscaped garden full of ginger torch and heliconia on the private property of a Rasta called Esau. Entry is overpriced, but grants a chance for a cool dip with the fish in the turquoise waters. The source of the Roaring River is about 400m further up the road, where the water foams up from beneath a matting of foliage.

This is also a quintessential counterculture lifestyle retreat that offers two very rustic but charming **cottages** (US$40-80) set in gardens at the edge of the tumbling brook (the 'waterhouse' cabin sits *over* the stream). Bamboo-enclosed toilets and showers are alfresco. Here you can also rent 'Esau's Mountain Retreat,' which is a separate cabin in the hills with fully equipped kitchen. Camping is US$10.

Also here is **Lovers Café** (mains US$3-8), which is known for its veggie feast, I-tal dishes, fruit juices and herbal teas.

Getting There & Away

Roaring River is at Shrewsbury Estate, about 2km north of the main crossroads in Petersfield (8km northeast of Savanna-la-Mar). You can catch a bus in Savanna-la-Mar as far as Petersfield. From there it's a hot walk or rough ride down the potholed road through the cane fields. Route taxis and coasters also run to Roaring River from Petersfield (US$1).

Organized tours to Roaring River are offered by companies in Negril (around US75).

FERRIS CROSS & PARADISE PARK

Ferris Cross is a major crossroads hamlet on the A2, 8km east of Savanna-la-Mar. Here the A2 turns southeast and follows the coast to Black River and the south coast. Another road – the B8 – leads northeast to Galloway, where it begins a steep climb to Whithorn and Montego Bay.

About a mile west of Ferris Cross, **Paradise Park** (955-2675; admission US$5; 9am-4:30 Mon-Sat) is an 800-hectare farm, where you can ride horses along the sand (US$30 per hour) and swim in a local creek.

SAVANNA-LA-MAR

pop 20,000

Savanna-la-Mar is the largest town in western Jamaica and the capital of Westmoreland parish. 'Sav,' as it is locally known, offers few attractions.

Sav is virtually a one-street town. Its axis is 2km-long Great George St. It was founded around 1730 and grew modestly as a sugar-shipping port during the colonial era. It has an unremarkable history except where Mother Nature is concerned, as numerous hurricanes have swept the town.

Information

National Commercial Bank (955-2623; Great George St)

Police station (918-1865; Great George St) Near the courthouse.

Post office (955-9295; Great George St)

Savanna-la-Mar Hospital (955-2133; emergency service 24hr) On the A2 on the northeast side of town.

Scotiabank (955-2601; Great George St)

Sights

The English colonialists never completed the **Savanna-la-Mar Fort** at the foot of Great George St. Parts of it collapsed into the swamps within a few years of being built. Its innards form a small cove where locals swim. A bustling daily market, specializing in vegetables and local fish, can be found by the fort.

The most interesting building is the **courthouse**, built in 1925 at the junction of Great George and Rose Sts, where there's a fountain made of cast iron, inscribed with the words, 'Keep the pavements dry.'

St George's Parish Church, opposite, was built in 1905. It's uninspired, but has a stately pipe organ that was dedicated in 1914.

At the north end of town by the roundabout known as Hendon Circle is the very handsome **Manning's School**, built in 1738 and named after a Westmoreland planter, Thomas Manning.

Sleeping & Eating

Lochiel Guest House (☎ 955-9344; Sheffield Rd; r US$20-30) On the A2, 2km east of town, this is another old stone-and-timber, two-story great house that looks delightful from the outside. Inside it's a bit run down, though some of its 14 rooms are appealing. All have utilitarian furniture and hot water in private bathrooms. Eight rooms in a modern annex offer better decor.

J's Jerk Centre (☎ 918-0159; 10 Rose St; mains US$3-5; lunch & dinner) A tiny outdoor place serving great jerk chicken and festival (a fried biscuit shaped like a sausage) plus steamed fish.

Hammond's Pastry (☎ 955-2870; 18 Great George St; mains US$1.50-5) Serves patties, pastries and the best traditional coco-bread around.

Old Fort Club Restaurant (☎ 955-3362; mains US$1.50-7) In the fort at the foot of Great George St. Serves Jamaican staples such as curried goat.

You can buy fresh fish and produce from the market at the base of Great George St, but the sanitary conditions aren't great.

Getting There & Away

Buses, minibuses and route taxis operate frequently along the A2/B8 between Montego Bay (US$3) and Negril (US$3). Public vehicles also depart on a regular basis from the Beckford St transportation center in Kingston (US$10, three hours).

South Coast & Central Highlands

Untrampled by the lockstep march of the resort-catered hordes, this region serves up an unspoilt Jamaica. The area is awash with natural splendor – majestic rivers, lugubrious swamps, gorgeous waterfalls, looming mountains, ominous cliffs, sandy beaches. It's one of the island's great ironies that a region so unsullied by mass tourism is so packed with sights and activities.

Atmospheric port town, Black River, is a gateway to the Great Morass, a swampy marsh and forest known as much for its thriving population of crocodiles as for its mangrove ecosystem. The surrounding coastal lands boast natural wonders such as the Font Hill Beach Park and Wildlife Sanctuary, Lover's Leap and one of Jamaica's loveliest waterfalls, YS Falls, and man-made attractions, like the Appleton Rum Estate and the Pelican Bar, an offshore restaurant perched on stilts. Yet the enduring appeal rests in the region's communities, from the hillside Maroon town of Accompong to the exceptionally hospitable beachside retreat of Treasure Beach to such vibrant fishing villages as Whitehouse and Alligator Pond.

The cool central highlands of Manchester parish are similarly disconnected from tourist trappings. You'll find rolling hills, bucolic valleys grazed by cattle in fields fringed by hedgerows and stone walls, and mountains where clouds drift through alpine forests of pine and oak. This is the breadbasket of the nation, supplying melons, peppers, scallions, carrots, tomatoes and corn to the entire island. Christiana and Mandeville, once the favored retreats of wealthy Jamaicans and Europeans, are prosperous communities providing a peaceful escape from the heat and hullabaloo of the coast.

HIGHLIGHTS

- **Treasure Beach** Slow down the pace at this serene, laid-back fishing community known for offbeat hospitality (p267)
- **Black River Great Morass** Explore Jamaica's longest river (p253) by small watercraft: see crocodiles in their mangrove ecosystem, eat at a riverside shack and discover hidden swimming holes
- **Accompong** Heed the call of the ancient *abeng* horn at this well-preserved Maroon village (p257) on the cusp of scenic Cockpit Country
- **YS Falls & Appleton Rum Estate** Soar over this majestic waterfall (p256) on a zip line, then delve into the island's largest rum distillery (p258) before sampling its wares
- **Peter Tosh Monument** Pay your respects to the Steppin' Razor at this modest yet poignant memorial (opposite)
- **Little Ochi** Watch fishermen pull in with the daily catch, then savor it in a beachside hut at Jamaica's finest seafood restaurant (p273)

- AREA: 2035 SQ KM
- TREASURE BEACH DEC DAILY HIGH TEMPERATURE: 30°C

HISTORY

People here have always been somewhat different from other Jamaicans. Miskito Indians were brought out to Jamaica from Central America to help track Maroons in the 18th century and eventually were given land grants in St Elizabeth. The Miskitos, along with others including 19th-century Scottish castaways and German settlers, are responsible for the high percentage of mixed-race peoples around Treasure Beach.

Jamaica's cool central highlands – rising northeast of St Elizabeth – were popular from the 19th century through the mid-1900s as a vacation retreat, when Christiana and Mandeville became social centers for the wealthy.

CLIMATE

The area has distinct climates associated with the temperate uplands and the warmer plains. The latter have a relatively balmy, dry climate, while the highlands are moist and refreshingly springlike.

GETTING THERE & AROUND

Route taxis and minibuses ply the coastal road but they only run infrequently, and to some areas only a few times per day. Service is much more reliable to and from Mandeville. The primary transportation centers for the region are Mandeville and Black River, where you can find long-distance transportation to Kingston, Negril and Montego Bay.

WHITEHOUSE & AROUND

The narrow coastal strip of southeastern Westmoreland parish is shadowed by the steep slopes of land known as Surinam Quarters. The sleepy fishing villages of Bluefields, Belmont and Whitehouse attract visitors for whom the sea means more than the boundaries of an all-inclusive. The peaceful beaches, with their colorful fishing boats drawn up on poles and nets hung out to dry, provide the perfect locale to exchange pleasantries with fisherfolk or disappear into a book for a day or two.

BLUEFIELDS

Bluefields was the site of Oristan, one of the first Spanish settlements in Jamaica, founded in 1519. Bluefields Bay provided safe anchorage for Spanish explorers, British naval squadrons and pirates. In 1670, infamous buccaneer Henry Morgan set out from Bluefields Bay to sack Panama City. Today it's a profoundly quiet place popular with escape artists and offering a nice collection of accommodations.

Surinam Quarters, inland from Bluefields, is named for the colonists who settled here after the English traded Surinam to the Dutch in exchange for Nieuw Amsterdam (New York) in 1667. Scots also settled in the area after the Battle of Culloden in 1745, and you'll see many Scottish place names around.

For local information, visit the **Bluefields People's Community Association** (☎ 955-8793; www.bluefieldsjamaica.org.jm; Belmont Sq) in Belmont. Internet access is also available.

Sights

One kilometer south of Bluefields lies the tiny inlet of Belmont, birthplace of reggae superstar Peter Tosh, who was murdered in 1987. You can pay your respects at the **Peter Tosh Monument** (admission US$5; 9am-5pm), a small mausoleum with a modest array of memorabilia. A casual place with few visitors, it's in stark contrast to the tourist maelstrom surrounding fellow Wailer Bob Marley's mausoleum in Nine Miles (see p175). Run by the Tosh family – his nonagenarian mother still lives on the property – the site also includes a gift shop selling cassettes and CDs as well as a small garden. In mid-October the annual **Peter Tosh Birthday Bash**, an informal local affair, features live roots reggae music played deep into the night.

Bluefields Beach Park (admission free; 8am-sunset), well signed from the A2, offers a relaxing stretch of sand and a nice collection of food stalls featuring locally caught fresh fish and plenty of Red Stripe. It can get crowded on weekends.

Tours

Travelers staying in the area can enjoy excellent day trips as well as excursions to regional attractions including YS Falls, the Black River Great Morass, Ipswich Caves and Alligator Pond. The following providers offer excellent customized trips; both of them offer German-language tours in addition to English.

Natural Mystic Tours (☎ 851-3962; www.geocities.com/naturalmysticja; Belmont; per person per day

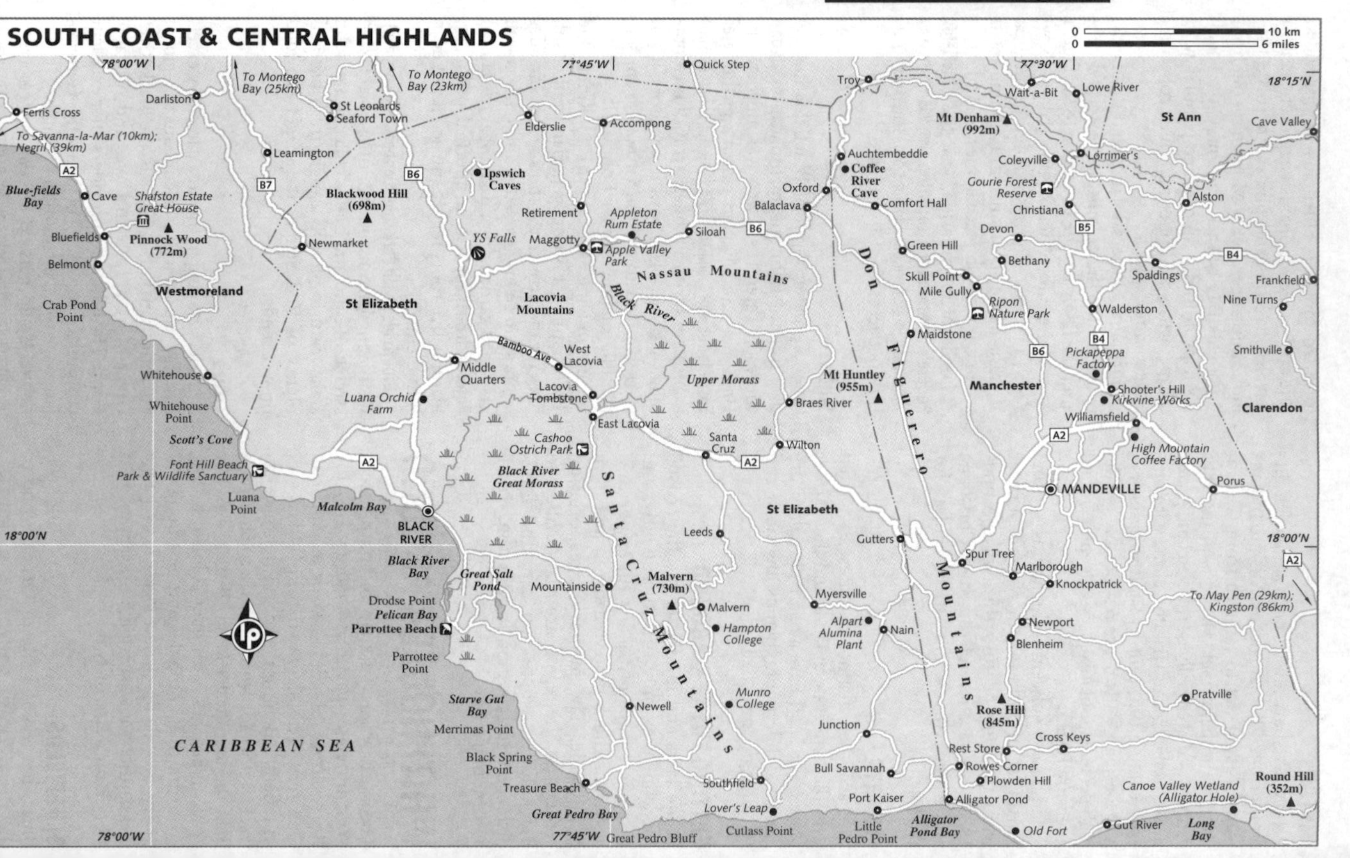
SOUTH COAST & CENTRAL HIGHLANDS
0 10 km
0 6 miles
78°00'W
77°45'W
77°30'W
18°15'N
18°00'N
CARIBBEAN SEA
Westmoreland
St Elizabeth
Manchester
Clarendon
St Ann
Nassau Mountains
Don Figuerero Mountains
Santa Cruz Mountains
Lacovia Mountains
Upper Morass
Black River Great Morass
Black River
MANDEVILLE
BLACK RIVER
To Savanna-la-Mar (10km); Negril (39km)
To Montego Bay (25km)
To Montego Bay (23km)
To May Pen (29km); Kingston (86km)
Ferris Cross
Blue-fields Bay
Cave
Bluefields
Belmont
Crab Pond Point
Darliston
Shafston Estate Great House
Pinnock Wood (772m)
Whitehouse
Whitehouse Point
Scott's Cove
Font Hill Beach Park & Wildlife Sanctuary
Luana Point
Leamington
Newmarket
St Leonards
Seaford Town
Blackwood Hill (698m)
Malcolm Bay
Luana Orchid Farm
Middle Quarters
Bamboo Ave
YS Falls
Ipswich Caves
Elderslie
Retirement
Maggotty
Apple Valley Park
Appleton Rum Estate
Accompong
Quick Step
Siloah
Balaclava
Oxford
Troy
Auchtembeddie
Coffee River Cave
Comfort Hall
Green Hill
Mt Denham (992m)
Wait-a-Bit
Lowe River
Coleyville
Gourie Forest Reserve
Christiana
Lorrimer's
Alston
Cave Valley
Spaldings
Frankfield
Nine Turns
Smithville
Devon
Bethany
Walderston
Skull Point
Mile Gully
Ripon Nature Park
Maidstone
Pickapeppa Factory
Shooter's Hill
Kirkvine Works
Williamsfield
High Mountain Coffee Factory
Porus
Mt Huntley (955m)
Braes River
Wilton
Santa Cruz
West Lacovia
Lacovia Tombstone
East Lacovia
Cashoo Ostrich Park
Great Salt Pond
Black River Bay
Drodse Point
Pelican Bay
Parrottee Beach
Parrottee Point
Starve Gut Bay
Merrimas Point
Black Spring Point
Treasure Beach
Great Pedro Bay
Great Pedro Bluff
Mountainside
Malvern (730m)
Malvern
Hampton College
Leeds
Newell
Munro College
Southfield
Lover's Leap
Cutlass Point
Gutters
Myersville
Alpart Alumina Plant
Nain
Junction
Bull Savannah
Port Kaiser
Little Pedro Point
Alligator Pond Bay
Alligator Pond
Spur Tree
Marlborough
Knockpatrick
Newport
Blenheim
Rose Hill (845m)
Rest Store
Rowes Corner
Plowden Hill
Cross Keys
Old Fort
Gut River
Canoe Valley Wetland (Alligator Hole)
Long Bay
Pratville
Round Hill (352m)
A2
B4
B5
B6
B7

US$100) Unique, off-the-beaten track tours including the popular 'Rastaman Hills' tour.

Shafston Tours (☎ 997-5076, 869-9212; www.shafston.com; Shafston Great House, Bluefields; day trips per person US$25, minimum 6 people) A good choice for outdoor pursuits such as river kayaking (US$50 per person) and hiking.

Sleeping & Eating

Catch the Vibes Guesthouse (☎ 851-3962; www.geocities.com/naturalmysticja/guesthouse; cottage s/d US$20/25) Located on a hill in Belmont Village, this tiny well-priced cottage is set in a flower garden with a great view over the sea. There's a basic kitchen and the local beach is only a five-minute walk away. A cooking service and dominoes instruction are provided on request. Natural Mystic Tours (p247) is based here.

Sunset Cottage (☎ 955-8007; r US$45) Located on the A2 in Bluefields, this simple, small immaculately kept hotel overlooking a rocky beach provides an excellent bargain for self-caterers. There are two rooms with two single beds and shared bathroom, one room with private bathroom, and a communal kitchen. There are also six apartments with kitchens and a cottage right on the sea. All units are cooled by fans and sea breezes, and there's a lovely gazebo perched over the water.

our pick **Shafston Estate Great House** (☎ 997-5076, 869-9212; www.shafston.com; all-inclusive per person US$50-85; P 💻 🏊) Poised on a hilltop with exquisite coastal views stretching as far as Savanna-la-Mar, this wonderfully creaky great house is a budget traveler's dream. In the original manor house there are 10 atmospheric, spacious rooms ranging from basic to modest; a few have bathrooms. For even cheaper digs, there are 13 simple yet charming rooms in a newer block with screened windows and clean, tiled communal unisex showers and bathrooms. Relax in a hammock, laze on a sundeck next to the pool and Jacuzzi, or chill out at the congenial poolside bar. To get here from the A2, take the dirt road opposite Bluefields police station, then it's a precipitous 3km climb over bad roads. Alternatively, gracious owner Frank Lohmann can arrange for airport transfers.

Horizon Cottages (☎ 955-8823; esaumary@hotmail.com; cottage US$110; P 💻 🏊) One of the first hotels in the area, this cozy spot right on the waterfront of Bluefields Bay features two wooden cottages, the Sea Ranch and the Rasta Ranch, each tastefully appointed with local artwork and featuring small kitchenettes and shared hot-water shower in the garden. The beach is private and kayaking is available.

For multiday rentals of exclusive and deluxe waterfront properties, contact **Sun Villas** (☎ in the USA 941-922-9191; www.sunvillas.com/south_coast.htm) or **Bluefields Villas** (☎ in the USA 202-232-4010; www.bluefieldsvillas.com). Both offer fully staffed, exquisitely furnished waterfront properties for between US$3500 and US$6300 per week in the high season.

Locally known for its crab backs, Dorrit's, a spacious roadside shack in Belmont, is the best place to eat in the area. It also does an excellent curried goat.

WHITEHOUSE

The small fishing village of Whitehouse is a great place to sample provincial coastal life. It stretches for about 2km along the A2, parallel to a series of beaches where motorized boats and pirogues are drawn up. The Whitehouse Fishing Cooperative supplies much of the island with wahoo, tuna, barracuda, bonito, snapper, kingfish, marlin and lobster taken on the Pedro Banks, about 130km out to sea.

The 2005 opening of the south coast's first large-scale all-inclusive resort was fiercely opposed by some local activists striving to preserve the region's unspoilt charm and traditional way of life. At last visit, however, the Sandals Whitehouse European Village & Spa was not doing particularly well and had not led to an influx of mass developments – for now.

Activities

You can hire a fishing boat to go **snorkeling** (per hr around US$15). Better yet, hop aboard with local fishermen for a trip to the fishing banks (typically up to four people for about US$20 per hour). Women should not go unaccompanied.

Sleeping & Eating

South Sea View Guest House (☎ 963-5172; info@southseaview.com; r without/with air-con US$70/80; ❄ 🏊) At the far southeast end of South Sea Park, this is a modern villa with 12 rooms, each with a bathroom, king-size bed, cable TV, phone and hand-painted tropical murals. There's a rocky cove good for bathing. Proprietor Norman Forrester opened this place, the first guest house in Whitehouse, more than two decades ago. He will arrange for guests to visit his 445-hectare fruit-and-vegetable farm at Cave Mountain in the high country overlooking Whitehouse.

Culloden Cove Villa (☎ 963-5344, 383-3872; lyons@cwjamaica.com; Little Culloden; per week US$1895) One-and-a-half kilometers to the northwest of Whitehouse, this excellent rental was formerly the site of the Culloden Café. These days you must come and stay in order to get some of the place's popular cuisine. The bright and breezy three-bedroom house features an atmospheric bar, shady veranda, beach access and plenty of books. A cook and 24-hour security personnel are included in the price. Stays are for one-week minimum.

Sandals Whitehouse European Village & Spa (☎ 640-3000; www.sandals.com; 3 nights all-inclusive d US$2350-3575; P ⊠ ✿ 🖵 ⛱) If your visions of Jamaica conjure up a quaint European village, this all-inclusive resort should hit the spot. It cost over US$100 million to build this place around three villages conceived to look like towns in France, the Netherlands and Italy. The resort has 360 well-appointed rooms – all with beachfront views – in nine categories spread over 20 hectares. The all-inclusive promise is fulfilled by its eight restaurants and six bars, as well as a full range of land and water sports, the largest swimming pool in Jamaica, and a long sandy beach.

Ruby's 24/7 (☎ 963-5686; mains US$3-6; 🕑 24hr) On the A2 in Whitehouse, Ruby's serves seafood and Jamaican fare on a shady patio.

Jimmyz Restaurant & Bar (☎ 390-3477; mains US$2.50-5; 🕑 breakfast, lunch & dinner Mon-Sat) On Fisherman's Beach in central Whitehouse, next to a pavilion where local fishermen sell their catch to wholesalers, this eatery is popular with old sea salts. The menu has fresh juices, including an exceedingly peppery ginger tonic, and dishes featuring steamed fish, chicken, 'sea puss' (octopus) and a particularly excellent spicy conch stew.

SCOTT'S COVE

About 8km east of Whitehouse, the A2 road sweeps around this deep little inlet marking the border of Westmoreland and St Elizabeth, where dozens of food and beer stalls line the shore. It's an excellent place to buy fried snapper and *bammy* – a pancake of fried cassava – with onions and peppers for a dollar or two, then take it for a picnic at Font Hill Beach, but there's nothing else to detain you.

FONT HILL BEACH PARK & WILDLIFE SANCTUARY

Although this **wildlife reserve and beach park** (☎ 396-4133; adult/child US$3/1.50; 🕑 9am-5pm), on almost 1300 hectares, east of Scott's Cove, is incongruously owned by the Petroleum Corporation of Jamaica, it has not tarnished its natural beauty…after realizing the oil it initially sought offshore didn't exist.

The sanctuary, which you can only visit accompanied by a guide, has scrubby acacia, logwood thickets and, closer to the shore, a maze of connected lagoons and swamps with a population of a couple of hundred crocodiles. The birding is fabulous, highlighted by a flock of bald plate pigeons as well as assorted black-billed whistling ducks, jacanas, herons and pelicans.

Two golden-sand beaches (connected by a trail) are fringed by a reef offering great snorkeling and bathing. Dolphins come into the cove, as do turtles for nesting season. Facilities include a small café and bar, changing rooms, picnic booths, volleyball, a boardwalk, an interpretive center and a marina. Horseback rides are also offered.

BLACK RIVER & AROUND

BLACK RIVER

pop 4000

Though capital of St Elizabeth and the parish's largest town, Black River has a transient feel to it. Its namesake river, on whose western banks it rests, spirits day-trippers off to the Great Morass to see crocodiles and eat at waterside jerk shacks, and those who stay in town use it simply as a base for visiting such nearby attractions as YS Falls and the Appleton Rum Estate.

Grant it more than a drive-by glance, however, and you'll get a sense of its more exalted past. The town's Georgian architecture attests to its 19th-century prosperity, when Black River exported local logwood from which Prussian blue dye was extracted for textiles. Locals proudly point out the Waterloo Guest House, which in 1893 became the first house in Jamaica to have electricity installed. The racetrack and spa that brought the wealthy have not survived, however.

Information

Black River Hospital (☎ 965-2212; 45 Main St) This is 1km west of town.

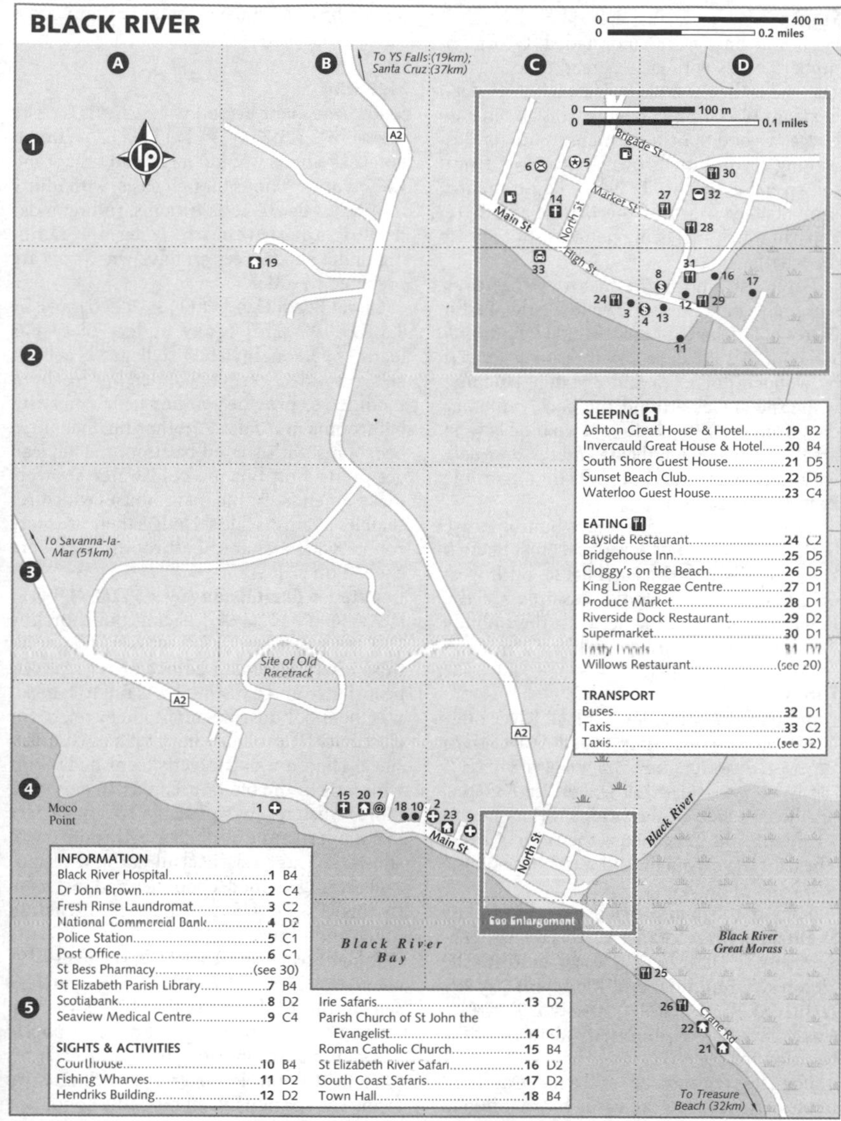

Dr John Brown (☎ 965-2305; 48 Main St) Medical clinic.

Fresh Rinse Laundromat (☎ 634-2166; High St; per load US$1) Self-service laundry.

National Commercial Bank (☎ 965-9027; 9 High St)

Police station (☎ 965-2232 or 119; North St)

Post office (☎ 965-2250) Immediately west of the police station.

St Bess Pharmacy (☎ 634-4526; 1A Brigade St; Mon-Sat)

St Elizabeth Parish Library (☎ 965-2270; Main St; internet access per 30 min US$1)

Scotiabank (☎ 965-2251; 6 High St)

Seaview Medical Centre (☎ 965-2978; 46 High St; 24hr)

Sights

High St is lined with colonnaded, Georgian timber houses with gingerbread trim. At the east end is the **Hendricks Building** (2 High St), dating from 1813. Immediately east is an old **iron bridge**, a good spot for watching crocodiles waiting for tidbits thrown by tourists from the riverside berths. Trawlers lie at anchor immediately south of the bridge and here you can watch fish being hauled ashore onto the wharfs.

Foremost among the historic structures worth checking out is the yellow-brick **Parish Church of St John the Evangelist** (cnr Main & North Sts), built in 1837. The airy interior is graced by wooden porticoes and a stately balcony, while the graves around the back cemetery date from the 17th century. Two blocks west are the porticoed **courthouse** and the **town hall**, with lofty pillars, and beyond that a simple **Roman Catholic church**.

Two of the most impressive buildings are both hotels: the 1894 **Invercauld Great House & Hotel** and the **Waterloo Guest House**, both west on Main St and splendid examples of the Jamaican vernacular style, with their shady wooden verandas and gingerbread trim.

Tours

A number of companies in Black River offer Great Morass boat tours. **South Coast Safaris** (☎ 965-2513, 965-2086; tour US$20, with lunch & visit to YS Falls US$33; tours 9am, 11am, 12:30pm, 2pm & 3:30pm), on the east side of the bridge, offers 60- to 75-minute journeys aboard the *Safari Queen*. The trips leave from the old warehouse on the east bank of the river.

Similar tours and prices are offered by **St Elizabeth River Safari** (☎ 965-2374, 965-2229; tours 9am, 11am, 2pm & 3:30pm), behind the Hendricks Building; and **Irie Safaris** (☎ 965-2221; fax 965-2466; 12 High St; tours every 90 min 9am-4.30pm), wharfside from a jetty just east of the bus station.

For a less regimented (and a more authentic) experience, you can easily hire a guide to take you upriver by canoe or boat for about US$15 to US$25 round-trip. Ask near the bridge in town. Or, if you're continuing on to Treasure Beach, you can hire a boat there for a round-trip tour (UA$60) that includes a stop at the Pelican Bar (p271) and a journey up the Black River.

Midday tours are best for spotting crocodiles; early and later tours are better for birding. Take a shade hat and some mosquito repellent.

Sleeping

South Shore Guest House (☎ 965-2172; 33 Crane Rd; camping US$12, r US$21-46; P) This 12-bedroom hotel has a breezy outdoor bar and restaurant. Rooms are spacious though basic, with utility furniture, fans, large bathrooms, and verandas fronting a narrow beach. It permits camping under shade trees on the lawn. Meals are prepared to order.

Sunset Beach Club (☎ 634-3839; 29 Crane Rd; s/d US$18/25; P) This funky budget place has loads of personality and privileged beach access. An old, cheerfully painted bus has been modified to provide two tiny bedrooms with bathrooms and fans. Another bus has three bedrooms with shared bathroom. They can get pretty hot, but the cold-water showers make amends. In the main house, which resembles a ramshackle ski lodge, there are more rooms with a shared bathroom. Meals are cooked on request.

Waterloo Guest House (☎ 965-2278; 44 High St; r US$30-50; P) Facing the shoreline and the photogenic hulk of a rusting ship, this rickety Georgian edifice offers real offbeat charm and a distinctive claim to fame: it was the first house in Jamaica to be wired for electricity. It probably hasn't changed much since. There are six meagerly furnished rooms with fans in the old house, plus 16 carpeted, more stylish rooms with cable TV and fridges in a modern annex. All have bathrooms with showers. There's a cheerful bar and restaurant serving seafood, chop suey and ice cream (mains US$3 to US$4.50; open for breakfast, lunch and dinner).

Ashton Great House & Hotel (☎ 965-2036; s US$50, d US$60-80, tr US$95; P) In a magnificent setting on a hill beside the A2 about 3km north of town, this large and atmospheric wooden house on more than 140 hectares once held dominion over a sprawling dairy farm. The spacious albeit modestly appointed rooms have phones, satellite TV and bathrooms. If there are few guests – a condition that seems to be the norm – the house can seem satisfyingly spooky at night, particularly as you sit on the grand balcony watching the bats flit by. There's a spacious pool with a children's section.

Invercauld Great House & Hotel (☎ 965-2750; 66 Main St; d US$59-97, ste US$85-155; P)

Built more than a century ago by an affluent Scottish businessman during Black River's heyday, this impressive house has gable roofs, bay windows, valances and intricate fretwork. It has 20 rooms – varying in size and mood – furnished with period antiques and replicas. More modern units have 32 rooms and suites with kitchens, balconies and cable TV. The hotel has an airy dining room, a cozy bar, a tennis court and a small pool.

Eating

Tasty Foods (☎ 634-4027; Market St; mains US$2.50-4; ⏰ lunch & dinner) This barnlike eatery is strictly Jamaican and seriously cheap. Keep an open mind and sample the red peas and chicken foot, stew pork and, for the culinary adventurer, cow head. Dessert anyone?

Waterloo Guest House (☎ 965-2278; 44 High St; mains US$3-5; ⏰ breakfast, lunch & dinner) Has a modest restaurant with an inexpensive Jamaican menu, plus an earthy bar serving ice-cream sodas and milk shakes.

Bayside Restaurant (17 High St; mains US$3-12; ⏰ lunch & dinner) This self-proclaimed 'pastry and pub' is a local favorite, serving an eclectic menu of Jamaican and continental fare plus pastries. Bayside Jerk & BBQ Centre is at the rear, overhanging the sea.

Riverside Dock Restaurant (☎ 965-9486; High St; mains US$4.50-8; ⏰ 10am-9pm Mon-Fri, 1-9pm Sat & Sun) This midrange riverside eatery, recently renovated with a bright color scheme, serves well-prepared dishes including seafood kebabs, lobster, guava-jerked chicken and roast pork with apple sauce. Service can be slow. You can book excursions with South Coast Safaris (opposite), which operates a desk here.

Willows Restaurant (☎ 965-2750; Invercauld Great House & Hotel; mains US$6-25; ⏰ breakfast, lunch & dinner) The fanciest place around, serving up Jamaican and continental favorites in elegant surrounds.

Cloggy's on the Beach (☎ 634-2424; Crane Rd; mains US$8-20; ⏰ lunch & dinner) This beachside joint is an all-round pleaser with its relaxed vibe, great bar ambience and excellent chow. It occasionally throws well-attended beach sound-system parties; ask the bartender for the lowdown. The menu features shrimp, lobster, conch and steamed and stewed fish.

Bridgehouse Inn (☎ 965-2361; 14 Crane Rd; mains US$8-15; ⏰ breakfast, lunch & dinner) Serves seafood and Jamaican dishes such as curried goat, washed down with health drinks made from beetroot juice and Irish moss. A variety of chicken dishes are also on offer.

There are stalls by the market and a bus station selling I-tal food. The best is **King Lion Reggae Centre** (☎ 965-9466; Market St), serving health foods and juices for under US$3.

There's a supermarket in the Hendricks Building, and another one 100m north. You can buy fruit, vegetables and meats at the open-air **produce market** (Market St), but hygiene here is questionable.

Getting There & Away

From Black River, public vehicles go to and from Santa Cruz (US$1.50), Savanna-la-Mar (US$2), Montego Bay (US$2.50) and Treasure Beach (US$1.75). The transportation center is behind the market, just west of the river. Taxis arrive and depart from a lot at the junction of Main and North Sts.

BLACK RIVER GREAT MORASS

There are many rivers to cross in this 200-sq-km wetland extending inland from the mouth of the Black River. For its singular scenery and its excellent wildlife-viewing opportunities, this is one of Jamaica's most satisfying explorations.

The best way to get a feel for the morass is to explore it by small watercraft or tour boat; quick excursions are easily arranged in Black River, but if you are heading on to Treasure Beach, lengthier forays up the river can be arranged there. Along the way, with the right guide, you can eat at delightful riverside shacks and discover hidden swimming holes – but beware of the crocodiles! The morass forms Jamaica's most significant refuge for crocodiles, and an estimated population of 300 live in the swamps. Several have made a habit of hanging out near the bridge in town, waiting for their next meal of raw chicken parts dispensed from the tour operators who have a vested interest in keeping them around.

The waters are stained coffee-brown by tannins from decomposed vegetation in the Great Morass, a complex ecosystem and a vital preserve for more than 100 bird species, including cinnamon-colored jacanas, egrets, whistling ducks, water hens and seven species of heron.

Locals go out in dugout canoes, tending funnel-shaped bamboo shrimp pots in the traditional manner of their West African forebears. These interconnecting waterways are

WHAT A CROC!

Saltwater crocodiles were so once common around the entire coast of Jamaica that an early bill advocated an 'alligator' be on the young country's coat of arms. Around the turn of the 20th century, this abundance began to draw international big game hunters, and, unsurprisingly, the population was gradually decimated. Happily, since 1971, crocodile hunting has been outlawed on the island.

Called an 'alligator' in Jamaica, the American crocodile *(Crocodylus acutus)* can now be found in a few protected areas along the island's south coast, most notably the Black River Great Morass, where it is estimated 300 patrol the waters, and Font Hill Wildlife Sanctuary, which is believed to be home to about 200. As long as these sanctuaries are protected, the alligators will be too, but the population will never return to its former numbers.

While the alligators can grow to an imposing 4m, they are relatively shy and eat mostly fish, deploying sharp, conical teeth well adapted for capturing slippery prey. They go for long periods without eating and can survive on less than 5kg of food a week. Unless they feel threatened, alligators leave visitors alone.

Early morning is a good time to see crocodiles, when they are sunning on the banks to replenish heat lost at night. A legacy of the dinosaur period, the crocodile maintains a body temperature of 25°C by alternating between shade, water and sun. They hunt at night and, when submerged, their beady eyes watch above the water.

navigable for about 30km upriver. Along the way, the mangroves suck water through long tendrils drooping into the water. Beyond the confluence of the YS, Middle Quarters and Black Rivers, the mangroves broaden into marshy meadows of tall sedges and reeds. Feisty game fish are plentiful, including snook and tarpon. On rare occasions, endangered manatees may even be seen near the river estuary.

For an excellent lunch experience, be sure to tell your guide that you want to visit **Sister Lou's River Stop** (lunch), on the Salt Spring tributary, where delicious stuffed crab backs (US$3.50) and pepper shrimp are served up. It's a great place to have a Red Stripe and watch the river drift by, or just watch local kids jump from a nearby bridge into the river.

MIDDLE QUARTERS

This small village on the A2, 13km north of Black River, is renowned for its women higglers (street vendors) who stand at the roadside selling delicious pepper shrimps – pronounced 'swimp' locally – cooked at the roadside grills. The shrimp are caught in traps made in centuries-old African tradition from split bamboo. US$3 will buy a spicy bagful.

If you're really hungry, do as Jamaican truckers do and pull into **Howie's Healthy Eating** (☎ 378-8714; mains US$2-6; 24hr), on the A2 at the turnoff for YS Falls. Here all sorts of good Jamaican cooking is done in big pots bubbling over wood fires. Choose from a number of soups and stews, fried fish and, of course, huge helpings of 'swimp.'

For a quick dip, stop by **Bubbling Spring** (☎ 755-3165, 850-1606; child/adult US$1/2; 8am-10pm), 1.5km south of Middle Quarters on the A2. Cool, slightly carbonated spring water is fed into long, shallow pools. Simple Jamaican fare is served.

At **Luana Orchid Farm** (☎ 361-8795), about 3km south of Middle Quarters, as many as 100,000 orchids are growing at various stages of development. It's not open as a tourist entity but visitors are welcome by prearrangement.

BAMBOO AVENUE

The soothing sound of a million leaves rustling in the wind is one of the quiet pleasures of this photogenic archway of towering bamboo. The 4km-long stretch of the A2 between Middle Quarters and Lacovia is shaded by dense 100-year-old stands of *Bambusa vulgaris*, the largest species of bamboo in Jamaica. Cool and pretty, Bamboo Avenue is the perfect place to stop for a coconut jelly, accompanied by a bag of pepper shrimp brought along from Middle Quarters. Several rest stops along the road, including the **TPDCo Travel Halt** (8:30am-5pm) with clean restrooms, offer coconuts, beer and snacks.

LACOVIA

This sprawling village extends for 3km east of Bamboo Avenue, and is divided into West Lacovia, Lacovia Tombstone and East Lacovia.

The only site of interest is the two side-by-side **tombstones** in the center of the junction in front of the Texaco gas station at Lacovia Tombstone. An unlikely legend says that the two young men who lie buried here killed each other in a tavern duel in 1738.

Carlyn Resorts (☎ 607-4826; East Lacovia; r US$15-20; P) is a wood-and-stone two-story structure with nine rooms. It's a stretch to call it a resort, with its small and basic fan-cooled rooms, but they're clean and have bathrooms (though no hot water). There's a small restaurant.

CASHOO OSTRICH PARK

This **park** (☎ 966-2222; adult/child US$3.50/2; 10am-4:30pm Tue-Sun), set on 40 hectares of farmland about 3km south of East Lacovia, has about two dozen African ostriches, as well as a large fruit orchard and herb garden and a petting zoo with an emu, donkeys, hens, ducks, geese and swans. There are also a kids' playground, bumper cars, swimming pool, badminton court, sand volleyball and a bar. You can saddle up for horseback rides (US$2). If you wish to bring a picnic, you'd do well to stop by Middle Quarters for some pepper shrimp.

It's wise to call ahead before making your way to the park, as sometimes the gates are locked and the place is deserted during posted 'open' hours. To get there, from the A2 in Lacovia take the turnoff at the Old Lacovia Bridge and follow the signs 1.5km to the village of Slipe.

SANTA CRUZ

pop 5500

Santa Cruz is a bustling market town and the most important commercial center in southwest Jamaica. During the past few decades it has grown modestly wealthy on revenues from the local bauxite industry. Before that ,Santa Cruz was a market center for horses and mules bred locally for the British army. A livestock market is still held on Saturday. While there's nothing in the town to detain you long, it's a good place to stop for money or a bite to eat.

Banks include **Scotiabank** (☎ 966-2230; 77 Main St) and **National Commercial Bank** (☎ 966-2204; 7 Coke Dr). **Dr Oliver Myers** (☎ 966-2106; 23 Coke Dr) has a clinic near the **police station** (☎ 966-2289), 200m south of the town center on the road to Malvern.

Hind's Restaurant & Bakery (☎ 966-2234; Santa Cruz Plaza, Main St; mains US$1-6; Mon-Sat) sells baked goods and is a clean, simple place to enjoy Jamaican fare such as brown stew and curried goat.

Paradise Patties (Shop 30, Beadles Plaza, Main St) sells veggie and beef patties for US$0.50. **Fruity's** (Shop 27, Philip's Plaza, Main St) serves delicious ice-cream cones.

Santa Cruz is a main stop for buses, minibuses and route taxis going between Kingston, Mandeville and Black River. They arrive and depart from the transportation center on the A2, at the east end of Santa Cruz.

NASSAU MOUNTAINS & SOUTH COCKPIT COUNTRY

The plains of St Elizabeth are bordered to the north by a low, narrow range of deeply forested hills that merge into the rugged Cockpit Country. Few roads penetrate the hills, where the sparse population is mostly involved in subsistence farming.

Between the Nassau Mountains and the Cockpit Country is the wide Siloah Valley, carpeted with sugarcane.

The Cockpit Country is easily accessed from the south via the hamlet of Troy. See p258 for more details, including trails and information on hiring guides.

MAGGOTTY

pop 1200

This dusty regional center, located 11km north of Lacovia, is laid out on a bend of the Black River at the western end of the Siloah Valley. It was named by the missionary Rev John Hutch after his English birthplace.

South of town there's excellent hiking in Black River Gorge, which features a series of 28 roaring cascades with intermittent pools that are good for swimming.

Sights & Activities

APPLE VALLEY PARK

Open only by appointment, this 169-hectare family **nature park** (☎ 963-9508; applevalleypark.com; adult/child Sat & Sun US$6/5; 10am-5pm), east of

Maggotty, surrounds an 18th-century great house. It has two small lakes and offers fishing and a variety of touristy activities that appeal to Jamaicans. There are paddleboat rides, go-karts, and kayaking on the Black River. Much of the park is a forest reserve good for birding. The owners also operate a tractor-pulled jitney from the old train station in Maggotty. You can spend the night at Apple Valley Guesthouse (below).

CYCLING

Based at Apple Valley Park, **Manfred's Jamaican Mountain Bike Tours** (☎ in Canada 705-745-8210; tour US$800) offers week-long tours of the south coast each week in January and February, with daily excursions geared to moderate riders. A support vehicle is provided. Over the week, you'll pedal 18km to 42km each day through glorious south-coast scenery to some of the region's most notable attractions, including YS Falls, Treasure Beach, Oxford Cave, Appleton Rum Estate and the Black River mangroves. Trips are offered in midwinter only and the cost excludes airfare but includes transfers, gratuity and accommodations. You can rent a bike (US$25/100 per day/week).

RIVER KAYAKING

Shafston Tours (☎ 997-5076, 869-9212; www.shafston.com; river kayaking per person US$50, minimum 6) offers kayaking tours on a pretty stretch of the Black River, which meanders through sugarcane fields and grassy bushland with some mild Class II rapids.

Sleeping & Eating

Apple Valley Guesthouse (per person camping/dm/d US$4.50/10/18) Patrick and Lucille Lee, the Chinese–Jamaican couple who run Apple Valley, also have bunks and private rooms in the 18th-century red-roofed great house south of town. It has five bedrooms and four bathrooms, plus a lounge. Guests have kitchen privileges at the guest house, but there is also an open-air restaurant (dishes US$2 to US$8) serving traditional Jamaican dishes. If you catch carp, silver perch or red snapper yourself, Lucille will cook it for you (US$2 per pound). Apple Valley Park is reached from behind the police station.

Poinciana Guest House (☎ 963-9676; r with shared/private bathroom US$20/30) Behind the post office 100m south of Apple Valley Park is this delightful old house on a hill. It has six modestly furnished rooms with bathrooms. There's hot water (when the heater works), a homey TV lounge and a communal kitchen. Additional rooms are in an annex. Meals are prepared. Enquire at the Happy Times Restaurant.

Valley Restaurant (☎ 963-9508; mains US$3-6; 11am-9pm Sat & Sun, weekdays by reservation) Opposite the Apple Valley Park, this air-conditioned restaurant offers Jamaican dishes, including vegetarian options.

Happy Times Restaurant (☎ 963-9807; Shakespeare Plaza; mains US$4; Mon-Sat) This place serves simple, well-prepared meals, including curried goat, snapper, curried chicken and brown-stew pork.

Getting There & Away

Public vehicles arrive and depart from opposite Shakespeare Plaza at the north end of Maggotty, connecting to Mandeville and Black River.

YS FALLS

Many rate this series of eight **cascades** (☎ 634-2454, 997-6360; www.ysfalls.com; adult/child US$15/6; 9:30am-3:30pm Tue-Sun, closed last 2 weeks in Oct & public holidays), hemmed in by limestone cliffs and surrounded by forest, as being the most beautiful in all of Jamaica. The cascades fall 36m from top to bottom, separated by cool pools perfect for swimming. The falls take their name from the original landowners, ranchers John Yates and Richard Scott. Water-lovers can float down a bamboo-shaded stretch of river on inner tubes for US$6, while the more adventurous can take a canopy zip line for US$30.

A tractor-drawn jitney takes visitors to the cascades, where you'll find picnic grounds, a tree house and a rope swing over the pools. Be careful! The eddies are strong, especially after rains when the falls are torrential. A stone staircase and pathway follow the cascades upriver. There are no lockers, however, so you'll need to keep an eye on your stuff while you bathe.

Admission includes a guide. There's a gift store, and **Mikey's Grill** (dishes US$2-4) serves fish and chicken dishes, plus burgers.

The falls are on the YS Estate, 5.5km north of the A2 (the turnoff is 1.5km east of Middle Quarters). The entrance is just north of the junction of the B6 toward Maggotty.

South Coast Safaris (☎ 965-2513, 965-2086) and **St Elizabeth River Safari** (☎ 965-2374, 965-2229) operate tours to YS Falls every half-hour between 9am and 3:30pm from Black River. You can also book tours with almost any company operating from Negril or Montego Bay.

Buses travel via YS Falls from Shakespeare Plaza in Maggotty. On the A2, buses, minibuses and route taxis will drop you at the junction to YS Falls, from where you can walk (it's about 3km) or catch an Ipswich-bound route taxi.

IPSWICH CAVES

These limestone caverns, about 8km north of YS Falls, are full of stalactites and stalagmites. The cave entrance is at Ipswich, an almost derelict hamlet on the railway line between Montego Bay and Kingston. At the entrance you can hire a guide to lead you into the chambers for a small fee (adult/child US$2/US$1). Natural Mystic Tours and Shafston Tours both lead excursions into the caves from Belmont and Bluefields respectively (see p247).

The turnoff is off the B6, about 3km north of YS Falls. You'll be glad of a 4WD.

ACCOMPONG

pop 1500

Six hundred meters above sea level, the village of Accompong, on the southwestern edge of Cockpit Country, is the sole remaining village in western Jamaica inhabited by descendants of the Maroons. It touts itself for that, but it's also a good base for exploring the region of Cockpit Country known as Me No Sen You No Come.

The village still enjoys aspects of quasi-autonomy and is headed by a 'colonel' (currently Sydney Peddie) elected by secret ballot for a period of five years. The colonel appoints and oversees a council, and it is considered proper etiquette to introduce yourself upon visiting (☎ 464-0651).

Local artisans still make *goombay* drums here. These – along with an array of medicinal herbs, calabashes and *abeng* horns – are for sale in the tiny red-and-green-painted **craft shop** as you enter town. The hand-carved *goombay* drum is box-shaped and covered with goatskin, and makes a wonderfully deep and resonant racket. A large one will set you back US$150.

Sights & Activities

Accompong is centered on the tiny 'Parade Ground,' where the Presbyterian church looks over a small **monument** that honors Cudjoe, the Maroon leader (the statue next to it is that of Leonard Parkinson, another Maroon freedom fighter). Opposite the monument, the **Accompong Community Centre & Museum** contains a motley miscellany of *goombay* drums, a musket, a sword, baskets and other artifacts from the Maroon era. Entry is included only as part of a community tour (US$15), which takes in a Maroon burial ground, a small herbal garden and the Kindah Tree, a stately mango tree, where the elders of the community congregate and which is considered sacred. If the museum's closed, call Mark Wright (☎ 398-7688) for a quick whip round the village.

There are several tours offered, including a one-hour trek down to the **Peace Caves** (about US$20), where Cudjoe signed the 1739 peace treaty with the British.

Festivals & Events

The traditional **Accompong Maroon Festival**, held each January 6, marks the signing of the 1739 peace treaty between war hero Captain Cudjoe of the Maroons with representatives of the King of England. The provisions of the treaty guaranteed the Maroons significant land holdings and personal freedom. In 2007 more than 15,000 visitors flocked to the small rural village for the festival, which features traditional dancing, drumming, mento bands and a wide variety of tonics and herbs. The festival culminates in a traditional march to the revered Kindah Tree, where a specially prepared Maroon dish of unsalted and unseasoned pork is consumed with yams, but a loud sound-system keeps the party going well into the night. For more information, call Maroon Attraction Tours (p258).

Sleeping & Eating

A&E (☎ 871-8848, 427-5438; r US$18) In the basement of a small restaurant-bar on the road to the cemetery, this tiny inn offers three small, simple but clean rooms with bathrooms. There's a TV lounge and a cheerfully appointed bar that provides a colorful place to sup with locals.

Baboo's Garden (☎ 475-3046; www.baboosgarden.com; r US$25) About a mile east of town, this new, solar-powered guest house features four thatched-roof bungalows whose balconies offer splendid views out over Cockpit Country. For US$125, the American owner offers transport from MoBay to Treasure Beach with a one-night stopover here.

Getting There & Away

Route taxis run from Shakespeare Plaza in Maggotty (US$2.50).

The route from Maggotty is well signed if you're driving, but the winding road is horribly potholed.

Maroon Attraction Tours (☎ 971-3900, 700-8805; 32 Church St, Montego Bay; tours US$50) offers customized excursions from Montego Bay. Ask for Kenneth.

APPLETON RUM ESTATE

You can smell the yeasty odor of molasses wafting from the **Appleton sugar estate and rum factory** (☎ 963-9215; factory tour & rum tasting US$12; Mon-Sat), well before you reach it, 1km northeast of Maggotty in the middle of the Siloah Valley. This is the largest distillery in Jamaica and the oldest: the factory has been blending the famous Appleton brand of rums since 1749. It is owned by J Wray & Nephew, Jamaica's largest rum producer.

The 45-minute tour of the factory details how molasses is extracted from sugarcane, then fermented, distilled and aged to produce rum, which you can taste in the 'John Wray Tavern.' Several dozen varieties – including the lethal Overproof – are available for sampling, and the well-stocked gift shop does brisk business with tipsy visitors who just can't get enough.

A motor-coach excursion, the Appleton Estate Rum Tour (US$85) departs MoBay daily, and from Ocho Rios and Negril several times each week. Some tours also include a stop at YS Falls. Contact **Caribic Vacations** (☎ in Montego Bay 953-9878, in Negril 957-3309, in Ocho Rios 974-9106) or Jamaica Estate Tours Ltd at the Appleton Rum Estate itself.

QUICK STEP

This remote mountain hamlet 13km north of Siloah offers magnificent views over the portion of the Cockpit Country known as the District of Look Behind. It's eerie and extremely foreboding, a chaos of honeycombed limestone cliffs hewn into bizarre shapes and cockpits (with deep forested bowls up to 150m across).

North of Quick Step the road peters out. Hiking trails lead into the heart of the Cockpits, but you are well advised to hire a guide through the Southern Trelawny Environmental Agency (p212). One trail leads to Windsor Caves, a full day's hike. It's easy to get lost and this is no place for that. *Don't attempt it alone!*

BALACLAVA

Balaclava sits atop a ridge at the east end of the Siloah Valley. If you're climbing uphill from the west, it's worth resting at the ridge crest to take in the view of the valley laid out below, smothered in sugarcane, as flat and green as a billiard table.

An attractive Anglican church and the disused railway station are about the only buildings of interest.

TROY & AROUND

Three kilometers northeast of Balaclava the B6 turns southeast for Mandeville; another road (the B10) leads north and climbs to Troy on the border with Trelawny parish. The latter is a spectacular drive as you climb up through a series of dramatic gorges, with the road clinging to the sheer face of the Cockpits.

Troy is the southeastern gateway to the Cockpit Country. It sits in a valley bottom and is surrounded by sugarcane fields. It is also a center for the cultivation of yams, which grow on tall runners. **St Silas church** is worth a look for its blue-tinted corrugated iron roof.

Auchtembeddie, 5km south of Troy, is a choice spot for spelunkers, who head to **Coffee River Cave**. It is totally undeveloped for tourism, but local guides will escort you for a negotiated fee.

A dirt road leads 3km north from Troy to Tyre, a hamlet on the edge of the Cockpits. Beyond Tyre the road fades into a bush-enshrouded trail. From here you can hike to Windsor (about 24km); see p214. Don't attempt it alone, as there are several forks and it is easy to get lost.

To hire a guide, contact the Southern Trelawny Environmental Agency (p212) in Albert Town, 17km northeast of Troy.

CHRISTIANA & AROUND

Around Christiana you'd be forgiven for imagining yourself in the Pyrenees or the highlands of Costa Rica. The air is crisp, clouds drift through the vales, and pine trees add to the alpine setting.

This is an important center for growing Irish potatoes. Cacao, yams, and coffee production are also important, and during picking season you can watch women with baskets moving among the rows, plucking cherry-red coffee berries.

CHRISTIANA

About 16km north of Mandeville at an elevation of 900m, the town of Christiana is the lovely heart of a richly farmed agricultural region of gently undulating hills and shallow vales.

The area was settled by German farmers during the 18th and 19th centuries. Moravian missionaries were also active during that era and a **Moravian church** commands the northern end of sinuous Main St. During the 19th century, Christiana became a hill-town resort popular with European dignitaries and Kingstonians escaping the heat of the plains.

Christiana is a fairly sleepy place (farmers go to bed early and get up around 4am or 5am), but if you're here on Thursday when the higglers come to sell their produce, the roads are so thick you can hardly drive through town. If you're in Christiana on a Thursday, stay through the evening for Higgler's Night.

Information

Christiana Health Centre (☎ 964-2749; Main St) Government-run; toward the south end of Main St.

Christiana Pharmacy (☎ 964-2424; Main St) Well stocked.

Dr Glen Norman Day (☎ 964-2361; Christiana Plaza) Clinic off Main St.

National Commercial Bank (☎ 964-2466; Main St)

Police station (☎ 964-2250; Main St)

Post office (☎ 964-2279; Main St) Next to the police station.

Scotiabank (☎ 964-2223; Main St)

Sights & Activities

CHRISTIANA BOTTOM

This beautiful riverside spot, in a valley bottom below the town, has a **waterfall** plus picnic spots framed by bamboo. Two **sinkholes** full of crystal-clear water offer refreshing dips. You can hike from the center of town, though the going at the lower reaches can be muddy and slippery. Take the road that leads east from the National Commercial Bank; it's 3km from here. Take the first left and then the second left.

GOURIE FOREST RESERVE

This forest reserve of pines, mahogany and mahoe growing atop and betwixt dramatic cockpits is 3km northwest of the town, near Coleyville. The park is laced with **hiking** trails. Gourie is most noteworthy for having Jamaica's longest cave system. Two **spelunking** routes have been explored. One of the routes is easy; the other is difficult and made more so by the presence of an icy river. Rubber-soled shoes are required and a guide is essential.

The **Forestry Department** (☎ 964-2065; Main St) rents two basic wooden cottages; you can get the keys from the caretaker at the reserve.

To get to Gourie from Christina, turn uphill (southwest) at the radio tower immediately south of the junction that leads west for Coleyville and Troy. Immediately take the left at a Y-fork, then right at the next Y-fork and follow the green wire fence.

Tours

Villa Bella Tours (☎ 964-2243; Hotel Villa Bella) offers excursions to the Oxford and Gourie Caves (US$40 for three hours), Quashie River sink cave and bush hike (US$55, minimum five persons), Lorimar Coffee Estate and the Moravian churches, plus bird watching trips to the Cockpit Country.

Festivals & Events

On Christmas Eve the streets here have traditionally been closed and farming families have poured in for a centuries-old Jonkanoo celebration called **Grand Market Night**, with men on stilts and general festivity in the streets. The festivities are sometimes cancelled; call Sherryl McDowell or Audrey Brown at Hotel Villa Bella (☎ 964-2243) for updates.

Sleeping & Eating

Hotel Villa Bella (☎ 964-2243; r US$60-85) The Villa Bella is a charming and cozy old country inn perched on a hill at Sedburgh, at the south end of town. This former grande dame retains its original mahogany floors (now somewhat squeaky) and 1940s furniture. The 15 recently renovated, exquisitely decorated rooms have cable TV and deep bathtub-showers. Rooms in the annex are smaller. Gracious and efficient service recalls the days when Christiana was a center for 'old-style tourism.' Facilities include a reading room and TV lounge. The hotel also offers one of the best and most reasonably priced dining experiences on the island. The superb menu merges Jamaican, Japanese and Chinese cuisines. Typical dishes include chicken teriyaki, Chinese-style poached fish in ginger and soy sauce, and sole Villa Bella (simmered in coconut milk, spices and lemongrass). Eat on the veranda or the garden terrace, where you can sip home-made ginger beer and admire the flower-filled garden. Afternoon tea is at 4:30pm. And the ackee breakfast is unsurpassed!

Main St has numerous undistinguished restaurants and pastry shops. **Akete Vegetarian Restaurant** (Main St; mains US$2-10; ⌚ breakfast, lunch & dinner) is recommended for I-tal food.

Getting There & Away

Christiana is well served by public transportation from both Kingston and Mandeville. A bus and minibuses also operate from Montego Bay and Ocho Rios via Albert Town.

SPALDINGS

Spaldings is a small, often mist-shrouded town set at about 900m elevation on the crest of the central highlands, about 5km southeast of Christiana. The hills are planted in market gardens. Ginger and yams are important local crops.

Spaldings is the site of **Knox College**, a highly rated coed religious school founded in 1940 by a progressive educator, the Rev Lewis Davidson, who believed that a school should serve to benefit its local community. Hence, the school has its own print works, farm and even a meat-processing plant.

The B4 continues east, dropping into the Rio Minho Valley.

Glencoe B&B (☎ 964-2286; s/d incl breakfast US$40/60) is a delightful piece of Old England at Nash Farm, 500m southwest of Spaldings. The two-story farmhouse has four quaint little upstairs bedrooms with mahogany floors, antiques and bathrooms with hot water. An enclosed veranda forms a wraparound lounge with a TV and a small library.

MANDEVILLE & AROUND

MANDEVILLE

pop 45,000

Imperturbable Mandeville lounges 610m above sea level on a plateau of the eastern flank of the Don Figuerero Mountains. Climbing up to Jamaica's fifth largest town, you're immediately conscious of the almost springlike coolness that marks Manchester Parish's capital and drew many British settlers in the 19th century. In the 1950s, these expats were joined by North Americans working in the bauxite industry, giving the town a cosmopolitan aura.

History

Established only in 1816, Mandeville began life as a haven for colonial planters escaping the heat of the plains. In the 19th century, the city prospered as a holiday retreat for wealthy Kingstonians, and attracted soldiers and British retirees from other colonial quarters. Many early expats established the area as a center for dairy farming and citrus and pimento production. Jamaica's unique seedless citrus fruit, the ortanique, was first produced here in the 1920s and is grown in large quantities.

North American bauxite company Alcan opened operations here in 1940 (in 2000 it sold its operations to a Swiss company, Glencore). Relatively high wage levels lured educated Jamaicans, bringing a middle-class savoir faire to the town.

Orientation

Mandeville is spread across rolling hills in a maze of wriggly streets. At its heart is a historic village green, called Cecil Charlton Park after a former mayor. The green is ringed by Park Cres, and from here the roads radiate out like spokes on a wheel. Manchester Rd leads southeast, Ward Ave leads west and Main St leads north.

Main St is the main artery and runs north to join Caledonia Rd; at the T-junction, Caledonia Rd leads east to Williamsfield; westward it runs back into town parallel to Main St and continues south as Perth Rd.

The Winston Jones Hwy (A2) skirts the town to the north and west before dropping eastward to Williamsfield and westward to St Elizabeth parish.

Information

BOOKSTORES

Booklands (☎ 962-9051; Manchester Shopping Plaza; ⌚ 8am-5pm Mon-Fri, to 3pm Sat) Meagerly stocked but with a decent selection of regional-interest titles.

EMERGENCY

Police station (☎ 962-2250, 119; Park Cres) On the north side of the green.

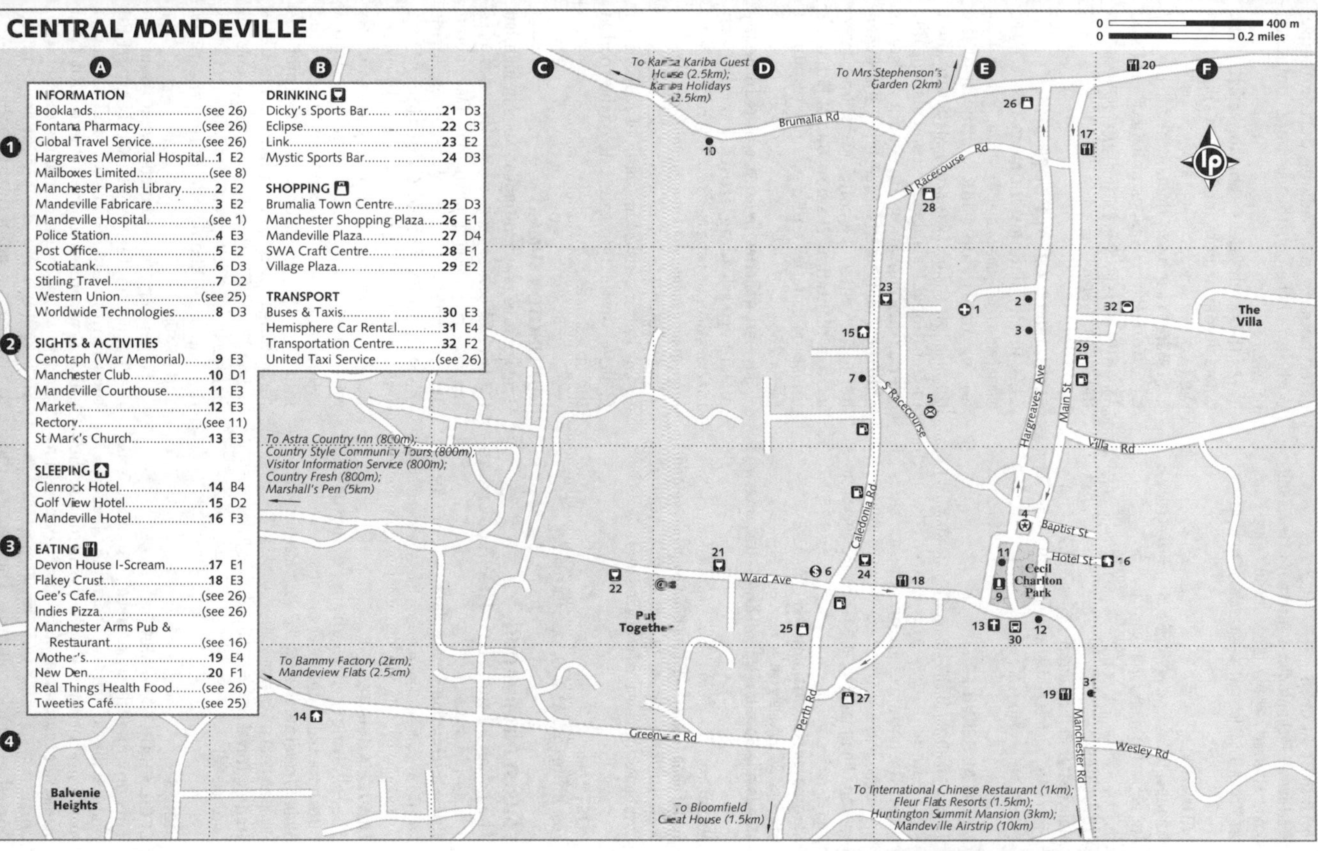

SOUTH COAST & CENTRAL HIGHLANDS

INTERNET ACCESS

Worldwide Technologies & Internet Cafe & Mailboxes Limited (☎ 961-1829; Suite 10, Central Plaza; per 30 min US$3) Internet is also available at the library.

LAUNDRY

Mandeville Fabricare (☎ 962-2471; 30 Hargreaves Ave; per load US$1; 🕑 8am-5pm)

LIBRARIES

Manchester Parish Library (☎ 962-2972; 34 Hargreaves Ave; internet per half hr US$1; 🕑 9:30am-4:30pm Mon-Fri, to 4pm Sat)

MEDICAL SERVICES

The two hospitals have emergency services. Although they are adjacent to each other, the entrances are on opposite sides of the racecourse.

Fontana Pharmacy (☎ 962-3129; Manchester Shopping Plaza)

Hargreaves Memorial Hospital (☎ 962-2040; Caledonia Rd) Privately run.

Mandeville Hospital (☎ 962-2067; 32 Hargreaves Ave)

MONEY

Scotiabank (☎ 962-1083; cnr Ward Ave & Caledonia Rd)

Western Union (☎ 962-1037; Brumalia Town Centre, Perth St) Receive or send money by remittance.

POST

Post office (☎ 962-2339; South Racecourse)

TOURIST INFORMATION

The Jamaica Tourist Board does not have an office in Mandeville.

Visitor Information Service (☎ 962-3725; 62 Ward Ave) The best information source is at the Astra Country Inn.

TRAVEL AGENCIES

The following agencies arrange domestic and international flight reservations:

Global Travel Service (☎ 962-2630; Manchester Shopping Plaza, 18 Caledonia Rd)

Sterling Travel (☎ 962-2203; Caledonia Plaza, Caledonia Rd)

Sights

CECIL CHARLTON PARK

This tiny English-style **'green'**, also known as Mandeville Sq, lends a charming village feel to the town center. On the north side is the **Mandeville Courthouse**, of cut limestone with a horseshoe staircase and a raised portico supported by Doric columns. The **Rectory**, the oldest home in town, adjoins the courthouse. Both it and the courthouse were completed in 1820.

On the south side is a **produce market**, and a **cenotaph** commemorating Jamaica's dead from the two world wars.

St Mark's Church, on the south side of Cecil Charlton Park, was established in 1819. The timber clerestory is impressive, as is the churchyard.

BLOOMFIELD GREAT HOUSE

This immaculate **historic home** (☎ 962-7130; bloomfield.g.h@cwjamaica.com; 8 Perth Rd; 🕑 noon-10pm Tue-Sat) stands atop a hill southwest of the town center. The two-story structure built in traditional Caribbean vernacular gleams after a fine renovation. It is about 170 years old (the exact date is uncertain) and began life as the center of a coffee estate and, later, a citrus plantation. It's now one of Jamaica's finest art galleries and a premier restaurant (see p265).

The **art galleries** feature works by many of Jamaica's leading artists, as well as an international repertoire. There are five arts-and-crafts studios and stores in the arcade downstairs.

The entrance is 200m south of Manchester College, on the opposite side of the road at the crossroads.

HUNTINGTON SUMMIT

The extravagant **Huntingdon Summit mansion** (☎ 962-2274; George's Valley Rd; admission free, donations accepted; 🕑 by appointment) in May Day, about 3km southeast of the town center, forms the yang to Bloomfield Great House's yin. The octagonal home is of palatial proportions, with wraparound plate-glass windows and artificial cascades that tumble into a swimming pool, from where waters feed into a pond in the lounge. The ostentatious furnishings reflect the catholic tastes of its owner, Cecil Charlton, a millionaire farmer, politician and self-promoter who served as the mayor of Mandeville during the 1970s and 1980s.

To get here, take Manchester Rd south to the T-junction; turn right onto Newport Rd then left onto May Day Rd, and left again after 1km onto George's Valley Rd (you can't miss the big green gates on the left). An appointment and a permit are required to visit; call ahead of time to book.

COMMUNITY TOURISM

You won't be long in the Mandeville area before you hear about 'community tourism,' an attempt to create opportunities for locals wishing to participate more fully in Jamaica's tourism industry, while fostering a deeper connection for visitors with the people of communities they might otherwise just pass through.

The dynamo behind the movement is Diana McIntyre-Pike, co-owner and manager of the Astra Country Inn and director of **Countrystyle Community Tours** (☎ 962-7758, 488-7207; www.countrystylecommunitytourism.com), a company geared towards providing alternatives to 'sea and sand' vacations. McIntyre-Pike helped to form the Central & South Tourism Committee, which sponsors special-interest tours, community guides, skills training and assistance with tourism development at the local level. She also runs the Countrystyle Institute for Sustainable Tourism, offering courses from community guide training to environmental waste management. 'Whatever development takes place, it must complement our lifestyle, not change our way of life,' she says.

The following tours were conceived to provide experience and insights that capture the 'real Jamaica.' Each day-tour includes lunch and refreshment:

- **Roots Jamaica** (US$50) introduces you to Jamaican hospitality. Spend a day in a country village, receive a community welcome and be entertained in a private home while sampling local food. Visit churches and community centers and listen as elders relate tales of the past.
- **Taste of Jamaica** (US$50) entails a day of village-hopping and learning to cook Jamaican cuisine in a natural setting with the community. Learn the old-time way of making bammy from cassava, taste sugarcane and plantain tarts, and sample fruits including naseberry, star apples and ortaniques. There's traditional coffee-making, a visit to Middle Quarters for some pepper shrimp, and the tour concludes with a meal at Little Ochie restaurant (p274) in Alligator Pond.
- **Jamaica Naturally** (US$50) unfurls nature at its best in six villages of the central and south areas of Jamaica. Along the way you'll enjoy the scenic splendor of Resource Village, Cut River, Alligator Pond, Bamboo Avenue, YS Falls, Black River and a dramatic conclusion at Lover's Leap.

In addition, Countrystyle offers 'community experience packages' for lengthier stays. Among them is a three-day all-inclusive package (including choice of one of the above day tours) for US$1000 (US$1200 per couple) and a seven-day B&B package (including all three tours) for US$1050 (US$2000 per couple).

Countrystyle Community Tours is affiliated with **Unique Jamaica** (www.uniquejamaica.com), a nationwide initiative to bring the values of community tourism to an ever-widening audience.

SOUTH COAST & CENTRAL HIGHLANDS

MARSHALL'S PEN

This impressive stone-and-timber **great house** (☎ 904-5454; admission US$10; by appointment), built in 1795, stands among beautifully landscaped gardens on a former coffee plantation turned cattle-breeding property on the northwest side of town.

The 120-hectare property is owned by Jamaica's leading ornithologist, Robert Sutton, and Anne Sutton, an environmental scientist. Robert can trace his ancestry to the first child born to English parents in Jamaica in 1655.

The Suttons' home has wood-paneled rooms brimming with antiques, leather-bound books, artwork and many other museum-quality pieces. You can tour the mini-museum by appointment only.

Marshall's Pen is splendid for birding: more than 100 species have been recorded here, including 25 of the 27 species endemic to Jamaica. It's a treat to don rubber boots and binoculars and set out with the Suttons and their several dogs swarming happily at your heels. Robert is coauthor with Audrey Downer of *Birds of Jamaica: A Photographic Field Guide*. Visiting in early morning or late afternoon is best.

To get to the property, take Oriole Close off Winston Jones Hwy, about 5km northwest of the town center (there's a sign for 'Somerset Quarries' at the junction). Turn left on Nightingale Dr and then, after about 100m, right on Mike Town Rd; the estate entrance – an unmarked stone gateway

– is about 400m further on the right. Take insect repellent.

Countrystyle Community Tours (see p263) offers tours by appointment.

MRS STEPHENSON'S GARDEN

This well-manicured **garden** (☎ 962-2909; fax 961-1486; 25 New Green Rd; admission US$2; by appointment) has been planned and planted, and pruned and mulched, by a stalwart who is a real artist. Carmen Stephenson's garden is a riot of color, a drunkenness of scents, difficult to dampen in even the wettest of weather. Keen amateur gardeners descend year-round to admire the layout or gasp at the collection that includes orchids and ortaniques. Casual visitors are welcome during daylight hours.

Activities

For golf, check out the **Manchester Club** (☎ 962-2403; mosquito_j@hotmail.com), the oldest golf club in the Caribbean. Located off Brumalia Rd, northwest of the town center, it has a nine-hole golf course that was laid out in the 1860s. A round costs US$25 and caddies are compulsory (US$15). The club also has three night-lit tennis courts and squash courts (both US$5 per hour).

Tours

Kariba Holidays & Leisure Tours (☎ 961-3829, 962-8006; Kariba Kariba Guest House, Winston Jones Hwy) offers tours locally and further afield.

Countrystyle Community Tours (☎ 962-7758; Astra Country Inn, 62 Ward Ave) has a 'Marvelous Mandeville' tour (per person US$60 full day, including lunch and transfers). It also offers tours further afield and specialist guides (see the boxed text, p263).

Festivals & Events

Manchester Horticultural Society Show (☎ 962-2909) is held in late May at Mrs Stephenson's Garden (above).

Manchester Golf Week is held in late July at the Manchester Club; contact the **Jamaica Golf Association** (☎ 975-4287) for details. The **Jamaica Horse Show** is held in July, and **Tennis Week** in August, both at the Manchester Club.

Sleeping

Glenrock Hotel (☎ 961-3279; glenrock@cwjamaica.com; 3 Greenvale Rd; s US$46, d US$53-60, ste US$65-75; P) In the process of a prolonged renovation at last visit, this congenial place has seven older (and cheaper) rooms with fans and louvered windows, plus bathrooms with hot water. Suites have king-size beds, cable TV, phones and kitchens with refrigerators.

Astra Country Inn (☎ 962-7758; 62 Ward Ave; r US$47-56, ste US$120;) On the western outskirts of town, this former nursing home contains 20 rooms (some with king-size beds) with cable TVs, including suites with kitchenettes. The Astra is home to an English-style pub, a pleasant dining room serving tasty Jamaican cuisine and the offices of Countrystyle Community Tours (p263), who will enhance your stay in Mandeville immeasurably.

Kariba Kariba Guest House (☎ 962-8006; 39 New Green Rd; r incl breakfast US$50) North of the town center, this beautiful fieldstone home run by a friendly English–Jamaican couple has five spacious rooms with balconies that share a bathroom. It has handsome tile and hardwood floors and a large lounge. Dinner and lunch cost US$5 each. The owner can point out nature trails and also leads customized excursions that give a good sense of rural Jamaican culture.

Fleur Flats Resorts (☎ 962-1053, in Canada 416-445-0209, in the USA 305-252-0873, in the UK 020-7964-0047; 10 Coke Dr; 1-/2-bedroom apt US$60/80) The spacious fully furnished apartments sleep up to four people in comfort. Rooms have TVs and phones. This family-oriented resort is a 20-minute walk from the town center.

Mandeview Flats (☎ 961-8439; mandeview.com/standard; 7 Hillview Dr, Balvenie Heights; s US$64-93, d US$75-93; P) With deeply satisfying views over Mandeville's surrounding undulating hillsides, this bright and gleaming small hotel offers 12 clean fan-cooled rooms. Each is done up in bright colors and has a TV. One has a kitchenette and can be combined with another to form a family suite. Breakfast is included; dinners are by arrangement.

Golf View Hotel (☎ 962-4477; www.thegolfviewhotel.com; 51/2 Caledonia Rd; s US$70-90, d US$75-95; 1-/2- bedroom ste US$110; P) This rambling, conference-oriented property with 60-odd rooms is centered on a small pool in a concrete courtyard. Rooms have contemporary decor, tile floors, fans, cable TVs, louvered windows and tub showers. Spacious suites have walk-in showers and four-poster beds.

Mandeville Hotel (☎ 962-2460; www.mandevillehoteljamaica.com; Hotel St; r $88-93, ste US$110-135, apt $195-255; P) The town's oldest hotel has been operating since 1875, yet an unimaginative 1970s renovation has cost it its character. It has 60 rooms of varying standards; all have cable TV and phone. Rooms to the rear are a bit dowdy. Spacious suites boast four-poster beds. Self-contained units with kitchenettes are also available. The restaurant overlooks a pool and is joined by a pub that gets rather crowded.

Eating

Tweeties Café (☎ 962-3426; 2 Perth Rd; breakfast US$2-4; 🕑 breakfast & lunch) Tweeties offers cheap breakfasts, as well as fish and chips, pizza and sandwiches in Brumalia Town Centre.

International Chinese Restaurant (☎ 962-1252; 117 Manchester Rd; mains US$5-25; 🕑 lunch & dinner) Filling portions of above-average Chinese fare are on offer at this casual spot.

New Den (☎ 962-3603; 35 Caledonia Rd; mains US$5-25; 🕑 lunch & dinner Mon-Sat) In the former home of a colonial family with an affinity for wickerwork, this refined Jamaican eatery serves up excellent fish and chips as well as curried or barbecued chicken. If you're especially hungry, try the mixed grill, which lets you pick any three grilled meat or fish dishes on the menu.

Country Fresh (☎ 962-7758; Astra Country Inn, 62 Ward Ave; mains US$7-15; 🕑 breakfast, lunch & dinner) With an emphasis on the authentic, this hotel-based restaurant grows much of its produce in a private garden. A set meal is offered; lunch and dinner can be made to order. Sandwiches and snacks cost US$2.

Manchester Arms Pub & Restaurant (☎ 962-9764; mains US$7-18; Mandeville Hotel, Hotel St; 🕑 breakfast, lunch & dinner) A broad menu of Jamaican and continental dishes is served here. It has a poolside barbecue each Wednesday night. Jamaican night is held on the last Wednesday of every month, with Jamaican food and entertainment, including a live mento band.

Bloomfield Great House Restaurant & Bar (☎ 962-7130; 8 Perth Rd; mains US$10-30; 🕑 lunch & dinner Mon-Sat) One of Jamaica's pre-eminent restaurants, this exemplifies the best of Caribbean fusion cuisine. Grab a seat on the veranda and sample the creative menu, which changes regularly and includes such house-made pastas as callaloo fettuccine, jumbo shrimp stuffed with jalapeno pepper and filet mignon. The lunch menu offers Caesar salad, pizza, fish and chips, and lighter fare. A Sunday champagne brunch is offered, as are free pick-up and drop-off from central Mandeville hotels. At the very least, drop by for a drink in the mahogany bar.

You can buy one half of the famous 'fish and bammy' at Clem Bloomfield's **Bammy Factory** (☎ 963-8636; 40 Greenvale Rd). **Flakey Crust** (11A Manchester Rd) sells fresh-baked breads, pastries and patties. **Devon House I-Scream** (Main St) has an outlet in Mandeville.

There are a dozen or so fast-food joints around town. A food court to the rear of the Manchester Shopping Plaza features **Indies Pizza** (☎ 961-1676; Shop 47); **Gee's Café** (☎ 962-2606; Shop 42), recommended for its Jamaican breakfasts; and the **Real Things Health Food Store** (☎ 962-5664). **Mother's** (Manchester Rd; patties US$0.40) is a good place to buy cheap patties and baked goods.

Fresh produce can be found at the market on the south side of Cecil Charlton Park, but hygiene is an issue.

Drinking & Entertainment

Mandeville is relatively devoid of an active nightlife. Locals have a humorous phrase to describe the town: 'newlyweds and nearly deads.'

Link (☎ 964-8799; 80 Caledonia Ave) This is a popular neighborhood bar where you're sure to make some friends. Entertaining karaoke nights are held on Thursday and Saturday, and on Sunday a DJ spins vintage reggae and American R&B.

Eclipse (☎ 962-2660; 33 Ward Ave; admission US$5) The only nightclub of note, it has live music out back and a disco inside. Friday is 'Ladies Nite,' with free entry.

Dicky's Sports Bar (Ward Ave; 🕑 4.30pm-midnight Mon-Thu, 4.30pm until last person leaves Fri-Sun) A classic Jamaican haunt with pool tables and the occasional sound-system party.

Mystic Sports Bar (Caledonia Rd) This sometimes-lively spot has pool tables.

The Manchester Arms (left) is a quiet English-style pub that's open late, while Bloomfield Great House (p262) has live musical entertainment on Friday night.

Shopping

SWA Craft Centre (☎ 962-0694; 7 N Racecourse) Behind the Manchester Shopping Plaza, this place trains young women to make a living from crochet, embroidery, weaving and so on. Its most appealing item is the famous 'banana patch' Rastafarian doll.

Getting There & Around

The airline **Timair** (☎ 952-2516; www.timair.com) serves the Mandeville airstrip, south of town, from MoBay.

Mandeville has direct bus, minibus and route-taxi services from virtually every major town in Jamaica. Most buses, and many minibuses and route taxis, depart and arrive from the transportation center, off Main St. Others depart and arrive near the market on the main square. Sample fares are US$3.50 to Kingston, US$5 to Savanna-la-Mar and US$6.50 to Montego Bay.

There is no local bus system. You'll find taxis near the market on Cecil Charlton Park. Otherwise, call **United Taxi Service** (☎ 961-3333; Manchester Shopping Centre).

Hemisphere Car Rental (☎ 962-1921; 51 Manchester Rd) rents cars.

GUTTERS & SPUR TREE HILL

Gutters, 16km east of Santa Cruz, sits astride the border of Manchester and St Elizabeth parishes at the foot of Spur Tree Hill. From here, the A2 road begins a long, steep switchback climb up the Don Figuerero Mountains to Mandeville.

At the top of the hill you can look out over the Essex Valley and the Santa Cruz Mountains. The valley floor is dominated by the Alpart alumina factory at Nain, 8km to the southeast, and aglitter at night.

You can admire the view midway up the hill at any of several roadside shacks.

WILLIAMSFIELD

In the village of Williamsfield, 300m below and northeast of Mandeville, at the base of the Winston Jones Hwy (A2), you can take a free tour of the **High Mountain Coffee Factory** (☎ 963-4211; Winston Jones Hwy; 10am-4pm Mon-Fri, tours by appointment). Here, coffee, herbal teas and liqueurs are produced by the Jamaica Standard Products Co under the three labels. It's adjacent to the old train station just west of the roundabout. The factory is tiny and the tour more of interest to coffee fanatics, but it has a tasting room and store.

The **High Mountain 10K Road Race** (☎ 963-4211), Jamaica's largest bicycle road race, is held here every January.

SHOOTER'S HILL

Shooter's Hill begins 3km northwest of Williamsfield and climbs steadily and steeply (430m in elevation) to Christiana. A lookout point midway offers splendid views. On the west side of the road, atop a hillock, is the Moravian-built **Mizpah Church** topped by a four-faced German clock.

Kirkvine Works, an alumina-processing plant at the base of Shooter's Hill, is owned and operated by Windalco. You can arrange free weekday tours in Mandeville through Astra Country Inn (p264), or through Mr J Neil at the **Kirkvine Works office** (☎ 961-7503, 962-3141). A day's notice is usually required. There's a strict dress code: long pants are required and feet must be covered (no sandals).

The **Pickapeppa Factory** (☎ 962-2928, 962-2809; www.pickapeppa.com; adult/child US$9/3), on the B6 at the foot of Shooter's Hill, offers 30-minute tours by appointment. The factory produces Jamaica's sinus-searing world-famous sauce, which graces most tables on the island. There's not much to see, other than workers stirring giant pots of simmering scallions and other vegetables.

MILE GULLY & AROUND

This village sprawls along a valley that runs northwest from Mandeville in the lee of the forested north face of the Don Figuerero Mountains. The B6 leads northwest from Shooter's Hill, winding, dipping and rising past lime-green pastures dotted with guango and silk-cotton trees and crisscrossed with stone walls and hedgerows.

The valley is pitted with caves, including **Oxford Caves**, near Mile Gully.

About 1km west of Mile Gully, at **Skull Point**, is a venerable blue-and-white 19th-century police station and courthouse at the junction for Bethany.

Ripon Nature Park (admission US$3), dating to 1730, in Mile Gully, produces citrus, flowers, coffee and cocoa and is being developed into a bird sanctuary, wild garden and ecopark by Derek O'Connor, owner of **Kariba Holidays & Leisure Tours** (☎ 962-8006) in Mandeville. The 5-hectare garden has more than 500 endemic species, including orchids. A palm-lined driveway leads to the vast and varied garden, accessible by trails and open for picnics. Fruit trees include giant plums. The hillsides are carpeted in ferns, and feature benches for quiet contemplation. Meditate among the fern-carpeted hillsides or check out the new hummingbird and butterfly garden, then cool off in the pool. A children' play park and horseback riding round out the activities.

The Bethany road climbs sharply and delivers you at the **Bethany Moravian Church** – a simple gray stone building dating to 1835, dramatically perched four-square midway up the hill with fantastic valley views. The church is rather dour close up, but the simple interior boasts a resplendent organ.

Another beautiful church – **St Simon's Anglican Church** – sits on a hillside amid meadows at Comfort Hall, 6km west of Mile Gully, with huge spreading trees festooned with old man's beard.

To the south of the B6, perched atop the Don Figuerero Mountains, at Maidstone, is **Nazareth Moravian Church**. One of the best-planned postemancipation 'free villages,' Maidstone was founded in 1840.

The annual **Emancipation Day Fair** is celebrated at Maidstone on August 1, with mento bands, Jonkanoo celebrations, and maypole and quadrille dancing.

Getting There & Away

Coasters and route taxis operate on the B6 between Mandeville and Maggotty via Mile Gully.

If you're driving from Mandeville, the B6 continues west about 8km to Green Hill and a T-junction. About 1.5km north (to the right) of the junction, en route to Balaclava, is a *very dangerous* spot: you'll climb a short hill that tempts you to accelerate. Unfortunately there's an unmarked railway crossing on the crest and a hairpin bend *immediately* after. Drive slowly!

TREASURE BEACH & AROUND

The coastal strip southeast of Black River is sheltered from rains for most of the year by the Santa Cruz Mountains, so there is none of the lush greenery of the north coast to be found here. Instead, you'll find acacia trees and cactus towering up to 9m. The region remains unsullied by tourism. Here one can slip into the kind of lazy, no-frills tropical lifestyle almost impossible to achieve elsewhere on the island's coast.

Dividing the plains north to south are the Santa Cruz Mountains, a steep-faced chain that slopes to the sea and drops 520m at Lover's Leap. The plains are hemmed in to the west by a range of hills called Surinam Quarters, whose scarp faces fall sharply to the coast; to the north by the Nassau Mountains and the Cockpit Country; and to the east by the Don Figuerero Mountains, a wedge-shaped upland plateau dominating Manchester parish. The base of the west-facing escarpment of the Don Figuereros forms the boundary between St Elizabeth and Manchester. Northeast of the Don Figuereros, the Mocho Mountains rise to Christiana and crest at Mt Denham (992m).

TREASURE BEACH

If Treasure Beach were any more laid-back it would risk floating off into the sea. With rocky headlands separating lonely, coral-colored sand beaches, the area is noted for its healthy supply of relaxed guesthouses and stylish boutique hotels. The sense of remoteness, easy pace, and graciousness of the local farmers and fisherfolk attract foreign travelers seeking an away-from-it-all, cares-to-the-wind lifestyle. Many have chosen to settle here – much to local pride.

Treasure Beach is the generic name for four coves – Billy's Bay, Frenchman's Bay, Calabash Bay and Great Pedro Bay. It's said that Scottish sailors were shipwrecked near Treasure Beach in the 19th century, accounting for the presence of fair skin, green eyes and reddish hair.

The area's residents are also known for their strong community spirit. Collectives like the Treasure Beach Women's Group and the Treasure Beach Foundation bring locals and expats together for effective projects relating to housing, education and local culture. There's a burgeoning cultural scene here, with artists, poets and other luminaries continuing to put down roots. Along with the Calabash Literary Festival, they continue to shape and guide a national literary dialogue.

With all the buzz that 'quiet' Treasure Beach is generating, it's no surprise that developers are hungrily buying up land, and it can be only a matter of time before the first major resorts appear. A citizens' committee meets each month to regulate impending development. But for the time being, it's just you and the sea.

Information

Jake's Place (p271) is an unofficial tourist information source. On the internet, a good starting point is www.treasurebeach.net.

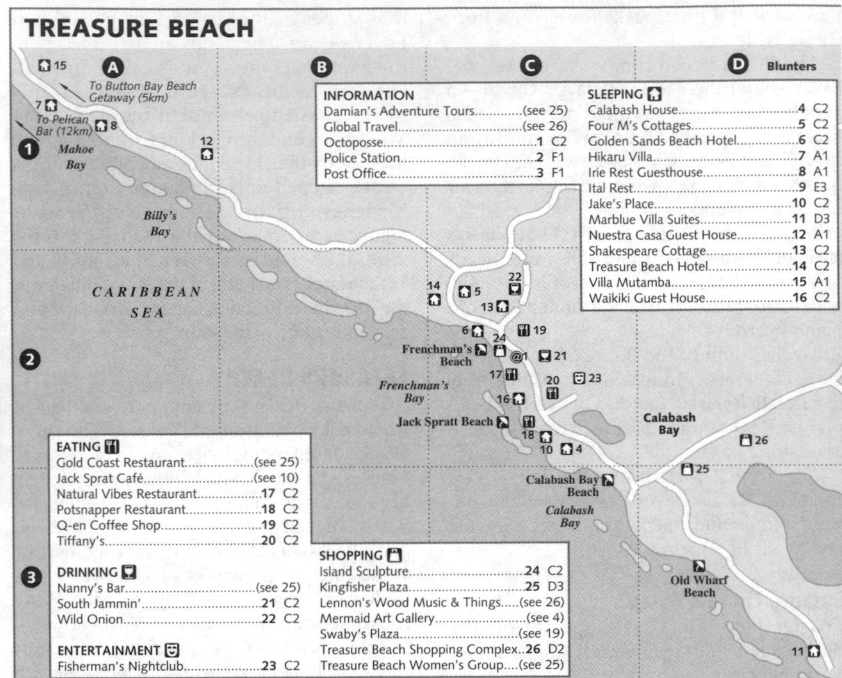

The nearest bank is in Southfield, 16km east of Treasure Beach. The post office is on a hillside beside the police station.

Dr Valerie M Elliott (☎ 607-9074; 🕑 7am-10pm Mon, Tue & Fri) Available on call.

Global Travel (☎ 965-0547; Treasure Beach Shopping Complex) Plane reservations and regional tours.

Octoposse (☎ 367-7501; per 30 min US$3; 🕑 7am-10pm Mon, Tue & Fri) Internet access.

Police station (☎ 965-0163) Between Calabash Bay and Pedro Cross.

Activities

The Treasure Beach region boasts many different ways to enjoy the outdoor activites, including gratifying beaches and excellent hiking. You will be able to wander for hours on the many footpaths that traverse their way over hill and dale and along the sea. Calabash Bay is backed by the Great Pedro Ponds, which are good spots for birding.

Bicycles can be rented at Jake's Place (see p271) and also at the **Q-en Coffee Shop** (☎ 326-9008; per 24hr US$7). Jake's also rents out kayaks. For bicycle, hiking, kayak or snorkeling tours, see opposite.

BEACHES

Four almost-empty fishing beaches beckon, all within easy walking distance of the accommodations around Calabash Bay. Water sports haven't yet caught on, although the waves are good for body-surfing. Beware! There is sometimes a vicious undertow at all area beaches. Ask a local where the safest swimming spots are.

The most visited is the folksy **Jack Spratt Beach**, at the western edge of Jake's Place. Large and brightly painted wooden fishing boats are pulled up on the sand, and there is invariably a fisherman or two on hand tending the nets. This is the safest beach for swimming. Nearby the Jack Spratt Café (p272) sells beer and excellent food at pleasant outdoor tables.

The next beach to the west is **Frenchman's Beach**, watched over by a landmark 'buttonwood' tree that has long attracted the attention of poets, painters and woodcarvers who ply their wares. This is also a great

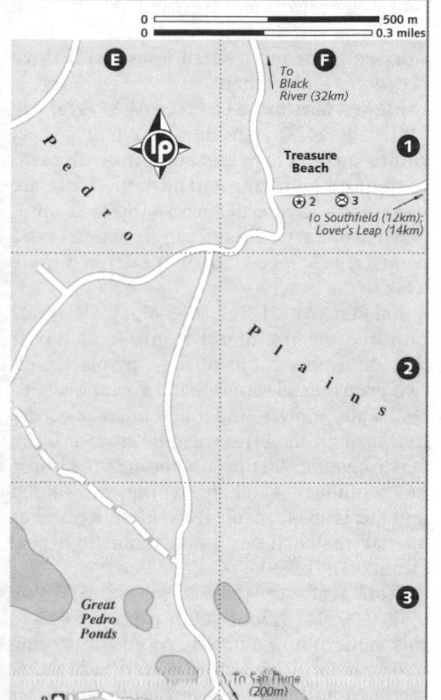

place to arrange trips to the Pelican Bar or Black River.

In the opposite direction from Jake's there's **Calabash Bay Beach**, with a few cook and rum shops and a sandy beach, and **Old Wharf Beach**, the most private of the bunch.

BOATING & FISHING

With a long and proud history of seafaring fishermen, it's no wonder that Treasure Beach is a great place from which to take to the sea. The best time to book a trip is during the early morning or late afternoon; the winds tend to pick up during the middle of the day. On bright moonlit evenings it is possible to take to the silvery waters for an enchanting tour of the coast.

Popular boating excursions include the Pelican Bar (p271), Black River Great Morass (p253), and Sunny Island and Little Ochie, both near Alligator Pond (p273). From Frenchman's Beach, boat captain and fisher **Dennis Abrahams** (☎ 435-3779, 965-3084; per person US$20, minimum 4; ⏲ 5pm) offers a sunset cruise by motorboat to Great Pedro Bluff and Billy's Bay, as well as fishing and on-demand trips to the Pelican Bar and Black River Great Morass. Other recommended captains include **Allan Daley** (☎ 423-3673, 366-7394) and **Teddy Parchment** (☎ 854-5442), who both offer customized four-hour boat tours for about US$30 per person (minimum four people).

Everyone with a boat in Treasure Beach is involved in some way with the pursuit of fishing, and it's easy to talk someone into taking you out to pull a trap or drop a line. Or you can book a fishing trip at Jake's (US$40 per hour for up to six people), which includes rods and bait. Fish frequently caught include grouper, kingfish and snapper; most restaurants are happy to prepare them for the night's dinner.

Tours

At Jake's Place (p271), the friendly staff are more than happy to arrange excursions and activities throughout the area. Julie Kolipulos offers day-long walking tours (US$30). At Jake's, a man calling himself simply **Andy** (☎ 438-1311; bicycle/kayak rental per day US$25/35) rents bicycles and kayaks and leads tours (from US$50).

Damian's Adventure Tours (☎ 965-3101, 965-3101; sandyboy9@yahoo.com; Kingfisher Plaza) offers

SOUTH COAST & CENTRAL HIGHLANDS

SCRUBS & RUBS IN TREASURE BEACH

Treasure Beach's fresh air and its soaring scenery provide a perfect environment for some rejuvenating body work, and visitors can enjoy the services of two excellent – and very different – practitioners. **Joshua Lee Stein** (☎ 965-0583, 965-0635; per hr US$60) offers massage at Jake's Place, but he also does the rounds of area hotels and guesthouses on his tricycle with folding massage table in tow. He gives discounts to students and seniors. For something different, **Shirley Genus** (☎ 421-8903, 863-3481; treatment US$80) offers a traditional Jamaican herbal steam bath and massage at Ital Rest (p270). Here, weary travelers can get the road rubbed out of them with a healing 'vibeful' massage in a hut filled with aromatic steam emanating from a herbal cauldron bubbling with fever grass, mint, eucalyptus and pimento (allspice).

TREASURE BEACH FOUNDATION

The **Treasure Beach Foundation** (☎ 965-3000; www.breds.org) – or Breds (short for brethren) – is dedicated to fostering heritage pride, sports, health and education among the community. Work includes restoring decrepit housing, sponsorship of both a soccer team and a basketball team, and the introduction of a computer lab at the local school.

Donations are welcome. Contact Jake's Place (opposite) for more information.

mountain biking locally, as well as hiking, snorkeling and overnight camping trips.

Festivals & Events

Treasure Beach Off-Road Triathlon (☎ 965-0635) Held in early May and sponsored by Breds.

Calabash International Literary Festival (☎ 922-4200; www.calabashfestival.org) A daring, acclaimed literary festival in late May at Jake's, drawing literary voices from near and far.

New Year's Eve Bonfire Party At Fisherman's Beach, this boisterous party is an institution.

Sleeping

Treasure Beach boasts one world-famous hotel and many restful guest houses that are as personable as the friendly folk who run them. There's a good selection of truly affordable lodging, making this one of the most economical places in Jamaica for an extended stay.

Speaking of sticking around, the area also features a great selection of spacious villas, many of them fully staffed. Some in this category provide bona-fide luxury and considerable style, while others are more modest and practical, providing good value for groups or families. Details of a variety of these can be found at www.treasurebeach.net and www.jamaica escapes.com.

BUDGET

Shakespeare Cottage (☎ 965-0120; r US$20-30) Two hundred meters east of the Treasure Beach Hotel, this choice budget option has five rooms with fans and bathrooms with cold water only. There's a communal kitchen.

Waikiki Guest House (☎ 965-3660, 345-9669; r/cottage/house US$20/35/50) An excellent budget option facing Frenchman's Beach, this cozy place has six rooms, each with fans and private cool-water bath; prices are negotiable. Waikiki also has a one-bedroom cottage, two two-story cottages and a small house with three bedrooms and kitchen.

Irie Rest Guesthouse (☎ 965-0034; Billy's Bay Way; d US$30; P ⊠ 💻) Another excellent budget choice, on offer here are six rooms with bathrooms and both fans and air-con. There are private patios, internet access and meals prepared to order. One room can sleep four (extra people are charged US$10). It's a five-minute walk to the beach.

Ital Rest (☎ 421-8909, 863-3481; r US$40) Four hundred meters inland from Great Bay is this atmospheric, out-of-the-way place with two exquisite all-wood thatched cabins with cool-water showers and toilets but no electricity. At night the breezy candle-lit rooms are very romantic. An upstairs room in the house has a sundeck. Kitchen facilities are shared and meals are available by request. It also has a small thatched bar and a fantastic herbal steam bath (p269).

Four M's Cottages (☎ 965-0131; camping US$10, s/d/tr US$40/60/80; ⊠) About 400m from the beach, this modern house has six rooms of varying size with hot-water bathrooms. Windows are screened and there are mosquito nets over some beds. Guests enjoy spending time in the kitchen with gracious host Effie Campbell. There are also good camping spots beneath shady trees.

Nuestra Casa Guest House (☎ 965-0152, 965-3565; www.billysbay.com; d US$50) This gem at Billy's Bay is run by Lillian Brooks, a delightful English lady, and her son Roger, a burly chap with a sense of humor. A wide veranda has rockers, and a rooftop sundeck is shaded by umbrellas. The reclusive three-bedroom house is tastefully decorated. Two rooms share a bathroom; a third has its own. All have lofty wooden ceilings. It's a tremendous bargain at these rates, which decrease for longer stays. Breakfasts are prepared by arrangement.

MIDRANGE

Golden Sands Beach Hotel (☎ 965-0167; golden sands guesthouse@yahoo.com; r US$45-50, cottages US$60-80; ⊠) With a seaside location some consider the best spot in Treasure Beach, this old favorite offers 20 modestly furnished rooms with bathrooms. Rooms vary; some have ceiling fans, others boast sea views, and one has hot water and air-con. There are also one- and three-bedroom cottages with air-con and TV.

Button Bay Beach Getaway (☎ 965-3873; www.buttonbayjamaica.com; s/d villa US$60/120; P) An outstanding, secluded option 20 minutes east of Treasure Beach, the Button Bay Beach Getaway is nestled cozily around its own private cove with an intimate outdoor pool. Rooms are modern yet comfortable with mesmerizing sea or mountain views from balconies or private terraces. There's a large villa laden with artwork available for families. Kayaking and a wide array of tours are available.

Calabash House (☎ 382-6384; www.calabashhouse.com; r/cottage US$75/275; P) A highly congenial spot run by an American expat, Calabash House offers airy rooms with bathrooms, each adorned with its own distinctive mosaic, as well as secluded beachside cottages with hammocks. The Mermaid Art Gallery fronts the hotel, which hosts several art workshops throughout the year as well as a literary festival in late May.

San Dune (☎ 377-7724; Great Bay; 1-2/3-4/5-6 people US$100/150/200;) A pleasing blend of old and new, this property surrounded by 12 hectares of farmland includes a 100-year-old cottage with fanciful lucy fretwork and four bedrooms, kitchen and veranda, and a new two-bedroom cottage with similar amenities. The owner, Maisie Campbell, just happens to be Jamaica's biggest scallion and onion farmer.

Treasure Beach Hotel (☎ 965-0110; s US$99, d US$107-145; P) This rambling property dotted with palms and nestled on a hillside overlooking the beach has 36 rooms including 16 spacious, deluxe oceanfront suites that have king-size four-poster beds, cable TVs, tile floors and patios. There are two swimming pools, a whirlpool, and a volleyball court; sailing and snorkeling are also offered. The Yabba Restaurant is on the premises.

Villa Mutamba (☎ 920-8194, 387-4112; www.villamutamba.com; d per week US$700) This exquisite villa overlooking Billy's Bay was built in 2004 by the great dub poet Mutabaruka. The place is infused with an exquisite, rootsy sensibility. It has a wildly romantic master bedroom, a loft suitable for kids and, most winningly, a balcony affording 180-degree views of Treasure Beach. To get to the house – it's located on the side of a steep hill – you must climb a formidable flight of stairs to reach the clifftop setting.

TOP END

our pick **Jake's Place** (☎ in the USA 965-3000, 800-688-7678, in the UK 020-7440-4360; www.islandoutpost.com/jakes; r US$95-195, cottages US$195-325; P) The most glistening gem in Treasure Beach's chest, this rainbow-colored retreat, run with panache by Jason Henzell wins the award for the 'chicest shack' between Negril and Kingston. There are 13 single rooms (many perched over the sea), four two-bedroom cottages, a three-bedroom villa (rooms can be rented separately) like a mini-Moroccan *ksar,* and a one-up/one-down house that features an exterior spiral staircase, terra-cotta tile floors, tile and glass-brick walk-in showers and exquisite handmade beds. The decor follows Greek and Islamic motifs: onion-dome curves, blood-red floors, and walls and rough-hewn doors inset with colored bottles and glass beads. Many beds are metal-frame antiques. Wi-fi is available. The exquisite pool – lamplit at night – is shaded by a spreading tree. Jake's has two restaurants. Local bands perform, moonlight poetry readings are hosted, and Jason arranges tours and activities (see p269).

our pick **Marblue Villa Suites** (☎ 840-5772, 848-0001; www.marblue.com; domicil/veranda ste US$159/299; P) One of Jamaica's most stylish small hotels this well-run and welcoming boutique hotel pampers its guests with thoughtful service and considerable streamlined luxury. Five one-bedroom villa suites are appointed with furniture designed by the owners, architect Axel and Andrea Wichterich. Each veranda suite features living areas that open to spectacular views of the sea. The three 'domicil' rooms provide good value. The Blue Parrot Tiki Lounge, weekly barbecues, two dramatic pools and superb cuisine round out the offerings.

Hikaru Villa (☎ 965-0442, in the USA 860-247-0759; www.villahikaru.com; villa per week US$2195;) This is a sumptuous, fully staffed beachfront villa with private tennis court and croquet lawn. There are four screened, fan-cooled bedrooms opening to a wide shaded patio that catches the near-constant sea breeze. Inside is a living room and dining area that seats eight. Just below the patio is a sheltered sunning terrace. Rates quoted here are for up to four people (add 10% for each extra person up to eight).

Eating

our pick **Pelican Bar** (☎ 354-4218; Caribbean Sea; morning-sunset; mains US$5-15) Built on a submerged sandbar 1km out to sea, this thatch-roofed eatery on stilts provides Jamaica's – and perhaps the planet's – most enjoyable spot for a drink. Getting there is half the fun: hire a local boat captain (you can book passage from Jake's for US$30). The clientele is a mix of enchanted travelers and repeat-business fishermen who while away the hours playing dominoes, talking on their cell phones, checking the cricket scores or exchanging pleasantries with the self-satisfied owner. In between Red Stripes, or perhaps before your meal of lobster, shrimp or fish, feel free to slip into the salubrious waters for a dip.

Gold Coast Restaurant (Kingfisher Plaza; meals US$2.50-4; Mon-Sat) There's always a sweet-smelling pot on the stove at this favorite local eatery. No-nonsense budget meals, ranging from curried conch to spicy shrimp, are served.

Natural Vibes Restaurant (mains US$3.50-12; breakfast & lunch) This unassuming spot offers bargain prices on local favorites such as lobster, chicken chop suey and beef stew. It's a good spot for a hearty Jamaican breakfast.

Tiffany's (☎ 965-0300; mains US$4-12; noon-10pm Tue-Sat) On the main road, this friendly restaurant offers comfortable ambience, rooftop dining and an eclectic menu that includes burgers, T-bone steaks, curried goat and salads.

Potsnapper Restaurant (☎ 393-0377; mains US$5-15; breakfast, lunch & dinner) With a steady supply of fresh fish from the morning's catch, this pleasant roadside eatery serves ackee and saltfish and porridge for breakfast, and seafood, pizza, curried goat and pepper steak for lunch and dinner.

Jake's Place (mains US$5-20; breakfast, lunch & dinner) Despite the easily distracted service, this atmospheric spot serves excellent fare in an open-sided wooden restaurant with low lighting and hip music. You can also dine poolside on the patio out back. The menu changes daily, but typical dishes include pumpkin soup, baked lamb, stuffed crab and chocolate cake. Filling lunches include vegetarian treats such as lima-bean soup.

our pick **Jack Sprat Café** (mains US$5-18; 7am-midnight) An excellent barefoot beachside eatery affiliated with Jake's, this appealing joint features vintage reggae posters and an old jukebox as well as a lively bar scene that spills onto the tree-shaded patio. Jack Sprat warms to any crowd or time of day, and offers a diverse menu of sandwiches, salads, crabcakes, smoked marlin and lobster as well as excellent jerk or garlic shrimp. A superb array of pizzas is available at night, and every meal should end with some of the superb ice cream.

Q-en Coffee Shop (☎ 326-9008; Swaby's Plaza) This small grocery store is also a good spot for Jamaican breakfasts.

Drinking & Entertainment

At night, Treasure Beach appears like a sleepy place – don't be fooled. Treasure Beach's hotspots party late into the night until the last person leaves. The **Fisherman's Nightclub** (☎ 379-9780), up a dirt road behind Tiffany's, is the oldest nightclub in town and the domain of local youth (mostly male) skanking to sounds from a selector (DJ); a pool hall and bar are at the back. On weekends, Wild Onion in Frenchman's Cove attracts a mix of locals and visitors with its spacious dance floor and pool tables. **South Jammin'** (☎ 965-0136) draws locals for darts, billiards and dominoes. Its dinner menu includes steamed fish, pepper steak, curried goat and lasagna. **Nanny's Bar** (Kingfisher Plaza) is a local haunt with a pool table; it stays open until the last person leaves. Jake's Place is the place to be for its infamous poolside cocktail hour. And of course, Jack Sprat Café is always lively and hosts small concerts, poetry readings and once-weekly outdoor movies.

For something quite different, allow one of the drivers from Jake's to take you on a country bar crawl. Over the course of a few hours you will visit local zinc-roofed rum shops and mingle with the community over overproof rum and dominoes.

Shopping

One of the best craft stores is on the front lawn at Jake's Place (p271).

Mermaid Art Gallery (☎ 382-6384) Part of the Calabash House hotel, this recently opened gallery specializes in excellent local woodwork and tie-dyed clothing.

Island Sculpture (☎ 831-6612) Opposite Swaby's Plaza, here a local called 'LT' crafts precious lignum vitae into abstract animal and mystical forms.

Lennon's Wood Music & Things (☎ 965-0476; Treasure Beach Shopping Complex) This shop sells music CDs.

Treasure Beach Women's Group (☎ 965-0748; treasurebeach@cwjamaica.com; Kingfisher Plaza) A wide range of gifts is sold here, including batiks, crafts made from calabash shells and other natural materials, swimwear, sandals and coffee.

Getting There & Around

There is no direct service to Treasure Beach from Montego Bay, Negril or Kingston. Take a minibus or route taxi to Black River (US$3), then connect to Treasure Beach (US$1.75). There are only three daily buses from Black River to Treasure Beach. It's best to enquire at the transportation yard the day before your desired departure. From Negril, you will have to transfer at Savanna-la-Mar to continue on to Black River.

Jake's Place and the more expensive hotels and villas arrange transfers from MoBay for US$100 (up to four people), car and motorcycle rental, and transfers by taxi.

Bicycles are rented by Andy at Jake's (see p269) and by the **Q-en Coffee Shop** (☎ 326-9008; per 24hr US$6.50).

MALVERN

Straddling the Santa Cruz Mountains at a refreshing 730m, this hamlet is a looping 24km drive northeast from Treasure Beach. Years ago Malvern was favored as a summer resort for its temperate climate. Today it's an agricultural and educational center.

In the 18th century these uplands became an important center for coffee cultivation. Sugar estates were absent and the harsh plantation system never took hold. Following emancipation, newly freed slaves settled as independent farmers and continued to grow coffee. In later years citrus farms became important, and cattle now grow fat on the lush pastures. Bauxite mining near Mandeville and Santa Cruz has brought further, much-evident prosperity to the region.

Malvern is dominated by the cream-colored **Hampton College** (it's a girls' school founded in 1858), about 1km south of Malvern Sq, the village center. **Munro College**, a boys' school founded in 1856, is 6km further south.

Mikarabee (☎ 966-5537, in the UK ☎ 01908-261888; www.mikarabee.com; per week US$2500; P) is a luxury villa with world-class views and spacious bedrooms. It has a game room, satellite TV, modern kitchen and fully equipped office. There's a graceful swimming pool and the services of a staff. To get there, go 3km toward the village of Retirement, and follow the road toward Elgin.

LOVER'S LEAP

You need a head for heights to stand by the cliff at **Lover's Leap** (☎ 965-6634; admission US$3; 10am-6pm), 1.5km southeast of Southfield, where the Santa Cruz Mountains plunge over 500m into the ocean. The headland is tipped by a red-and-white-hooped solar-powered **lighthouse**.

Far below, waves crash ashore on jagged rocks and wash onto **Cutlass Beach**. You can hike with a guide (US$20 per group): it's a stiff one-hour down. With luck you may see wild mountain goats.

Lover's Leap is named for two young slaves who supposedly committed suicide here in 1747. Legend says the woman was lusted after by her owner, who arranged for her lover to be sold to another estate. When the couple heard of the plot, they fled and were eventually cornered at the cliffs, where they chose to plunge to their deaths.

A children's play area, souvenir shop, small museum and restaurant are atop the cliff.

On the road to the site, **Lover's Leap Guesthouse** (☎ 965-6004; P) offers well-appointed rooms (US$30 to US$50), some with Jacuzzis, and has a small restaurant serving simple meals and snacks.

ALLIGATOR POND

Alligator Pond, hidden at the foot of a valley between two steep spurs of the Santa Cruz and Don Figuerero Mountains, is about as far from packaged tourism as you can get. Although Kingstonians crowd in on weekends, this large fishing village remains undiscovered by foreign travelers and offers a genuine offbeat Jamaican experience.

The hamlet is set behind a deep-blue bay backed by dunes. The main street is smothered in wind-blown sand. Each morning, local women gather on the dark-sand beach to haggle over the catch delivered by fishermen, whose colorful old pirogues line the long shore. Local youths surf wooden planks.

The **Sandy Cays**, about 32km offshore, are lined with white-sand beaches. The snorkeling and scuba diving are good at **Alligator Reef**, about a 20-minute boat ride from shore.

Venus Sunset Lounge & Accommodation (☎ 965-4508; r US$25), 2km east of Alligator Pond, has four simply furnished rooms with fans, shared bathroom and cold water. It has a thatched bar and basic restaurant overlooking a tiny beach.

A better option is the **Sea-Riv Hotel** (☎ 962-7265; r US$25-40; P), on the black-sand beach next to the mouth of a river. There are 18

SOUTH COAST & CENTRAL HIGHLANDS

appealing, fan-cooled rooms. The resort offers water sports and many in-the-know guides.

our pick **Little Ochie** (☎ 965-4449; www.littleochie.com; mains US$7-15; 7am until last guest leaves) is *the* place to eat in Alligator Pond – if not the entire southeast coast. Since 1989 Evrol 'Blackie' Christian has been running this seafood mecca on the beach with such verve and style that it was only a matter of time until it became famous. The place has tremendous atmosphere, with thatched tables and chairs on the beach, including some built into thatched-roof old boats raised on stilts. Watch the fishermen pull up on the beach with their catch before you go inside to place your order – name your fish and exactly how you want it cooked. Specialties include fish tea, curried conch, roast fish, lobster prepared seven different ways, and aphrodisiac tonics such as 'Stallion Punch.' Try the steamed snapper simmering in creamy sauces of fresh vegetables served with oven-hot bammy or the sumptuous jerk lobster and shrimp dishes. You'll never want to leave.

Minibuses and route taxis operate between Alligator Pond and the Beckford St transportation center in Kingston (about US$10), and from Mandeville via Gutters (about US$5).

LONG BAY

Long Bay, to the east of Alligator Pond, is a near-pristine spot. Virtually the entire 24km shoreline, which is hemmed in by mountains, is composed of mangroves and reeds that make up the Long Bay Morass – a nirvana for birders. There are crocodiles, too, and the swamp is a last refuge for endangered manatees.

Given boardwalks and an interpretive center, the morass could be an ecotourist mecca. The area begs for national-park status to head off the developers. The cattle that have invaded the wetlands have introduced exotic species of flora, and locals continue to kill marine turtles that come ashore to lay eggs.

The area is uninhabited, with the except-ion of a meager facility at **Gut River**, 10km east of Alligator Pond. Here a mineral spring emerges from a deep cleft and feeds a pond where the occasional flash reveals mullet and big crabs 6m down. The pool grows more shallow toward its mouth, where the water is trapped behind a sand spit that hides a lonely red-sand beach. On Sunday people crowd in for a 'bashment (dancehall show) on the beach,' with ear-splitting reggae. When they leave, garbage is strewn everywhere and nobody bothers to clean it up.

God's Well is a sinkhole that drops to a cave at about 50m. Scuba divers occasionally test the waters (God's Well is for experienced divers only – the first diver to tackle it died). Believe it or not, divers have even been known to do the 'Suicide Run,' a 3km swim to the ocean through the seemingly impenetrable swamps. Yes, the chance of bumping into a crocodile is very real, but locals advise: 'Dem alligators no problem, mon…Dem coward. 'Im see you come close, mon, 'im swim fast, fast can go!'

Long Bay extends to Alligator Hole, also known as the Canoe Valley Wetland (see p109), where you can swim with manatees.

A taxi from Alligator Pond costs about US$10 round-trip. A minibus travels to Gut River from Mandeville on weekends.

Directory

CONTENTS

ACCOMMODATIONS

From the lazy, beach-oriented playgrounds of the resort centers to the offbeat, atmospheric towns of the western and southern coasts, Jamaica offers a compelling range of accommodations for every budget and style. If you're traveling on a shoestring, head to a simple guest house, where rooms can be had for US$30 to US$60. Midrange hotels are priced up to US$150: if this is your budget, you'll enjoy a wide range of choice in appealing small hotels, many with splendid gardens, sea views or both. If traveling with your family or a group, consider one of the hundreds of villas available to rent across the island. And if you've decided to splurge on something sumptuous, Jamaica's luxury hotels rank among the finest in the world.

Throughout this book and unless otherwise stated, prices (given in US dollars) are for double rooms in high season and refer to European Plan, or room only with bathroom. Don't forget to check if the quoted rate includes tax and service charge; if not, the compulsory 6.25% to 15% GCT (and possibly a 10% to 15% service charge) may be added to your bill.

Low season (summer) is usually mid-April to early-December; the high season (winter) is the remainder of the year, when hotel prices increase by 40% or more and popular hotels are often booked solid. All-inclusive packages are usually based on three-day minimum stays.

Even out of high season, it is advisable to book top-end hotels and all-inclusive resorts well in advance. You should make reservations directly with hotels, preferably by phone or email, or use a travel agent, hotel representative or online reservation service. Online services to consider include **Travelocity** (www.travelocity.com) and **Expedia** (www.expedia.com).

All-Inclusive Resorts

All-inclusive resorts offer a cash-free, self-contained vacation: you pay a set price and (theoretically) nothing more once you arrive.

PRACTICALITIES

- Electricity is 110V, 50Hz. Sockets throughout Jamaica are usually two or three pin – the US standard.
- The *Jamaica Gleaner* is the high-standard newspaper; its rival is the *Jamaica Observer*. The best domestic magazine is Air Jamaica's *Sky Writings*.
- There are 30 radio stations and seven TV channels; most hotels have satellite TV.
- The video system used is NTSC, the same as in the US.
- Metric and imperial measurements are both used. Distances are measured in meters and kilometers, and gas in liters, but coffee (and ganja) is most often sold by the pound.

BOOK YOUR STAY ONLINE

For more accommodation reviews and recommendations by Lonely Planet authors, check out www.lonelyplanet.com/hotels. You'll find the true, insider lowdown on the best places to stay. Reviews are thorough and independent. Best of all, you can book online.

Some of the resorts are undeniably classy. The prospect of leaving your wallet in the room safe and testing your all-you-can-eat-and-drink capacity each night *does* carry a certain appeal. If this sounds like your kind of holiday, you have many options.

The all-inclusive experience, however, precludes discovering the colorful, gritty, off-the-beaten-track Jamaica, and mingling with locals. All-inclusive meals and drinks discourage many guests from exploring Jamaica's wonderfully diverse independent restaurants and nightspots. Most resorts offer excursions, and you're free to explore on your own, but a majority of guests never leave the property.

Rates for all-inclusive resorts presented in this book are guidelines based on each resort's unpublicized 'rack' or 'standard' rate. You will likely spend considerably less depending on the source of booking, season and current specials. Most resorts perpetually publicize special rates; further discounts can be found either on their websites or on booking sites like Expedia and Travelocity.

The major all-inclusive resort chains include the following:

Couples (in the USA ☎ 800-268-7537 or 954-416-1280, in the UK ☎ 1582-794-420; www.couples.com)

Franklyn D Resorts (in the USA ☎ 888-337-5437, in the UK ☎ 1582-792-260; www.fdrholidays.com) Family-oriented resort that also operates the Pebbles resort.

Riu (in the USA ☎ 888-666-8816, in Canada ☎ 866-845-3765, in Spain ☎ 34-971-269-460; www.riu.com)

Sandals (in the USA ☎ 800-726-3257 or ☎ 305-284-1300, in Canada ☎ 800-545-8283, in the UK ☎ 0207-823-8758; www.sandals.com) Also operates Beaches.

Superclubs (in the USA ☎ 800-467-8737 or ☎ 954-925-0925, in Canada ☎ 800-701-5923, in the UK ☎ 0208-339-4150; www.superclubs.com) Also operates Breezes, Starfish, Grand Lido and Hedonism resorts.

B&Bs

A B&B (bed and breakfast) is usually a lodging where the owner plays live-in host and provides breakfast in the quoted room rate. In Jamaica, some establishments purporting to be B&Bs actually charge for breakfast, and true B&Bs are few and far between.

Camping

Jamaica is not developed for campers, and it is unsafe to camp anywhere in the wild. Many budget properties will let you pitch a tent on their lawns for a small fee. Some even rent tents and have shower, toilet and laundry facilities.

Guest Houses

Most guest houses are inexpensive, and are good places to mix with the locals. Some are self-contained apartments, and some are indistinguishable from hotels or faceless motels. The best offer economical, unusual and comfortable lodging off the beaten track.

Companies that represent guesthouses in Jamaica include these ones:

Carolyn's Caribbean Cottages (☎ 382-6384; www.carolynscaribbeancottages.com) Operates a wide range of cottages islandwide.

Port Antonio Guest House Association (☎ 993-7118; www.go-jam.com) Represents guest houses in Portland parish and across Jamaica.

Homestays

You can make your own arrangements to stay with individuals or families who do not rent rooms as a normal practice. The following agencies coordinate homestays:

Countrystyle Community Tours (☎ 962-7758; countrystyle@mail.infochan.com; PO Box 60, Mandeville) Can arrange homestays in central Jamaica as part of community tours.

Southern Trelawny Environmental Agency (☎ 610-0818; www.stea.net; 3 Grants Office Complex, Albert Town) Coordinates homestays in the wild and woolly Cockpit Country.

Hotels

Jamaican hotels run the gamut, from simple roadside lodgings to wildly expensive palaces. Anyone who wants to support the local economy should seek out independent hotels. **Insiders Jamaica** (www.insidersjamaica.com), a website created by the Jamaica Tourist Board (JTB), promotes small hotels and inns.

For something different, Jamaica offers travelers some quintessentially Caribbean boutique hotels that are unpretentious and gracious. Some of the best are available through **Island Outpost properties** (in the USA ☎ 800-688-7678, in the UK ☎ 800-6887 6781; www.islandoutpost.com; 2107 N Decatur Rd Ste 432, Decatur GA 30033, USA).

Villa Rentals

Jamaica boasts hundreds of private villas for rent, from modest cottages to lavish beachfront estates. They range from one to eight bedrooms in size and offer additional living space such as living rooms, dining areas, patios or verandas. Most have their own pool and are fully staffed. They're cost-effective for those traveling with family or a group of friends.

Rates start as low as US$100 per week for budget units with minimal facilities. More upscale villas begin at about US$750 weekly and can run to US$10,000 or more for a sumptuous multibedroom estate. Rates fall as much as 30% in summer. A large deposit (usually 25% or more) is required.

Two good starting points are the **Caribbean Villas Owners Association** (☎ 877-248-2862; www.cvoa.com) and the **Jamaican Association of Villas & Apartments** (JAVA; ☎ 974-2508; www.villasinjamaica.com; PO Box 298, Ocho Rios).

Here are other villa-rental companies:

Caribbean Way (☎ 877-953-7400, in North America ☎ 514-393-3003; www.caribbeanway.com; Ste 1305, 740 Notre Dame W, Montreal, Quebec, Canada H3C 3X6).

Sun Villas (☎ 888-625-6007, in the USA ☎ 941-922-9191; www.sunvillas.com; 1410 South Lake Shore Dr, Sarasota, FL 34231)

Villascaribe (☎ 800-645-7498, in North America ☎ 678-417-0081; www.villascaribe.com)

ACTIVITIES

For an island its size, Jamaica packs an impressive punch with sports and outdoor activities for those who bored of bumming on the beach. Reefs beckon for diving, mountains for hiking, rivers for rafting, and the island is renowned for a dozen golf courses. For more on outdoor activities, see p53.

BUSINESS HOURS

Most business offices are open 8:30am to 4:30pm Monday through Friday. Very few offices are open Saturday.

Most stores open at either 8am or 9am and close at 5pm, though on Saturday they close at noon. Generally shops are closed on Sunday, except pharmacies, which are open every day.

CHILDREN

All-inclusive resorts such as Franklyn D Resort, FDR Pebbles, Beaches (Boscobel, Negril and Whitehouse) and Starfish (Trelawny) cater to families and have an impressive range of amenities for children.

Lonely Planet's *Travel with Children*, by Cathy Lanigan, gives you the lowdown on preparing for family travel.

Practicalities

Many hotels offer free accommodations or reduced rates for young children in their parents' room; many provide a babysitter/nanny by advance request. Increasingly, resorts and upscale hotels offer free childcare centers.

It's a good idea to prearrange necessities such as cribs, babysitters, cots and baby food at hotels other than family resorts.

Many car-rental agencies in Jamaica do not offer safety seats. One agency that does is Island Car Rentals (p294).

Breastfeeding in public is regarded as something of a spectacle.

Sights & Activities

Negril, Ocho Rios and Montego Bay are perhaps the best towns for children. Each is replete with kid-friendly attractions and activities, most notably Dunn's River Falls (outside Ocho Rios), Kool Runnings Water Park (Negril), Aquasol Theme Park (Montego Bay) and horseback riding (all three).

CLIMATE CHARTS

One of Jamaica's greatest allures is its idyllic tropical maritime climate. Coastal temperatures average a near-constant 26°C to

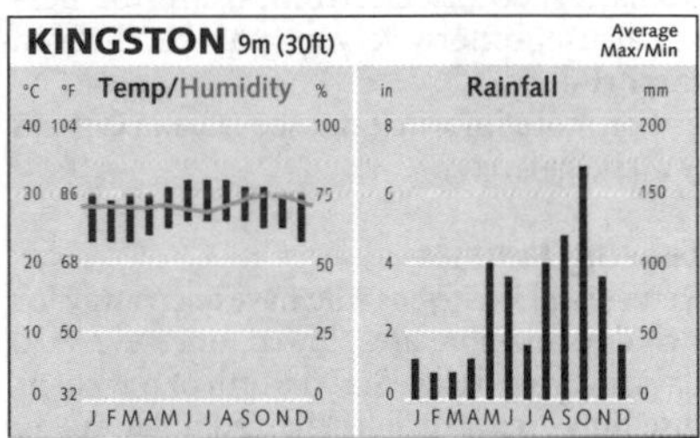

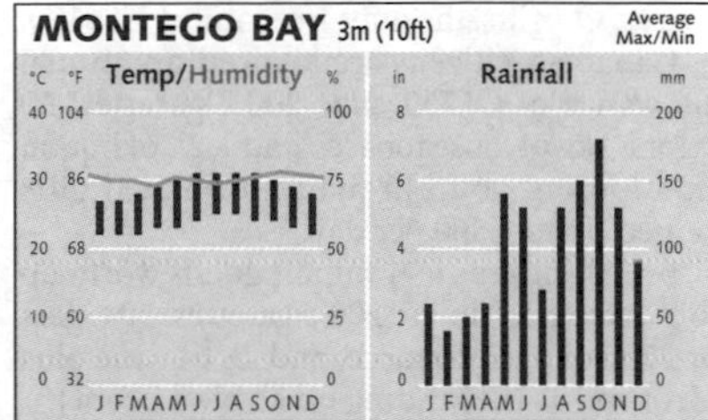

30°C year-round. Temperatures fall steadily with increasing altitude but even in the Blue Mountains average 18°C or more.

The annual rainfall averages 1980mm, but nationwide there are some considerable variations, with the east coast receiving considerably more rain than elsewhere on the island. Parts of the John Crow and Blue Mountains receive an average of 7620mm a year. By contrast, the south coast sees little rain and in places is semi-barren.

A 'rainy season' starts in May or June and extends through November or December, with the heaviest rains in September and October. Rain can fall at any time of year, however, and normally comes in short, heavy showers, often followed by sun.

Jamaica lies in the Caribbean 'hurricane belt.' Officially the hurricane season lasts from June 1 to November 30; August and September are peak months.

See also p13.

CUSTOMS

Entering Jamaica

You are allowed to import the following items duty-free: 25 cigars, 200 cigarettes and two liters of alcohol. You may bring a 'reasonable' amount of duty-free goods for personal use; anything deemed in excess of 'reasonable' may incur an import tax.

You may need to show some proof that laptop computers and other expensive items (especially electronics) are for personal use; otherwise you may be charged import duty.

For more information, see **Jamaica Customs** (www.jacusto ms.gov.jm).

Leaving Jamaica

Returning US citizens who have been away for two days or more are allowed, once every 30 days, to bring back US$600 worth of merchandise duty-free. You'll be charged a flat rate of 10% duty on the next US$1000 worth of purchases. On gifts, the duty-free limit is US$100.

Canadian citizens are allowed an annual allowance of C$750, plus 200 cigarettes, 50 cigars, 1kg of loose tobacco and 1.2L of liquor. In addition, you can mail unsolicited gifts valued up to C$60 per day.

British citizens may import goods worth up to £145 in addition to 200 cigarettes, 50 cigars or 250g of loose tobacco, and 2L of wine plus 1L of spirits (depending on alcohol proof).

Australians can bring back A$900 of gifts and souvenirs, plus 250 cigarettes or 250g of tobacco, and 2.25L of alcohol.

DANGERS & ANNOYANCES

The Jamaica Tourist Board publishes a pocket-size pamphlet, *Helpful Hints for Your Vacation*, containing concise tips for safer travel. Use the **JTB hotline** (☎ 888-991-9999) for emergency assistance.

The **US State Department** (☎ 202-647-5225; www.travel.state.gov) publishes travel advisories that advise US citizens of trouble spots, as does the **British Foreign & Commonwealth Office** (☎ 020-7008-0232; www.fco.gov.uk; Travel Advice Unit, Consular Division, Foreign & Commonwealth Office, 1 Palace St, London SW1E 5HE).

Crime

Jamaica has the highest murder rate for any country not in the throes of war (the nation had a record 1574 murders in 2007, a 17% rise on the previous year), and Kingston and Spanish Town have the worst reputations in the Caribbean for violent crime. Although the vast majority of violent crimes occur in ghettoes far from tourist centers, visitors are sometimes the victims of robbery and scams. Crime against tourists has dropped in recent years, however, and the overwhelming majority of visitors enjoy their vacations without incident.

Most crime against travelers is petty and opportunistic. Take sensible precautions with your valuables. Steer clear of ghettoes, where you are very likely to get into serious trouble. Try to avoid walking at night in Kingston and downtown Montego Bay, but if you do, stick close to main thoroughfares. Take taxis when possible, preferably arranged by the hotel's front desk.

Keep hotel doors and windows securely locked at night, and lock car doors from the inside while driving. Don't open your hotel door to anyone who can't prove their identity. If you're renting an out-of-the-way private villa or cottage, check in advance with the rental agency to establish whether security is provided. And don't assume you're entirely safe at all-inclusive resorts: readers have reported security issues even there.

Carry as little cash as you need when away from your hotel. Keep the rest in a hotel safe. You can rely on credit cards and traveler's checks for most purchases, but you'll need

PREVENTING CHILD-SEX TOURISM IN JAMAICA

Tragically, the exploitation of local children by tourists is becoming more prevalent throughout Jamaica. Various socio-economic factors make children susceptible to sexual exploitation, and some tourists choose to take advantage of their vulnerable position.

Sexual exploitation has serious, lifelong effects on children. It is a crime and a violation of human rights.

Jamaica has laws against sexual exploitation of children. Many countries have enacted extraterritorial legislation that allows travelers to be charged as though the exploitation happened in their home country.

Responsible travelers can help stop child-sex tourism by reporting it. It is important not to ignore suspicious behavior. Cybertipline is a website where sexual exploitation of children can be reported. The website can be found at www.cybertipline.com. You can also report the incident to local authorities and if you know the nationality of the perpetrator, report it to their embassy.

Travelers interested in learning more about how to fight against sexual exploitation of children can find more information on the ECPAT International website at www.ecpat.org.

Beyond Borders is the Canadian affiliate of ECPAT. It aims to advance the rights of children to be free from abuse and exploitation without regard to race, religion, gender or sexual orientation. Its website can be found at www.beyondborders.org.

ECPAT – USA (End Child Prostitution and Trafficking) is part of a global network working on these issues with over 70 affiliate organizations around the world. The US headquarters is located in New York, and can be contacted on ☎ +1-718-935-9192. Its website can be found at www.ecpatusa.org.

cash for most transactions in rural areas and at gas stations.

Many local police are members of the communities they serve and cannot always be trusted to be impartial.

Driving Hazards

Driving in Jamaica is dangerous. Licenses can be bought without taking a driving test, and the roads are governed by an infatuation with speed completely incongruous with the rest of Jamaican life. Look out for people along the roads or animals that might dash in front of you, and pay extra attention at roundabouts, where driving on the left is not always adhered to. Pedestrians should beware of the many drivers who would as soon hit you as slow down.

For tips on driving conditions, see the Transportation chapter, p285.

Drug Trade

Ganja (marijuana) is everywhere in Jamaica and you're almost certain to be approached by hustlers selling drugs. Cocaine is also widely available (Jamaica is the major stop on the Colombia–US drug route). The street sale of drugs is a sad pandemic that has corroded society and led to frightening levels of violence.

Despite their ubiquity and cultural eminence, drugs are strictly illegal and penalties are severe. Roadblocks and random searches of cars are common, undertaken by well-armed police in combat gear (professionalism is never guaranteed, and 'dash' – extortion – is often extracted to boost wages). If you *do* buy drugs, don't be stupid enough to try to take any out of the country. If you're caught, you will *not* be getting on your plane home, however small the amount. A night (or a lengthy sentence) in a crowded-to-bursting Jamaican lockup is bad for your health!

Harassment

Usually the traveler's biggest problem is the vast army of hustlers (mostly male) who harass visitors, notably in and around major tourist centers. A hustler is someone who makes a living by seizing opportunities, and the biggest opportunity in Jamaica is you!

Hustlers walk the streets looking out for potential buyers of crafts, jewelry or drugs, or to wash cars, give aloe-vera massages or offer any of a thousand services. A sibilant 'ssssst!' to catch your attention is the first indication that hustlers have their eyes on you.

It's important to be polite but firm in repressing unwanted advances; never ignore them, which can be taken as a grave insult.

Aggressive persistence is the key to their success and trying to shaking them off can be a wearying process. Hustlers often persist in the hope that you'll pay just to be rid of them. A good defensive gambit is to play like a savvy local: 'Cho mon, doan't harass de touris'!' or pretend to be a tourist from a non-English-speaking country (few Jamaicans speak Croatian). If harassment continues, seek the assistance of a tourist police officer or the local constabulary.

DISABLED TRAVELERS

Very few allowances have been made in Jamaica for travelers with disabilities. Useful resources include these ones:

Council for Persons with Disabilities (☎ 922-0585; 4 Ellesmere Rd, Kingston 5)

Disabled Peoples' International (☎ 967-9439; caribbean.dpi.org; PO Box W123, Woods Centre, St John's, Antigua)

Disabled People's Organisations of the Caribbean (☎ 967-9439; Ministry of Labour Building, IF North St, Kingston)

EMBASSIES & CONSULATES

Unless otherwise noted, details are for embassies.

Jamaican Embassies & Consulates

Canada Ottawa High Commission (☎ 613-233-9311; fax 613-233-0611; hc@jhcottawa.ca; Standard Life Bldg, Suite 402, 275 Slater St, Ottawa, Ontario KIP 5H9); Toronto Consulate General (☎ 416-598-3008; jcgtoronto@attcanada.net; Suite 402, 214 King St W, Toronto, Ontario M5H 1KA)

Germany (☎ 49 30 85 99 450; info@jamador.de; Schmargendorfer Strasse 32; 12159 Berlin)

UK (☎ 207-823-9911; hc@jhcuk.com; Jamaican High Commission, 1-2 Prince Consort Rd, London SW7 2BZ)

US Miami Consulate General (☎ 305-374-8431; fax 577-4970; 842 Ingraham Bldg, 25 SE Second Ave, Miami, FL 33131); New York Consulate General (☎ 212-935-9000; fax 935-7508; 2nd fl, 767 Third Ave, New York, NY 10017); Washington (☎ 202-452-0660; fax 202-421-0081; 1520 New Hampshire Ave NW, Washington, DC)

Embassies & Consulates in Jamaica

If your country isn't represented in this list, check 'Embassies & High Commissions' in the yellow pages of the Greater Kingston telephone directory.

Australia (Map pp80–1; ☎ 926-3550, 926-3551; 64 Knutsford Blvd, Kingston High Commission, Kingston 5)

Canada Kingston High Commission (Map pp80–1; ☎ 926-1500; 3 West Kings House Rd, Kingston); Montego Bay Consulate (Map p184; ☎ 952-6198; 29 Gloucester Ave, Montego Bay)

France (Map pp80–1; ☎ 978-0210; 13 Hillcrest Ave, Kingston 6)

Germany (Map pp80–1; ☎ 926-6728; 10 Waterloo Rd, Kingston 10)

Italy (Map pp80–1; ☎ 968-8464; 10 Surbiton Rd, Kingston 10)

Japan (Map pp80–1; ☎ 929-7534; 1 Kensington Crescent, Kingston 5)

Netherlands (Map pp80–1; ☎ 926-2026; 53 Knutsford Blvd, Kingston 5)

Sweden (Map pp80–1; ☎ 941-3761; Unit 3, 69 Constant Spring Rd, Kingston Consulate, Kingston 10)

Switzerland (Map pp80–1; ☎ 978-7857; 22 Trafalgar Rd, Kingston Consulate, Kingston 10)

UK Kingston High Commission (Map pp80–1; ☎ 510-0700, 926-9050; bhckingston@cwjamaica.com; 28 Trafalgar Rd, Kingston); Montego Bay Consulate (☎ 912-6859, Montego Bay)

US Kingston (Map pp80–1; ☎ 929-4850, 926-6440 after hours; kingstonacs@state.gov; Life of Jamaica Bldg, 16 Oxford St, Kingston); Montego Bay Consulate (Map p184; ☎ 952-0160, 952-5050; usconsagency.mobay@cwjamaica.com; St James Plaza, 2nd fl, Gloucester Ave, Montego Bay)

FOOD

Some Eating sections in destination chapters of this book are divided into budget, midrange and top-end categories. We define a midrange restaurant as one where a main dish at lunch or dinner costs between US$10 and US$20. Budget and top-end places cost, respectively, less than US$10 and over US$20. For the full story on eating in Jamaica, see the Food & Drink chapter, p42.

GAY & LESBIAN TRAVELERS

Jamaica is an adamantly homophobic nation. Sexual acts between men are prohibited by law and punishable by up to ten years in prison and hard labor. Some reggae dancehall lyrics by big-name stars like Beenie Man, Bounty Killer, Buju Banton and Sizzla seem intent on instigating violence against gays. Law enforcement in most cases fails to prosecute perpetrators of gay bashing: when gay-rights activist Brian Williamson was stabbed to death by a mob in June 2004, police maintained that he was a robbery victim. In 2007, Mandeville was the scene of several gay-bashing incidents, and a policeman who came out of the closet was forced to go into hiding.

The debate over institutional homophobia in Jamaica heated up in 2004 with the release of a report by Human Rights Watch detailing the abuse meted out to sexual minorities and people living with HIV/AIDS. As a form of protest, most gays refuse to visit the island; those who do find that they cannot express their sexuality openly without an adverse – and often dangerous – reaction.

J-Flag (helpline ☎ 978-8988; www.jflag.org) is Jamaica's first human-rights organization created to serve the needs of sexual minorities.

The following organizations can provide assistance in planning a trip:

International Gay & Lesbian Travel Association (☎ 954-776-2626, 800-448-8550; www.iglta.com; 4431 N Federal Hwy No 304, Ft Lauderdale, FL 33308, USA)

Purple Roofs (www.purpleroofs.com/caribbean/jamaica.html) Lists gay-friendly accommodations in Jamaica.

HOLIDAYS

New Year's Day January 1
Ash Wednesday February
Good Friday & Easter Monday March/April
Labour Day May 23
Emancipation Day August 1
Independence Day August 6
National Heroes' Day October 19
Christmas Day December 25
Boxing Day December 26

INSURANCE

However you're traveling, it's worth taking out travel insurance. Everyone should be covered for the worst possible case: an accident, for example, that requires hospital treatment and a flight home.

Consider purchasing a travel insurance policy that covers theft, loss of baggage and medical treatment. You might also consider trip-cancellation insurance if you have booked a prepaid package with cancellation penalty clauses. Any travel agent can recommend an appropriate package.

INTERNET ACCESS

Many upscale hotels provide in-room, dial-up access for laptop computers. Wireless networks are making their first appearances in the best hotels. Most town libraries now offer internet access (US$1 for 30 minutes), though you may find there's only one or two terminals and waits can be long. Most towns also have at least one commercial entity where you can get online.

LEGAL AGE

- Consent (heterosexual): 16
- Drinking: 18
- Driving: 16
- Voting: 18

LEGAL MATTERS

Jamaica's drug and drunk-driving laws are strictly enforced. Don't expect leniency because you're a foreigner. Jamaican jails are Dickensian hellholes! If you are arrested, insist on your right to call your embassy in Kingston to request its assistance.

MAPS

The Jamaican Tourist Board (JTB) publishes a *Discover Jamaica* road map (1:350,000). No topographical details are shown.

The best maps are Hildebrandt's Jamaica map (1:300,000) and ITMB Publishing's maps (1:250,000), available online or at travel bookstores.

The most accurate maps are the Jamaica Ordnance Survey maps published by the **Survey Department** (☎ 922-6630; 231-1/2 Charles St, PO Box 493; Kingston 10).

MONEY

The unit of currency is the Jamaican dollar, the 'jay,' which uses the same symbol as the US dollar ($). Jamaican currency is issued in bank notes of J$50, J$100, J$500 and J$1000. The official rate of exchange fluctuates daily; see the inside front cover for exchange rates at the time of going to press.

Prices for hotels and valuable items are usually quoted in US dollars, which are widely accepted.

For international transfers, **Western Union** (☎ 926-2454, 888-991-2056; www.westernunion.com; 7 Hillview Ave, Kingston 5) has offices islandwide.

ATMs

Most of the city bank branches throughout Jamaica have 24-hour automated teller machines (ATMs) linked to international networks such as Cirrus or Plus. In more remote areas, look for ATMs at gas stations.

Black Market

Young Jamaican men are eager to change Jamaican dollars in street transactions. It's strictly illegal, however, and not worth it: the black-market rate is rarely more than 5% lower than the official exchange rate, and many black-marketeers are scam artists.

Cash

It's a wise idea to always have some 'J' on hand throughout your island visit. Carry small bills: it can be hard to get change for any note over J$100. US dollars are widely accepted, but you'll be given change in Jamaican dollars. Almost any commercial entity will change dollars for you.

Credit Cards

Major credit cards are widely accepted throughout the island. To report lost or stolen credit cards from Jamaica, call **American Express** (☎ 800-877-3060), **MasterCard** (☎ 800-307-7309) or **Visa** (☎ 800-847-2911).

Moneychangers

Virtually every town and village has at least one licensed moneychanger. They offer rates slightly lower than banks and charge a processing fee of between 2% and 5% of the transaction. All kinds of outlets operate as 'cambios,' including supermarkets and general stores.

Tipping

A 10% tip is normal in hotels and restaurants. Some restaurants automatically add a 10% to 15% service charge to your bill. Check your bill carefully, as the charge is often hidden. Some all-inclusive resorts have a strictly enforced no-tipping policy. Outside Kingston, tourist taxi drivers often ask for tips but it is not necessary; Juta (route) taxis do not expect tips.

Traveler's Checks

Traveler's checks are widely accepted in Jamaica, although some hotels, restaurants and exchange bureaus charge a hefty fee for cashing them.

Immediately report lost traveler's checks to **American Express** (in the USA ☎ 800-221-7282, in Jamaica ☎ 800-877-3060) or **Thomas Cook** (☎ 800-223-7373).

POST

When sending mail to Jamaica always include the addressee's name, address or post-office box, town and parish, plus 'Jamaica, West Indies.'

You can have mail addressed to you marked 'Poste Restante' care of a major central post office. You should have a letter or package addressed with '(your name), Poste Restante, General Post Office,' then the town and parish, plus 'Jamaica, West Indies.'

Every town has a post office and most villages have postal agencies.

Airmail letters worldwide cost J$60 to J$90 per 15 grams. Domestic letters cost J$30 for up to 230 grams. Jamaica Post's website, www.jamaicapost.gov.jm, lists rates.

Airmail to North America usually takes about two weeks, and a week longer to Europe. If you're in a rush, try FedEx (www.fedex.com) or DHL (www.dhl.com), with offices in most major cities.

SHOPPING

Jamaica offers a wide range of arts, crafts and duty-free items, plus food items and drinks such as Blue Mountain coffee, rum liqueurs and other gourmet products.

Tens of thousands of Jamaicans make a living as artists selling to tourists. Much of the artwork is kitsch; paintings and carvings of Bob Marley or Rasta men, fish and animals, often painted in rainbow hues and touched with pointillist dots. There's plenty of first-rate art, however, at galleries islandwide.

Good buys include colorful bead jewelry, baskets and other straw goods, including straw hats, and woodcarvings. Look for 'jippi-jappa' hats (pronounced hippy-happa) from St Catherine parish, beautifully woven from fine strips of palm leaf in the style of Panama hats.

Never pay the asking price for crafts. Haggle! It's expected. Expect to settle on a price at least 20% below initial asking price. Don't waste energy haggling in most shops, however, as prices there are generally fixed.

TELEPHONE

Jamaica has a fully automated digital phone system operated by **Cable & Wireless Jamaica** (☎ 888-225-5295; www.cwjamaica.com), which has offices islandwide where you can make direct calls.

Major hotels have direct-dial calling; elsewhere you may need to go through the hotel operator or call from the front desk. Hotels add a 15% government tax, plus a service charge, often at outrageous rates.

Cell Phones

You can bring your own cell phone into Jamaica, but if your phone is locked by a specific carrier, don't bother. A good option is to purchase an inexpensive cellular phone (from US$35) and a prepaid phonecard. Cards are sold in denominations of up to J$1000 and you'll find them at many gas stations or stationery shops.

Cell-phone providers include **bMobile** (☎ 888-225-5295; www.cwmobile.com/jamaica) and **Digicel** (☎ 888-344-4235; www.digiceljamaica.com).

Phone Codes

If you wish to call Jamaica from abroad, dial your country's international dialing code, then ☎ 876 (Jamaica's country code), and the seven-digit local number.

Jamaican numbers mostly have seven digits, which you dial for calls within the same parish. For calls to other parishes, dial '1' then the seven-digit number.

Phonecards

Public phones require a prepaid phonecard, available from Cable & Wireless Jamaica offices, retail stores, hotels, banks and other outlets. The card is available in denominations up to J$500. For international calls, Cable & Wireless WorldTalk cards can be used from any phone.

TIME

In autumn and winter, Jamaican time is five hours behind Greenwich Mean Time, and the same as in New York (Eastern Standard Time). Jamaica does not adjust for daylight saving time. Hence, from April to October, it is six hours behind London and one hour behind New York.

TOILETS

There are very few public toilets, and those that do exist are best avoided. Most restaurants have restrooms, but many require that you make a purchase before they'll let you use them.

TOURIST INFORMATION

The **Jamaica Tourist Board** (JTB; www.visitjamaica.com) has offices in key cities around the world. You can request maps and literature, including hotel brochures, but they do not serve as reservation agencies.

Tourist Offices Abroad

Canada (☎ 416-482-7850; jtb@jtbcanada.com; 1 Eglington Ave E No 616, Toronto M4P IL3)
Germany (☎ 2104-832974; jamaica@travelmarketing.de; c/o Fast Forward-Marketing, Schwarzbachstrasse 32, 40822 Mettmann)
Italy (☎ 648-90-12-55; sergat@rmnet.it; c/o Sergat Italia, Via Nazionale 230, 00184 Rome)
Japan (☎ 3-3400-2974; tourist-board@jamaica.co.jp; Strategic Tower Bldg 2F, 2-11-1 Shibuya, Shibuya-ku, Tokyo 150-0002)
Netherlands (☎ 34-843-0829; info@ontdekjamaica.nl; Postbus 2073, 3441 DB Woerden)
UK (☎ 207-224-0505; jamaicatravel@btconnect.com; 1-2 Prince Consort Rd, London SW7 2BZ)
USA (☎ 800-233-4582, 305-665-0557; jamaicatrv1@aol.com; Ste 1101, 1320 South Dixie Hwy, Coral Gables FL 33146)

Local Tourist Offices

The JTB has offices in **Kingston** (☎ 929-9200; info@visitjamaica.com; 64 Knutsford Blvd, Kingston 5), **Montego Bay** (☎ 952-4425; Cornwall Beach) and **Port Antonio** (☎ 993-3051; City Centre Plaza, Harbour St).

VISAS

No visas are required for entry to Jamaica for citizens of European Union countries, the USA, Canada, Mexico, Australia, New Zealand, Japan or Israel.

Nationals of the UK, Ireland, USA and Canada may stay for six months. Nationals of Austria, Belgium, Denmark, Finland, Germany, Iceland, Israel, Italy, Luxembourg, Mexico, the Netherlands, Norway, Sweden, Switzerland, Turkey and Commonwealth countries (except Sri Lanka and Pakistan) may stay for three months. Nationals of Argentina, Brazil, Chile, Costa Rica, Ecuador, France, Greece, Japan, Portugal and Spain may stay for 30 days.

All other nationalities require visas (citizens of most countries can obtain a visa on arrival, provided they are holding valid onward or return tickets and evidence of sufficient funds).

Immigration formalities require every person to show a return or ongoing airline ticket when arriving in Jamaica.

WOMEN TRAVELERS

Many Jamaican men display behavior and attitudes that might shock visiting women, often expressing disdain for the notion of female equality or women's rights.

If you're single, it may be assumed that you're on the island seeking a 'likkle love beneat' de palms.' Protests to the contrary will likely be met with wearying attempts to get you to change your mind. If you go along with the flirting, your innocent acceptance will be taken as a sign of acquiescence. Never beat about the bush for fear of hurting the man's feelings.

Many women welcome these advances, as evidenced by the proliferation of 'rent-a-dreads' – semiprofessional good-time guys, or gigolos – on the arms of North American and European women. Expect to be the moneybags in any romantic encounter.

Rape is not uncommon in Jamaica and occasionally involves female tourists. Women traveling alone can reduce unwanted attention by dressing modestly when away from the beach. You should avoid walking alone at night and otherwise traveling alone in remote areas.

See also p38.

WORK

Visitors are admitted to Jamaica on the condition that they 'not engage in any form of employment on the island.' Professionals can obtain work permits if sponsored by a Jamaican company, but casual work is very difficult to obtain.

Transportation

CONTENTS

GETTING THERE & AWAY

ENTERING THE COUNTRY

Expect a wait in the immigration halls at the airports in Kingston and Montego Bay. There are often only two or three immigration officers on hand to process the planeloads of passengers and often multiple flights land within minutes of each other, increasing the burden on officials. See p283 for information about visa requirements.

Passport

US citizens traveling to and from the Caribbean by air or sea are now required to have a passport or another secure, accepted document in order to enter or re-enter the USA.

Canadian citizens do not need passports for visits of up to six months. However, they *do* need two pieces of identification, including proof of citizenship or permanent residency, such as a passport, birth certificate or driver's license with photo ID. Other visitors must arrive with a passport. British citizens need passports that will still be valid six months after their arrival.

AIR

Airports & Airlines

Jamaica's international airports are in Montego Bay and Kingston. For flight arrival and departure information, call the airports, visit their websites or call the airline directly.

The majority of visitors to Jamaica arrive at **Donald Sangster International Airport** (☎ 952-3124; www.mbjairport.com), about 3km north of Montego Bay.

There's a Jamaica Tourist Board (JTB) information booth in the arrivals hall and a 24-hour money-exchange bureau immediately beyond immigration. There is also a transportation information desk plus desks representing tour companies, hotels and rental cars immediately as you exit customs. A **police station** (☎ 952-2241) is outside.

Ensure your luggage is locked and never leave valuables in unlocked pockets.

The adjacent terminal serves domestic flights. The terminals aren't linked by walkways and are a sweaty 10-minute walk apart. The charter airlines, including Air Jamaica Express, provide connecting shuttles.

Norman Manley International Airport (☎ 924-8452, 888-247-7678; www.manley-airport.com.jm) is 18km southeast of Kingston downtown.

There's a JTB desk in the arrivals hall, a money-exchange bureau before customs, and a taxi information booth as you exit customs. Beyond customs there's a bank and Island Car Rentals. Ahead is the JUTA taxi office, a **police station** (☎ 924-8002), an ATM, a telephone office and the Otahetis Café.

The following major airlines have offices in Jamaica:

Air Canada (www.aircanada.com) Kingston (☎ 924-8211); Montego Bay (☎ 952-5160, 888-991-9063)

THINGS CHANGE...

The information in this chapter is particularly vulnerable to change. Check directly with the airline or a travel agent to make sure you understand how a fare (and ticket you may buy) works and be aware of the security requirements for international travel. Shop carefully. The details given in this chapter should be regarded as pointers and are not a substitute for your own careful, up-to-date research.

CLIMATE CHANGE & TRAVEL

Climate change is a serious threat to the ecosystems that humans rely upon, and air travel is the fastest-growing contributor to the problem. Lonely Planet regards travel, overall, as a global benefit, but believes we all have a responsibility to limit our personal impact on global warming.

Flying & Climate Change

Pretty much every form of motor travel generates CO_2 (the main cause of human-induced climate change) but planes are far and away the worst offenders, not just because of the sheer distances they allow us to travel, but because they release greenhouse gases high into the atmosphere. The statistics are frightening: two people taking a return flight between Europe and the US will contribute as much to climate change as an average household's gas and electricity consumption over a whole year.

Carbon Offset Schemes

Climatecare.org and other websites use 'carbon calculators' that allow jetsetters to offset the greenhouse gases they are responsible for with contributions to energy-saving projects and other climate-friendly initiatives in the developing world – including projects in India, Honduras, Kazakhstan and Uganda.

Lonely Planet, together with Rough Guides and other concerned partners in the travel industry, supports the carbon offset scheme run by climatecare.org. Lonely Planet offsets all of its staff and author travel.

For more information check out our website: lonelyplanet.com.

Air Jamaica (www.airjamaica.com) Kingston (☎ 888-359-2475)
Air Jamaica Express (www.airjamaica.com/express.asp) Kingston (☎ 888-359-2475); Montego Bay (☎ 952-4300; 9 Queens Dr); Ocho Rios (☎ 726-1344)
American Airlines (www.aa.com) Kingston (☎ 800-744-0006; 26 Trafalgar Rd); Montego Bay (☎ 800-744-0006)
British Airways (www.britishairways.com) Kingston (☎ 929-9020; 25 Dominica Dr); Montego Bay (☎ 952-3771)
BWIA West Indies Airways (www.bwee.com) Kingston (☎ 800-538-2942; 33 Tobago Ave)
Cayman Airways (www.caymanairways.com) Kingston (☎ 926-1762; 23 Dominica Dr)
COPA Airlines (www.copaair.com) Kingston (☎ 926-1762, 926-1763; 23 Dominica Dr); Montego Bay (☎ 952-5530)
Cubana (www.cubana.cu) Kingston (☎ 978-3410, 978-3406; 22 Trafalgar Rd); Montego Bay (☎ 952-0527, 940-2345)
International AirLink (www.intlairlink.com) Montego Bay (☎ 940-6660)
Northwest Airlines (www.nwa.com) Montego Bay (☎ 800-225-2525)
US Airways (www.usairways.com) Montego Bay (☎ 800-622-1015)

Tickets

The cost of plane tickets to Jamaica varies widely, depending on such variables as time of year, weather and traffic in the region. Higher fares normally apply in 'high season,' from mid-December through mid-April, with even higher fares for peak times such as Christmas and around the New Year. You can save 20% or more by traveling in low season; weekday flights offer savings, too.

Airlines often run specials fares, so it's worth checking their websites or calling directly. Before you book, compare ticket prices on online travel sites. Some discount online services are likely to quote rates offered to wholesalers and consolidators, for which special conditions and restrictions apply (see p290). Here are some that we recommend:

- www.cheaptickets.com
- www.expedia.com
- www.itn.net
- www.lowestfare.com
- www.orbitz.com
- www.travelocity.com

DEPARTURE TAX

Jamaica's departure tax is US$22. In most cases this fee is paid with your plane ticket, but if not it will be collected when you check in for your flight. You can pay in either Jamaican or US currency, but credit cards are not accepted.

The travel agencies usually can't match rock-bottom fares, but offer greater security. Firms such as **STA Travel** (☎ in the USA 800-781-4040, in the UK 0870-160-0599; www.statravel.com) have offices worldwide and specialize in low fares for students, although no discount fares are available to Jamaica from North America.

If you plan on visiting additional Caribbean destinations, consider buying an air pass that permits any number of stopovers (see p288).

Charter Flights

Charter flights from the US, Canada, UK and Europe offer another option for getting to Jamaica. Fares are often cheaper than on regularly scheduled commercial airlines, but you usually have to go and come back on a specific flight, and you'll probably have no flexibility to extend your stay.

Although charter companies do most of their business booking package tours that include both accommodations and airfare, they will often find themselves with a few empty seats on planes they've chartered. The seats will sometimes be sold for bargain prices a week or two prior to departure.

In the USA you can sometimes find these seats advertised in the travel pages of larger Sunday newspapers, such as the *New York Times* and the *Boston Globe*.

Travel agencies that specialize in discount travel can also be helpful.

Asia & Africa

There are no direct flights; travelers fly via London or the USA.

In Asia, there are several offices of **STA Travel** (Bangkok ☎ 0-2236 0262; www.statravel.co.th; Hong Kong ☎ 2736 1618; www.statravel.com.hk; Japan ☎ 0353-912 922; www.statra vel.co.jp); Singapore ☎ 6737 7188; www .statravel.com.sg).

Another resource in Japan is **No 1 Travel** (☎ 0332-056 073; www.no1-travel.com); in Hong Kong try **Four Seas Tours** (☎ 2200 7760; www.fourseastravel .com/english).

Rennies Travel (www.renniestravel.com) and **STA Travel** (www.statravel.co.za) have offices throughout Southern Africa. Check their websites for branch locations.

Australia & New Zealand

Travelers from Australia or New Zealand must fly via the USA, where you can connect to flights to Jamaica. Fares from Australia to Los Angeles begin at about A$1850. From New Zealand, fares to Los Angeles begin at about NZ$2650.

Direct service between Australia, New Zealand and California is provided by the following airlines:

Air New Zealand Auckland (☎ 0800-737-000); Sydney (☎ 02-8235-9999; www.airnz.co.nz)
Delta Airlines Auckland (☎ 09-379-3370); Sydney (☎ 02-9262-1777)
Qantas Auckland (☎ 09-357-8900); Sydney (☎ 02-9957-0111)
United Airlines Auckland (☎ 09-307-9500); Sydney (☎ 02-9237-8888)

You can also fly via Santiago, Chile, or Buenos Aires, Argentina.

For online bookings, try www.travel.com .au, www.travel.co.nz, www.zuji.com .au or www.zuj i.co.nz.

These are tour agencies that specialize in the Caribbean:

Caribbean Bound (☎ 02-9267 2555; www.caribbean .com.au; Suite 102, 379 Pitt St, Sydney 2000, NSW, Australia)
Contours (☎ 03-9670 6900; www.contourstravel.com .au; Lvl 6, 310 King St, Melbourne, Victoria 3000, Australia)
Flight Centre Australia (☎ 133 133; www.flightcentre .com.au); New Zealand (☎ 0800 243 544; www.flight centre.co.nz)
STA Travel Australia (☎ 1300 733 035; www.statravel .com.au); New Zealand (☎ 0508 782 872; www.statravel .co.nz)

Canada

Air Canada (☎ 888-247-2262; www.aircanada.com) serves Montego Bay from Montreal, Halifax, Kingston and Winnipeg in winter, and Montego Bay from Toronto daily year-round. **Air Jamaica** (☎ 888-359-2475, in the USA 800-523-5585; www.airjamaica.com) flies nonstop from Toronto. Fares from Toronto to Montego Bay begin at about C$800.

Canadian Universities Travel Service (☎ 866-246-9762; www.travelcuts.com) sells discount airfares. The agency has 25 offices throughout Canada.

Check with the following companies for information on charter flights and package charters to Jamaica:

Air Transat Holidays (☎ 800-587-2672; www .airtransat.com) Charters to Montego Bay from Toronto, Quebec and Montreal.
Conquest Tours (☎ 866-266-7974; www.conquest vacations.com)

TRANSPORTATION

GG Tours (☎ 416-487-1146; www.ggtours.ca) Charters to Kingston from Toronto.
Signature Vacations (☎ 416-967-1112; www.signaturevacations.com) Charters to Montego Bay from Toronto.
Sunquest Vacations (☎ 416-485-6060, 877-485-6060; www.sunquest.ca) Charters to Montego Bay from Toronto and Ottawa.
Tours Maison (☎ 800-361-8835; www.toursmaison.ca) Charters to Montego Bay from Montreal.

The Caribbean

Air Jamaica (www.airjamaica.com; hub Kingston; ☎ Europe ☎ 020-8570-7999; Jamaica ☎ 888-359-2475; North America & the Caribbean ☎ 800-523-5585) uses Montego Bay as a hub for connecting its US flights with the Caribbean destinations of Antigua, Bahamas, Barbados, Bonaire, Havana (you can reserve flights between Jamaica and Cuba in the USA, but you must purchase your ticket in Jamaica), Curaçao, Santo Domingo, Grenada, St Lucia and Turks and Caicos. Many flights are operated by Air Jamaica's domestic airline, **Air Jamaica Express**.

Other airlines flying within the Caribbean include the following:
ALM/Dutch Caribbean (☎ 876-926-1762; www.flydca.com; hub Curacao) Serves Montego Bay and Kingston from Curacao.
BWIA (☎ 800-538-2942; www.bwee.com; hub Trinidad) Serves Kingston from Antigua, Barbados and Trinidad.
Cayman Airways (☎ 876-926-1762, 876-926-7778; www.caymanairways.com) Serves Montego Bay and Kingston from Grand Cayman and Cayman Brac.
Sky King (☎ 649-941-5464; www.skyking.tc) Serves Kingston from Turks and Caicos.

AIR PASSES

Air Jamaica's Caribbean Hopper Program enables travelers flying on an Air Jamaica flight from a US city to visit three or more islands (economy US$399, first class US$699) that are within their Caribbean and Central American network, which includes anywhere in Jamaica, Turks and Caicos (Providenciales), Grand Cayman, the Bahamas, Cuba, Panama City, Bonaire, Barbados, Grenada and St Lucia. The minimum stay is three days and the maximum is 30. No backtracking is allowed.

American Airlines offers the American Eagle Caribbean Explorer pass, which allows travelers from the USA, Canada and Mexico who fly to the American Eagle hub in San Juan to then explore 23 other Caribbean destinations. Tickets must be purchased seven days in advance and travel must begin within 14 days of arrival in San Juan. Tickets are nonrefundable and some holiday blackout dates apply.

BWIA (☎ 020-8577-1100; www.bwee.com) offers a Caribbean Travelers Air Pass to anyone flying into the Caribbean on a BWIA international flight. This pass (economy US$399; first class US$599) lets passengers travel within 30 days to any of the airline's Caribbean destinations. On this 30-day pass, the itinerary must be set in advance and there's a US$20 charge to make changes. Each destination can be visited only once, other than for connecting flights.

Continental Europe

The following carriers provide direct flights. Typical return fares to Montego Bay are €550 low season and €800 high season.
Condor (☎ 01802-337135; www.condor.de) Serves Montego Bay from Frankfurt.
Iberia (☎ 902-400-500; www.iberia.com) Serves Montego Bay from Vienna, Dusseldorf, Munich, Stuttgart, Frankfurt and Hamburg.
LTU (☎ 800-888-0200; www.ltu.de) Serves Montego Bay from Dusseldorf.
Martinair (☎ 020-60-11-767; www.martinair.com) Serves Montego Bay from Amsterdam.

In France, recommended travel agencies include these ones:
Anyway (☎ 08 92 89 38 92; www.anyway.fr)
Lastminute (☎ 08 92 70 50 00; www.lastminute.fr)
Nouvelles Frontières (☎ 08 25 00 07 47; www.nouvelles-frontieres.fr)
OTU Voyages (www.otu.fr) This agency specializes in student and youth travelers.
Voyageurs du Monde (☎ 01 40 15 11 15; www.vdm.com)

In Germany, try:
Expedia (www.expedia.de)
Just Travel (☎ 089-747-3330; www.justtravel.de)
Lastminute (☎ 01805-284-366; www.lastminute.de)
STA Travel (☎ 01805-456-422; www.statravel.de) For travelers under the age of 26.

Other recommended travel agencies in Continental Europe include the following:
Airfair (☎ 020 620 5121; www.airfair.nl) A reputable agency in the Netherlands.
Barcelo Viajes (☎ 902 11 62 26; www.barceloviajes.com) In Spain.

CTS Viaggi (☎ 064-62-04-31; www.cts.it) In Italy, specializing in student and youth travel.
Nouvelles Frontières (☎ 902-17-09-79; www.nouvelles-frontieres.es)

In Spain try the following:
Viajes Marsans (☎ 913 43 30 00; www.marsans.es) Offers charter flights to Montego Bay from Madrid.

UK

The following airlines offer direct flights to Jamaica. Typical fares average about £875 in the low season, and £950 in the high season.

Aeroflot (Eire ☎ 06-47-2299; UK ☎ 020-7355 2233; infres@aeroflot.co.uk; 70 Piccadilly, London W1V 9HH) Weekly service to Montego Bay from Ireland.
Air Jamaica (UK ☎ 020-8570 7999; www.airjamaica.com) Serves Kingston and Montego Bay from London-Heathrow.
British Airways (☎ 0870-850 9850; www.britishairways.com) Serves Kingston and Montego Bay from London-Gatwick.
Virgin Atlantic (☎ 0870/380-2007; www.virgin.com) Serves Kingston and Montego Bay.

It can be cheaper to instead fly via the USA, changing aircraft in New York or Miami (return fares between London and Miami can be as low as £250 in low season). Airlines that fly to the USA from the UK include **American Airlines** (☎ 800-433-7300; www.aa.com), **British Airways** (☎ 020-8897 4000; www.britishairways.co.uk), **Delta Airlines** (☎ 800-221-1212; www.delta.com), **United Airlines** (☎ 084-5844 4777; www.unitedairlines.co.uk) and **Virgin Atlantic** (☎ 800-862-8621; www.virgin.com).

For discount tickets from the UK, try the following travel agencies:

Council Travel (☎ 020 7437 7767; 29a Poland St, London W1V)
London Flight Centre (☎ 020-7244 6411; www.topdecktravel.co.uk; 125 Earls Court Rd, London SW5)
STA Travel (☎ 087-0160 0599; www.statravel.co.uk; 86 Old Brompton Rd, London SW7)
Trailfinders (☎ 020-7937 5400; www.trailfinders.co.uk; 215 Kensington High St, London W8)

For additional low-fare options, look in the magazine *Time Out* and the Sunday papers for ads.

CHARTER FLIGHTS

Jamaica is a major charter destination from the UK. All charter flights are into Montego Bay. They are usually considerably cheaper than scheduled fares, although departure and arrival times are often inconveniently scheduled in the middle of the night. You should be able to find fares as low as £300 in the low season, and £650 in high season.

Good resources include **Charter Flight Centre** (☎ 020-7854 8434; www.charterflights.co.uk) and **Dial a Flight** (☎ 087-0566 6666; www.dialafl ight.co.uk).

Leading charter operators to Jamaica include the following:

British Airways Holidays (☎ 01293-617000; www.britishairways.com/holidays)
Caribtours (☎ 020-7751 0660; www.caribtours.co.uk)
Cosmos Holidays (☎ 08704-435285; www.cosmosholidays.co.uk)
Thomas Cook Airlines (☎ 0884-855-0515; www.thomascookairlines.co.uk) Charters to Montego Bay from London-Gatwick.
Thomas Cook Signature (☎ 0870-443 4582; www.thomascooksignature.com)
Thomson Holidays (☎ 0870-165 0079; www.thomson-holidays.com)

USA

The most popular routings are via Miami (90 minutes) and New York (three hours, 20 minutes). Jamaica is also served by direct flights from about a dozen other cities.

Fares quoted around press time for round-trip travel to Montego Bay originating on a weekend averaged about US$600 low season and US$750 high season from New York, and US$500 low season and US$650 high season from Miami. These should be considered only ballpark figures.

The following carriers fly from the US to Jamaica:

Air Jamaica (☎ 800-523-5585; www.airjamaica.com) Direct flights from Atlanta, Baltimore, Boston, Chicago, Fort Lauderdale, Houston, Los Angeles, Miami, Newark, New York, Orlando, Philadelphia and Washington DC.
Air Transat (☎ 866-847-1112; www.airtransat.com) Has regular service to Montego Bay from Toronto and Montreal.
American Airlines (☎ 800-433-7300; www.aa.com) Flies to Kingston and Montego Bay from Miami, New York and Boston.
Continental Airlines (☎ 800-523-3273; www.continental.com) Flies to Kingston and Montego Bay from Newark.
Delta (☎ 800-221-1212; www.delta.com) Flies to Montego Bay from Atlanta.
Northwest Airlines (☎ 800-225-2525; www.northwestairlines.com) Flies to Montego Bay from Detroit, Minneapolis and Memphis.
United Flies to Montego Bay from Chicago.
US Airways (☎ 800-428-4322; www.usairways.com) Flies to Montego Bay from Charlotte, Fort Lauderdale and Philadelphia.

CHARTER FLIGHTS

These flights generally offer the lowest fares for confirmed reservations (as much as one-third lower than regular airline prices). Some of the key operators to Jamaica include the following:

Adventure Tours (☎ 800-999-9046; www.adventuretoursusa.com) Charters to Montego Bay from Denver.

American Trans Air (☎ 800-435-9282; www.ata.com) Charters to Montego Bay from Dallas.

Apple Vacations (☎ 800-365-APPLE, 847-640-1170; www.applevacations.com) Charters to Montego Bay from Chicago, Detroit, St Louis and Milwaukee.

Funjet Vacations (☎ 800-558-3050; www.funjet.com) Charters to Montego Bay from Chicago, St Louis, Detroit, Houston and Milwaukee.

GWV International (☎ 800-225-5498; www.gwvvacations.com) Charters to Montego Bay from Boston.

MLT Vacations (☎ 800-328-0025; www.mltvacations.com) Charters to Montego Bay from Minneapolis.

Sunburst Holidays (☎ 800-MONTEGO, 800-666-8346; www.sunburstvacations.com) Charters to Montego Bay from Boston.

Trans Global Vacations (☎ 800-338-2160; www.tgvacations.com) Charters to Montego Bay from Minneapolis.

Vacation Express (☎ 800-486-9777; www.vacationexpress.com) Charters to Montego Bay from Atlanta, Charlotte, Cincinnati, Louisville, Nashville and Washington.

Vacations by Sun Country (☎ 800-752-1218; www.suncountry.com) Charters to Montego Bay from Minneapolis.

DISCOUNT & LAST-MINUTE TICKETS

Discount travel agencies in the USA are known as consolidators (though you won't see a sign on the door saying 'Consolidator'). San Francisco is the ticket consolidator capital of America, although some good deals can be found in Los Angeles, New York and other big cities.

A number of discount ticket agencies sell reduced-rate tickets to the Caribbean. Online, try **Airfares For Less** (☎ 800-627-8468; http://martintravelservices.com/airfares/); **Cheapairlines** (☎ 800-852-2608; www.cheapairlines.com) and **Discount Airfares** (www.discount- airfares.com).

If you can fly on very short notice (usually within seven days of booking), consider buying a ticket from a 'last-minute' ticket broker. These companies buy surplus seats from airlines at hugely discounted prices. Discounts can be as great as 40%.

Last Minute Club (☎ 416-449-5400, 877-970-3500; www.lastminuteclub.com) specializes in air and hotel packages to the Caribbean. Also check out **Moment's Notice** (☎ 888-241-3366; www.moments-notice.com).

SEA

Jamaica is a popular destination on the cruise roster, mainly for passenger liners but also for private yachters. Arrival by freightliner is even an option.

For maps and charts of the Caribbean, contact **Bluewater Books & Charts** (☎ 954-763-6533, 800-942-2583; www.bluewaterweb.com; 1811 Cordova Rd, Fort Lauderdale, FL 33316). The **National Oceanic & Atmospheric Administration** (☎ 301-713-9312; chartmaker.ncd.noaa.gov) sells US government charts.

Cruise Ship

More than 800,000 cruise-ship passengers sail to Jamaica annually, making it one of the world's largest cruise-ship destinations. While the ships get bigger, the amenities also grow and today your ship can have everything from climbing wall and inline skating rink to nightclubs and waterfalls. Most ships hit four or five ports of call, sometimes spending a night, other times only a few hours.

The typical cruise-ship holiday is the ultimate package tour. Other than the effort involved in selecting a cruise, it requires minimal planning – just pay and show up – and for many people this is a large part of the appeal. While the majority of mainstream cruises take in fine scenery along the way, the time spent on the islands is generally limited and the opportunities to experience a sense of island life are more restricted.

Port visits are usually one-day stopovers at either Ocho Rios or Montego Bay, with Falmouth expected to become a port of call in 2009. Most cruises last one to two weeks and will include other western Caribbean destinations such as Cozumel and Progreso in Mexico, Grand Cayman, and Key West and Miami FL. Cruise lines featuring Jamaica as a port of call include the following (all phone numbers are in North America).

Carnival Cruise Lines (☎ 800-327-9501; www.carnival.com)

Celebrity Cruises (☎ 800-722-5941; www.celebritycruises.com)

Costa Cruise Lines (☎ 800-462-6782; www.costacruises.com)

Holland America (☎ 800-426-0327; www.hollandamerica.com)

Princess Cruises (☎ 800-774-6237; www.princess.com)

OFF THE BOAT

Cruise-ship passengers who show interest in the local culture and put money directly into the hands of small merchants are more appreciated by Jamaicans than those who stay wrapped in the cocoon of organized land tours or see nothing beyond the duty-free shops.

While the cruise-lines' optional land tours are conveniently packaged to take in many of the island's sightseeing highlights, they also move quickly and tend to shield visitors from interaction with the local people. In addition, a fair percentage of the money paid for these tours stays with the organizers rather than going into the local economy. If you venture out on your own, you're likely to enjoy a richer cultural experience. If you want to tour the island, consider hiring a local taxi driver, who will likely shed light on local issues and give you a more colorful tour. Wander the streets of the main town, poke into little shops, eat at local restaurants and buy souvenirs from street vendors, or veer off the beaten track. Visit small businesses and chat with the owners, buy local rums and other souvenirs in small shops instead of on board – you'll help fuel the local economy (and save money in the process).

Radisson Seven Seas Cruises (☎ 877-505-5370; www.rssc.com)
Royal Caribbean International (☎ 888-398-9819; www.royalcaribbean.com)

COST

The cost of a cruise-ship trip can vary widely, depending on season and vacancy. While it will save you money to book early, keep in mind that cruise lines want to sail full, so many offer excellent last-minute discounts, sometimes up to 50% off the full fare. You'll pay less for a smaller room, but beware that the really cheap cabins are often claustrophobic and poorly located (be sure to ask before booking).

Some cruise lines provide free or discounted airfares to and from the port of embarkation (or will provide a rebate if you make your own transportation arrangements), while others do not. Meals, which are typically frequent and elaborate, are included in the cruise price. Alcoholic drinks are usually not included and are comparable in price to those in bars back home. Guided land tours are almost always offered at each port of call, generally for about US$40 to US$100 each. Most cruises end up costing around US$200 to US$400 per person per day, including airfare from a major US gateway city. Port charges and government taxes typically add on about US$150 per cruise. Be sure to check the fine print about deposits, cancellation and refund policies, and travel insurance.

BOOKING A CRUISE

When it comes to figuring out what cruise to take, read whatever you can, ask around for referrals, then call some travel agencies. Agents most knowledgeable about cruises usually belong to Cruise Lines International Association (CLIA), an organization of cruise lines that works with about 20,000 North American travel agencies. Check out **Cruise Critic** (www.cruisecritic.com), which gives ship profiles, reviews of the different cruise-ship companies and details about bargains and special deals.

For travelers with physical limitations, **Flying Wheels Travel** (☎ 507-451-5005, 800-535-6790; www.flyingwheelstravel.com) specializes in booking disabled-accessible Caribbean cruises.

Several agencies in the US deal specifically in booking Caribbean cruises. They are often a great source of information on special deals. Here are some we recommend:

Cruise Outlet (☎ 800-775-1884; www.thecruiseoutlet.com)
Cruise.com (☎ 888-999-2783; www.cruise.com)
Cruise411 (☎ 800-553-7090; www.cruise411.com)
Cruises at Cost (☎ 800-274-3866; www.cruisesatcost.com)
World Wide Cruises (☎ 800-882-9000; www.wwcruises.com)

Freighter

Several freighters that ply between North America and Europe call in on Jamaica, and some take paying passengers. Most have plush cabins and passengers are well looked after by stewards. Book early!

Ford's Freighter Travel Guide (☎ 818-701-7414; 19448 Longelius St, Northridge, CA 91324, USA) lists freight ships that take some passengers.

The following agencies specialize in freighter cruises:

Freighter World Cruises (☎ 626-449-3106; www.freighterworld.com; Suite 335, 180 South Lake Ave, Pasadena CA 91101)
Hamburg-Sud Reiseagentur (☎ 040-370 5155; Ost-West Strasse 59-61, 20457 Hamburg, Germany)
Maris USA (☎ 203-222-1500, 800-996-2747; www.freightercruises.com; 215 Main St, Westport CT 06880, USA)
NSB Frachtschiff-Touristik (☎ 0421-338-8020; www.nsb-reisebuero.de; Cioenstrasse 22, D-28195 Bremen, Germany)

Private Yacht

Many yachters make the trip to Jamaica from North America. If you plan to travel in summer, keep fully abreast of weather reports; mid to late summer is hurricane season.

Upon you arrival in Jamaica, you *must* clear customs and immigration at either Montego Bay (Montego Bay Yacht Club), Kingston (Royal Jamaican Yacht Club, Port Royal), Ocho Rios (St Ann's Bay) or West Harbour in Port Antonio. In addition, you will need to clear customs at *each* port of call in Jamaica.

You'll need the regular documentation for foreign travel (see p283).

GETTING AROUND

AIR

There are four domestic airports: Tinson Pen in Kingston, Boscobel Aerodrome near Ocho Rios, Negril Aerodrome, and Ken Jones Aerodrome at Port Antonio.

Montego Bay's Donald Sangster International Airport has a domestic terminal adjacent to the international terminal. It's a bit of a walk – Air Jamaica Express provides a shuttle.

In Kingston, most domestic flights use Tinson Pen, 3km west of downtown, but it's a 40-minute ride to the domestic airstrip from Norman Manley International Airport.

Airlines in Jamaica

Air Jamaica (Jamaica ☎ 800-359-2475; North America & the Caribbean ☎ 800-523-5585; UK ☎ 20-8570-7999; www.airjamaica.com) offers a daily service between Kingston and Montego Bay, and between Montego Bay and Ocho Rios through its domestic air service, Air Jamaica Express.

Typical one-way fares (for purchase outside Jamaica) are US$60 for Kingston to Montego Bay (seven daily) and US$56 for Montego Bay to Ocho Rios (two daily).

TimAir (☎ 952-2516, 979-1114; www.timair.net; domestic terminal, Donald Sangster International Airport) has charter flights between its hub in Montego Bay and Kingston (US$205), Mandeville (US$175), Negril (US$179), Ocho Rios (US$362) and Port Antonio (US$599). Rates are for two passengers; fares go up or down for fewer or more passengers.

Helicopter

You can charter a four-passenger Bell Jetranger helicopter for transportation to any airport or for personalized tours from **Island Hoppers** (☎ 974-1285; www.jamaicahelicoptertours.com; 120 Main St, Ocho Rios; tours per person 20-/30-/60-minutes US$360/520/1000, minimum 3 paid seats). Tours depart from Montego Bay and Ocho Rios.

BICYCLE

Mountain bikes and 'beach cruisers' (bikes with fat tires, suitable for riding on sand) can be rented at most major resorts (US$15 to US$30 per day). However, road conditions are hazardous and Jamaican drivers are not very considerate to bicyclists. For serious touring, bring your own mountain or multipurpose bike. You'll need sturdy wheels to handle the potholed roads.

BOAT

The ferry that has long sailed from the Kingston waterfront to Port Royal was not in service at the time of research.

See p290 for details on cruising in Jamaican waters.

BUS & PUBLIC TRANSPORTATION

Traveling by public transportation could be the best – or worst! – adventure of your trip to Jamaica. An extensive transportation network links virtually every village and comprises several options that range from standard public buses to private taxis, with minibuses and route taxis in between.

For the adventurous traveler who doesn't mind getting up close and personal with fellow passengers without the comfort of air-conditioning and is unfazed by the wild and often dangerous maneuverings of the drivers, this is the cheapest way to get around Jamaica. There is usually no set timetable – buses leave when the driver considers them full – and passengers are crammed in with little regard for comfort. Guard your luggage carefully against theft.

Public buses, minibuses and route taxis depart from and arrive at each town's transportation station, which is usually near the main market. Locals can direct you to the appropriate vehicle, which should have its destination marked above the front window (for buses) or on its side.

Don't expect drivers to be able to make change for large bills. Carry a supply of Jamaican coins and bills in denominations of J$50 and J$100.

Public buses and minibuses are regulated by the **Ministry of Transport & Works** (☎ 754-2584; www.mtw.gov.jm; 138 Maxfield Ave, Kingston 10).

See p295 for more information about public transportation.

Classes

BUSES

Large buses are few and far between in Jamaica due to the narrow twisting roads. Throughout the island, there are bus stops at most road intersections along routes, but you can usually flag down a bus anywhere except in major cities, where they only pause at designated stops. When you want to get off, shout 'One stop!' The conductor will usually echo your request with, 'Let off!'

MINIBUSES

Private minibuses, also known as 'coasters,' have traditionally been the workhorses of Jamaica's regional public transportation system. All major towns and virtually every village in the country are served.

Licensed minibuses display red license plates with the initials PPV (public passenger vehicle) or have a Jamaican Union of Travelers Association (JUTA) insignia. JUTA buses are exclusively for tourists. They usually depart their point of origin when they're full; they're often overflowing, with people hanging from the open doors.

ROUTE TAXIS

These communal taxis are the most universal mode of public transportation, reaching every part of the country. They operate like minibuses, picking up as many people as they can squeeze in along their specified routes.

Most route taxis are white Toyota Corolla station wagons marked by their red license plates. They should have 'Route Taxi' marked on the front door, and they are not to be confused with similar licensed taxis, which charge more. A rule of thumb: avoid any taxi that lacks the red license plate.

Costs

Taking public transportation is terrifically inexpensive. Buses and minibuses charge in the neighborhood of US$1 per 50km, and route taxis charge about US$2 to US$3 per 50km.

CAR & MOTORCYCLE

Automobile Associations

There is no national roadside organization to phone when you have car trouble. Most car-rental agencies have a 24-hour service number in case of breakdowns and other emergencies. If you do break down, use a local mechanic only for minor work; otherwise the car-rental company may balk at reimbursing you for work it hasn't authorized. If you can't find a phone or repair service, seek police assistance. *Never* give your keys to strangers.

Driver's License

To drive in Jamaica, you must have a valid International Driver's License (IDL) or a current license for your home country or state, valid for up to six months. In the USA you can obtain an IDL by applying with your current license to any Automobile Association office.

Fuel & Spare Parts

Many gas stations close at 7pm or so. In rural areas, stations are usually closed on Sunday. At time of research, gasoline cost about US$1.85 per liter. Most gas stations only accept cash for payment, although a growing number of modern gas stations in the larger towns accept credit cards.

Rental

Several major international car-rental companies operate in Jamaica, along with dozens of local firms. Car-rental agencies are listed in the local yellow pages.

High-season rates begin at about US$45 per day and can run as high as US$125, depending on the vehicle. Cheaper rates apply in the low season. Some companies include unlimited distance, while some set a limit and charge a fee for excess kilometers driven. Most firms require a deposit of at least US$500, but accept a credit-card imprint. Keep copies of all your paperwork. Renters must be 21 years old (some companies will rent only to people aged 25 or older).

You can reserve a car upon arrival, but in the high season be sure to make your reservation in advance. Reconfirm before your arrival.

Before signing, go over the vehicle with a fine-tooth comb to identify any dents and scratches. Make a note of each one before you drive away. You're likely to be charged for the slightest mark that wasn't noted before. Don't forget to check the cigarette lighter and interior switches, which are often missing.

Most of the companies rent out modern Japanese sedans. A big car can be a liability on Jamaica's narrow, winding roads. Some companies also rent 4WD vehicles, which are highly recommended if you intend to do *any* driving away from main roads.

Stick shift is preferable because frequent and sudden gear changes are required when potholes and kamikaze chickens appear out of nowhere. Remember that you'll be changing gears with your *left* hand. If this is new to you, you'll soon get the hang of it.

Jamaica's largest and most reputable car-rental company is **Island Car Rentals** (www.islandcarrentals.com); Donald Sangster International Airport (☎ 952-7225); Kingston (☎ 926-8012; 17 Antigua Ave); Norman Manley International Airport (☎ 924-8075); North America (☎ 800-892-4581); Ocho Rios (☎ 974-2666). Eleven categories of cars cost US$44 to $99 daily.

Major international companies, with rates comparable to those of Island Car Rentals, are represented by these offices in Jamaica:

Avis (www.avis.com); Donald Sangster International Airport (☎ 952-0762); Norman Manley International Airport (☎ 924-8293)

Budget (www.budget.com); Norman Manley International Airport (☎ 759-1793); Ocho Rios (☎ 974-1288)

Hertz (www.hertz.com); Donald Sangster International Airport (☎ 979-0438) Norman Manley International Airport (☎ 924-8028)

Thrifty (www.thrifty.com; Donald Sangster International Airport ☎ 952-5825)

Local rental agencies often provide better daily rates than the international chains, but the cars are sometimes road-worn. Reputable agencies include these ones:

Beaumont's Car Rentals Kingston (☎ 926-0311;56c Brentford Rd); Montego Bay (☎ 971-8476; www.beaumonts-car-rental.com; 34 Queens Dr)

Caribbean Car Rentals (☎ 926-6339; www.caribbeancarrentals.net; 31 Hope Rd, Kingston)

Triple-A-Car Rental (☎ 974-2859; www.tripleacar.com; 180 Main St, Ocho Rios)

Insurance

Check in advance whether your current insurance or credit card covers you for driving while abroad. All rental companies will recommend damage-waiver insurance, which limits your liability in the event of an accident or damage. This costs about US$12 to US$40 per day and is a valuable investment.

Road Conditions

Jamaica's roads run the gamut from modern multilane highways to barely passable tracks. You can expect any road with the designation 'A' before its number to be in fairly good condition. 'B' roads are in general much more narrow and often badly potholed, but still passable in the average rental car. Minor roads, particularly those in the Blue Mountains and in the Cockpit Country, can be hellish. If you plan to drive off the major routes, it's essential to have a stalwart 4WD vehicle.

Signage on main roads is good, but directional signs are few and far between as soon as you leave the main roads. Many B-roads are not shown on maps. And what may appear on a map to be a 30-minute journey may take several hours. More often than not there are no signs to indicate sharp curves, steep ascents or work in progress. In addition roads are often poorly lit, if at all.

Road Hazards

Jamaican drivers rank among the world's rudest and most dangerous. Cars race through towns and play chicken with one another, overtaking with daredevil folly. Jamaica has the third-highest auto fatality rate in the world, behind Ethiopia and India. Use extreme caution and drive defensively, especially at night when you should be prepared to meet oncoming cars that are either without lights or blinding you with their high-beams. Use your horn liberally, especially when approaching blind corners.

Road Rules

Always drive on the left. Remember: 'Keep left, and you'll always be right.' Here's another local saying worth memorizing: 'De left side is de right side; de right side is suicide!' Even these dictums may go out the window when you find yourself negotiating a roundabout.

Jamaica has a compulsory seatbelt law.

Speed limits range from 50km to 80km and vary from place to place across the island.

HITCHHIKING

Hitchhiking is common enough among Jamaicans but, because public transportation is absurdly cheap, few tourists stick out their thumbs.

Hitchhiking is never entirely safe in any country in the world and we don't recommend it. Travelers who decide to hitchhike should understand that they are taking a small but potentially serious risk. If you choose to take that risk, you will be safer if you travel in pairs and let someone know where you are planning to go.

LOCAL TRANSPORTATION

Bicycle

Bicycle rentals are commonly available in resort towns (US$15 to US$30 per day) but the frenetic nature of Jamaican traffic may preclude you from having the pleasant experience that you had in mind.

If you want to do any serious riding, consider bringing your own bike. However, you need to be prepared to fix your own flats and broken chains. Bike shops are virtually nonexistent.

Buses

Kingston's **municipal bus system** (Jamaica Urban Transport Co Ltd; ☎ 749-3196; fares US$0.35-0.50; 🕑 5am-10pm) operates a fleet of Mercedes-Benz and Volvo buses, including some for the disabled. Buses stop only at official stops.

Students, children, disabled persons and pensioners pay half the full fare.

Motor Scooter & Motorcycle

Dozens of companies hire motorcycles and scooters; they're available at any resort town. These companies are far more lax than the car-rental companies; you may not even have to show your driver's license. If you are not an experienced motorcycle driver, it might be better to rent a scooter, which is far easier to handle. Scooters cost about US$35 per day and motorcycles cost about US$45 a day; note that the deposits can be high.

Road conditions in Jamaica are hazardous. If the rental agency has helmets available, *wear one!*

Route Taxi

Route taxis, which are generally white Corolla station wagons with red PPV plates, provide vital transportation on both the local and national level. You can generally flag them down anywhere. See p293 for more information.

Taxi

Licensed taxis – called 'contract carriages' – have red PPV license plates (those without such plates are unlicensed). They're expensive, but affordable if you share the cost with other passengers.

Jamaica Union of Travelers Association (JUTA; juta@cwjamaica.com; Kingston ☎ 926-1537; Montego Bay ☎ 952-0813; Negril ☎ 957-9197) operates islandwide and is geared almost exclusively to the tourist business. Other taxicab companies are listed in the yellow pages and in the regional chapters of this book.

The Transport Authority has established fixed rates according to distance (different rates apply for locals and tourists, who pay more). Licensed cabs should have these posted inside. Taxis are also supposed to have meters, but many don't use them.

The following were typical fares in 2007, based on up to four people per taxi:

Route	Fare
Around Montego Bay	US$15-20
Kingston-Ocho Rios	US$120-150
Kingston-Port Antonio	US$100-120
Montego Bay-Ocho Rios or Negril	US$100
Norman Manley International Airport-Kingston (Uptown)	US$25
Donald Sangster International Airport-Montego Bay	US$8

TRAIN

Although Jamaica was the proud home to the first railway lines outside Europe and North America, those railway tracks marked on the maps are all that's left of them. The railway system was shut down in 1992. Talks of putting the trains back into operation have come to naught.

TRANSPORTATION

Health

CONTENTS

Obviously prevention is the key to staying healthy while abroad. Travelers who receive the recommended vaccines and follow commonsense precautions usually come away with nothing more than a little diarrhea – a rite of passage to any tropical holiday.

From the medical standpoint, Jamaica is generally safe as long as you're reasonably careful about what you eat and drink. The most common travel-related diseases, such as dysentery and hepatitis, are acquired by consumption of contaminated food and water. Mosquito-borne illnesses are not a significant concern on the island, except during outbreaks of dengue fever.

BEFORE YOU GO

Bring medications in their original containers, clearly labeled. A signed, dated letter from your physician describing all medical conditions and medications, including generic names, is also a good idea. If you're carrying syringes or needles, be sure to have a physician's letter documenting their medical necessity.

INSURANCE

If your health insurance does not cover you for medical expenses abroad, consider supplemental insurance. US travelers can find a list of medical-evacuation and travel-insurance companies on the **US State Department website** (www.travel.state.gov/medical.html). Find out in advance if your insurance plan will make payments directly to providers or reimburse you later for overseas health expenditure.

RECOMMENDED VACCINATIONS

Since most vaccines don't produce immunity until at least two weeks after they are given, visit a physician four to eight weeks before your departure. Ask your doctor for an international certificate of vaccination (known as the yellow booklet), which will list all the vaccinations you've received. It's mandatory for countries requiring proof of yellow-fever vaccination upon entry, but it's a good idea to carry it wherever you travel.

RECOMMENDED VACCINATIONS

Chickenpox For travelers who've never had chickenpox; two doses one month apart. Possible side effects are fever or a mild case of chickenpox.

Hepatitis A Recommended for all travelers; one dose before trip, and a booster six to 12 months later. Side effects may include soreness at injection site, headaches or body aches.

Hepatitis B Recommended for long-term travelers in close contact with the local population; three doses over six months. Side effects may include soreness at injection site or low-grade fever.

Measles One dose, recommended for travelers born after 1956 who've had only one measles vaccination. Side effects could include fever, rash, joint pains or allergic reactions.

Rabies For travelers who may have contact with animals and may not have access to medical care; three doses over three to four weeks. Possible side effects: soreness at injection site, headaches, body aches (and it's expensive).

Tetanus-diphtheria For all travelers who haven't had a booster within 10 years; one dose lasts 10 years. There may be some soreness at injection site.

No vaccinations are required to enter Jamaica unless you have visited any of the following locations within the previous six weeks: Asia, Africa, Central and South America, Dominican Republic, Haiti or Trinidad and Tobago. Check with the **Jamaica Tourist Board** (JTB; www.visitjamaica.com) or your travel agent before departure to see what current regulations may be. Yellow fever is not a threat in Jamaica, but immunization may be required of travelers arriving from infected areas, chiefly in Africa and South America.

MEDICAL CHECKLIST

Recommended items for a personal medical kit:

- acetaminophen/paracetamol (Tylenol) or aspirin
- adhesive or paper tape
- antibacterial ointment (eg Bactroban) for cuts and abrasions
- antibiotics
- antidiarrheal drugs (eg loperamide)
- antihistamines (for hay fever and allergic reactions)
- anti-inflammatory drugs (eg ibuprofen)
- bandages, gauze and gauze rolls
- DEET-containing insect repellent for the skin
- iodine tablets (for water purification)
- oral rehydration salts
- permethrin-containing insect spray for clothing, tents and bed nets
- pocketknife
- scissors, safety pins and tweezers
- steroid cream or cortisone (for poison ivy and other allergic rashes)
- sunblock
- syringes and sterile needles
- thermometer

INTERNET RESOURCES

There is a wealth of travel health advice on the internet. **Lonely Planet** (www.lonelyplanet.com) is a good place to start. The **World Health Organization** (www.who.int/ith/) publishes a superb book called *International Travel and Health*, which is revised annually and is available online on its website at no cost. Another website of general interest is **MD Travel Health** (www.mdtravelhealth.com), which provides complete travel health recommendations for every country, updated daily, also at no cost.

It's usually a good idea to consult your government's travel health website before departure, if one is available.

Australia (www.smartraveller.gov.au)
Canada (www.hc-sc.gc.ca/english)
UK (www.doh.gov.uk/traveladvice)
USA (www.cdc.gov/travel)

FURTHER READING

If you're traveling with children, Lonely Planet's *Travel with Children* may be useful. *ABC of Healthy Travel* by E Walker et al, and *Medicine for the Outdoors* by Paul S Auerbach, are other valuable resources.

IN TRANSIT

DEEP VEIN THROMBOSIS (DVT)

Blood clots may form in the legs during plane flights, chiefly because of prolonged immobility, and the longer the flight, the greater the risk. Though most blood clots are reabsorbed uneventfully, some may break off and travel through the blood vessels to the lungs, where they could cause life-threatening complications.

The chief symptom of deep vein thrombosis is swelling or pain in the foot, ankle or calf, usually but not always on just one side. When a blood clot travels to the lungs, it may cause chest pain and difficulty in breathing. Travelers with any of these symptoms should immediately seek medical attention.

To prevent development of deep vein thrombosis on long flights, you should walk about the cabin, perform isometric compressions of the leg muscles (ie contract the leg muscles while sitting), drink plenty of fluids and avoid alcohol and tobacco.

JET LAG & MOTION SICKNESS

Jet lag is common when crossing more than five time zones, and is characterized by insomnia, fatigue, malaise or nausea. To avoid jet lag, try drinking plenty of fluids (nonalcoholic) and eating light meals. Upon arrival, get exposure to natural sunlight and readjust your schedule (for meals, sleep etc) as soon as possible.

Antihistamines such as dimenhydrinate (Dramamine) and meclizine (Antivert, Bonine) are usually the first choice for treating motion sickness. Their main side effect is drowsiness. A herbal alternative is ginger, which works like a charm for some people.

IN JAMAICA

AVAILABILITY & COST OF HEALTH CARE

Acceptable health care is available in most major cities and larger towns throughout Jamaica, but may be hard to locate in rural areas. Most travelers will find the quality of health care will not be comparable to that in their home country. To find a good local doctor, your best bet is to ask the management of the hotel where you are staying or contact your embassy in Kingston or Montego Bay (see p280).

Many doctors and hospitals expect payment in cash, regardless of whether you have travel health insurance. If you develop a life-threatening medical problem, you'll probably want to be evacuated to a country with state-of-the-art medical care. Since this may cost tens of thousands of dollars, be sure you have insurance to cover this before you depart (see p296).

Many pharmacies are well supplied, but important medications may not be consistently available. Be sure to bring along adequate supplies of all prescription drugs.

INFECTIOUS DISEASES

Dengue Fever

Although extremely rare, dengue fever is present in Jamaica, notably in Portland parish and around Kingston. Dengue is a viral infection transmitted by Aedes mosquitoes, which bite mostly during the daytime and are usually found close to human habitations, often indoors. They breed primarily in artificial water containers such as jars, barrels, cisterns, metal drums, plastic containers and discarded tires. As a result, dengue is especially common in densely populated, urban environments.

Dengue usually causes flulike symptoms that can include fever, muscular aches, joint pains, headaches, nausea and vomiting, often followed by a rash. The experience of body aches may be quite uncomfortable but most cases resolve uneventfully within a few days. Severe cases usually occur in children under 15 who are experiencing their second dengue infection.

There is no treatment for dengue fever except to take analgesics such as acetaminophen or paracetamol (Tylenol) and drink plenty of fluids. Severe cases may require hospitalization for intravenous fluids and supportive care. There is no vaccine.

Hepatitis A

In Jamaica hepatitis A is the second most common travel-related infection (after traveler's diarrhea). Hepatitis A is a viral infection of the liver that is usually acquired by ingestion of contaminated water, food or ice, though it may also be acquired by direct contact with infected persons. The illness occurs throughout the world, but the incidence is higher in developing nations. Symptoms may include fever, malaise, jaundice, nausea, vomiting and abdominal pain. Most cases resolve without complications, though it occasionally causes severe liver damage. There is no treatment.

The vaccine for hepatitis A is extremely safe and highly effective. If you get a booster six to 12 months later, it lasts for at least 10 years. You really should get it before you go to any developing nation. Because the safety of hepatitis A vaccine has not been established for pregnant women or children under age two, they should instead have a gammaglobulin injection.

Hepatitis B

Like hepatitis A, hepatitis B is a liver infection that occurs worldwide but is more common in developing nations. Unlike hepatitis A, the disease is usually acquired by sexual contact or by exposure to infected blood, generally through blood transfusions or contaminated needles. The vaccine is recommended for long-term travelers (on the road for more than six months) who expect to live in rural areas or have close physical contact with locals. Additionally, the vaccine is recommended for anyone who anticipates sexual contact with the local inhabitants or possible medical, dental or other treatments while abroad, especially if a need for transfusions or injections is expected.

Hepatitis B vaccine is safe and highly effective. However, three injections are necessary to establish full immunity. Several countries added hepatitis B vaccine to the list of routine childhood immunizations in the 1980s, so many young adults are already protected.

HIV/AIDS

In 2005 around 1.5% of all Jamaican adults carried HIV, and that percentage is believed to have risen. The Caribbean is the second-worst affected region in the world, after sub-Saharan Africa. Be sure to use condoms for all sexual encounters. If you think you might visit a piercing or tattoo parlor, or if you have a medical condition that might require an injection, make certain you bring along your own sterile needles.

Jamaica has a toll-free **AIDS/STD Helpline** (☎ 888-991-4444, 967-3830; 🕒 10am-10pm Mon-Fri).

Jamaica AIDS Support (JAS; Kingston ☎ 978-2345; 4 Upper Musgrave Ave; Montego Bay ☎ 952-9817; 1st fl, Van Haze Bldg, 16 East St; Ocho Rios ☎ 974-7236; www.jamaicaaidssupport.com; McDowell Bldg, Pineapple Pl) operates a hospice and provides assistance for anyone infected with HIV.

The website of the **National AIDS Committee** (☎ 967-1100; www.nacjamaica.com; 2-4 King St, 4th fl, Oceana Bldg, Kingston) is an informative resource.

Sexually Transmitted Diseases

There's a high prevalence of venereal disease in Jamaica. Gonorrhea and syphilis are the most common; sores, blisters or rashes around the genitals and discharges or pain when urinating are common symptoms. Symptoms for women may be less marked or not observed. Syphilis symptoms eventually disappear, but the disease continues and can cause severe problems, even death, in later years. The treatment of gonorrhea and syphilis is by antibiotics.

While sexual abstinence is the only certain preventative, using condoms is also effective. High-quality condoms are readily available in Jamaica's resort areas, but less so in the smaller towns.

Tetanus

This potentially fatal disease is present in Jamaica as in other tropical areas. It is difficult to treat, but is preventable with immunization. Tetanus (lockjaw) occurs when a wound becomes infected by a germ that lives in the feces of animals or people; clean all cuts, punctures or animal bites. The first symptom may be discomfort in swallowing, or stiffening of the jaw and neck, followed by painful convulsions of the jaw and whole body.

TRAVELER'S DIARRHEA

Throughout most of Jamaica, tap water has been treated and is safe to drink, but in some far-flung rural areas it is safest to avoid it unless it has been boiled, filtered or chemically disinfected (with iodine tablets). To prevent diarrhea, eat fresh fruits or vegetables only if cooked or peeled; be wary of dairy products that might contain unpasteurized milk; and be highly selective when eating food from street vendors.

If you develop diarrhea, be sure to drink plenty of fluid, preferably an oral rehydration solution containing lots of salt and sugar. A few loose stools don't require treatment, but if you start having more than four or five stools a day, you should start taking an antibiotic (usually a quinolone drug) and an antidiarrheal agent (such as loperamide). If diarrhea is bloody or persists for more than 72 hours, or is accompanied by fever, shaking chills or severe abdominal pain, you should seek medical attention.

ENVIRONMENTAL HAZARDS

Animal Bites

Do not attempt to pet, handle or feed any animal, with the exception of domestic animals known to be free of any infectious disease. Most injuries caused by animals are directly related to a person's attempt to touch or feed them.

Any bite or scratch by a mammal, including bats, should be promptly and thoroughly cleansed with large amounts of soap and water, then an antiseptic such as iodine or alcohol should be applied. The local health authorities should be contacted immediately regarding possible post- exposure rabies treatment, whether or not you've been immunized against rabies. It may also be advisable to start an antibiotic, since wounds caused by animal bites and scratches frequently become infected. One of the newer quinolones, such as levofloxacin (Levaquin), which many travelers carry in case of diarrhea, would be an appropriate choice.

Various fish and other sea creatures can sting or bite dangerously (see p300). Jamaica has no venomous snakes.

Bedbugs, Lice & Scabies

Bedbugs often live in dirty mattresses and bedding. Spots of blood on bedclothes or on the wall around the bed can be read as a suggestion to find another hotel.

Lice, which are easier to see, cause itching and discomfort. They make themselves at home in your hair (head lice), clothing (body lice) or pubic hair (crabs). You catch lice through direct contact with infected people or by sharing combs, clothing and the like. Powder or shampoo treatment will kill the lice.

Likewise, scabies – an infestation of microscopic mites – is acquired through sexual contact, bed linen, towels or clothing. The first sign – severe itching caused by an infestation of eggs and feces under the skin – usually appears three to four weeks after exposure (as soon as 24 hours for a second exposure) and is worse at night. Infestation appears as tiny welts and pimples, often in a dotted line, most commonly around the groin and the lower abdomen, between the fingers, on the elbows and under the armpits. Treatment is by pesticidal lotions.

At the same time as using the treatment, you must wash *all* your clothing and bedding in hot water.

Cuts & Scratches

Skin punctures can easily become infected in hot climates and may be difficult to heal. Treat any cut with an antiseptic. Where possible, avoid bandages and Band-Aids, which can keep wounds wet. Coral cuts are notoriously slow to heal, as the coral injects a weak venom into the wound. Clean any cut thoroughly with sodium peroxide if available.

Food

Salads and fruit should be washed with purified water or peeled where possible. Ice cream is usually OK, but beware of street vendors who sell ice cream that has melted and been refrozen. Thoroughly cooked food is safest, but not if it has been left to cool or has been reheated. Shellfish such as oysters and clams should be avoided as well as undercooked meat, particularly in the form of mince. Steaming does not make shellfish safe to eat. Wash your hands before eating.

Mosquito Bites

To prevent bites wear long sleeves, long pants, hats, and shoes rather than sandals. Bring a good insect repellent, preferably one containing DEET, which should be applied to exposed skin and clothing but not to the eyes, mouth, cuts, wounds or irritated skin. In general, adults and children over 12 should use preparations that contain 25% to 35% DEET, which usually lasts for about six hours. Children between two and 12 years of age should use preparations containing no more than 10% DEET, applied sparingly, which will usually last for about three hours. Products that contain lower concentrations of DEET are as effective, but for shorter periods of time. Neurological toxicity has been reported from DEET, especially in children, but appears to be extremely uncommon and generally related to overuse. Compounds containing DEET should not be used on children under the age of two.

Insect repellents containing certain botanical products, including eucalyptus oil and soybean oil, are effective but last only 1½ to two hours. Products based on citronella are not effective.

For additional protection, you can apply permethrin to clothing, shoes, tents and bed nets. Permethrin treatments are safe and remain effective for at least two weeks, even when items are laundered. Permethrin should not be applied directly to skin.

Don't sleep with the window open unless there is a screen. If sleeping outdoors or in accommodations that allow entry of mosquitoes, use a bed net, preferably treated with permethrin, with edges tucked in under the mattress. The mesh size should be less than 1.5mm. If the sleeping area is not otherwise protected, use a mosquito coil, which will fill the room with insecticide through the night. Wristbands impregnated with repellent are not effective.

No-See-'Ums

These well-named irritants are almost microscopically small fleas that hang out on beaches and appear around dusk (especially after rain), and have a voracious appetite. Their bite is out of all proportion to their size. Most insect repellents don't faze them. A better bet is a liberal application of Avon's Skin So Soft, a cosmetic that even the US Army swears by.

Sea Creatures

Spiny sea urchins and coelenterates (coral and jellyfish) are a hazard in some areas. If you're stung by a coelenterate, apply diluted vinegar or baking soda. Remove tentacles carefully, and not with bare hands. If you get stung by a stinging fish, such as a stingray, immerse the limb in water at about 45°C.

Local advice on where to swim is the best way to avoid contact with jellyfish. If you get stung, dousing with vinegar will deactivate any stingers that have not 'fired.' In addition to calamine lotion, antihistamines and analgesics may reduce the reaction and relieve the pain.

Sun

To protect yourself from excessive sun exposure, you should stay out of the midday sun, wear sunglasses and a wide-brimmed sun hat, and apply sunscreen with a sun protection factor (SPF) of 15 or higher, with both UVA and UVB protection. Sunscreen should be generously applied to all exposed parts of the body approximately 30 minutes before sun exposure and should be reapplied after swimming or vigorous activity. Travelers should also drink plenty of fluids and avoid strenuous exercise when the temperature is high.

You'll sweat profusely in Jamaica. Don't rely on feeling thirsty to indicate when you should drink water. Not needing to urinate, or very dark yellow urine, is a sign of dehydration. You'll lose quite a bit of salt through sweating. Salt deficiency is characterized by fatigue, lethargy, headaches, giddiness and muscle cramps, and in this case salt tablets may help. Vomiting or diarrhea can also deplete your liquid and salt levels. Anhydrotic heat exhaustion, caused by an inability to sweat, is quite rare. Unlike other forms of heat exhaustion, it is likely to strike people who have been in Jamaica's hot climate for some time, rather than newcomers.

Long, continuous periods of exposure to high temperatures can leave you vulnerable to heat stroke, a sometimes fatal condition that occurs if the body's heat-regulating mechanism breaks down and the body temperature rises to dangerous levels.

The symptoms are feeling unwell, not sweating very much (or at all) and a high body temperature. Where sweating has ceased, the skin becomes flushed and red. Severe throbbing headaches and lack of coordination will also occur, and the sufferer may be confused or aggressive. Eventually the victim will become delirious or convulse. Hospitalization is essential, but meanwhile get victims out of the sun, remove their clothing, cover them with a wet sheet or towel and fan them continually.

Prickly heat is an itchy rash caused by excessive perspiration trapped under the skin. It usually strikes people who have just arrived in a hot climate and whose pores have not yet opened sufficiently to cope with increased sweating. To alleviate symptoms, keep cool and bathe often, use a mild talcum powder, or resort to air-con.

Don't underestimate the power of the tropical sun, no matter how dark your skin color. You can get sunburned surprisingly quickly, even on cloudy days. Use a sunscreen of SPF 15 or more. Build up your exposure to the sun gradually. A hat provides added protection, and you should also use a barrier cream for your nose and lips. If you do get burned, calamine lotion and aloe vera will provide soothing relief.

Avoid booze by day, as your body uses water to process alcohol. Drink water, or coconut water straight from the husk.

Water

Water is generally safe to drink from faucets throughout the island except in the most far flung rural regions. It is safest, however, to stick with bottled water. It's a good idea to avoid ice, particularly ice sold at street stands as 'bellywash,' 'snocones' or 'skyjuice,' shaved-ice cones sweetened with fruit juice.

Unless you're certain that the local water is not contaminated, you shouldn't drink it. Vigorous boiling for one minute is the most effective means of water purification. At altitudes greater than 2000m, boil for three minutes. In Jamaica's backwaters, clean your teeth with purified water rather than tap water.

Another option is to disinfect water with iodine pills. Instructions are usually enclosed and should be carefully followed. Or you can add 2% tincture of iodine to one quart or liter of water (five drops to clear water, 10 drops to cloudy water) and let it stand for 30 minutes. If the water is cold, longer times may be required. The taste of iodinated water may be improved by adding vitamin C (ascorbic acid). Iodinated water should not be consumed for more than a few weeks. Pregnant women, people with a history of thyroid disease and those allergic to iodine should not drink iodinated water.

A number of water filters are available on the market. Those with smaller pores (reverse osmosis filters) provide the broadest protection but they are relatively large and are readily plugged by debris. Those with somewhat larger pores (microstrainer filters) are ineffective against viruses, although they remove other organisms. Manufacturers' instructions must be carefully followed.

Worms

Parasitic worms are common in rural tropical areas. They can be present on unwashed vegetables or in undercooked meat, and you can pick them up through your skin by walking barefoot. If left untreated, they can cause severe health problems.

CHILDREN & PREGNANT WOMEN

In general, it's safe for children and pregnant women to go to Jamaica. However, because some of the vaccines listed in this chapter are not approved for use in children and pregnant women, these travelers should be particularly careful not to drink tap water or consume any questionable food or beverage. When traveling with children, make sure that all their routine immunizations are up to date. It's sometimes appropriate to give children some of their vaccines a little early before visiting a developing nation. You should discuss this with your pediatrician. If pregnant, you should bear in mind that, should a complication such as premature labor develop while you're abroad, the quality of medical care available may not be comparable to that in your home country.

The yellow fever vaccine is not recommended for pregnant women or children less than nine months old. If arriving from a country with yellow fever, these travelers should obtain a waiver letter, preferably written on letterhead stationery and bearing the stamp used by official immunization centers to validate the international certificate of vaccination.

Language

CONTENTS

UNDERSTANDING PATOIS

When Jamaicans speak patois, the discussion may be incomprehensible to visitors. It might sound like a chaotic babble without rules. But don't be mislead: there are rules. They're just different from those of traditional English grammar.

Some words are unexpectedly present, for example, where others are unexpectedly missing. New words are invented and slip into general parlance as quickly as others fall from grace, and vowel sounds go sliding off into diphthongs. Like Yorkshire folk, Jamaicans often drop their 'h's' (thus, *ouse* instead of 'house') and add them in unexpected places (for example, *hemphasize*). Jamaicans usually drop the 'h' from 'th' as well: hence, *t'ree* for 'three,' and *t'anks* for 'thanks.' 'The' is usually pronounced as *de* and 'them' as *dem*. They also sometimes drop the 'w,' as in *ooman* (woman).

Jamaicans also often flip letters, as in *flim* for 'film,' and *cerfiticket* for 'certificate.' They rearrange syllables and give them their own inflections. In patois, the word 'up' is used to intensify meaning: thus, cars *mash up*. Patois words are usually spelled phonetically, so their written form reflects their sound quite closely.

In order to express the mood of the moment, 'Jamaica talk' infuses words with intonation, repetition, gesture, imagery and drama. It is not a static, written language, but an oral, vital thing that infuses life into inanimate objects. Thus, one does not forget to mail a letter; instead, *dat letter jus' fly out of mi mind*. A waiter does not simply drop a tray full of crockery; *dat wurtless t'ing jump right out of mi hands*. Among people who believe in *duppies* (ghosts), such reasoning can permit individuals to disclaim responsibility for their actions.

Such animate imagery, a carryover of West African proverbs, infuses Jamaica talk with life and is used to crystallize sayings based on the wisdom of experience, often using living creatures as teachers. In the context of a society torn from its roots and oppressed, the islanders have evolved countless sayings that express simple warnings about behavior and interpersonal relationships. Thus, 'Every day you goad donkey, 'im will kick you one day.' Or, 'When you go to donkey's house, doan't talk about ears' and 'If you play with puppy, 'im lick your mouth.'

Jamaican patois is liberally laced with sexual innuendo and slang, often of an extremely sexist nature. Cuss words abound, especially the word *rass*, an impolite term that originally meant 'backside' or 'arse'; its meaning now varies according to circumstance. It's a word visitors to Jamaica should know, as it's one of the most commonly used (and misunderstood) words. Generally it is a term of abuse, as in *Im a no good rass!* (mild), or when used with the most offensive (yet common) Jamaican derogatory term, *Im a rass blood claat* (a menstrual pad). It can also be used as an endearment *(Hey, rass, gi mi smallers)* or in a similar vein to describe a superlative *(Dat gal pretty to rass, mon!)*.

Patois is not gender specific. Everyone and everything is simply *im* or *dem*. Possessive pronouns such as 'my' and 'mine' are often replaced with *a fi*, which can also be an intensifier, as in *A fi mi bike* (It's *my* bike). Plurals are often either ignored (as in 'five finger') or signified by the word *dem*,' as in *De byah dem go to school* (The boys have gone to school). Note how the present tense is used to convey a past action.

Since you'll not be able to walk far without being asked for money, it helps to know enough patois to comprehend what you're hearing. Expect to hear *Gi mi a smallers no bass* (Give me some money now boss); *bass* means 'boss' and is often used to address persons in authority or those able to dispense favors.

There are several Jamaican pocket guides to understanding patois, including *Memba de Culcha: Chief Words, Phrases, Proverbs & Riddles in Jamaican Dialect* by Cecily Reece-Daly.

COLONIAL CARRYOVERS

Many words in the Jamaican lexicon have been carried over from early English colonial days, reflecting true Shakespearean English. The language is imbued with terms that are otherwise considered archaic. One of the most obvious is 'chain,' the old English measurement (22 yards), which is still used liberally, though rarely accurately. Similarly, you may find yourself being served a drink in a 'goblet.'

A few terms derive from slave days. Thus visitors can expect to be called *massa* (master) or 'mistress.' The term 'pickaninny' is still used for children, despite its racist connotations in Western culture; for example, the bus conductor might say *pickney stan' up an gi big people seat.*

AFRICAN HERITAGE

Scores of words have been passed down from Africa, mostly from the Ashanti, Cormorante and Congolese languages. Thus, a Jamaican may refer to a fool as a *bo-bo*. A commonly used African word is *nyam*, which means 'to eat.'

SAYINGS & PROVERBS

Jamaicans use plenty of metaphors and proverbs. They will tell you *Cockroach no business in a fowlyard* (Mind your own business). If a Jamaican tells you, *De higher monkey climb, de more 'im expose*, he or she is telling you that your boasting is transparent and that you're acting pretentiously, exposing more than you should.

Some phrases you'll hear may not mean what they suggest. *Soon come*, for example, is a common refrain, but don't hold your breath! The phrase *really* means the subject will arrive eventually – almost the opposite of what you would expect. Likewise, *jus' up de road* or *jus' a likkle distance* can mean miles or the other side of town.

The most common greeting you'll hear is *Everyt'ing cool, mon?* or *Everyt'ing irie?*

'JAMAICA TALK'

A good preparatory source is the movie *Dancehall Queen*, with dialogue in thick, at times impenetrable, Jamaican dialect. Here are some words you'll be sure to hear while strolling through the streets.

ago – to be intent on doing something, as in 'Me ago duntown.'
agony – a sexual act, or a style of dancing that suggests it
almshouse – anything negative
arms house – a violent posture, common during sound-system clashes
atops – Red Stripe beer

Babylon – the establishment, white society
bakra – a slave owner, white man
baldhead – a non-Rasta; person of unsound viewpoint
bandulu – a hustler, criminal, or the act of being swindled
bangarang – a commotion, sometimes associated with rival, deafening sound-system noise
bankra – a basket
bashment – a large dance or party; anything fabulous
batty – a bottom or rear end, as in 'Yu batty too big, mon!' (as heard from a woman who doesn't give a damn for a propositioner's looks)
batty boy – a gay man
batty riders – tight lycra hot pants for showing off one's *batty*, favored by dancehall queens
bawl – to call out, especially in anguish
beenie – small
big up – to inflate or promote oneself, as in 'Big up yo chest, mon!'
blood – a respectful greeting, as in 'Wh'appen blood?' Also a swear word, most often used with *claat* (see p300)
bly – a chance or opportunity; sometimes a feeble excuse
Bobo dread – a Rastafarian follower of Prince Emanuel Edwards
bomba – commonly used abusive term, usually allied with *claat*, as in 'Get de bomba-claat car out mi way!'
boonoonoonoos – fabulous, greatest; street or beach party
boops – a man who keeps a woman in idle splendor (men, watch out if a woman tells you, 'Mi wan' you fi mi boops')
brawta – additional
breadkind – any starchy vegetable used as a side dish in lieu of bread
bredda – a friend, usually male
bredren – male friends
brownings – brown-skinned women; also a 'well-heeled' woman showing off her status
buck – to meet someone
bumper – a rear end or backside
burn – to smoke ganja
busha – an overseer of a slave plantation
byah – a boy

carry go bring come – to spread gossip
chalice – a Rastafarian's holy ganja pipe (also known as a *cutchie*)
charged – stoned or drunk
check – to appreciate, especially a point of view or a person's physical attraction; also to pay a visit
chillum – a pipe for smoking ganja
cho – an expression to signify that the speaker is becoming annoyed
chronic – particularly potent ganja
claat, clawt – one of the strongest and most frequently heard Jamaican expletives (see p300)
coolie – someone from India
cool runnings – no problem
cool yu foot – slow down, relax
copasetic – cool, *irie*
cork – full
cotch – to relax, rest; also means to brace or support something, as well as a place to sleep
cris – from 'crisp,' meaning attractive or top-notch; 'Im a cris, cris t'ing!' ('He's handsome!')
cris-biscuit – anything *cris* or excellent
crub – to dance salaciously, as in 'wining'
culture – used to signify that something is Rastafarian
cuss-cuss – an argument
cutchie – ganja pipes

dally – the opposite of to linger; to go
dawta – a respectful term for a young woman
de – the
degeh – measly or pathetically small, usually used in a derogatory sense
deh-deh – to be someplace, as in 'Mi deh-deh!' ('I'm here!')
deportees – used cars, imported from Japan
dibby-dibby – pathetic, especially a competitor's weak sound system
do – please, as in 'Do, me a beg yu'
don – a male authority figure
downpresser – a Rastafarian term for an oppressor
dread – a Rastafarian; also a terrible situation
dunzer – money; also known as *smallers*
duppy – a ghost

facety – cheeky, impertinent, as in 'Yu facety to rass, gal!' ('You're rude, girl!')
fiyah – a Rastafarian greeting
flex – how one behaves; to party wildly

ganga-lee – a gangster
ganja – marijuana; also known as 'de 'oly 'erb,' 'wisdom weed,' 'colly weed,' *kaya*, *sensie* and *tampie*
ginnal – a swindler or con artist
gorgon – a person to be feared
gow – an empty boast
gravilishas – greedy
grind – see *flex*
guidance – a Rastafarian parting term, meaning 'May God be with you'
gwan – go away
gyal – a woman

heartical or **'eartical** – an esteemed person, someone with integrity; authentic
herb or **'erb** – marijuana (see *ganja*)
higgler or **'iggler** – a market vendor, usually female; also a person who bargains
him or **'im** – any singular pronoun: he, she, him, her, it
hottie-bottie or **'ottie-bottie** – an attractive woman

Idren – brethren, used by Rastafarians to mean friends
irie – alright, groovy; used to indicate that all is well; also a greeting ('Everyt'ing irie?')
iron bird – an airplane
I-tal – natural foods, health food, purity
iyah – a greeting

Jah – God; an Old Testament name, popular with Rastafarians
Jamdung – Jamaica (also known as Jah-Mek-Ya, as in 'God's work')
janga – shrimp, crayfish
Joe Gring – a man with whom a woman has an affair while her husband or boyfriend is away
Jook – to pierce or stab

kaya – marijuana (see *ganja*)
kingman – a husband
kiss me neck – to express surprise
kiss mi – not an invitation, but a common profane exclamation, as in 'Kiss mi rass!'

labba labba – talk
labrish – gossip
leggo beast – rowdy person
let off – to give
level vibes – no problem
lick – to smoke; to be in vogue; to strike a blow
lick shot – a gun fired at a dancehall to express appreciation
lion – upright, usually describes a righteous Rastafarian
lovers rock – romantic reggae

maarga – thin (from meager), as in 'Da boy deh maarga' ('That man there is skinny')
mantel – good-looking man, usually one who's promiscuous
market mammie – a higgler
mash up – to have an accident
massah – mister; derived from 'master' of slavery days and now used for any male, particularly one in authority
massive – a noun used to describe a crowd
matey – girlfriend who is one of several sexual partners
men – used in the singular for a gay man

mule – childless woman
myal – white magic, used to do good, that incorporates use of herbal medicines and control of *duppies*

naa – won't, as in 'Mi naa go dung deh' ('I won't go down there')
natty – dreadlocks; also 'natty dread'; also used for a Rastafarian
nuff – plentiful; also used as a greeting with 'respect,' as in 'Nuff respect!'

obeah – illegal black magic that incorporates use of herbal medicines and witchcraft
one love – parting expression meaning unity

peeny-wally – insect that flashes phosphorescent
pickney – child or children, shortened version of 'pickaninny'
pollution – people living in spiritual darkness
posse – a group of young adults who form a clique
prentice – a young man
punny printers – extremely tight *batty riders*

queen – a respectful term for a woman, usually a Rastafarian woman

ragamuffin – a no-good person
ramp – to annoy someone or interfere, as in 'De gyal ramp wid me!'
rass – a backside; also one of the most violent cuss words
reach – to arrive, as in 'De bus not reach yet, mon!'
reality – ghetto reality or a hard life
reason – to debate or discuss
red-eye – an envious or greedy person
renk – foul-smelling; extreme rudeness
respect – commonly used greeting and farewell
rhaatid – like *rass*, but a gentler and more commonly used expletive; its meaning depends on intonation and facial expression, but usually expresses surprise
riddim – Jamaica's reggae has it
risto – a member of the elite (derives from aristocrat)
roots – coming from the people or communal experience
roughneck – a scoundrel or ragamuffin
rude boy – a ghetto criminal or vandal
runnings – whatever is happening; also means crafty business schemes
rush – to be the focus of things

samfi-man – a con man
satta – an invitation to sit, usually to meditate
sensie – marijuana (see *ganja*)
sipple – slippery
skank – to con; also an early 1970s dance move
sketel – a beautiful and promiscuous woman, one with many boyfriends
skin-out – to abandon whatever one is doing to have sex, usually at a stageshow
skylark – to dawdle or idle
slack – sexually explicit lyrics
smaddy – somebody
smallers – money; also known as *dunzer*
soke – to fool around, as in 'No soke wi' mi' ('Don't mess with me')
stageshow – a live music event
stoosh – airs of superiority, condescending behavior
structure – one's body, as in 'A fi mi structure!' ('It's my body!')
sufferer or **suffrah** – a poor but righteous person
swimp – shrimp

talawah – small but powerful, as in 'De byah likkle but 'im talawah'
tampie – marijuana (see *ganja*)
tea – any hot drink
ting – a thing or woman, as in 'A mi ting, she' ('That's my girlfriend'); also used for genitals (male or female)
trace – to cuss someone
trash – to dress up, to be well turned out

wine – a sensuous dance movement
wolf – a Rastafarian imposter
work – sex

yard – a Jamaican's home
yardie – a gangster-type from the ghettoes, used by Jamaicans to mean anyone from Jamaica
yush – a greeting used by *rude boys*

Glossary

The following are common nouns and other terms used in this book.

abeng – goat horn
all-inclusive resort – resort hotel where all activities, meals, beverages, entertainment, etc are included in the room rate
Antilles – the Caribbean islands
Arawak people – indigenous pre-Columbian inhabitants of Jamaica

Babylon – term used by *Rastafarians* for oppression or corruption; sometimes used to denote the police

calabash – gourd whose hardened shell serves as a vessel for holding liquid
cay – coral isle
charcoal-burners – people who eke out a meager living burning mangrove to make charcoal
cimaroon – Spanish term for an escaped slave
cockpits – limestone hillocks separated by canyons
custos – colonial-era representative of the Crown at parish level

dancehall – type of reggae, popularized through the 1980s, in which DJs perform over prerecorded music; a place where dancehall is performed (usually an open space)
dancehall queen – female habitué of *dancehall* clubs
DEA – US Drug Enforcement Agency
dreadlocks – uncut, uncombed hair, as worn by *Rastafarians*
dub – remixed version of a recording with the vocal removed

endemic – native, or regularly found here; usually refers to species of flora and fauna

free colored – offspring of white slave owners and black slaves; accorded some special rights

General Consumption Tax (GCT) – charge of between 6.25% and 15% on most hotel bills and some restaurant bills or store purchases
go-go – exotic dancing; staple of Jamaican nightlife

Jamintel – Jamaica International Telephone
JLP – Jamaica Labour Party
JTB – Jamaica Tourist Board
JUTA – Jamaica Union of Travelers Association

Maroons – community of escaped slaves who resisted the British during the colonial period; also their contemporary descendants
mento – first indigenous Jamaican music
MoBay – slang for Montego Bay
NEPA – Negril Environmental Protection Area
NRCA – Natural Resources Conservation Authority
Nyahbinghi – Rastafarian council site; also a type of drum

Ochi – slang for Ocho Rios

PADI – Professional Association of Dive Instructors
parish – one of 14 political districts
pirogue – canoe hollowed out of a large tree trunk; long wooden fishing boat
PNP – People's National Party

ragga – type of digital reggae epitomizing *dancehall* music since 1985
Rastafarian – adherent of the religious philosophy Rastafarianism, whose main tenets hold that those of African descent are one of the 12 lost tribes of Israel, that Emperor Haile Selassie is divine, and that he will lead Rastafarians to *Zion*; also called a Rasta
rum shop – local bar, usually utilized by the working class

Sandals – large chain of *all-inclusive* resort hotels
soca – combination of soul and calypso music
sound system – mobile disco using giant speakers, such as a *dancehall*
spliff – joint; marijuana rolled in paper
SuperClubs – large chain of *all-inclusive* resort hotels

toaster – DJ who talks or sings over a record in a *dancehall*

Xaymaca – *Arawak people*'s term for Jamaica

yabbas – earthenware pots

Zion – the Promised Land (Ethiopia) in the *Rastafarian* religion

Behind the Scenes

THIS BOOK

This is the 5th edition of Lonely Planet's *Jamaica* guide, written by Richard Koss. The 1st, 2nd and 3rd editions of this book were researched and written by Christopher Baker. Michael Read wrote the 4th edition, with contributions from Norman C Stolzoff, PhD. This guidebook was commissioned in Lonely Planet's Oakland office, and produced by the following:

Commissioning Editors Jay Cooke, Jennye Garibaldi, Marina Kosmatos
Coordinating Editors Laura Stansfeld, Louisa Syme
Coordinating Cartographer Owen Eszeki
Coordinating Layout Designer Aomi Hongo
Managing Editor Imogen Bannister
Managing Cartographer Alison Lyall
Managing Layout Designer Celia Wood
Assisting Editors Gennifer Ciavarra, Melissa Faulkner, Martine Power, Tom Smallman, Helen Yeates
Assisting Cartographers Barbara Benson, Mick Garrett, Karen Grant
Cover Designer Marika Kozak
Project Manager Craig Kilburn
Language Content Coordinator Quentin Frayne

Thanks to Nina Collins, Rachel Imeson, Laura Jane, Lisa Knights, Adam McCrow, Malcolm O'Brien, Susan Paterson

THANKS

RICHARD KOSS

Heartfelt thanks go to everyone at Lonely Planet, especially to Jennye Garibaldi for hiring me to cover Jamaica and for all her hard work creating my brief, and to Marina Kosmatos for her guidance and good humor (and humour). Also to Laura Stansfeld and Louisa Syme for their patience, dedication and organizational dexterity; to Helen Yeates, Gennifer Ciavarra and Martine Power for their eagle eyes and editorial diligence; and to Owen Eszeki for his cartographic acumen. Someday, I will show up in Melbourne and buy you all drinks at the Ding Dong Lounge.

I couldn't begin to list all the people who helped me in Jamaica, but I am especially indebted to Diana McCaulay at the Jamaica Environment Trust, Claudia Cole at the Jamaica Tourist Board, and Matt Snow, the JTB's rep back in NYC. Also to Frank Lohmann for the ride from Bluefields to Treasure Beach, and Dennis Rappaport for helping me get my car checked at the auto body shop in St Ann's Bay (Hertz charged me for the dent anyway, bless 'em).

I am also grateful for the company, during the last week of my trip, of Anja 'I can't believe you wait till we're in the water before saying you've never been kayaking!' Mutić and Gary Campbell,

THE LONELY PLANET STORY

Fresh from an epic journey across Europe, Asia and Australia in 1972, Tony and Maureen Wheeler sat at their kitchen table stapling together notes. The first Lonely Planet guidebook, *Across Asia on the Cheap,* was born.

Travelers snapped up the guides. Inspired by their success, the Wheelers began publishing books to Southeast Asia, India and beyond. Demand was prodigious, and the Wheelers expanded the business rapidly to keep up. Over the years, Lonely Planet extended its coverage to every country and into the virtual world via lonelyplanet.com and the Thorn Tree message board.

As Lonely Planet became a globally loved brand, Tony and Maureen received several offers for the company. But it wasn't until 2007 that they found a partner whom they trusted to remain true to the company's principles of traveling widely, treading lightly and giving sustainably. In October of that year, BBC Worldwide acquired a 75% share in the company, pledging to uphold Lonely Planet's commitment to independent travel, trustworthy advice and editorial independence.

Today, Lonely Planet has offices in Melbourne, London and Oakland, with over 500 staff members and 300 authors. Tony and Maureen are still actively involved with Lonely Planet. They're traveling more often than ever, and they're devoting their spare time to charitable projects. And the company is still driven by the philosophy of *Across Asia on the Cheap*: 'All you've got to do is decide to go and the hardest part is over. So go!'

SEND US YOUR FEEDBACK

We love to hear from travellers – your comments keep us on our toes and help make our books better. Our well-travelled team reads every word on what you loved or loathed about this book. Although we cannot reply individually to postal submissions, we always guarantee that your feedback goes straight to the appropriate authors, in time for the next edition. Each person who sends us information is thanked in the next edition – and the most useful submissions are rewarded with a free book. See the Behind the Scenes section.

To send us your updates – and find out about Lonely Planet events, newsletters and travel news – visit our award-winning website: **www.lonelyplanet.com/contact**.

Note: we may edit, reproduce and incorporate your comments in Lonely Planet products such as guidebooks, websites and digital products, so let us know if you don't want your comments reproduced or your name acknowledged. For a copy of our privacy policy, go to www.lonelyplanet.com/privacy.

godfather of Wray and Nephew. And thanks, finally, to Latrell for not chewing up the furniture while I was away.

OUR READERS

Many thanks to the travelers who used the last edition and wrote to us with helpful hints, useful advice and interesting anecdotes:

Sophia Batson, Malcolm Bridges, George and Amy Brockman, Jill Browning, Stephen Burnell, Scott Buschkuhl, Petr Cernoch, Frank Cousins, Jen Cromer, Joe Cummings, Susan Drinkwater, Virginia Kay, Amir Kraitzer, Chris Leary, Mandy Leask, Leslie Lehmann, Janet Lovell, Emily Mariko-Sanders, Paolo Mariotti, Ward Matthews, Katharina Osika, Jay Panetta, Aristea Parisi, Rahul Parson, Andrea Piampiani, Arlene Poste, Dr Christa Rottscheidt, Michael P Snow, Thomas Spear, Pierre St-Cyr, Dale Suiter, Denise Tonsberg, Hayley Trickey, Rosanna Trifogli, Barbara van Lint, Chris van Oosten, Hubert Vollmer, Maria Wennerberg, Jill White, Ted White, Alexis Wolton, Pepe Zahl, Asier Zendoia

ACKNOWLEDGMENTS

Many thanks to the following for the use of their content:

Globe on title page ©Mountain High Maps 1993 Digital Wisdom, Inc.

Index

INDEX

C

000 Map pages
000 Photograph pages

D

E

000 Map pages
000 Photograph pages

000 Map pages
000 Photograph pages

12am
1am
2am
3am
4am
5am
6am
7am
8am
9am
10am
11am
12pm
International Date Line
Mon
Sun
ARCTIC OCEAN
CHUKCHI SEA
BEAUFORT SEA
Queen Elizabeth Is (Can)
Ellesmere Is (Can)
Banks Is (Can)
Victoria Is (Can)
BAFFIN BAY
Greenland (Denmark)
GREENLAND SEA
NORWEGIAN SEA
Russia
Alaska (US)
Baffin Is (Can)
Iceland
NORTH SEA
HUDSON BAY
BERING SEA
GULF OF ALASKA
Canada
LABRADOR SEA
United Kingdom
Ireland
8.30am
NORTH ATLANTIC OCEAN
United States
Azores (Port)
Portugal
Spain
NORTH PACIFIC OCEAN
Bermuda (UK)
Morocco
Midway Is (US)
Canary Is (Sp)
GULF OF MEXICO
Mexico
The Bahamas
Cuba
Haiti
Hawaii (US)
Eastern Caribbean Islands
CARIBBEAN SEA
Mauritania
Mali
Cape Verde
Guatemala
Nicaragua
Senegal
Guinea
Burkina Faso
Panama
Venezuela
Guyana
Liberia
Ghana
Galapagos Is (Ecuador)
Colombia
Suriname
GULF OF GUINEA
EQUATOR
Ecuador
Kiribati
Ascension (UK)
Samoa
2.30am
Peru
Brazil
Tahiti
French Polynesia (Fr)
Tonga
Cook Is (NZ)
Bolivia
SOUTH ATLANTIC OCEAN
Pitcairn Is (UK)
Easter Is (Chile)
Paraguay
Chile
Uruguay
New Zealand
Argentina
Tristan da Cunha (UK)
Gough Is (UK)
12.45am
Chatham Is (NZ)
SOUTH PACIFIC OCEAN
Falkland Is (UK)
South Georgia & South Sandwich Is (UK)
Bouvet Is (Norway)

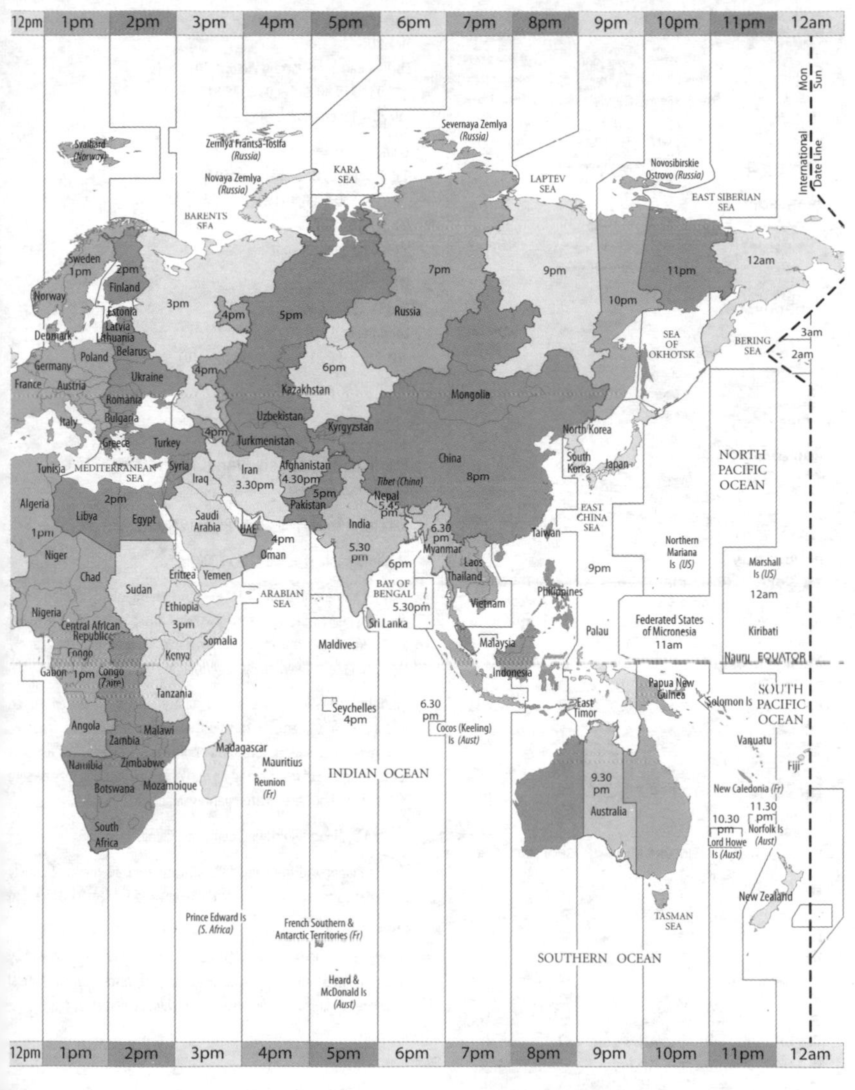
12pm 1pm 2pm 3pm 4pm 5pm 6pm 7pm 8pm 9pm 10pm 11pm 12am
Mon
Sun
International Date Line
Svalbard (Norway)
Zemlya Frantsa-Iosifa (Russia)
Novaya Zemlya (Russia)
Severnaya Zemlya (Russia)
KARA SEA
LAPTEV SEA
Novosibirskie Ostrovo (Russia)
EAST SIBERIAN SEA
BARENTS SEA
Sweden 1pm
2pm
Finland
Norway
Estonia
Latvia
Lithuania
Denmark
Belarus
Poland
Germany
France
Austria
Ukraine
Romania
Bulgaria
Italy
Greece
Turkey
Tunisia
MEDITERRANEAN SEA
Syria
Iraq
Iran 3.30pm
Afghanistan 4.30pm
Pakistan
5pm
Nepal 5.45 pm
India
5.30 pm
Algeria
Libya
2pm
Egypt
1pm
Saudi Arabia
UAE
4pm
Oman
Niger
Chad
Sudan
Eritrea
Yemen
Ethiopia 3pm
Somalia
Nigeria
Central African Republic
Congo
Gabon
1pm
Congo (Zaire)
Kenya
Tanzania
Angola
Zambia
Malawi
Namibia
Zimbabwe
Botswana
Mozambique
South Africa
Madagascar
Mauritius
Reunion (Fr)
3pm
4pm
5pm
Russia
7pm
9pm
11pm
12am
10pm
6pm
Kazakhstan
Uzbekistan
Turkmenistan
Kyrgyzstan
Mongolia
China
8pm
Tibet (China)
North Korea
South Korea
Japan
SEA OF OKHOTSK
BERING SEA
3am
2am
NORTH PACIFIC OCEAN
EAST CHINA SEA
Taiwan
6.30 pm
Myanmar
Laos
Thailand
Vietnam
6pm
BAY OF BENGAL
5.30pm
Sri Lanka
ARABIAN SEA
Maldives
Philippines
9pm
Northern Mariana Is (US)
Marshall Is (US)
12am
Palau
Federated States of Micronesia 11am
Kiribati
Nauru EQUATOR
Malaysia
Indonesia
Papua New Guinea
East Timor
Solomon Is
SOUTH PACIFIC OCEAN
Seychelles 4pm
6.30 pm
Cocos (Keeling) Is (Aust)
INDIAN OCEAN
Vanuatu
Fiji
New Caledonia (Fr)
9.30 pm
Australia
11.30 pm
Norfolk Is (Aust)
10.30 pm
Lord Howe Is (Aust)
New Zealand
TASMAN SEA
Prince Edward Is (S. Africa)
French Southern & Antarctic Territories (Fr)
Heard & McDonald Is (Aust)
SOUTHERN OCEAN

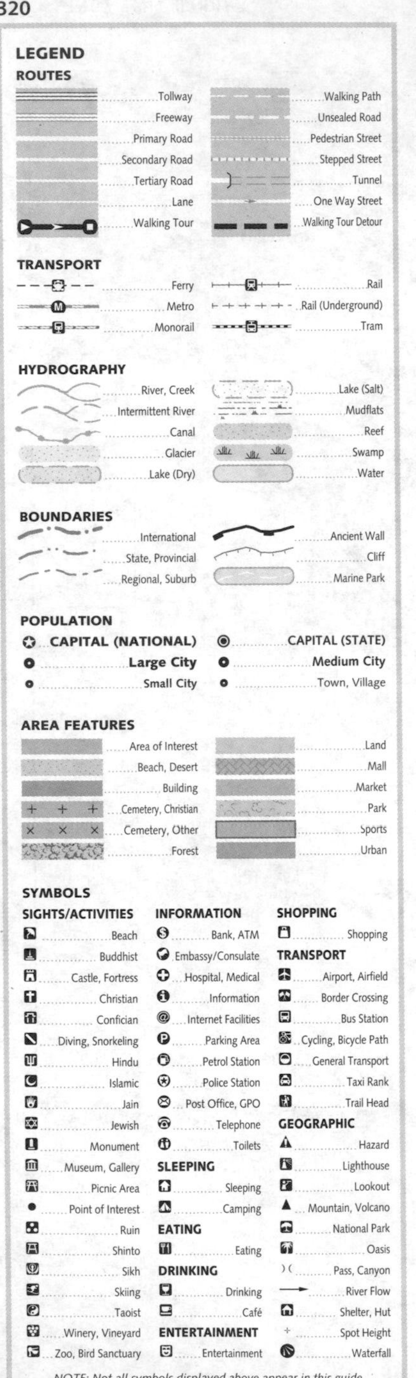

LONELY PLANET OFFICES

Australia

Head Office
Locked Bag 1, Footscray, Victoria 3011
☎ 03 8379 8000, fax 03 8379 8111
talk2us@lonelyplanet.com.au

USA

150 Linden St, Oakland, CA 94607
☎ 510 250 6400, toll free 800 275 8555
fax 510 893 8572
info@lonelyplanet.com

UK

2nd fl, 186 City Rd,
London EC1V 2NT
☎ 020 7106 2100, fax 020 7106 2101
go@lonelyplanet.co.uk

Published by Lonely Planet Publications Pty Ltd
ABN 36 005 607 983

Cover photograph: Jamaican mango hummingbird feeding on a bleeding heart vine, Montego Bay © Rolf Nussbaumer / Alamy. Many of the images in this guide are available for licensing from Lonely Planet Images: www.lonelyplanetimages.com.

Printed by Hang Tai Printing Company, China.